Studies in Archaeology

THE EARLY MESOAMERICAN VILLAGE

Edited by
Kent V. Flannery

The Early
Mesoamerican Village

This is a volume in

Studies in Archaeology

A complete list of titles in this series appears at the end of this volume.

The Early Mesoamerican Village

Edited by
KENT V. FLANNERY

Museum of Anthropology
University of Michigan
Ann Arbor, Michigan

ACADEMIC PRESS

A Subsidiary of Harcourt Brace Jovanovich, Publishers

New York   London   Toronto   Sydney   San Francisco

All royalties from the sale of this book accrue to
account 300587, The James B. Griffin Fund, for the
support of graduate student research in archaeology
at the University of Michigan.

ACADEMIC PRESS, INC.
111 Fifth Avenue, New York, New York 10003

United Kingdom Edition published by
ACADEMIC PRESS, INC. (LONDON) LTD.
24/28 Oval Road, London NW1

Library of Congress Cataloging in Publication Data
Main entry under title:

The Early Mesoamerican village.

    Includes bibliographies and index.
        1.   Indians of Mexico--Antiquities.   2.   Indians
of Central America--Antiquities.   3.   Mexico--Antiqui-
ties.   4.   Central America--Antiquities.   5.   Cities
and towns, Ruined, extinct, etc.--Mexico.   6.   Cities
and town, Ruined, extinct, etc.--Central America.
I.   Flannery, Kent V.
F1219.E18   930'.1'028   75-13088
ISBN 0−12−259852−0

PRINTED IN THE UNITED STATES OF AMERICA
82   9 8 7 6 5 4 3 2 1

To the Memory of

MATTHEW W. STIRLING

1896–1975

*a pioneer in the excavation
of early Mesoamerican villages*

Contents

List of Contributors

Numbers in parentheses indicate the pages on which the authors contributions begin.

ELIZABETH BRUMFIEL (234), Museum of Anthropology, University of Michigan, Ann Arbor, Michigan

ROBERT D. DRENNAN (345), R.S. Peabody Foundation, Andover, Massachusetts

TIMOTHY K. EARLE (196), Department of Anthropology, University of California, Los Angeles, California

KENT V. FLANNERY (1, 13, 31, 34, 51, 68, 72, 103, 159, 162, 173, 286, 333, 369), Museum of Anthropology, University of Michigan, Ann Arbor, Michigan

JOYCE MARCUS (79), Museum of Anthropology, University of Michigan, Ann Arbor, Michigan

JANE W. PIRES-FERREIRA (286, 292, 306, 311), Museum of Anthropology, University of Michigan, Ann Arbor, Michigan

STEPHEN PLOG (136, 255), Department of Anthropology, Southern Illinois University, Carbondale, Illinois

NANETTE M. PYNE* (272), Museum of Anthropology, University of Michigan, Ann Arbor, Michigan

ROBERT G. D. REYNOLDS (180), Department of Geography, University of Michigan, Ann Arbor, Michigan

DAVID L. ROSSMANN (95), Center for Demographic and Population Genetics, The University of Texas Health Science Center at Houston, Houston, Texas

MICHAEL E. WHALEN (75), Museum of Anthropology, University of Michigan, Ann Arbor, Michigan

MARCUS C. WINTER (25, 34, 62, 227, 306), Centro Regional de Oaxaca, I.N.A.H., Colonia Reforma, Oaxaca, Mexico

ALAN ZARKY (117), Museum of Anthropology, University of Michigan, Ann Arbor, Michigan

*Present address: Department of Near Eastern Languages and Literature, University of Washington, Seattle, Washington.

Chapter 1

RESEARCH STRATEGY AND FORMATIVE MESOAMERICA *

KENT V. FLANNERY

> One can still not confidently predict even on what prob-
> lem 60% of his data is going to bear before going into an
> intensive excavation project. [Richard E.W. Adams
> 1969: 36]
>
> Current lack of concern with the development of planned
> research designs generally obviates the recovery of data
> pertinent to questions which derive from current
> theoretical interests.
>
> The methodology most appropriate for the task of iso-
> lating and studying processes of cultural change and
> evolution is one which is regional in scope and executed
> with the aid of research designs based on the principles of
> probability sampling. [Lewis R. Binford 1964: 425–426]

"The Near East," Sir Mortimer Wheeler once remarked at lunch, "is the land of archeological sin." Such a statement could have been made only by a man who had never worked in Mesoamerica.

How sad that Sir Mortimer could not have been with David Grove, Jorge Angulo, and me on that sunny morning in the 1960s when we came across a Mesoamerican archeologist at work on a Formative site in the Central Mexican Symbiotic Re-

*A great deal of the data on early villages in Oaxaca is presented here for the first time. It was made possible by National Science Foundation grants GS-1616, GS-2121, and GS-42568, and the collaboration of the Instituto Nacional de Antropologia e Historia (Mexico). We thank these institutions for their support and encouragement.

gion. Four stalks of river cane, stuck loosely in the ground, defined a quadrilateral (though not necessarily rectangular) area in which two *peones* picked and shoveled to varying depths, heaving the dirt to one side. On the backdirt pile stood the archeologist himself, armed with his most delicate tool—a three-pronged garden cultivator of the type used by elderly British ladies to weed rhododendrons. Combing through every shovelful of dirt, he carefully picked out each figurine head and placed it in a brown paper shopping bag nearby—the only other bit of equipment in evidence. This individual was armed with an excavation permit that had been granted because, in the honest words of one official, "he appeared to be no better or worse than any other archeologist who had worked in the area." When questioned, our colleague descended from the backdirt pile and revealed that his underlying research goal was to define the nature of the "Olmec presence" in that particular drainage basin; his initial results, he said, predicted total success.

As Grove, Angulo, and I rattled back along the highway in our Jeep, each of us in his own way sat marveling at the elegance of a research strategy in which one could define the nature of a foreign presence in a distant drainage basin from just seven fragmentary figurine heads in the bottom of a supermarket sack. All through that day and the next, I could not shake the feeling that we had looked through a tiny window into the heart of some unexpected Truth. And then, over a beer on the plaza of some forgotten nearby *pueblo*, it came to me. In terms of scientific method, what we had done, we and 50 years of our predecessors in the archeology of Formative Mesoamerica, was only a fraction of a brownie point better than what we had seen going on between those four stalks of river cane.

This is a book about Formative villages and some of the ways they can be studied. The area considered is the southern half of Mexico and the western part of Guatemala, two regions that belong to the culture area called Mesoamerica. The time period covered is roughly that of 1500 to 500 B.C., a millenium of great importance in Mesoamerican prehistory. It was at the start of this period that true, permanent villages of pole-and-thatch (wattle-and-daub) houses first became widespread in Mesoamerica. Out of this initial stage of agriculturally based villages, the later high civilizations of Mesoamerica developed. With the appearance of these "primary village farming communities," Mesoamerica first became definable as a culture area, distinct from the desert food-gatherers to the north and the tropical forest peoples to the south. Thus, a major concern of Mesoamerican archeologists, since at least the 1920s, has been to find

out as much as possible about the early Mesoamerican villages for which this book is named.

But there is a tremendous credibility gap between what Mesoamerican archeologists say they are interested in, and what they really do. The only way I can think to illustrate this is to present a parable. I will reduce myself and all my colleagues in the archeology of Formative Mesoamerica to a series of three imaginary characters to whom, for the sake of hurting no one's feelings, I will attribute some of the real events of the last two decades in Mesoamerica.

Mesoamericanists at Work: A Modern Parable

The first protagonist to be presented is a composite character whom I will call the "Real Mesoamerican Archeologist," or "R.M.A." for short. I have worked side by side with R.M.A. for nearly 18 years, and I like him. Like so many Mesoamerican archeologists, he is amiable, friendly, loyal, kind, and hospitable. He is totally in love with Mesoamerica, with its food, its drink, its people. He still believes in the romance of archeology; his eyes glisten and his voice grows husky as he looks at an Olmec jade. He is open and incredibly generous with his unpublished data. He would rather spread out all his sherds on the table for you than eat dinner, but he would rather drink beer with you than spread out all his sherds. He may not be able to remember the best route back to his site, but he never forgets which stall on the plaza has the best *carnitas*. In his off-hours, away from the site, he is still a Mesoamericanist; that is, he belongs to a group that includes some of the most colorful characters and greatest beer drinkers, hell raisers, folk singers, pub crawlers, satyrs, nymphomaniacs, and storytellers in all of archeology.

R.M.A. is an anthropologist, and his goals are those of anthropological archeology. As far as the

Formative is concerned, what he wants to do is ambitious and commendable.

> I want to pick a valley which is a real hydrographic unit: you know, define it by the boundary of the watershed. Then I want to do a real settlement pattern survey. Then pick some really good sites, get the whole sequence. I want to know the ecological adaptation of the early villages to the area, and get some data on social and political organization. Make some real solid population estimates. Then I want to define the relationship of my area with the valleys of Puebla and Morelos, the Gulf Coast, highland Guatemala. Really pin down the trade wares and outside influences. Maybe even work on how the "village Formative" turned into the "temple Formative." I'd really like to reconstruct the whole Formative way of life.

But if you had visited R.M.A. in the field, you would gradually have begun to wonder how his research strategy could accomplish the goals he had set for himself. During the first field season, he completed his intensive survey, which consisted of recording all those mounds which require four-wheel drive to get over. On one of the mounds near the Río San Jacinto, he found some "good stuff—you know, zoned rocker stamping and white-rim black ware," and decided to give it a test. He put in two pits of the type I like to call "telephone booths"—each 1.5 by 1.5 m, and carried 5 m to sterile soil by horizontal 20-cm levels. It's dark down inside a telephone booth, but if you poke around sometimes you can feel which way the cultural strata are running—at least, in the case of the coarser deposits like, say, pea gravel. One pit, his "richest," had a really interesting feel because it was dug in the slopewash off the edge of the site, and the strata crossed all his arbitrary levels at a 45° angle.

During his second season, R.M.A. put a 20-m trench right through the center of the site. In order to "refine" the stratigraphy this time, his arbitrary levels were only 10 cm deep, though admittedly 20 m long. Since the center of the site

was a buried artificial mound, his trench went through 5 m of Classic pyramid fill composed of basketloads of Early Formative, Middle Formative, and Late Formative debris. R.M.A. was delighted with the tremendous variety of sherds, which included some types never found before in the region.

Back at his lab, he divided a long table into chalked sections corresponding to his arbitrary levels, and laid out the whole sequence. Over a beer, I asked him if he didn't think it was unusual to find fragments of Early Classic Thin Orange pottery side-by-side with the limbs of hollow Formative figurines. "You have to expect a little intrusion," he explained. "You can't see all the gopher burrows after 2000 years."

I have to hand it to R.M.A., because he turned that 5 m of totally mixed mound fill into a seriated sequence of pottery types which looked—when presented as a graph of frequency polygons, or "battleships"—totally convincing. He did it by observing which attributes showed some difference from one level to another, by combining these into modes, and combining these again into types. Never have the esthetic qualities of sampling error been more tastefully displayed. R.M.A. identified most of the pottery types on the basis of published reports from nearby valleys, but, in the end, he had six unidentified types left over. These he lumped together to form a new phase, which he named "San Jacinto" and placed at the very beginning of the sequence. The sequence from Mound 1 of the Río San Jacinto project went into one of R.M.A.'s now-famous preliminary reports. (They are famous because R.M.A. has produced more preliminary reports, and fewer final reports, than anyone outside Near Eastern prehistory.) As usual, his report was reviewed by his former professor, the Great Synthesizer, or "G.S.," as we will call him in the pages that follow. G.S. began in archeology just like R.M.A., but he soon learned that center-digging mounds wasn't where it was at. Writing about other people's center-digging of mounds was where it was at; and especially the center-digging of his former students, who were gentlemanly about their unpublished data. In addition, G.S. had once discovered a carbonized corncob on his backdirt pile, which directed his theoretical interests to "the ecological approach." Thus, he was in a better position to put the Río San Jacinto pottery sequence in an "ecological perspective" than almost any other reviewer. G.S.'s review of R.M.A.'s report was thoughtful and kindly disposed, but just as I feared, he also thought it peculiar that Teotihuacán Thin Orange should occur in all levels in association with limb fragments of hollow Olmec figurines. Nevertheless, he concluded by saying that "this volume is a welcome addition to the all-too-scanty literature on the Formative of the middle Río San Jacinto basin."

When I last saw R.M.A., he was serving his 3-year stint as a department chairman—chafing behind his desk, itching to get back to the field. In the interim, he was sending one of his students to the drainage of the Río San Pedro, which adjoined the San Jacinto. R.M.A. had never personally been to the San Pedro but, given the richness of Mesoamerica, he knew his student would find "good stuff" there. His orders were to survey intensively just as R.M.A. had, to pick a good mound, test it with telephone booths, center-trench it, lay out the pottery sequence, seriate it, and compare it with the sequence from San Jacinto. The strategy was so original that the student had had no trouble obtaining a National Science Foundation Doctoral Dissertation Improvement Grant.

"I'd like to have you talk to the kid before he goes to the field," said R.M.A. "I've had him read a lot of your articles . . ."

"Sure, I'll be glad to."

". . . and he disagrees with nearly all of them."

With that preparation, I must now introduce you to the student, for he is the third of the principal characters in this parable. I will call him the "Skeptical Graduate Student," or "S.G.S." He is obnoxiously smart, and has only a vestigial respect for established authority. Idealism sticks out all

over him. His edges are rough. He understands the New Math. I knew he was going to make some wise remark, and I was trying to think of a suitable put-down in advance when he asked politely, "Tell me, Mr. Science, do you really think that a person can define the ecological adaptation of a Formative people, reconstruct their way of life, figure out their social and political organization, and uncover their relationship with other Formative peoples by putting a couple of telephone booths into a mound?"

"I don't think so," I admitted.

"Then why do people go on doing it?" he asked.

"I've sort of been wondering about that myself."

"I've been reading Binford," he began. I stiffened a little at that, because these religious fanatics always make me nervous. "He says," S.G.S. went on, "that the methodology most appropriate for the task of isolating and studying processes of cultural change and evolution is one which is regional in scope, and executed with the aid of research designs based on the principles of probability sampling."

Smart-ass kid, I thought to myself.

"Do you know Binford personally?" he finally asked.

"Yes," I answered. "I was with him the day he fed 5000 undergraduates with a few loaves of bread and a newspaperful of fish."

Archeological Research Strategy

By now the crafty reader will have guessed that the three allegorical characters introduced in the parable above are all part of one personality. All of us engaged in Formative archeology have varying degrees of each—skeptical graduate student, real Mesoamerican archeologist, and great synthesizer—carrying on a dialectic inside our heads. Periodically, each of us senses that the methodology and research strategy we use in the field cannot possibly yield the kinds of information we claim in the grant proposals we are after. But for how long can we continue to blame this on the shortcomings of the sites themselves, or fatalistically rationalize, as does R.E.W. Adams (1969) in the quote at the beginning of this book, that "one can still not confidently predict even on what problem 60% of his data is going to bear before going into an intensive excavation project"?

Let us momentarily yield the floor to the Skeptical Graduate Student, and he will direct us to a paper by Stuart Struever (1969) entitled "Archeology and the study of cultural process: Some comments on data requirements and research strategy." In this paper, Struever, an archeologist working in the midwestern United States, outlines a research program that is "regional in scope" and "based on the principles of probability sampling" as Binford (1964) has suggested. Struever's ideas are founded, not on some idealistic a priori notions of what archeology should be in the future, but on what he has actually been doing during a 15-year project in a 19-mile stretch of the lower Illinois River basin. He sees such a project proceeding along three main lines:

1. Reconstructing subsistence–settlement systems.
2. Obtaining population measures for geographic areas and for a series of prehistoric socio-political units, ranging from household to polity.
3. Inferring aspects of prehistoric social structure.

These are precisely the things that our friend R.M.A. claims to be interested in, but which he has not the remotest idea of how to accomplish. This is because, although he knows that the Formative was a time of "village farming communities," he does not dig sites and analyze sites as if they were village farming communities. He digs them and analyzes them as if they were huge layer cakes of discarded sherds.

In this book, we will focus on the village, although it was only one of a number of settlement types during Formative times. The village is crucial because it was the "home base" from which other settlement types—maguey roasting camps, hunting camps in caves, fishing stations, field huts in cornfields, and so on—were usually founded. As we shall see, the village is the key to Formative social structure from family to regional polity. And the number of Formative villages that have been dug *as if they were villages* can still be counted on the fingers of one hand after 50 years of Formative archeology. But, by using some of the "building blocks of society" outlined in Struever's article, and adding a few others which are specific to Mesoamerica, we can make a start toward constructing a model of how the early Mesoamerican village operated.

The Units of Society

For Struever, the smallest observable unit of the village is the *activity area*, a single locus of activity of one or more members of the community. Perhaps comparably small is the *feature*, which includes nonportable facilities, such as a hearth or storage pit. On the next level, we Mesoamericanists may add those portions of the house floor, often composed of several features and/or activity areas, which make up the *male and female work areas* of the household as described in Chapter 2. The next larger unit is the *house*. To this, Marc Winter (Chapter 2) has added a new category—the *household cluster*—which consists of the house and all the surrounding storage pits, burials, middens, and features that can be reliably associated with that same household.

Beyond the level of the individual household, we may find, at least in some villages, the *courtyard group*—several houses sharing a common patio. In larger villages, there may be still another unit—the *barrio* or residential ward—composed of related courtyard groups whose architecture, material remains, and other attributes may distinguish them from neighboring barrios. Beyond this is the *village* itself, discussed in Chapter 3. This is not unlike Struever's unit, the *maximum local aggregate*, which he defines as "the maximum number of people who together occupy a single settlement at some time during a total settlement cycle."

Beyond the level of the individual village, the definition of units becomes even trickier. Struever has isolated a unit called the *maximum subsistence-settlement unit*, which "includes all people integrated at one or more intervals in the functioning of a subsistence-settlement system ... It sometimes occurs that people who at no time in the settlement cycle live together in one settlement still belong to a single maximum subsistence-settlement unit. This would be the case in some redistributive systems." It would also be the case in a situation where all the villages in a single valley raised and exchanged different staple products, even where the economy was not redistributive.

For the purposes of our analyses here, we will consider *all the villages in a single valley* to constitute the maximum subsistence-settlement unit. In Early Formative Mesoamerica, these regional groupings of villages had two main arrangements: *linear* (along linear river systems) and *nonlinear*. These will be considered in Chapters 6 and 7.

But even if we consider each valley or each drainage basin a maximum subsistence-settlement unit, there is still a larger polity. For each valley in Formative Mesoamerica was linked into a larger economic and social unit by *interregional networks of exchange* and *pan-Mesoamerican networks of sacred lore and ritual paraphernalia*. These important but poorly understood interregional networks will be considered in Chapters 10 and 11. It is our contention that they laid the Formative groundwork for the later Classic "symbiotic networks" linking various regions of Mesoamerica (Sanders 1956).

Our framework for the early Mesoamerican village thus runs from the smallest observable unit— the individual activity area in or around the house—through the household, the village, and the regional network of villages within a valley, to the relationships between valleys. But this satisfies only the "regional basis" required by Binford. It remains to consider the rationale for "probability sampling."

Sampling Designs

When R.M.A. excavates Formative sites, he operates within what is sometimes called the "normative" theoretical framework. For him, each artifact, each feature, and each site is the physical manifestation of a series of shared ideas, values, and beliefs—the "norms" of a prehistoric culture. The description of change in these shared ideas through time and space becomes his major objective. If R.M.A. is interested in the Early Formative period, he puts a pit in an Early Formative site and then reports that the Early Formative is "typified" by whatever he finds in that pit. "Early Formative villages of the middle San Jacinto drainage are characterized by neckless jars with a red band at the rim, obsidian blades, volcanic tuff metates, Type A figurines, ash lenses, brown gopher burrows, and intrusive Classic burials whose heads extend outside the excavated area."

Just like the normative theorist described by Struever, our friend R.M.A.

> attempts to reconstruct prehistoric cultures in terms of a series of normative concepts expressed in a list of typical artifact, feature, and even settlement forms. Therefore, a single excavation of undetermined size in a village site can be expected to yield an artifact and feature sample from which these typical forms can be identified. Similarly, any site of a particular cultural phase, thoroughly investigated, is regarded as *typifying* sites of that phase. [Struever 1969: 2]

When R.M.A. visited me in the field in 1967, he was fascinated by the diversity and specialization in the modern villages in the Valley of Oaxaca. "Isn't it great," he commented, "the way Atzompa makes green pottery and Coyotepec black pottery, San Juan Guelavía makes baskets, Ejutla makes woven mats, Teotitlán makes blankets and Santo Tomás Jalieza makes belts." Yet if R.M.A. were to work on the Formative in the same valley, he would excavate one "good" site and generalize from that to the "Formative culture" of the whole region. For some reason, Formative villages are not expected to have the diversity of today's, although the archeological record suggests that they frequently do. Thus, R.M.A.'s normative framework deprives him of one of the major sources of information available to the archeologist: variation.

This is the second point made by Binford (1964) and expanded by Struever (1969). Only by discovering the *ranges of variation* among artifacts, features, houses, villages, and regions can the archeologist hope to determine which differences between these units are functional and which are accidental. And in regions where villages were specialized in their agricultural or craft activities, the word "typical" may in fact be meaningless, insofar as certain categories of artifacts or features are concerned.

"But how can I recover the full range of variation for all those things?" R.M.A. complains. "I can't dig every square foot of every site in the valley. Even if I lived that long, I couldn't get enough research funds to do it." Of course not; he has to take a sample, just as all archeologists do. But there are ways of taking a sample which permit you to draw highly probable conclusions about the range of variation, and ways which don't.

"I know," says R.M.A. "Random sampling, and so on. I'm so sick of hearing about it I could retch. I'm just not interested in doing anything that complicated."

Now we have to be careful, because R.M.A. is getting annoyed. So we point out to him that every simple mathematical act he performs every field season—calculating the percentage of white pottery to black, drawing frequency polygons, comparing levels at two nearby sites, estimating the number of burials in the village—is, whether he realizes it or not, predicated on the assumption that his sample is unbiased. And R.M.A. has never taken an unbiased sample in his life.

What makes the situation all the more ironic is that taking an unbiased sample is really much easier than R.M.A. thinks; he has been unduly frightened by the polemics of the "new archeology." In fact, drawing an unbiased sample may take less time than the system the Real Meso-american Archeologist usually uses for deciding where to dig, which requires waiting all day until he sees which part of the site gets the most shade. In Chapter 5, Stephen Plog evaluates several methods of sampling for Formative sites within a valley. In Chapter 3, Marc Winter evaluates one method for sampling within a Formative site. Neither method requires much more math than R.M.A. typically uses on his pottery seriation graphs. Each is based on a principle that is almost childlike in its simplicity: Each site, or each house or feature in each site, must be given an equal opportunity to be found.

When we explained this to the Great Synthesizer over lunch at the Faculty Club, he frowned thoughtfully and said, "Now let me see if I have this all straight in my mind. You're saying that we should make the *region*, and not the individual site, our basis for analysis. If we can't survey the whole region intensively, we should sample it in such a way that we can reasonably predict how many sites of each phase—and what *types* of sites— there should be in the whole region. We should then pick a series of sites which will give us the full range of . . . of . . ."

"Subsistence–settlement activities."

"Right. And when we excavate, we should sample the prehistoric village in ways which will increase our chances of seeing the *range* of activities carried out in it. Our units of collection should be houses and features within 'natural' or 'cultural' strata. Within those, we should look for activity areas that reflect the different roles of the individuals within a household, and the different activities of different households."

"Something like that," I agreed.

"Well," said the G.S. tolerantly, "it seems to me that what you are saying is no more, and no less, than what we have been saying for years. Of course, the rhetoric is different nowadays, but if you'll look at my 1938 article in *American Antiquity*, you'll see that, admittedly in different words, I was arguing for exactly the procedure you've just outlined."

I looked at my peas and carrots.

"What you've rediscovered, in your own very humble way," he went on, "is that we must have a spatially bounded universe with a series of populations in it, and that we must draw samples from those populations in such a way as to recover data on the nature and sources of variation. And that's no more, and no less, than what I like to call The Basic Paradigm of Good Archeology."

"How would you like some peas and carrots shoved up your nose?" I inquired pleasantly.

The Goals of This Book

Obviously, no archeologist in a real field situation starts out by working on features and activity areas. First he must survey and locate the sites, then select those to be excavated. Only after he has begun excavation will he start recovering the smallest "building blocks of society." But this book is not a field-methods manual, and it will therefore not adhere to the exact sequence of events followed by an archeologist in the field. Instead, it will consider the units of the early Mesoamerican village in the order given in the preceding pages, from smallest to largest. Its ultimate goals are two. The first is to explore some analytical procedures for sampling and studying Formative cultures on the activity area, house, *barrio*, village, region, and interregional levels. In the course of this exploration, the various contributing authors will try out each of these procedures on actual data from Formative Mesoamerica. This will make possible our second goal: to present a model of Early Formative society which is based on substantive data, and which can hopefully be tested and refined in the future on the basis of still better data.

At the outset, the reader should be warned about two shortcomings of the book. First, the analytical procedures we have used here in no sense constitute the only ones that could have been used; there are many acceptable alternative forms of analysis. Second, in many cases, we could not test our procedures adequately, because the primary data on Formative Mesoamerica were so incomplete. Often, the substantive data were either not collected or at least not published in ways that allowed us to analyze them as we wanted to. In these cases, we have indicated how the data might have been collected or presented in order to increase our chances for success.

Because of the unevenness of the primary literature, we have been unable to cover all of Mesoamerica. Our substantive examples are drawn mainly from the highland valleys of Mexico, Puebla, Tehuacán, and Oaxaca; the lowland Grijalva depression; and the coastal plains of southern Veracruz/Tabasco and Chiapas/western Guatemala. We should perhaps apologize in advance for drawing so heavily on the unpublished raw data of the University of Michigan's Oaxaca project, but, in the case of some topics, it was the only region from which we had sufficiently detailed information at our disposal. We have tried to balance this by using other areas as heavily as the available published data permit.

The idea for this book first came to the surface during a seminar at the University of Michigan in the late 1960s. There Richard I. Ford, 12 skeptical graduate students, and I tried with limited success to apply locational analysis (cf. Haggett 1965) to a variety of archeological problems. The idea grew during our 1969 field season in the Valley of Oaxaca, as I tried to figure out how to cope with 40 acres of Early Formative houses at the village of San José Mogote, and Marc Winter tried to figure out how to sample an entire hamlet near Santa María Atzompa. Finally, things came to a head in 1970 during a seminar on problems in Mesoamerican prehistory at Ann Arbor. There I suddenly realized that those of us interested in sampling Formative Mesoamerica on all levels had reached the critical mass necessary to begin. I drew up a table of contents and we allocated the work, which continued during a settlement pattern seminar organized in 1971 by Ford. In the course of writing the volume, we have tried wherever possible to restrict ourselves to the Early and Middle stages of the Formative (1500–500 B.C.), bringing

TABLE 1.1 Relative Chronology for Formative Mesoamerica (showing those regions, sites, and phases mentioned in the text)

	Valley of Mexico	Valley of Puebla	Valley of Tehuacán	Valley of Oaxaca	Southern Veracruz	Tabasco	Central Chiapas	Pacific Coast of Guatemala	Guatemala Highlands
100 (A.D.)			Palo Blanco	Monte Albán II			VI(Horcones)		Miraflores
A.D./B.C.									
100	Late Ticomán	Acatepec ← ← ←				Castañeda		Crucero	
200		→ → →					V(Guanacaste)		
300	Early Ticomán			Monte Alban I	Remplás				
400						Franco	IV(Francesa)	Conchas 2	Las Charcas
500	Late Zacatenco		Santa María	Rosario	Palangana	(La Venta III – IV)	III(Escalera)		
600	Early Zacatenco	← ← ← ←							
700	El Arbolillo	→ → → →		Guadalupe		Puente	II(Dili)	Conchas 1	
800					Nacaste	(La Venta II)		Jocotal	Arévalo
900	Bomba	Moyotzingo → → →			B San Lorenzo				
1000	Justo	→ → →		San José	A	Palacios (La Venta I)	I(Cotorra)	Cuadros	
1100									
1200	Ayotla		Ajalpan		Chicharras				
1300				Tierras Largas	Bajío	Molina		Ocós	
1400					Ojochi				
1500									
1600			Purrón	Espiridión					
1700									

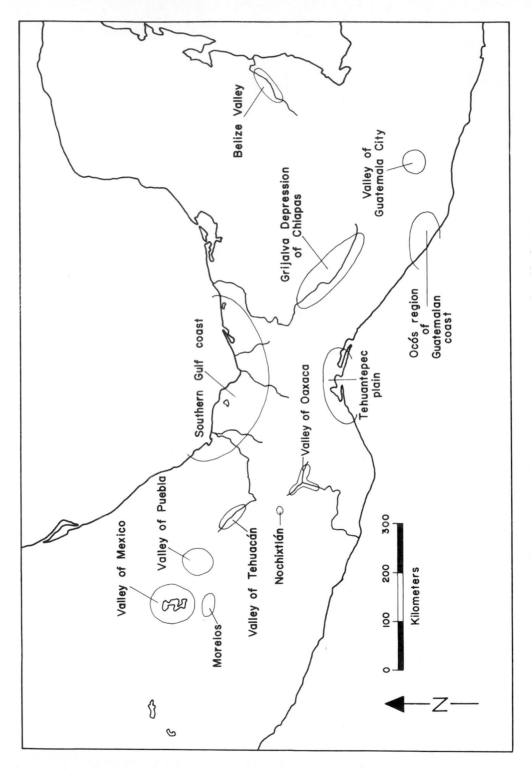

Figure 1.1 Map of Mesoamerica, showing regions mentioned in the text.

in the Late Formative (500 B.C.–A.D. 100) only where it was necessary to show trends through time. Ideally, we would like to see the whole battery of techniques applied to a single region at a single time period.

Two of the authors (Pires-Ferreira and Winter) have worked on the Valley of Oaxaca project since 1967, with ample time to try out the techniques they describe in this volume. Two others (Drennan and Plog) joined the project in 1970; three more (Brumfiel, Whalen, and Pyne) in 1971; and one more (Marcus) in 1972. The remaining authors were participants in one or more seminars with Ford or myself. In addition, Earle, Plog, and Winter are all veterans of the long-term project at Vernon, Arizona, directed by the late Paul S. Martin.

It is no accident that in selecting my collaborators for this book, I turned to the Pepsi generation. None of them has been in archeology long enough to become jaded, or convinced that the things we have tried to do here cannot, in fact, be done. Yet they are skeptical, too; one of the criteria for selection was the number of times each had given me the finger in class. The longer I work with them, the more convinced I become that Formative Mesoamerica cannot be left to the Mesoamericanists. It is too important, and too much fun. Indeed, so long as its excavators "can still not confidently predict even on what problem 60% of their data is going to bear," the early Mesoamerican village should be kept on the list of endangered species.

Acknowledgments

Perhaps my introduction has given outsiders reason to suspect that virtually no good archeological research has been done on the Mesoamerican Formative. Thank heaven, things aren't really that bad, or we would have had no data with which to construct our model at all. Not only are there some examples of very exciting work in the literature but, in addition, our colleagues in many parts of Mesoamerica have generously provided us with unpublished data that filled in gaps or explained seemingly anomalous phenomena. There is no way we can thank them all; we can barely mention the hard core. For the Valley of Mexico, we have relied heavily on Jeffrey R. Parsons, Richard Blanton, William T. Sanders, José Luis Lorenzo, Paul Tolstoy, and Christine Niederberger; for the State of Puebla, Richard S. MacNeish, Melvin L. Fowler, Jörg Aufdermauer, and Heinz Walter; for Morelos, David Grove; for the Grijalva and the Chiapas Coast, Gareth W. Lowe, Thomas A. Lee, and Carlos Navarrete; and for the Gulf Coast, Michael D. Coe, Richard A. Diehl, and Edward B. Sisson. Each of these archeologists gets a gold star and our apologies for the way we may have manhandled his data on the Formative.

I also would like to thank Jean Baardsen for typing the manuscript, Werner Riedl for his fine line drawings, and John Rick and George Stuber for printing the photographs. Further thanks go to Robert Whallon, Henry Wright, and Richard Ford for their constructive criticism of an earlier draft. Indeed, very special thanks go to Whallon, our resident wizard of the computer, for checking over all the mathematics in the entire volume and providing several important statistical definitions.

References

Adams, R.E.W.
    1969   Maya archaeology 1958–1968, a review. *Latin American Research Review* IV: 3–45.
Binford, L.R.
    1964   A consideration of archaeological research design. *American Antiquity* 29: 425–441.
Haggett, P.
    1965   *Locational analysis in human geography*. London: Edward Arnold.
Sanders, W.T.
    1956   The central Mexican symbiotic region: A study in prehistoric settlement patterns. In *Prehistoric settlement patterns in the New World*, edited by G.R. Willey. *Viking Fund Publications in Anthropology* No. 23. New York: Wenner–Gren. Pp. 115–127.
Struever, S.
    1969   Archeology and the study of cultural process: Some comments on data requirements and research strategy. Revised version of paper presented at symposium, "Cultural Process and the Evolution of Civilization," held at the School of American Research, Santa Fe, N.M. (Joseph R. Caldwell, Chairman). Mimeograph.

Chapter 2

ANALYSIS ON THE HOUSEHOLD LEVEL

Introduction

Very little is known about the households of Mesoamerica's earliest villagers. This fact can be demonstrated in absolute terms, by a simple search through the literature: There is not a single published plan of a complete Early Formative house. It can also be established in comparative terms, by flipping through the North American archeological literature and noting how much more is known about house plans from the Woodland period of the Midwest or the Pueblo period of the Southwest. Why should we know so much less about the people who *originated* village life on the North American continent?

Perhaps I can best illustrate the point with another parable about my friend, the Real Mesoamerican Archeologist, and his Skeptical Graduate Student. The parable is based on a true incident, although all the names have been changed to protect the guilty.

The incident took place during one of my visits, late in R.M.A.'s first field season at Mound A in the Río San Jacinto drainage. R.M.A. and S.G.S. were having an argument—not a new one, but the same one they had been having since the first day of the season. As usual, R.M.A. had told S.G.S. he didn't need his advice, because he'd been excavating mounds "back when S.G.S. was watching Howdy Doody." And as usual, S.G.S. had replied that R.M.A.'s excavation technique actually *reminded* him of watching Howdy Doody. In fact, S.G.S. went on, R.M.A.'s parental condescension "made him think of Buffalo Bob." To which the Real Mesoamerican Archeologist replied that S.G.S.' theories made *him* think of buffalo *chips*.

It was a classic confrontation. R.M.A. taught at an Ivy League university which did not believe in allowing its students to work as field assistants for other archeologists, on the grounds that it "destroyed their individual initiative." On the other hand, neither did he believe in taking his own students to the field, because "you can't fire your own students." Hence, most of his own students made it to their Ph.D. qualifying exams with their individual initiative intact. Their first field experience was when they were sent off to Mexico to excavate a site for their doctoral dissertation. "Of course," said R.M.A., "they'll probably screw up a little at first, but the area's so rich they're bound to come up with something." In years to come, this philosophy was destined to put him on the Mexican government's list of Ten Most Wanted Men.

That's where S.G.S. came in. He was someone else's graduate student, from a Midwestern university, and hence eminently fireable. All his previous field training had been on Woodland sites, where he had spent most of his time on his knees scraping carefully with a trowel for the ephemeral remains of pole-and-thatch structures. Seen through such Woodland eyes, R.M.A.'s field technique struck S.G.S. as akin to digging the foundations for a highway overpass. On the other hand, the Real Mesoamerican Archeologist had an appreciation for the magnitude of earth that would have to be moved at San Jacinto, and he was getting impatient at S.G.S.' insistence that every rodent burrow be pedestaled for cross-sectioning.

"We'll never find any architecture in this mound," said the Skeptical G.S., "until we stop digging by artificial 20-cm levels."

"We found a hearth, didn't we?" said R.M.A.

"Sure. Right in the profile. A meter from the surface and 4m above sterile soil. It's just hanging up there in the air, like the Goodyear blimp."

"What did you expect? Did you think we'd find an old Indian curled up beside it, trying to keep warm?"

"We could at least have tried to find an associated floor."

"All right," said R.M.A.—tired now, looking at his watch, seeing that it was nearly 4:00 and feeling worn-out and thirsty—"let's compromise.

Finish the trench my way, and let me get started on the pottery analysis. While I do that, you go back to the profile and dig any way you want—get the hearth, the floor, the whole house, the upstairs bedroom, anything."

And so, while I had a beer and R.M.A. began his pottery analysis, S.G.S. cut the profile of the trench back half a meter and reexcavated. He did indeed find the house floor associated with the hearth, a 20-cm level of hard-packed earth capped with clay. Above this was another 20-cm level, this time of collapsed wall debris including masses of burned daub with impressions of wattle. Below the floor extended a series of very nice postmolds, at least 15 cm deep and tapered. The Skeptical Graduate Student even managed to correlate these architectural features with R.M.A.'s arbitrary levels, so that R.M.A. could date them with his ceramics.

R.M.A. wrote the final report. It's on the shelf of every Mesoamericanist's library. But turn to Pages 614 and 615 if you want to discover an amazing fact, known only to a handful of archeologists.

R.M.A. analyzed his pottery in great detail, by arbitrary level, using it as the basis for a highly detailed chronology. The chronology is a fine one, with a series of six phases labeled A through F. In his conclusions, R.M.A. states that houses of Phase C (900–800 B.C.) were "characterized by lines of slender posts." Houses of Phase D (800–700 B.C.) had stamped clay floors, but the post pattern was unknown. Houses of Phase E (700–600 B.C.) "were of wattle-and-daub construction, probably similar to those described for Phases C and D." None of this seems particularly remarkable until you notice that Phase D was defined on the basis of ceramics from a depth of 120–140 cm, the level at which S.G.S. found the house floor. The level above (100–120 cm), containing the burnt daub, falls in ceramic Phase E; the postmolds, at a depth of 140–160 cm, belonged to ceramic Phase C. Thus, the reader is presented with something truly remarkable: a wattle-and-daub house that lasted through three periods, and whose postmolds were 300 years older than its roof.

Mesoamerica does this to us. Its bewildering richness brings on a kind of archeological amnesia. Take the case of George Vaillant, who arrived in the Valley of Mexico in the late 1920s after working at Pecos pueblo with the masterful A.V. Kidder. Vaillant dug his way through Zacatenco, Ticomán, and El Arbolillo without recovering a single house. In his book *Aztecs of Mexico* (1941), he referred occasionally to all three sites as "middens." Perhaps, in some strange way, Vaillant regarded Zacatenco as equivalent to the stratified refuse heaps that occurred *outside* the rooms at Pecos. Vaillant noted burnt chunks of cane-impressed daub in this refuse, but whatever he had learned from working with architecture at Pecos evidently faded from his mind as Zacatenco began to rain figurines.

One archeologist who did not suffer such amnesia was a young student of Fay-Cooper Cole's, trained in Midwestern archeology on the Kincaid Project, who arrived at Pánuco, Veracruz, in 1948. There, in deposits of the Middle Formative Chila phase, Richard S. MacNeish scraped down to expose a curving line of four postmolds crossing his trench. These were among the earliest traces of Formative architecture then known, and their curving pattern was confirmed by MacNeish's later discovery of a clay house model from the Middle Formative Aguilar phase. This miniature house not only had the rounded corners implied by the curving postmold line, but also gave many other details of the Middle Formative houses of the Pánuco River area:

> The floor plan of the house is apsidal with a door in one of the longer sides. The walls of the house are vertical, smoothed, and painted white. At the apex of the roof there is depicted a long pole, which at either end fits into forked poles (evidently roof supports or pillars coming

from within the house). Brushing or scratching on the surface of the roof radiates out from this exterior ridge pole and evidently is meant to depict thatch or grass. This roof overhangs the walls. [MacNeish 1954: 601]

In the years since 1948, more traces of early Mesoamerican houses have turned up, but we still have no idea of either the range of dwellings within a region or the range of differences between regions. It stands to reason that there should have been differences between houses adapted to the arid highlands and those adapted to the humid lowlands, yet, at the moment, it is easier to list their similarities than their differences. From cool, dry Tehuacán all the way to the hot, wet Guatemalan coast, one can find houses with upright wooden posts, stamped clay floors, and walls of finger-sized canes that were lashed together, daubed with mud, and surfaced with a thin layer of whitewash or limey clay.

Nor do we have any evidence on the origins of the "typical" Early Formative house just described. No one has yet been able to trace it back to an earlier, preceramic area. The closest thing to a "house" so far recovered from late preceramic times is an apparently oval structure from site Ts-381 in the Tehuacán Valley (MacNeish n.d.). The site, in a tributary canyon some 2 km west of the village of Chilac, belongs to the Abejas phase and dates to ca. 3000 B.C. There MacNeish recovered part of an oval shelter 3.9 m by 5.3 m in extent, with its base excavated 60 cm into sterile clay. The flat "floor area" within the excavated base was only 6 sq m in extent—about one-fourth the size of the smallest Early Formative houses for which we have any evidence (see pp. 16–23). On the basis of the postmold pattern, MacNeish (personal communication) reconstructs the shelter as having a central ridge pole supported by two uprights only 15 cm in diameter, and accompanied by "leaners" coming in at an angle from the sides of the shelter. No evidence of daub or plastered mud was found, and a dozen more test excavations at the site failed to produce another shelter. In other words, as late as 3000 B.C., we still have no evidence for the 24–35 sq m, rectangular, wattle-and-daub house with four corner posts which was so abundant in Mesoamerica by 1000 B.C.

In this chapter, Marc Winter and I discuss analysis on the *household level* of the early Mesoamerican village. Our discussion will proceed through four units of analysis: (*1*) the house itself; (*2*) the "household cluster," a term coined by Winter for the house plus its associated burials, storage features, activity areas, and so on; (*3*) the individual activity areas and features themselves; and (*4*) possible "male" and "female" work areas, composed of groups of associated features, artifacts, and activity areas.

The Early Mesoamerican House

KENT V. FLANNERY

Between 1350 and 850 B.C., the one-room, thatch-roofed, wattle-and-daub house became the most common residential structure in Mesoamerica's early villages. In addition to having served as a shelter for its occupants, such a house can serve the archeologist as a unit for analysis if he manages to isolate it from its surrounding debris, intrusive features, and the like. The variation between houses within a village can be one of our best sources of information about the variation between families—variation in subsistence, division of labor, craft activity, social status, and so on.

This section is intended as a brief sampling of the data on early houses in Mesoamerica, together with some of the ways they can be handled analytically. By attempting to restrict myself to the Early Formative (1500–850 B.C.), I hope to avoid the much greater complexity of house types that occurs from Middle Formative times on. In some regions, because of the limited available data, I have no choice but to draw on a few Middle Formative examples.

The Valley of Oaxaca

I will begin my discussion with the Valley of Oaxaca, since that is the area I know best. From Oaxaca, we have recovered the remains of perhaps 20 Early Formative dwellings in various stages of preservation (Figures 2.1–2.4). Our sample from the Middle Formative, only partially analyzed at this writing, is slightly smaller (Flannery *et al.* 1970).

Apparently, the first step in construction of an Early Formative house was the excavation of the floor area. Where houses were built on a level surface, this excavation was usually not more than 10 cm deep. Where houses were built on a slope, the uphill side was excavated as deeply as necessary (sometimes as much as 40 cm) in order to level the floor. The Early Formative villagers thought nothing of excavating that far even into bedrock when it was relatively soft, and then digging the postholes even deeper. Usually (but not always) the floor was dampened and stamped hard, like the "puddled adobe" technique of the American Southwest. And usually (but not always) this layer of stamped clay was given a light surface of clean and relatively fine sand. In most cases, it seems likely that this was stream-bed or river-bed sand, often including tiny rounded particles of water-worn gravel. Probably the sand kept house floors from getting muddy in the rainy season.

Such floors are easiest to recognize in profile:

Figure 2.1 House 1 in Area A at Tierras Largas, Oaxaca, before excavation. The floor area appears as a rectangle of dark organic debris in the center of the photograph.

Figure 2.3 South half of House 13 at San José Mogote, Oaxaca, showing pattern of multiple small posts, and doorway area framed by stones (lower right). [Excavation: J. Marcus]

Figure 2.2 Debris left *in situ* on floor of House 1 in Area A at Tierras Largas, being uncovered during the course of excavation.

A   B   C

Figure 2.4 Fragments of burnt daub from Early Formative houses in Oaxaca. (A), plastered corner fragment; (B) cross-section of fragment showing impressions of canes lashed together in bundles; (C) fragment showing impressions from rope tied around upright post.

They appear as a 1–2-cm layer of very compact clay, covered by anywhere from 2 to 10 mm of sand. Frequently the sand has in it patches of ash from cooking fires, or countless tiny resharpening or retouch flakes from flint tools made or repaired in the house. Often, the sand layer is easy to separate from the overlying earth and debris with the blade of a trowel. When one of our archeologists came down on such a sand layer from above, he was usually able to follow it to the edge of the house, where the sand gave out and the underlying stamped clay curved upward slightly, due to the excavation of the floor area by the Formative

house builders. Once having discovered the edge of the house, our archeologists searched for a corner; for, once a corner has been located, one can reasonably estimate the area that must be opened up to expose the entire house.

Early Formative villagers in Oaxaca experimented with a number of different arrangements for the upright posts that supported the roof. We have detected a number of possible trends through time. In the period we call the Tierras Largas phase (1400–1150 B.C.), there was a tendency to use small posts (10–15 cm in diameter) and more of them (up to an estimated 20–25 posts per house in some cases). This might be because these early houses developed out of still-earlier shelters (like MacNeish's structure at Ts-381) which used multiple small "leaners." At any rate, during the subsequent San José phase (1150–850 B.C.) there was a trend toward the use of fewer posts and larger ones (20–25 cm in diameter). The four corner posts in a San José phase house were normally the largest, and where additional posts were added for stability or to frame a doorway, they were usually smaller (15 cm or less).

It is not always possible to tell where the posts in a poorly preserved house were set; probably they were often "robbed" from an abandoned house to use elsewhere. Of course, when the postholes are in bedrock, they are easy to recover; when set in mottled, multicolored midden, they can be tremendously elusive and ambiguous. We had our best luck when, after removing the layer of sand, we were able to scrape the clay floor and the surrounding surface with trowels, and spray both with a fine film of water from a crop sprayer (Figure 2.3). Often this is just enough to highlight the color differences between the floor and the postmolds (which may actually occur outside the "floor area"). But gopher burrows may also look like small postmolds, so each potential mold had to be cut in profile.

Sometimes the Early Formative builders outlined the house with a wall foundation of cobbles or small boulders. Sometimes they used this only along one wall, and sometimes they merely framed a corner or a posthole with stones. In a few cases, posts evidently became loose and had to be wedged with a stone, which was then left in the posthole to be discovered by the archeologist. Best of all, the post sometimes burned, learing its carbonized base in the ground. By the San José phase, 100% of the identifiable burnt posts we recovered were of pine. Pine grows straight, and has enough resin to repel termites; this probably made it the preferred construction material in spite of the fact that, in some cases, it could be obtained only by a 20-km round trip up the mountains.

The houses just described had a rectangular ground plan, varying from 3 X 5 m to 4 X 6 m or (rarely) even 5 X 7 m in size. How the roof was constructed is unknown. A large burned daub fragment from one San José phase house (Figure 2.4) provided us with a series of pole and rope impressions; the latter suggest that horizontal roof joists were lashed to upright corner posts with rope just under a centimeter thick. Presumably the roof was thatched with grass; burned samples of reed canary grass (*Phalaris* sp.) indicate that this may have been one material used.

The walls of Early Formative houses in Oaxaca were built of finger-sized reeds or canes lashed together in bundles. Once again, *Phalaris* seems to have been used, although *Phragmites* is also a possibility for some of the larger canes. Over these "wattle" walls went a layer of clay "daub" which was smoothed and sometimes even burnished. Some burned fragments show that house corners were square. Although some builders were content to leave the clay surface smoothed or lightly burnished, many others added a layer of limey whitewash, apparently over the entire house. This whitewash, which has sufficient lime in it to react to hydrochloric acid, often has the thickness and gloss of a pottery slip; its color varies from true white to ivory, yellowish, or pinkish white. We have not yet determined whether the difference between plain and whitewashed houses is functional (for example, between residences and cook shacks) or social (that is, between higher- or lower-status families).

Early Formative houses had a door (roughly 1 m wide) on one of the long sides. Unless this door is framed by stones, as for example in House 13 in Area A at San José Mogote (Figure 2.3), it can be difficult to find. Often, there may be no more to indicate its presence than a sunken area of very hard-packed earth, the "well-worn path" between the house and its dooryard.

During the lifetime of an Early Formative house, the occupants might make a number of modifications. Posts might be moved or replaced as they deteriorated or became loose; others might be reinforced by "leaners." Often, because of the addition of ramadas or lean-to's, the ground surface around the house became as hard-packed as the floor. These gradual modifications over time complicate the pattern of archeological evidence in the ground, and can result in house plans that are genuinely enigmatic. House 4 at the site of Tomaltepec (Figure 2.5) can serve as an example of a residence with two superimposed floors, each virtually indistinguishable from hard-packed areas outside the house, and a series of postmolds that is undoubtedly far in excess of what the house would have had at any one time. In the words of the excavator, Michael Whalen:·

> House 4, an early San José phase wattle-and-daub structure reminiscent of the preceding Tierras Largas phase house construction style, is represented by a roughly rectangular arrangement of postholes associated with two superimposed packed earth floors. Although lacking the sand layers found in some contemporary structures in the region, the floors were both well preserved and well defined, consisting in each case of a thin (3 cm.), essentially flat layer of hard-packed, slightly clayey earth. The lowest of the floors rested directly on virgin soil. These surfaces, however, were not limited to the area enclosed by the wall posts. Rather, the exterior surfaces—which were virtually identical to the interior ones—clearly extend for more than a meter on the north, east, and west sides of the house, at which points they had been disturbed by later activity. On the south side, the surface extends for at least three meters beyond the wall posts. Later intrusive features precluded accurate determination of the entire exterior (unroofed) surfaced area associated with the house, but it was *at least* 30–35 square meters (excluding the area of the house itself). Additional postholes, suggesting lean-to's or other small associated structures, occur both inside and outside of the house, as the accompanying plan indicates.
>
> The long axis of the house is oriented roughly east–west (79°-259°), with what may be a doorway and associated windscreen near the center of the south wall. The dimensions of the house are approximately 4.7 meters by 2.2 meters, thus enclosing some 10.3 square meters. A preliminary estimate of unroofed to

roofed surfaced area of this Early Formative house, then, is at least 3:1.

> Chipped stone, shell fragments, bone, burned daub, charcoal, and ceramics were recovered from the several floor surfaces, both inside and outside of the house. Two associated bell-shaped storage pits and one large cylindrical pit were also recovered on the east side of the house [Whalen 1974:2]

Having thus described a sample of Early Formative houses from the Valley of Oaxaca, let us now look briefly at the architectural data from a few early villages in other regions of Mesoamerica. Rather than attempting a comprehensive review, we have picked five widely spaced regions with contrasting environment. In spite of their differences, these regions provide examples of almost all the construction features mentioned here. Most common are pieces of burnt wall clay with reed or cane impressions on one or more sides; these have been called "cane impressions," "wattle-and-daub chunks," or "briquettes" (Willey *et al.* 1965:511). Second in frequency are reports of stamped-clay floors. Third in frequency are reports of isolated postmolds or partial lines of posts.

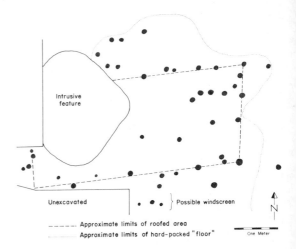

Figure 2.5 Plan of House 4 at Tomaltepec, Oaxaca, showing a complex postmold pattern which presumably results from gradual post replacement and modification during the lifetime of the house.

The Tehuacán Valley, Puebla

Villages of the Ajalpan phase (1500–850 B.C.) and the first half of the Santa María phase (up to ca. 500 B.C.) produced burnt daub fragments similar to those from Oaxaca (MacNeish 1962). To give only one example, the small village of Las Canoas (ca. 750 B.C.) yielded 160 such "briquettes." Measurable cane impressions were between 11 and 25 mm in diameter and set very close together. Considerable grass had been mixed into the clay daub. While the Las Canoas houses generally had smoothed and burnished (but unwhitewashed) walls, at least a few houses from the neighboring site of Coatepec had lime whitewash as thick as a pottery slip. One of the Coatepec daub chunks came from a nicely squared house corner with a small area cut out of it, possibly for fitting against a corner pole or roof joist (Flannery 1964:74).

The Valley of Mexico

Recently, Tolstoy and Fish (1973) have recovered a series of partial house plans from the Early Formative village of Coapexco, located at 2600 m on the lower slopes of Mt. Ixtaccihuatl in the Valley of Mexico. Of all these houses, the largest and most elaborate was Structure 4 (Figure 2.6). Depending on certain assumptions concerning the ratio of roofed area to unroofed courtyard, Structure 4 can be estimated between 4 by 4 m and 6 by 7 m.

> The floor, though badly destroyed in parts, is an extremely well-defined, hard layer of packed mud with ground-in fragments of pumice, black volcanic sand, gravel and sherds. Some of these inclusions must have been purposefully added and the resulting material, several cm thick in places, often give the appearance of a deliberately created pavement. In N-S cross-section, the central section of this surface is sunk below contemporary ground, bending upward on both edges. On the north

side, the pavement curls up and over the rise and tread of 30-cm-high rounded shelf or bench. On the south edge, this floor rises more gradually to a rim like that of a basin, some 15 to 20 cm above the level interior. These two rims, the northern and the southern, are essentially straight but converge toward each other on the downhill (western) side of the flat area which they define and which thus tapers westward, toward what we infer to have been the entrance. We are uncertain, however, whether this tapering (trapezoidal?) outline defines the roofed area, or whether the latter extends somewhat beyond these boundary features to the north and south, as does the pavement itself, which forms an irregular, broken edge some 50 to 100 cm south and north of this trapezoidal depressed section. In the second case, the upward curls of the paved area would define interior benches rather than the edges of the structure itself. The latter then could have had a more "normal," perhaps rectangular, outline, instead of the unusual trapezoidal or oval shape which we are compelled to postulate otherwise. [Tolstoy and Fish 1973:12–13]

All in all, the area around Structure 4 yielded parts of one house, an associated paved courtyard, postmolds from a lean-to or overhang near the house entrance, and parts of a second house (Structure 5). The houses at Coapexco sometimes had foundations of fieldstone, with or without adobe lumps. In addition, some smoothed chunks of daub, presumably from walls, were covered with red specular hematite pigment.

Elsewhere in the Valley of Mexico, early architectural data are more fragmentary. At Zacatenco, Vaillant suspected the houses were of wattle and daub, owing to "the rarity of stones . . . coupled with the amount of dirt in the rubbish" (Vaillant 1930:38). He uncovered an oval "oven" of *tepetate* slabs and wattle and daub at El Arbolillo (Vaillant 1935: 157, and Figure 6, no. XI), and it seems likely that the houses were of similar construction. By the end of the Early Formative, some buildings at the site of Zohapilco (Tlapacoya) had foundations of planoconvex adobe bricks (Christine Niederberger, personal communi-

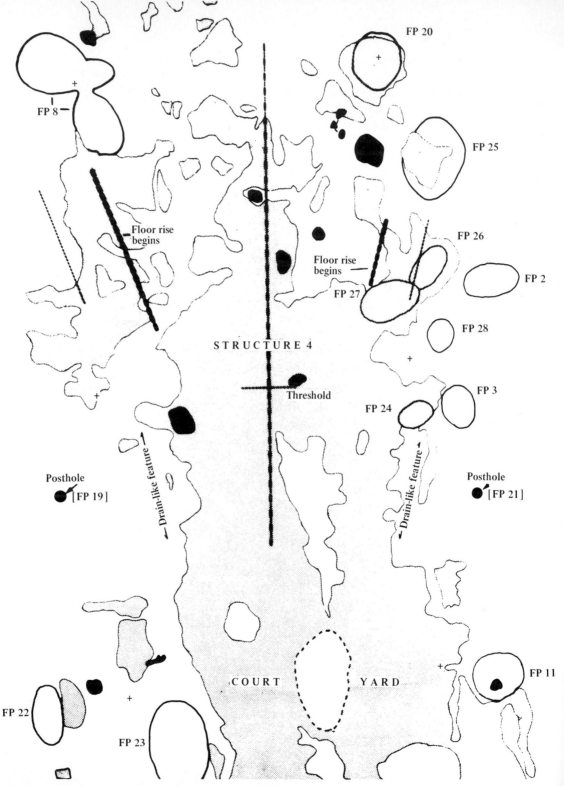

Figure 2.6 Partial plan of Structure 4 at Coapexco, Valley of Mexico, showing floor rise, postholes, drain-like features, courtyard, and associated pits. The stippled area indicates a floor-like surface of packed mud, pumice, sand, gravel, and sherds. [After Tolstoy and Fish 1973: Figure 4.]

cation); but some of these *might* be from public buildings rather than ordinary residences.

The Central Depression of Chiapas

At Chiapa de Corzo during the Early and Middle Formative, houses were of wattle and daub with "well-finished adobe surfaces" (Lowe 1959:11, 73); by this, we assume Lowe refers to plastered daub rather than adobe bricks. By 500 B.C., at least some of these houses were provided with field-stone foundations. Lowe ventures that such houses "were probably square or rectangular in outline," though he does not state specifically whether fragments from right-angle corners were found.

The Guatemalan Pacific Coast

Middle Formative (Conchas phase) houses at La Victoria (Coe 1961:116) were archeologically represented by daub chunks with impressions of "finger-sized" canes lashed so tightly together that they touched. The walls were plastered with clay and whitewashed, but in contrast to the Puebla–Oaxaca region, the corner fragments show that house corners were rounded.

Some additional architectural evidence came from Early Formative (Cuadros phase) levels at nearby Salinas La Blanca, where three postmolds from the same house were found at one point in excavation Cut 2. Unfortunately, since Cut 2 was a classic example of "telephone booth" excavation (see Chapter 1), we know little about the house except that it had a reddish to grayish-brown clay floor with a thick layer of charcoal on the surface. Two of the postmolds were 70 cm apart in the south part of the excavation, while the third lay almost 3 m away to the northwest. Post diameters were 10–15 cm, tapering to a pointed base. The floor was slightly basin-shaped in cross-section, but it had been dug into an area already raised high above the humid surrounding plain by earlier accumulations of house clay, midden debris, and mollusk shells (Coe and Flannery 1967:Figure 6).

Pánuco, Veracruz

The Middle Formative clay house model discovered by MacNeish at Pánuco has already been described (p. 15). It is interesting that Pánuco houses, like those from the Guatemalan coast, had rounded rather than square corners. The one set of four postmolds found by MacNeish were 15–18 cm in diameter and spaced roughly 30 cm apart. In other words, the house was probably one with a large number of small posts rather than a small number of large ones.

Summary

It is difficult to summarize a subject about which so little is known. Raoul Naroll (1962) has estimated that, in villages of "Neolithic" type, an average of about 10 sq m of roofed area per person are present. If we accept this average for Meso-america, where early houses ran from 15–35 sq m in extent, I would have to conclude that these dwellings were intended for nuclear families.

Wattle-and-daub construction seems to have been pan-Mesoamerican, but there was considerable variety in post pattern. Houses also varied as to whether they were whitewashed or simply mud-plastered. Most houses in the Mexican highlands had square corners, while several lowland areas—from Pánuco to the Guatemalan Pacific Coast—had houses with round corners. In both cases, the door seems to have been on one of the long sides.

I have omitted any discussion of features or activity areas associated with houses. That is because there is a larger unit—the "household cluster," to be defined by Marcus Winter later—which seems to be a more appropriate context in which to discuss both features and activity areas.

The Beginnings of Adobe Architecture

I have also omitted any discussion of adobe brick construction. So far as I can tell, on the basis

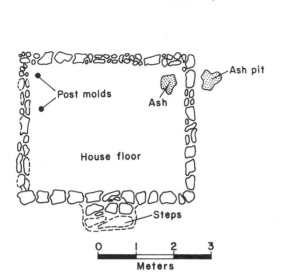

Figure 2.7 Plan of Middle Formative adobe house from the site of Cuanalán, Valley of Mexico. [Redrawn from Sanders 1965: Figure 13a.]

of present evidence, the first use of adobe brick probably occurred in connection with public buildings during the second half of the Early Formative. In some regions, adobe lumps or bricks were used instead of field stones to provide the foundations for wattle-and-daub houses late in the Early Formative. However, not until Middle Formative times did the use of adobe brick for residences become widespread; and even then, adobe residences coexisted with wattle-and-daub houses, perhaps suggesting that social status might be reflected in the choice of building materials.

For example, in his excavations at Moyotzingo in the Valley of Puebla, Aufdermauer (1970:15) has evidence for wattle-and-daub huts as far back as 1330 B.C., but no evidence for "solid adobe architecture" before 600 B.C. In Oaxaca, where wattle-and-daub houses appeared between 1400 and 1300 B.C., the first planoconvex ("bun-shaped") adobes were used in public buildings between 900 and 800 B.C. (Flannery *et al.* 1970:30).

Rectangular adobes did not appear until 500–400 B.C., somewhat too late to be relevant to our discussion of Mesoamerica's earliest villages.

At Moyotzingo, once adobe architecture appeared, there was a gradual displacement of wattle-and-daub houses from the upper slopes of the site where they had once been common. Soon only the lower slopes had wattle-and-daub residences, while the higher areas featured the solid adobe architecture that Aufdermauer (1970:15) interprets as elite residences.

Eventually, even non-elite residences would come to be of adobe. A very nice example of this was recovered by William T. Sanders' project at the Middle Formative village of Cuanalán in the Valley of Mexico (see Figure 2.7). According to Sanders:

> One complete house and part of another were excavated. Both houses had hard-packed earth floors and walls constructed of irregular lumps of adobe laid in earth mortar and covered by mud plaster. The completely excavated house consisted of a single room four meters square with an earth ramp or stairway entrance on the southern side and a lean-to kitchen on the northern side. Hillside communities of this period have heavy rock debris; the fragments are similar to those used in Classic and post-Classic walls. This would suggest a pattern in Cuanalán times similar to the post-Classic and modern and related to the distribution of raw materials, with adobe houses in the plainside communities and stone houses in piedmont and hilly terrain. Similar rock debris occurs on all Formative sites in hilly areas. [Sanders 1965:94]

Cuanalán (500–400 B.C.) is really too late to qualify as an "early village," but this house shows striking similarities in size (16 sq m) and shape to earlier one-room houses of wattle-and-daub construction. The meter-wide door and the localized ash deposits both inside and outside are all familiar. In addition, some houses at Tierras Largas had isolated postmolds nearby which may have been from some kind of lean-to.

The Archeological Household Cluster in the Valley of Oaxaca

MARCUS C. WINTER

The concept of the "household cluster" has proved useful for organizing and comparing Formative period data from the Valley of Oaxaca. Excavations at the site of Tierras Largas (Winter 1970, 1972) showed that three kinds of facilities—*houses, bell-shaped storage pits,* and *graves*—consistently occurred in spatial concentrations separated by open areas. These three main facilities were sometimes accompanied by *other types of pits, ovens,* or *midden deposits*. In the Valley of Oaxaca, pits, burials, and other features generally occur outside but within a few meters of the house structures. I will here consider these concentrations of features to be material manifestations of prehistoric households. A typical household cluster might consist of one house, two to six large storage pits, one to three graves, and various additional features, separated from the nearest contemporary cluster by an open area of 20–40 m (see Figure 2.8).

The distinction between "household cluster" and "household" should be stressed. A household cluster consists of archeological remains, while a household consists of a group of people who interact and perform certain activities. Through analysis of the archeological data, we can reconstruct the composition of prehistoric households, compare the activities carried out by household members, and study the relations between different households.

It was not always possible in the Tierras Largas excavations to find *all* the elements just listed in any one household cluster. For example, one excavated area, *Area G*, yielded several bell-shaped pits and evidence of a house (represented by some postholes and burned daub), yet no burials or ovens. In that particular case, however, only

28 sq m of contiguous area were excavated. I estimate that cultural features comprising a single Early or Middle Formative household cluster at Tierras Largas may be scattered over an area of about 300 sq m, and thus predict that an expanded excavation of Area G would yield additional household cluster evidence.

The household cluster concept is useful because it provides a context in which pits, burials, house remains, and other features can be understood not simply as isolated cultural features, but as manifestations of a specific segment of society. Much work needs to be done to clarify the nature of Formative households, and to test the validity of the household cluster concept at different sites and over several regions. At this point, however, it seems to be a productive means of organizing data for studying a unit of Formative society on an analytic level between that of the house or the activity area and that of the community.

Features within Household Clusters

The House

Flannery (this chapter) has already mentioned the range of variation in Early Formative houses. At Tierras Largas, these were usually 18–24 sq m in extent and rectangular, with square corners. There is considerable variation in the amount and condition of debris found on house floors. Some house floor areas excavated at Tierras Largas appeared to have been swept clean at the time of abandonment, or perhaps later.

In contrast, two houses with floors sunk 30–50 cm into soft bedrock yielded abundant artifacts and refuse. One of these, *House 2* (ca. 900 B.C.)

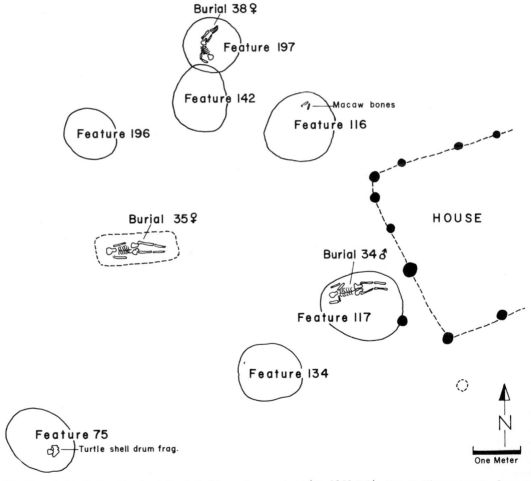

Figure 2.8 Household Cluster No. 1 of the Late Tierras Largas phase (ca. 1250 B.C.), Area B, Tierras Largas, Oaxaca, showing partial posthole pattern of house; bell-shaped pits; and human burials.

contained what appeared to be an accumulation of refuse and debris including sherds, utilized chert and obsidian flakes, fragments of bone needles, and some pieces of animal bone. This debris may represent a gradual accumulation of artifacts that were discarded, stamped into the floor, and covered over when sand was brought in for filling in small depressions, or for resurfacing the floor. If this is true, then one can argue that the artifacts and refuse on the floor indicate the following activities as having been carried out in House 2:

1. Cutting and scraping tasks, represented by utilized chert and obsidian flakes.
2. Sewing or basketry production, represented by bone needles.
3. Production of cutting tools, represented by waste flakes.
4. Production or modification of hunting tools (?), represented by a single stone projectile point.
5. Cooking and food consumption, represented by animal bones and by fragments of cooking pots and fire-blackened pottery braziers.

House 1 at Tierras Largas (ca. 900 B.C.) also contained abundant artifacts and refuse, apparently having been used as a refuse dump after abandonment. More than 25 whole and reconstructable late San José phase vessels and a dozen figurines were found in the house fill, along with many more fragmentary pieces. The refuse accumulation also included utilized chert and obsidian flakes, bone tools, broken shell ornaments, carbonized seeds, and animal bones. It seems unlikely that this tremendous quantity of refuse was present when the house was occupied, and I suspect that much of it represents debris discarded around the time of abandonment. In this case, the artifacts and refuse would not necessarily represent activities carried out in the house proper, although they might represent activities carried out within the spatial bounds of the same household cluster. Some tools, resting directly on the floor sand, may still be useful guides to the activities carried on in the house (see Figures 2.15 and 2.17).

Bell-Shaped Pits

Bell-shaped pits are among the most characteristic features found within household clusters at Formative sites in the Valley of Oaxaca, and their contents have provided abundant information on domestic activities. These features have a relatively small, restricted opening below which they expand outward toward the flat or slightly rounded base. At Tierras Largas, Formative period bell-shaped pits frequently occurred in the soft, decomposed bedrock, so their form and contents could be isolated easily during excavation.

It seems likely that food storage was the major function of these pits. Many had basal diameters of 1.0 to 1.5 m and could have held a metric ton of maize—the amount used by an average rural family in the Valley of Oaxaca in the course of a year. A few exceeded 4 cu m in volume. Pollen analysis by Suzanne K. Fish showed that samples taken from bell-shaped pits at Tierras Largas contained a higher percentage of maize pollen than did samples from other contexts.

Hall, Haswell, and Oxley (1956) have shown that such subterranean pits can be used effectively for grain storage for years. When capped with a flat rock (as some Oaxaca pits evidently were) and sealed with clay, they inhibit insect growth through lack of oxygen. Probably they were used until the sides began to cave in, then replaced with a new pit. When five or six pits occur in a house cluster, it is likely that some were used in sequence rather than simultaneously.

Bell-shaped pits in household clusters were, however, used for storing more than food. Two such pits excavated at Tierras Largas contained artifacts that may have been abandoned while in storage. One contained two whole ground-stone *manos*, two *metates*, a large jar, a figurine fragment, and a carbonized piece of wood, perhaps part of an implement. Another contained deer long bones, apparently material for making bone handles and other tools. Thus, household items and implements were sometimes stored in bell-shaped pits.

Most of the bell-shaped pits excavated at Tierras

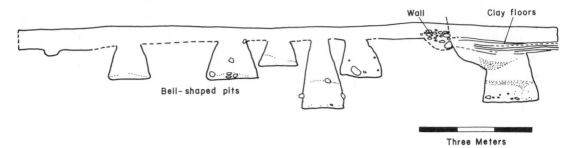

Figure 2.9 North–south cross-section through San Francisco Acatepec, Puebla, showing stone wall foundation; clay floor; and a group of bell-shaped storage pits. Ca. 260–90 B.C. [Redrawn from Walter 1970.]

Largas contained refuse rather than unbroken tools, and they appear to have been abandoned at a later stage in the cycle of use than those found with unbroken tools. Though originally used for storage, most pits were eventually used as refuse containers and/or human graves. Pits probably were abandoned under two sets of conditions. On the one hand, the natural process of water seepage caused the collapse of bedrock walls. Such pits were simply filled with refuse, and new ones constructed. On the other hand, some pits seem to have been abandoned in conjunction with the burning and leveling of a house. Several pits at Tierras Largas contained large quantities of burned daub along with other debris. This suggests the abandonment of some house sites after intentional or accidental burning of the house structure, followed by the sweeping of house debris into the pit.

Bell-shaped storage pits are common features at other Valley of Oaxaca sites like San José Mogote and San Sebastián Abasolo (Flannery *et al.* 1970), and they were extremely widespread in highland Mesoamerica, from the Valley of Mexico to Guatemala City. Even a casual search of the literature reveals that, in many other regions, they occur in such dense concentrations as to suggest groups like those we found in our household clusters. Let us look briefly at a few of these areas.

In the Valley of Puebla, both the Early Formative village of Moyotzingo (Aufdermauer 1970) and the Late Formative village of San Francisco

Acatepec (Walter 1970) had many bell-shaped pits. Those at Moyotzingo (1330–740 B.C.) contained sherds, figurine fragments, burnt daub, obsidian tools and waste flakes, animal bones, and carbonized plant remains including maize and avocado. Those at Acatepec (260–90 B.C.) contained black earth with carbonized plants and animal bones, burnt daub, sherds, and occasional grinding stones. In particular, one of Walter's profiles from Acatepec shows a stone wall, a clay floor, and a series of pits strongly suggestive of a household cluster (see Figure 2.9).

Walter also gives some interesting data to support our interpretation of these as pits for maize storage: In two cases at Acatepec, pocket gopher burrows running from sterile soil and entering a bell-shaped pit had been deliberately plugged with small stones by the Formative villagers (Walter 1970:28).

Some pits at both Moyotzingo and Acatepec had been used for burials, further suggesting their proximity to houses. At the Early Formative village of Ajalpan in the Tehuacán Valley, MacNeish (1962: Figure 6) discovered a bell-shaped pit which, in its final stages, had been used for a burial accompanied by a large hollow figurine. In addition, it seems likely that the now-famous *pozos troncocónicos* of the site of Tlatilco (Piña Chán 1958: Lám. 17–18) are further examples of this kind of feature. Farther to the south, Chiapa de Corzo in the Central Depression of Chiapas is reported to have bell-shaped pits dating to the Middle Formative Escalera phase (Borhegyi 1965a:9, Footnote).

At the Middle Formative site of Las Charcas in the Kaminaljuyú area of highland Guatemala, Borhegyi (1965a,b) reports "bottle-shaped pits" excavated 2–4 m deep through sterile surface soil into the underlying volcanic ash. Thus, the Las Charcas villagers used the volcanic ash much as the Tierras Largas farmers used the soft, decomposing gneiss bedrock beneath their village. The Las Charcas pits are said to have occurred in "concentrations," and some were sealed with stone slabs (like their counterparts at Tierras Largas and Abasolo in Oaxaca). At a late stage in their use cycle, many were filled with household debris including burnt daub with pole impressions, ashes, carbonized corncobs and fruit seeds, animal bones, cooking pots, and discarded *metates* and *manos*; some also had burials.

In short, the bell-shaped storage pit might have been a common feature of nearly every village in highland Mesoamerica between 1500 and 500 B.C. We would be willing to predict that, where concentrations of such pits occur, careful search probably will turn up a house within 10 m to one side or another.

Human Burials

Human burials are the third major element in the definition of the household cluster. The usual context is a shallow grave within 10 m or less of a house, or sometimes in a convenient bell-shaped pit that happened to be open at the time. This spatial association of burials with dwellings and pits suggests that the buried individuals were probably occupants of the nearest house. Adult individuals of both sexes (sometimes accompanied by dog burials), children, and infants have been found in the context of household clusters—although, perhaps not unexpectedly, nowhere can we be sure that we have all the members of a household. Nor do we know why some persons were buried fully extended in specially prepared graves while others were stuffed into a bell-shaped pit. Because this section is not intended as a discussion of burial

analysis, I will do no more than to stress that data on the sex and age of each burial must be provided by a physical anthropologist if we are ever to reconstruct the household that produced the household cluster.

Although household clusters as such are not defined for Vaillant's Formative sites in the Valley of Mexico, he specifically states that one burial at Ticomán (Skeleton 22) was "stuffed head down into an abandoned oven or storage cist, with mudded walls" (Vaillant 1931:317). A burial from El Arbolillo (Skeleton 148) also "was found with its upper body inserted in a sort of pit or oven" (Vaillant 1935:155). These examples sound very much like some Oaxaca burials, and suggest that, in the Valley of Mexico, it was also customary to bury the dead within the household cluster, sometimes inside an open storage pit. I have already mentioned the burials inside bell-shaped pits at Ajalpan, Moyotzingo, and Acatepec in Puebla, and from Las Charcas in Guatemala (see p. 28).

Ovens

Three main types of ovens have been found in association with household clusters. These include (*1*) hemispherical and (*2*) rectangular ovens dug below the ground surface, and (*3*) circular above-ground ovens with domed mud roofs and shallow, basin-shaped floors. Ovens range in diameter from roughly 60 cm to over 1 m. They are frequently characterized by red, burned floors and sides, and sometimes by concentrations of burned rocks, ash, or charcoal-stained sand. Specific functions of ovens remain to be determined, but it is possible that some served to roast foods such as *Agave* hearts or wild game; indeed, the roasting of *Agave* or "century plant" hearts in earth ovens is one of Mesoamerica's oldest and most persistent activities (Flannery 1968). None of the ovens we recovered appeared to be a pottery kiln, and none occurred inside houses.

Parenthetically, we might add that, between 1200 and 500 B.C., houses in Oaxaca usually did not contain hearths. This is presumably because cooking was done in large pottery braziers, which could be moved from place to place, inside or outside, as they were needed. Fragments of such braziers occur on house floors(Figure 2.15), in middens, or dumped into bell-shaped pits. Like the ovens, they suggest that a lot of cooking was done in the vicinity of the house, much of it out of doors.

In other regions of Mesoamerica, earth ovens may have been more common than they were in Oaxaca. For example, from El Arbolillo, Vaillant reported "a fire pit made of slabs of stone and tepetate, set in a square of some 20 centimeters, interior dimension," as well as several ovens (Vaillant 1935:155). He also discovered "an oval construction, 65 by 80 centimeters, made by lining an excavation with slabs of tepetate and erecting a superstructure of wattle and daub" (Vaillant 1935:157). This may have been still another type of oven.

At Coapexco in the Valley of Mexico, Tolstoy and Fish discovered cooking pits of several sizes both inside and outside an Early Formative house designated as Structure 3.

> Two interior features are contemporaneous with Structure 3: a hearth-like arrangement of rocks set in the floor of the NW portion of the structure, and, in the SE corner, a small subfloor pit (Feature Pit 7) with a modeled clay rim and a fill of black earth, ashes and rocks. The first of these features could have functioned as a support for hot food or a brazier (the absence of charcoal, ashes or other evidence of heat seems to exclude its use as a true fireplace). The second, measuring 50 X 40 cm across and 13 cm in depth, could have held burning coals. The two features, however, do not seem to add up to adequate intra-mural cooking facilities for a household. It seems likely, therefore, that major cooking took place outside, in some larger feature such as Feature Pit 10. The latter is somewhat deeper than Feature Pit 7 (ca. 50 cm), appears to be contemporary with Structure 3, and is located about 1 m south of what may have been the entrance of the latter. [Tolstoy and Fish 1973:12]

Figure 2.10 Features exposed in bedrock during excavation below Houses 16 and 17 at San José Mogote, Oaxaca. Shown are postholes, drainage canals, and large cistern. Ca 1150–1000 B.C. [Excavation: J.W. Rick]

Other Features

Three additional types of features have been found in association with household clusters:

1. Refuse middens sometimes occur. However, since trash was often used to fill low spots in courtyards, and fresh trash may have been removed from the immediate living area, such middens are not necessarily diagnostic features of household clusters.
2. Drainage ditches were found in association with houses at both San José Mogote and Tierras Largas. They probably functioned to divert rain run-off, in one case to a bedrock cistern (Figure 2.10). Drains were common features at early Mesoamerican villages, the most spectacular example being the basalt-lined system at San Lorenzo, Veracruz (Coe 1968: Figures 12–13).
3. Pits of various shapes and sizes sometimes occur with household clusters. The relatively large cylindrical pits may have served functions similar to bell-shaped pits; the function of the various smaller pits have not been determined.

Future work undoubtedly will expand the list of features found with household clusters, and provide more information on their functions. In the meantime, let us offer one example of how household cluster data might be recorded, using actual data from the site of Tierras Largas. *Household Cluster No. 1 of the Late Tierras Largas Phase*, discovered in Area B, appeared as follows (Figure 2.8):

1. *House*: Partial plan of an estimated 4-by-6-m rectangular house, with the floor slightly below ground level.

   Construction: Wattle and daub, with white, limey clay surfacing.

   Post pattern: Numerous small posts, set less than a meter apart (roughly 4 posts per 3 m).

2. *Associated features*: 8 bell-shaped pits were found to the west of the house; they had an average storage capacity of 1.5 cu m. Apart from domestic refuse, some of the significant remains found in the pits are as follows.

   Feature 75. 1 bone needle; 1 frag. turtle shell drum (*Dermatemys*).

   Feature 86. Frags. burnt daub; 13 maize kernels; 1 avocado seed.

   Feature 116. Frags. burnt daub; cut wing bones of macaw.

   Feature 117. Burial 34; corncob; more than 70 frags. burnt daub.

   Feature 134.

   Feature 142.

   Feature 196.

   Feature 197. Burial 38.

3. *Burials*: 3 were discovered to the west of the house. None had any grave goods.

   Burial 34. Adult male, over 40 years, extended supine in bell-shaped pit (Feature 117).

   Burial 35. Adult female, 20–30 years, extended supine in grave.

   Burial 38. Adult female, prone, legs slightly flexed, in bell-shaped pit (Feature 197).

4. *Other refuse* in this household cluster included 14 fragments of *metates* and *manos*, as well as bones of deer, cottontail, jackrabbit, gopher, and mud turtle.

5. *Inferences*: Members of this household engaged in the usual activities of agriculture, hunting, and food preparation. In addition, they participated in ceremonial activity to the extent of preparing macaw feathers and using a Gulf Coast turtle shell drum (see Chapter 11, this volume). Several adult household members died during occupation of the cluster. However, the large amounts of burnt daub included in Feature 117 with Burial 34 suggest that the house may have been abandoned and destroyed after the death of that middle-aged male individual.

The Early Formative Household Cluster on the Guatemalan Pacific Coast

KENT V. FLANNERY

As Winter points out (p. 25), the effectiveness of the household cluster as an analytic level needs to be tested in various regions of Mesoamerica. At the same time, because of the way early Mesoamerican villages have usually been reported, it is almost impossible for us to test the concept on other sites by means of the archeological literature. It is for this reason that we have relied so heavily—perhaps too heavily—on our own sites, when interregional comparisons are so clearly needed.

Now I would like to attempt a reconstruction of the household cluster at an early village far distant from Oaxaca, and in a completely different environment. The site is Salinas La Blanca, near Ocós on the tropical Pacific Coast of Guatemala. When the site was originally excavated in 1962, most of the analytic framework described in this chapter had not yet been formulated. Salinas La Blanca was analyzed by arbitrary stratigraphic level, by "cut," and by mound (Coe and Flannery 1967). It is so difficult to reconstruct household clusters from such data that I would hesitate to do so, had I not been present at the original excavation.

The site of Salinas La Blanca consists of two low mounds on the left bank of the Naranjo River, approximately 2 km upstream from the river's present entry into a coastal estuary. Each mound seems to have formed through the gradual accumulation of debris from household activities. The eastern mound, still unexcavated, covers less than .25 ha. The western mound, only 25.0 m distant, may once have covered more than .5 ha. Our excavation of this western mound totaled 15.0 sq m, or less than a .3% sample of the mound.

I have no way of estimating how many households would have occupied the village at one time. In 1962, two households from one extended family, represented architecturally by four thatched houses, lived on the west mound. One household of five persons occupied three houses and a courtyard, covering 400 sq m; a second household of two persons, occupying a single house, lay 50 m to the north. These figures may be compared with Winter's estimate of 300 sq m for a household cluster, and 30 m for the distance between household clusters, at Tierras Largas (see p. 228). Both sets of figures imply considerable use of open space, with households widely separated. This is understandable when one sees how that open space is used at Salinas La Blanca today: here borrow pits are dug, fishing nets are spread out to

dry, canoes are repaired, fish are cleaned, and refuse is discarded.

Now let us consider the levels at Salinas La Blanca dating to the Early Formative Cuadros phase (1000–850 B.C.). Our .3% excavation was placed near the exact center of the mound, believed a priori to be the area most likely to produce a house. At a depth of roughly 3 m, one level did yield three postmolds from a single house; all other Cuadros phase levels consisted of sherd midden, shell midden, outdoor hearths, borrow pits, and the kinds of features one might expect to find in the space between houses. So repetitive were these deposits that I now suspect they could be considered standard features of a Cuadros phase household cluster. Let me, therefore, tentatively reconstruct an "idealized" household cluster from Salinas La Blanca.

Central to the household cluster would be the house itself. The village of Salinas La Blanca was founded on the edge of a mangrove swamp. The houses were protected from flooding by the artificial raising of the area with loads of clay. By heaping alternate layers of domestic refuse, red and gray clay together, villagers produced a platform or low rise on which the house could be safely placed. The single house we found (Figure 2.11) had a basin-shaped foundation which was shallowly dug into such an artificial rise; over this went a floor of hard-packed clay. The upright posts were small (10–15 cm) and set fairly close together (70 cm apart in one case). Overall size of the house is unknown, but at least one dimension was greater than 3 m. By the time the house was abandoned, the upper surface of the floor had patches of ash and charcoal from domestic cooking activity. In places, what appeared to be casts of corncobs, beans, squash stems, and avocado pits suggested that many foodstuffs were stored in the house. At one ash-free point on this floor lay an oval lens of clay where

impressions in the clay of a twilled mat or *petate* were found ... although the original had long since deteriorated. Immediately un-

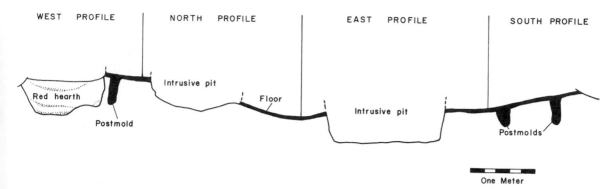

WEST PROFILE   NORTH PROFILE   EAST PROFILE   SOUTH PROFILE

Red hearth

Intrusive pit

Floor

Intrusive pit

Postmold

Postmolds

One Meter

Figure 2.11 Cross-section of Early Formative house floor, postmolds, and red hearth from Cut 2, Salinas La Blanca, Guatemala. [Redrawn from Coe and Flannery 1967: Figure 6.]

derlying these impressions were abundant casts of leaves, as well as the cast of a maize cob. [Coe and Flannery 1967:19]

It is possible that this feature was a bed consisting of a layer of leaves placed on the floor and covered with a *petate*, recalling the mats on the floor of House 2 at San José Mogote and House 1 at Tierras Largas (see below). Today, however, most villagers in the Ocós area sleep in hammocks.

The second major feature of the Salinas La Blanca house cluster would be the large, red, outdoor hearth. From the numbers of these we found, I would estimate there were at least three per house. The nearest such hearth to the house just described was only a few centimeters from one postmold; there were at least two more at distances of 3 m or so. These hearths, evidently dug in a courtyard near the house, were 1.0–1.5 m in diameter and up to 60.0 cm deep. Devoid of artifacts, the red hearths most frequently contained very small pebbles, crab claws, and shells of the mollusk *Agaronia testacea*. The marsh clam *Polymesoda radiata* also seems to have been opened in this way, by heating it over hot coals or heated pebbles.

"Borrow pits" were a third feature of the household cluster. These pits, probably dug for the purpose of obtaining clay for daubing walls or other constructions, were up to 2.0 m in diameter and 1.5 m deep. They occurred at some distance

from the house (and possibly in the open areas between household clusters as well).

A fourth feature of the Salinas La Blanca household cluster would be the sherd or sherd-and-shell midden. These tended to occur on ancient sloping surfaces, probably the nearest slope leading down from the house platform. Some middens were almost solid marsh clam shells and sherd fragments, with little or no intervening dirt. Thousands of the sherds were from neckless jars or *tecomates*, and hundreds of these had a limey crust on the interior, which suggests they were used for boiling or steaming maize in lime water (Coe and Flannery, 1967:81). One even had a calcined crab pincer still adhering to it. From their frequency, I would expect that each household cluster had one to two of these sherd-and-shell middens.

Without a larger sample of houses from the Cuadros phase, we have no way of knowing which household activities were universal, which regionally specialized, which unique, and so on. However, a few tentative comparisons and contrasts with Mexican highland household clusters can be drawn.

In both areas, low places or downhill slopes at some distance from the house were used as sherd dumps. However, the tremendous emphasis on below-ground storage reflected in the bell-shaped pits of Oaxaca, Puebla, Kaminaljuyú, and the Valley of Mexico finds no counterpart at Salinas La Blanca. Instead of the *Agave*-roasting pits of the arid highlands, some Cuadros phase households used clam-baking hearths. In both areas, house-holders soaked corn in lime water and ground it with a *metate*; but the Cuadros villagers may have stored more of it inside their houses than in outdoor facilities.

Obviously, attempting to reconstruct household clusters from most published site reports on early Mesoamerican villages would be a risky and highly speculative exercise. I suspect, however, that if in the future the Real Mesoamerican Archeologist were to present his primary data in that form, it might greatly enrich our understanding of the similarities and differences between regions, be-tween villages within regions, and between house-holds within villages.

Analyzing Household Activities

KENT V. FLANNERY and MARCUS C. WINTER

Perhaps the smallest spatial unit of archeological analysis is the *activity area*, and we have deferred it until now because we feel it makes more sense to discuss it in terms of the household cluster. Activity areas are spatially restricted areas where a specific task or set of related tasks has been carried on, and they are generally characterized by a scatter of tools, waste products, and/or raw mate-rials; a feature, or set of features, may also be present. Even where activity areas are not clearly present, Mesoamerican archeologists have generally recognized *activity sets*—"tool kits" used for the performance of a specific task.

For example, in his excavations at Ticomán in the Valley of Mexico, George Vaillant (1931:416–419) found two burials accompanied by what seem to be kits for specific craft activities, both dating to the Late Formative period (Figure 2.12). Skeleton 17, an elderly male (?), had been buried with what Vaillant described as a "leather-worker's kit." Among the tools

> were found two spongy horn grainers or chisels, much worn and with both ends shaved down to edges. These might have been used to detach the flesh from the hide. Their function

> was supplemented by three small obsidian scrapers. For perforating holes in the leather there were three large bone awls made from deer radii, the distal portions of which were smoothed to a point. Two bodkins were used presumably to push the thread or sinew through the holes perforated by the awls. A small shovel-tipped tool of bone has no ex-plicable use unless for fine work in the prepara-tion of the hide or as an implement for weaving mats and baskets. [Vaillant 1931:313]

Burial 17 also had in his lap a set of 16 pocket gopher mandibles, which may well have been part of the same tool kit; each contains one sharp, chisel-ended incisor tooth. (Vaillant considered them too "brittle" to be utilitarian, but this is an underestimate of the gopher incisor.)

Skeleton 34, also an elderly male, was buried with a kit of 15 stone and 11 bone tools for "finer work, like perhaps the tailoring of a hide." Inter-estingly, Skeleton 34 is shown as having been buried in a seated, upright position with the tools near his feet—a position that suggests to us that he was buried in a bell-shaped pit whose outlines Vail-lant did not detect. The tool kit is described as follows:

Thirteen obsidian blades and flakes provided for the cutting of the material. Two small bone awls served to perforate it and a needle equipped with an eye took care of the sewing. Six bird fibulae [sic]* were probably blanks from which other needles could be manufactured. A hollow bone cut at one end might have been a needle case, and a battered bone, much used, served no explicable use. Needles with eyes were almost always associated in graves with blades of obsidian, so that there must have been a tailoring industry, although whether it was in hide or textiles cannot be decided on the archeological evidence. [Vaillant 1931:313–314]

Three other Middle or Late Formative burials at Ticomán were accompanied by tool kits which, although not as elaborate as those with Skeletons 17 and 34, also seem to be "sets of tailoring implements." All three burials were male. One middle-aged female, Skeleton 48, also had a single bone bodkin and an obsidian blade. On the basis of Vaillant's data one could at least propose—as a hypothesis for future testing—that, at any one time, there were several households at Ticomán engaged in leather working or tailoring as a part-time specialty. Moreover, one could propose that this particular task was more often than not a male activity.

Such clues to the organization of household activity cannot be obtained from a study of the artifacts alone. They can be obtained only from contextual data, such as activity areas or activity sets. For more data on the household tools of the Formative Valley of Mexico, we can refer the reader to an important synthesis by Paul Tolstoy (1971).

Variation between Households

Although Mesoamerican archeologists have very rarely carried out definitive functional analyses of Formative tools (as, for example, microscopic

*This is a misidentification by Vaillant. The bones are not even all bird bones, and one appears to be a dog fibula. All do, however, look like good needle blanks.

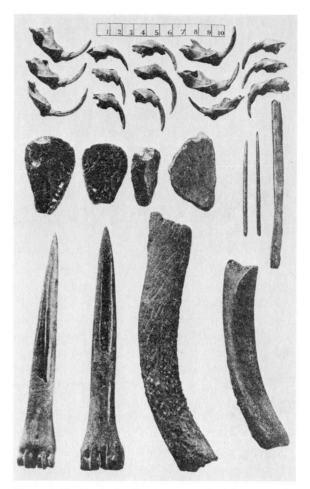

Figure 2.12 Formative "leather-worker's kit" associated with Skeleton 17 at Ticomán, Valley of Mexico. Top three rows: 15 gopher mandibles. Fourth row, left to right: 3 obsidian scrapers; 1 frag. pottery disc; 2 small bone bodkins; 1 bone chisel. Bottom row, left to right: 2 awls of deer metapodial; 2 hide grainers of deer antler. [After Vaillant 1931: Plate XCI.]

edge-wear analyses of stone artifacts), they have usually done a good job of describing and illustrating the tools they have found. Such are the continuities of rural Mesoamerican Indian life that ethnographic analogy has frequently been used, with considerable justification, in the interpretation of Formative artifacts. Customarily, variation in artifact assemblages has been presented by site and level, or by site and time period.

Once houses or household clusters have been identified, however, still another kind of variation is available for study: *the variation in activities between households*. In this section, we will briefly discuss the variation between households at 1500–500 B.C. in the region we know best, the Valley of Oaxaca. Wherever possible, we will point out what seem to be analogous activity areas or tool kits from other Formative sites mentioned in the archeological literature. Our discussion is intended to raise possibilities, rather than to be exhaustive.

Household Activities in Formative Oaxaca

We have no way of estimating the adequacy of our Oaxaca sample. We have drawn on the 3 best-preserved houses from Barrio del Rosario, Huitzo; the 10 best-preserved houses at San José Mogote; the 6 best-preserved household clusters at Tierras Largas; a single house from San Sebastian Abasolo; 2 houses from Santo Domingo Tomaltepec; and our 30 best-preserved bell-shaped pits. The data from this sample have encouraged us to *tentatively* divide household activities in early Oaxacan villages into four categories, as follows:

1. *Universal household activities.* These are activities represented either by tools, features, or activity areas, for which there was some evidence at every reasonably complete house in our sample; we might predict, therefore, that these activities were carried out by every household in the valley.

2. *Possible household specialization.* Some types of tools seemed to be of nearly universal distribution, but the activity areas where they were manufactured were found at only one or two houses. We interpret these as activities carried out at every village, but perhaps by only one or two households in each village.

3. *Possible regional specialization.* Some activities are represented at only two of our five excavated villages; at those two villages, however,

they are represented at virtually every house. Such activities may be regional specialties which were carried out by certain villages in only one part of the valley, with virtually every household in those villages participating.

4. *Possibly unique specializations.* Certain activities are known from only one village in our sample. At each of these villages, however, they are present in more than one house or household cluster. We suspect that at least one of these activities may be unique to a single residential ward or *barrio* at the largest early village in the valley. Let us now give a few examples of each of these categories.

Universal Household Activities

Food procurement, preparation, and storage apparently were carried on by every household during the period 1500–500 B.C. No extensively excavated household cluster failed to yield evidence of the following: (*1*) fragments of grinding stones (*metates* and/or *manos*); (*2*) storage pits; (*3*) fragments of large storage jars, some with a 5- or 10-gallon capacity; (*4*) bones of cottontail rabbit; (*5*) carbonized kernels or cupule fragments of maize; and (*6*) fragments of pottery charcoal braziers. Where any of these ingredients were missing, we suspect it was because the house or household cluster could not be extensively excavated because of disturbance, poor preservation, or lack of time. What this suggests is that each household was probably autonomous in terms of certain basic subsistence practices during the millenium between 1500 and 500 B.C., regardless of any part-time specialization.

Nevertheless, there is a degree of variation between households, even in "universal" subsistence practices, that deserves mention. For example, virtually every flotation sample from a house floor or storage pit contained corn kernels and seeds of prickly pear fruit (*Opuntia*). The presence of beans (*Phaseolus*) or avocado pits (*Persea*), however, was quite variable. Barrio del Rosario Huitzo yielded many beans, San Sebastián Abasolo many avocados; Tierras Largas had only modest amounts of either. Our samples are too numerous for this merely to be the result of sampling error. More likely, there was variation in the species chosen for cultivation by each household.

Similarly, although virtually every house contained cottontail bones, and usually bones of dog and mud turtle as well, amounts of deer bone varied considerably. Houses at San José Mogote and Tierras Largas had high numbers of deer bone, while Huitzo and Abasolo had less. Perhaps the greatest variety in hunted species occurred at Fábrica San José, a piedmont barranca site with good access to mountain hunting lands. Clearly, a village's physical location strongly influenced its access to certain kinds of game (see Chapter 4); in later periods, status considerations determined how much deer meat a household received (Spores 1965:969).

While grinding stones and storage jars were common in households, it was decidedly uncommon to find them complete and in good shape. Occasionally, they were forgotten and left behind in good condition, as in Feature 57 at Tierras Largas. This feature consisted of two parts. Feature 57a was a small bell-shaped pit that contained a complete *mano* and *metate*, a large complete jar, a broken figurine, a piece of carbonized wood or matting, and a portion of a second jar. Feature 57b consisted of a complete *mano* and *metate* lying on a small pile of sand which probably resulted from the digging of the adjacent pit.

Certain kinds of tool preparation may also be classified as universal household activities. Particularly common in all houses were a series of chipped-stone tools and waste debris, including cores and core fragments of locally available chert or quartz. Most of the tools are small utilized flakes and flake fragments, though large (approximately 5 cm long) flakes with secondary retouch are sometimes found. Most, if not all, households seem to have had access to local stone, and each household may have produced its own cutting and scraping tools. Antler tines (also present in some household clusters) were evidently used for pressure flaking.

Not quite as common were obsidian flakes and, at least as early as 1050 B.C., prismatic obsidian blades. Apparently important for cutting tasks, obsidian seems to have been available to all households, though no obsidian sources occur in the Valley of Oaxaca (in this regard, see Chapter 10).

Bone needles made from split deer long bones occur with many household clusters, and may have been used for sewing, basket making, or some other tasks. Some houses had several needles, but no "kits" of needles (such as those at Ticomán) have been found.

Another common household tool was the *piscador* or "cornshucker." Made from a sharpened deer metapodial, this awl-like tool is identical to *piscadores* used today by Oaxaca farmers to slit open cornhusks, or remove kernels from cobs; the wear pattern is identical as well.

Analogous Activities in Other Areas

A glance at Paul Tolstoy's descriptions of utilitarian artifacts from the Valley of Mexico (Tolstoy 1971) suggests that many of the same tools—*metates, manos,* antler tine pressure flakers, deer metapodial cornhuskers, and so on—must have characterized early villages in that region as well. The same is true of MacNeish, Nelken-Terner, and Johnson's (1967) descriptions of tools from early villages at Tehuacán, Puebla. Perhaps the most striking difference is that villagers in the valleys of Mexico, Puebla, and Tehuacán made hundreds of chipped stone points for lances or atl-atl darts, while Oaxacan villagers seem to have done virtually all their deer hunting without chipped-stone projectile points. Despite such regional differences, and despite our lack of information on the horizontal (house-by-house) distribution of utilitarian artifacts in areas such as the Valley of Mexico, the available data leads us to suspect the general range of "universal household activities" was similar in all these regions.

If we turn to the tropical lowlands, there are also some noticeable regional differences. Perhaps the clearest is the fact that, in some coastal areas, it was fishing, rather than land-mammal hunting, that contributed the bulk of the animal bone in the household cluster. Nevertheless, such artifacts as *metates, manos, piscadores,* and antler tine pressure flakers were still common at lowland villages like Chiapa de Corzo (Lee 1969) or San Lorenzo (Coe, personal communication). Indeed, such regional differences as occur do not alter our overall impressions that households of 1500–500 B.C. were (*1*) generally autonomous with regard to food procurement, preparation, and storage, but (*2*) interdependent with regard to a series of part-time crafts that only certain households conducted (see p. 36).

Possible Household Specialization

Certain kinds of flint tool manufacture may have been carried out by specific households within each village, not as a full-time specialty but as a form of interhousehold cooperation between relatives and affines. For example, Feature 184 at the village of Tierras Largas was a bell-shaped pit that contained an unusually high number of small chert flakes and flake fragments, undoubtedly the waste debris from stone tool manufacture by pressure retouch. Over 300 pieces were recovered, along with a bifacial tool that was probably broken during manufacture. Perhaps each small village had one or two persons sufficiently skilled at pressure flaking to provide the rest of the village with certain tools. Our evidence from other pits and houses would suggest that the average villager rarely did more than pick up a conveniently sharp flake and use it without deliberate retouch.

Certain kinds of bone tool manufacture ma have been similarly organized. Feature 140 at Tierras Largas was a bell-shaped pit that contained

Figure 2.13 Artifacts from Early Formative celt-working activity areas at San José Mogote, Oaxaca; a, b, and c were all found together. (a) Partially finished celt; (b) finished but unused celt; (c) and (d) quartz cobbles used first for pecking out celts, then polishing them (with the smooth facet shown on face of cobble).

an unusual cache of deer bone, including at least one complete, unmodified long bone, and several other long bones that had been cut to produce socket-type handles, bone rings, and other tools. Although all households used bone tools, this was the only feature that indicated that one or two households might have done a great deal of the village's bone tool manufacture.

Ground-and-polished celt manufacture also may have been a household specialty; several residential wards at San José Mogote had such households. One, dating to ca. 1150 B.C., contained a finished celt, a partially completed celt, and a large quartz pebble which clearly had been used to polish the celt bits (Figure 2.13). Nearby was a stone pounder which probably had been used to peck out the shape of the celt before polishing. The celts were of green metamorphic rock, while the polisher was of even harder quartz.

Analogous Activities in Other Regions

The "leather-working kits" included with certain burials at Ticomán in the Valley of Mexico (see pp. 34–35) suggest that that activity may have been a household specialization. Out of Vaillant's sample of 43 adult burials, only 5 males had such kits (and 1 female had what *might* be a smaller version). Or stated differently, 5 out of the 16 middle-aged to elderly burials definitely identified as "male" had leather-working kits. Leather working, therefore, might have been carried on by fewer than a third of the households at Ticomán.

Possible Regional Specialization

Certain kinds of shell ornament production may have been restricted to households in the northwestern, or Etla, region of the Valley of Oaxaca during Early Formative times. Two villages in that region—Tierras Largas and San José Mogote—have evidence of shell working in almost every house of the period 1150–850 B.C. that has been extensively excavated. Very few houses from other excavated villages of that time period have yielded shell-working activity areas, although finished shell ornaments appear at all other villages.

A "typical" shell-working activity area at San José Mogote would be an area of 1–2 sq m, small enough to suggest that a single individual (rather than a group) was at work. Such areas were usually in the corner of a house, and they were littered with small flint chips and fragments of cut and discarded shell. They would usually include 1 or more chert knives or burins (for cutting shell) and from 1 to 10 small chert drills or perforators (for drilling shell) (see Figure 2.14). They would also usually include fragments of ornaments which broke in the process of manufacture, as well as "undesirable" parts trimmed off such shells as *Spondylus* (spiny oyster) or *Pinctada* (pearl oyster).

Certain kinds of feather working may have had a similar regionally restricted distribution. Two (or possibly three) Early Formative bell-shaped pits from different household clusters at the village of Tierras Largas yielded the bones of macaw—most likely the military macaw (*Ara militaris*), whose blue-green feathers were widely prized in Pre-Columbian times. Wing bones seem to have been

cut in such a way as to preserve the feathers. Since Early Formative villages in other parts of the valley have not produced macaw remains, the accumulation and/or working of these feathers may have been restricted to the Etla region, or possibly even restricted to households at Tierras Largas alone.

Salt making was restricted to villages near saline springs, our best-studied example being Fábrica

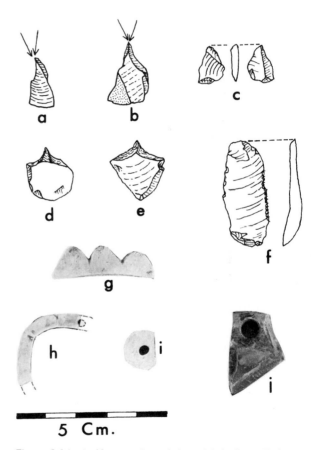

5 Cm.

Figure 2.14 Artifacts and workshop debris from Early Formative shell-working activity areas at San José Mogote, Oaxaca. (a) and (b) Chert burins for cutting shell; (c) chert graver; (d) and (e) small chert drills; (f) utilized chert flake; (g) fragment of cut and engraved shell ornament; (h) broken fragment of mother-of-pearl holder for magnetite mirror; (i) fragment of shell bead; (j) broken fragment of drilled pearl oyster.

San José (Drennan 1972). As early as 1300 B.C., the area was visited briefly, probably to obtain salt, but no houses were built. During the Middle Formative, the production of salt by boiling brackish spring water in pottery jars was evidently a common activity, with many jars retaining a mineral crust. Another small site called Las Salinas, founded near a saline spring not far away, may have been a salt-making village at 900–800 B.C.

Analogous Activities in Other Regions

Salt making was probably one of Formative Mesoamerica's most widespread regional specializations. Suitable localities varied from the brackish springs of the Tehuacán Valley and the shores of saline Lake Texcoco in the Valley of Mexico to the fossil lagoons and estuaries of the coastal lowlands. In Chapter 4, Alan Zarky discusses the tiny Guatemalan coastal hamlets which apparently produced salt from dry former estuary beds.

The manufacture of metates from suitable volcanic rock may have been a regional specialization in still other areas. At the Early Formative village of Coapexco, near Amecameca in the Valley of Mexico, Tolstoy and Fish (1973:18) report atypically large numbers of *metates* and *manos*, including numerous unfinished specimens in and around the houses.

Formative sites near obsidian flows in other parts of Mesoamerica may have had similar regional specializations. Shook and Proskouriakoff (1956) mention *obsidian-working areas* at Middle Formative sites near Guatemala City; the Valley of Mexico is rich in such areas, but, so far, none have been reported for the early village period in which we are interested. Places near which early obsidian working might be expected include Guadalupe Victoria, Puebla; Otumba, Valley of Mexico; Zinapécuaro, Guanajuato; and El Chayal, Guatemala (see Pires-Ferreira, Chapter 10 of this volume).

We cannot help feeling that there must be many more such regional specializations in early villages than are reported in the literature. Perhaps, at the time, the excavators who ran across them assumed that they would not be of interest to anyone else.

Possibly Unique Specializations

Magnetite mirror production may have been restricted to one set of households in one residential area at the village of San José Mogote during the period 1150–850 B.C. Rare examples of finished mirrors have been found at four other villages—Fábrica San José, Hacienda Blanca, Tomaltepec, and Tierras Largas—but no areas of mirror manufacture have been found anywhere outside a small area (Area A) on the eastern edge of San José Mogote. On one small field in this area, intensive surface collection turned up more than 500 fragments of magnetite, hematite, and related iron ores.

A "typical" magnetite working area at San José Mogote might be an area 1–2 sq m in extent, once again suggesting that production was by individuals rather than groups. In addition to scattered lumps of unused iron ore (presumably rejected because of flaws or inappropriate cleavage planes), such an activity area might include a number of small flat mirrors, about the size of a thumbnail, which had broken during manufacture. Polishers of quartz or hematite (both of which are harder than magnetite) were sometimes present. Nearby might be found "mirror holders" of pearl oyster—shell artifacts with spaces just the right size for a small magnetite mirror. Whether these "holders" were made by the same individuals who made the mirrors is not yet clear. However, some shell working was carried on in the same household clusters with the magnetite working.

Mirror-polishing activity areas were typically inside houses. What is more, in Area A at San José Mogote, as many as four stratigraphically superimposed levels contained such activity areas, suggesting that four generations of households had the same part-time specialty. In no other Early Formative residential ward have such mirror-working areas so far been discovered.

We are sure that similar situations—spatially restricted, specialized activities which span several generations in the same residential area—must occur at other early Mesoamerican villages, but

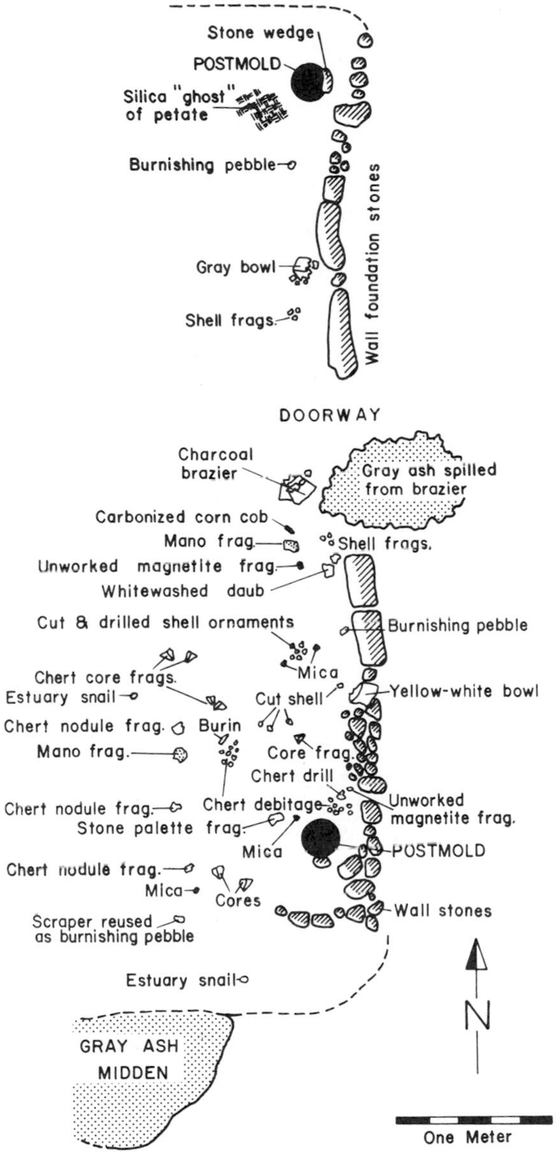

they are hard to find in the literature. Indeed, we have written this chapter largely in the hope that fellow archeologists will bring new activity areas and new tool kits to our attention, or point out to us ones we have overlooked.

The Recording of Household Activities

The preceding is an abridged and highly oversimplified review of a very complex topic. On the theory that one concrete example is worth a thousand words of discussion, let us consider one actual house in particular.

House 2 in Area C at San José Mogote (Figure 2.15), dating to approximately 1000 B.C., is a convenient example. Only the eastern half of the house had been preserved. The long axis of the house ran north-south, with a door on the east side, and with a midden to the south of (and slightly downhill from) the house. Here is how that house might be reported:

Number: House 2.

Length: Approximately 5 m (N–S) from corner post to corner post.

Width: Unknown (west half disturbed by modern adobe makers).

Post pattern: Two corner posts (in the NE and SE corners) represented by postmolds, both framed by lines of stones. Post diameters, 20 cm.

Construction: Wattle and daub, with white, limey clay surfacing. A row of foundation stones lines the east side, except in the doorway, which is 1.1 m wide. Two particularly large stones flank the doorway. Charred *Phalaris* (reed canary grass) present, probably from roof thatch. Floor, stamped clay with a light surface of clean sand.

Major items plotted on floor: Impression, containing silica exoskeleton of twilled *petate* or sleeping mat, near NE corner. Restorable outleaned wall bowl (Vessel 3), near wall N. of door. Restorable cylindrical bowl (Vessel 1),

Figure 2.15 East half of House 2 in Area C at San José Mogote, Oaxaca, with artifacts and features plotted *in situ*. (West half not preserved.)

near wall S. of door. Restorable pottery char-coal brazier (Vessel 2), lying crushed in front of doorway. Nearby is a small charred corn-cob. The spilled ash from Vessel 2, when floated, produced six corn kernels, many cob fragments, two prickly pear fruit seeds, one burnt cane fragment, and two unidentifiable seeds.

Activity areas: Apparent shell-working area, covering about 1.5 sq m in SE corner. The arti-facts include three fragments of chert nodules; two cores and five core fragments; and two separate concentrations of chert waste flakes 60 cm apart. One of the latter includes a chert burin, while the other includes a chert drill. There are numbers of cut and drilled shell ornament fragments and shell waste, primarily freshwater mussel. Two unused shells of *Cerithidium* (an estuary snail) and one *Ano-malocardia* shell are present. Apparently the worker started with chert nodules and raw shell, made his own flake cores, then made his own burins and drills from the flakes, and finally worked the shell. Included in this activity area are several possibly unrelated items, including an unworked chunk of iron ore (another occurs near the door); a stone palette fragment; a broken fragment of ground stone *mano* (another occurs near the door); and two quartz pebble burnishers, one made on a former scraper.

Associated feature: A gray ashy midden outside the house, to the south and downslope. When floated, it produced 17 maize kernels, many cob fragments, 1 possible cucurbit seed, and 3 chile pepper seeds.

Possible "Male" and "Female" Work Areas in Oaxaca Houses

Now we must raise one more possibility, which cannot yet be confirmed because our sample of houses is too small. That is the possibility that there may be an intermediate level of analysis be-

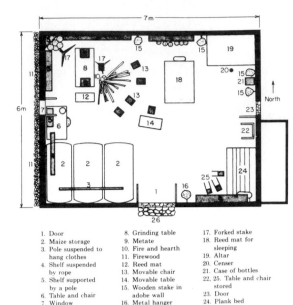

1. Door	8. Grinding table	17. Forked stake
2. Maize storage	9. Metate	18. Reed mat for
3. Pole suspended to	10. Fire and hearth	sleeping
hang clothes	11. Firewood	19. Altar
4. Shelf suspended	12. Reed mat	20. Censer
by rope	13. Movable chair	21. Case of bottles
5. Shelf supported	14. Movable table	22, 25. Table and chair
by a pole	15. Wooden stake in	stored
6. Table and chair	adobe wall	23. Door
7. Window	16. Metal hanger	24. Plank bed
		26. Stoop

Figure 2.16 Modern highland Maya house from Zinacan-tan, Chiapas, Mexico, conceptually divided into men's and women's work spaces. [After Vogt 1969: Figure 32.]

tween the activity area or feature, and the house or household cluster. That level would be the "male" or "female" work area.

A very nice ethnographic model for such work areas can be drawn from Evon Vogt's study of the highland Maya of Zinacantan, Chiapas (Figure 2.16). According to Vogt (1969: 83-84):

Although Zinacanteco houses contain no in-terior walls or partitions, they are conceptually divided into "rooms" or living spaces. These are defined by the location of the hearth and associated objects that are owned and used by the women, and by the location of the interior house altar and associated objects owned and used by men. The house altar is nearly always constructed against the wall; others are located in corners but with one edge against the wall opposite the hearth. In houses without interior altars, the men's possessions still tend to be clustered in the living space opposite the hearth.

The hearth, with a fire that almost never dies (except when the members of the household are away for extended periods of time), is a focal point for women's work, as well as for family interaction, since men and children sit by the fire for warmth and also eat near the fire.

On the basis of Vogt's data, one could predict that a future archeologist, excavating a Zinacanteco house that had been hastily abandoned, would find objects owned and use by men near the altar, objects owned and used by women near the hearth. However, some men's objects could well occur intermingled with women's objects because of the family interaction near the hearth, just mentioned.

There are obvious problems in applying the Zinacanteco model to houses of the Formative period. For example, Early Formative houses in the Valley of Oaxaca usually had no hearths; instead, they had portable pottery braziers which could be moved from place to place within the house. Moreover, very few early houses show anything resembling an altar; one or two Early Formative household clusters in Oaxaca had possible ritual features, but we will defer their discussion until Chapter 11.

On the other hand, we have no doubt that even these early households had "objects owned and used by men" and "objects owned and used by women," and the distribution of these within the house well might have been patterned. Thus, early houses could have been "conceptually divided" into work areas with men's tools and male-related features, work areas with women's tools and female-related features, and areas of overlap due to family interaction.

Our candidates for women's tools include *metates* and "two-hand" *manos*; pottery charcoal braziers; pots showing a crust where maize had been soaked in lime; some hammerstones for food preparation; deer bone cornhuskers; spindle whorls; sewing (as opposed to leather-working) needles; and so on. We suspect that most of the flint chipping was done in male work areas, and that antler tine pressure flakers, projectile points, and many kinds of chert bifaces and scrapers were men's tools. On the basis of the Ticomán data already

mentioned, we suspect many bone hide-working tools (fleshers, beamers, etc.) also were used by men, along with tools for land clearance (celts), weapon manufacture (shaft smoothers, burins), and a variety of extractive tasks. Men also may have used some kinds of small "one-hand" *manos*, as well as hammerstones for celt manufacture.

In at least some early houses from Oaxaca, we do note a tendency for our presumed "women's tools" to occur to one side of the midline as one enters the house, while presumed "men's tools" occur to the other side. In House 1 at Tierras Largas (Figure 2.17), most chert cores, scrapers, areas of retouch flakes, and at least one biface lay in front of or to the left of the door as one would enter. All bone needles, deer bone cornhuskers, and pierced sherd discs (probably spindle whorls) lay in front of or to the right of the door as one would enter. In addition, a gray ash deposit from cooking activity occurred in the "right half" of the house, and contained a needle and a deer bone cornhusker.

Most of the chert working in House 2 at San José Mogote (Figure 2.15) also was concentrated to the left of the door as one entered: cores, nodules, debitage, and utilized flakes. In front of the door was a smashed charcoal brazier with food debris, and more food remains occurred to the right of the door. Coextensive with, and possibly related to, the chipped stone scatters was a shell-working area, only one of many craft areas associated with presumed "men's tools" in early Oaxaca villages. It was most often in these "men's work areas" that burins and drills were made, shell and mica were cut and drilled, and ritual ornaments polished or burnished. One suspects, therefore, that this was an activity carried on by males in their free time, away from the hunt or the *milpa*. Obviously, to demonstrate this convincingly we need a much larger sample of houses; our sample is not yet statistically significant.

Indeed, obtaining an adequate sample of men's and women's work areas will be difficult, for only a small percentage of houses are sufficiently undisturbed; in many, the floor debris is so kicked

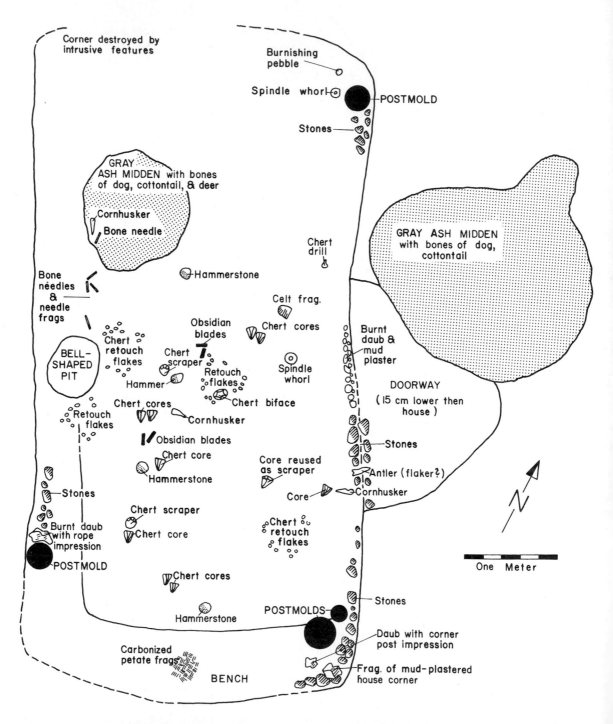

Figure 2.17 Plan of House 1 in Area A at Tierras Largas, Oaxaca, with selected artifact categories plotted on floor and intrusive features omitted. Late San José phase, ca. 900 B.C.

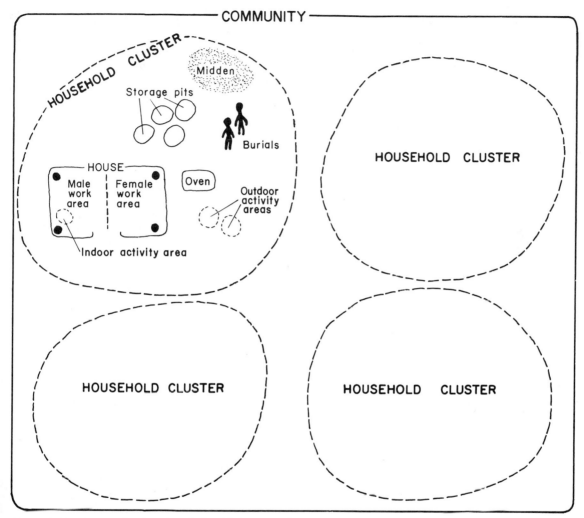

Figure 2.18 Diagram showing the relationship between the analytical levels of activity area; feature; male or female work area; house; household cluster; and community.

around that the areas are blurred. Nevertheless, we believe that the search for this intermediate analytic level is worth the effort, in terms of its potential for illuminating sexual division of labor in the Formative (Figure 2.18).

References

Aufdermauer, J.
  1970 Excavaciones en dos sitios preclásicos de Moyotzingo, Puebla, *Comunicaciones* No. 1:9-24. Fundación Alemana para la Investigación Científica, Puebla.

Borhegyi, S. F.
  1965a Archaeological synthesis of the Guatemalan highlands. In *Handbook of Middle American Indians*, vol. 2, edited by R. Wauchope and G. R. Willey. Austin: University of Texas Press, Pp. 3-58.
  1965b Settlement patterns of the Guatemalan highlands. In *Handbook of Middle American Indians*, vol. 2, edited by R. Wauchope and G. R. Willey. Austin: University of Texas Press. Pp. 59-75.

Coe, M. D.
1961   La Victoria: An early site on the Pacific coast of Guatemala. *Papers of the Peabody Museum of Archaeology and Ethnology* vol. LIII. Harvard University, Cambridge, Mass.
1968   San Lorenzo and the Olmec civilization. In *Dumbarton Oaks Conference on the Olmec*, edited by E. P. Benson, Washington, D.C.: Dumbarton Oaks. Pp. 41–71.

Coe, M. D., and K. V. Flannery
1967   Early cultures and human ecology in south coastal Guatemala. *Smithsonian Contributions to Anthropology* No. 3. Smithsonian Institution, Washington, D.C.

Drennan, R. D.
1972   Excavations at Fábrica San José, Oaxaca, Mexico. Mimeographed preliminary report. Ann Arbor, Mich.

Flannery, K. V.
1964   The middle formative of the Tehuacán Valley. Unpublished Ph.D. dissertation, University of Chicago.
1968   Archeological systems theory and early Mesoamerica. In *Anthropological archeology in the Americas*, edited by B. J. Meggers. Washington, D.C.: Anthropological Society of Washington, Pp. 67-87.

Flannery, K. V., M. C. Winter, S. Lees, J. Neely, J. Schoenwetter, S. Kitchen, and J. C. Wheeler
1970   Preliminary archeological investigations in the Valley of Oaxaca, Mexico, 1966–1969. Mimeographed preliminary report. Ann Arbor, Mich.

Hall, D. W., G A. Haswell, and T. A. Oxley
1956   *Underground storage of grain.* British Colonial Office, Pest Information Laboratory, Dept. of Scientific and Industrial Research. London: H. M. Stationery Office.

Lee, T. A., Jr.
1969   The artifacts of Chiapa de Corzo, Chiapas, Mexico. *Papers of the New World Archaeological Foundation* No. 26. Provo, Utah.

Lowe, G. W.
1959   Archaeological exploration of the upper Grijalva River, Chiapas, Mexico. *Papers of the New World Archaeological Foundation* No. 2 (Pub. no. 3). Provo, Utah.

MacNeish, R. S.
1954   An early archaeological site near Pánuco, Vera Cruz. *Transactions of the American Philosophical Society* 44(n.s.): 539–641.
1962   *Second annual report of the Tehuacán archaeological-botanical project.* R. S. Peabody Foundation for Archaeology, Andover, Mass.
n.d.   Excavations at site Ts-381. Manuscript to appear in a future volume of *The prehistory of the Tehuacán Valley*. Austin: University of Texas Press.

MacNeish, R. S., A. Nelken-Terner, and I. W. Johnson
1967   *The Prehistory of the Tehuacán Valley*, edited by R. S. MacNeish, Vol. 2. *Nonceramic Artifacts.*

Naroll, R.
1962   Floor area and settlement population. *American Antiquity* 27:587–589.

Piña Chán, R.
1958   Tlatilco. Vol. I. *Serie Investigaciones.* Instituto Nacional de Antropología e Historia. Mexico, D. F.

Sanders, W. T.
1965   The cultural ecology of the Teotihuacán Valley. Dept. of Anthropology, Pennsylvania State University, University Park. Mimeograph.

Shook, E. M., and T. Proskouriakoff
1956   Settlement patterns in Meso-America and the sequence in the Guatemalan highlands. In *Prehistoric settlement patterns in the New World*, edited by G. R. Willey. *Viking Fund Publications in Anthropology* No. 23. New York: Wenner-Gren. Pp. 93–100.

Spores, R.
1965   The Zapotec and Mixtec at Spanish contact. In *Handbook of Middle American Indians*, vol. 3, edited by R. Wauchope and G. R. Willey. Austin: University of Texas Press. Part 2, pp. 962–987.

Tolstoy, P.
1971   Utilitarian artifacts of central Mexico. In *Handbook of Middle American Indians*, vol. 10, edited by R. Wauchope, G. F. Ekholm, and I. Bernal. Austin: University of Texas Press. Part 1, pp. 270– 96.

Tolstoy, P., and S. K. Fish
1973   Excavations at Coapexco, 1973. Mimeographed preliminary report. Dept. of Anthropology, Queens College (C.U.N.Y.), New York.

Vaillant, G. C.
1930   Excavations at Zacatenco. *Anthropological Papers* Vol. 32: Part 1. American Museum of Natural History, New York.
1931   Excavations at Ticomán. *Anthropological*

Papers Vol. 32: Part 2. American Museum of Natural History, New York.

1935   Excavations at El Arbolillo. *Anthropological Papers* Vol. 35: Part 2. American Museum of Natural History, New York.

1941   *Aztecs of Mexico*. New York: Doubleday, Doran.

Vogt, E. Z.

1969   *Zinacantan: A Maya community in the highlands of Chiapas*. Cambridge, Mass.: Belknap Press (Harvard University).

Walter, H.

1970   Informe preliminar sobre una excavación realizada en el sitio preclásico de San Francisco Acatepec, Puebla, Mexico. *Comunicaciones* No. 1:25–36. Fundación Alemana para la Investigación Cientifica, Puebla.

Whalen, M. E.

1974   Excavations at Sto. Domingo Tomaltepec,

Oaxaca, Mexico. Mimeographed preliminary report. Dept. of Anthropology, University of Michigan, Ann Arbor.

Willey, G. R., W. R. Bullard, J. B. Glass, and J. C. Gifford

1965   Prehistoric Maya settlements in the Belize valley. *Papers of the Peabody Museum of Archaeology and Ethnology* Vol. LIV. Harvard University, Cambridge, Mass.

Winter, M. C.

1970   Excavations at Tierras Largas (Atzompa, Oaxaca): A preliminary report. In Preliminary archeological investigations in the Valley of Oaxaca, Mexico, 1966–1969, edited by K. V. Flannery. Mimeographed preliminary report. Ann Arbor, Mich.

1972   Tierras Largas: A formative community in the Valley of Oaxaca, Mexico. Unpublished Ph.D. dissertation, University of Arizona, Tucson.

Chapter 3

ANALYSIS ON THE COMMUNITY LEVEL

Introduction

The subject of sampling whole communities can perhaps best be introduced by another parable concerning my colleague, the Real Mesoamerican Archeologist. Like most archeologists of his generation, R.M.A. was raised on the writings of Sir Mortimer Wheeler, Kathleen Kenyon, and other British archeologists who are justifiably famous for their meticulous field techniques. Many of these techniques date back to General Pitt-Rivers, who not only adapted military organization to the running of his field crews, but laid out his excavations with the orderliness of an army parade ground. Both R.M.A. and I had long admired photographs of British excavations in India and the Near East which showed dozens of 5-m squares separated by neat, 1-m baulks, left as "witness sections" and as roads for wheelbarrows. From the air, as one of my colleagues is fond of remarking, such excavations look just like ice-cube trays.

R.M.A.'s second crucial excavation in the Río San Jacinto drainage was at a shallow mound which he intended to dig with such military precision "in order to find houses"; the latter goal was of course at the urging of his graduate student, S.G.S. R.M.A. put a 2-by-2-m square in the center of the site, but it hit no architecture. Accordingly, he put a systematic series of 2-m squares, spaced exactly 10 m apart, over the entire site—a total of 20 squares in all. None hit architecture, but the regularly spaced pattern looked great on the aerial photograph. R.M.A.'s preliminary report concluded, "after extensive testing on a ten-meter grid it can safely be assumed that no houses have been preserved on the site."

Two years later, as part of an irrigation project in the San Jacinto drainage, government hydrology crews bulldozed the same mound. Happily, a team of salvage archeologists was right behind the bulldozer as it worked, recovering whatever data might be saved. The first swath through the low mound, shearing to a depth of 25 cm, uncovered 2 house floors, which were quickly mapped. The second swath hit 3 more; the third and fourth as well. While the bulldozer operator waited, the map grew to 10 houses, then 15. Finally it was over. And here comes the part that S.G.S. makes me tell over and over, whenever R.M.A. is out of the room: The site had been a planned village of 16 houses, arranged in 4 rows of 4 each, spaced exactly 10 m apart. In fact, spaced with exactly the military regularity of R.M.A.'s 10-m grid—so that when his first pit missed the first house, it was predestined that he would miss them all.

The regular grid, or "ice-cube tray," may have a lot to recommend it in terms of orderliness and aesthetic quality, but, for some archeological tasks, it is far from the optimum strategy. For sampling some communities to recover house patterns, as described later, transect samples or random sampling squares may actually be a more efficient approach.

In this chapter, Marc Winter and I examine two sampling problems which occur on the community level: (*1*) How can I get a representative sample of the surface remains of a Formative community, and (*2*) How can I excavate a representative sample of a Formative community? The examples we give are only a few of the hundreds of possible alternative strategies, and they may not be even the best alternatives. The intensive surface pickups I describe probably will not work very well in the tropical forest. Perhaps Winter's random sampling quadrats could substitute for surface collection in some lowland areas.

In the course of writing this chapter, we discovered that neither we nor anyone else knew very much about the size of the "average" early Mesoamerican village. For some types of sampling, it is absolutely necessary to know the site size beforehand. Joyce Marcus accordingly took on the job of scanning the literature for village sizes, with interesting and sometimes unexpected results.

Many of Mesoamerica's early villages are small and shallow, with little or no evidence of houses

visible on the surface; some, in fact, consist superficially of little more than a plowed field, a grove of prickly pear, or a stand of sugar cane. Though superficially unimpressive—and hence usually passed over when the time comes for site selection—these shallow sites can be gold mines of information for the Mesoamerican archeologist. Only at such sites can he hope to achieve enough horizontal exposure of the deposits to really see in detail the "anatomy" of a village—the layout of the houses and their relationship to pits, burials, work areas, and other features. At deeper sites, the labor and expense of removing overburden from such an area would usually be prohibitive. To be sure, some shallow sites have been plowed to bedrock, and are useless for the kinds of analysis we describe here. But the fact is that the Real Mesoamerican Archeologist usually dismisses small, shallow sites as "unimportant" before he knows whether or not they are, and then spends most of his season trenching mound fill.

In 1969, Marc Winter excavated a small, shallow site in Oaxaca in what is perhaps the first serious attempt to apply the principles of probability sampling to extensive horizontal exposure of Formative deposits. His efforts produced the first maps that even approximate the layout of a Formative village (cf. Figures 8.3–8.5). For although the small site Tierras Largas (near Atzompa, Oaxaca) had been plowed for hundreds of years, the postholes and storage pits, burials and house floors had been excavated into bedrock by the Formative villagers of 3000 years ago.

The Real Mesoamerican Archeologist visited us while Winter was at work, and he could barely disguise his boredom. "If this is the best site you can come up with, you ought to work with *me* next year," he said. "In my area, we've got Formative sites 5 m deep."

"It happens," said Winter, "that we have already tested one site that is 7 m deep, and that, within 20 minutes' drive, there is another stratified site over 17 m deep. We chose this site precisely because it's only 30 cm to bedrock."

"You gotta be kidding," said R.M.A. "And what the hell is this weird pattern of pits all over the place?"

"That's a 3.7% random sample of the village."

"Gross," said R.M.A.

With the patience of an international diplomat, Winter showed R.M.A. the early results of the sample—six Early Formative houses, each with its three to five storage pits and a few burials, each with its household inventory *in situ* on the floor of the house. They were the first Early Formative houses R.M.A. had ever seen. They are the last he will ever see. As he left on the train, hurrying back to his 5-m mound on the Río San Jacinto, he had only one last comment.

"Thirty centimeters," he said with clear exasperation, "is not even enough to cover the *base* of a colossal basalt head."

In one of the sections that follow, Winter presents a synopsis of his sampling program for Tierras Largas in 1969—the year when he filled the role of the Skeptical Graduate Student. Winter never claimed his program was perfect, and it is certain that he would make modifications in it if he were to do it again. At the time, however, it came to grips with a problem never seriously attacked by my friend, R.M.A.: What was the layout of a small Early Formative village, and what can we infer about its social organization on the basis of that layout?

Sampling by Intensive Surface Collection

KENT V. FLANNERY

Archeologists would agree that the cultural debris lying on the surface of a site in some way reflects what is buried below. However, few attempts have been made to discover just how closely one can predict from detailed knowledge of surface distributions what he will find if he digs. [Redman and Watson 1970:279]

One of the most obvious first steps in sampling on the community level is to sample the remains lying on the surface of the ancient community. Although all archeologists do this at one time or another, there is little agreement on what surface collections can tell us. On one hand, we have the optimistic statement of Redman and Watson (1970:280) that "surface and sub-surface artifact distributions are related so that a description of the first will allow prediction of the second." On the other hand, we have the statement by my friend the Real Mesoamerican Archeologist (per-

sonal communication, 1970) that "surface remains are just that—the junk you find on the surface—and nothing more. And I say, screw them."

R.M.A.'s skepticism is understandable. He happens to know that, in 1967, inspired by the Hatchery West study to be described later, some of us conducted the *total* systematic surface pickup of a preceramic open-air site in the Valley of Oaxaca. The work was directed by Frank Hole, a seasoned veteran of many field campaigns, with Marcus Winter and Suzanne K. Fish. After mapping the site, which occupied 1.5 ha (hectares) of an old alluvial fan flanked by two dry arroyos, Hole and his crew laid out a grid of 5-by-5 m squares over the entire surface of the site and picked up *everything* by square: Projectile points, bifaces, choppers, grinding stone, fire-cracked rock, waste flakes all went into the bag. They then drew contour maps showing the relative densities of various materials over the whole 1.5 ha. It was with some interest that R.M.A. watched us complete the map of projectile point distribution, and he was truly impressed when their distribution formed a giant ring completely encircling the site.

"I haven't read a lot of that French structuralism," he admitted, "but could you have a circular village like Levi-Strauss finds in Amazonia? Or did all the projectile points wind up in some kind of circular defensive moat around the site?"

"Worse than that," said Hole. "We just spent 2 weeks and about 300 man-hours discovering that the site is on a slight rise, so the projectile points tend to appear all around the edges where they were eroded by the arroyos."

"Furthermore," said Winter, "another 50 man-hours of analysis enabled us to propose the following law-like generalizations.

1. Artifacts on the surface tend to move downhill.
2. When sheet erosion takes place, it moves the lighter waste flakes farther than it moves the heavy grinding stones."

After all that, one can hardly blame R.M.A. for never again even bothering to wash his surface collections. Had he spent another week with us, however, and seen the results of the next 50 man-hours of work, he would have observed that many of the contour maps *did* provide clues to the subsurface nature of the site. Clear areas of flint working, seed grinding, and butchering did appear, and guided the subsequent excavations so that even preceramic "architecture" was eventually discovered (Flannery *et al*. 1970:22–24). Our suggested path lies somewhere between R.M.A.'s pessimism and Redman and Watson's optimism: Systematic intensive surface collections *can* work, but they don't *always* work. And for some purposes, they give very ambiguous results because of the nature of the archeological site.

In the sections that follow, we give four concrete examples of communities sampled by systematic surface collection. The first is a shallow, midwestern U. S. site. The second is a deeply stratified

Near Eastern *tell*. The third is a small early Mesoamerican village. The fourth is a large, very complex, deeply stratified Formative ceremonial-civic center.

Hatchery West, Illinois, U.S.A.

In 1963, Lewis R. Binford and a team of archeologists from the University of Chicago (Binford *et al*. 1970) arrived at the Hatchery site, a Woodland occupation on the east bank of the Kaskaskia River near Carlyle, Illinois. Prior to actual excavation of the site, they undertook one of the most ambitious "intensive surface collections" ever attempted in North America. First, the area was photographed from the air and a local farmer was hired to plow the site, bringing large quantities of material to the surface. Second, the site was staked off in a grid of squares 6 m on a side. Third, the crew waited for summer rains to wash down the freshly plowed fields, thereby cleaning and exposing the utmost amount of material. Fourth, all exposed artifactual material in every square was collected and bagged by square. Finally, the material from each square was counted and analyzed, and a series of contour maps drawn to show the density and distribution of artifact classes over the surface of the site (Figure 3.1). On the basis of these distributions, areas of the site were selected for excavation.

These excavations brought to light a number of interesting relationships between the buried features of the site and what lay on the surface. First, there was little correspondence between the areas of highest sherd density and the Woodland houses; the houses usually occurred in areas of light surface sherd density (1–5 sherds per 6-m square), while the areas of densest surface sherds (16–20 per square) apparently overlay midden or dump areas. These areas of "rich" surface remains are precisely those which our old friend R.M.A. would be most likely to excavate, thereby missing most of the architecture. Second, distribution of major classes of material (sherds, flint tools, fire-cracked

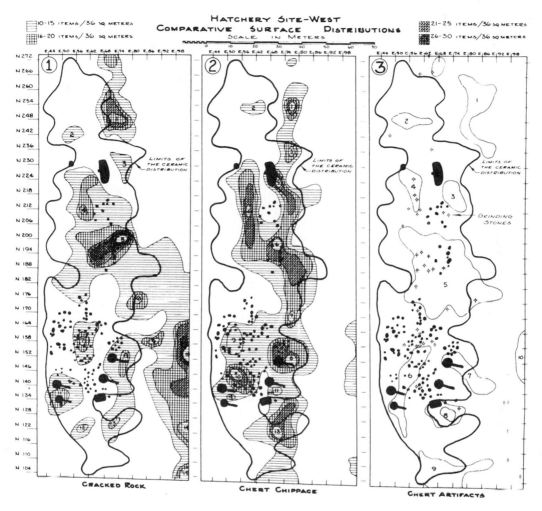

Figure 3.1 Contour maps of densities of various materials (cracked rock, chert chips, and artifacts) on the surface at Hatchery West, Illinois. [After Binford *et al.* 1970: Figure 3.]

rock, grinding stones, etc.) showed so little overlap or "isomorphy" over the site that the authors concluded that the collection of a "representative sample" of cultural items from any one location on the site would be "impossible" (Binford *et al.* 1970:15). The distribution maps, however, did provide nice clues to the subsurface makeup of the site: Woodland houses in the light sherd-density areas, middens in the high sherd-density areas, and preceramic occupations in areas with no sherds but high concentrations of cracked cobbles.

It should be pointed out that such a program proved effective at Hatchery West partly for three reasons. One, the site is relatively small (3.7 acres, or less than 2 ha), so the total collection could be made in 4 days by an average crew of 17 persons. Two, the site is shallow (average depth, 45 cm), and therefore one could expect some immediate correspondence between surface and subsurface features. Three, although the site has several time periods represented and many prehistoric pits which have undoubtedly brought older material to the surface, it had not been subjected to the kind of massive earth moving and borrow-pit digging seen in Mesoamerican sites with monumental architecture.

Çayönü and Girik-i-Haciyan, Turkey

In 1968, Charles L. Redman and Patty Jo Watson undertook controlled surface collections at two *tells* or large, stratified archeological mounds near Diyarbakir, Turkey (Redman and Watson 1970). Both sites were so large (up to 250 m in diameter) and so rich in surface material that a *total* surface collection—like that conducted at Hatchery West—was beyond the time and manpower at the expedition's disposal. Moreover, the sites were up to 5 m high, and it was likely that some amount of material from the lower levels had been redeposited in the upper levels. Some sort of sampling program was clearly in order.

The sampling designs used by Redman and Watson include two described by Stephen Plog in his study of regional sampling (Chapter 5, this volume): (*1*) the simple random sample and (*2*) the stratified unaligned systematic sample.

1. For the mound of Çayönü, the authors laid out a grid of 5-by-5 m squares, using a table of random numbers (see p. 64). This is very like the system used by Marcus Winter to sample Tierras Largas (see pp. 62–67), and it had two disadvantages. First, the taking of a simple random sample makes it necessary to define the boundaries of the site before beginning. Second, as so often happens in random sampling, in the Çayönü case, there were areas where squares tended to cluster in groups of two to six, and other areas where no squares were selected at all. Redman and Watson therefore had to add nine additional squares to fill in these "blank areas."

2. To correct for the problems of simple random sampling, Redman and Watson used a stratified unaligned systematic design at the mound of Girik-i-Haciyan (Figure 3.2). Once again, they began with a grid of 5-m squares; but this time they oriented the grid along the major north-south, east-west axes of the site, and squares were selected with reference to these axes. Blocks of nine squares (units three squares on a side) were chosen as the "strata" which give the design its name, and, within each block, one square was chosen at random by selecting its north-south, east-west coordinates from a random number table. This had two advantages. First, it insured good distribution of sample squares over the whole site (with no "blank" areas). Second, it made it unnecessary to define the limits of the site before beginning, as the grid could be expanded indefinitely in four directions.

In the case of both Çayönü and Girik-i-Haciyan, Redman and Watson drew contour maps of the artifact distributions like those produced by Binford and his co-workers at Hatchery West. Later test excavations, in their opinion, showed a good correspondence between surface distributions and buried remains. At Çayönü, a test in the area of highest surface sherd density produced 10,000 pot sherds but no architecture to a depth of 50 cm. Another test, in an area of high flint blade density and no sherds, produced a preceramic house only 50 cm below the surface. Note, however, that these good correspondences are *between surface remains and the upper levels of the site*; understandably, they tell us little about the deeply buried levels. This is no criticism of the technique, only a simple recognition of the limitations of *any* kind of surface collection on a deep, stratified site.

Coapexco, Valley of Mexico

Lying at 2600 m (8580 feet) on the lower slopes of the Ixtaccíhuatl volcano, Coapexco is probably the highest Early Formative site in Mesoamerica. The site appears as two distinct concentrations of surface material, the "Upper Ridge" and "Field 1"

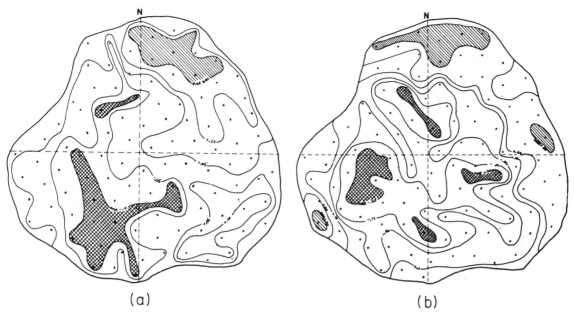

Figure 3.2 Contour maps of densities of sherds and chipped stone on the surface of Girik-i-Haciyan, Turkey. (a) Ratio of painted to plain pottery (hatching means relatively more painted ware; cross-hatching means relatively more plain-ware); (b) ratio of chipped stone to pottery (hatching means relatively more chipped stone; cross-hatching means relatively more pottery). [After Redman and Watson 1970: Figures 7–8.]

areas, separated by some 500 m of dissected mountainside. The site was originally found on survey by Jeffrey Parsons, who regarded the two concentrations as small hamlets, half a kilometer apart. Tolstoy and Fish (1973), the excavators, found Early Formative sherds scattered on the surface throughout the intervening area, and raise the possibility that Coapexco is one large site. While we have no first-hand information to resolve this question, our inclination is to regard Coapexco as two small hamlets. To consider it one site would make it 50 ha, which as Marcus' synthesis (this chapter) indicates, would leave Coapexco second only to San Lorenzo, Veracruz, as the largest Early Formative site in Mesoamerica. It seems unlikely that this high, isolated site, with no visible ceremonial mounds, was such a major population center.

The "Upper Ridge," an area of 2.5 ha of relatively high sherd density, is about the size of Blan-

ton's smaller hamlets in the Ixtapalapa region (Table 3.6). Here, Tolstoy's crew of 3–6 persons carried out an intensive surface pickup. Two fields, measuring approximately .5 ha each, were mapped at a scale of 1:50 with contour intervals of 5.0 cm. Most of that surface was then gridded with 4-by-4 m squares oriented to the long axis of the Upper Ridge.

> 572 such squares were laid out. Of these, 525 were totally collected for sherds, figurines and chipped stone, and 489 were also collected for "other stone" (ground stone, fire-cracked rocks and unworked stone, most of it, if not all, consisting of manuports). The larger items in the "other stone" category, as well as all items, regardless of size, bearing traces of workmanship or use as tools, were plotted *in situ* before being bagged. [Tolstoy and Fish 1973:5–6]

Tolstoy's group then drew contour maps showing the surface densities of various categories of

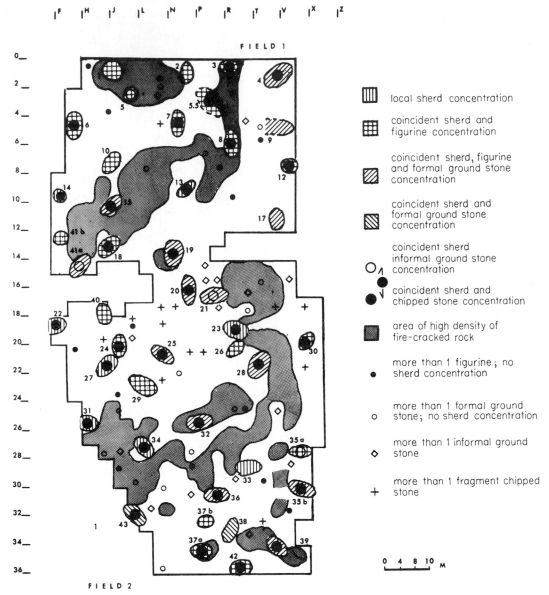

Figure 3.3 Contour maps of surface concentrations of various materials, Upper Ridge, Coapexco site, Valley of Mexico. [After Tolstoy and Fish 1973: Figure 2.]

material, not unlike the maps already described for Hatchery West (see Figure 3.3). The contours indicated some 50 concentrations of surface material, 31 of which are described by Tolstoy and Fish as "hot spots" of potsherds, figurine parts, chipped stone, and ground stone. The authors reasoned that these "hot spots" could indicate the former locations of houses, a prediction they tested with north–south and east–west excavation trenches. The results of this test are shown in Table 3.1.

TABLE 3.1   Relationship between Surface Concentrations and Subsurface Structures or Features at Coapexco[a]

Trench	Length in meters	Number of concentrations of cultural material				
		Earlier appearing on surface	Revealed in trench	Not seen earlier on surface	Visible on surface, not seen in trench	Total structures suggested by all indicators[b]
EWT 1	56	—	4	4	—	4
EWT 2	84	4	7	5	2	6
EWT 3	20	—	—	—	—	—
NST 1	34	3	5	3	1	6
NST 2	28	2	4	2	—	4
NST 3	28	1	3	2	—	3
NST 4	32	3	7	4	—	5–7
Total	*282*	*13*	*30*	*20*	*3*	*28–30*

[a]After Tolstoy and Fish 1973:9. EWT = East-West trench; NST = North-South trench.

[b]Total estimated number of structures differs from total number of observed concentrations because some concentrations seen in the trenches represent feature pits.

Basically, the trenches at Coapexco showed that the relationship between surface and subsurface features is somewhat complex. Some concentrations seen on the surface turned out to be features, rather than houses. Some houses appeared right where the surface concentrations indicated they would be. Still other houses appeared which had not been indicated on the surface. Moreover, the number of houses per hectare, as suggested by all indicators (surface and subsurface), was far in excess of the density seen in modern urban centers. This seemed to be a clear reflection of the time span involved, with newer houses built beside older houses that were being abandoned. Tolstoy and Fish eventually concluded the following:

1. Some surface "hot spots" do predict the approximate locations of buried houses.
2. Other "hot spots," however, indicate the location of features.
3. The number of houses predicted by surface "hot spots" will be far greater than the number occupied at any one time.
4. Concentrations of fire-cracked rock are most dense outside of, and between houses, and hence probably related to outdoor (cooking?) activities.
5. An "attenuation effect" results when heavy overburden reduces surface evidence of a buried structure.
6. A "merger effect" results when some concentrations become indistinct through inclusion in neighboring concentrations of high density.
7. Not all refuse concentrations existing at 25 cm below the surface can be detected on the surface itself.

In summary, the results of the Coapexco experiment indicate that, on reasonably shallow sites, controlled surface pickup *can* indicate the locations of houses before excavation begins. However, not all these houses will be contemporary, and some may turn out to be features. Numerous intervening variables—depth, overburden, erosion, length of occupation, and so on—will complicate the making of any reliable predictions of population size. And finally, if all these problems exist on relatively small areas of no great depth, what can be expected from large sites that are 5–10 m deep?

San José Mogote, Oaxaca, Mexico

One of the largest and most complex Formative sites in Mesoamerica for which we have any kind of "controlled surface pickup" is San José Mogote in the Valley of Oaxaca. The sampling design and its results are less than ideal, since the site is many times larger than any of those discussed so far, and the man-days of labor available were relatively few. We feel, however, that both the failures and the successes of the experiment will help in the planning of future surface pickups, and we present them for what they are worth.

San José Mogote is a very large site (covering more than 100 ha) with a long sequence spanning the period from Early Formative to Proto-Classic. In places, the site must be 4 to 5 m deep, and in the course of building earthen mounds, the later occupants moved and reused tons of earlier deposits. Thus, in addition to problems of sheer size, we were faced with the fact that some of the Early and Middle Formative sherds on the surface come not from primary deposits but from late Formative and Proto-Classic mound fill.

Virtually the whole of the analysis reported here was carried out in the final 2 weeks of the 1967 field season by Richard Orlandini, Chris Moser, and myself. It was Orlandini's responsibility to design the sampling technique, bearing in mind what had been done at Hatchery West, but with concessions made for the enormity of the site and its prodigious surface yield. From the beginning, Orlandini knew that he had only 2 weeks, and that, as he put it, "it would take a fleet of moving vans to carry away all the sherds from the surface." He had no time to lay out a grid over such an area, and even the laying out of 5-by-5-m squares would be time-consuming. Orlandini reasoned that it would be faster to lay out *circles* 5 m in diameter, using a variant of the "dog leash" technique proposed by Binford (1964). A survey pin would be driven in the ground and then the archeologist, using a 2.5 m string as the radius,

could quickly lay out a 5-m circle with powdered lime. These circles would provide us with a uniform-sized unit for collection.

Our need was for coverage of the whole site, without "blank areas" or clusters—ideally, by means of the stratified unaligned systematic design used at Girik-i-Haciyan by Redman and Watson. Having no grid and no axes, we used as our "strata" the individual maize or alfalfa fields that covered the site. Depending on its size, each individual field received 2–5 circles, located where they would do the least damage to the crop—a concession to the fact that the maize was then 3 feet high, and the farmers understandably nervous. Placing the circles where plants had failed to sprout or had been trampled by cattle was as close as we could come to generating a "random pattern." We began by scattering the circles 100 to 200 m apart; and near the periphery of the site, where circles were monotonously similar in content, we left it at that. Near the center of the site, where variation in content was greater, we kept adding circles until they were only 50–100 m apart. In all, Orlandini made 90 circles (and 2 more were added in 1970, bringing the total to 92). This gave us a total sample area of about 1840 sq m—less than one five-hundredth of the site, yet providing us with an estimated 25,000 sherds.

The method of collection was as follows. After Orlandini laid out each circle, a local workman was assigned to it with orders to pick up every scrap of material within the circle, even to scraping the surface clean with a trowel. In one pile, he placed all pot sherds; in another, all fragments of flint or chert, bone, shell, mica, magnetite, and so on. In a third pile, he placed all heavy stone, varying from pounders or *metates* and *manos* to obvious cut stone from architectural façade or stone rubble used in building fill. As he finished, Moser and I arrived and recorded the contents of his circle on a standardized form. For items such as chipped stone, the actual counts were used; for sherds, we used symbols to indicate whether the yield was light (under 50 sherds), medium (50–100), or heavy (over 100 sherds) *for each time period*.

Our reasons for conducting the intensive surface pickup were to define the approximate limits of the site for each time period, to locate functionally different activity areas where possible, to distinguish between areas of public buildings and areas of ordinary private houses, and to select areas for future excavation. In the process of analysis of the circles, therefore, we had to make the following simplifying assumptions:

1. Large, well-preserved sherds present in large numbers (sometimes including rim-to-base sections) were taken to indicate primary deposits below the surface.
2. Small, worn, rounded and eroded sherds present in large numbers were taken to indicate secondary deposits—in other words, sherds reused in construction fill or redeposited by pit-digging.
3. Extremely fancy pottery (such as funerary urn fragments, bridge-spouted vessels, or bowls with glyphs) were taken to indicate the presence of either public architecture or cemeteries.
4. Chunks of burned wattle and daub were taken to indicate small domestic structures.
5. Fragments of adobe brick indicated large private houses or modest public buildings.
6. Fragments of cut-stone facing, or masses of the kind of stone rubble used in building fill, were taken to indicate public buildings of more massive nature.
7. Circles with very few sherds but with high densities of plaster fragments were taken to indicate patios or plazas (where lower deposits were sealed off).
8. High frequencies of common maize-grinding stones (often occurring in areas of high wattle-and-daub frequency) were taken to indicate residential areas.
9. High concentrations of magnetite chunks and mirror fragments; onyx chips, drill plugs, and polishers; and numerous shell fragments with chert drills or burins in evidence were taken to indicate areas of craft activity.

Although any of these assumptions could be wrong, they (or others like them) are needed for the interpretation of surface remains. By using them, for example, one could interpret a given circle as follows:

> This is an area of Late Formative public buildings, as indicated by primary Late Formative sherd refuse; cut stone; rubble; and adobe fragments, with some fancy pottery. The fill of the structures is Early Formative debris, now rounded and eroded, but perhaps not from very far away. (The circle immediately to the west, for example, has primary Early Formative deposits with wattle-and-daub house fragments, *metates*, and *manos*.)

Table 3.2 gives an example of how the form for a given circle would be made out. Figure 3.4 shows the surface distribution of sherds of various time periods at San José Mogote. It was on the basis of such maps that areas were later selected for excavation. Not all of them have been excavated, and the final evaluation of the survey results must await that excavation.

It might legitimately be asked, how much can one predict from a sample comprising less than one five-hundredth of a site, and which falls short of the ideal "stratified unaligned systematic" spacing? In fact, in spite of the crudeness of the sample and the haste with which it was done, the number of predictions is large, and a number already have been verified.

Materials of the Early Formative can be picked up over an area roughly 450 m on a side, giving us a village that can be estimated at 20 ha in extent. Within this area, surface materials reflect at least three different kinds of predicted residential patterns: (*1*) an area of fancy "public buildings" with

TABLE 3.2   Abridged Version of Form Filled Out for Each 5-m Circle, Controlled Surface Pickup, San José Mogote, Oaxaca, Mexico[a]

Category of material	Code number of circle						
	1	4	12	21	34	42	85
Sherds, San José phase	x	xx			xxx		
Sherds, Guadalupe phase	xx	x			x	x	x(Re)
Sherds, Rosario/M.A. I	xxx	x	x(Re)	?	xxx	xxx	x
Sherds, Monte Albán II	xx	x	x(Re)	?	x	x	
Urn fragments	1		1				
Sea shells					1		
Iron ore		1					
Mica	3		1				
Obsidian			1		1		
Ground stone fragments		1			Hammer stone	Onyx waste	6
Chert fragments or flakes	10	5	14	20	26	4	11
Chipped stone tools	1	2				1	3
Adobe fragments							1
Burnt daub					xx		1
Construction stone		xxx		x		x	x
Other				Rubble mound fill	Comal frags.		

[a] x = present; xx = very common; xxx = heavily represented; (Re) = appears to be redeposited. After Flannery, Orlandini, Moser, and Varner (unpublished).

a relatively low percentage of chipping debris and utilitarian ground stone—this area was excavated in 1969 and did in fact contain such buildings, although some were earlier than predicted; (2) an area of ordinary wattle-and-daub houses with higher frequencies of chipping debris and utilitarian ground stone—this area was transect sampled in 1969 and does appear to contain such houses, though most are 200 years later than the public buildings mentioned; (3) an area of some 2 ha or more, near the eastern limits of Early Formative settlement, with a disproportionately high surface yield of worked and unworked magnetite, mica, quartz, and marine shell—this area had been excavated in 1966 and 1967, and the houses there did provide evidence of the craft activities that one would predict from the sample (Flannery et al. 1970:38–58).

During the Middle Formative, San José Mogote grew to cover more than 40 ha, and some of the areas previously mentioned were covered over and surrounded by literally tons of rubble and black clay (to fill in low areas for settlement) or adobe and earthen platforms. Circles in these areas show primary Middle Formative sherd refuse, adobe fragments, and redeposited fill of both Early and Middle Formative times. One area, tested in 1969, yielded a Middle Formative public building with adobe walls.

From Late Formative times, surface materials can be picked up over an area of perhaps 100 ha. The sample circles indicate that outlying areas were covered with "ordinary" houses accompanied by masses of utilitarian grinding stones. The "downtown" area was another matter. Here we would predict that the zone of public buildings had shifted to the east and that the public buildings now included massive rubble-filled structures faced with dressed stone; on the eastern limits of the "downtown" area was an elite cemetery with

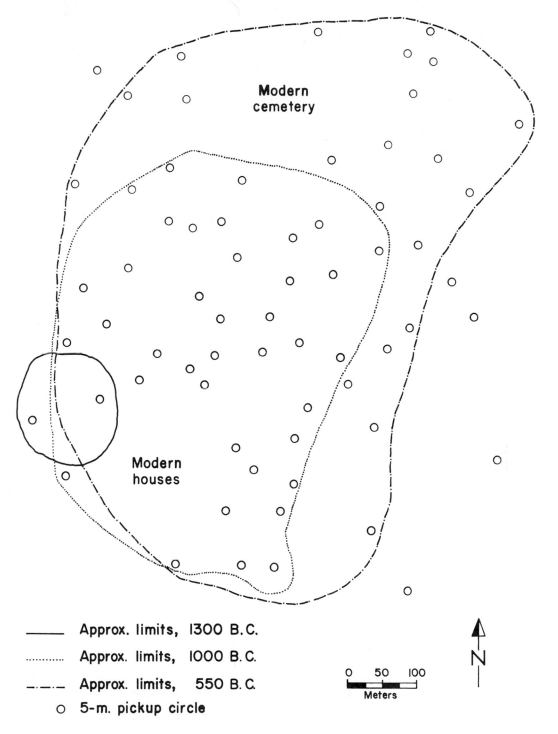

Modern
cemetery

Modern
houses

—————— Approx. limits, 1300 B.C.

⋯⋯⋯⋯⋯ Approx. limits, 1000 B.C.

—·—·— Approx. limits, 550 B.C.

○ 5-m. pickup circle

0   50   100
Meters

N

Figure 3.4 Growth of San José Mogote, Oaxaca, through time, as indicated by densities of surface sherds of various time periods. [After Flannery, Orlandini, Moser, and Varner, unpublished.]

hundreds of bridge-spout vessels as offerings. These predictions remain to be confirmed by excavation.

Summary

On the basis of the foregoing, we suggest that systematic, intensive surface studies of Formative villages can yield valuable information even when the sampling design is less than ideal, the time is too short, and the site is so complex that one must assume a lot of disturbance and secondary disposition. They can yield such information, however, only if one approaches the whole study with healthy skepticism, aware that a great deal of the pattern on the surface has resulted from erosion, gravity, monumental construction and disturbance, plowing, looting, and modern occupation. Indeed, in many cases, the use of extremely sophisticated sampling techniques might—because of these sources of disturbance—yield data no better than a relatively simple sampling design. This is something we hope can be worked out over the next decade by our pessimistic friend R.M.A.

Excavating a Shallow Community by Random Sampling Quadrats

MARCUS C. WINTER

The site of Tierras Largas covers the tip of a low piedmont spur overlooking the floodplain of the Atoyac River some 5 km north of Oaxaca City. Surveys in 1966 and 1968 suggested that Early and Middle Formative remains probably covered no more than 2 ha, and generally were less than 50 cm thick above bedrock. The site seemed an ideal place in which to make extensive horizontal excavations for the purpose of recovering the overall layout and house plans of what would be, by Parsons' and Blanton's definitions (Blanton 1972) a "Formative hamlet."

Tierras Largas was mapped in 1968, and, in 1969, I was confronted with the task of obtaining a sufficiently large and representative sample to reveal the village plan. Apart from a few prominent mounds (which we suspected might postdate the periods of interest to us), there were no traces of houses visible on the surface: The entire Formative area was, in fact, a featureless plowed field bisected by a dirt road.

Our first concern was to establish whether the site had been plowed beyond the point of usefulness. Three test pits, placed 20 m apart, revealed that it had not; and in fact, by pure luck, one of these test pits hit what appeared to be a floor or courtyard surface that was intact and undisturbed. Clearly, however, we could not depend on such luck to find the remainder of the Formative houses, or to form the basis for an estimate as to how many there might be. Some type of probability sampling was called for, and I decided to use the least complicated: a "simple random sample by squares" (see Plog, Chapter 5, this volume). This required (*1*) the definition of a sample universe, (*2*) the selection of sampling units, and (*3*) the determination of a sample size.

Definition of the Sample Universe

The boundaries of the area to be included in the random sample were determined by several factors. A primary consideration was the surface distribution of sherds of the Early Formative San José phase (1150–850 B.C.). Since the initial research aims called for a study of the San José phase village layout, sherds of other phases were not used in defining the universe. In the process of excavation, a still earlier period of the Early Formative (the Tierras Largas phase, 1400–1150 B.C.) was discovered.

Approximate extent of San José phase sherds had been noted in brief visits to Tierras Largas in 1968, and a more careful examination of surface sherds was made in preparation for sampling. The area encompassed by the distribution of these sherds was tentatively considered part of the San José phase village area, although the relationship between surface sherds and primary subsurface deposits was unknown at the time. The idea was to include all areas in the sample universe where San José phase primary deposits might possibly be present beneath the surface, and distribution of surface sherds seemed to be a reasonable criterion for delimiting a finite area.

Some parts of the site showed a gradual decrease in San José phase surface sherds, particularly on the east, northeast, and southwest. To ensure adequate coverage, the sample universe boundaries in these areas were extended 10 to 30 m beyond the obvious limit of San José phase sherds. In most other areas, the sample universe was easily bounded by changes in surface contour which roughly correlated with the limit of San José phase sherds. On the northwest, this boundary was formed by the edge of the piedmont spur. The western boundary was formed by the base of an artificial terrace from a later period, and the southeast boundary by the slope on the edge of the piedmont spur.

Several large areas within the limits of San José phase surface sherds were omitted from the sample universe. These included badly disturbed areas, such as a road that cuts through the site, and the area next to the road on the south where part of the site had been scraped away for use as fill in road construction. Visible mounds were also omitted from the sample universe, since their exca-

vation was considered to be a separate problem to be dealt with later, and most presumably postdated the San José phase. An area of earlier test excavation (Area A) was also excluded.

Selection of Sampling Units

Excavation of Area A had shown that, given the relative shallowness of the site, 2-by-2-m squares were large enough to clearly reveal subsurface deposits. Smaller squares would have been difficult to excavate in some places, and would have posed some problems in interpreting excavated deposits. Consequently, the 2-by-2-m unit was chosen as the size for sample squares.

In order to determine the number of sample squares to be excavated, it was necessary to know exactly how many 2-by-2-m squares occurred within the sample universe. A north-south (magnetic) grid of 2-by-2-m squares was laid out and extended towards the limits of the San José phase sherd scatter. Some of the site boundaries, particularly along the road, formed irregular areas, and it was necessary to know exactly how many 2-by-2-m squares could be placed there. As the metal stakes were placed and the areas measured on the ground, the information was recorded on graph paper, eventually producing a site outline.

Next, the squares inside the sample universe were numbered, beginning with the south side of the block of squares on the east side of the road, and numbering from east to west. The block of squares west of the road was then numbered, resulting in a total of 5307 sample squares in the universe.

Determination of Sample Size

After defining the sample universe of 5307 2-by-2-m squares (21,228 sq m), it was necessary to determine what proportion should be excavated. I decided to use a simple random sample, partly to avoid the possible complications and error of a more elaborate sampling technique, and partly because there did not seem to be any obvious reason for using something more elaborate. The sample could have been stratified on the basis of natural or modern features, such as distance from the top of the piedmont spur or side of the road, but this seemed unwarranted since it would not have been based on differences in the archeological material. In retrospect, it might have been useful to draw a "stratified systematic unaligned sample" of squares for excavation at Tierras Largas (see Plog, Chapter 5, this volume, and Redman and Watson 1970). Among other things, use of a stratified systematic unaligned sample provides against clustering of sample units and the occurrence of large unsampled areas on the site. It would be worthwhile to use this approach at another small Formative village in the Valley of Oaxaca and compare the results with the outcome of the simple random sample used at Tierras Largas.

Sample size was set up in terms of locating Formative houses. One house (House 1, in Area A) already had been excavated, and when it was originally recognized beneath the plow zone as a dark stain including sherds, burned daub, and other debris, it had covered an area of nearly 22 sq m (see Figure 2.1). House 1 was assumed to be "fairly typical" in size, since its dimensions did not diverge greatly from those of Formative houses previously recovered at the sites of Huitzo and San José Mogote.

The next step was to estimate the number of San José phase houses in the sample universe. There was no good basis for an accurate estimate, so 8 to 40 houses were used as a reasonable guess. If about 5 people lived in each house, the village population would have been 40 to 200 people. These estimates seemed to be within a reasonable range for a small Formative village like Tierras Largas. Using the estimates, the amount of area covered by houses would be:

Minimum: 8 houses X 22 sq m each = 176 sq m;
Maximum: 40 houses X 22 sq m each = 880 sq m.

Proportions of the sample universe (21,228 sq m) covered by houses would be:

Minimum: 176 sq m/21,228 sq m = .008 or .8%;
Maximum: 880 sq m/21,228 sq m = .041 or 4.1%.

Thus, evidence of houses was expected to occur in less than 5% of the sample universe or in less than 5% of the 2-by-2-m squares in the sample universe.

Sample size needed to determine the actual rate of occurrence of houses was then found, using tables published by Arkin and Colton (1963:22–23, 147). With a population size close to 5000 squares and an expected rate of occurrence of not over 5%, a sample size of 197 was chosen since this would yield a 95% confidence level with reliability of ±3% (Arkin and Colton 1963:147). A sample size of 195 is adequate for a population of 5000, but I increased the size to account for a slightly larger population. (In retrospect, it would have been convenient to use a sample size of 200, simply to facilitate calculations with a round number.) After the sample size had been determined, 197 actual sample squares at the site were chosen for excavation from a table of random numbers (Arkin and Colton 1963:158, beginning with the second thousand). Table 3.3 presents a list of the selected sample squares, arranged numerically in ascending order. Locations of sample squares are shown in Figure 3.5. The square numbers were used for provenience designations during excavation and analysis. Since 197 sample squares were excavated in a universe of 5307 squares, the sample proportion is 3.71% of the universe.

Excavation of Sample Squares

Sample squares were excavated with trowels, ice picks, and paintbrushes by teams of two workmen. Where squares hit open areas with no features, such as courtyards or nearly sterile areas, they were excavated to bedrock or sterile sandy clay,

TABLE 3.3 List of 197 Sample Squares Selected Randomly and Excavated at Tierras Largas

				Sample square numbers					
22	610	1248	1932	2423	2997	3488	3804	4324	4850
59	650	1301	1961	2439	2998	3493	3811	4343	4856
78	678	1314	1995	2461	3010	3497	3832	4358	4879
131	751	1392	1998	2488	3085	3510	3839	4363	4896
156	754	1403	2013	2490	3086	3564	3892	4367	4936
159	756	1437	2018	2522	3126	3574	3930	4413	4980
262	830	1501	2062	2529	3144	3578	3932	4430	5014
264	852	1562	2186	2544	3145	3615	3969	4471	5026
298	854	1582	2222	2556	3148	3660	4064	4499	5045
368	883	1596	2234	2611	3168	3666	4094	4547	5080
374	927	1612	2243	2629	3180	3673	4103	4604	5090
400	946	1614	2250	2690	3187	3682	4105	4631	5106
427	963	1665	2260	2738	3205	3683	4106	4724	5107
459	1023	1678	2273	2777	3225	3685	4124	4733	5127
466	1028	1769	2302	2782	3257	3724	4125	4746	5223
499	1030	1784	2304	2802	3262	3731	4153	4768	5225
548	1037	1792	2319	2836	3328	3733	4171	4785	5228
566	1205	1849	2322	2851	3464	3764	4240	4786	—
588	1212	1850	2344	2873	3482	3792	4264	4827	—
604	1222	1863	2377	2986	3487	3796	4312	4829	—

and appropriate notes were made. However, when primary deposits of possible Formative material were encountered, such as pits, burials, activity areas, or the corners or edges of houses, excavation was stopped and the material was covered with plastic sheets and dirt to await the next stage of excavation.

This final stage of excavation involved the greater horizontal exposure of areas around sample squares which appeared to contain primary deposits of Formative material. Ten such areas (Areas B through K) were added to previously investigated Area A. The extent of each area is listed in Table 3.4. Not all the areas yielded useful primary Formative deposits, but all produced information useful in understanding various aspects of occupation of the site.

With the excavation of these 11 larger areas, a total of 1490 sq m of horizontal area were uncovered (Table 3.4). The sample universe from which sample squares were randomly chosen for excavation covered slightly over 2 ha (21,228 sq m). However, the sample universe was not a single contiguous unit, because certain areas covered by mounds, destroyed by road construction through the site, and excavated prior to random sampling (Area A) were omitted from the universe. In all, about .6 ha (6036 sq m) of site area was omitted from the sample universe for these reasons (Table 3.5). Thus, the total area *outlined* by the periphery of the sample universe was 27,264 sq m, or about 2.7 ha.

The sample universe was defined primarily on the basis of surface occurrence of Early Formative sherds. To assure adequate coverage, some areas were included in the universe even though no Early Formative sherds were found on their surface. Omitting these areas, but including disturbed or inaccessible portions—that is, the mounds and road cut—yields an estimated figure of 2.0 to 2.5 ha for the Early Formative occupation based on *surface sherd distribution*. Thus, our total excavations sampled no more than 6% of the site. Small as this figure sounds, it appears from a

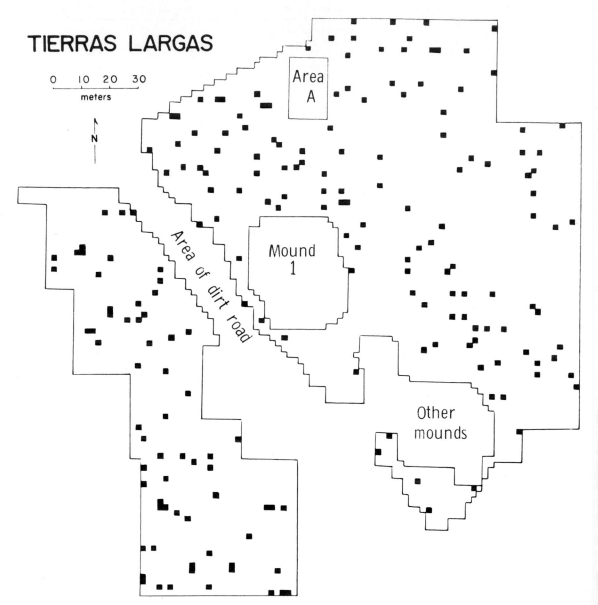

Figure 3.5 Sample universe at Tierras Largas, showing locations of 197 2-by-2-m sample squares selected randomly and excavated.

TABLE 3.4 Sizes of Excavated Areas at Tierras Largas[a]

Area designation	Number of 2-by-2-m squares	Designations of sample squares in area	Total excavated area (square meters)	Total excavated area excluding sample squares (square meters)
Area A	77	none	308	308
Area B	30	2851; 2986	120	112
Area C	22	1998; 2222	88	80
Area D	15	2377; 2529	60	52
Area E	12	3892	48	44
Area F	4	3724	16	12
Area G	7	1612; 1665	28	20
Area H	6	5080	24	20
Area I	6	678	24	20
Area J	5.5	610	22	18
Area K.	5	2836	20	16
Total	*189.5*	*all above*	*758*	*702*

[a]197 2-by-2-m sample squares were excavated, totaling 788 square meters. A grand total of 1490 sq m in all was excavated at Tierras Largas.

casual search of the literature that it is a great deal more than is usually sampled at Formative sites.

The sampling program at Tierras Largas showed that, during any one period, the village was composed of a series of 8-12 household clusters (see Chapter 2), separated by courtyards or open work areas 20-40 m across. Each household cluster covered 300 sq m or more, and each was composed of at least one house and a series of pits, burials, ovens, drainage ditches, or other features, as well as activity areas. Because of the way the sample was taken, one can estimate the numbers of houses, pits, burials, and so forth, that would be found if the entire community could be excavated. Each estimate consists of a range of numbers at the 95% confidence level. In Chapter 8, we will discuss the growth of Tierras Largas through time, and present a series of maps showing what the village might have looked like during several different periods.

TABLE 3.5 Within-Site Areas Omitted from the Sample Universe at Tierras Largas and Not Excavated[a]

Area designation	Number of 2-by-2-m squares	Total area (square meters)
Mound 1	310	1240
Small mound group	353	1412
Road-cut, bank along road, and area scraped away for road fill	769	3076
Total	*1432*	*5728*

[a]Area A (308 sq m) was omitted from the sample universe but excavated before the sample program was initiated. Thus, a total of 6036 sq m of within-site area was omitted from the sample universe.

Excavating Deep Communities by Transect Samples

KENT V. FLANNERY

Not all sites can be sampled efficiently by the methods described by Winter (pp. 62–67). At deeper sites—like the 5-m mounds so beloved by the Real Mesoamerican Archeologist—2-by-2-m squares like those used by Winter at Tierras Largas would quickly turn into deep, dark, and uninformative "telephone booths." This is, in fact, how R.M.A. often excavates; but even he isn't fully satisfied with it.

As Stephen Plog's section on site survey (Chapter 5) makes clear, for some purposes, transect samples are more efficient than either quadrats or sample squares. One case in which they might be more efficient is the sampling of very deeply stratified Formative sites. A "transect" through such a site would be a long trench, ideally connecting two points selected at random. All features recovered in the trench would be recorded, and an idea of their relative frequency could be built up, once a statistically meaningful proportion of the site had been sampled by such transects.

Although the "ideal" method would be to select a series of random points on opposite sides of the site and connect them with trenches, it is unlikely that many archeologists of R.M.A.'s generation could bring themselves to make such trenches. Many would cross the site at odd angles (see Figure 5.4), and the result would look very disorderly and unplanned to a generation raised on the writings of Sir Mortimer Wheeler. Moreover, the archeological officials of most Latin American countries would probably take a dim view of the appearance of such an excavation, unless the rationale behind it could be convincingly spelled out. Perhaps a future generation of skeptical graduate students will have the nerve (and permis-

sion) to sample some deep Formative sites this way. In the meantime, most archeologists will continue to make trenches that follow an orderly grid, the cardinal compass points, or some site axes—and which, therefore, will have many of the defects of orderly grid square samples.

As a preview of what transect sampling might have to offer, let us now examine several transects through Formative sites in Mexico. These were "profiles" cut fortuitously by local adobe makers—not made according to any random sampling design, but not placed according to any cardinal-point grid either. They cross deeply stratified archeological deposits at compass directions far from the cardinal points, and their content, at least, gives us an idea of what transect trenches might provide in the way of raw data.

Ajalpan, near Tehuacán, Puebla

Mesoamerican archeologists have frequently used fortuitous cut banks, looter's holes, or arroyos as a way of getting a "preview" of buried deposits before excavating. One of the field workers who has used these most extensively is Richard S. Mac-Neish, and one of the best examples is his site of Ajalpan.

The village of Ajalpan lies in a zone of mesquite, short grass, and prickly pear groves along the east bank of the Río Salado in the central valley of Tehuacán, Puebla. The Formative archeological site runs for several hundred meters along the alluvial plain just south of town, at an elevation of 1230 m (4050 feet). Since the matrix of the site is excellent brick clay, local brickworkers had made an enormous quarry in the area when MacNeish arrived in 1962. Literally hundreds of meters of nearly vertical cut banks were available for examination; one could wander at will through a maze of "transects" in the Formative village, selecting areas with interesting features or good stratigraphy for excavation. As MacNeish (1962:19-20) reports:

> The primary excavation was made in the northern part of this area at site Ts 204. Here the walls of a peninsula-like cut revealed good stratigraphy of the Formative period. . . . To insure good stratigraphic control of our excavation we first cleared off three sides of a block nine by ten by ten meters. Then we completely excavated a six by six by nine meter portion of this block by stripping off the horizontal natural strata against the profiles. In this manner, we could usually see and strip off strata or floors from two or three vertical profiles. This technique insured maximum control and avoided digging by arbitrary levels.

In the course of this excavation, MacNeish recovered three superimposed house floors and one bell-shaped storage pit which later had been used for a burial, as in the case of many Tierras Largas pits (see Chapter 2).

Barrio del Rosario Huitzo, Oaxaca

Barrio del Rosario is the northernmost *barrio* of the village of San Pablo Huitzo, located at 17° 17' N. Lat., 96° 54' W. Long. in the Valley of Oaxaca. The setting is a narrow stretch of semiarid valley at an elevation of 1969 m (5563 feet), near the confluence of an intermittent tributary stream with the main Atoyac River. Formative deposits underlying the *barrio* cover an estimated 2.7 ha; the central 13% of the site consists of a mound about 50 by 70 m in extent, which rises 5 m above the courtyards of the present houses of Huitzo (and has cultural deposits known to continue for 2 m more below the courtyards.) This mound—which was evidently somewhat larger before brickmaking

activities were carried out on it—is a *tell* in the Near Eastern sense, with a long stratigraphic sequence of private and public buildings. It is the massive adobe architecture of the "public" and/or "elite residential" buildings that raised this "downtown area" above the rest of the site (Flannery *et al.* 1970:27).

Under normal conditions, the internal makeup of such a mound would be difficult, if not impossible, to predict before excavation. A typical procedure used in Mesoamerican archeology would be to clear off the vegetation (mostly mesquite trees and grass) and put a test trench into it from one side in search of walls. That proved unnecessary in this case, because the removal of earth for adobe brick had exposed a continuous, nearly vertical face almost 60 m long—a kind of rough-and-ready version of the transect sample. All that remained was to cut the profile to a truly vertical condition and shave it with razor-sharp trowels and square-ended shovels. This was accomplished in a matter of days in 1967, using a house painter's scaffold and a plumb bob. The profile was then sprayed with a light mist of water from a crop sprayer, and the color changes leapt out at us: dozens of meters of earthen platforms, house floors, pits, postholes, burials, and refuse middens, constituting a long cross-section of the village, from which we could select as many features as we wanted for excavation. All we were deprived of was the kind of statistical manipulation of the data that would have been possible had the profile(s) been placed by means of a true random transect design.

As the profile at Huitzo dried, we photographed and later outlined with an ice pick all the visible stratigraphic breaks in color, soil texture, and type of material. While these were still fresh, we constructed a grid of 1-by-1-m squares over the whole profile, using mason's string (Figure 3.6). The horizontal lines were established by mason's bubble level, the vertical lines by plumb bob. The whole profile was then drawn and numbers were assigned to all houses, platforms, walls, pits, burials, and middens that were visible.

Figure 3.6 Sample transect through archeological deposits at Barrio del Rosario, Huitzo, Oaxaca, divided into 1-by-1-m squares. Visible are house floors, platforms, and bun-shaped adobe brick walls.

After this drawing was complete, we examined the whole profile and selected the 5-m-wide section that contained the widest variety of houses and features. This became the "control" section, whose stratigraphy was known in advance and whose features were numbered even before excavation; it was to be totally screened through half-centimeter mesh, with all categories of material saved, and samples of every ashy layer kept out for carbonized seed flotation. Starting at the top of the profile, we cut this "control" section back only half a meter (to insure the minimum amount of dipping or rising of the various strata) and excavated downward exclusively by "natural" or "cultural" levels.

Each *type* of archeological deposit presented a different set of problems, for which a separate set of techniques was required. Although we are far from satisfied with the procedures used, let us examine these in detail.

When a *wattle-and-daub house* collapses, it often forms a puddle of debris 4 by 6 m in extent and up to 30 cm thick. In the profile of a "transect trench," this will appear as a lens of clay debris varying from 3 to 7 m in length, depending on how the house has been sectioned. At Huitzo, we first scraped the top of the lens with trowels to prepare it for excavation. We then dug through the upper 20 cm or so of the lens with trowels and ice picks; this zone usually contained burned fragments of clay daub with cane impressions, especially near walls. Most of the daub falls within a meter or less of the wall, but some fragments roll even to the center of the house.

Below this layer of collapsed daub, and sometimes mixed with it, are the pot sherds and artifacts left *in situ* on the floor of the house at the time of abandonment. The problems of distinguishing these from materials thrown in after abandonment and before wall collapse have already been discussed by Winter in the preceding section. From here on, the techniques we used were the same as his: to plot all artifacts *in situ*, carefully troweling down to the sand floor through the light film of ash tramped onto it by the occupants of the house. Finally, the sand would be removed and the earth below it sprayed, to bring out the different color of any postmolds that might be present. These would be drawn in plan view, then pedestaled and cross-sectioned. When they contained charcoal from a burned post, it would be saved for wood identification and radiocarbon dating. The light film of ash from the top of the sand floor also would be saved for flotation. This was our version of "Midwestern" archeology.

We also scraped the top surfaces of *refuse midden* to separate them from the deposits above. Excavated slowly by trowel, each midden would then be screened to remove all artifacts, animal bones, and avocado seeds. The dirt passing through the half-centimeter screen would be saved in large baskets lined with newspaper, and allowed to dry in the shade in preparation for flotation.

The *"public" or "elite residential" platforms* at Huitzo were excavated by our version of "Near Eastern" archeology. We cut down to them from above with small picks, stopping just 10 cm above the platform. The last 10 cm were removed with trowels and ice picks. Carefully the top of the platform was scraped, then brushed with a whisk broom. Then, using ice picks or sharpened screwdrivers, a crew of experienced workmen began peeling away the fill from the top and sides of the platform, working back from the sprayed profile a little bit at a time. As they proceeded, they outlined any adobe bricks present by picking out half a centimeter of the surrounding mortar with the tip of an ice pick. Arriving at any plastered face of the structure, they peeled the earth to within a

centimeter of the plaster and let it dry; after this, it could be flicked off the surface of the plaster with the point of a trowel. A final step was to scrape and spray the top of the platform in a search for postholes.

By treating the ready-made "transect" at Huitzo in this fashion, we recovered:

1. A detailed drawing of a 20-m cross-section of the central part of the Formative village, in which the stratigraphic relationships of public and private buildings and their various middens, pits, and associated features were known.
2. Remains of five "public" or "elite residential" platforms whose internal construction could be seen.
3. Parts of lenses left by the collapse of four private houses, three of which had house floors with artifacts *in situ* and sometimes postmolds. The houses thus sampled could then be compared (with each other, and with houses at other sites) in terms of architecture, artifact categories, trade goods, foodstuffs, and activity areas.
4. Several middens rich in identifiable seeds, animal bones, and discarded trade goods, whose stratigraphic relationship to the houses could be demonstrated through the section drawing.

San José Mogote, Oaxaca

The site of San José Mogote has already been described in a previous section (pp. 58–59). The setting is a spur of the Oaxaca piedmont which projects out, like a low peninsula, toward the Atoyac River at an elevation of about 1610 m (5280 feet). Like Barrio del Rosario Huitzo, San José Mogote had been the scene of earth removal for local adobe brickmaking. In this case, brickmakers had exposed two vertical cut banks or "transects"—one 99.5 m long, the other 37.5 m long. In 1969, we eventually extended the latter to 93 m, at which point it intersected the former, giving us a continuous cross-section of the village some 192.5 m long. This cross-section—which contained more than a dozen house lenses with floors, and many associated middens, pits, and burials— was excavated with the same combination of "Midwestern" and "Near Eastern" techniques used at Huitzo (Flannery *et al*. 1970:38).

Because the profile at San José Mogote was so long, it was possible, in some cases, to pick up areas where an entire "household cluster," in Winter's terms (see Chapter 2), had been cross-sectioned: The transect passed through a house, then its adjacent midden and one of its bell-shaped storage pits, then a burial in almost certain association. It is very unlikely that such a phenomenon would have occurred in the much shorter "transect" at Huitzo, and this fact argues for long transects.

Two additional features, seen at San José Mogote but not at Huitzo, also argue for long transects: arroyo fill and slope wash. From the 192.5-m section, it was clear that the original surface on which Early Formative occupation had begun was a sloping hillside covered with gullies and small arroyos. The villagers had placed their houses on the high points, with burials and some storage pits part of the way down the slope. The arroyos were unused, but had partially filled with erosion products of all periods.

Late in the Middle Formative, a massive program had been initiated to fill these arroyos level with the high points, in order to expand settlement. To this purpose, earlier debris was scraped up and dumped into the arroyos, sometimes stabilized with rough adobe retaining walls. The stratigraphy of these vast areas was thus totally mixed; in places, one could have dug to a depth of 5 m without finding a single object that was still in its original context. Moreover, an examination of the section drawings showed that areas of arroyo fill or slope wash—both useless for the kinds of analyses we hoped to do—made up 80% of the deposits in that part of San José Mogote, while undisturbed primary deposits were only 20%. This well may be typical of hillside Formative sites. It means that, if one has no previously cut profile from which to select a place for his initial test pit, *that pit has only about one chance in five of hitting primary deposits*.

How many Formative archeologists have been victims of these unfavorable odds? I know of half a dozen Formative sites whose whole *sequence* is based on redeposited fill, and of at least one archeologist who has done it six times. He needs only four more to qualify for his Mickey Mouse ears.

Two Possible Village Subdivisions: The Courtyard Group and the Residential Ward

KENT V. FLANNERY

Before leaving the community level of analysis, we should consider two possible subdivisions of early Mesoamerican villages. Both are vaguely and poorly defined because of small sample size. Their existence has not been confirmed either by extensive excavation or by stylistic analysis of intravillage partitioning, and my discussion of them will be highly tentative. Nevertheless, they deserve mention because they may represent intermediate analytical levels, between the household cluster and the community.

As all Mesoamerican archeologists are aware,

present-day Indian villages in Mesoamerica are frequently divided into *barrios* or residential wards. The barrio constitutes an organizational unit at the subcommunity level; each barrio in a village has a series of communal or ceremonial activities which it plans and carries out relatively independently of other barrios. Unless there are status differences between two barrios, such that houses in one might be architecturally more elegant than in the other, one usually does not "see" the division between barrios. They become clear only when one barrio is engaged in an activity not shared by other barrios, such as a craft specialization, or a barrio-specific ceremony.

Although *barrio* is a Spanish term, there are good ethnohistoric grounds for believing that Pre-Columbian cities, towns, and villages in Mesoamerica were usually divided into residential wards. Even if one goes back 1000 years before the conquest, one finds that cities like Teotihuacán were divided into wards of craft specialists like potters, obsidian workers, and perhaps merchants (Millon 1967). Such evidence extends far back into the Formative period. We have already mentioned Aufdermauer's (1970:15) evidence that, shortly after 600 B.C., the village of Moyotzingo, Puebla, was divided into at least two residential areas: Large solid houses of adobe brick appeared on the summit of the low hill, while the lower slopes were covered with wattle-and-daub huts. That such residential wards can sometimes be detected even on the surface is indicated by Coe's (1963) map of Naranjito, a late Formative village on the Guatemalan Pacific Coast (see Figure 3.11). At Naranjito there seemingly were eastern and western residential areas, with the "higher-status" houses in the western area. Both at Moyotzingo and Naranjito, public buildings were spatially associated with the somewhat more elegant residences.

However, such ward divisions need not have been associated with social rank, particularly in the early village period of interest to us here. At San José Mogote in the Valley of Oaxaca (see pp. 58–59) there appear to have been at least four residential wards, and possibly more, between

1150 and 850 B.C. They occurred on low natural rises at the site, and they were separated by ancient erosion gulleys into which the occupants threw their trash. One residential ward, in Area C, lies at the west edge of the site. A second, in Area B, lies 100 m to the east, on top of a separate natural rise. A third, in Area A, lies 300 m still further to the east, near what was at that time the eastern edge of the village. The architectural differences between these contemporary residential wards are not striking, but there are some differences in craft activities (cf. Pires-Ferreira, Chapter 10) and perhaps ceramic design preferences (cf. Pyne, Chapter 9).

Obviously, such residential wards are more easily detectable at large villages, or long narrow communities strung out along watercourses. But what about small, compact hamlets of 1–2 ha or so, perhaps consisting of 8–12 households? Winter's work at Tierras Largas (pp. 227–229) would suggest that such small communities were probably *not* divided into residential wards. In fact, such hamlets may have been about the size of (or even smaller than) a residential ward at a large village like San José Mogote. It may be that 8–12 households was a minimal social unit, below which subdivision for organizational reasons was neither practical nor desirable. If so, it might help explain the enormous prevalence of 1–2 ha hamlets detected by Marcus in her section of this same chapter (pp. 79–89). However, it also raises a typological question: If both hamlets and individual residential wards at larger villages were about 1–2 ha in size, how do we know whether a given 1–2 ha site (like Tierras Largas) was a separate community, or just an outlying barrio* of a larger village (like San José Mogote)? An answer is easy to come by: We don't yet know, and it may be

---

*Outlying barrios are common not only in present-day, "dispersed" Indian communities, but in the later periods of the archeological record. For example, during the Post-Classic period in the Valley of Oaxaca, Bernal (personal communication) describes the community of Zaachila as consisting of a central nuclear town surrounded by large outlying barrios at distances of 3–5 km.

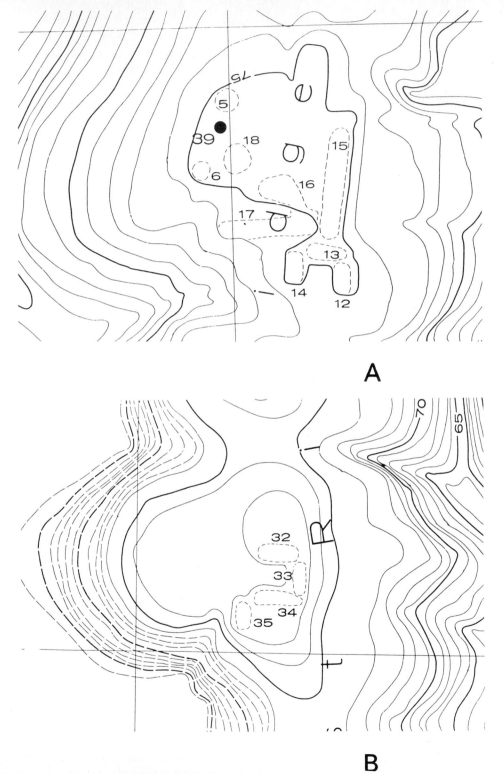

Figure 3.7 San Lorenzo, Veracruz. Possible groups of three house mounds sharing a common courtyard. (A) Mounds 12, 13, and 14, northwest ridge; (B) Mounds 32, 33, and 34, southwest ridge. [After Coe 1968b.]

very hard to find out, so we will defer the question until Chapter 6.

It is possible, however, that even small hamlets of 8–12 households were subdivided into what might *very tentatively* be called "courtyard groups." These would consist of groups of 3 to 4 households, all sharing the same courtyard or open work space. Examinations of Winter's maps for the late Tierras Largas phase and the late San José phase at Tierras Largas (Figures 8.3–8.4) do suggest such groupings.

Between 1250 and 1150 B.C., Tierras Largas was a hamlet of about 10 households, occupying 2.2 ha. Between 950 and 850 B.C., it was a hamlet of perhaps 8 households, occupying 1.5 ha. At both periods, household clusters were separated by open areas which appear by simple inspection to be roughly rectangular in shape; these were 30–40 m across at 1250 B.C., only 20 m across at 900 B.C. Wherever the outlines of the house are clear, the long axis of the structure seems to flank the courtyard. Simple inspection also suggests that there may have been houses on three sides of each courtyard, the fourth side being left open.

Obviously, since no real test of this arrangement has been carried out, we could be reading the courtyard pattern into the data. We cannot help being influenced by the knowledge that, in later periods of the Formative, public buildings were often arranged around three or four sides of a rectangular patio. However, supporting data for a "courtyard group" of three to four households comes from San Lorenzo, Veracruz. An examination of Coe's (1968b) map of San Lorenzo reveals several groups of house mounds arranged around three sides of a courtyard (Figure 3.7). The mounds themselves are roughly 5–7 by 10–12 m in extent, with courtyards 10 m across. Since these particular mounds have not been excavated, we cannot state their time period with any confidence. They presumably fall somewhere between 1150 and 500 B.C., and they may have been for elite houses.

As this impressionistic discussion suggests, the concepts of "residential ward" and "courtyard group" need a great deal of work before their validity as analytical levels can be determined. If future analysis proves them to be useful, the sequence of units in large villages would perhaps run: house, household cluster, courtyard group, residential ward, community. To accomplish this will take hard work. And to show which segment of Formative society is reflected by each of these analytical levels would be a Skeptical Graduate Student's dream come true.

Zoning within an Early Formative Community in the Valley of Oaxaca★

MICHAEL E. WHALEN

Previous sections of this chapter have discussed the household cluster, the courtyard group, and

*The work upon which this paper is based was supported by National Science Foundation Doctoral Dissertation Improvement Grant GS-40325, and by a Ford Foundation Grant for Field Training in Archeology made to the University of Michigan.

the residential ward as units of analysis within early villages. This section presents one example of the division of an early village into functionally different zones involving some of these analytic units.

Recently completed excavations at Santo Domingo Tomaltepec in the Tlacolula district of the Valley of Oaxaca (Whalen 1974) have isolated three possible zones of this Early Formative community. These are (A) an area of relatively higher status residences, including a stone-and-adobe house platform; (B) an area of relatively lower status residences, such as wattle-and-daub houses; and (C) a cemetery area, apparently disassociated from any other contemporary cultural feature. Before proceeding to a discussion of these three zones, let us briefly consider the community itself.

Tomaltepec is a small, fairly shallow site (some 2 ha in area and .5 to 1.5 m deep) with only the most meager surface indications—ceramic or otherwise—of Early Formative occupation, although Late Formative sherds are relatively abundant. The site is located on the high terrace of a tributary stream in the piedmont zone, near the point where the stream emerges from a mountain canyon. Recent surveys show this to be a fairly typical settlement choice for Early Formative sites in the western Tlacolula valley (S. Kowalewski, personal communication), though it contrasts sharply with the Atoyac River sites in the Etla region (see Flannery, Chapter 6, this volume). The topography of the terrace, which merges with a ridge of piedmont, had a considerable effect on village patterning, as will shortly be apparent. A population of 25 to 40 persons residing in 5 to 8 household clusters is estimated for the Early Formative period. Specifically, the occupation of greatest interest at Tomaltepec dates to the early part of the San José phase (1150–1000 B.C.), the ceramic assemblage still including distinctive material from the antecedent Tierras Largas phase.

Accordingly, each of the three above-mentioned zones will be briefly described, and finally the structure of the whole community will be considered.

Area A: A Relatively Higher-Status Residential Area

This area consists of two superimposed structures: (*1*) a wattle-and-daub house of the usual Early Formative type (House 9), and (*2*) a slightly later stone-and-adobe house platform (Structure 11), which was erected partly over the remains of the earlier house.

House 9 is of essentially the same elevation as the relatively lower-status house (House 4) to be considered presently, and, by all indications, was much the same sort of wattle-and-daub structure. Bell-shaped storage pits of roughly equivalent capacity were associated with each house. A marked difference between the two structures, however, was noted in the fill of the two pits (which, by all indications, consisted of contemporary trash from the immediate area of each house).

The pit associated with House 9 in Area A yielded an assemblage of chipped stone tools and debitage in which the proportion of imported obsidian to local chert was considerably higher than in House 4 samples. In addition, the House 9 pit yielded more substantial quantities of animal bone, including deer and rabbit. In addition, more marine shell was recovered from the House 9 area and pit than from any other single contemporary location at Tomaltepec.

However, it should be emphasized that while the occupants of House 9 possessed objects which, in terms of transportation "costs" could be designated relatively more "expensive" (e.g., sea shell and obsidian), there is no indication that House 9 was dissimilar in *kind* to the relatively lower-status structure, House 4. The essential difference here, in other words, would seem to be one of degree.

The second (and slightly later) structure in the relatively higher-status residential zone, however, was different in kind. This was a stone-and-adobe house platform (Structure 11). Structure 11 measured some 4 by 8 m, with vertical walls rising approximately 1 m above the ground surface. Due to later leveling for the superimposition of a Middle Formative platform, nothing remained of the house that once stood atop Structure 11. However, the vast quantities of domestic refuse associated with the structure most strongly suggest a residential rather than a ceremonial–civic function. Almost certainly, Structure 11 is unique at Tomaltepec, differing from other contemporary houses, which were not set on platforms.

Domestic refuse associated with Structure 11 includes impressive quantities of obsidian and animal bone, a vast increase in both cases over similar material associated with House 9. In comparison with House 4, an entirely different order of magnitude of consumption is in evidence at Structure 11. In addition, a partly finished marine shell ornament as well as several large fragments of unaltered shell were found in association with Structure 11, implying production as well as consumption of "high cost" items.

Area A would thus seem to have remained a relatively higher-status residential area through two successive construction phases. Reference to Figure 3.8 shows Area A on the southeastern edge of the community, near the drop-off from the terrace to the stream. Tomaltepec, in other words, does not fit the widespread, preconceived notion of a Mesoamerican community organized around centrally placed high-status residences or public buildings. Indeed, it may be that, at this stage of cultural evolution, the precise location within the village chosen by relatively higher status families was not a matter of great significance, and that community plans were relatively informal.

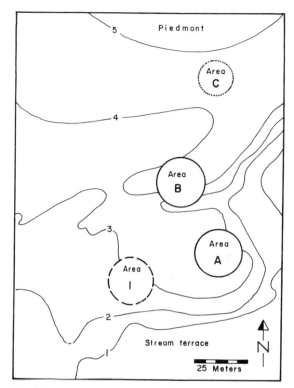

Figure 3.8 Santo Domingo Tomaltepec, Oaxaca. Map of Early Formative village showing spatial relationship of areas mentioned in the text. Known household cluster (—); probable household cluster(— — —); cemetery area (. . . .).

Area B: A Relatively Low-Status Residential Area

As previously indicated, Area A is almost certainly unique at Tomaltepec. In contrast, test excavations suggest that Area B generally typifies the remainder of the community. House 4, the wattle-and-daub structure located in Area B, has already been described in Chapter 2 of this volume (p. 20). Excavated in association with the house floor itself was a bell-shaped storage pit, the contents of which have already been referred to (Chapter 2). Much less animal bone, much less

obsidian, virtually no marine shell, and a higher proportion of tools and debitage of locally available chert were recovered. These associations and the nature of the house itself, when taken in comparison with House 9, lead to our designation of Area B as part of a relatively lower-status residential zone.

Area C: A Specialized Cemetery Area

Area C, an Early Formative cemetery area, lay to the north of the community in a zone that was technically beyond the "limits of the site" as defined by surface survey. Because the area had never been used for houses, middens, or features of any kind, no Early Formative ceramics occurred on the surface. However, excavation of an area of 110 sq m produced 60 San José phase burials representing some 70–80 adult individuals of both sexes. No infants or children were present in the cemetery. Although secondary burials had been added in a number of cases, no burial had been excessively disturbed by any other contemporary burial; the implication is that some system of burial location must have existed. Furthermore, uniformity of burial position was nearly absolute, most skeletons being prone, face down, with head to the east.

At San José Mogote, Tierras Largas, and San Sebastián Abasolo in the Valley of Oaxaca, numerous burials were found in household clusters. However, a high proportion of these (especially at San José Mogote and Abasolo) were children and infants. The discovery of an adult cemetery at Tomaltepec brings up a possibility to be investigated in future years: that initiated adults were usually buried in a special cemetery, while children dying too young for initiation were usually buried in the vicinity of the house.

Intracommunity Spacing

The relationship between Areas A, B, and C at Tomaltepec is shown in Figure 3.8. A fourth area, Household Location 1, is also shown to the west of Area A. By all indications, the household in this location more closely resembled that discovered in Area B than either of the residences in Area A. No other area tested yielded any evidence of houses on platforms.

Each known and probable household location, then, is represented in Figure 3.8 by a circle of 20 m in diameter. This distance both approximates the size of Early Formative household clusters as estimated by Winter (Chapter 2) and reflects the

dispersion of House 4 and associated features in Area B, the most extensively excavated area of the site. In each case, the known or presumed location of the house itself is near the center of the circle.

Based upon his work at Tierras Largas, Winter (1972:85–87) has suggested that (*1*) household clusters were approximately evenly spaced; (*2*) in the Tierras Largas and early San José phases, spacing between the margins of household clusters was some 20 m; and (*3*) distance between cluster centers averaged 40 m. Reference to Figure 3.8 indicates that these spacing principles also are applicable to the village at Tomaltepec.

The centers of House 9 and Structure 11 (both in essentially the same location in Area A) lie between 40 and 45 m from the center of House 4 (Area B). Likewise, if circles of 20 m in diameter are drawn around House 4 and House 9/Structure 11 and are taken to represent household cluster boundaries, some 20 to 25 m remains between the two clusters. Testing in this between-cluster area produced little or no Early Formative debris, all of which accords well with Winter's spacing principles. Similarly, both House 4 and House 9/Structure 11 lie between 40 and 50 m from Probable Household Location 1. The edge of a circle of 20 m in diameter drawn around Probable Location 1 is separated by 20–25 m from the House 9/Structure 11 household cluster boundary, and by some 33 m from the House 4 cluster boundary. Finally, the Area C cemetery is located some 30 m north of Area B, with no intervening evidence of household clusters. Apparently, therefore, roughly the same distance considered adequate for separating ordinary households was considered adequate for (*1*) separating higher-status residences from the nearest household and (*2*) segregating cemetery areas from the nearest household.

Finally, it should be pointed out that further household clusters of ordinary type are believed to occur to the northwest of Area B and Household Locality 1, in areas that could not be thoroughly investigated, owing to a lack of time and funds.

Summary and Conclusions

At some Early Formative sites in the Valley of Oaxaca, it is possible to distinguish a zone of public buildings, distinct from that of ordinary residences. At Barrio del Rosario Huitzo, for example, such a zone constituted 13% of the surface area of the site (cf. Chapter 3, this volume).

Tomaltepec could conceivably be divided into (*1*) a small zone of higher-status residences in the southeast corner of the site; (*2*) a much larger zone of lower-status residences which surrounded the first zone on the west and north; and (*3*) a cemetery beyond the northern limits of the village as defined by surface ceramics. However, such zonation was certainly less formal than the zonation of later Classic and Post-Classic Mesoamerican communities. Not only was the segregation of the cemetery and the higher-status residence no greater than that between ordinary households, but there is a good chance that the precise location of the higher-status residence within the community was a matter of no great consequence.

The Size of the Early Mesoamerican Village

JOYCE MARCUS

This section deals with a simple-sounding question: What size were Early Formative Mesoamerican villages? As so often happens with the simplest archeological questions, I have been unable to find the answer anywhere in the literature. Most Mesoamerican archeologists have simply not provided us with reliable measurements of Formative villages. Even when the absolute area of the site is known, it is often not clear what size it was at any one period.

Notable exceptions are the surveys conducted by Sanders (1965), Parsons (1971), and Blanton (1972) in the eastern Valley of Mexico. These investigators paced out the scatters of surface sherds of all periods for each of their sites, calculating the size of the site in hectares for each time period with the aid of large-scale aerial photographs. Although methodical and relatively complete surveys are known from other regions, they are not in the same format as the Valley of Mexico data, and hence not exactly comparable. Usually, the surveys in other regions give only the maximum size reached by the site, which is not precise enough in the case of multiperiod sites.

Even more imprecise is the conversion of site size into population estimates. Both Parsons and Blanton have attempted such conversions, applying a constant range of persons-per-hectare based on modern villages, and using the density of surface debris as a guide to whether the "small" or "large" end of that constant range applies. Both have been very consistent and rigorous about applying this methodology. However, as Tolstoy and Fish (1973) point out, two variables intervene between hectarage and population: (*1*) duration of occupation and (*2*) the effective thickness of overburden. Tolstoy and Fish therefore recommend "that population estimates be based on estimated number of households rather than on estimated amounts of surface refuse" (Tolstoy and Fish 1973:20).

This is precisely the unit that Winter (Chapters 2 and 8, this volume) has used for calculating the population of Oaxaca villages. Even this method, however, has logistic difficulties. For one thing, the length of occupation seriously affects one's estimates. As Tolstoy and Fish (1973) point out, what we want is an estimate of the "momentary population" for each village, not the number of houses built over a 300-year phase as defined on the basis of ceramics.

To give one example: Winter's original calculations suggested that, during the San José phase (1150–850 B.C.), about 12–22 houses were built at Tierras Largas, Oaxaca (Flannery 1972:44). No sooner had Flannery quoted these figures than Winter refined the ceramic chronology to make the period divisible into "Early San José" (1150–1000 B.C.) and "Late San José" (1000–850 B.C.) subphases. This cut the "momentary population" of houses virtually in half, with an estimated five falling in Early San José and eight in Late San José (see Table 8.1, Chapter 8). Thus, as Winter (1972) points out, even when one's data result from a statistically sound sampling program, there is still an important role to be played by old-fashioned common sense.

In the tables that follow, I summarize site size and population estimates for Early and Middle Formative villages from four different regions—two in the highlands and two in the lowlands. No two areas were surveyed the same way, and some estimates are in number of persons while others are in number of households. Parsons, Blanton, and Winter all assume an average of five persons per household, based on Colonial censuses. I need not remind the reader that we have no Formative censuses, but I have no other figure to suggest.

Two site size distributions are evident in the tables. One appears to be a normal, unimodal distribution; the other is strongly discontinuous. This phenomenon will receive further comment at the end of this section. It prepares us nicely for the discussion of complex settlement systems to be undertaken by Flannery in Chapter 6.

The Eastern Valley of Mexico

The Valley of Mexico is a good starting point, since it contains examples of both normal and strongly discontinuous site size distributions. Let us contrast two areas that have been intensively surveyed, the Ixtapalapa peninsula (Blanton 1972) and the Texcoco plain (Parsons 1971).

The Ixtapalapa Peninsula

Only three sites are known from the Early Formative period (Table 3.6). By the Middle Formative, the number had increased to four, ranging in size from 3.0 to 12.5 ha (Table 3.7). Compared with other regions, all these sites could be considered medium-sized; there were no tiny 1-hectare hamlets, nor any exceptionally large nucleated villages. We note with interest that three sites stayed the same size during the entire 500-year period, a situation also observed by Winter (Chapter 8, this volume) for hamlets in Oaxaca.

The three Middle Formative sites excavated by George Vaillant (1930, 1931, 1935) in the Guadalupe hills area of the Valley of Mexico would all fit comfortably into the Ixtapalapa size distribution. As estimated by Flannery (1964) from Vaillant's

TABLE 3.6   Size and Population Estimates for Three Early Formative Sites (1150–850 B.C.), Ixtapalapa Peninsula, Valley of Mexico[a]

Site	Estimated number hectares	Estimated population		Classification (after Blanton)
		Minimum	Maximum	
Ayotla	9	90	225	Village
Ix–EF–2	3	30	75	Hamlet
Ix–EF–3	4	40	100	Hamlet
Totals	*16*	*160*	*400*	

[a]This represents the total number of sites recovered for this period in the area surveyed. After Blanton (1972:317).

TABLE 3.7 Size and Population Estimates for Four Middle Formative Sites (850–550 B.C.)
Ixtapalapa Peninsula, Valley of Mexico[a]

Site	Estimated number hectares	Estimated population		Classification (after Blanton)
		Minimum	Maximum	
Ayotla	9	90	225	Village
Ix–MF–2	3	30	75	Hamlet
Ix–MF–3	4	40	100	Hamlet
Ix–MF–4	12.5	125	313	Village
Totals	*28.5*	*285*	*713*	

[a]This represents the total number of sites recovered for this period in the area surveyed. After Blanton (1972:318), with the correction of a typographical error in the classification of Ix–MF–3 (cf. 1972:40–41).

published contour maps, El Arbolillo should have covered roughly 5.1 ha; Zacatenco and Ticomán should each have covered 2.5 ha. For certain areas of the Valley of Mexico, therefore, it appears that the pattern is one of medium-sized hamlets or small villages in Blanton's classification, without any notable extremes.

The Texcoco Plain

No Early Formative sites are known from the Texcoco region. The sample of 19 sites from the Middle Formative period, however, provides a striking contrast to the Ixtapalapa region. Of 19 sites, 14 were tiny hamlets of 1 ha or less (Table 3.8). Four other sites were hamlets of 2–5 ha,

TABLE 3.8 Size and Population Estimates for 19 Middle Formative Sites (850–550 B.C.),
Texcoco Region of the Valley of Mexico[a]

Site	Estimated number hectares	Estimated population		Classification (after Parsons)
		Minimum	Maximum	
Tx–MF–1	1	10	50	Hamlet
Tx–MF–2	1	10	50	Hamlet
Tx–MF–3	5	10	50	Hamlet
Tx–MF–4	1	10	50	Hamlet
Tx–MF–5	4	20	100	Hamlet
Tx–MF–6	1	10	50	Hamlet
Tx–MF–7	4	10	50	Hamlet
Tx–MF–8	2	10	50	Hamlet
Tx–MF–9	1	10	50	Hamlet
Tx–MF–10	1	10	50	Hamlet
Tx–MF–11	1	10	50	Hamlet
Tx–MF–12	1	10	50	Hamlet
Chimalhuacán	45	600	1200	Large nucleated village
Tx–MF–14	1	10	50	Hamlet
Tx–MF–15	< 1	10	50	Hamlet
Tx–MF–16	1	10	50	Hamlet
Tx–MF–17	1	10	50	Hamlet
Tx–MF–18	1	10	50	Hamlet
Tx–MF–19	< 1	10	50	Hamlet
Totals	*74*	*790*	*2150*	

[a]This represents the total number of sites recovered for this period in the area surveyed. After Parsons (1971: Table 6).

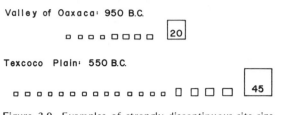

Figure 3.9 Examples of strongly discontinuous site size distributions in Oaxaca and the Valley of Mexico (size in hectares; all sites drawn to same scale).

falling somewhere in the Zacatenco-El Arbolillo range. All these hamlets were dwarfed by a single site at Chimalhuacán, Tx-MF-13, which covers 45 ha and is classified by Parsons (1971) as a "large nucleated village." This site is nearly 10 times larger than the second largest site in the area, producing a strongly discontinuous distribution (Figure 3.9). If one momentarily disregards Chimalhuacán, the mean size of all the other 18 sites in the region is only 1.6 ha. This means, according to Parsons' estimates, that a single site accounts for 60% of the area covered by Middle Formative debris and 55–77% of the estimated Middle Formative population.

The site at Chimalhuacán lies at 2240-m elevation, on the edge of Lake Texcoco; most of the 18 hamlets are well up in the piedmont zone near small streams. However, this difference in environmental setting hardly seems adequate to explain the observed size difference. All four Ixtapalapa sites have a lakeshore setting, and not one even approaches Chimalhuacán in size. Not even the well-known site of Tlatilco, estimated at 30 ha by Sanders (1965:166) and Parsons (1971:180), comes close. Rather, the Texcoco pattern is one that seems to be duplicated in other regions and other environments (see pp. 83–84), and will almost certainly have to be explained in terms of sociopolitical organization.

The Valley of Oaxaca

Compared to the eastern Valley of Mexico, the Valley of Oaxaca has been less intensively sur-

veyed, and the techniques of the survey have been somewhat different (Bernal 1965; Flannery *et al.* 1970). In 1971, Richard Blanton (1973) began for the first time to apply to the Valley of Oaxaca the same survey methodology he, Parsons, and Sanders had applied to the Valley of Mexico. It is expected that his results will eventually provide truly comparable data from the two different regions.

In the meantime, village measurements must be made using Flannery's preliminary survey results, coupled with Winter's various estimates of the number of households per hectare at Tierras Largas (Winter 1972, and Chapter 8 of this volume). These figures are arrived at empirically by Winter from his own excavations, using (*1*) estimates derived from house floor evidence found in sample squares; and (*2*) estimates derived from household cluster evidence found in sample squares; and (*3*) estimates based on spacing patterns between houses excavated. The final estimate takes into account all three of the above figures. It is worth noting that the number of households per hectare does *not* remain constant through all periods (see Winter, Chapter 8, this volume). In addition, Drennan's (1972) estimates for the partly contemporary site of Fábrica San José—figures that are also empirically derived—show that the number of households per hectare may also vary *between* villages at the same time period. For all these reasons, population estimates (in households) are given only for those early Oaxacan villages which actually have been excavated.

Late Tierras Largas Phase

More than a dozen sites of the Tierras Largas phase (1400–1150 B.C.) are known so far from the Valley of Oaxaca; a sample of 10 sites dating to the second half of the phase are shown in Table 3.9. Virtually all are hamlet size, and most probably amounted to no more than 5–10 households. Even the largest, San José Mogote, probably covered no more than 3 ha; at least 300 sq m (.03 ha) of this, however, consisted of public buildings. Public buildings were definitely absent at Tierras Largas during this phase, and are not

TABLE 3.9 Tentative Size and Population Estimates for a Sample of Ten Late Tierras Largas Phase Sites (1300-1150 B.C.), Valley of Oaxaca[a]

Site	Estimated number hectares	Estimated number households	Classification[b]
San Lázaro Etla	1–2	?	Hamlet
Reyes Etla	.5–1.0	?	Hamlet
San José Mogote	2–3	10–30	Large hamlet/ small village
Hacienda Blanca	1–2	?	Hamlet
Tierras Largas	2.24	10	Hamlet
Hac. Experimental	.5–1.0	?	Hamlet
S.B. Coyotepec	1–2	?	Hamlet
Emiliano Zapata	1–2	?	Hamlet
S. Ana Tlapacoyan	1–2	?	Hamlet
S.D. Tomaltepec	1–2	?	Hamlet

[a]This does *not* represent the total number of sites for this phase.
[b]After Parsons 1971.

known for any other site of the period. It is not yet known to what extent the presence of public architecture affects the number of households per hectare.

Late San José Phase

More than a dozen sites of the San José phase (1150–850 B.C.) are also known. Our sample of 10 sites from the second half of that phase, given in

Table 3.10, now shows a discontinuous pattern similar to that of the Texcoco plain during the Middle Formative. Nine of the sites are hamlets between .5 and 2.0 ha in size. A single site, San José Mogote, covers 20 ha—10 times the size of the next largest site (Figure 3.9). Assuming that Winter's estimates of households per hectare for Tierras Largas can be extrapolated to San José Mogote, this means that one site accounts for more than half the area occupied and roughly half

TABLE 3.10 Tentative Size and Population Estimates for a Sample of Ten Late San José Phase Sites (1000–850 B.C.), Valley of Oaxaca[a]

Site	Estimated number hectares	Estimated number households	Tentative classification[b]
B. del R. Huitzo	1–2	5–10	Hamlet
S. Marta Etla	.5–1.0	?	Hamlet
S. Lázaro Etla	1–2	?	Hamlet
San José Mogote	20	80–120	Large nucleated village
Hacienda Blanca	1–2	?	Hamlet
Las Salinas	.5	?	Hamlet
Tierras Largas	1.59	8	Hamlet
Emiliano Zapata	1–2	?	Hamlet
S. Ana Tlapacoyan	1–2	?	Hamlet
S. S. Abasolo	1–2	5–10	Hamlet

[a]This does *not* represent the total number of sites for this phase.
[b]After Parsons 1971.

TABLE 3.11   Tentative Size and Population Estimates for a Sample of Eight Rosario Phase Sites (600 B.C.),
             Valley of Oaxaca[a]

Site	Estimated number hectares	Estimated number households	Tentative classification[b]
B. del R. Huitzo	2.7	?	Hamlet
San Lázaro Etla	1–3	?	Hamlet
San José Mogote	40	100–140	Large nucleated village
Hacienda Blanca	1–3	?	Hamlet
Fábrica San José	2	10–12	Hamlet
Tierras Largas	3	9–10	Hamlet
Cuilapan	1–3?	?	Hamlet
S. Ana Tlapacoyan	3	?	Hamlet

[a]This does *not* represent the total number of sites for this phase.
[b]After Parsons 1971.

the households in our sample. Once again, the estimate for San José Mogote does not make allowances for the presence of substantial public buildings at that site.

Rosario Phase

The strongly discontinuous distribution of villages continues into the Middle Formative Guadalupe and Rosario phases (850–500 B.C.). However, the complexity of these sites makes size estimates impossible without intensive surface sampling of the type described earlier in this chapter. Hence, we are limited to a sample of only eight sites from the Rosario phase (Table 3.11).

The number of sites larger than 2 ha is greater than in previous periods, but as Winter's estimates show, the actual number of households in each hamlet may not be much greater (see Chapter 8). Fábrica San José, excavated by Drennan, had 10–12 households in 2 ha; Tierras Largas, excavated by Winter, had 9–10 households in 3 ha. San José Mogote reached 40 ha, still more than 10 times the size of the next largest village.

By the Rosario phase, the problem of public buildings (ceremonial, civic, or both) becomes serious. An indeterminate (but probably very large) area of San José Mogote was composed of such buildings. At Barrio del Rosario Huitzo, at least

13% of the community (3500 m^2 out of an estimated 2.7 ha) was taken up by substantial stone architecture (Flannery *et al.* 1970). At Tierras Largas, there is no conclusive evidence for public buildings, but the center of the site had a partly investigated structure which may have been an elite residence (Winter 1972). Fábrica San José, according to Drennan (1972), appears to have had no public buildings in the Guadalupe or Rosario phases. Such figures suggest that (*1*) size alone is a poor indicator of whether or not a village is likely to contain public buildings, and (*2*) we cannot measure residential population very accurately when we do not know the area occupied by public buildings.

The Southern Gulf Coast

The southern Veracruz-Tabasco lowland might be yet another region of strikingly discontinuous site size distribution—or so it appears on the basis of the admittedly meager published data. From the Chontalpa district of Tabasco, Sisson (1970) reports 18 sites dating to two Early Formative phases, Molina (1350–1150 B.C.) and Palacios (1050–900 B.C.). All sites are considered "small, probably a cluster of houses on a natural levee"

(Sisson 1970), and would presumably be classed as "hamlets" in Parsons' or Blanton's terminology.

For the large mode of the distribution, we must turn to Coe's (1968a,b) work in the region of San Lorenzo, Veracruz. This area features a complex of three Early Formative sites, all within a few kilometers of each other. As measured by Rossmann (Chapter 4, this volume), the site sizes are as follows:

San Lorenzo: 52.9 ha
Tenochtitlán: 23.0 ha (?)
Potrero Nuevo: 4.6 ha
Total: 80.5 ha

With the exception of Tenochtitlán, these sites are believed by Coe to have reached peak size between 1150 and 900 B.C., contemporary with Sisson's 10 small Palacios phase villages (see Rossmann's discussion of the problem of estimates for Tenochtitlán). Whether one considers San Lorenzo alone, or the whole 80-ha complex as a unit, the implied size disparity is fully as great as that between Parsons' Chimalhuacán site and its tiny Middle Formative contemporaries. However, we also should consider the possibility of a three-tiered size distribution on the southern Gulf Coast. As pointed out by Earle (Chapter 7, this volume), there may well be "secondary ceremonial centers" —sites like Los Soldados and Estero Rabón, to mention only two—intermediate in size between "primary centers" like San Lorenzo and the tiny

hamlets discovered by Sisson. The problem is that we have no accurate measurements on any of the possible secondary centers.

The Pacific Coast of Guatemala

One of the few areas of the coastal lowlands for which we have size estimates of early villages is the Ocós region of Guatemala (Coe and Flannery 1967). It must be admitted at the outset that the estimates are less than ideal. The area is tropical forest, and it could not be surveyed by the intensive methodology used in the Valley of Mexico; the sample falls far short of the total universe of sites. Even when a site was located, its overall size was hard to estimate because of the difficulty of finding surface sherds in high tropical grass or mangrove swamp (Flannery, personal communication). In this chapter, I will restrict myself to the seven most reliable Early Formative sites (Table 3.12) and the six most reliable Middle Formative sites (Table 3.13).

All the sites are hamlets, none larger than 3 ha, and some as small as 200–300 sq m. In view of Winter's estimate of 300 sq m for a typical household cluster at Tierras Largas (Chapter 2, this volume), it is possible that some of the smallest Ocós area sites consist of a single household cluster, or at most a single "courtyard group" (Flannery, this chapter). Even the largest site, La Victoria (Coe

TABLE 3.12 Tentative Size and Population Estimates for a Sample of Seven Early Formative Sites (1350–850 B.C.) from the Guatemalan Pacific Coast [a]

| Site | Estimated number hectares | Estimated household | | Tentative classification |
		Minimum	Maximum	
Salinas la Blanca	1–2	3	8	Hamlet
SM–10	3	10?	12?	Hamlet
SM–12	.03	1	?	One household?
SM–20	.2	?	?	Hamlet
La Victoria	<3	<10	<12	Hamlet
SM–41	3	10?	12?	Hamlet
SM–52	.03	1	?	One household?

[a]This does *not* represent the total number of sites known for the area at this time period. After Coe and Flannery (1967).

TABLE 3.13   Tentative Size and Population Estimates for a Sample of Six Middle Formative Sites (850–500 B.C.) from the Guatemalan Pacific Coast [a]

Site	Estimated number hectares	Estimated households		Tentative classification
		Minimum	Maximum	
SM–19	.02	1	?	One household?
SM–28	.8	?	?	Hamlet
SM–31	.8	?	?	Hamlet
SM–37	.8	?	?	Hamlet
La Victoria	3.0	10	12	Hamlet
SM–53	.8	?	?	Hamlet

[a]This does *not* represent the total number of sites known for the area at this time period. After Coe and Flannery (1967).

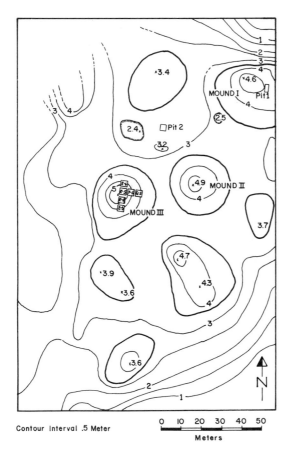

Contour Interval .5 Meter

0 10 20 30 40 50
Meters

Figure 3.10   La Victoria, Guatemala. Distribution of low mounds indicating locations of probable Middle Formative household clusters. [Redrawn from Coe 1961: Figure 3.]

1961) is thought to consist of no more than 10–12 households scattered over an area of roughly 3 ha during the Middle Formative Conchas phase. In fact, Coe's household estimates for La Victoria are remarkably close to Winter's estimates for Tierras Largas in the Guadalupe phase (see p. 228). However, one reason the Ocós area sites are so small *may* be that some are specialized fishing hamlets within a larger and more complex regional system (see Flannery, Chapter 6, this volume).

The site of La Victoria originally consisted of 10–12 low mounds, 8 of which were mapped by Coe (see Figure 3.10). Each mound ranges from 20 to 40 m in diameter, and the mean distance between mounds is 47 m, with a range of 36–60 m. Coe's excavations in Mound III (35 m in diameter) yielded evidence of clay floors and burnt daub, while his Pit 2 (placed midway between Mounds I and III) produced no evidence of architecture. The most economical explanation is that the mounds indicate where the household clusters were, and the spaces between are equivalent to the 30–40 m-gaps between Middle Formative household clusters at sites like Tierras Largas. Evidently, the mounds accumulated because the houses at La Victoria were built on clay platforms to keep them off the muddy alluvium.

We cannot leave the Guatemalan Coast without mentioning one more site, even though it is somewhat later than the period of our interest. This is the site of Naranjito in the Department of Santa

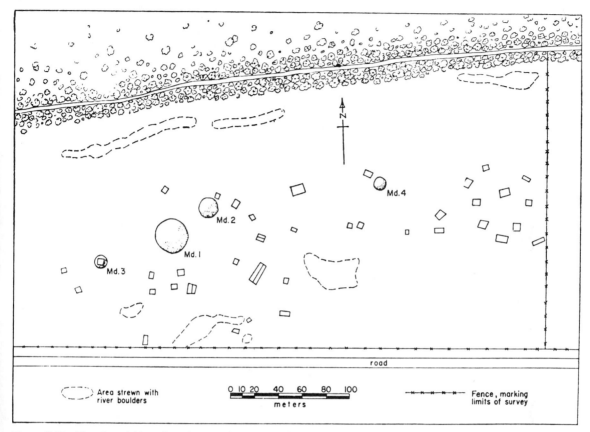

Figure 3.11 The site of Naranjito, Santa Rosa, Guatemala, showing house mounds visible on the surface. [After Coe 1963: Figure 1.]

Rosa, reported by Coe (1963). Because Naranjito is a pure, one-period site of the Late Formative Crucero phase (300 B.C.–A.D. 200), all house mounds can be regarded as contemporary for the sake of analysis.

Naranjito covers 6–7 ha. Almost 50 house mounds are visible on the surface, and 39 of these appear in the portion of the site mapped by Coe and T. Patrick Culbert (Figure 3.11). Individual house size runs from 2 by 3 m at the smallest to 9 by 18 m at the largest. More importantly, the mounds occur in two groups which could constitute different residential wards. The eastern group, consisting of at least 13 houses, is more closely spaced and includes neither "temple mounds" nor houses with internal partitions. The western group includes the largest houses, 3 of which are divided by internal walls, and it partially surrounds a series of "temple mounds" up to 4 m high. Coe suggests that this western group may represent a high-status residential area.

The Upper Size Limits of Early Villages

As a number of anthropologists have pointed out, the pressures for village fissioning are very strong in prestate societies (cf. Carneiro 1961).

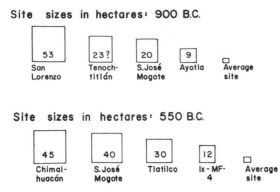

Figure 3.12 Some large Early and Middle Formative villages, compared with average sites of those same periods (size in hectares; all sites drawn to same scale).

Since we do not consider any of the cultures of the 1500–500 B.C. period in Mesoamerica to have been "states," we are not surprised that perhaps 90% of the carefully measured sites of that period were less than 2 ha in size. The characteristic fissioning of prestate societies makes 1-ha hamlets easy to explain. What requires explanation is the way certain villages were able to reach 20–50 ha, remain nucleated, keep the peace, and overcome the natural tendency to fission. In view of this, it may be useful to examine the population estimates made for some of the "monsters" of the early village period (Figure 3.12).

Early Formative

Probably the largest site of its time period was San Lorenzo, Veracruz, which reached 53 ha by 900 B.C. The number of house mounds visible on the surface "indicates a population of about a thousand persons" (Coe 1968a: 57). Coe assigns another 1000 persons to nearby Tenochtitlán and about 250 persons to Potrero Nuevo, each located less than 3 km from San Lorenzo. His total estimate for the region is a population that "may never have exceeded 2500 souls," in a total habitation area of about 80 ha. This implies a within-site density of 31 persons per hectare, or perhaps 6–7 households per hectare. This density is roughly comparable to Winter's Early Formative estimates for Tierras Largas in the Valley of Oaxaca (see

Tables 3.9 and 3.10), which were arrived at independently. However, a large (but unmeasured) percentage of San Lorenzo was taken up by clay platforms, plazas, and basalt monuments.

San Lorenzo is about twice the size of San José Mogote (20 ha), a Oaxacan site of the same time period. For San José Mogote, we have estimated 80–120 households, perhaps representing a population of 400–600 persons. This is somewhat lower than Coe's estimate for Tenochtitlán.

Middle Formative

Unfortunately, we have no accurate measurement for the habitation area of La Venta, Tabasco, possibly the largest site of the period 850–500 B.C. The largest reliably measured site, Chimalhuacán in the Valley of Mexico, covers 45 ha. San José Mogote in the Valley of Oaxaca covered 40 ha by 550 B.C., but some percentage of that area was taken up by public buildings. Parsons, using calculations based on surface sherd density, estimates 600–1200 persons for Chimalhuacán. Flannery, using Winter's empirical data from Tierras Largas, estimates San José Mogote at 100–140 households (perhaps 500–700 persons). The site of Tlatilco in the Valley of Mexico might have reached 30 ha during the Middle Formative (Sanders 1965:166; Parsons 1971:180), but there are no reliable population estimates.

Chiapa de Corzo, Chiapas, was another large site of this period. There are no reliable period-by-period measurements of the site, but Lowe (1959: Figure 3) presents a map showing those excavations at Chiapa de Corzo which turned up Chiapa I or II deposits. Assuming continuous occupation between all these areas by the end of Chiapa II (800–500 B.C.), Middle Formative Chiapa de Corzo would have covered 49 ha. This estimate rests on somewhat shaky assumptions, however, and is almost certainly too large.

Summary and Conclusions

Early Mesoamerican villages showed a considerable range in size. The overwhelming majority—

perhaps as many as 90%—were small hamlets. In terms of actual population, such hamlets probably ranged in size from a single household to 10–12 households, totaling perhaps 50–60 persons.

Certain early villages, however, reached sizes that were more than 10 times the average for their region. Some of these were 20–30 ha; the largest seem to have been 45–55 ha, and had populations estimated at somewhere around 1000–1200 inhabitants. This figure might be near the upper population limit that could be integrated into single communities in Mesoamerica prior to the rise of the state.

There are at least two different size distributions detectable in the Early and Middle Formative: "normal" and strongly discontinuous. In the "normal" situation, villages may be 3, 6, 9, or 12 ha in size, with no obvious extremes. The discontinuous situation occurs in conjunction with some of Mesoamerica's largest early villages: a 20–40-ha "monster" may be surrounded by 1–2-ha hamlets. Such distributions occur without reference to any particular environmental zone. They may therefore result from social and political factors, and some of these factors might well be necessary preconditions for the rise of the state. This being the case, they are deserving of the most careful future scrutiny.

References

Aufdermauer, J.
1970   Excavaciones en dos sitios preclásicos de Moyotzingo, Puebla. *Comunicaciones* No. 1:9–24. Fundación Alemana para la Investigación Científica, Puebla.

Arkin, H., and R. R. Colton
1963   *Tables for statisticians*. New York: Barnes & Noble.

Bernal, I.
1965   Archaeological synthesis of Oaxaca. In *Handbook of Middle American Indians*, vol. 3, edited by R. Wauchope and G. R. Willey. Austin: University of Texas Press. Pp. 788–813.

Binford, L. R.
1964   A consideration of archaeological research design. *American Antiquity* 29:425–441.

Binford, L. R., S. R. Binford, R. Whallon, and M. A. Hardin
1970   Archaeology at Hatchery West, Carlyle, Illinois. *Memoirs of the Society for American Archaeology* No. 24.

Blanton, R. E.
1972   Prehispanic settlement patterns of the Ixtapalapa peninsula region, Mexico. *Occasional Papers in Anthropology* No. 6. Dept. of Anthropology, Pennsylvania State University, University Park.
1973   The Valley of Oaxaca settlement pattern project. Mimeographed preliminary report. Hunter College (C.U.N.Y.), New York.

Carneiro, R. L.
1961   Slash-and-burn cultivation among the Kuikuru and its implications for cultural development in the Amazon basin. *Antropologica*, Suppl. 2:47–67.

Coe, M. D.
1961   La Victoria: An early site on the Pacific coast of Guatemala. *Papers of the Peabody Museum of Archaeology and Ethnology* Vol. LIII. Harvard University, Cambridge, Mass.
1963   A late Preclassic village in Santa Rosa, Guatemala. *Middle American Research Records* III:119–124.
1968a   San Lorenzo and the Olmec civilization. In *Dumbarton Oaks Conference on the Olmec*, edited by E. P. Benson. Washington, D.C.: Dumbarton Oaks. Pp. 41–78.
1968b   Map of San Lorenzo, an Olmec site in Veracruz, Mexico. Dept. of Anthropology, Yale University, New Haven, Conn.

Coe, M. D., and K. V. Flannery
1967   Early cultures and human ecology in south coastal Guatemala. *Smithsonian Contributions to Anthropology* No. 3. Smithsonian Institution, Washington, D.C.

Drennan R. D.
1972   Excavations at Fábrica San José, Oaxaca, Mexico. Mimeographed preliminary report. Ann Arbor, Mich.

Flannery, K. V.
1964   The Middle Formative of the Tehuacán Valley. Unpublished Ph.D. dissertation, Dept. of Anthropology, University of Chicago.
1972   The origins of the village as a settlement type in Mesoamerica and the Near East: A comparative study. In *Man, settlement, and urbanism*, edited by P. J. Ucko, R. Tringham, and G. W. Dimbleby. London: Duckworth. Pp. 23–53.

Flannery, K. V., M. Winter, S. Lees, J. Neely, J. Schoenwetter, S. Kitchen, and J. C. Wheeler
 1970   Preliminary archeological invesgitations in the
        Valley of Oaxaca, Mexico, 1966–1969. Mime-
        ographed preliminary report. Ann Arbor,
        Mich.
Lowe, G. W.
 1959   Archaeological exploration of the upper
        Grijalva River, Chiapas, Mexico. *Papers of the
        New World Archaeological Foundation* No. 2
        (Pub. no. 3). Provo, Utah.
MacNeish, R. S.
 1962   *Second annual report of the Tehuacán archae-
        ological-botanical project.* R. S. Peabody
        Foundation for Archaeology, Andover, Mass.
Millon, R.
 1967   Teotihuacán. *Scientific American* **216**:38–48.

Parsons, J. R.
 1971   Prehistoric settlement patterns in the Tex-
        coco region, Mexico. *Memoirs* No. 3. Museum
        of Anthropology, University of Michigan,
        Ann Arbor.
Redman, C. L., and P. J. Watson
 1970   Systematic, intensive surface collection.
        American Antiquity **35**:279–291.
Sanders, W. T.
 1965   The cultural ecology of the Teotihuacán Val-
        ley. Mimeographed preliminary report. Dept.
        of Anthropology, Pennsylvania State Univer-
        sity, University Park.

Sisson, E. B.
 1970   Settlement patterns and land use in the north-
        western Chontalpa, Tabasco, Mexico: A Pro-
        gress report. *Cerámica de Cultura Maya*
        6:41–54.
Tolstoy, P., and S. K. Fish
 1973   Excavations at Coapexco, 1973. Mimeo-
        graphed preliminary report. Queens College
        (C.U.N.Y.), New York.
Vaillant, G. C.
 1930   Excavations at Zacatenco. *Anthropological
        Papers* Vol. 32: Part 1. American Museum of
        Natural History, New York.
 1931   Excavations at Ticomán. *Anthropological
        Papers* Vol. 32: Part 2. American Museum of
        Natural History, New York.
 1935   Excavations at El Arbolillo. *Anthropological
        Papers* Vol. 35: Part 2. American Museum of
        Natural History, New York.
Whalen, M. E.
 1974   Excavations at Sto. Domingo Tomaltepec,
        Oaxaca, Mexico. Mimeographed preliminary
        report. Dept. of Anthropology, University of
        Michigan, Ann Arbor.
Winter, M. C.
 1972   Tierras Largas: A Formative community in
        the Valley of Oaxaca, Mexico. Unpublished
        Ph.D. thesis, Dept. of Anthropology, Uni-
        versity of Arizona, Tucson.

Chapter 4

THE VILLAGE AND ITS CATCHMENT AREA

Introduction

With Chapter 4, we move from the community to a unit of analysis one step larger. That unit is the *catchment area*: the zone of resources, both wild and domestic, that occur within reasonable walking distance of a given village.

The term "site catchment analysis" was introduced into the literature by Claudio Vita-Finzi and Eric Higgs (1970:5) as "the study of the relationships between technology and those natural resources lying within economic range of individual sites." The concept of site catchment rests on the assumption that, other things being equal, "the further the area is from the site, the less it is likely to be exploited, and the less rewarding is its exploitation (unless it is peculiarly productive) since the energy consumed in movement to and from the site will tend to cancel out that derived from the resource. Beyond a certain distance the area is unlikely to be exploited from that site at all: in

terms of the technology available at the time, its exploitation becomes uneconomic" (Vita-Finzi and Higgs 1970:7).

This assumption is supported with ethnographic data from several sources. One is Richard Lee's study of Kalahari Bushman hunter-gatherers (Lee 1967), which suggests that women are unlikely to forage farther than 10 km from the base camp in search of plant foods; small groups of men may travel farther in pursuit of game, but, in such cases, they may make a separate overnight camp away from the base camp. Another source is Chisholm's study of European peasant agriculture, which concludes that it is "exceptional" for farmers to travel more than 3-4 km to their fields (Chisholm 1968). Accordingly, in their application of site catchment analysis to the Late Paleolithic and early Neolithic period of the Eastern Mediterranean, Vita-Finzi and Higgs drew circles with a 5-km radius around the sites to be analyzed, reasoning that most resources used by a prehistoric group would have come from the 7900-ha "catchment areas" thus produced—especially for groups whose major subsistence activity was agriculture. Within each circle, they next calculated the number of hectares of "arable," "potentially arable," "grazing," "marsh," and "dune" lands available, and expressed each as a percentage of the total catchment area. The percentages then led them to conclusions about the nature and function of each site; for example, sites whose catchment areas had low percentages of arable land were thought to be largely nonagricultural. The sites of Nahal Oren and el-Wad were regarded as "unlikely" spots for agricultural settlement because arable or potentially arable land "does not at best exceed 20 percent" of the total catchment circle (Vita-Finzi and Higgs 1970:16).

Vita-Finzi and Higgs were aware that walking time (rather than actual distance) is the critical factor, and that catchment areas will vary according to region and economy. As a further refinement of their method, they adopted a scheme of "weighting" sections of the catchment area according to their distance from the site. The weighting factor is derived from Virri's (1946) studies which "illustrate how both net and gross yields per hectare decline with distance from the farmstead" in Finland (Vita-Finzi and Higgs 1970:29). To apply the weighting factor suggested by Vita-Finzi and Higgs, one must draw concentric circles with radii of 1, 2, 3, 4, and 5 km around the site, then calculate the area occupied by each type of land. Land within 1 km of the site is weighted 100% (fully exploited). Land between 1 and 2 km is given a 50% weighting, land between 2 and 3 km a 33% weighting, and so on (Vita-Finzi and Higgs 1970: Table 3).

Site catchment analysis provides an interesting and reasonably objective method for comparing sites, both within the same region and between regions. Indeed, the considerable attention Vita-Finzi and Higgs' article has already received among Old World archeologists is an accurate reflection of its importance to the field. As with all pioneering efforts, however, there are some problems both in the assumptions made in the original article, and in its specific application to the Mt. Carmel area. These problems only increase when one leaves the Upper Paleolithic camps and early Neolithic villages discussed by Vita-Finzi and Higgs, and turns to Formative Mesoamerica.

For several compelling reasons, we feel these complications must be considered here. For one thing, there are in archeology both pioneers and latecomers. Some of the latecomers in catchment analysis, understandably excited by the pioneer article, have shown a tendency to follow it as slavishly as if it were a cookbook; misguided conclusions are the main result. This was surely not Vita-Finzi and Higgs' intent when they presented the original article. Its place in the literature is secure, and our critique can only strengthen it.

The Problem of Arable Land Percentages

First, we may question the assumption that sites are nonagricultural if arable land constitutes only a small percentage of their catchment area. There are two reasons for this. To begin with, when one is dealing with small communities in the first place, a very small percentage of a 7900-ha catchment may be agriculturally sufficient. Some of today's races of Mexican maize produce a metric ton per hectare, which is roughly the amount consumed during the course of a year by an Indian family of 2 adults and 3 children (see p. 106). Thus, a village of 70 families totaling 350 persons could support itself on less than 1% of its 7900-ha catchment area; and most early Mesoamerican villages, as revealed in the previous chapter, had fewer than 70 households. Similarly, if wild emmer wheat in Palestine yields 500–800 kg per hectare (Zohary 1969), a village of 50 families could support itself (at the rate of a metric ton per family) on no more than 100 ha—about 1.3% of its 7900-ha catchment area.

The second reason for questioning the assumption is that a figure of 5–10% arable land, while superficially small, may in fact be far higher than the percentage for the region as a whole. There are many Pueblo sites in the southwestern United States whose 5-km catchments include less than 10% arable land. Be assured: They were farmers. If one were to consider the entire region in which the sites occur, he would often find the overall percentage of arable land was less than 1%.

Consider Vita-Finzi and Higgs' map of Nahal Oren and Iraq El-Baroud as another example (Vita-Finzi and Higgs 1970: Figure 4). As the authors point out, Nahal Oren's 7000-ha catchment area includes only 8% arable land. The site, however, just happens to immediately overlook the only patch of arable land to the coastal side of the mountains shown on the entire map—in other words, 100% of the arable land below 200-m elevation. This is a strip of wadi alluvium more than a kilometer long. If one drew a circle of 1-km radius around Nahal Oren, he would have to conclude that arable land was in fact highly selected for, because it occurs within that circle of "100% exploitation" in much higher frequency than it does on the map as a whole. The fact is that 8% of 7000 ha (560 ha) could produce enough wheat to supply a population many times greater than that estimated for Nahal Oren.

Thus, we would not see the relevant question as "What is the percentage of arable land within a circle of 5-km radius?" Instead, we would ask two different questions: (1) "Is the percentage of arable land in the 5-km circle significantly higher than the percentage of arable land in the region as a whole?" and (2) "Could the number of persons we estimate for the site have been supported by the amount of arable land within the 5-km circle?" If the answer to both questions is "yes," one should probably not attach too much importance to a low absolute percentage of arable land within the catchment circle.

Our two questions, however, require different methodologies to answer. Question 1 can be handled as Alan Zarky recommends later in this chapter, with the use of simple statistics. In this approach, one treats a given catchment circle as a sample drawn from a regional universe. He calcu-

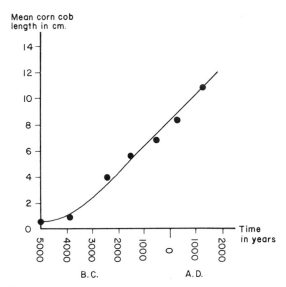

Figure 4.1 Increase in mean corncob length through time in ancient Mexico, from 5000 B.C. to the present. [Redrawn from Kirkby 1973: Figure 48a.]

lates the proportions of various land use areas within both the sample and the universe. He then asks, using the chi-square statistic, "Did the founders of the site draw a sample that reflects the overall makeup of the regional universe, or did they select for one or another type of land?"

Question 2 requires two estimates: one for the population of the site, and one for the yield of the available land. In the case of Formative Mesoamerica, one can estimate the population in terms of households per hectare after test excavation (cf. Winter, Chapter 3) or persons per hectare based on surface remains (cf. Blanton 1972). The yield of the land, in kilograms of maize per hectare, can be tentatively estimated from two charts published by Anne Kirkby (1973: Figures 48a,b). Kirkby first graphed the mean length of corncobs at various periods from 5000 B.C. to A.D. 1500 (Figure 4.1), based on data from Tehuacán presented by Mangelsdorf, MacNeish, and Galinat (1967). She then derived a curvilinear regression relating mean corncob length in centimeters to corn yield in metric tons per hectare (Figure 4.2), based on four seasons of field work in Oaxaca. By combining

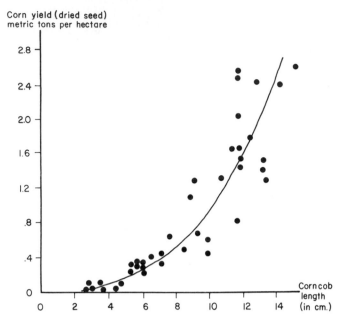

Corn yield (dried seed)
metric tons per hectare

Figure 4.2 Mean yield of maize in metric tons of dried seed per hectare for different lengths of corncobs measured in the Valley of Oaxaca, 1966–1970. [Redrawn from Kirkby 1973: Figure 48b.]

these two charts, we can arrive at rough estimates for those ancient periods when maize was less productive than today. For example, maize at 1000 B.C. would have had a mean cob length of about 6 cm, which suggests a yield of 300 kg per hectare on the best alluvial soils of the Puebla–Oaxaca region. Although these figures are by no means sacred, several of us have found them useful in our contributions to this chapter.

Other Problems

There are various problems involved in the "weighting" of concentric catchment circles, especially in Mesoamerica. In some parts of that region today, farmers' landholdings are dispersed into nearby valley-floor fields, more distant piedmont fields, and very distant mountain fields—a kind of insurance against annual disaster in any one physiographic zone. We do not know if this pattern existed in the Formative, but if it did, any "weighting" of zones by us would be highly subjective.

We agree with Vita-Finzi and Higgs that "beyond a certain distance" some areas are "unlikely to be exploited from that site at all." In Formative Mesoamerica, for example, some mountain deer-hunting localities could not be exploited economically from valley-floor villages; hunting camps in the mountains were founded for this purpose. Technically, these were "different sites." However, as I will argue later in this chapter, they functioned as temporary annexes to the village, to which the deer meat was eventually brought back. Thus, while one *could* say that a certain resource was located at an inconvenient distance from Village A, it could *not* be concluded that the village did not use it; Camp B might make it readily available at certain times of the year.

Finally, a consistently raised objection to site catchment analysis is that of changing environments. How justifiable is it to reason, from a land-use map of the 1970s, back to the environment of 10,000 or even 1000 years ago? Might not the proportions of the various zones have been very different? As we see it, this is a question that will always be with us, not merely in site catchment analysis but in all phases of archeology. One has two choices: He can throw up his hands in defeat, or he can reconstruct the prehistoric environment to the best of his ability and plunge ahead. Vita-Finzi and Higgs have plunged ahead, and we will follow their example.

An Outline of the Chapter

In accord with the discussion above, three different approaches to site catchment—covering three different environmental zones—will be presented in this chapter. First, Rossmann analyzes the tropical Gulf Coast, using the format pioneered by Vita-Finzi and Higgs, complete with the differential weighting of more distant catchment rings; to this he adds a comparison of crop yield with estimated population. This approach takes the catchment circle as given, and reconstructs the resource use. Flannery's section on temperate Oaxaca and Tehuacán takes the resources as given, and reconstructs the size of the catchment circle. Zarky's section on the Guatemalan Coast takes the

regional universe as given, and deduces the resources by treating the catchment circles as samples drawn by prehistoric man. If the papers show anything in common, it is that early Mesoamerican villages in most regions drew on the land at a level well below the potential carrying capacity of their respective environments (cf. Sahlins 1972). This makes the exceptions all the more interesting (pp. 246–248).

Actually, there is a fourth site catchment analysis in this volume: Elizabeth Brumfiel's study of the Texcoco region, in the temperate Valley of Mexico. Brumfiel's paper is deferred until Chapter 8 because she uses site catchment as the stepping stone to a new level of analysis. In her treatment of the relations between regional population and catchment yield, Brumfiel demonstrates the utility of site catchment analysis, not as an end in itself but as the takeoff point for another whole series of studies. This is reassuring evidence that site catchment will survive the pruning of some of its lower-level assumptions, and take up a permanent place in the archeologist's arsenal.

A Site Catchment Analysis of San Lorenzo, Veracruz

DAVID L. ROSSMANN

The sites of San Lorenzo, Potrero Nuevo, and Tenochtitlán are located near the Coatzacoalcos River in southern Veracruz, Mexico. They were occupied during the Early and Middle Formative periods and again during the terminal Classic, after a hiatus of 1300 years. Excavations were conducted at San Lorenzo by Michael D. Coe in 1966, 1967, and 1968. Along with the excavations, an extensive program, including mapping by photo-

grammetry, soil sampling, ethnographic observation, and studies of present patterns of land use, was carried out on a 75-sq-km area surrounding the three sites (Coe 1968a,b; 1969a,b). It is on the results of that survey that this site catchment analysis is based. I also had at my disposal large-scale land-use maps of the San Lorenzo area which were printed at Yale University but are not widely available (Coe 1968c).

The San Lorenzo Region

The area is low-lying, warm, and tropical. The extensive alluvium left by the Coatzacoalcos and its tributaries is interrupted by backswamps, oxbow lakes surviving from old river courses, and gently rolling hills. Some of these hills, which do not flood in the rainy season, were obvious choices for Formative village sites.

Some precipitation occurs throughout the year, but March, April, and May have the least rainfall. The rainy season runs from June to October; September is the wettest month. From July through November, much of the land is flooded by the rains, and the people use dugout canoes for transportation.

San Lorenzo and Potrero Nuevo reached their greatest areal extent during the San Lorenzo phase (1150–900 B.C.). Tenochtitlán was also occupied during this period, but its maximum extent was reached during the Late Classic Villa Alta phase. Indeed, so much Villa Alta overburden covers Tenochtitlán that the extent of its San Lorenzo phase deposits cannot be accurately measured. The population we will assume for Tenochtitlán during the San Lorenzo phase is based on a comment by Coe and is probably too large, but we have no other estimate to offer. Based on the number of house mounds visible on the surface, Coe (1968b) estimates that San Lorenzo would have had a population of about 1000 persons during the San Lorenzo phase. He assigns another 1000 to Tenochtitlán and perhaps 250 persons to Potrero Nuevo. It is this time period for which our analysis is intended.

The analysis map (Figure 4.3) was reproduced from Coe (1968c). The extent of the site of San Lorenzo was defined for purposes of the analysis as the 70-m contour line; for Potrero Nuevo, the boundary is the 24-m contour line. For Tenochtitlán, the boundary is partially the 30-m contour line, but as this contour encloses more than the site itself, the boundary was chosen only to include most of the monuments listed for the site on Coe's map.

In constructing the kilometer circles for the catchment analysis, certain simplifying assumptions were made. Since the defined site of San Lorenzo is roughly 1.17 km long by .75 km wide, the site was abstractly defined as covering a circle with a diameter of 1 km. Tenochtitlán is roughly .97 km by .35 km, and it was defined as a circle with a diameter of .6 km. As suggested earlier, however, this is the maximum extent of Tenochtitlán and may be substantially larger than the area occupied during the Early Formative. Potrero Nuevo, with dimensions of .44 by .24 km, was defined as a circle of diameter .3 km. This definition is also appealing in that the largest site, San Lorenzo, has the largest catchment, which one would expect. The division of the area between sites when catchment circles overlap was made purely by the geometric intersection of those circles, half being given to one site and half to the other. No attempt was made to weight this division in favor of the larger site, but, effectively, this was done by a geometrical artifact: The catchment is a function of the abstractly defined circular area of each site.

Catchments were defined for each site up to a distance of 5 km from the edge of the site. At this point, the catchments extend considerably beyond the survey area. It will thus have to be assumed that the proportions calculated from the survey area approximate the true proportions of each type of land in the entire catchment of each site.

Coe (1969b), from soil sample studies and field ethnography, has defined four different soil types for the area. *Tierra de primera*, or first-class soil, occurs on the natural levees along the rivers; on the map (Figure 4.3), these areas are designated with the number two (2). Away from the levees is *tierra de potrero*, a very acid, low-lying soil. This is mostly a grassland that is under water for nearly half the year; these areas are designated by the number three (3) on the map. In the uplands, above the 24-m contour, occur two types of soil, *tierra barreal* and *tierra grava*. The *tierra barreal* is a rich, clayey soil which is slightly acid. *Tierra grava* is a mixture of sand and gravel and is largely

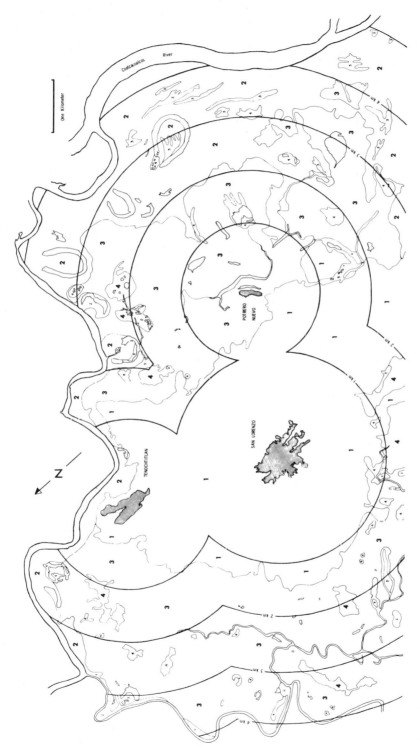

Figure 4.3 Site catchment circles of 1–5-km radius for San Lorenzo, Potrero Nuevo, and Tenochtitlán, Veracruz. Numbers indicate soil types. [Base map from Coe 1968c.]

97

the product of artificial fill in the archeological sites. Tropical forest grows in these areas. Both types of soil are designated *lomas* and are indicated by the number one (1) on the map. Also on the map are areas numbered four (4); these are swampy regions, and usually occur in the *tierra de potrero* savannas. Other features on the map are the rivers and lakes.

Soil types were used to define the environmental zones because they correspond quite closely both with the crops that can be grown and with the natural flora and fauna in the area. The present inhabitants grow two crops of corn in a year. The wet season or *temporal* crop is grown in *milpas*, small cornfields in the *lomas*. The dry season or winter corn, *tapachol*, can be grown both in *milpas* and on the river levee. But the levee land, because it is flooded for half the year, can produce only one crop. The yield is greater on the levee per crop—3.15 metric tons per hectare versus 2.25 metric tons per hectare for *lomas* fields. And this land can be used every year, while the *milpas* must lie fallow for 3 to 6 years after a year or two of production. So while a given *milpa* can produce 4.5 metric tons of corn per hectare per year compared to the 3.15 tons for levee land, over time, a unit of levee land is more productive. There are two other major crops grown: *tonamil*, which is grown only in the *lomas* from August to November, and *chamil*, which can be grown in both *lomas* and *tierra de primera* from March to June.

The most important source of animal protein for present-day inhabitants of the area is fish, which are caught mostly from the oxbow lakes in the savannah. Local farmers also hunt deer, peccary, and armadillo. In November and December, they take some of the large number of migratory ducks and geese on the lakes and ponds in the *tierra de potrero*.

West, Psuty, and Thom (1969) provide detailed information on the localization of faunal resources in Tabasco, an area a little farther to the south. From this work, we may draw some analogies to the exploitation of fauna in the various biotopes at San Lorenzo. In rain forest similar to that which occurs on the *lomas* at San Lorenzo, birds, reptiles, monkeys, squirrels, opossums, and anteaters are available. More important, however, are the larger mammals in this area, such as peccary, brocket deer, and tapir. Smaller mammals, such as the forest rabbit, armadillo, and porcupine, are also present. In areas of secondary growth after slash-and-burn agriculture has been abandoned in a *milpa*, white-tail deer are found, along with an increased number of rabbits, rodents, and game birds. These areas are also confined to the *lomas* at San Lorenzo. On the savannas, or *tierra de potrero*, are white-tail deer, rabbits, quail, and rodents, though most of these animals tend to stay near the forest edge. Along the river margins—the *tierra de primera* at San Lorenzo—live the agouti and cavy, two large rodents, as well as raccoons and otters. In the marshes, fish, reptiles, amphibians, and birds predominate. There are turtles, clams, snails, crustaceans, and substantial numbers of migratory waterfowl.

The Analysis

The catchment analysis used here follows the original paper by Vita-Finzi and Higgs (1970) rather than the chi-square method of Zarky (this chapter). I attempted to calculate the amount (in hectares) of various types of land available to each of Coe's three sites. This was done for successively larger catchment circles of 1, 2, 3, 4, and 5 km, measured from the periphery of the circle defined as the occupied area of the site. Using a planimeter on Coe's large-scale soil map (Coe 1968c), the area in hectares of each of the five categories of land for each kilometer ring were obtained, and percentages of each type of land per kilometer per site were calculated to derive the catchment of each site. These data appear in Table 4.1.

There are rather large differences between sites, and between different kilometer catchments for a single site. For the total Tenochtitlán catchment,

TABLE 4.1 Site Catchments in the San Lorenzo Area: Area (in Hectares) and Percentage of Catchment Circle for various soil and land types

	Lomas (1)	Tierra de primera (2)	Tierra de potrero (3)	Marshes (4)	Water (5)	Total
San Lorenzo (area of site, 52.99 ha)						
Area within 1 k of site						
Area	1163.01	.0	16.64	23.81	2.82	1206.28
Percentage	96.41	.0	1.38	1.97	.23	
Area within 2 k of site						
Area	1463.81	.0	365.57	104.71	20.74	1954.83
Percentage	74.88	.0	18.70	5.36	1.06	
Area within 3 k of site						
Area	1504.51	.0	711.94	117.25	51.46	2385.16
Percentage	63.08	.0	29.85	4.92	2.16	
Area within 4 k of site						
Area	1504.51	64.00	965.12	143.36	69.38	2746.37
Percentage	54.78	2.33	35.14	5.22	2.53	
Area within 5 k of site						
Area	1504.51	64.26	974.08	143.36	69.38	2755.59
Percentage	54.60	2.33	35.35	5.20	2.52	
Potrero Nuevo (area of site, 4.61 ha)						
Area within 1 k of site						
Area	151.30	6.66	367.62	1.02	18.18	544.78
Percentage	27.77	1.22	67.48	.19	3.34	
Area within 2 k of site						
Area	336.86	62.47	903.68	44.80	31.75	1379.56
Percentage	24.42	4.53	65.50	3.25	2.30	
Area within 3 k of site						
Area	404.70	489.22	1245.70	92.67	90.12	2322.41
Percentage	17.43	21.07	53.64	3.99	3.88	
Area within 4 k of site						
Area	404.70	1127.17	1405.96	104.70	117.77	3160.30
Percentage	12.81	35.67	44.49	3.31	3.73	
Area within 5 k of site						
Area	404.70	1362.43	1423.11	104.70	117.77	3412.71
Percentage	11.86	39.92	41.70	3.07	3.45	
Tenochtitlán (Maximum area[a], 23.04 ha)						
Area within 1 k of site						
Area	366.08	50.94	139.78	2.82	1.28	560.90
Percentage	65.27	9.08	24.92	.50	.23	
Area within 2 k of site						
Area	429.57	130.04	513.28	46.08	6.48	1125.45
Percentage	38.17	11.55	45.61	4.09	.58	
Area within 3 k of site						
Area	429.57	172.54	778.50	63.49	15.95	1460.05
Percentage	29.42	11.82	53.32	4.35	1.09	
Area within 4 k of site						
Area	429.57	191.48	881.41	63.49	16.97	1582.92
Percentage	27.14	12.10	55.68	4.01	1.07	
Area within 5 k of site						
Area	429.57	193.53	882.69	63.49	16.97	1586.25
Percentage	27.08	12.20	55.65	4.00	1.07	

[a] As Tenochtitlán reached its maximum extent in Villa Alta times, this figure is probably significantly larger than the San Lorenzo phase occupation (see text).

over half the land is *tierra de potrero* savanna and about a quarter of it is upland *lomas*. But in the 1-km catchment for this site, nearly two-thirds is upland *lomas*, while less than a quarter is savanna. The total catchment for San Lorenzo is nearly the reverse. Over half is upland *lomas*, with about one-third savanna. Here in the 1-km catchment, over 95% of the land is upland *lomas*. The total catchment for Potrero Nuevo contains about 40% each of *tierra de primera* and *tierra de potrero* savanna. But in the 1-km catchment of this site, over two-thirds of the land is savanna, while only about 1% is river levee *tierra de primera*.

When examining the catchments from an agricultural perspective, the distance from the site must be considered, as land closer to the site is more accessible. A "weighting factor," as derived by Vita-Finzi and Higgs (1970:28), was used. The total hectares for each land type for each kilometer band were multiplied by an appropriate weighting percentage, and adjusted hectare areas were produced. Percentages of each category of land in each kilometer catchment were then calculated, as in Table 4.1. The adjusted data appear in Table 4.2.

The result of this weighting is that the proportion of land nearer the site is overrepresented in the total catchment percentages. For Tenochtitlán, there is about an equal representation of *lomas* and savanna, together about 85% of the land. The disparity between *lomas* and savanna has been reduced from the unweighted data, in favor of the savanna. For San Lorenzo, the weighting results in nearly three-quarters of the land being upland *lomas*, with a reduction in savanna representation from about a third to a fifth. It is the *tierra de primera* that suffers the greatest reduction at Potrero Nuevo, changing from a little less than 40% to less than 15%, while the savanna contribution rises from 40% to 50%. The total hunting catchments for each site are probably better represented by the unweighted data.

The site catchment analysis suggests some possible differences among sites. First, let us consider the sites as separate villages.

San Lorenzo, with nearly three-fourths of its (adjusted) catchment in *lomas*, had at least 1327 ha of a soil type that today yields an average of 4.5 metric tons per hectare per year when double-cropped by slash-and-burn cultivation. Even if three-fourths of the *lomas* were fallow in any one year, the remaining fourth would produce about 1500 metric tons of maize—enough, according to Coe's (1969b:14) estimates, to feed about 7500 persons, which is seven and one-half times the population he estimates for San Lorenzo. Of course, the race of Early Formative maize used may not have matched today's yields (cf. Kirkby 1973: Figure 48), but San Lorenzo also had another (adjusted) 16 ha of *tierra de primera*. This large village probably also exploited the wild game of the *lomas*, both in the tropical forest and in those abandoned plots taken over by secondary growth. They also had available the fish and waterfowl resources of the savannah, though on a smaller scale.

Potrero Nuevo, with over 50% of its (adjusted) catchment in savanna, would seem to have had less of an agricultural advantage. However, roughly one-quarter of its catchment (an adjusted 383 ha) was rich *tierra de primera* which today yields 3.15 metric tons of maize per hectare per year. At today's rates, such a quantity of land would produce about 1200 metric tons, more than 20 times the amount needed by the population of 250 estimated for the site by Coe (1968b). Potrero Nuevo's large areas of savanna also give it considerable access to fish and waterfowl, and it had a somewhat smaller area (an adjusted 269 ha) of *lomas* for hunting and slash-and-burn cultivation.

As already stressed, our speculations about Tenochtitlán's catchment must be limited because we do not know the actual area occupied in Early Formative times. Our weighted estimates, based on the eventual maximum size of the village, indicate a more even balance between *lomas* (40%) and savanna (45%) than is characteristic of its neighboring villages. Even if three-fourths of its *lomas* were fallow in any one year, at today's rates, the remaining fourth would produce nearly 450 metric

TABLE 4.2 Site Catchments in the San Lorenzo area [a]

	Lomas (1)	Tierra de primera (2)	Tierra de potrero (3)	Marshes (4)	Water (5)	Total
San Lorenzo						
Area within 1 k of site						
Area	1163.01	0.0	16.64	23.81	2.82	1206.28
Percentage	96.41	0.0	1.38	1.97	.23	
Area within 2 k of site						
Area	1313.41	0.0	191.11	64.26	11.78	1580.56
Percentage	83.10	0.0	12.09	4.07	.75	
Area within 3 k of site						
Area	1326.98	0.0	306.56	68.44	22.02	1724.00
Percentage	76.97	0.0	17.78	3.97	1.28	
Area within 4 k of site						
Area	1326.98	16.00	369.86	74.97	26.50	1814.31
Percentage	73.14	.88	20.39	4.13	1.46	
Area within 5 k of site						
Area	1326.98	16.05	371.65	74.97	26.50	1816.15
Percentage	73.07	.88	20.46	4.13	1.46	
Portrero Nuevo						
Area within 1 k of site						
Area	151.30	6.66	367.62	1.02	18.18	544.78
Percentage	27.77	1.22	67.48	.19	3.34	
Area within 2 k of site						
Area	244.08	34.57	635.65	22.91	24.97	962.18
Percentage	25.37	3.59	66.06	2.38	2.60	
Area within 3 k of site						
Area	266.69	176.82	749.66	38.87	44.42	1276.46
Percentage	20.89	13.85	58.73	3.05	3.48	
Area within 4 k of site						
Area	266.69	336.30	789.72	41.87	51.33	1485.91
Percentage	17.95	22.63	53.15	2.82	3.45	
Area within 5 k of site						
Area	266.69	383.35	793.15	41.87	51.33	1536.39
Percentage	17.36	24.95	51.62	2.73	3.34	
Tenochtitlán						
Area within 1 k of site						
Area	366.08	50.94	139.78	2.82	1.28	560.90
Percentage	65.27	9.08	24.92	.50	.23	
Area within 2 k of site						
Area	397.83	90.49	326.53	24.45	3.88	843.18
Percentage	47.18	10.73	38.73	2.90	.46	
Area within 3 k of site						
Area	397.83	104.66	414.94	30.25	7.04	954.72
Percentage	41.67	10.96	43.46	3.17	.74	
Area within 4 k of site						
Area	397.83	109.39	440.66	30.25	7.29	985.42
Percentage	40.37	11.10	44.72	3.07	.74	
Area within 5 k of site						
Area	397.83	109.80	440.92	30.25	7.29	986.09
Percentage	40.34	11.13	44.71	3.07	.74	

[a] In this chart, the data given in Table 4.1 have been adjusted by weighting land closer to the site more heavily than land farther from the site, after the method of Vita–Finzi and Higgs (1970).

tons of maize per year if double-cropped. This is enough to feed more than twice the population of 1000 estimated for Tenochtitlán by Coe (1968b), an estimate that may be somewhat on the high side. In addition, Tenochtitlán had nearly 400 ha of primary- and secondary-growth hunting territory in the *lomas*, as well as the fish and waterfowl of the savanna marshes and oxbow lakes.

Thus, although the types of resources available to each village were the same, the relative amounts were quite different. At today's rates of production, none of the three villages would have any trouble sustaining the population estimated for it by Coe. However, if the race of maize used in the Early Formative was less productive, or if the growing of two crops per year on the *lomas* was not yet customary, the figures would be sharply reduced. If, for example, San Lorenzo phase corn yielded only 250 kg per hectare (Kirkby 1973: Figure 48) and only one crop per year were grown on the *lomas*, San Lorenzo would need to have kept 800 ha (or about 60% of its weighted *lomas* area) in cultivation every year in order to feed 1000 persons. This would imply a greatly reduced fallow cycle and much more stress on the environment than suggested by using today's figures. It is perhaps the kind of stress suggested by Drennan in Chapter 11 (this volume) in his discussion of the decline of San Lorenzo.

Problems with the Analysis

I would like now to discuss some problems arising from this analysis, many of which are inherent in the original Vita-Finzi and Higgs catchment methodology.

One of these is the changing of the landscape. The numerous oxbow lakes in the savanna at San Lorenzo indicate that the Coatzacoalcos River has shifted its course many times in the 3000 years since the Early Formative. Such changes would affect the amount of *tierra de primera* in the vicinity of each site. They might also obliterate small villages located on or near the river alluvium.

In other words, the landscape to which we have applied our planimeter is not exactly the landscape the Early Formative farmers looked out on.

A second problem is that our catchment figures show an almost inverse ratio between size of village and amount of *tierra de primera*. San Lorenzo, by far the largest site, has access to the least river levee land. Following the assumptions of the original Vita-Finzi and Higgs article, we would have to conclude that Early Formative farmers valued *lomas* land highly and cared little about *tierra de primera*. Yet, according to Coe (1969b), it is precisely these permanently cropped levee lands that are most sought by the present caciques of the area:

> With the exception of a few community *parcelas* which are set aside for the use of the primary school in each settlement, much of this land is in private hands.... In the village of Tenochtitlán, for instance, the most powerful family has arisen through a gradual acquisition of such lands. [Coe 1969b:15]

As Coe points out, the treatment of this permanent cropland as private property strikingly contrasts with the shifting slash-and-burn plots of the *lomas*, which are seen largely as *ejido*, or communal land. In other words, the raw catchment data could easily be misinterpreted unless one had relevant ethnographic data at his disposal. It seems likely that the real reason Formative villages are so squarely in the *lomas* is that the lower-lying areas flood virtually every year. And the river levee lands, though a more distant part of the catchment, may have played a more important role than their actual percentage would indicate.

Still a further problem is that of site typology. San Lorenzo was a major ceremonial–civic center, while Potrero Nuevo and Tenochtitlán were smaller villages. It may therefore be that San Lorenzo could command the resources of the river levee almost as a form of tribute, regardless of their actual distance from the site. Indeed, an interesting possibility is raised by Coe's reference to *parcelas* of *tierra de primera* which are today "set aside for the use of the primary school." Because plots of levee land do not shift as do slash-and-burn fields in the *lomas*, they can be permanently designated for the support of certain social institutions. Comparable plots might well have been set aside to maintain Early Formative institutions—chieftainship, pyramidal mound construction, the production of sumptuary goods by artisans.

Unfortunately, the raw figures and percentages of the catchment analysis are mute on such subjects. Indeed, there is a serious possibility that Potrero Nuevo and Tenochtitlán should not be considered as separate villages, but as outlying tributary *barrios* of San Lorenzo. In this case, the whole region considered here could probably be regarded as one giant catchment area.

Summary and Evaluation

Site catchment analysis, as originally proposed by Vita-Finzi and Higgs, can be profitably applied to Formative communities. Given some reasonable estimates of the productivity of aboriginal agriculture, it can provide guidelines for the area needed to sustain Formative populations. It does not, however, tell us all we need to know about the institutions that governed the way resources were used by those communities. To draw conclusions about settlement choices purely on the basis of percentages of various land types could be misleading, unless independently derived data on those institutions are available. Site catchment analysis probably gives us a good rough sketch of the resources within walking distance of a village. What it does not give us is a sketch of the network of interrelationships by which those resources were manipulated. We know, for example, that less than 1% of San Lorenzo's weighted catchment was *tierra de primera*. What we do not know is how much of a handicap this was to a society capable of bringing in 10-ton basalt blocks through 50 km of jungle and swamp.

Empirical Determination of Site Catchments in Oaxaca and Tehuacán

KENT V. FLANNERY

Nestled as they are among the gray-green mountains where Mesoamerican agriculture may have originated, the highland valleys of the Puebla–Oaxaca region provide a laboratory for the study of the Formative. Since MacNeish's initial test pits in 1960, the area has seen nearly 15 years of continuous work by Mexican, German, Canadian, and U.S. institutions. In this section, I will examine site catchments in two valleys, those of Oaxaca and Tehuacán. My approach will be one long-since discarded by the vanguard of the New Archeology: I will examine the facts and ask them to speak for themselves.

The original Vita-Finzi and Higgs framework for site catchment, applied by Rossmann in the preceding section, starts with a specified catchment area and asks "What resources should be available within it?" I will reverse this by beginning with the empirical data on plant, animal, and mineral resources found at Formative villages in Oaxaca and Tehuacán and ask "From how far away must they have come?" In this approach, one does not decide whether or not a village was farming by calculating the percentage of good farm land within 5 km; one decides by finding out whether the remains in the site are from wild or domestic plants. Admittedly, in addition to being reactionary, this does tend to cut off a certain amount of stimulating debate.

Philosophy aside, it must be granted that conditions for this kind of inductive analysis could not be better in the Puebla-Oaxaca highlands. The climate is arid to semiarid, the soils often mildly alkaline. Animal bones are preserved, pollen survives, and carbonized seeds often rest in a matrix of soft, decomposed clay from wattle or adobe brick. It is a far cry from the destructively acid soils of the tropical Gulf Coast, where even the most dedicated ecologist is greeted by deer bone with the consistency of wet graham crackers.

Empirical Data on Subsistence

Recovery of empirical data on subsistence in this region involves some of the simplest techniques known to archeology. It consists basically of recovering animal bones, plant remains, and pollen grains, something the Real Mesoamerican Archeologist does almost every time he digs. His main complaint is that he can't find anyone to analyze them after he's dug them up.

Palynologist James Schoenwetter has found that a 150-cc sample of earth is usually adequate for a 100-grain pollen count at most Early and Middle Formative sites. Scraped up with a clean trowel, good samples can be taken from house floors, postholes, storage pits, or the fill of burial vessels. Schoenwetter takes his samples in paper bags, which can be sealed yet still allow evaporation of the soil moisture which sometimes causes mold spores to grow when samples are kept in plastic bags.

As far as faunal remains go, it all depends on the size of screen you use. A man with a trowel will find most of the deer and dog bone. A 5-mm mesh will stop cottontail and gopher bones. A 1.5-mm mesh (roughly the size of window screen) will recover quail toes, tiny lizard and fish vertebrae, and stray pack rat molars. Anything smaller than that will be hard to identify, and even harder for a prehistoric man to hunt.

It is with the recovery of plant remains that the Real Mesoamerican Archeologist most often throws up his hands. For even in Puebla and Oaxaca, early Mesoamerican villages do not have preservation like that of dry caves; the plant remains are all carbonized, and must be recovered by flotation. R.M.A. has seen photographs of the power-driven froth flotation machine used by Cambridge University in Israel (Jarman, Legge, and Charles 1972). He doesn't have one, doesn't know where to buy one, and doesn't know how to build one. "If I had one of those, I'd use it," he says.

"But otherwise?"

"God, I just—I don't know. I'd *like* to, of course, but . . ."

"But you think flotation is something complicated, like operating a nuclear reactor."

"Well . . ." he hesitates.

"What if I told you," I say, "that flotation can be done with a plastic washtub, right at the site, with no fancy equipment at all? Then you wouldn't have any excuse, would you?"

"Well . . . I don't really have a plastic washtub." And so R.M.A., who can use an alidade as well as a professional surveyor, shirks a procedure that can be carried out by an illiterate. Finally he yields: "Write it down for me." And I write it down on the brown paper bag he hands me, partly covered by his field notes for that day. I will repeat it here for anyone else whose budget will not permit the purchase of a froth flotation machine.

"Gray ash and black ash are good bets for flotation samples; so is ashy brown earth with visible charcoal flecks. White ash is usually not so good, because the burning is too complete and the oxidation too strong to promote carbonization. Take as big a sample as you can. A 2-kilo sherd bag is good, but a 5-gallon wicker basket lined with newspaper is better. Let the sample dry for a

Figure 4.4 Archeological flotation at Abasolo, Oaxaca. Workmen stir a solution of water, earth, and sodium silicate, pouring the floating charcoal into a fine screen.

a couple of teaspoons of sodium silicate ('water glass') to each liter of water. The silicate acts as a deflocculant, to disperse the clay and bring the charcoal to the surface clean. Pour in some cupfuls of dirt from the sample, stir, and when you think all the carbon is floating, pour it off into a screen before it starts to waterlog (Figure 4.4). Be generous with the water, and pour only carbon, not mud, into your screen. When the screen is full, let it dry for a day in the shade, slowly. And *there* are your carbonized seeds (Figure 4.5).

"Remember, a 5-mm mesh will only stop avocado pits and corncob fragments. A 1.5-mm mesh will stop chile pepper seeds. But if you want the chenopods, amaranths, and smaller field weeds, you have to turn to carburetor mesh."

R.M.A. looks at my scrawled instructions. "If I get *that* much charcoal," he shrugs, "I think I'll just send it along to the radiocarbon lab."

week, very slowly, in the shade; if it dries in the sun, the seed coat shrinks faster than the inner seed, and it cracks.

"Now fill a plastic washtub with water, and add

Site Catchments in the Valley of Oaxaca

The Valley of Oaxaca, with an average elevation of 1500 m, is semiarid and semitropical. Four

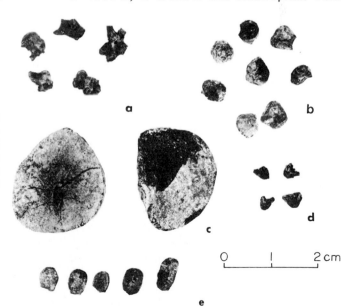

Figure 4.5 Carbonized plant remains recovered by flotation at Huitzo, Oaxaca. (a) Cupule-bearing fragments from shattered maize cobs; (b) maize kernels; (c) two cotyledons of domestic avocado seed; (d) seeds from the fruit of the prickly pear cactus; (e) cotyledons of domestic bean.

0   1   2 cm

physiographic zones are of relevance to our discussion of site catchment:

1. *The low alluvium*. This is a narrow strip that represents the present flood plain of the Atoyac River. Aboriginally it would have been characterized by a forest of willow (*Salix*), alder (*Alnus*), and baldcypress or ahuehuete (*Taxodium*).
2. *The high alluvium*. This is a level alluvial plain, representing the Pleistocene floodplain of the Atoyac, and constituting the "valley floor" where most agriculture is practiced today. Aboriginally it would have been characterized by mesquite (*Prosopis*) and other legume trees, except where cleared for farming.
3. *The piedmont*. This is an apron of gentle slopes near the base of the mountains, once covered with a thorn forest of prickly pear (*Opuntia*), organ cacti, maguey (*Agave*), and legume trees (*Cassia, Leucaena*).
4. *The mountains*. This is a zone of steep slopes with an aboriginal cover of oak, pine, pinyon, manzanita (*Arctostaphylos*), and abundant fruit and nut trees.

In general, early villages in the Valley of Oaxaca are located either on piedmont spurs or low rises near the Atoyac River, or in the upper piedmont along well-watered tributary barrancas. A few are at specific resource localities like salt springs or pottery clay beds. An example of the riverside locality would be San José Mogote, discussed in earlier chapters of this book. An example of an upper piedmont locality would be its satellite settlement, Fábrica San José.

The pitfalls of using straight percentages for the site catchments of early Mesoamerican villages can be illustrated by comparing these two Oaxacan sites. In a recent paper, Robert Drennan (1975) draws circles of 2.5-km radii around San José Mogote and Fábrica San José. The circle around San José Mogote includes 76% high alluvium, 24% piedmont, and no mountain areas. The circle around Fábrica San José includes only 12% high

alluvium, 73% piedmont, and 15% mountains. Clearly, the difference in high alluvium between the two catchment areas is striking; San José Mogote has more than six times as much. Might we conclude from this that agriculture was less important at Fábrica San José, or that the latter village practiced piedmont dry farming while San José Mogote cultivated the humid alluvium?

Consider the following figures. A circle with a 2.5-km radius includes 19.6 sq km, or 1960 ha. Twelve percent of that would be 235 ha. If we refer to the regression diagrams of Anne Kirkby (1973), already mentioned in the introduction to this chapter (Figures 4.1–4.2), we find that, at 1000 B.C., the maize of the Oaxaca–Puebla region would have had a mean cob length of about 6 cm and a consequent yield of about 300 kg per hectare. Thus, the alluvium within the Fábrica San José catchment circle was theoretically capable of producing 70.5 metric tons of maize at 1000 B.C. Given an average annual consumption of about 1 metric ton of maize per household in the Valley of Oaxaca (Susan H. Lees, personal communication),* this would have supplied 70 households. Even assuming that two-thirds of the alluvium lay fallow every year, some 23 households could have been supported. However, Drennan's estimate for the number of households at Fábrica San José throughout its occupation is only 10–12. Such a population could have been supported by the yield from 40 ha of alluvium in a good year—17% of the alluvium, and only 2% of the total circle of 2.5-km radius. Thus, both the conclusions given at the end of the previous paragraph would have been too hasty.

Let us now focus on the village of San José Mogote. Four field seasons of excavation at that site have produced enough carbonized seeds (iden-

*Kirkby (1973) uses a figure of 2 metric tons of maize per household, but this represents the average amount *produced*, including "salable excess" used to obtain other foodstuffs. Lees' estimate is based on the actual *consumption* by households she studied in Oaxaca. Readers who wish to use Kirkby's estimate need only multiply the number of hectares required by 2.

tified by C. Earle Smith), wood charcoal (identified by Wilma Koschik), pollen (identified by James Schoenwetter), and animal bones (identified by the writer) to begin a definition of its catchment area. In addition, mineral resources such as chert (studied by Michael Whalen), magnetite (studied by Jane W. Pires-Ferreira), and pottery clay (studied by William O. Payne) have, in many cases, been traced to the nearest source. The result is that we can now go through the list of commodities whose use is empirically demonstrated for the Early Formative San José phase (1150-850B.C.) and determine from how far away they must have come. We will begin with those nearest at hand (Figure 4.6).

1. *Within the village.* Several foodstuffs presumably were available within the village itself, necessitating a trip of no more than a few hundred meters. These would have included domestic dogs (common) and turkeys (very rare). Because the site is on a piedmont spur, edible wild fruits like prickly pear (*Opuntia*) and hackberry (*Celtis*) may have invaded the secondary growth on vacant lots just as they do today. Moreover, for many months following the harvest season, villagers would have had foodstuffs like maize stored in bell-shaped pits near their houses.

2. *From the river* (1 km). With a walk of less than 1 km to the river, villagers could obtain mud turtles (*Kinosternon*); reed canary grass (*Phalaris*) for roof thatching, mat weaving, and basketry; and sand for floor surfacing and adobe making. Opossum (*Didelphis*) and raccoon (*Procyon*) also frequent this zone.

3. *On the alluvium* (within 2.5 km). Within a radius of 2.5 km, the villagers had available to them more than 1400 ha of high alluvium with an estimated productive potential of over 400 metric tons of maize (cf. Table 6.1, Chapter 6). Carbonized seed samples show that teosinte (*Zea mexicana*) also grew in the cornfields and crossed with local maize, whether by accident or design. This is presumably also the zone where chiles (*Capsicum*) and

squashes (*Cucurbita*) were grown, and possibly avocados (*Persea*) as well. San José Mogote could have grown enough of these basic staples for its estimated 80–120 households without going outside the 2.5-m circle; this zone also would have produced the highest density of edible field weeds like chenopods, amaranths, and *Portulaca*. The wild food resources of the high alluvium, where not cleared for agriculture, included mesquite pods (*Prosopis*) and cottontail rabbit (*Sylvilagus*).

4. *On the piedmont* (0–5 km). Some 24% of San José Mogote's 2.5-km. catchment circle is piedmont, and the area is greatly increased by expanding the radius to 5 km. The food resources of the upper piedmont (between 2.5 and 5.0 km) are greater than those of the lower piedmont, making the additional travel worthwhile; but most of them are only seasonally available. The *Agave* or century plant, the edible prickly pear stem, the cottontail rabbit, and the jackrabbit (*Lepus mexicanus*) are available most of the year, as are small birds like quail (*Cyrtonyx montezumae*), dove (*Zenaidura macroura*), and pigeon (*Columba fasciata*). Seasonally available are hackberries, the *nanche* or West Indian cherry (*Malpighia*), and the fruit of the prickly pear and organ cactus. It is not yet known whether the *Agave* and prickly pear were cultivated at this time, or collected wild, or both.

5. *The mountains* (5–15 km). We have now arrived at a 5-km distance from the village, the threshold beyond which agricultural activity is considered to yield "decreasing returns." However, the mountain zone, even at distances of 15 or 20 km, was crucial to villagers of the San José phase. Every carbonized upright or roof beam identified from houses of this phase is of pine, which had to be brought from the mountains above 2000 m in elevation. In addition, pine was the preferred fuel used in charcoal braziers—predominating as much as 5 to 1 over oak, which also comes

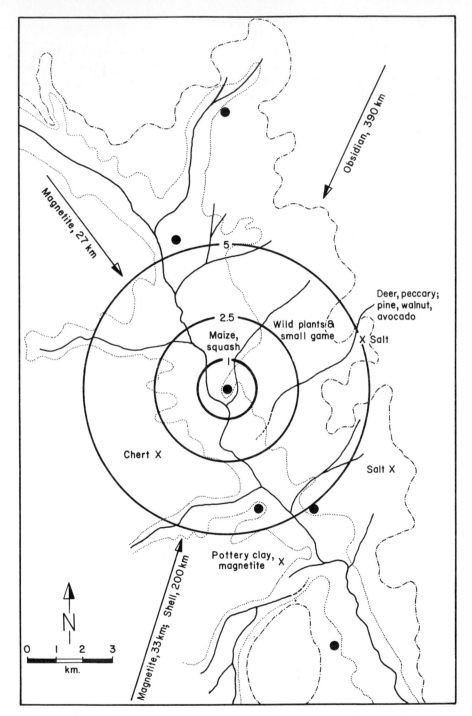

Obsidian, 390 km

Magnetite, 27 km

Deer, peccary;
pine, walnut,
avocado

X Salt

Wild plants &
small game

Maize,
squash

Chert X

Salt X

Pottery clay, X
magnetite

Magnetite, 33 km; Shell, 200 km

N

0 1 2 3
km.

Figure 4.6 The northeast Valley of Oaxaca. Site catchment circles with radii of 1.0, 2.5, and 5.0 km are centered on the village of San José Mogote. Dotted line (. . . .) indicates the transition from the alluvium to the piedmont; dashed line (— · —) indicates the transition from the piedmont to the mountains. Various local resources are shown.

from the mountain zone. Thus the villagers, who theoretically could have picked up mesquite, willow, and alder as firewood from nearer their homes, chose instead to make round trips of more than 10 km to obtain mountain woods.

For a society with few domestic animals, the mountains were also a vast reservoir of meat. White-tail deer (*Odocoileus virginianus*) and collared peccary (*Tayassu tajacu*) were the chief game animals, but the mountains also had abundant rabbits, doves, and pigeons of the same species found on the piedmont. Acorns (*Quercus* sp.) and black walnuts (*Juglans* sp.) were harvested in the mountains, and ended up in the carbonized debris at San José Mogote. In addition, some tiny avocado seeds may have been from wild trees in the same zone.

6. *Specific mineral resources* (3–50 km). Salt, chert, pottery clay, and magnetite were specific mineral resources which also can be dealt with in catchment terms. Salt was available from the springs at Fábrica San José, only 5 km away, or at Las Salinas, 6.5 km distant. Unlimited chert was available near Matadamas, 3 km to the west and across the river, which seems to have been the source most frequently used by San José Mogote (M. Whalen, personal communication). The basic clay used for the eight major pottery types of the San José phase is a decomposition product of Pre-Cambrian gneiss, available for 70 km along the western piedmont of the valley. The small Early Formative hamlet of La Nopalera occurs at a particularly fine clay source 6–7 km southwest of San José Mogote, near where Atzompa potters still get their raw material (S. Kowalewski, personal communication). The white slip used for some pottery types, however, was a more iron-free kaolinite clay which does not occur so close at hand; at least one suitable deposit is available at a fossil hot spring near Mitla, some 40 km east of Oaxaca City. Clearly, a circle of 5 km radius

would have provided the villagers with most of their basic mineral needs (salt, sand, lime, chert, clay), but not with more exotic minerals.

Magnetite, used in the manufacture of small iron-ore mirrors, was such an exotic mineral. One source did in fact lie only 6 km away at Loma Salinas, not far from the pottery clay beds mentioned earlier; the two major sources utilized by San José Mogote, however, lay 27 km to the north and 33 km to the south. Mirrors from all three sources were traded to other regions of Mesoamerica (see Pires-Ferreira, Chapter 10 of this volume).

7. *Exotic materials from distant regions* (200 km?). Finally, we come to a series of items at San José Mogote which may have been brought from more than 200 km away. These include marine shells from the Pacific Ocean; freshwater mussels from the Gulf Coast drainage; fish spines; shark teeth; and jadeite or nephrite. Although certainly not common, such items were important in the ceremonial life of the community.

Summary: Catchments and Levels of Exclusivity

Based on the empirical data from San José Mogote, one could therefore envision its catchment area as consisting of a series of ever-widening concentric circles. San José needed a circle of less than 2.5 km radius to satisfy its basic agricultural requirements. A radius of 5 km probably satisfied its basic mineral resource needs and provided important seasonal wild plants. However, it needed a circle of perhaps 15-km radius to supply necessary deer meat, house construction material, and preferred types of firewood. In order to engage in trade with other regions, it collected exotic materials from a still larger circle of perhaps 50-km radius. And to satisfy the requirements of a complex ceremonial system, it relied on exotic materials from a circle perhaps 200 km in diameter.

The implications of these ever-widening circles become clear when one views San José Mogote's catchment area alongside those of its neighbor vil-

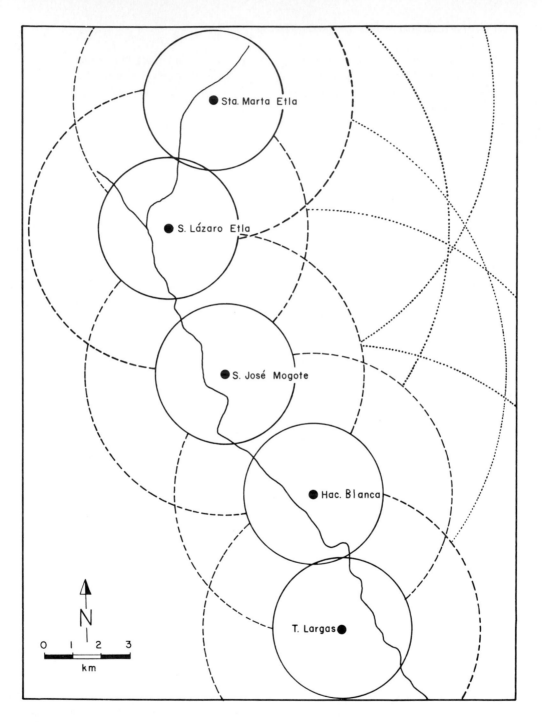

Figure 4.7 Early Formative villages along the Atoyac River in the northeastern Valley of Oaxaca. Catchment circles with radii of 2.5 km (solid line —), 5.0 km (dashed line – – –), and 7.5 cm (dotted line . . . .) are indicated.

lages, San Lázaro Etla to the north and Hacienda Blanca to the south (Figure 4.7). Circles with a radius of 2.5 km drawn around each site do not overlap; they are exclusive. When circles of 5 km radius are drawn, however, San José Mogote's overlaps with those of its two nearest neighbors. When circles of 7.5-km radius are drawn, each site's catchment overlaps with those of its *four* nearest neighbors. By the time we reach 50 km, all exclusivity is gone, and we are talking about one catchment area for the entire Valley of Oaxaca.

These concentric levels of decreasing exclusivity bring to mind Richard Ford's study of a Tewa Pueblo in New Mexico (Ford 1968). There, the innermost catchment circle consists of a small area of river bottom land and fringing upland where the village is located, cultivation takes place, and ancestors are buried; this area would be defended, by violence if necessary, against intrusion by outsiders. Beyond this is a zone of piedmont where both men and women forage, expecting to encounter neighbors from nearby villages. Still farther out lies a zone where women do not venture, but where men hunt deer and visit mountaintop shrines. This very large zone of mountains and piedmont is shared amicably with even more distant neighbors, speaking different dialects. We would not be at all surprised to learn that early Mesoamerican villagers treated their concentric catchment circles the same way.

Because the relationship between site catchment and village spacing is discussed in Chapter 6, we will mention it here only as a warning. Since major sites of the San José phase tend to be spaced about 5 km apart on the upper Atoyac River, it would be tempting to see this spacing as the result of a need for each village to maintain exclusive rights to an inner circle of 2.5-km radius. This temptation must be resisted. As shown in Chapter 6, such a circle was far larger than all but the largest of the villages would have needed; had agricultural factors alone determined the spacing, sites could have been much closer together than they actually were.

The Village and the Seasonal Camp: An Example from Tehuacán

We must now consider a further complication for the conception and analysis of catchment areas. Until now, we have acted as if villagers subsisted mainly on those foodstuffs available within a few hours' walk of the village. That is not strictly true. In some regions, empirical data suggest that, at various seasons of the year, groups of farmers left the village and set up temporary camps in good foraging localities, where they collected wild foods for eventual transport back to the village. Orchard crops also may have been grown nearby. In effect, these camps served as annexes to the village, where resources normally out of convenient walking distance were brought temporarily within reach.

Clearly, such camps have implications for the "weighting" of successive circles on the basis of distance from the village. In the preceding section, Rossmann (following Vita-Finzi and Higgs 1970: Table 3) has weighted land within 1 km of the site as 100% utilized, land between 1 and 2 km as 50%, land between 2 and 3 km as 33%, and so on. A seasonal camp made 15 km from the village, however, might in effect raise part of that very distant circle to a level of utilization approaching that of the immediate environs of the village. In such a situation, it is the intermediate distances (for example, 5, 6, 7 km) that would be least exploited.

Let us therefore examine the relationship between a village and a seasonal camp in the valley of Tehuacán, Puebla. Both sites belong to the Middle Formative period known as the Santa María phase, and their occupations fall somewhere between 800 and 500 B.C. For the purposes of this discussion, we will consider only the innermost 1 km, or "100% utilized," circle.

The city of Tehuacán lies at roughly the same elevation as Oaxaca, but the valley steps down rapidly to the south via a series of travertine terraces to below 1000 m. For the purposes of this analysis, the major physiographic zones to be considered are as follows:

1. *The arroyo of the Río Salado.* This is the entrenched bed of a mildly alkaline river, and originally would have been filled with thickets of quebracho (*Acacia unijuga*) and chintoborrego (*Vallesia glabra*).
2. *The alluvial valley center.* This level plain, where most agriculture is conducted today, would originally have been a mesquite grassland with low shrubs like the coyotomate (*Castela tortuosa*).
3. *The broader piedmont slopes on the east edge of the valley.* Like the piedmont of the Oaxaca Valley, this zone of relatively gentle slopes would originally have been covered by thorn forest. North of Ajalpan, the vegetation is temperate and somewhat thinner. South of Ajalpan, where the valley dips below 1200 m, the vegetation becomes arid tropical thorn forest with a broad canopy closing 1.5 m above the ground. The high, spiny thickets, filled with edible wild plants to be described later, are dominated by species of Leguminosae, Bursuraceae, and Anacardiaceae intermixed with dense stands of columnar cacti (Smith 1965).
4. *The mountains.* As in the case of Oaxaca, a zone of higher mountains, once covered with oak and pine, rises above the eastern piedmont of Tehuacán. Acorns and wild avocados would have been available in this zone.

Las Canoas (Ts 367)

The Middle Formative village of Las Canoas occupied the east bank of the Río Salado in the central alluvial valley of Tehuacán (MacNeish *et al.* 1970). Surface survey by jeep and on foot reveals that diagnostic Early Santa María phase sherds occur in clusters, varying from 50 by 50 m to 100 by 100 m in extent, confined to a narrow strip set back 100 m from the river. Although this strip runs for a distance of approximately 1 km from

the site of Ajalpan (Ts 204) to Coatepec (Ts 368), clusters are widely spaced (200–300 m apart). Ajalpan, Canoas, and Coatepec all are closely related; thus it is not clear whether three separate sites are involved, or one long narrow community that moved downriver from north to south as it grew. With the wisdom of hindsight, I would now tend to consider the Early Santa María surface scatters as reflecting widely spaced household clusters or courtyard groups, perhaps 5–10 in all. Zone D2 at Las Canoas, a lens of burnt wattle and daub 10–12 cm thick and covering approximately 16 sq m, was probably the remains of a single house.

Canoas lies at 1200 m elevation, and a circle of 1 km radius drawn around it includes only two resource zones: the alluvial plain (90%) and the narrow trench of the Río Salado (10) (see Figure 4.8). Within 1 km, however, there are available some 300 ha of alluvium, theoretically enough to produce 90 metric tons of maize of the size calculated for 1000 B.C. (see Figures 4.1–4.2). This is more than enough to support the population we estimate for Las Canoas. Hence, it seems likely that most of the crops known for the Early Santa María phase (maize, squash, avocado, chile, amaranth, and several kinds of fruit trees) were grown within a kilometer of Las Canoas.

The site yielded abundant fragments of animal bone. Domestic dogs, available within the village, were the most common animals eaten. Second in frequency were bones of cottontail and jackrabbit, both available within a kilometer of Las Canoas. Pocket gophers, which probably occurred right in the cornfields, also came from nearby. In terms of kilograms of meat, however, the animal providing the largest portion was the white-tail deer; and, as in the case of Oaxaca, this species was probably hunted in the mountains to the east, well outside the 1-km radius (Flannery 1967).

Zone VII, Coxcatlán Cave (Tc 50)

Coxcatlán Cave (MacNeish 1962) is a large rockshelter overlooking a dry arroyo in the upper pied-

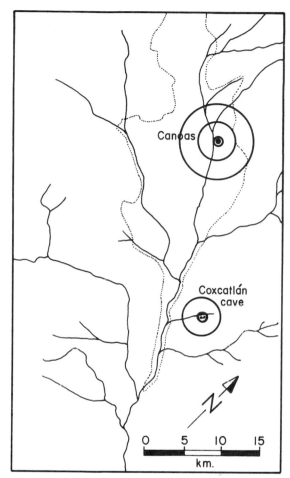

Figure 4.8 The Tehuacán Valley. Catchment circles with radii of 2.5 and 5.0 km are centered on Las Canoas village and Coxcatlán Cave. Dotted line (. . . .) indicates the transition from the alluvium to the piedmont.

mont, 20 km south of Las Canoas. Its elevation is between 900 and 1000 m. In contrast to the Canoas area, which once would have been temperate mesquite grassland, the Coxcatlán region is an arid tropical thorn forest with dozens of edible plant species not available in the vicinity of Canoas. It is also superb deer range. Zone VII, one of 28 cultural strata excavated in the rockshelter, was a Santa María phase deposit with extensive refuse areas, artifacts, storage pits, and grass bedding left by its seasonal occupants.

It seems likely that Zone VII represents a series of camps made by persons who came from, and later returned to, a village. While at the rockshelter, they harvested plants and hunted wild animals. In all honesty, it cannot be convincingly argued that Las Canoas was the specific village from which the Zone VII foragers came, as there are many other Santa María phase villages in the valley. However, Las Canoas was one of the nearest villages whose ceramics date it to approximately the right time period.

If one draws a circle of 1-km radius around Coxcatlán Cave, he comes up with a very different set of resources from those in the alluvial valley. This difference is reflected in the hundreds of plant fragments preserved by dessication inside the rockshelter (Smith 1967). They include the fruits of local trees or shrubs like the chupandilla (*Cyrtocarpa procera*), cozahuico (*Sideroxylon* sp.), buckthorn (*Condalia mexicana*), susí (*Jatropha neopauciflora*), and possibly wild avocado (*Persea americana*); seeds of foxtail grass (*Setaria* sp.); the *Agave*, represented by nearly 500 chewed quids; the prickly pear (*Opuntia* spp.); several varieties of organ cacti, like the cardón (*Lemaireocereus weberi*); pods of the pochote or silk-cotton tree (*Ceiba parvifolia*); and pods of tree legumes like the mesquite (*Prosopis*) and guaje (*Leucaena*). In addition, Santa María phase villagers collected wild grasses for bedding, canes for basketry and matting, the cholulo berry (*Zizyphus pedunculatus*) for soap making, and possibly medicinal plants like venenillo (*Thevetia peruviana*). Several seasons of the year are represented, with April–May occupation heaviest, and smaller occupations in September, November, and February. It is believed that these represent multiple visits whose deposits coalesced under the weight of overburden, rather than one continuous year-long occupation.

This impression of multiple visits is supported by the faunal data. The nearly 200 bone fragments from Zone VII occurred in two isolated groups. In the west end of the rockshelter lay one scatter, composed mainly of deer. No bones occurred in the intervening central area. The east end of the

TABLE 4.3 Calendar of Economic Activities and Foods Eaten in the Tehuacán Valley during the Middle Formative

Month	Activities	Foods eaten in village
January	Small bands of hunters pursue deer intensively, especially in thorn forest near Coxcatlán; this is the heart of the relatively lean dry season, and maguey and prickly pear leaves may also have been gathered.	Deer; dog; small game; corn and chile stored from October harvest; perhaps dried squash seeds stored from November harvest; perhaps maguey (quids) and prickly pear leaf (cooked).
February	Deer, having been hunted since October, are probably getting scarcer; small bands gather pochote, which now ripens in the Coxcatlán hills. Maguey and prickly pear may also have been gathered.	Dogs; some game; corn, chile, and perhaps squash seed stored from harvest; raw and/or cooked kernels of pochote; perhaps maguey (quids) and prickly pear leaf (cooked).
March	By now, most of the deer not killed between October and February have probably moved as far from human settlement as possible. The last of the pochote pods are gathered; perhaps also maguey and prickly pear. Fields were probably being cleared, and perhaps, then as now, a minor crop of maize may have been planted in anticipation of an early beginning to the rainy season.	Dog; some game; some stored domestic plants; some pochote; perhaps maguey (quids), prickly pear leaf; possibly other nonseasonal wild plants like tuber of pochote.
April	Amaranth harvest begins. Wild cactus fruits bloom and begin to be collected; ciruela fruits ripen; avocado and white zapote are harvested from slopes above Coxcatlán; large trapping-and-harvesting bands sent out from villages begin to arrive at seasonal campsites in the thorn forest, such as Zone VII of Coxcatlán Cave.	Dog; perhaps some game; amaranth; fruits of prickly pear, cardón, ciruela, avocado, zapote blanco; some stored domestic plants.
May	Large trapping-and-collecting bands are settled in the Coxcatlán thorn forest. Cottontail are trapped in great numbers, along with skunks and some other small game; fruits of ciruela, avocado, zapote blanco, and various cacti are collected. Amaranth is still being harvested. The first rains may begin this month and, if so, some planting of maize begins.	Rabbits; other small game; dogs; some deer and peccary; amaranth; fruits of ciruela, avocado, zapote blanco, prickly pear, and cardón cactus; some stored domestic plants.
June	The rainy season begins in full force. Large bands encamped in the Coxcatlán thorn forest are finishing their seasonal stay and returning to the valley villages to begin the planting of maize and squash and the harvest of whatever maize was planted in March. Cottontails are trapped in large numbers, and other game (both large and	Rabbits and other small game; dogs; iguanas and smaller lizards; some deer and peccary; fruits of prickly pear and cardón; mesquite beans; stored amaranth; some corn, probably both green and stored.

114

small is taken. Plant collectors are still concentrating on cactus fruits, but their focus now begins shifting toward the valley floor, where mesquite beans are now ripe. June is usually a peak rainy month.

Month	Description	Diet
July	Planting of corn and squash continues. Probably by now, all the scattered hunting-collecting bands have returned to their villages to participate in planting along the river floodplains and in wet barrancas. Collecting centers on mesquite beans; trapping of rabbits, gophers, and other small game continues. The rains slacken somewhat.	Rabbits and other small game; dogs; iguanas and small lizards; mesquite beans; stored corn and amaranth.
August	This month is usually the midsummer lull in precipitation. Chile is planted to take advantage of the September rains. Mesquite beans are gathered. Rabbits and other small game are trapped, and probably some hunting of larger game is done in the inactive period before the fall maize harvest.	Rabbits and small game; dog; some deer and peccary; iguana and smaller lizards; mesquite beans; stored corn and amaranth.
September	The rains return in full force; September is usually another month of peak precipitation. Small bands begin to drift back to the Coxcatlán thorn forest to collect fruit of the chupandilla, which ripen at this time. Cottontails, other small game, lizards, and perhaps some deer and peccary are hunted or trapped. Toward the end of the month, the harvest of green corn may begin, on the valley floor and in the wet barrancas.	Rabbits; dog; large and small game; iguanas and smaller lizards; chupandilla fruit; stored domestic plants; fresh green corn.
October	Rains end. The main harvest of ripe corn and squash probably occupies all or most able-bodied villagers this month. Some chupandilla may still be collected. Toward the end of the month, small bands of hunters begin to settle in the Coxcatlán thorn forest in anticipation of fall deer hunting.	Dog; small game; perhaps some deer; ripe corn, green corn, and squash; some chupandilla.
November	Harvest of squash, tomatoes, and chile. Berries of the cholulo are collected for soapmaking. Small bands are now hunting deer in the mountains and the Coxcatlán thorn forest.	Dog; deer; some small game; corn, squash, chile.
December	Intensive hunting of deer in the mountains and thorn forest by small bands of men. At this time, gathering of maguey and prickly pear leaves may possibly begin.	Deer; dog; perhaps some small game; some corn, squash, and chile; possibly also maguey (quids) and young prickly pear leaves.

zone was so thick it was removed in two levels of 15 cm each; the upper and lower sections showed interesting seasonal differences.

In the west scatter, bones of roasted *Ameiva* (a race-runner lizard) indicated a rainy season camp. The same was true of the lower 15 cm of the east scatter, where these lizards also were represented. The upper 15 cm of the east scatter had no such rainy season indicators, but included deer whose antlers were in their fully hardened (dry season) condition. This dry season deposit had the highest frequency of deer bone, amounting to the remains of at least three individuals. Other animals hunted during the Zone VII occupation were collared peccary, cottontail rabbit, spotted skunk, black iguana, and an unidentified bird. No domestic dog bones occurred at all—a striking absence in view of their numbers in the remains of the Las Canoas village.

Santa María Phase Site Catchment

By now, it must be clear how the presence of seasonal camps complicates our analysis of Middle Formative catchment at Tehuacán. We presumably would be correct in inferring that maize agriculture was uppermost in the minds of the Las Canoas villagers, based on the fact that a circle of 1-km radius around the site includes 90% alluvial farmland. We would err, however, if we went on to infer that Las Canoas had little access to chupandilla, cozahuico, buckthorn, susi̇́, cardón, and other thorn-forest plants simply because those resources occur beyond the 5-km limit of "diminishing returns." Santa María phase villagers got around that problem by founding camps in lush collecting areas that were more than a day's round trip away. There—for a week, a month, or part of a season—several families had a whole new set of resources at their doorstep.

Conversely, the Tehuacán example warns us not to draw conclusions about village subsistence based solely on cave remains. Within a 1-km radius of Coxcatlán Cave, the percentage of good alluvial

farmland is zero, yet there were agricultural products preserved in the camp: corn, squash, chiles, amaranth, and fruits like the ciruela (*Spondias mombin*) and white zapote (*Casimiroa edulis*). It is likely that some of these domesticates were grown in barrancas near the rockshelter, but many were probably carried there from the village when the trip was made. To calculate the percentage of domesticated to wild products solely on the basis of cave debris (cf. MacNeish 1967) almost certainly overrepresents the wild species; the cave camps, after all, were founded in part to harvest wild products. The percentage of maize in flotation samples from villages will almost surely be higher than its percentage at contemporary cave camps, just as the percentage of domestic dog bones will be higher in a Santa María phase village than in a Santa María phase camp.

In order to draw conclusions about a given early Mesoamerican village, one must consider not only its own immediate catchment area but those of its associated seasonal camps. Even when those camps have not been discovered, the presence of products from distant resource zones may hint at their existence, as in the case of the Oaxacan villages already described. That is why we feel that empirical data, in the form of plant and animal remains from the village itself, should be used in the definition of its catchment area.

The relations between a village and its satellites, like seasonal hunting or harvesting camps, leads naturally into the topic of complex settlement systems. We have chosen to defer that topic until Chapter 6. Before leaving the Tehuacán Valley, however, let us present a model for the timing of seasonal use of site catchment areas around villages and camps of the Santa María phase. The model is based on empirical data from Las Canoas and Coxcatlán Cave, combined with data on the seasonal availability of plant species in the Tehuacán Valley. It is presented in the form of a month-by-month calendar of subsistence activities for villagers of the Santa María phase (Table 4.3).

Summary and Conclusions

Site catchments in the valleys of the Oaxaca-Puebla highlands can be visualized as a series of concentric rings. The innermost ring around the village, not shared with neighboring villages, provided most of the agricultural products. A second and larger ring, shared with two neighboring villages, brought in many mineral resources, wild plants, and small game. A third and still larger ring, shared with as many as four neighboring villages, provided larger game, construction materials, and exotic materials for trade. At strategic points in this outer ring, there were placed seasonal campsites which, acting as temporary annexes to the village, gave more distant wild resources and orchard crops the same accessibility as those in the innermost ring.

While factors of site catchment helped to determine the exact location of the village on the landscape, they apparently did not determine the spacing between villages. The few figures at our disposal suggest that each village, given its size, had more exclusive or unshared land than it needed. Thus social factors, not explained by catchment analysis, must have influenced village spacing. These factors are dealt with in Chapters 6 and 7. It is this interplay between social distance, subsistence needs, and the geometry of location that makes the complex settlement systems of the Formative such an interesting challenge.

Statistical Analysis of Site Catchments at Ocós, Guatemala

ALAN ZARKY

In this section, I will present an alternative to the site catchment method of Vita-Finzi and Higgs (1970). This alternative method will then be applied to the Formative villages of the Ocós region of Guatemala. Since this is a tropical lowland area, the approach also may offer some useful contrast with Rossmann's analysis of tropical lowland Veracruz (this chapter).

The alternative approach offered here does not reason directly from the percentages of various environmental zones within a catchment area to the main subsistence activities at a site. As Flannery points out in the introduction to this chapter, such reasoning could be highly misleading in the case of prehistoric villages. To take an extreme case, let us imagine a village located on a small oasis in the Nubian Desert. A standard site catchment analysis might show that water occupied only 1% of its 5-km-radius catchment circle, while blowing sand dunes occupied 99%. It would be erroneous, however, to argue from this that the occupants of the site were interested primarily in blowing sand dunes. The point is that, if located anywhere else in the entire region, the catchment would include *less* than 1% water.

In terms of basic assumptions, the Vita-Finzi and Higgs model takes site location as given, and then asks "What resources could be exploited within easy walking distance of this site?" The model for Oaxaca presented by Flannery in this chapter takes empirical data on plant, animal, and mineral remains as given, and then asks "How far from the

TABLE 4.4   Three Hypothetical Distributions for Sixty Archeological Sites in a Region of Hills, Mesas, and Flatlands

Landform	Percent of total area	Expected percent of sites	Expected number of sites	Observed number of sites	Observed percent of sites	Percentage difference between expected and observed
Part A						
Hills	25	25	15	15	25	0
Mesas	25	25	15	15	25	0
Flatlands	50	50	30	30	50	0
						0
Part B						
Hills	25	25	15	5	8.3	16.7
Mesas	25	25	15	10	16.7	8.3
Flatlands	50	50	30	45	75.0	25.0
						50.0
Part C						
Hills	25	25	15	10	16.7	8.3
Mesas	25	25	15	15	25	0
Flatlands	50	50	30	35	58.3	8.3
						16.7

site would its occupants have had to go in order to obtain these resources?" The approach offered here takes the proportions of various environmental zones within a large study area as given. It then asks "For each smaller catchment area, which environmental zones are represented in significantly higher percentages than they exhibit in the study area as a whole?" The method therefore requires tests for significance which should yield levels of confidence not provided by the alternative methods mentioned earlier. Such tests for significance may well show that prehistoric villages were located to take advantage of certain resources, even when such resources constitute only a small percentage of the total catchment area of the site.

The Methodology

To illustrate the method, let us use a hypothetical example, taken largely from Plog (1968).

Imagine an area with 60 archeological sites and the landforms (*1*) hills, (*2*) mesas, and (*3*) flatlands. If sites were located randomly, without selection for any one landform, we would expect the percentage of sites within any zone to be proportional to the percentage of the total study area which that zone made up, as in the case represented by Table 4.4 (Part A). If, on the other hand, the prehistoric population had considered flatlands advantageous and hills and mesas undesirable locations, we might find a configuration like that of Table 4.4 (Part B).

The total percentage point difference between the expected and observed sites can be used as an indicator of how important a factor, such as a given landform, was in site selection. The 50% difference in the deliberately exaggerated case shown in Part B of Table 4.4 is presumably significant, but what if the difference between observed and expected is much smaller? We already have suggested the desirability of any technique giving a certain level of confidence in our conclusions as to whether a particular factor is being selected for or not. Now, does Part C of Table 4.4 indicate a genuine (though slight) selection among land-forms, or is it a result of either (*1*) minor, random influences on site selection, or (*2*) random errors in our sampling, owing to problems of survey?

To answer this question, we turn to a test from inferential statistics that can tell us the likelihood that the results found could be due to chance factors, even if certain expectations (for example, sites located in proportion to zonal area) were true. This also then tells us how probable it is that we would be wrong if we concluded that there were systematic deviations in our data (for instance, deliberate selection for certain zones among those under consideration). If this probability is small enough, we will accept the latter conclusion.

This test is known as the *one-sample chi-square test* (Siegel 1956).* It is computed by comparing the observed and expected numbers within each category, using the formula

$$\chi^2 = \sum \frac{(o-e)^2}{e}$$

where

Σ = summation
o = the observed data (using the raw counts, not percentages)
e = the expected data (using the raw counts, not percentages)

and the number of degrees of freedom (*df*) = *n*–1 where *n* = the number of categories in which the data are observed.

Using Part C of Table 4.4, we derive a χ^2 of 2.5 with 2° of freedom, and, upon looking it up in a table of chi-squares, we learn that the deviations

*The chi-square test does assume independence of observation (sites), which might not be a valid assumption in the case of a complex settlement system (see Flannery, Chapter 6, this volume). However, unless sites are highly clustered (so that we, in effect, inflate our sample size by counting several sites in a zone where there is just one site system), this should not be a major problem.

from our expected data are not extreme enough to conclude that sites are distributed other than in proportion to zone size (there is a greater than 20% probability that such a conclusion would be wrong). On the other hand, using Part B of the table, we derive a χ^2 of 15.83 which, with 2° of freedom, is highly significant; we can conclude that zone selection is going on, with less than .01 probability of our being wrong.

Variations in the Method

Let us now consider some variations and additional modifications that might be made in this approach, along with some of its complications and pitfalls. The test just used takes into account only the zone in which the site is actually located, whereas a walk of 1 or 2 hours might bring prehistoric villagers within reach of the resources of other zones. In considering a given zone, therefore, we might want to include not only (*1*) the sites actually within that zone but also (*2*) all sites within some convenient travel distance of that zone. Such distances might be variable; we have Vita-Finzi and Higgs' suggestion of 5 km for farmers, but Lee (1968) suggests a 6-mi radius for Bushman hunter–gatherers, and Woodburn (1968) a 1-hour walk for Hadza foragers. Thus, when computing the proportion of a total study area occupied by various environmental zones, we might consider expanding each zone to include those sites from which it could be reached conveniently; this is what I have done for the Ocós region (later in this section).

If, for a given environmental factor, we want to argue that what would be important in site location is not merely having the catchment area include the critical zone (as in the case of some water resources), but to include as much as possible (as in the case of some soil zones suitable for agriculture), the technique again would have to be altered slightly. Rather than counting the number of sites whose catchment areas are included in the zone, we would measure the actual square area of all catchment areas included within each zone. These would then be the figures used in computing percentage point differences. However, it would be illegitimate to test the data with chi-square, since the numbers would not represent discrete observations (sites) but, rather, arbitrary units of area. By having to measure instead of simply count, this method would be significantly more difficult, but, for many variables, the added realism of the implicit model would make it worthwhile.

As an additional modification for realism, it would be desirable to use population figures, rather than number of sites, if this data were available. Percentage point difference would be valuable, but testing with chi-square would probably be a questionable procedure, since the numbers of persons living together at a site are not really independent and would guarantee significance for almost any table. One could, instead, use analysis of variance to see whether average site population differs significantly across zones, and if not, proceed as before, using the number of sites.

In addition to the above-mentioned limitation in use of chi-square, there is the problem that sometimes the numbers in the "expected" cells will be too small to make the statistic valid. An alternative approach is therefore to test any one zone of the environment against all others to see if the proportion of sites located there is significantly higher than would be expected from the proportion of the entire study area which that zone makes up. This can be done with the *binomial test* to be used later in this section (see also Siegel 1956). It would be statistically illegitimate to make repeated tests of all combinations of a variable (such as mesa against flatland and hills, hills against mesa and flatland, and so on) but, if there is one area the investigator has a priori interest in testing, this would be an acceptable method.

A further pitfall is that, if one is testing a variable that happens to be highly correlated with another (for example, rainfall and altitude), significant results may show up for one variable when it is the other that was in fact selected for. For this reason, it is necessary to test for as many relevant

variables as there are satisfactory data. One could then construct a table using all variables simultaneously to suggest which are actually causally linked and which only incidentally related. Use of such a table also might indicate whether selection for interacting variables were occurring (if, for example, neither altitude nor rainfall alone were selected for, but actually a particular combination of the two; for discussion, see Plog and Hill 1971). For a hypothetical example of how this might appear, see Table 4.5. Looking at either variable alone, it would be difficult to determine what is happening. When they are combined, it appears that rainfall is the important factor. Within each rainfall zone, the distribution of sites is roughly proportional to the size of each altitude zone; within each altitude zone, however, sites are disproportionately congregated in the high rainfall zone.

Related Settlement Pattern Studies

Although this particular approach previously has not been applied to Formative Mesoamerica, related studies using comparable assumptions and statistics have been undertaken in the American Southwest. In a pioneering effort, regrettably still unpublished, Fred Plog (1968) explored several methods of testing the importance of environmental factors to settlement patterns. He first suggested what might be an alternative to the approach I describe in this section, measuring the importance of an environmental variable by the amount of "selectivity" in site distribution by means of a coefficient of variation, which shows the extent to which sites are either evenly distributed over environmental zones or concentrated in one zone. Plog tested for temporal changes in selectivity, but the approach would not be valid for a synchronic study with one data set, as it, like the Vita-Finzi and Higgs model, does not take into account the expected distribution based upon relative sizes of zones.

Another approach explored by Plog was to test

TABLE 4.5　Example of Chart Used to Compare Effects of Two Different Environmental Variables on Archeological Settlement [a]

		Archeological sites		
Variable	State	Percent expected	Percent observed	Percentage difference
Altitude alone	high	20	40	+ 20
	medium	40	30	− 10
	low	40	30	− 10
Rainfall alone	high	30	55	+ 25
	low	70	45	− 25
Altitude and rainfall considered together	high rain, high altitude	15	27	+ 12
	high rain, medium altitude	5	9	+ 4
	high rain, low altitude	10	20	+ 10
	low rain, high altitude	5	3	− 2
	low rain, medium altitude	35	23	− 12
	low rain, low altitude	30	18	− 12

[a]Hypothetical data; see text.

whether or not spacing between sites was different across zones defined on the basis of environmental variables. This attacks a different aspect of settlement patterns and should be regarded as complementary to, rather than conflicting with, the approach mentioned earlier. It would certainly be interesting to know if certain aspects of the environment, whether or not they tended to attract settlement, tended to affect the interaction between sites insofar as this is reflected in their spacing. To investigate this, Plog matched different degrees of spacing against the different zones using a *k-sample chi-square test* (Siegel 1956). It would also be possible to use actual site-to-site distances or the nearest-neighbor statistic (see Earle, Chapter 7, this volume), using analysis of variance to test for significant differences across zones. Fred Plog's approach thus provides an initial link between the environmental and social aspects of settlement patterns, as discussed at the beginning of this chapter.

An Application to the Ocós Region, Guatemala

The time now has come for a substantive application of the method proposed here. Unfortu-

nately, few studies of Formative Mesoamerica have been published in sufficient detail to provide suitable raw data. Even the area I have chosen does not have a complete and intensive site survey. Such sites as have been found, however, are located on a map that also indicates the present boundaries of some eight contrasting environmental zones, and the text of the report lists the major resources of these zones.

Ocós lies at the coastal end of a 50-km alluvial plain which extends from the base of the Sierra Madre de Guatemala to the Pacific Ocean. The region is tropical, with an average annual rainfall of 1000 mm (40 in.). The 5-by-1-km transect briefly surveyed by Coe and Flannery (1967) has a maximum elevation of 5 m above sea level. As pointed out by Flannery (Chapter 6, this volume), their survey area did not cover all settlement types within the complex coastal system, but only those sites near the coast. Most Formative sites were small hamlets, none larger than 3 ha and some as small as 300 sq m (Marcus, Chapter 3, this volume). Locations of all sites by period are given in Figures 45–47 of Coe and Flannery (1967).

Our first problem becomes the definition of a region for analysis. By including too much or too little area in the defined region, one can obtain highly skewed results. Based upon the area most extensively surveyed and the lower number of sites far inland, I delineated an area bordered by the Río Suchiate on the west, the border of Coe and Flannery's map on the east, the Pacific Ocean, and a line parallel to the coast 7 km inland (Figures 4.9–4.11). Within this area, Coe and Flannery defined some eight general biotopes (sometimes inaccurately referred to as "microenvironments"), which I have reduced to six categories, as follows:

1. Beach (including "beach sand" and "low beach scrub").
2. Mangrove forest.
3. Riverine vegetation.
4. Tropical savanna.
5. Former estuaries (including "salt *playas*" and "*madresal* groves").
6. Agricultural land (including "mixed tropical forest" and "cleared fields and second growth").

Note that I did not consider the present-day "marine estuary and lagoon system" because it is thought to have come into existence since the Formative (Coe and Flannery 1967).

Using a polar planimeter, the total percentage of the study area occupied by each of these environments was computed,* with the following results:

Environment	Percentage
Beach	9.1
Mangrove	22.5
Riverine	5.4
Savanna	6.2
Former estuary	1.9
Agricultural	54.9

Site Catchment Sizes in the Ocós Region

In determining the sizes of site catchments in the Ocós region, I drew on an earlier, unpublished

*Following our discussion above, the perimeter of each environment was increased by .5 km to take into account those sites lying outside but within easy walking distance.

paper by Philippides (n.d.). In attempting to draw 5-km circles around the tiny Formative sites of that region, Philippides noticed an enormous overlap of circles, caused by the close spacing of hamlets. He immediately realized that, owing to the agricultural richness of the area and the low maize requirements of the smaller sites, circles that large are unrealistic.

> The Vita-Finzi and Higgs analysis for the Mt. Carmel prehistoric settlements suggests theoretical circles within a 2-hour perimeter, i.e., 5 km. Due to the distinctly different conditions of environment and subsistence systems in Ocós, one would be justified in arbitrarily reducing the radius of the catchment circle from 5 to 1 km. . . . However, even this limit was shown to be perhaps exaggerated, because the majority of circles overlap in almost all cases. For this reason, additional circles of 0.5 km. radius were used, which could possibly be a better approximation to the actual situation. [Phillippides n.d.]

Independent evidence suggests that such .5 km radii are not unreasonable. For example, Early Formative refuse at the site of Salinas La Blanca included more than 30 fragments of a land crab (*Cardisoma crassum*) that is abundant in mangrove and *madresalar* habitats. Not a single fragment of this crab occurred in Early Formative refuse at La Victoria, less than 3 km away. Salinas La Blanca lies at the very edge of the *madresalar*, while La Victoria is more than .5 km from a similar biotope. As far as small game is concerned, residents of each site evidently picked up only what was in the immediate environs of the village.

A circle with a radius of .5 km includes some 75 ha of land. Let us suppose that, during any given year, two-thirds of that would be unused, leaving 25 ha of farm land. At 1 metric ton per hectare—a conservative estimate of today's yields in the Ocós region—such a catchment area would yield enough maize each year to feed 25 families. No Early or Middle Formative hamlet in the survey area is thought to have been that large. Given all the above considerations, I have tentatively

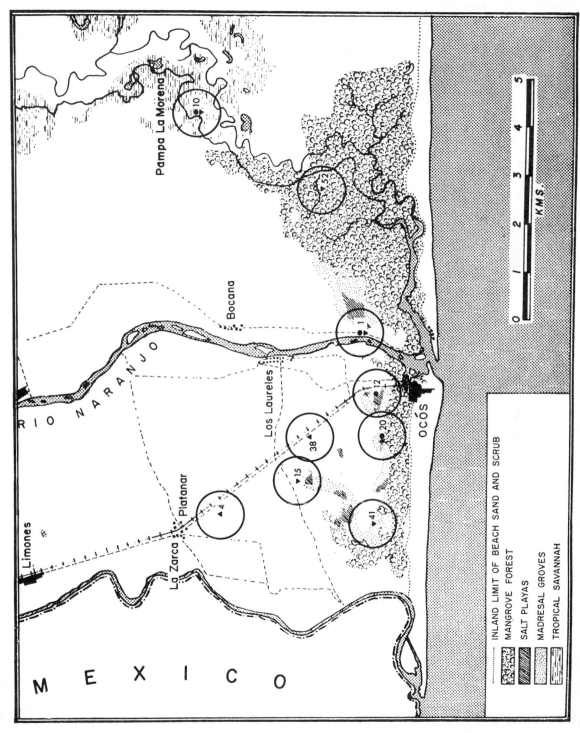

Figure 4.9 Early Formative hamlets at Ocós, Guatemala, showing catchment circles with .5-km radius. [Base map from Coe and Flannery 1967: Figure 45.]

123

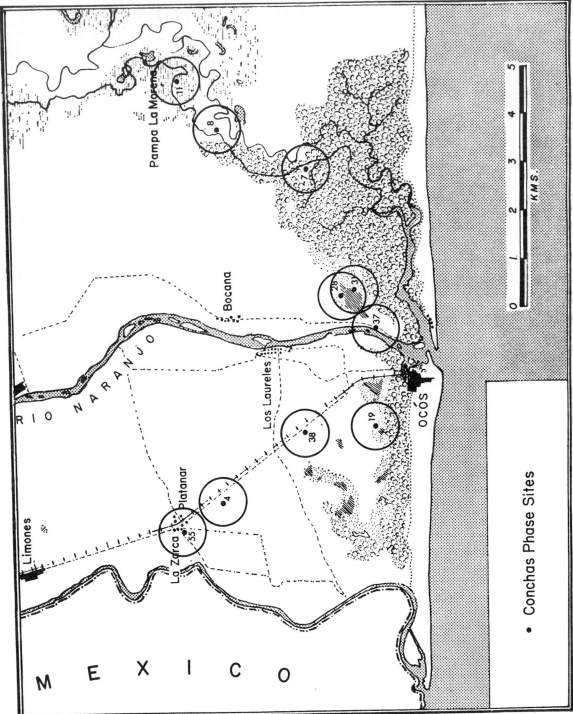

Figure 4.10 Middle Formative hamlets at Ocós, Guatemala, showing catchment circles with .5-km radius. Environmental zones as in Figure 4.9.

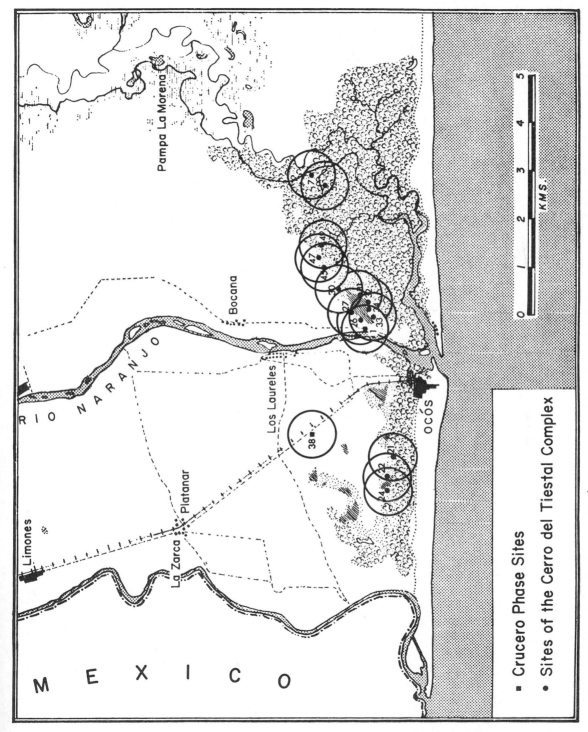

Figure 4.11 Late Formative hamlets at Ocós, Guatemala, showing catchment circles with .5-km radius. Environmental zones as in Figure 4.9.

- ■ Crucero Phase Sites
- ● Sites of the Cerro del Tiestal Complex

TABLE 4.6 **Statistics on Observed and Expected Sites by Environmental Zone for Various Segments of the Formative Period, Ocós Region Guatemalan Pacific Coast**[a]

	Beach	Mangrove forest	Riverine vegetation	Tropical savanna	Former estuaries	Agricultural land	Sum of absolute values
Early Formative							
Number of expected sites	.82	2.02	.49	.56	.17	4.94	9
Number of observed sites	0	2.75	.25	.5	1.25	4.25	9
Percent of expected sites	9.1	22.5	5.4	6.2	1.9	54.9	100
Percent of observed sites	0	30.5	2.7	5.5	13.9	47.2	100
Percent of difference	−9.1	+8	−2.7	−.7	+12	−7.7	*40.2*
Middle Formative							
Number of expected sites	.91	2.25	.54	.62	.19	5.49	10
Number of observed sites	0	2.25	.25	1	1.25	5.25	10
Percent of expected sites	9.1	22.5	5.4	6.2	1.9	54.9	100
Percent of observed sites	0	22.5	2.5	10	12.5	52.5	100
Percent of difference	−9.1	0	−2.9	+3.8	+10.6	−2.4	*28.8*
Late Formative							
Number of expected sites	1.54	3.74	.92	1.05	.32	9.33	17
Number of observed sites	0	6.25	.58	0	3.58	6.58	17
Percent of expected sites	9.1	22.5	5.4	6.2	1.9	54.9	100
Percent of observed sites	0	36.8	3.4	0	20.9	38.5	100
Percent of difference	−9.1	+14.3	−2	−6.2	+19	−16.4	*67*

[a]Figures may not add exactly to given totals, owing to slight rounding error.

accepted Philippides' figure of .5 km for the main catchment radius for each hamlet in this study.

The Statistical Analysis

The raw data for the analysis were handled as follows. Sites whose .5-km-radius catchment area included only one of the six environmental zones listed earlier were counted as one site for that zone. Those whose catchment area included two zones were counted as ½ site for each zone; those whose catchment included three zones as 1/3 for each zone, and so on. For example, Coe and Flannery's village SM-26 contributed ¼ site each to the riverine, former estuary, agricultural, and mangrove forest zones (Coe and Flannery 1967: Figure 47). This is a good approximation to computing the actual amount of a catchment area encompassing the different zones, and allows the poten-

tial use of chi-square, since actual site numbers, rather than arbitrary square area units, are used. The observed numbers of sites for each zone then could be compared with the expected numbers, based on the percentage of the total sample area that each environmental zone make up. The results are summarized in Table 4.6.

The largest positive selection seems to be for former estuary environments in all periods. By contrast, the beach zone is consistently underrepresented, suggesting that ocean resources were not a determining factor in settlement location (or that trips of several kilometers to the sea were no hindrance). As to changes through time, Table 4.6 is slightly ambiguous. The percentage point difference between observed and expected site numbers decreases between Early and Middle Formative times (from 40.2 to 28.8), then increases again (to 67.0) during Late Formative times. This would suggest a change from more, to less, and then to still more selectivity in site location through time. The changes are not great (since the potential difference is 200%), and it is questionable whether they are statistically significant. However, independent archeological data support the trend seen in the data, and provide a reasonable basis for interpretation.

Early Formative

During the Early Formative, hamlets occurred with greater than expected frequency in the former estuary and mangrove zones. This is reasonable on two counts, since the former estuaries were functioning during that period. They served, first, as the route of canoe transportation through nearly impassable mangrove forest and largely uncleared tropical forest; and, second, as a source of food. The empirical data from Salinas La Blanca, for example, indicate that Early Formative farmers harvested marine catfish, gar, snook, red snapper, grunt, mojarra, jack, needlefish, sleeper, oyster, marsh clam, and mussel from the estuary; in a single stratum of one small excavation, "well over 100 kilos of fish meat may be represented" (Coe and Flannery 1967:76).

Middle Formative

The Middle Formative was a period of population dispersal. Although the estuaries maintained their importance (and indeed probably served as routes of dispersal), the discrepancy between observed and expected sites by zone is less. In particular, the savanna was colonized more heavily than in previous periods, and there was no overrepresentation of sites along the margins of the mangrove forest.

Late Formative

By Late Formative times, the total discrepancy between observed and expected site percentages had increased to 67%. Most of the discrepancy can be accounted for by heavy overrepresentation in the former estuary zone (+ 19%) and on the mar-

gins of the mangrove forest (+ 14.3%), which amounts to the same thing. Here, however, the estuarine resource explanation used for the Early Formative will no longer work, for these former estuaries were drying up. As the Pacific Coast prBogrades, such estuaries turn into salt *playas* and eventually are colonized by the *madresal (Avicennia nitida)*, a salt-tolerant mangrove (Coe and Flannery 1967:13-14). Late Formative Crucero phase sites and (to an even greater extent) Terminal Formative Cerro del Tiestal sites cluster heavily on these salt *playas*, and from "a significant number" of these sites come examples of ceramics usually associated with salt making:

> Such objects are typical of many regions where primitive salt making from brine was carried out. It is possible, therefore, that sites of the Cerro del Tiestal complex were saltmaking stations which supplied the large Late Formative sites farther inland. [Coe and Flannery 1967:91]

Such an explanation accounts for the high selectivity of Late Formative sites. It also underscores the fact that, by that period, the Ocós survey transect may contain only one specialized site type out of many that made up the coastal settlement system (see Chapter 6 of this volume).

A Binomial Test for Significance

Unfortunately, owing to the very small expected values in several cells, a chi-square test for the entire table cannot be utilized. This is a result of the somewhat small total number of sites, and especially of the large number of environmental zone types, some very small in area. Since we approached this data in a vacuum, and thus with no a priori expectations, a test of individual differences of proportion would be statistically illegitimate, based as it would be on expectations from the data.

Purely as an example, however, we can perform a *binomial test* to see whether the 3.58 site catchment areas located in former estuaries during the Late Formative are significantly higher than the proportion we would expect, based on Early Formative patterns. For this we use the formula:

$$p = \Sigma p(x)$$

where

$$p(x) = \binom{N}{x} P^x \, Q^{N-x}$$

and

$p(x)$ = the probability of obtaining x number of site in a given zone, given N and P

P = the expected proportion of cases (in this case, 14%)

Q = 1 − P (in this case, 86%)

N = the observed number of sites (in this case, 17)

x = 4, 5, 6, . . . 17 (i.e., the cases that would diverge even farther from the expected than the results obtained)

$$\binom{N}{x} = \frac{N!}{x! \, (N-x)!}$$

$$N! = N \times (N-1) \times (N-2) \times \ldots \times 1$$

The result in this case ($p = .208$) indicates that the chances are about 1 in 5 that one could obtain results diverging even farther from the expected than ours merely through random sampling errors or fluctuations. Thus, it would be difficult to prove there was increased selection for salt *playa* locations through time in this case.

Problems Encountered in the Analysis

Obviously, sample size is one of the major problems involved in a chi-square approach to site catchment. Only with a sufficiently large total number of sites, and expected values for each cell, can statistically meaningful tests be made.

Another problem lies in the interpretation of results. For example, applying the binomial formula,

just displayed, with the value $P = .019$ (the expected proportion based on the amount of former estuary area within the study regon) indicates highly significant selectivity for former estuaries for all three major divisions of the Formative. However, as we have seen, the *reasons* for this selectivity probably varied through time, as estuaries turned slowly to salt *playas*.

In addition, there is an apparent discrepancy between the results of the test for change through time, just described, and a subjective look at the maps, which clearly suggest a marked trend for tighter concentration around the salt *playas* culminating in the Late Formative. Such a discrepancalls not for rejecting either the intuitive or the statistical approach a priori but, instead, for a reexamination of all the assumptions that went into each, for they are probably answering different questions. In this case, the .5-km radius—adequate for hamlets maintaining a balance between farm land and fishing resources—is probably too large for the analysis of salt-making stations. The intuitively obvious trend, upon reexamination, seems not to be for more sites to be close to salt *playas* but for close sites to be even closer. Tighter catchment circles would reveal this statistically.

Finally, our catchment analysis is subject to one of the same problems facing the Vita-Finzi and Higgs method: changing landscape. We must never forget that the present estuaries of the Guatemalan Coast did not exist when these sites were occupied, that base levels and river courses have changed with each major earthquake, and that the *Avicennia* groves where sites occur today were estuaries where channel catfish swam 3000 years ago.

References

Blanton, R. E.
1972   Prehispanic settlement patterns of the Ixtapalapa peninsula region, Mexico. *Occasional Papers in Anthropology* No. 6. Dept. of Anthropology, Pennsylvania State University, University Park.

Chisholm, M.
1968 *Rural settlement and land use.* 2nd ed. London: Hutchinson.

Coe, M. D.
1968a Map of San Lorenzo, an Olmec site in Veracruz, Mexico. Dept. of Anthropology, Yale University, New Haven, Conn.
1968b San Lorenzo and the Olmec civilization. In *Dumbarton Oaks Conference on the Olmec*, edited by E. P. Benson. Washington, D.C.: Dumbarton Oaks. Pp. 41–78.
1968c Soil and land use maps of San Lorenzo, Veracruz, Mexico. Dept. of Anthropology, Yale University, New Haven, Conn.
1969a The archaeological sequence at San Lorenzo Tenochtitlán, Veracruz, Mexico. Paper read at annual meeting of Society for American Archaeology, Milwaukee, 1 May 1969.
1969b Photogrammetry and the ecology of the Olmec civilization. Paper read at Working Conference on Aerial Photography and Anthropology, Cambridge, Mass., 10–12 May 1969.

Coe, M. D., and K. V. Flannery
1967 Early cultures and human ecology in south coastal Guatemala. *Smithsonian Contributions to Anthropology* No. 3. Smithsonian Institution, Washington, D.C.

Drennan, R. D.
1975 Fábrica San José and Middle Formative society in the Valley of Oaxaca, Mexico. Unpublished Ph.D. dissertation, Dept. of Anthropology, University of Michigan, Ann Arbor.

Flannery, K. V.
1967 Vertebrate fauna and hunting patterns. In *The prehistory of the Tehuacán Valley.* Vol. 1. *Environment and subsistence*, edited by D. S. Byers. Austin: University of Texas Press. Pp. 132–175.

Ford, R. I.
1968 An ecological analysis involving the population of San Juan Pueblo, New Mexico. Unpublished Ph.D. dissertation, Dept. of Anthropology, University of Michigan, Ann Arbor.

Jarman, H. N., A. J. Legge, and J. A. Charles
1972 Retrieval of plant remains from archaeological sites by froth flotation. In *Papers in economic prehistory*, edited by E. S. Higgs. Cambridge, Eng.: Cambridge University Press. Pp. 39–48.

Kirkby, A. V. T.
1973 The use of land and water resources in the past and present Valley of Oaxaca. *Memoirs* No. 5. Museum of Anthropology, University of Michigan, Ann Arbor.

Lee, R. B.
1967 !Kung Bushman subsistence: An input-output analysis. In *Human ecology, an anthropological reader*, edited by A. P. Vayda. New York: Natural History Press.
1968 What hunters do for a living, or, how to make out on scarce resources. In *Man the hunter*, edited by R. B. Lee and I. DeVore. Chicago: Aldine. Pp. 30–48.

MacNeish, R. S.
1962 *Second annual report of the Tehuacán archaeological-botanical project.* Andover, Mass.: R. S. Peabody Foundation for Archaeology.
1967 A summary of the subsistence. In *The prehistory of the Tehuacán Valley.* Vol. 1. *Environment and subsistence*, edited by D. S. Byers. Austin: University of Texas Press. Pp. 290–309.

MacNeish, R. S., F. A. Peterson, and K. V. Flannery
1970 *The prehistory of the Tehuacán Valley.* Vol. 3. *Ceramics.* Austin: University of Texas Press.

Mangelsdorf, P. C., R. S. MacNeish, and W. C. Galinat
1967 Prehistoric wild and cultivated maize. In *The prehistory of the Tehuacán Valley.* Vol. 1. *Environment and subsistence*, edited by D. S. Byers. Austin: University of Texas Press. Pp. 178–200.

Philippides, D.
n.d. Site catchment analysis for the Ocós area in coastal Guatemala. Unpublished ms, Dept. of Anthropology, University of Michigan, Ann Arbor.

Plog, F. T.
1968 Archeological surveys: A new perspective. Unpublished Master's thesis, Dept. of Anthropology, University of Chicago.

Plog, F. T., and J. N. Hill
1971 Explaining variability in the distribution of sites. In *The distribution of prehistoric population aggregates*, edited by G. J. Gumerman. *Prescott College Anthropological Reports* No. 1. Prescott, Arizona.

Sahlins, M. D.
1972 *Stone age economics.* Chicago/New York: Aldine–Atherton.

Siegel, S.
1956 *Nonparametric statistics for the behavioral sciences.* New York: McGraw Hill.

Smith, C. E., Jr.
  1965   Flora, Tehuacán Valley. *Fieldiana:Botany,* 31(4):107–143. Field Museum of Natural History, Chicago.
  1967   Plant remains. In *The prehistory of the Tehuacán Valley.* Vol. 1. *Environment and subsistence,* edited by D. S. Byers. Austin: University of Texas Press. Pp. 220–255.

Virri, T. J.
  1946   Maanjake-olojen Vaikutuksesta Maataloustuctantous. *Maatalous Agronomien Yhdistkysen Julkaisa,* pp. 6–11.

Vita-Finzi, C., and E. S. Higgs
  1970   Prehistoric economy in the Mt. Carmel area of Palestine: Site catchment analysis. *Proceedings of the Prehistoric Society* 36:1–37.

West, R. C., N. P. Psuty, and B. G. Thom
  1969   *The Tabasco lowlands of southeastern Mexico.* Baton Rouge: Louisiana State University Press.

Woodburn, J.
  1968   An introduction to Hadza ecology. In *Man the hunter,* edited by R. B. Lee and I. DeVore. Chicago: Aldine. Pp. 49–55.

Zohary, D.
  1969   The progenitors of wheat and barley in relation to domestication and agricultural dispersal in the Old World. In *The domestication and exploitation of plants and animals,* edited by P. J. Ucko and G. W. Dimbleby. London: Gerald Duckworth & Co. Pp. 47–66.

Chapter 5

SAMPLING ON THE REGIONAL LEVEL

Introduction

In Chapter 3, we confronted the problem of sampling whole communities. Now we must move to the *supracommunity* or *regional* level, in which the relationships of various communities to each other must be considered. In this chapter, we will deal with the problem, "How do I get an adequate sample of sites?"—surely one of the earliest to be faced by an archeologist starting a new project. In later chapters, we will move to two more questions in which Mesoamericanists have expressed an interest: "What pattern is discernible in the distribution of sites in my sample?" and "What was the probable relationship between these sites and between the social units that occupied them?"

Many Mesoamerican archeologists—among them W. T. Sanders, R. S. MacNeish, J. R. Parsons, and R.E. Blanton—have taken as their *region* an entire highland valley, or a definable subdivision of a val-

ley. Rather than "sampling," these archeologists have surveyed the entire region—field by field, meter by meter, often using large-scale aerial photographs and multiple crews of five to six persons each. They know they have an adequate sample because they collect the entire site "universe" (in statistical terms), setting aside for the moment the obvious limitations of site preservation and human error. This is the ideal. If every archeologist could do this, we would not even have bothered to discuss sampling on the regional level in this chapter.

Unfortunately, most Mesoamerican archeologists do not have budgets of $50,000 to $100,000; nor do they have the time or the manpower to survey entire valleys. Most must content themselves with finding some percentage of the sites in their chosen region—all the major ceremonial centers, perhaps most of the larger villages, and some undetermined fraction of the tiny hamlets and seasonal camps. If you ask them whether or not they have

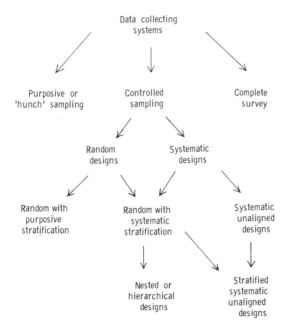

Figure 5.1 Diagram showing the relationships of different kinds of sampling designs: from the "hunch" sampling of the Real Mesoamerican Archeologist, through the controlled sampling of his Skeptical Graduate Student, to the complete surveys of Sanders, Parsons, and Blanton (see text). [Redrawn from Haggett 1965:Table 7.2.]

an adequate sample, either they say "I hope so," or they shrug and say "I don't know." Both answers are correct. They do hope so, and they don't know.

One of the reasons they don't know is that their reconnaissance amounts to what Peter Haggett (1965) calls "purposive" or "hunch" sampling (see Figure 5.1). Often, such surveys are strongly determined by where the good roads or clearings are, where the local guides happen to have been, and which mounds are visible the longest distance under certain lighting conditions. Mesoamericanists are well aware of the incompleteness of such surveys, and usually very honest about them. A particularly frank statement by the very man most often credited with inventing settlement pattern studies comes to mind:

> Our survey of the valley was not complete in the sense of a rigorous, careful, on-foot exploration of all the bottom lands. . . . Such a staggering task was beyond our strength. [Willey *et al.* 1965:576]

In this chapter, we will make two basic suggestions, which we hope sound reasonable. First: If you can survey your entire region meter by meter, do so in preference to sampling. Second: If you can't do that—if, for example, you can only survey a 20% sample—for heaven's sake, do it in such a way that you have some idea of the reliability of your results. One way to do that is by using some kind of probability sampling. Admittedly, that sounds as if it should take longer than the way you were planning to do it. Believe it or not—as Stephen Plog's section of this chapter perhaps will demonstrate—it doesn't really take much more time than you were already planning to spend. The real payoff, however, is that, if your survey is done that way, there are further statistical manipulations to which you can legitimately subject your data; if not, your analysis ends there. In later sections, we will consider some of the further manipulations possible with total or systematically sampled survey data (see, for example, pp. 236–248).

Probability Sampling and Regional Surveys

The Real Mesoamerican Archeologist doesn't like probability sampling. He regards it as (*1*) a waste of energy, (*2*) too time-consuming, (*3*) not as reliable as his intuition, and (*4*) not applicable to complex societies. He even has reservations about applying it to such "simple" political units as Formative villages. He and I have had acrimonious debates on the subject, neither of us backed up by very much data or mathematical expertise, and each of us continually harrassed by the Skeptical Graduate Student, who claims to have both. I really feel I should introduce this chapter by describing one classic argument we all had during the 1966 field season. It centered around a critique that W. J. Mayer-Oakes and R. J. Nash had recently presented, which R.M.A. was fond of misquoting (at least, S.G.S. and I agree that he was frequently misquoting).

The argument began in the Quinta Las Rosas, a now-defunct "nocturnal center" on the outskirts of Veracruz. The Quinta was famous for its colonial tile and for the fact that the shower was in the center of the patio; customers who arrived before 9:00 P.M. were treated to a parade of 12 nubile young ladies scrubbing down behind a translucent shower curtain, before their evening exercise. Lukewarm drinks were served in tile booths, under ceiling fans that did little more than stir up the tropical moths. Everyone in the place used eye makeup, but it was particularly disturbing on the male waiter, who also used spray glitter on his temples. There was a 100-record Wurlitzer in one corner, and, in the subdued light, the patio took on the look of a small basketball court redecorated for the senior prom. On one wall was a recessed shrine with glowing altar candles and the hand-lettered prayer: "Oh Thou who wert Conceived without Sin, help us to Sin without Conceiving."

While the waiter filled our order, R.M.A. drew on a paper napkin the outline of the Río San Jacinto drainage and the pattern of sites he had found so far. Reaching the end of the paper, he concluded, "and to the south, it looks as if there were no more Formative sites—just Early Classic, and some small Post-Classic sites."

Near his elbow, the Skeptical Graduate Student quickly added, "but we can't be sure of that, because our sample of sites is inadequate and our survey so far has been very haphazard and unsystematic."

Now, short of calling attention to a whole projectile point on his backdirt pile, there is probably no easier way to make a Real Mesoamerican Archeologist angry than by telling him that his survey techniques are inadequate. In fact, R.M.A. is still overheated from having read Binford's 1964 article "A consideration of archaeological research

design." Fortunately, he believes that he saw Binford subjected to the ultimate put-down. He tells the story often. In fact, he tells it every time his Skeptical Graduate Student brings up the subject of sampling.

"It was at the 1964 meetings of the American Anthropological Association, held in Detroit," he says. "Everybody was talking about Binford's article. Well, Bill Mayer-Oakes and Ronald Nash had tried out some of his techniques on Bill Sanders' Teotihuacán survey area, and they presented a critique . . ." (Mayer-Oakes and Nash 1964, 1965).

At this point, the Skeptical Graduate Student always rolls his eyes straight up at the ceiling and shakes his head in disbelief. The action was not lost on R.M.A., but he was interrupted by the waiter, who had just brought three rum-and-cokes. Three young ladies followed the waiter, circling our table with little attempt at subterfuge. One was clearly trying to see if R.M.A.'s lap would support her full body weight; I doubted it, but I've been wrong before.

"What Mayer-Oakes and Nash did was to take Bill Sanders' survey map of the Teotihuacán Valley, showing the location of all 500-odd sites he had found," R.M.A. went on. "To this, they applied the 'stratified random sampling program' that Binford had recommended. First, the 750-sq-km valley was divided into seven 'strata' or environmental zones: the Río San Juan delta, the Patlachique Range, Cerro Gordo, the lower valley, middle valley, upper valley, and northern valley. They then gridded the whole map with squares .6 km on a side, and selected a 20% sample of those squares at random. The sample was allocated so that various 'strata' received squares in proportion to their area—more squares in the biggest areas, and so on. Finally, they placed their grid with its sample areas over the map of Sanders' sites, to see how many they would have found." He smiled triumphantly. "And you know what they found? Do you know?"

"I can't imagine."

"They missed Teotihuacán. For God's sake, the largest Pre-Columbian city in the New World, 20 sq km, an estimated 125,000 population, and they missed it. Now why, for God's sake, should I use a technique that won't even find Teotihuacán? I could find it with my eyes shut and my hands tied behind my back."

"Yeah, it is hard to miss," I admitted.

"Well, they did it. And what's more, as Mayer-Oakes and Nash pointed out, the 20% stratified random sample recovered *none* of Sanders' 'Proto-Classic urban sites', *none* of his 'Cuanalán phase large villages', and only *one* of his 'Zacatenco phase hamlets'."

"Not too good, I guess."

R.M.A. adjusted his position slightly to accommodate the ample young lady who now occupied his left knee. "And do you know what Mayer-Oakes and Nash concluded?"

"Lay it on me."

"They said, and here I am going to quote them exactly to the best of my memory, 'given the same amount of time, we believe that an archeologist working by instinct (parenthesis) i.e., expertise (close parenthesis) could certainly locate a greater number of sites' (Mayer-Oakes and Nash 1965:16). Now, isn't that what I do every day? Hell, I found 33 sites last week without a table of random numbers."

The Real Mesoamerican Archeologist sat back in satisfaction while we finished our rum-and-cokes and ordered a round for our newly arrived companions. We hadn't heard from the Skeptical Graduate Student yet, which was unusual, but I figured he was too smothered under the weight of the young lady in his lap to reply. I was wrong, of course; he's never that out of breath.

"I have never," said S.G.S., "heard such a gross distortion of what went on at that session of the meeting."

"How would you know? You weren't even born yet."

"I was there," said S.G.S. "That was back when I was a Skeptical *Under*graduate Student. As I

remember, Mayer-Oakes and Nash were rather temperate in their criticism, and even said, 'it seems clear that Binford's theoretical framework and specific sampling techniques offer much of interest and value to archeologists working anywhere' (Mayer-Oakes and Nash 1965:21).

I wondered if Sonia, Rosa, and Yolanda were taking notes. In fact, I was wondering how they would score on a surprise quiz on sampling design.

"It seems to me," S.G.S. went on, "that you and several others who heard that talk have a complete misconception of what a 20% random sample is supposed to do. Somehow you seem to think that its purpose is to find a lot of sites—more than Sanders could find in his total survey, or more than I could find in a comparable period by racing around the Teotihuacán Valley with a bag over my head, picking up sherds.

"That isn't what it's supposed to do at all.

"And you, and many others, missed Binford's most important comment, since it came at the end of the conference session during a three-way conversation between Mayer-Oakes, Deetz, and Ascher."

"I don't remember a thing," said R.M.A.

"Mayer-Oakes had, in the interests of impartial scholarship, provided Binford with a copy of his results before the talk. It showed the following recovery of sites by the 20% sample (Mayer-Oakes and Nash 1965:13):

Aztec sites
   (i) Urban—4
   (ii) Rural—61
Toltec sites
   (i) Urban—2
   (ii) Rural—30
Classic Teotihuacán sites
   (i) Urban—1
   (ii) Rural—23
   (iii) Traces of occupation—11
Proto-Classic Hamlets—5
Cuanalán hamlets—1
Zacatenco hamlets—1
Pre-Classic hamlets—1
Preceramic sites—1

"These Binford communicated to the assembled crowd."

"What a memory," I marveled.

"Then Binford compared these with the totals for each type of site found by Sanders. And do you know what?"

"I can already guess."

"Virtually every type of site recovered by the 20% stratified random sample—'rural Toltec sites', 'rural Aztec sites', and so on—was recovered in approximately the proportion it contributed to the whole site universe. If one type of site made up, say, 40% of the total 500-odd sites, it also made up about 40% of the sites recovered by the sample. As Binford put it: 'the results are an excellent confirmation of the value of stratified random sampling'."

"Fantastic."

"You see," S.G.S. went on, "what the critics misunderstood was that probability sampling is *not a discovery technique*. It isn't a better way to find lots of sites. As Mayer-Oakes and Nash themselves said, 'we are not saying that Sanders has done a better survey, because . . . he has sampled more than 20% of the area, and it is not as if we can pit one approach against the other . . . this is about what we would find with 20% areal coverage'" (Mayer-Oakes and Nash 1965:14). Surveying the entire area is always preferable to surveying only 20% of it. But what you and most other people do is survey about 20% in a haphazard fashion. We can never know if you have recovered each site type in the same frequency with which it occurs in the total universe of sites. On the other hand, if you took a 20% sample according to probability sampling techniques, you could multiply each type of site by 5 and have some confidence—*in fact, a mathematically definable confidence*—that the results would approximate the real site universe."

R.M.A. sighed impatiently.

"A 20% random sample isn't designed to find Teotihuacán," S.G.S. continued, "or any other type of site that is unique or represented by only a few examples. If, in a universe of 500 sites, there are only five 'Zacatenco phase hamlets', then such sites make up only 1% of the universe; the chances are that, in a 20% sample, you might recover only one of them. In the case of 'Cuanalán phase large villages', there are only two in the whole universe; small wonder the sample didn't recover any at all. Probability sampling isn't the best way to find sites—it's just the best way to get a *representative* sample of sites, if you can't go for the whole universe as Sanders did."

"It's too complicated and it takes too long," R.M.A. replied. "And as Mayer-Oakes and Nash pointed out, 'increasing the areal coverage to find the rarer types of sites is a waste of time and resources' " (Mayer-Oakes and Nash 1965:14).

"Why would it take any longer than your techniques?" asked S.G.S. "We spend most of our time pushing the Jeep out of the mud anyway."

Sitting in the slowly moving shadow of the ceiling fan, listening to Sonia prattle in one ear and S.G.S. in the other, I realized that opinions would always differ on what had happened in Detroit. Some people had gone away feeling vindicated, pleased to hear that traditional survey techniques would recover more sites, that probability sampling wouldn't find unique features like Cuanalán phase large villages or the Pyramid of the Sun. Others had gone away convinced that only probability sampling would produce reliable, statistically valid samples whose confidence levels could be defined in mathematical terms. There was no hope of rapprochement.

"Let's go home," I said, and R.M.A. rose unsteadily.

"You go on," said S.G.S. "I'm staying to take Rosa up on a very interesting suggestion she just made."

"Her? You think she's the best in the place?" R.M.A. demanded incredulously. "Don't you think you should try a 20% stratified sample of the whole universe of girls before you decide?"

"As an archeologist," smiled S.G.S., "my instinct (parenthesis) i.e., expertise (close parenthesis) tells me that she is unique at the 99% confidence level."

All of which, I think, goes a long way toward explaining the applicability of probability sampling. There are times and places where your knowledge is limited, and drawing a systematic random sample is the only justifiable procedure. In other times and places, with some prior knowledge, your instincts tell you when you already have a really great site.

In the section that follows, Stephen Plog attacks the problem of sampling a completely unknown valley. He uses the same approach as Mayer-Oakes and Nash: Three areas of the Valley of Oaxaca which had previously been intensively surveyed are "blanked out," and various sampling techniques are applied to them. These include all four of the major sampling techniques described by geographer Peter Haggett—simple random, stratified, systematic, and stratified systematic unaligned. Plog then evaluates the "efficiency" of the various sampling techniques for predicting the total number of sites from a 10% sample. Without giving away the results, we can advise the Real Mesoamerican Archeologist to be of good cheer: The simplest and least sophisticated sampling techniques give results that do not differ significantly from those of more complex techniques. To the best of my knowledge, this is the first time these four techniques have been evaluated, relative to each other, for their efficiency in recovering reliable samples of Mesoamerican archeological sites.

Of course, the 8-sq-km city of Monte Albán was not found in any of Plog's samples. But then, it's unique.

Relative Efficiencies of Sampling Techniques for Archeological Surveys *

STEPHEN PLOG

Probability sampling is particularly useful in archeological settlement pattern studies in Mesoamerica, where archeologists rarely have the time, money, or desire to study the entire land area that is the subject of their investigation. However, many archeologists are reluctant to apply such techniques because there have been almost no objective tests of the efficiency of such sampling programs (but see Mayer-Oakes and Nash 1965).

An intensive site survey of three blocks of land in the Valley of Oaxaca during the summer of 1970 provided the opportunity to test four major

*The research described here was made possible by an Undergraduate Research Participation Grant (GY-7576) from the National Science Foundation to the University of Michigan (1970).

types of sampling strategies against "real" archeological data. The three areas—located in the Etla, Zaachila, and Valdeflores regions—were walked field by field, and all sites were recorded. This survey was conducted by D. M. Varner, R. D. Drennan, L. C. Kuttruff, and myself. The actual experience of slogging through mud, wading rivers, and climbing thorn-forested slopes provided an appreciation for the practical difficulties of Mesoamerican surveys which, I hope, prevents this section of the chapter from being an exercise in "ivory tower" archeology.

Basically, what I have done is to "blank out" the three survey areas, "sample" them by several different strategies, and then compare the results of the sampling with the actual pattern of sites we

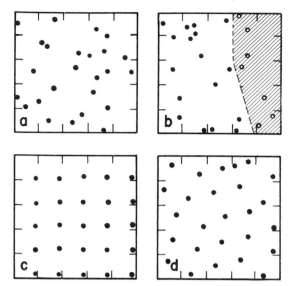

Figure 5.2 Alternative sampling designs. (a) Simple random; (b) stratified random; (c) systematic; (d) stratified systematic unaligned. [Redrawn from Haggett 1965: Figure 7.4.]

found. The efficiency of each technique—relative to alternative techniques—is judged in terms of the precision with which a 10% sample would make possible a prediction of the total number of sites in each survey area.

In this section, I will describe the sampling techniques to be used in the tests, and discuss their nonstatistical and statistical advantages and disadvantages, both in theory and in practice. Second, the data to be used for the tests will be discussed. Third, a series of sampling tests will be run on the data. The effect of different sampling techniques on the estimation of a population parameter will be examined. Also, an attempt will be made to determine the effects of settlement pattern and site size on the estimation.

The Four Types of Sampling Designs

The four types of samples taken were simple random, stratified, systematic, and stratified systematic unaligned. Two of these sampling techniques

already have been mentioned in Chapter 3 (this volume). All four are defined in simple terms and illustrated graphically by geographer Peter Haggett, whose diagram we have reproduced as Figure 5.2. His definitions are as follows (Haggett 1965:195–196):

(i) In *simple random sampling* a sample of N individuals is drawn from the areal population at a series of random co-ordinates. The two axes of the area are numbered and a location is chosen by a pair of random co-ordinates. For example, the random numbers ninety-eight and twenty-six would give a location ninety-eight units north by twenty-six units east; or a grid reference of 9826 in terms of a standard reference system. (Fig. 5.2a) shows the location of twenty-four points drawn by simple random sampling for a hypothetical study area.

(ii) In *stratified sampling* the study area is divided into natural segments (such as cropland and woodland) and the individuals in the sample are drawn independently from each segment. Within each segment the location of the points is determined by the same randomization procedure as in simple random sampling. (Fig. 5.2b) shows such a sample for twenty-four points. In this case the number of individuals has in each segment been made proportional to its area; sixteen points in the left-hand segment (two-thirds of the area) and eight points in the right-hand segment (one-third of the area).

(iii) In *systematic sampling* a grid of equally spaced locations is defined with one individual at each location. (Fig. 5.2c) shows a simple case for twenty-five individuals. Here the grid is square and at right angles to the sides of the study area. The origin of the grid is decided by the randomization of the original grid point.

(iv) A *stratified systematic unaligned sample* (Fig. 5.2d) is a composite design derived from the preceding sampling designs by Berry (1962:7) with the theoretical advantages of (a) randomization, and (b) stratification, together with the useful aspects of (c) systematic samples. By avoiding alignment of the sample points, it also avoids the possibility of error caused by periodicities in the phenomena. . . . The study area . . . is systematically divided into a regular checkerboard of sub-areas. Beginning with the corner sub-area, a point, I, is determined by random numbers, the x- and y-axes of the sub-area being numbered zero to nine so that a random number between zero and ninety-nine gives a co-ordinate position with respect to both axes . . . the x co-ordinate being kept constant all along the row, but the y co-ordinate varied from a random-numbers table. As these numbers . . . are drawn, the points move up and down with respect to the y-axis but remain in the same position with respect to the x-axis. . . . When both the first row and column are completed, a new corner point must be generated, point II. . . . The random x co-ordinate of point X_1 and the random y co-ordinate of point Y_1 are combined to locate point II. This point is then the starting point for a new row and a new column, which in their turn, are used to generate a new corner point, point III. This process continues until all columns and rows are full.

The Test for Sampling Efficiency

The test I used for sampling efficiency is the *F-test*, the same measure used by Berry (1962) in his comparisons of sampling strategies. Basically, the *F*-test is a method for determining whether or not the variances of two samples are equal. The variance is a measure of the degree of dispersion or spread of the observations in a sample from the average of these observations. In this study, the "observations" in each of my samples were groups of 100 predictions of the number of sites in an area which were obtained for one combination of sampling method, sampling design, and size of sampling unit. The formula for the *F*-test is:

$$F = \frac{(S_1)^2}{(S_2)^2}$$

where $S_1{}^2$ = the variance of the first sample and $S_2{}^2$ = the variance of the second sample.

The Sampling Methods Used

Two different methods were used for dividing the areas into sampling units. The first type of sampling unit used was *quadrats*, or squares of equal size. Two different sizes of squares were used in

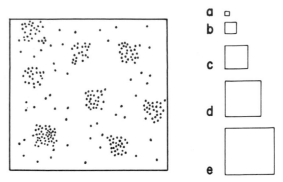

Figure 5.3 Diagram showing the differences that can result from using sample quadrats of different sizes. In the case of this hypothetical settlement pattern, sampling with smaller quadrats (a and b) would suggest slight clustering, with intermediate quadrats (c) strong clustering, and with large quadrats (d and e) regularity. [Redrawn from Haggett 1965: Figure 7.6.]

each area. The smaller units were squares .5 km on a side, and the larger units were 1.0 km on a side. Hereafter, these will be referred to as *small quadrats* and *large quadrats*. (For a look at the way quadrat size can affect sample results, see Figure 5.3.) The size of the units was chosen arbitrarily. The second type of sampling unit used was *transects*. Lines were drawn parallel to the shortest side of each survey area at constant intervals. The short side was used only because this divided the area into more sampling units. For one set of samples, an area 75 m to each side of the line was taken as the sampling unit, and thus the lines were drawn at a distance of 150 m from each other. For another set of samples, an area 150 m to each side of the line was used as the sampling unit, so that the lines were spaced 300 m apart. Again, the size of the units was chosen arbitrarily. Hereafter, the different units will be referred to as *small transects* and *large transects*.

There are many additional ways of structuring both quadrat and line samples. For quadrat samples, two adjacent sides of the survey area could be used as an axis with points marked off at intervals. Coordinates then could be drawn randomly, and quadrats constructed with the points as their center. For transect samples, one side of the survey area could be used as an axis with points along it. A point then could be drawn randomly, and a line drawn from that point parallel to the adjacent side of the axis. However, the use of permanent units, which could be numbered, greatly facilitated the repetitive drawing of samples and calculation of the estimate (for a look at some alternative transect sampling designs, see Figure 5.4).

Another type of sampling method, *point samples*, was not used in this study. There were two reasons for excluding it. First, it is felt that point samples are inefficient for archeological survey purposes because of the travel time involved. (For much the same reasons, it is easier to walk transects across an area than to travel to a large series of small random quadrats.) The smaller the sampling unit, the greater the time involved in traveling

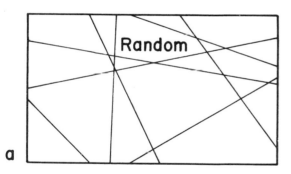

a

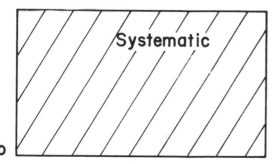

b

Figure 5.4 Alternative transect sampling designs. (a) Random; (b) systematic. [Redrawn from Berry and Baker 1968:Figure 6.]

between units if the sampling intensity is equal. This becomes particularly important where roads are poor or nonexistent or where travel by vehicle is impossible, and thus travel between points is slow. Second, it is felt that point samples may be viewed as one extreme of quadrat samples.

All four designs for drawing samples were used with the quadrat sampling method: simple random, stratified, systematic, and stratified systematic unaligned. All of these except the last also were used with the transect method. A stratified systematic unaligned design is not possible with transects as they are structured in this study.

For the *simple random samples*, the areas were gridded into squares, and each sampling unit in the population was assigned a number, moving consecutively from left to right and from the top to the bottom rows of squares. Similarly, the transects were assigned numbers from left to right. Then, using a random numbers table, the desired number of sampling units were chosen. This is similar to the program used by Winter at Tierras Largas (Chapter 3, this volume).

With the *stratified designs*, each survey area was divided into a number of strata or subgroups equal to the number of sampling units to be chosen. That is, only one sampling unit was drawn in each stratum. All stratification was done systematically, that is, geographical areas of equal size were used as the strata. This is in contrast to purposive stratification in which some characteristic of the population, such as the distribution of environmental zones, is used as the basis for stratification. The sampling procedure within each stratum was carried out as in the random sampling outline described earlier. Also, sampling within each stratum was representative. The ratio of units sampled within each stratum to the number of sampling units in the stratum was equal to the ratio of the total number of units sampled (or n) to the total number of sampling units (or N). This ratio, n/N, is called the *sampling fraction*. For one of the survey areas, the Valdeflores area, it was impossible to make the strata sizes equal. In this case, the sampling fractions within each stratum were kept equal when possible.

For the *systematic samples*, the first sampling unit was chosen at random, and the remaining units chosen at intervals of approximately N/n from the original unit. The same sampling grid as that constructed for the simple random samples was used.

The *stratified systematic unaligned design* used was an altered version of the one described by Haggett (1965:197) and Berry (1962:7). First, the survey area was divided into a number of strata equal to the number of units to be sampled. Within each stratum, each quadrat was assigned a coordinate, such as (3,2) as if it were a point. The unit in the lower left-hand corner of the stratum was assigned the coordinate (1,1), the unit above it (1,2), the unit to the right of it (2,1), and so on. Thus the units were treated as integer points on an axis. The remaining process is the same as that described by Haggett. A coordinate is chosen randomly for the stratum in the lower left-hand corner of the survey area. For the bottom row of strata, the *x*-coordinate of the unit to be sampled is kept constant, while the *y*-coordinate in each stratum is chosen randomly. For the far left column of strata, the *y*-coordinate is kept constant for all strata, and the *x*-coordinate is chosen randomly for each stratum. The coordinates to be sampled for all other strata are determined by taking the *x*-coordinate of the stratum to the immediate left and the *y*-coordinate of the stratum immediately below.

Sampling designs and methods may be compared both statistically and nonstatistically. Nonstatistical criteria for comparison vary with the purpose of the research. For instance, if one desires to measure the spatial variability of some phenomena, both stratified and systematic designs are better than a simple random design because they provide better areal coverage. Systematic samples are easier to draw and carry out. However, if there are any periodicities in the distribution of the phenomena, the regularly spaced units of the sys-

tematic sample may land at the same point in the pattern every time, resulting in a biased picture of the spatial variation of the phenomena (see the introduction to Chapter 3). Stratified systematic unaligned samples provide the advantages of the other designs, while avoiding the danger of periodicities in the data (Berry 1962:6–10).

Quadrat samples "are subject to the problem of 'modifiable units' " (Berry 1962:4). That is, different size units can be chosen, with different results from each size. As will be seen later, this is also true of the transect method. However, in the case of quadrat samples, the variations in the results may be useful in supplying data concerning the scale of the pattern under investigation (Greig-Smith 1964:54–93; Haggett 1965:198). A disadvantage of the transect method in the field is the difficulty of keeping a straight course. This is especially true when there are obstacles such as rivers to cross.

Statistical means also may be used for comparing different sampling techniques. Comparisons can be made of the precision of different sampling techniques, where "precision" is defined as *the squared standard error of the mean of a distribution of sample estimates obtained by repeated applications of a sampling procedure to a group of data*. Comparison also may be made between the accuracy of sampling techniques where "accuracy" is defined as *the difference between the mean of the distribution of sample estimates and the true population mean*. (It is realized that there are additional statistical problems in using sampling techniques. For instance, for systematic and stratified samples as they are structured here, one cannot calculate the variance for each individual sample. This problem will not be dealt with here.)

At least three methods, using precision, accuracy, or a combination of both, have been suggested for comparing sampling techniques. Deming (1950:17) suggests the use of *the inverse of the standard error of the mean of the sampling distribution*. The disadvantage of this is that, for simple random samples, the standard error is a biased estimate of the true standard error when the estimates of all possible samples are not available, although the bias is small in most cases. Berry (1962:8), Haggett (1963:111), and Stuart (1962:22) use *the squared standard error of the sampling distribution* for comparison. The squared standard error is an unbiased estimate of the true squared standard error of the mean for simple random samples when all possible samples are not available. An alternative method is to include a measure of the accuracy of a technique by measuring the squared standard error of the individual sample means from the true population mean rather than from the mean of the sampling distribution (Cochran 1953:15; Hansen, Hurwitz, and Madow 1953:57). This is called *the mean square error of the estimate*. However, it has been shown that, when the difference between the mean of the sampling distribution and the population mean is less than 25% of the standard deviation, it may be ignored without any significant effect on the results of the comparison (Hansen, Hurwitz, and Madow 1953:58).

Efficiency is a term used for comparisons of the precision of two or more sampling techniques. A sampling design or sampling method is more "efficient" than another design or method if its squared standard error is less than the squared standard error of the other technique. Theoretically, both systematic and stratified sampling should result in more efficient estimates of a population characteristic than simple random sampling.

Stratification results in a more efficient estimate if the strata are internally homogeneous in regard to the characteristic being measured. That is, the variation in the population can be explained to a large degree by variation between strata. When this occurs, some of "the samples possible under simple random sampling are impossible with stratified sampling, and with effective stratification these tend to be the more extreme samples that contribute more heavily to the sampling variance" (Hansen, Hurwitz, and Madow 1953:47).

An example makes this fact easier to understand. Suppose we have 16 sampling units of some size, with 4 units with 4 sites, 4 units with 3 sites, 4 with 2 sites, and 4 with 1 site, and thus a population average of 2.5 sites per unit. If a random sample of 4 units is drawn for the purpose of estimating the average number of sites per sampling unit, the most extreme possible samples would give averages of 4 sites per unit and 1 site per unit. However, if 4 strata were created in the population, with 1 stratum containing all the units with 4 sites, another stratum containing all the units with 3 sites, and so on, all possible samples of 4 units would have the population average of 2.5 sites per unit. This is an extreme example, but it illustrates the gain in precision that can result from stratification if the within-stratum populations are homogeneous. The amount of gain thus depends on how well the strata divide the population into homogeneous groups.

Systematic sampling may result in gains in efficiency in much the same way as stratification. It excludes some possible combinations of samples. When the sampling units are chosen at some interval from each other, this in effect stratifies the population into groups of the same size as the interval (Cochran 1953:206). For instance, if we have 15 sampling units, choose 1 at random, and then choose 2 more at an interval of N/n or 5 from the random unit, there are only 5 possible samples: 1-6-11, 2-7-12, 3-8-13, 4-9-14, and 5-10-15, where the figures refer to the number of the sample units. The strata consist of the first 5 sampling units, the second 5 sampling units, and the third 5 sampling units. There is always 1 unit from each stratum in a sample. The difference between systematic and stratified samples is that the systematic "occur at the same relative position in the stratum, whereas with the stratified random sample the position in the stratum is determined separately by randomization within each stratum. The systematic sample is spread more evenly over the population, and this fact has sometimes made systematic sampling considerably more precise than stratified random sampling" (Cochran 1953:206). However, systematic sampling precision is dependent on the properties of the population, and while it may result in gains in estimation precision, it may also result in precision which is worse than simple random sampling (Cochran 1953:214).

Tests of the relative efficiencies of sampling techniques are abundant in the literature. Ten samples drawn with each design by Cochran (1953:212–213) on an artificial population show that both stratified and systematic samples provide more efficient estimates than simple random samples. Cochran (1953:222–223) also presents data taken from tests by Yates (1948), Finney (1948, 1950), Osborne (1942), and Johnson (1943). The data used in the tests by Yates were altitudes read at intervals of .1 mile from an ordnance survey map, soil temperatures, and potato yields. When the precision of systematic samples is compared with the precision of stratified samples with strata size equal to that of the systematic samples and one sampling unit drawn per stratum, the systematic sample is more precise. The ratios of the squared standard error of the stratified sample to the squared standard error of the systematic sample are 2.99, 2.42, 1.45, 1.26, and 1.37. With stratified samples with strata twice the size of the systematic strata and thus two sampling units drawn per strata, systematic samples are again more efficient, with ratios of 5.68, 4.23, 2.07, 1.65, and 1.90 in five tests. Osborne and Finney used forest cover and timber volume for their test data. The sampling method used was transects. Three comparisons of the first type of stratification (strata sizes equal to those of the systematic samples) with systematic samples show systematic samples to be more efficient, with ratios of 1.07, 1.19, and 1.39. Five comparisons of the second type of stratification with systematic samples also show systematic samples to be more precise, with ratios ranging from 1.35 to 4.42. Johnson made similar tests using data from seedbeds. Comparison was between only systematic samples and stratified samples of the second type. Three tests gave ratios of 1.89, 2.22 and .93.

Schumacher and Chapman (1942:63–64) report results of a comparison between simple random samples and stratified samples of the second type. They used the quadrat sampling method. Eleven samples of each kind were drawn from an artificial population of numbers. The ratio of the squared standard error of the simple random samples to the squared standard error of the stratified samples was 8.39.

Berry (1962:10–11) has conducted tests using land-use data from two areas. Point samples were used for all the tests. In tests from one area (Coon Creek), four stratified systematic unaligned samples were compared with four stratified samples with strata four times as big as those of the stratified systematic unaligned design and with four points per stratum, and with the expected squared standard error of simple random samples. The relative efficiency of the stratified systematic unaligned samples over the simple random samples was 21.5. The relative efficiency of the former method over the stratified samples was 5.65, 2.3, and 3.4 for different land-use categories. Similar tests were run on data from the Montford area but at a lower sample intensity. Here the differences were not as great. The squared standard errors were as follows: simple random samples (expected) 13.4, systematic unaligned samples 10.2, stratified samples 11.3, checkerboard systematic samples 12.8, systematic traverses 13.5, and random traverses 11.0. Four samples were drawn with each design.

Extensive tests comparing point, quadrat, and transect samples have been made by Haggett (1963:108–114) using land-cover data from England. He drew 64 simple random samples with each method at five different intensities. At all five intensities, the mean error—the deviation of the sample means from the population mean—of the transect samples was less than that of both the point and quadrat samples. Haggett also drew three simple random and three stratified samples for comparison, using the quadrat method. The ratio of the squared standard error of the simple random to the squared standard error of the stratified samples was 5.38.

In summary, these results show systematic and stratified systematic unaligned samples to be more efficient than stratified and simple random samples, and stratified samples to be more efficient than simple random samples at a given sampling intensity. Also, on the basis of Haggett's data, transect methods are more efficient than quadrat methods. One set of tests by Berry shows point samples to be more efficient than transect samples, but his tests were much less extensive than Haggett's.

A few points should be made about these tests. First, the squared standard error of a sampling distribution, like most statistics, is subject to sampling error (Cochran 1953:12). Thus, it seems unwise simply to calculate the ratio of the squared standard error of one sampling design to the squared standard error of another sampling design, and consider it a measure of the relative efficiency of the two designs. At least some recognition should be made of the number of samples involved in computing the squared standard error. For instance, if an *F*-distribution is used to test the hypothesis that the squared standard errors of the sampling designs are equal for the tests by Berry, with a .05 significance level, all the hypotheses except one are accepted. Only the expected squared standard error of the simple random sample and the squared standard error of the stratified systematic unaligned sample can be considered significantly different. I am not trying to ignore the fact that the relative efficiencies of the designs are consistent in their direction—that is, that the squared standard errors of systematic samples are usually less than the squared standard error of the stratified samples and so on—but am simply saying that the ratio of the two squared standard errors is not a fair measure of the absolute magnitude of

the differences, especially when the statistics are based on only a few samples.

A second point is that, when comparisons are made between systematic or stratified systematic unaligned and stratified designs, it would be best to use equal strata sizes for each design so that only one sampling unit is chosen from each stratum for both designs. The tests of stratified designs by Berry use strata that are four times as large as those used in the stratified systematic unaligned designs. Thus, the comparison is not between the most efficient types of each sample but, rather, involves a less efficient type of stratified sample.

If the comparisons between systematic and stratified designs are restricted to those *F*-tests involving populations with two-dimensional space (these would seem to be more similar to archeological survey data), and to those tests involving the most efficient type of stratified design, we are left with five comparisons. Three are from Finney (1948, 1950) and two from Yates (1948). The ratios of stratified to systematic are 2.99, 1.37, 1.07, 1.19, and 1.39. For comparisons between simple random designs and others, we have Haggett's and Berry's data left, if less efficient stratified designs are used. We have ratios of simple random to stratified sampling of 2.17, 3.18, and 1.19; ratios of simple random to stratified systematic unaligned of 21.5 and 1.22; and a ratio of simple random to systematic of 1.05. Although only one of these ratios (21.5) is statistically significant, when more than one ratio is available for a comparison, they are consistent in the direction of the ratio. Also, most of the ratios indicate that gains in efficiency from different designs are small. Again, the predicted decreasing order of efficiency is from (*1*) stratified systematic unaligned or (*2*) systematic, to (*3*) stratified, and then to (*4*) simple random. Also, we expect the transect sampling method to provide more efficient estimates than the quadrat sampling method.

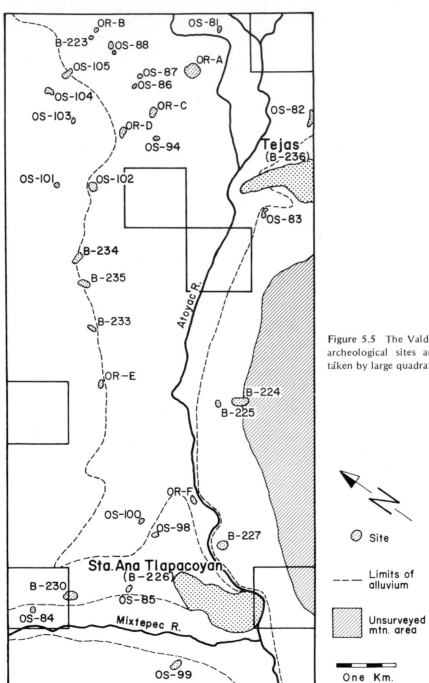

Figure 5.5 The Valdeflores survey block, showing archeological sites and a 10% stratified sample taken by large quadrats.

Site

Limits of alluvium

Unsurveyed mtn. area

One Km.

The Data

The data used for the tests are from three rectangular blocks of land in the Etla, Zaachila, and Valdeflores regions of the Valley of Oaxaca (Figures 5.5–5.7); their sizes and the number of sites found in each are given in Table 5.1. Each block was drawn so as to include all the major environmental zones and types of agricultural land in its area. Because the width of the valley varies considerably, not all blocks are of the same size.

Although occupations of all time periods from Early Formative through late Post-Classic were found, virtually all sites were multicomponent, with the most frequent period recovered being Monte Albán IIIB–IV (A.D. 700–800). Since my aim in this study is merely to see how efficient various sampling techniques are for recovering sites in totally unknown, unsurveyed areas, I will concern myself with total numbers of sites and not with individual time periods as was done by Mayer-Oakes and Nash (1965; see discussion on pp. 133–134).

The Valdeflores survey block, in the extreme south of the valley, is an area of predominantly canal irrigation on sandy alluvium with two major rivers. A total of 33 sites were plotted, with an average site size of 4.75 ha.

The Zaachila survey block, just south of the city of Oaxaca, lies in the broadest part of the valley in a region of well irrigation and dry farming on predominantly clay alluvium. Here, 21 sites were plotted, with an average site size of 14.8 ha; but if the largest site in the block, Cuilapan de Guerrero, is not included in the calculations, the average site is only 3.4 ha.

The Etla survey block, north of Oaxaca City, is an area of highly productive irrigation (mainly by canal) and dry farming, on predominantly clay alluvium. In this much smaller sample block, which actually had the highest density of sites per square kilometer, 17 sites were recovered. Average site size was 8.65 ha; but if the largest site in the block, San José Mogote, is not included in the calculations, the average site is only .92 ha.

I also calculated the distances between each site and its "nearest neighbor." Since nearest-neighbor analysis is defined and discussed by Timothy Earle in Chapter 7 (this volume), I will treat it only briefly here. The outcome of such analysis is a statistic called the *nearest-neighbor coefficient*, which suggests (on the basis of distances to nearest neighbor) whether site patterns are random, clustered, or evenly spaced. Briefly, a nearest-neighbor statistic of 0.00 indicates total clustering; 1.00 indicates random patterning; and 2.15 indicates perfectly even spacing (see Earle, p. 197 of this volume, for a fuller explanation). Ideally, of course, the nearest-neighbor coefficient should be calculated not for sites of all periods as a whole but period by period, as is done in Chapter 7. For the three sample blocks under consideration here, all coefficients are at or near randomness, as follows:

Valdeflores	.90
Zaachila	1.00
Etla	1.13

As suggested, however, a great deal of that approach to randomness probably results from treating together sites of all time periods.

Frequency distributions of the number of sites per sampling unit for the populations from which the samples were drawn are presented for each area in Tables 5.11–5.13 at the end of this section of Chapter 5.

The Tests

As mentioned earlier, each sampling design was used with both quadrat and transect sampling

TABLE 5.1 The Three Sample Survey Blocks in the Valley of Oaxaca, Giving Area of Each Block and Number of Sites Recovered

Sample block	Size in sq km	Total number sites
Valdeflores	55	33
Zaachila	54	21
Etla	18	17

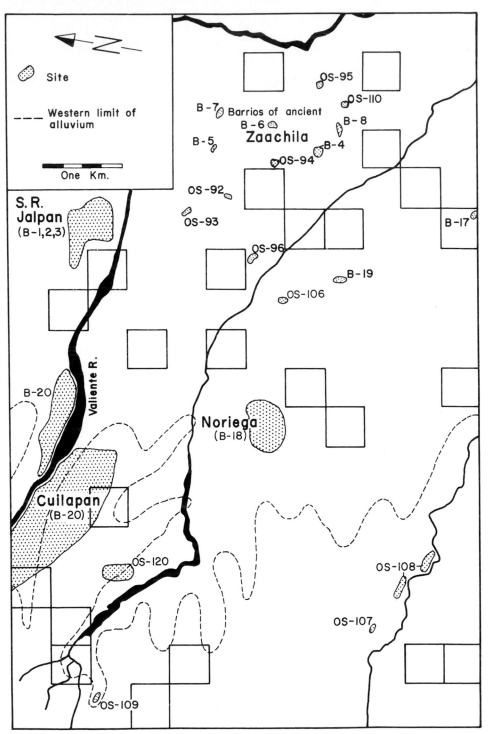

Figure 5.6 The Zaachila survey block, showing archeological sites and a 10% simple random sample taken by small quadrats.

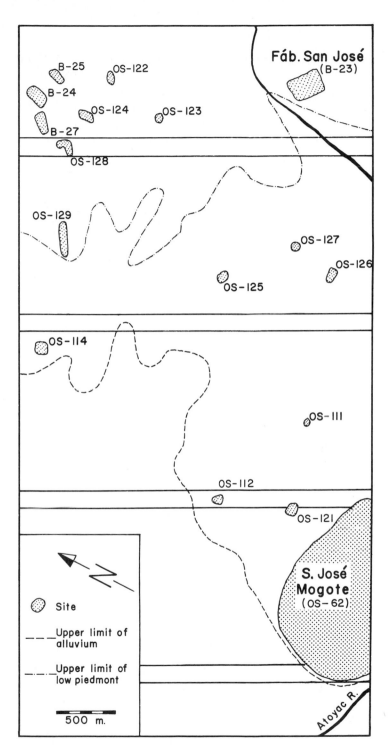

Figure 5.7 The Etla survey block, showing archeological sites and a 10% systematic sample done by small transects.

methods (except for the stratified systematic un-aligned design, which was used only with the quad-rats), and two sizes of sampling units were used with each design. In most cases, for each sampling method, 200 samples were drawn with each sam-pling design—100 with each size of sampling unit.

The exceptions to this were in cases in which all possible samples for a particular design in one of the areas totaled less than 100. This occurred pri-marily with the systematic samples. For instance, in the Zaachila area, there were 216 quadrats of the small size (squares .5 km on a side). For each sample, 24 quadrats were chosen. If the first unit is chosen randomly, and the remainder are taken at an interval of N/n or 9, there are only 9 possible different samples. The individual sampling units for each sample were chosen without replacement.

The sample intensity was chosen arbitrarily. It was decided that a sample of approximately 10% would be taken. An exact 10% sample was not possible in some cases because of indivisibilities of the sampling units. However, in all cases, it was possible to keep the sample intensity between 10% and 11.1%. It is felt that these intensities are simi-lar enough to be regarded as equivalent.

The question that was "asked" of the samples was: How many sites are there in the area? Many other population characteristics could have been measured and estimated, rather than the number of sites in an area. However, it was felt that the discovery of a *representative number of sites in an area* is one general purpose of most surveys, re-gardless of the other variables that they may also be designed to measure. In addition, one central problem of applying sampling techniques to arche-ological survey data is the *distribution of the data both in regard to their normality and to their spatial distribution*. The use of the absolute num-ber of sites present in solving this problem is as helpful, in this regard, as any internal charac-teristic of the sites would be. Whether or not the use of other measurements in the tests would alter the results is a problem for future research.

For example, if a precise measurement of pop-ulation through time is desired for an area, one might want to look at the average area per site in particular time periods (or for an area such as the American Southwest, the total number of rooms per time period). The relative precision of the designs and methods in estimating these charac-teristics may differ from their relative precision in estimating the total number of sites.

Once the samples were drawn from the three Oaxaca survey blocks, the number of sites in each block, as predicted by each sample, was calculated. It was originally assumed that this could be accom-plished by multiplying the number of sites found by each sample by the reciprocal of the sampling fraction, N/n. However, this results in a far too high estimate of the number of sites. It was dis-covered that this bias occurs when an individual site is so large as to be located in more than one sample unit. To obtain an unbiased estimate of the number of sites in an area, the percentage of the total area of the site in each sample unit it "in-habits" must be calculated. Only that fraction of the site area in the sample unit must be included when the estimation is calculated.

An alternative method, which also results in an unbiased estimate, is to simply consider a site inha-biting two sample units as having 50% of its area in each unit, a site inhabiting three sample units as having 33% of its area in each unit, and so on. Since the last method also gives an unbiased esti-mate of the total number of sites—and since it is easier to use—it was used for all the samples. Once the number of estimated sites was calculated for each sample, the mean estimate and the squared standard error of the mean were calculated for each group of 100 samples.

The mean estimates and their squared standard errors are given in Tables 5.2–5.4, along with the number of samples for each test and the sampling fraction. In Table 5.5 are given the ratios between the squared standard errors of all pairs of sampling designs for each area. In Table 5.6 are the ratios of the squared standard error of each type of sam-pling design drawn with large sample units to the squared standard error of the same design drawn with small sample units. In Table 5.7 are the ratios

TABLE 5.2 Sample Data for the Valdeflores Area

Sampling design and method	Mean estimate	(Standard error)^2 of the mean	Number of samples	Sampling fraction
Simple random, small quadrats	37.88	186.13	100	24/220
Simple random, large quadrats	32.34	278.59	100	6/55
Stratified, small quadrats	30.64	167.39	100	24/220
Stratified, large quadrats	35.83	264.91	100	6/55
Systematic, small quadrats	34.42	147.70	100	24/220
Systematic, large quadrats	33.26	248.57	55	6/55
Stratified systematic unaligned, small quadrats	32.45	194.16	100	24/220
Stratified systematic unaligned, large quadrats	32.93	293.30	100	6/55
Simple random, small transects	34.04	196.64	100	8/73
Simple random, large transects	32.33	226.77	100	4/37
Stratified, small transects	33.69	143.30	100	8/73
Stratified, large transects	35.04	181.98	100	4/37
Systematic, small transects	32.81	163.81	73	8/73
Systematic, large transects	32.25	176.46	37	4/37

of quadrat designs to the same type of design drawn with transects.

Since, in all but four cases, the difference between the estimated mean and the actual population mean is less than 25%, no consideration of the accuracy of the sampling techniques is made in the comparisons.

Results

The results of my tests are not completely consistent with the results, just reported, from tests based on nonarcheological data. Based on the latter, I would expect that all ratios in Table 5.5, with the possible exception of the ratio between stratified and systematic samples (2/3), would be

greater than 1.0. It is clear that they are not. For my tests:

1. *Stratification results in the most consistent gain in efficiency over simple random sampling, providing greater precision in 9 of 12 cases.* If, for each of the 12 cases, we test the hypothesis that the squared standard error of the stratified samples is equal to the squared standard error of the simple random samples, none of the 12 ratios are high enough to reject the hypothesis (a .05 significance level is used, and this level will be used in all *F*-tests that follow). As expected from the other sampling tests, it is suggested that, while gains in precision from stratification are consistent, they are small.

TABLE 5.3 Sample Data for the Zaachila Area

Sampling design and method	Mean estimate	(Standard error)^2 of the mean	Number of samples	Sampling fraction
Simple random, small quadrats	24.90	129.12	100	24/216
Simple random, large quadrats	18.84	166.93	100	6/54
Stratified, small quadrats	21.69	114.21	100	24/216
Stratified, large quadrats	19.95	176.68	100	6/54
Systematic, small quadrats	21.09	147.26	9	24/216
Systematic, large quadrats	21.00	346.00	9	6/54
Stratified systematic unaligned, small quadrats	24.40	149.01	100	24/216
Stratified systematic unaligned, large quadrats	22.14	185.07	100	6/54
Simple random, small transects	21.41	98.19	100	6/60
Simple random, large transects	20.55	158.21	100	3/30
Stratified, small transects	18.68	80.69	100	6/60
Stratified, large transects	23.52	156.68	100	3/30
Systematic, small transects	21.04	63.98	10	6/60
Systematic, large transects	20.96	130.94	10	3/30

2. *Systematic designs provide less consistent gains in efficiency over simple random sampling, having a smaller squared standard error in 7 of 12 cases.* In only 2 of these 7 instances is the gain in efficiency statistically significant.* Systematic samples cannot be considered to provide consistently more precise estimates than simple random samples. The most notable fact about the systematic samples is the variability in precision. Their precision relative to stratified systematic unaligned samples for the large quadrat samples in the Zaachila area gives the highest ratio in the table. Their precision relative to simple random samples for the large quadrats in the Zaachila area gives the lowest ratio in the table.

*Some of the squared standard errors being compared in the tables are from populations (all possible samples of a given type of sampling technique were obtained) and some are from samples (all possible samples were not drawn). When the squared standard errors of a population and a sample are compared, statistical significance is determined by defining the 95% confidence interval for the squared standard error of the sample of estimates and then seeing if the squared standard error of the population of estimates falls within this interval. If it does not fall within the interval, the difference between the squared standard errors is considered statistically signifi- cant. Also, in some cases, the squared standard errors of two populations of estimates are compared. The difference between such values must be considered statistically significant since there is no sampling error. For all comparisons of the squared standard errors of two samples of estimates, the F-test is used.

TABLE 5.4 Sample Data for the Etla Area

Sampling design and method	Mean estimate	(Standard error)^2 of the mean	Number of samples	Sampling fraction
Simple random, small quadrats	15.96	121.35	100	8/72
Simple random, large quadrats	16.25	218.01	100	2/18
Stratified, small quadrats	18.66	151.19	100	8/72
Stratified, large quadrats	17.00	199.97	81	2/18
Systematic, small quadrats	17.03	86.36	9	8/72
Systematic, large quadrats	17.00	292.51	9	2/18
Stratified systematic unaligned, small quadrats	16.86	126.16	100	8/72
Stratified systematic unaligned, large quadrats	17.00	207.71	27	2/18
Simple random, small transects	14.76	99.14	100	4/40
Simple random, large transects	14.40	207.73	100	2/20
Stratified, small transects	17.48	108.99	100	4/40
Stratified, large transects	16.75	172.71	100	2/20
Systematic, small transects	16.97	154.48	10	4/40
Systematic, large transects	17.00	208.89	10	2/20

3. *Stratified systematic unaligned samples show no gain in efficiency*. Their squared standard error is higher than that of stratified samples in 5 of 6 cases, and higher than systematic samples in 4 of 6 cases. Their precision is little different from that of simple random sampling.

The results in Table 5.6 are a direct contrast with the results of Table 5.5. The ratios in Table 5.6 are consistent in all 21 cases. *The smaller sampling units are more efficient than the larger sampling units, and 12 of the 16 cases not involving a comparison between the squared standard errors of 2 populations show significant differences between large and small units, using an F-test.* The mean gain in efficiency is especially large for systematic samples.

Comparisons of the squared standard error of a sampling design used with different sampling methods also offer more consistent results.

4. *Transect samples, as expected, are more efficient than quadrat samples in 15 of 18 cases.* However, the ratios are not as high as those of Table 5.5, with none of the 13 cases not involving a comparison between population values being statistically significant. However, I do not feel that this is a fair test of the relative precision of quadrat and transect methods. In all the comparisons, there are fewer sampling units with the transect method, as in the Etla area where there are 72 small quadrats but only 40 small transects. As I have shown, *the greater the number of sampling units, the greater the precision of the estimate*. If a

TABLE 5.5 Ratios between the (Standard Error)^2 of Sampling Designs[a]

Survey area and sampling method	1/2	1/3	1/4	2/3	2/4	3/4
Valdeflores:						
Small quadrats	1.11	1.26	.96	1.13	.86	.76
Large quadrats	1.05	1.12	.95	1.07	.90	.85
Small transects	1.37	1.20	—	.87	—	—
Large transects	1.25	1.29	—	1.03	—	—
Zaachila:						
Small quadrats	1.13	.88	.87	.78	.77	.99
Large quadrats	.94	.48	.90	.51	.95	1.87
Small transects	1.22	1.53	—	1.26	—	—
Large transects	1.01	1.21	—	1.20	—	—
Etla:						
Small quadrats	.80	1.41	.96	1.75	1.20	.68
Large quadrats	1.09	.75	1.05	.68	.96	1.41
Small transects	.91	.64	—	.71	—	—
Large transects	1.20	.99	—	.83	—	—

[a]The numbers at the top of the table represent the sampling designs as follows: 1 = simple random, 2 = stratified, 3 = systematic, 4 = stratified systematic unaligned.

TABLE 5.6 Ratios between Sampling Units of Different Sizes[a]

Survey area and sampling method	Random	Stratified	Systematic	Stratified systematic unaligned
Valdeflores, quadrat	1.50	1.58	1.68	1.51
Valdeflores, transect	1.15	1.27	1.08	—
Zaachila, quadrat	1.29	1.55	2.35	1.24
Zaachila, transect	1.61	1.94	2.05	—
Etla, quadrat	1.80	1.32	3.39	1.65
Etla, transect	2.10	1.58	1.35	—

[a]Ratio = (standard error)^2 of large sample units/ (standard error)^2 of small sample units.

TABLE 5.7 Ratios between Sampling Methods[a]

Survey area and size of sampling unit	Random	Stratified	Systematic
Valdeflores, small	.95	1.17	.90
Valdeflores, large	1.23	1.46	1.41
Zaachila, small	1.32	1.42	2.30
Zaachila, large	1.06	1.13	2.64
Etla, small	1.22	1.39	.56
Etla, large	1.05	1.16	1.40

[a]Ratio = (standard error)^2 of quadrats/ (standard error)^2 of transects.

comparison is made between the methods where the number of sampling units are more equivalent, that is, between the large quadrat samples of the Zaachila area (with 54 sampling units) and the small transect samples from the same area (with 60 sampling units), the difference is greater. The ratios are 1.70 for the simple random design, 2.19 for the stratified design, and 5.41 for the systematic design. All three ratios are statistically significant.

Table 5.7 points out the wide range of variation in systematic samples again, with two ratios for systematic samples greater than 2.00, while the next highest ratio in the table is 1.46. The two lowest ratios in the table also occur with systematic samples.

Additional Tests

Another set of tests were run in order to answer several other questions. Research by Haggett and Board (1964:409–410) has shown that the degree of accuracy of sample based estimates of land-use areas varies directly with the proportion of an area covered by the phenomenon in question and inversely with its fragmentation. Haggett (1965:198) also has suggested that the difference in results between the two areas that Berry (1962) used for his tests may be due to the different type of areal pattern Berry analyzed. In one area, large blocks of woodland were used for the tests; in the other, small blocks of cultivated land were used. Finally, Berry and Baker (1968:94) state that

> if the spatial distribution being studied is *random*, each of the procedures will give unbiased estimates with approximately equal variances. . . . If *linear trends* are present in the data, stratified and systematic sampling will be more precise than random sampling; further, stratified sampling will be more precise than systematic because it permits within strata errors to be cancelled out.

In order to test these ideas, the effect of two variables—*site size* and *settlement pattern*—on the sampling results was investigated. First, all sites in the Etla area were reduced to dots on the map, while the settlement pattern as measured by nearest-neighbor analysis was held constant. For the next three tests, the original site size was used, while the settlement pattern was changed. In the first two of these tests, the sites were arranged in clustered patterns or in hexagonal (very evenly spaced) patterns, again as measured by nearest-neighbor analysis. The actual nearest-neighbor coefficients were .55 and 2.05, respectively. (As mentioned earlier, the original nearest-neighbor coefficient was 1.13.) For the third test of settlement pattern, it was desirable to arrange the sites in a linear pattern. A line was drawn between randomly chosen points on each of the short sides of the area. The line was drawn between the short sides of the area so that the transects would not run parallel to the linear trend; this would cause the squared standard error of the estimate to be high, since theoretically one transect could hit all the sites while the remainder found none. It is assumed that, where linear trends may be present (for instance, along river systems), the approximate direction of the trend can be estimated. The sites then were placed along the line within .5 km to either side. If the sites were already within this limit, they remained where they were. Sites outside the limit were placed randomly within it.

These tests were run only in the Etla area. It was chosen solely because it was smaller than the others, as this made the actual manipulation much easier. Only the small sampling units (squares .5 km on a side) were used for the tests. As before, 100 samples were drawn for each design used with each sampling method, except when all possible samples for a design totaled less than 100. For each combination of sampling design and sampling method, the same 100 samples were used for each type of settlement pattern and for each of the two types of site sizes.

All analyses rest on the assumption that the effect of any other variables on the sampling results is constant.

The results of the tests are shown in Tables 5.8 through 5.10. The squared standard error of all the samples for the different tests are given in Table 5.8. In table 5.9 are the squared standard error ratios between pairs of designs for all tests. The ratios between the squared standard error of a sampling design for each of the test runs and the squared standard error of the same design originally (original squared standard error in the denominator) are given in Table 5.10.

Results

The area covered by a phenomenon and its areal distribution did affect the precision of the samples. *The reduction in site size increased the squared standard error of all but one sampling design.* If the hypothesis that "the squared standard errors of the sample designs are equal when the site size is reduced" is tested, two of the four increases not involving a comparison between two population values are significant. *A clustered settlement pattern also increases the squared standard error of the sample designs and decreases the precision in five of seven cases.* Three of the four increases not involving a comparison between two population values are significant.

Both hexagonal and linear settlement reduce the squared standard error of the sampling designs. The reduction occurs with all sampling designs for the linear settlement pattern, and all but one design for the hexagonal settlement pattern. The increase in precision is greater for the linear settlement pattern in five of seven cases, but the differences between the two are small. The squared standard errors of the designs are significantly different from the original squared standard errors in three of five cases for the linear pattern and four of five cases for the hexagonal pattern for the comparisons not involving two population values. A general trend can be noted between the size of the nearest-neighbor coefficient and the squared

standard error of the samples. *As the nearest-neighbor coefficient increases, that is, goes from clustered to random to hexagonal settlement patterns, the squared standard error of the sampling designs decreases and thus precision increases.*

These tests also can be used for evaluating the hypotheses of Berry and Baker (p. 153). The hypothesis that, "if the phenomena being studied are randomly distributed, the sampling designs will have approximately equal squared standard errors" is supported. Using the original sampling tests from the 3 areas, if the hypothesis of equal squared standard errors between designs is tested, only 9 of the 51 ratios not involving a comparison between 2 population values are significant. Thus, 42 of the pairs can be considered statistically equal. The hypothesis for linear trends in the data states that, *when linear trends are present, stratified and systematic samples will give more precise estimates than random samples, and stratified samples will be more precise than systematic samples.* For quadrat samples, stratified and systematic samples give significantly greater precision than simple random samples, but only systematic samples are more precise for the transect samples. Stratified samples provide significantly greater precision than systematic samples for the quadrat samples, but not for the transect samples. Thus, the evidence for evaluating the hypothesis is mixed. Additional hypotheses can be suggested from these tests for future research. For example, *if the sites are clustered, then stratified and systematic samples will provide greater precision than simple random samples. If the data are very evenly spaced, simple random samples will provide greater precision than stratified or systematic samples for quadrat sampling methods.* Another hypothesis is that, "the smaller the site size, the greater the precision of quadrat samples relative to transect samples."

One final question of interest which these tests can help to answer is whether or not the precision of one sampling design will vary less than the precision of other sampling designs as the nature of

TABLE 5.8   (Standard Error)^2 for Sampling Tests with Modified Settlement Pattern and Site Size

Sampling design and sampling method	Original	Clustered	Hexagonal	Linear	Site size reduced
Simple random, quadrats	121.35	211.34	77.79	91.92	156.85
Stratified, quadrats	151.19	149.42	80.98	55.60	146.91
Systematic, quadrats	86.36	140.89	167.73	56.05	150.75
Stratified systematic unaligned, quadrats	126.16	186.77	64.07	54.85	180.13
Simple random, transect	99.14	154.82	83.52	55.99	235.26
Stratified, transect	108.99	136.14	66.30	77.85	361.81
Systematic, transect	154.48	87.44	51.55	48.21	401.11

TABLE 5.9   (Standard Error)^2 Ratios among Sampling Designs for Modified Variable Tests[a]

Modified variable and sampling method	1/2	1/3	1/4	2/3	2/4	3/4
Original, quadrats	.80	1.41	.96	1.75	1.20	.68
Original, transects	.91	.64	—	.71	—	—
Clustered, quadrats	1.41	1.50	1.13	1.06	.80	.75
Clustered, transects	1.14	1.77	—	1.56	—	—
Hexagonal, quadrats	.96	.46	1.21	.48	1.26	2.62
Hexagonal, transects	1.26	1.62	—	1.29	—	—
Linear, quadrats	1.65	1.64	1.68	.99	1.01	1.02
Linear, transects	.72	1.16	—	1.61	—	—
Site size reduced, quadrats	1.07	1.04	.87	.97	.82	.84
Site size reduced, transects	.65	.59	—	.90	—	—

[a]The numbers at the top of the table represent the sampling designs as follows: 1 = simple random, 2 = stratified, 3 = systematic, 4 = stratified systematic unaligned.

TABLE 5.10   (Standard Error)^2 Ratios between Modified Variable Tests and Original Tests[a]

Sampling design and sampling method	Clustered	Hexagonal	Linear	Site size reduced
Simple random, quadrats	1.74	.64	.76	1.29
Stratified, quadrats	.99	.54	.37	.97
Systematic, quadrats	1.63	1.94	.65	1.75
Stratified systematic unaligned, quadrats	1.48	.51	.43	1.43
Simple random, transects	1.56	.84	.56	2.37
Stratified, transects	1.25	.61	.71	3.32
Systematic, transects	.57	.33	.31	2.60

[a]Ratio = variance of modified variable/original variance.

the population changes. Such a design would be of value when planning probability samples where little is known about the nature of the population characteristics. For the quadrat samples, the precision of the stratified and systematic samples vary approximately equally as the population characteristics are changed, while both vary less than the precision of the simple random samples, although not significantly. The precision of the simple random sample varies less for the transect samples, with stratified sample precision varying less than the precision of the systematic samples. However, again the differences are not statistically significant. Thus, no single sampling design seems to provide a precision that uniformly varies less than that of other designs as the population characteristics change.

Summary and Conclusions

It has been shown that the nature of archeological data is such that rules derived from theory or from tests on other data regarding the relative precision of estimation of different types of sampling techniques must not be applied indiscriminately. While stratification provided greater precision than simple random samples in 9 of 12 cases, F-tests show that the gains were not statistically significant. This was expected from the results of previous tests in other fields. However, systematic samples resulted in less consistent gains in precision over simple random samples, and cannot be considered more efficient. Also, stratified systematic unaligned samples were less efficient than either stratified or systematic designs, and

TABLE 5.11   Frequency Distribution for Populations, Valdeflores Area

Sites per sampling unit	Small quadrats	Large quadrats	Small transects	Large transects
.00	169	26	29	8
.14	13	0	4	0
.17	0	0	3	0
.25	4	7	0	3
.33	0	0	1	0
.50	14	4	16	8
.64	0	0	2	0
.67	0	0	1	0
.75	0	0	0	1
1.00	14	8	9	6
1.14	1	0	0	0
1.17	0	0	1	0
1.25	0	1	0	1
1.33	0	0	2	0
1.50	4	3	1	3
1.64	0	0	1	0
1.67	0	0	1	0
1.75	0	0	0	3
2.00	1	2	2	1
2.50	0	1	0	1
3.00	0	3	0	2
Totals	220	55	73	37
	$\bar{x} = .14982$	$\bar{x} = .60000$	$\bar{x} = .45192$	$\bar{x} = .89189$
	$\sigma^2 = .12439$	$\sigma^2 = .71273$	$\sigma^2 = .27765$	$\sigma^2 = .67750$

TABLE 5.12   Frequency Distribution for Populations, Zaachila Area

Sites per sampling unit	Small quadrats	Large quadrats	Small transects	Large transects
.00	172	29	20	7
.05	0	0	10	0
.08	12	0	0	0
.09	0	0	0	5
.17	0	5	2	0
.20	0	0	1	0
.22	0	0	6	0
.25	12	0	2	0
.33	3	3	0	1
.42	0	0	0	5
.50	2	7	4	0
.67	0	1	3	0
.75	0	0	2	0
1.00	15	4	5	6
1.33	0	0	0	1
1.42	0	0	0	1
1.50	0	0	4	0
1.67	0	0	1	0
2.00	0	4	0	2
2.33	0	0	0	1
3.00	0	1	0	1
Totals	*216*	*54*	*60*	*30*
	$\bar{x} = .09699$ $\sigma^2 = .06769$	$\bar{x} = .38907$ $\sigma^2 = .43510$	$\bar{x} = .35067$ $\sigma^2 = .22368$	$\bar{x} = .69867$ $\sigma^2 = .62005$

provided about the same precision as simple random samples.

The largest and most consistent gains in precision resulted from a decrease in the size of the sampling units. The use of transect samples rather than quadrat samples resulted in the next largest and most consistent gains. However, it has been suggested that transect samples might be even more efficient than the results of the tests showed. Thus, a change in the type of sampling design must be seen as only a third alternative for increasing the precision of estimation.

It has been shown that the size of archeological sites, and their pattern of distribution, can have significant effects on the precision of estimation of total site numbers. It is believed that these tests will make the results of this study applicable to a wider range of situations, for instance, (*1*) in the southwestern United States, where settlements are smaller than those of Mesoamerica, or (*2*) in parts of Mesoamerica where it is known from the outset that there may be linear trends in the data, owing to the effect of river systems.

The hypothesis that, "with random distribution of the data, the squared standard errors of different sampling designs will be approximately equal" has been positively tested. The hypothesis of increasing relative precision from simple random, to systematic, to stratified designs, in that order—if linear trends exist in the data—has received mixed support at best. Also, three additional hypotheses have been offered concerning the relative efficiency of sampling techniques as site size and settlement pattern vary.

It has been shown that no sampling design provides precision in estimation which varies signifi-

TABLE 5.13 Frequency Distribution for Populations, Etla Area

Sites per sampling unit	Small quadrats	Large quadrats	Small transects	Large transects
.00	46	5	16	5
.11	0	0	9	0
.13	7	0	0	0
.20	0	0	0	5
.25	4	0	0	0
.33	0	0	1	0
.50	5	3	3	3
.83	0	0	1	0
1.00	8	7	4	2
1.13	1	0	0	0
1.33	0	0	4	0
1.50	0	2	0	1
1.83	0	0	1	0
2.00	0	0	0	1
2.17	0	0	1	0
2.50	0	0	0	1
3.00	0	0	0	1
3.50	1	0	0	1
5.50	0	1	0	0
Totals	72	18	40	20
	$\bar{x} = .23667$ $\sigma^2 = .26545$	$\bar{x} = .94444$ $\sigma^2 = 1.46914$	$\bar{x} = .42425$ $\sigma^2 = .33976$	$\bar{x} = .85000$ $\sigma^2 = 1.11250$

cantly less than other designs with changes in settlement pattern or settlement size.

This study was meant to provide an initial attempt at the application of the rules of probability sampling to archeological survey data. The conclusions must be tested further before their validity can be established. Tests using data from other areas of the world would be particularly helpful. Perhaps the major question, for which this study has not supplied even an initial answer, is whether or not the relative precision of sampling techniques varies with the intensity of the sample. This, too, is a problem for future research.

Although *some* of the expectations of probability sampling were not confirmed by these tests, an inference by anyone that probability sampling does not work for archeological data, and there-

fore should not be used, would be unwarranted. Even if *all* the expectations had not been confirmed, the use of probability sampling in archeological research would still be of critical importance. Probability sampling is the only way selection bias can be avoided, and the only means through which the reliability of the sample data can be known. If the reliability of the data is unknown, then the reliability of inferences drawn on the basis of these data must be questioned. What this study suggests is that, for surveying unknown areas, the simplest sampling designs well may be the most practical.*

*For additional information on the use of sampling techniques in archeology, the reader should consult Mueller's (1974) study.

The Trouble with Regional Sampling

KENT V. FLANNERY

"There are two problems with Plog's paper," said the Real Mesoamerican Archeologist, after I had read him a preliminary draft. "One is that he doesn't tell me what to do if I miss Teotihuacán in my sample. The other is that he doesn't tell me how to sample the Gulf Coast jungle or the Petén rain forest." R.M.A. has a point, and I will deal with his objections in reverse order.

Plog's tests admittedly were run in one of Meso-america's ideal environments: the arid or semiarid highlands, where one can see through the sparse vegetation and practically identify individual trees on the aerial photographs. Attempting to sample the lowland Maya jungle by .5 km^2 quadrats would border on lunacy. Even if you succeeded in actually doing it, no one would ever believe you.

As we see it, the only hope for probability sampling in such tropical wilderness areas would be to use *transect samples* (see discussion in Chapter 3 and in Plog's section of this chapter). In some respects, the surveys some Mayanists have conducted along trails in the Petén area are a form of "transect" (e.g., Bullard 1960). So are the long *"brecha* strips" surveyed north and south from Tikal (Puleston and Callender 1967). They differ from true transect samples in that they were neither selected according to formal probability sampling procedures, nor designed to sample a predetermined percentage of a bounded universe of sites. However, the Tikal *brecha* strip surveys suggest that transects can be made even in the Petén vegetation, and Plog's results show that transect sampling is actually more efficient than quadrats.

As for Teotihuacán, we yield to R.M.A.: It is unlikely that we can understand the Valley of Mexico without it. To this dilemma, William T. Sanders (personal communication, 1973) has

offered a solution, based on R.M.A.'s own observation that "you couldn't miss it if you tried." It seems to Sanders that, for any of the later periods of Mesoamerican prehistory, there is likely to be a size hierarchy of sites, rather like a demographic pyramid (Figure 5.8). At the apex will be a few huge sites, whose monumentality makes them impossible to miss. Below this will be a larger number of intermediate sites, smaller but still relatively easy to find by traditional Mesoamerican survey techniques. At the base of the pyramid will be large numbers of small, unobtrusive sites which might well be overlooked by any but the most intensive survey.

Perhaps our old friend R.M.A. could enjoy the best of both worlds by doing two kinds of survey, simultaneously or sequentially. He himself could traverse the region in his customary way, locating Teotihuacán and probably a good proportion of the medium-range sites with mounds. At the same time, his Skeptical Graduate Student could draw a 20% stratified random sample of the region by small quadrats (see Plog, this chapter), thus providing him with an accurate basis for estimating the numbers of smaller sites of various types and

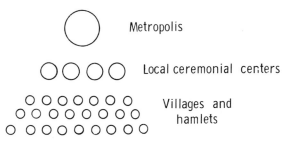

Figure 5.8 The "population pyramid" of archeological sites (see text).

periods, as well as the strata (or environmental zones) in which they were most likely to occur. Each would be doing the kind of survey he loved best, and the outcome certainly would be more useful than the results obtained by either archeologist working alone.

References

Berry, B. J. L.
  1962 Sampling, coding, and storing flood plain data. *Agriculture Handbook* No. 237. Farm Economics Division, Economic Research Service, U.S. Department of Agriculture.
Berry, B. J. L., and A. M. Baker
  1968 Geographic sampling. In *Spatial Analysis*, edited by B. J. L. Berry and D. F. Marble. Englewood Cliffs, N.J.: Prentice-Hall. Pp. 91–100.
Binford, L. R.
  1964 A consideration of archaeological research design. *American Antiquity* 29:425–441.
Bullard, W.
  1960 Maya settlement pattern in northeastern Peten, Guatemala. *American Antiquity* 25:355–372.
Cochran, W. G.
  1953 *Sampling techniques*. New York: John Wiley.
Deming, W. E.
  1950 *Some theory of sampling*. New York: John Wiley.
Finney, D. J.
  1948 Random and systematic samples in timber surveys. *Forestry* 22:1–36.
  1950 An example of periodic variation in forest sampling. *Forestry* 23:96–111.
Greig-Smith, P.
  1964 *Quantitative plant ecology*. London: Butterworth's.
Haggett, P.
  1963 Regional and local components in land-use sampling: A case study from the Brazilian Triángulo. *Erdkunde* 17:108–114.
  1965 *Locational analysis in human geography*. London: Edward Arnold.
Haggett, P., and C. Board
  1964 Rotational and parallel traverses in the rapid

integration of geographic areas. *Annals of the Association of American Geographers* 54:406–410.
Hansen, M. H., W. M. Hurwitz, and W. G. Madow
  1953 *Sample survey methods and theory*. Vol. 1. New York: John Wiley.
Johnson, F. A.
  1943 A statistical study of sampling methods for tree nursery inventories. *Journal of Forestry* 41:674–689.
Mayer-Oakes, W. J., and R. J. Nash
  1964 Archeological research design—a critique. Paper presented at the 63rd Annual Meeting of the American Anthropological Association, 21 November 1964.
  1965 Archeological research design—a critique. Dept. of Anthropology, University of Manitoba. Mimeograph.
Mueller, J. W.
  1974 The use of sampling in archaeological surveys. *Memoirs of the Society for American Archaeology* No. 28.
Osborne, J. G.
  1942 Sampling errors of the systematic and random surveys of cover-type areas. *Journal of the American Statistical Association* 37:256–264.
Puleston, D. E., and D. W. Callender, Jr.
  1967 Defensive earthworks at Tikal. *Expedition* 9:40–48.
Schumacher, F. X., and R. A. Chapman
  1942 Sampling methods in forestry and range management. *Bulletin* No. 7. School of Forestry, Duke University, Durham, N.C.
Stuart, A.
  1962 *Basic ideas of scientific sampling*. New York: Hafner Publishing.
Willey, G. R., W. R. Bullard, Jr., J. B. Glass, and J. C. Gifford
  1965 Prehistoric Maya settlements in the Belize Valley. *Papers of the Peabody Museum of Archaeology and Ethnology* Vol. LIV. Harvard University, Cambridge, Mass.
Yates, F.
  1948 Systematic sampling. *Philosophical Transactions of the Royal Society* (Series A) 241:345–377. London.

Chapter 6

ANALYSIS ON THE REGIONAL LEVEL: PART I

Introduction

As we suggested in Chapter 5, the question "How do you know you have an adequate sample of sites?" draws a predictably heated response from the Real Mesoamerican Archeologist. On the other hand, he is all smiles when you ask him "What pattern is discernible in the distribution of sites in your sample?" Then he rolls out his maps, as he did for me one snowy January morning in his office at the university, and easily points out the pattern by inspection.

"All the early sites are down here by the San Jacinto River," he said, "where the best agricultural land is. By the Late Formative, we have a couple of hilltop sites with stone masonry architecture, probably located on high points that could be easily defended. All in all, we have about 38 Formative sites of all sizes and periods."

"You can't fool him on settlement patterns," said the Skeptical Graduate Student, looking over his shoulder. "There's *nothing* he likes better than a lot of black dots on a map."

"Especially when I have a Bonafide Genius to help ink them in," said R.M.A. And then, for my benefit, he added: "The Little Guru here is mad because I wouldn't let him add a bunch of dashed lines linking them up, like MacNeish did in his *Science* article."

"I wanted to model the whole settlement *system*," S.G.S. complained. "*He's* completely hung up at the level of *pattern*."

"System—pattern—what's the difference?" shrugged R.M.A. "It's a word. Like Don Lehmer says, a fancy package for what used to come in a plain brown wrapper." He had started to unroll his map depicting the Classic settlement pattern.

"Look," said S.G.S., and we looked. He was pointing to a lone snowflake that glistened momentarily on the office window.

"Every snowflake," said S.G.S. with almost unbearable condescension, "is composed of ice crystals. Every ice crystal has the same shape, and can be described in a few short phrases. Yet no two snowflakes are the same, and the amount of verbiage needed to describe its final shape is 10, maybe 20 times that needed to describe an ice crystal. You know what the first crystal looked like, and you can describe the final pattern of the flake. What you can't describe, and can't even understand, is the set of rules that generated that particular pattern. That's the *system*. That's the part you're *missing*. In the same way, you know what the first village at San Jacinto looked like, and you can describe the final pattern of sites, but you don't have the remotest idea how that original village gave rise to that particular pattern."

There was silence in the office while the Real Mesoamerican Archeologist watched the snowflake melting back to its primordial elements.

"Why the hell don't you go down the hall and get us three cups of coffee?" he said casually, rolling up his map of the Classic before we had a chance even to see the dots.

Evolution of Complex Settlement Systems

KENT V. FLANNERY

Throughout the early chapters of this book, we have acted as if the village were the only type of settlement known during the millenium 1500–500 B.C. In reality, the village was accompanied by a multitude of less permanent settlements, camps, and special-purpose stations. We also have been cavalier in our use of the term "village," mentioning only in passing that some of our colleagues have made further distinctions like "hamlet," "nucleated village," "dispersed village," and "town." We have already stated our reasons for choosing to focus on the village, but, having reached the level of *regional settlement systems*, we can no longer ignore the distinctions our colleagues have made.

Perhaps from the very beginning, Formative societies exhibited patterns of settlement that were complex, consisting of several kinds of contemporaneous sites integrated into an overall regional network. Such complex regional patterns began growing from the moment the first village was founded in their area. They evolved through time, as the original village gave rise to daughter communities which were smaller, or larger, or more specialized, or less specialized, and which maintained their ties to the parent community. The study of these complex settlement patterns now has fascinated four consecutive academic generations of Mesoamerican archeologists and shows no sign of diminishing returns (cf. Parsons 1972).

But this is a chapter on settlement *systems*, and it would seem appropriate to make explicit the distinction between these and settlement *patterns*, for the two are not synonyms. A settlement pattern, as its name implies, is the pattern of sites on the regional landscape; it is empirically derived by sampling or total survey, and is usually studied by counting sites, measuring their sizes and the distances between them, and so on. A settlement system, on the other hand, is the set of "rules" that generated the pattern in the first place. It cannot be empirically derived, but at least some of the rules can be deduced by simulation or the use of probabilistic models. Indeed, we have put the term "rules" in quotation marks because, as will be stressed later, it is meant not in a jural or deterministic sense but a probabilistic one.

Thus, the sentence "Early Formative villages lie strung out along the Río San Jacinto" describes a pattern of settlement. The sentences "No village ever seems to have been founded within a mile of another" and "Daughter communities were usually founded some four miles upstream from the parent community" are probabilistic statements that indirectly reflect some of the rules of the settlement system.

In this section, we will give three brief examples of the complex regional patterns associated with early Mesoamerican villages. We will discuss the site typologies used, and the ways in which the various types of sites are thought to have been integrated. Moving on, we will touch on the appearance of administrative hierarchies within regional patterns. Finally, we will arrive at the question of how one gets at the system behind the pattern, at the set of rules that shape random processes into a highly structured network of interrelated settlements. We will barely introduce that topic, for it is to be followed by three studies giving more substantive archeological examples of patterns, as well as some suggested methodologies by which the underlying system might be uncovered.

Site Typologies

One of the first steps in the analysis of any settlement pattern is the development of a site typology, a classification that reflects the differences in size, function, features, and other attributes of sites dating to the same period. By far the greatest concern with producing objective site typologies has come from workers in the Valley of Mexico.

Sanders began in the mid-1950s by defining the village as "a nucleated community with populations running at least into the hundreds and in which at least 75 percent of the population derive at least 75 percent of their income from agriculture or some other extractive activity" (Sanders 1956:117). A town, on the other hand, was defined as "a rural community in which the bulk of the population is still dedicated to farming but in which trade and craft specialization are added as secondary activities, reducing the percentage of population dedicated to agriculture to below 75 percent" (Sanders 1956:117). Sanders' use of the term "extractive activity" allowed for both farming villages and fishing villages, but his town–village dichotomy, having been based on ethnographic data, presented certain logistic problems for archeological survey. First, one could rarely tell from surface remains whether or not craft specialists represented 26% (or more) of the population. Second, it presented a situation in which a specialized salt-producing community with a population of 101 could be classed as a "town," while a neighboring community of 800 farmers remained a "village." Based as it was on the "Central Mexican Symbiotic Region" (the Valleys of Mexico, Toluca, Tlaxcala–Puebla, and Morelos), where craft specialists tended to be concentrated in towns and cities, the dichotomy was less applicable to areas like Oaxaca, which tend to have craft-specialist villages. Finally, the phrase "populations running at least into the hundreds" excluded 90% of all known Early Formative villages (see Chapter 3). Thus, over the next decade, Sanders and his associates—most notably Jeffrey Parsons (1971)—set about providing a longer and more detailed series of definitions of settlement types.

In the early 1970s, Parsons (1971) and his colleague Richard Blanton (1972) published settlement pattern studies on areas of the Valley of Mexico which present that expanded series of definitions. Glossing over some of the differences between the two reports, their relevant site typology is as follows.

1. *Primary regional center*, defined by Parsons as

having several thousand inhabitants, and by Blanton as being nucleated and architecturally complex, with a population over 2000.

2. *Secondary regional center*, defined by Parsons as having many hundreds to a few thousands of inhabitants, and by Blanton as between 1000 and 2000 inhabitants, nucleated, and with large-scale ceremonial–civic architecture.

3. *Segregated elite district*, defined by Parsons (1971:22) as "an isolated residential area, situated in a topographically prominent situation, in which is concentrated a high proportion of ceremonial–civic architecture." Similar, but lacking the residential aspect, is an *isolated ceremonial–civic precinct*.

4. *Nucleated village*. Both Parsons and Blanton describe this type as lacking large-scale ceremonial–civic architecture. Blanton used 100–1000 inhabitants as a rule of thumb for villages, while Parsons used 100–1500, with villages of over 500 persons classed as "large."

5. *Dispersed village*, defined by Parsons but not recovered in Blanton's survey, is as its name implies merely a spread-out version of the *nucleated village*.

6. *Hamlet*, defined by Parsons as a community of under 100 persons and by Blanton as 10–100 persons, lacking any obvious ceremonial–civic architecture. Here, Blanton calls to mind MacNeish's (1969) dichotomy between villages and hamlets in the Tehuacán Valley: *Villages* have "houses arranged around plazas or mounds" while *hamlets* are "small groups of houses not associated with plazas or mounds."

7. *Isolated residence*, defined by Blanton but not recovered in Parsons' survey, consists of one nuclear or extended family with an assumed population of 5–10 persons.

8. *Camp*, defined by Parsons as a small, scattered, seasonal or temporary site with no permanent architecture. Camps have been divided by MacNeish (1964) into those produced by *microbands* (2–5 persons, for a day

or two to most of a season) or *macrobands* (15–20 persons, for all or most of a season).

Clearly, even this expanded list of settlement types would not cover all the sites found in Formative Mesoamerica. One would have to add such things as *flint quarries* or *chipping stations; kill sites* or *butchering stations; salt-making sites; maguey-roasting camps; fishing, shrimping,* or *shellfishing camps; dams; agricultural terrace areas;* and so on through a vast list of site types. We present a partial list in the hope that it will keep the village in perspective, in spite of our decision to focus this book on that one particular settlement type.

Most of the communities discussed in this book would be classed as "hamlets" or "villages" in the Parsons–Blanton typology; a few perhaps would be considered "regional centers." In most cases, lacking more specific data, we have simply regarded hamlets and villages "as the small and large ends of a size continuum, and their differences in public architecture as being more a matter of degree than kind" (Flannery 1972a:38-39). Where further data are available, we have made typological distinctions along the lines suggested by Parsons·and Blanton. As stated in a previous paper, we are attracted by the functional aspects of the Blanton–MacNeish division into villages (with public architecture) and hamlets (without), given its implications about the ritual integration of the two types. In practice, however, the division is hard to apply "because (a) its proof requires more extensive excavation than most sites have received, and (b) there are already hints that even small hamlets may have some kinds of 'public' buildings, like community shrines, or the 'visitors' reception huts' of the Tiv" (Flannery 1972a:38). For these reasons, in this book, we generally use "village" as a generic term for any small, permanent community.

Still another problem in the application of the settlement typologies just described is that class differences are based partly on population figures, which are estimated from surface debris. Both

Parsons and Blanton, for example, present rules of thumb for calculating population from "light," "medium," and "heavy" sherd densities. Tolstoy and Fish (1973) recently have pointed out that many other variables—such as degree of erosion, deflation, or depth of overburden—intervene between population and surface sherd density. We may never know the exact relationship between households and surface sherds, but Parsons and Blanton, preferring to light one small candle rather than curse the darkness, have given us the only estimates we have.

Integration of Settlement Types

We already have stated at the outset of this book that the village was the base on which most other settlement types were founded. Therein lies one key to the integration of the various types, and we will now consider a few examples.

The Tehuacán Valley

Villages, microband camps, and macroband camps characterized the Early and Middle Formative of the Tehuacán Valley. In Chapter 4, we discussed the relationship between Las Canoas, a Santa María phase village, and Zone VII of Coxcatlán Cave, a Santa María phase macroband camp. A similar relationship existed during the early Ajalpan phase (1500–1150 B.C.) between the village of Ajalpan (Ts 204) and the microband camp in Zone J of Purrón Cave (Tc 272). Indeed, in this case, the relationship is even clearer, since Ts 204 is the only early Ajalpan phase village known in the valley, and the pottery of Zone J at Purrón Cave seriates between that of Zones G and H at Ts 204 (MacNeish, Peterson, and Flannery 1970:239 and Figure 147). Ajalpan is therefore the only known village from which the Zone J campers could have come.

As shown by Figure 6.1, Purrón Cave lies in the mountains some 25 km south of Ajalpan. Using

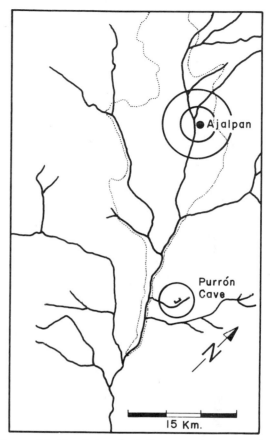

Figure 6.1 The Tehuacán Valley, showing the Early Formative village of Ajalpan and the Purrón Cave campsite. Catchment circles with radii of 2.5 and 5.0 km are given. Dotted line indicates limit alluvium.

Vita-Finzi and Higgs' (1970) figures, this would represent a 10-hour walking distance, with a round trip consuming 20 hours. Thus, a foraging party could not leave Ajalpan, reach the Arroyo Lencho Diego where Purrón Cave is located, and return the same day if they expected to do any substantial amount of wild plant collecting. A trip spanning several days would have been necessary. The empirical data suggest that a camp was made in Zone J during the late rainy season (C. Earle Smith, Jr., personal communication), for more than a few days but considerably less than a full season. Most of the wild plants collected were species that could not have been gathered within 2 km of the Ajalpan village, although many would have been available within 5 km. The Purrón encampment was, therefore, like an extension of Ajalpan's catchment area.

The full array of settlement types from the millenium 1500–500 B.C. (Early Ajalpan, Late Ajalpan, and Early Sta. María phases) would include hamlets, small villages, large villages, winter microband camps, summer and fall macroband camps (MacNeish 1964). In MacNeish's scheme, the integration of these types would have been as follows. Hamlets, lacking ceremonial–civic structures, were tied to villages through their sharing of such facilities at the latter sites. In addition, at various seasons of the year, foraging parties sent

out from villages and hamlets hunted and collected wild plants in the mountains. When their collecting areas were more than a day's round trip from the community, the foragers camped in caves, rockshelters, or in the open (Figure 6.2).

The Valley of Oaxaca

The Valley of Oaxaca shared many settlement types with Tehuacán. In addition to hamlets and villages, a microband camp of the Tierras Largas phase occurred in a cave near Mitla. One small hamlet, perhaps consisting of only 2–3 households, appeared at a salt spring during the San José phase; another tiny hamlet was located in an area of the piedmont where both magnetite and high-quality pottery clay are available (unpublished surveys by

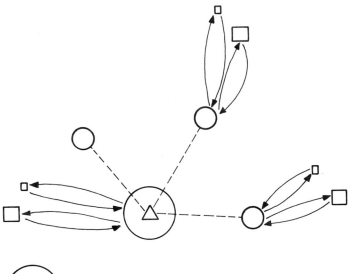

Figure 6.2 Simplified diagram showing the hypothetical integration of various Early Formative settlement types in the Tehuacán Valley. [Redrawn from MacNeish 1964.]

△ within ○   Village (with public bldgs.)

○   Hamlet

□   Summer–fall macroband camp

▫   Winter microband camp

------   Participation in use and maintenance of public bldgs.

———▸   Travel to and from camps

S. Kowalewski and D. Varner). As suggested in Chapter 4, all these small, resource-oriented hamlets were located more than 5 km from the largest village and major consumer in their region. Nearer resources, which could perhaps be reached by a round trip of less than half a day, had no permanent settlement. Our model for the integration of these various settlement types is given in Figure 6.3.

The Chiapas–Guatemala Coast

The Pacific Coast of Chiapas and Guatemala provides us with an even more complex situation. In the relatively simple Oaxaca and Tehuacán cases just given, villages were linked to a small series of seasonal camps and tiny specialized hamlets out-side their immediate catchment areas. On the Chiapas–Guatemala Coast, the entire piedmont and coastal plain formed an integrated system of regional centers, inland farming villages, coastal fishing–farming hamlets, and island fishing or shell-fishing stations, each eventually linked to seasonal camps and salt-making stations (Lowe 1966; Green and Lowe 1967; Gareth Lowe and Carlos Navarrete, personal communication). In Chapter 4, Alan Zarky undertook a site catchment analysis of the coastal fishing–farming hamlets. A look at the overall system shows how misleading it would be to extrapolate from this narrow estuary belt to the entire coast (as Coe and Flannery [1967] did).

1. The great Formative regional center for the area is of course *Izapa*, located inland near Tapa-

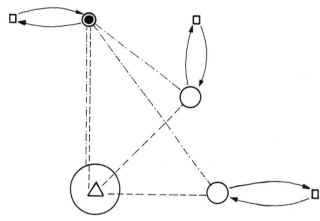

Figure 6.3 Simplified diagram showing the hypothetical integration of various Early Formative settlement types in the Valley of Oaxaca.

△ Village (with public bldgs.)

◯ Hamlet

◉ Resource-specific hamlet (salt, pottery clay, etc.)

▢ Microband camp

- - - - - Participation in use and maintenance of public bldgs.

⟶ Travel to and from camps

–·–·–·– Trips made to obtain specific resources

chula where the rainfall is higher but land clearance also a heavier task. Founded very early in the Formative, Izapa grew from a hamlet to a primary regional center by Late Formative times.

2. Smaller villages with an inland, maize-farming emphasis include *Altamira*, also founded well back in the Early Formative.

3. As one approaches the lagoon-estuary system at the margins of the coastal plain, several new types of sites appear. *Aquiles Serdán* is an example of a nucleated village of house mounds around remnants of a fossil lagoon, its debris including mortars and *metates* for corn grinding as well as bones from 20 species of fish. Other estuary regions had only small hamlets like *Salinas La Blanca* and *La Victoria*, already discussed in Chapter 4. There are suggestions that these small hamlets may have used ceremonial–civic facilities at larger inland villages with pyramidal mounds (Coe 1961).

4. Out in the coastal swamps and estuaries occur still other site types. *Islita* is one of a group of tiny islands in the mangrove swamps near Mapastepec; there, excavations by Navarrete showed that "shells are rare and a fishing economy is indicated, perhaps based on shrimp-taking then as now" (Lowe 1966:454). On the other hand, the nearby site of *Islona de Chantuto*, occupied in the late preceramic and Early Formative, has so many layers of mollusks that past excavators have referred to it as a "shell midden" (cf. Lorenzo 1955).

5. Small mounds of scraped-up saline earth along the margins of extinct estuaries, like the *Cerro del Tiestal* sites mentioned in Chapter 4, may be salt-making stations which supplied salt to villages farther inland. Judging by the debris, they may have been only seasonally occupied.

6. Some piedmont sites, like *El Campito* near Pijijiapan, have monumental rock carvings in Middle Formative style. It is not clear from published descriptions whether these carvings occur with villages or with settlements like Parsons' "segregated elite districts."

Exactly how all these settlement types were integrated is a complex and incompletely answered question, but it seems likely that all shared in an economic network in which maize moved seaward while fish, shellfish, and salt moved inland. Moreover, it is likely that the situation was complex from the very beginnings of the Formative. There can be no clearer example of a situation in which no one site could be used to "typify" the Formative of a particular region. Our tentative model for the integration of these coastal sites is given in Figure 6.4.

Evolution of Site Hierarchies

One other aspect of complex settlement systems emerges from the Parsons–Blanton typology and our model for the Chiapas–Guatemalan Coast: the existence of an administrative hierarchy. The germ of a hierarchy is already implicit in the relationship between village and microband camp, since one is only a seasonal satellite of the other, but it is not an *administrative* hierarchy. With the designation of "primary regional centers," "secondary regional centers," and "villages," an administrative hierarchy becomes explicit. The addition of hierarchical data to the analysis converts survey maps from a pattern of dots, like those produced by Plog in the preceding chapter, to a series of tiered levels like those discussed by Earle in the chapter that follows.

The processes by which site hierarchies arise are poorly understood. In some areas, like the Valley of Oaxaca, primary regional centers of the Early and Middle Formative often turn out to be among the oldest communities in the area. Such sites grow, erect ceremonial–civic structures, and increase their administrative functions while giving rise to "daughter communities" that may never develop similar functions. It may be that, as societies with ranking evolved, senior lineages of higher rank tended to remain at the parent community while cadet lineages of lower rank founded the

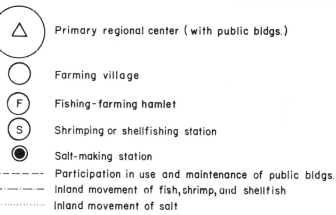

Figure 6.4 Simplified diagram showing the hypothetical integration of various Formative settlement types on the Pacific Coast of Chiapas and western Guatemala.

newer sites. This would help explain the observed archeological pattern in Oaxaca but, of course, it does not explain why ranking evolved in the first place.

It also can be observed that older, more multi-purpose communities tend to take administrative priority over younger, more special-purpose communities, and that larger sites tend to show evidence of more administrative functions than smaller sites; but none of these low-level generalizations really explains the hierarchy.

One series of models which have long been used by geographers and only belatedly tried by archeologists are those provided by central place theory (cf. Johnson 1972; Flannery 1972b: Figure 5; Marcus 1973). Despite the proven utility of the central place model as a heuristic device, few ideas introduced into archeology have met with more antagonism. There are perhaps two reasons for this. One is that many Real Mesoamerican Archeologists rejected the model out of hand on the grounds that it was developed by geographers working with Western, market-based societies featuring a "maximizing" economy. The other reason is that many Skeptical Graduate Students accepted the model with an overenthusiasm that could only be compared to that of a child with a new toy. Let me now try to walk a line between these two positions.

It is true that Walter Christaller (1933), the geographer usually credited with initiating central place studies, was dealing with a Western economy. The settlement pattern he observed in southern Germany was one in which central market towns were spaced roughly equidistant from each other, each primary center having in turn "a wreath of satellite places of lesser importance" around it, also with a roughly predictable spacing, and so on down the hierarchy of centers. Struggling to deduce the settlement system that had produced this pattern, Christaller came up with a series of statements for the relationship between a rural hinterland and the central places whose goods and services it required. Assuming (1) uniform distribution of population and purchasing power, (2) uniform terrain and resource distribution, (3) equal transport facility in all directions, and (4) all central places performing the same functions and serving areas of the same size, the most economical spacing of such service centers would be equidistant.

Because a hexagon is the most economical geometric form for the equal division of an area between a number of points, many of Christaller's "wreaths of satellite places" formed hexagonal patterns or "lattices" around primary centers. However, as Johnson's (1972) study shows, it is not necessary to have perfect hexagons to show statistically significant structuring of settlement owing to the service functions of major centers; indeed, it is not really even necessary that the lattices be six-sided. Some of the most ill-informed

attacks on central place studies have come from critics who spent far too much time on the details of geometry, and ignored statistically defensible clues that the "service functions" of primary and secondary regional centers had begun to strongly override site catchment factors in determining the growth and development of sites. We will not pursue this point here, because Timothy Earle's substantive example in Chapter 7 says it better.

It is unlikely that central place models will ever play a major role in Early Formative archeology, for outside of the Veracruz–Tabasco lowlands, there are very few areas with striking site hierarchies. By Middle Formative times, however, more areas show hierarchies; and they become widespread in the Late Formative and Classic periods (Figure 6.5). In defense of the Real Mesoamerican Archeologist, we must agree that such hierarchies do not imply Western marketing techniques or maximization policies. As Earle's study shows, equidistant spacing can as easily be caused by *competition between regional centers for the support and tribute of the rural hinterland*. And the crucial service functions of the early Mesoamerican central place were more likely *ceremonial and civic* than economic. As Earle demonstrates, all that is necessary to produce a three-tiered site hierarchy with a strong tendency toward equidistant spacing at the upper tier is a chiefdom level of sociopolitical organization, with competition for tribute between neighboring caciques.

Finally, it would be a mistake to conclude that hierarchy is lacking if archeological analysis of a settlement pattern fails to reveal clear and definite tiers of the type defined by Christaller. For there are at least two kinds of central place hierarchies, that of Christaller and that of Lösch (1954; and cf. Haggett 1965:124). In Christaller's hierarchy there are definite steps or tiers, in which (1) all centers in a particular tier are the same size and have the same service functions, and (2) all higher-order centers possess all the functions of the lower-order centers. Lösch's hierarchy is a more nearly continuous sequence of centers without distinct tiers,

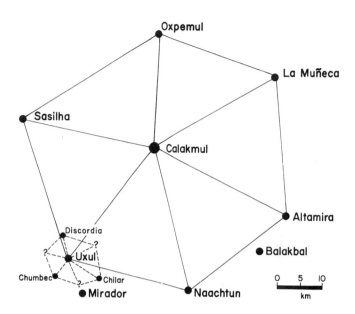

Figure 6.5 Application of a central place model to the Classic Maya lowlands. Six virtually equidistant secondary ceremonial centers form a hexagonal pattern around Calakmul, a primary Maya center of the Late Classic period. In turn, tertiary centers may have formed smaller hexagonal patterns around secondary centers like Uxul. [After Marcus 1973:Figure 5.]

in which (*1*) settlements of the same size need not have the same function, and (*2*) larger centers need not have all the functions of the smaller centers. Marcus (1974) already has shown that the lowland Classic Maya probably had a more Löschian hierarchy, and Earle (Chapter 7, this volume) implies the same for the Gulf Coast when he suggests that smaller Olmec centers, such as Potrero Nuevo, may have provided local administrative services that did not concern major centers like San Lorenzo.

Evolutionary Models for Settlement Systems

It is a difficult but important leap from complex settlement patterns to the complex settlement systems that generated them. As geographer Peter Haggett (1965:96) points out, "one of the problems of the Christaller and Lösch models of settlement is that they are essentially static, whereas we know in reality that the central place hierarchy is complicated by time." The same is true even of settlement patterns without a conspicuous hierarchy.

Haggett discusses two kinds of models for settle-

ment evolution over time—*deterministic* and *probabilistic*. In the deterministic model, settlement is never random; it spreads gradually according to a set of definite guidelines built into the system. In the probabilistic model, on the other hand, growth is simulated by random processes, but those "are in turn restricted by the operation of certain 'rules' based on empirical observations of settlement behaviour" (Haggett 1965:97).

In our opinion, the probabilistic model offers the greater promise for Formative Mesoamerica. So many factors were involved in the founding of early villages that the full story will never be known, and although Formative behavior was not random, the interactions of countless variables frequently make it appear so on the surface. However, by empirical observation, a good many of the "rules" or "principles" that influenced settlement choices can be discovered. It is in this sense, and not the deterministic sense, that we use the term "rules" in our definition of settlement system.

In this chapter and the one that follows, we will examine the evolution of two kinds of settlement patterns characteristic of Formative Mesoamerica. One is the growth of linear patterns of villages along correspondingly linear river systems. The other is the growth of dispersed (nonlinear) patterns of villages, with a site hierarchy and detectable regularity in spacing between sites of certain tiers. These are not the only two patterns observable in early Mesoamerica, but they are two of the most interesting and contrastive.

Before proceeding to some actual cases, let us briefly consider the way a deterministic model might view these two contrasting patterns. The two models in Figure 6.6 are borrowed from Haggett's summary of Bylund's work in Sweden (Bylund 1960; Haggett 1965: Figure 4.6), and can serve as examples.

Model A illustrates the evolution of regional settlement by dispersal from a centrally located original village through four temporal stages. At T_1, only the original village exists. At T_2, four daughter communities have budded off. Each of these gives rise to two granddaughter communities at T_3, and so on. Settlement expands symmetrically in all directions at the same rate, producing a pattern too uniform to match any known Formative Mesoamerican case. Nevertheless, the model portrays the kind of growth that might in time come to include a primary center surrounded by lattices of secondary centers with associated tertiary villages. In a probabilistic model, daughter and granddaughter communities could be founded at random anywhere in the system, but factors of distance, spacing, and location would help determine whether they were likely to plateau at the level of village or grow to be regional centers. In Chapter 7, Timothy Earle analyzes such a system in the Valley of Mexico, using the nearest-neighbor statistic to discover spacing regularities at different levels of the site hierarchy. These regularities suggest that, in a nonlinear, hierarchical system, each level has its own set of "rules" or "principles," simultaneously imposed on a system that also has aspects of randomness.

Model B in Figure 6.6, although originally designed for a coastal situation, can be used to portray the growth of settlement along a linear river and its tributaries. At T_1, there is only one village

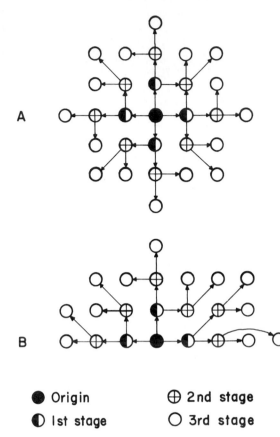

● **Origin**   ⊕ **2nd stage**
◐ **I st stage**   ○ **3rd stage**

Figure 6.6 Hypothetical models of colonization and settlement pattern evolution. (A) Dispersal from a centrally located original village through four temporal stages; (B) the growth of settlement along a linear river and its tributaries. [Redrawn from Haggett 1965:Figure 4.6, after Bylund 1960.]

on the main river. At T_2, it gives rise to three daughter communities: one upstream, one downstream, and one on a major tributary. At T_3, settlement has spread still farther upstream and downstream on the main river, and colonization of new tributaries continues. Note that not until very late in the evolution of the system are there as many villages on tributaries as on the main river. Once again, the symmetry and determinism of the model are such that the model matches no "real" pattern observed in Formative Mesoamerica.

The remainder of Chapter 6 deals with the probabilistic alternatives to this linear river model. In the section that follows, I will point out that, although T_1 communities frequently do settle in the center of the floodplain, T_2 communities are likely to occur farther from the original settlement than in Model B, with T_3 settlements filling the intervening gaps. This may be simply a way of saying that T_2 settlements could be founded at random anywhere in the system, but those that satisfied certain "principles" survived to be discovered by archeologists.

Finally, in what is perhaps the clearest example of a probabilistic approach, Robert Reynolds applies a Markovian model to the evolution of linear settlement along the Grijalva River. In that study, Reynolds is led empirically to a series of observations about spacing between villages—observations phrased as statements of probability, yet surely reflecting the kinds of "rules" or "principles" that keep complex settlement systems from being a set of wholly random processes.

Linear Stream Patterns and Riverside Settlement Rules

KENT V. FLANNERY

In many parts of Mesoamerica, Formative settlements sprang up along linear river systems, forming long strings of villages whose arrangement is quite different from the dispersed or hexagonal patterns discussed by Earle in Chapter 7. Such systems occur along the Pánuco River in Veracruz, the Atoyac River in the Valley of Oaxaca, the Grijalva River in the Central Depression of Chiapas, and many others. Although archeologists have been aware of such linear patterns for some time, few efforts have been made to search for the general rules that produced them. The Real Mesoamerican Archeologist has simply assumed, with some justification, that Formative farmers settled near rivers because there was good humid bottom land and fresh drinking water to be had there. Granting this fact, however, there are still many interesting questions to be asked about linear river settlement systems, of which four will be raised here:

1. Why are Formative villages located on a par-

ticular *side* of the river, for example, on the left bank rather than the right bank?
2. What determines the *spacing* between Formative villages sharing the same river?
3. What is the relationship between nearest-neighbor pairs of villages that are on opposite sides of the river?
4. Given that linear settlement systems are one-dimensional (as opposed to the two-dimensional dispersed or hexagonal systems studied by Earle), how does one perform *central place studies* on them? Indeed, how do central places arise in systems that have no "center"?

Principles of Bank Selection

In the late 1950s, geographer Andrew Burghardt addressed himself to one aspect of our first problem, namely "the question of why the larger river cities are on a particular bank of the river" (Burghardt 1959:305). Burghardt used the great river systems of the central United States—the Mississippi, Missouri, Ohio, and others—as his testing ground because, in that area, the drastic effects of topography were lessened and "in many locales desirable sites were available on both banks." Moreover, many of the river towns in this area were so recent that the reasons for their choice of riverbank were a matter of historical record.

Burghardt came to a number of conclusions that are of relevance to Formative Mesoamerica. Some of these might have been predicted intuitively: (*1*) that river towns are often founded as ports (in the case of major rivers), crossing points, or both; (*2*) that if the river was predominantly a routeway (as in the case of the Grijalva River in central Chiapas), port towns appeared at very regular travel distances along it; (*3*) that if it was predominantly a barrier (as in the case of the Atoyac River in central Oaxaca), towns developed on either or both banks at convenient crossing points or fords; and so on. But one principle discovered by Burghardt, which is not so intuitively obvious, may in fact be the most important for Formative Mesoamerica: (*4*) *Local factors being equal, the side of the river chosen by a town may depend on where its more distant sustaining hinterland is located.* In the case of the Midwestern rivers, towns dependent on supplies from the industrial East settled mainly on the east bank; those supported mainly by the products of the farmers and fur trappers to the west settled on the west bank. Obviously, this principle should be taken into consideration in analyzing the "catchment areas" of streamside villages (see Chapter 4, this volume).

Burghardt went on to propose two more principles, governing the competition between riverbank towns: (*5*) At a particular locale, if the original town developed on the more favorable bank, no competitor arose across the river; but if it did not, a competitor did develop and usually superseded the initial settlement; and (*6*) the larger river towns show an interesting uniformity of spacing along the rivers, which "may be considered to be a variation on the 'central place' location of towns" (Burghardt 1959:322). Thus, some of the same spacing principles underlying central place theory presumably apply to linear systems as well.

Site Hierarchy on the Linear Belize River System

A convenient example of how central place principles might apply to linear systems can be drawn from the work of Willey and his co-workers (1965) in the Belize Valley of British Honduras. The area provides a classic example of linear patterning along a river, which Willey refers to as "ribbon strip" settlement.

By the Spanish Lookout phase (Late Classic, A.D. 700–900) there had developed along the Belize River a site hierarchy which was divided by Willey and his associates into three levels of sites, as follows:

1. *Major ceremonial centers*, with sizeable steep "temple" mounds and lower "palace" platforms arranged around more than one plaza, and usually with ball courts, plain or carved stelae. This type would include such sites as Benque Viejo (Xunantunich), Cahal Pech, and Baking Pot.
2. *Minor ceremonial centers*, which have at least one pyramidal temple-type mound of small to medium size, as well as lower buildings around a single plaza or court. This type would include such sites as Actuncan, Nohoch Ek, Cayo Y, Spanish Lookout, and Barton Ramie.
3. *House-mound groups*, which lack the features of Type 2 and presumably were only residential in nature.

Type 3 settlements, as might be expected, outnumbered everything else. In addition, there were approximately twice as many Type 2 settlements (minor ceremonial centers) as Type 1 settlements (major ceremonial centers). Using this fact, and drawing on the principles of equidistant spacing as set forth in central place theory, one can construct a model for the expected arrangement of major and minor centers between Benque Viejo and Barton Ramie during the Spanish Lookout phase.

Such a model is presented in Figure 6.7(a). In this figure, we have drawn the "ribbon strip" of the Belize Valley as if it were an absolutely straight line for 26 km between the two sites just mentioned. The most efficient spacing is considered to be a model arrangement in which Type 1 settlements are placed equidistant along the river, with a pair of evenly spaced Type 2 settlements between each pair of major centers. Thus, Benque Viejo, Cahal Pech, and Baking Pot should lie 10 km apart, with minor centers every 3.3 km between them.

In Figure 6.7(b), we present the observed arrangement of Spanish Lookout sites, taken from Figure 2 of Willey *et al*. (1965). Obviously, the "ribbon strip" does not form a straight line, and there are substantial river meanders and topographic variations that our model smoothed out. In spite of these meanders and variations, the observed pattern of sites is remarkably close to the expected arrangement given in our model.

Settlement patterns in the Belize Valley therefore support Burghardt's suspicions about the applicability of central place principles to linear river systems. However, the Belize example does not date to the early village period which is our main concern in this book. Let us therefore turn back to the Formative to pursue some of Burghardt's additional questions.

The Etla Region of the Valley of Oaxaca

One region where early villages follow the linear course of a river is the northwestern, or Etla, arm of the Valley of Oaxaca (Flannery *et al*. 1970). The Etla region is in fact the upper valley of the Atoyac River, running northwest to southeast for

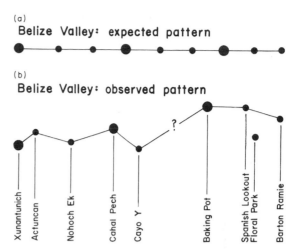

Figure 6.7 Linear settlement along the Belize River during the Spanish Lookout phase. (a) The expected pattern of major and minor ceremonial centers based on central place theory; (b) the observed pattern of Late Classic centers [based on Willey *et al*. 1965:Figure 2.]

approximately 30 km at an average elevation of 1600 m above sea level. The climate is temperate and semiarid, with 500–700 mm of annual rainfall.

The region's three major physiographic zones—high alluvium, piedmont, and mountains—already have been described in Chapter 4. Needless to say, it is the high alluvium that was the major attraction for early farmers, and the principal Early Formative villages in the Etla region occur on piedmont spurs or low hills immediately overlooking the floodplain. Since the band of alluvium is relatively narrow, these sites form a linear pattern paralleling the Atoyac.

The Atoyac is a river too small for navigation and, in the dry season, it is crossed with no difficulty. Nineteenth-century travelers report that it was swift and difficult to cross in the rainy season, however, and even today it may rise dramatically in spite of the lowering of the local water table owing to modern irrigation. In August of 1969, the Atoyac overflowed its banks, flooding parts of the city of Oaxaca, sweeping away the main bridge to Monte Albán, and making it abundantly clear why the early villagers had settled on low hills.

Site Spacing

It will certainly be some time before the expansion of Early Formative settlement in the Etla region is understood in detail, for many separate processes are involved. One general process, however, resembles the model shown in Figure 6.8. At the beginning of the Formative (T_1), the first and oldest village was founded near the Atoyac, virtually in the center of the Etla Valley. At the next stage (T_2), daughter villages were founded midway between the original parent village and the northern and southern limits of the valley. At a subsequent stage (T_3), new villages were founded midway between the original village and each of its previous (T_2) daughter communities. All were riverside villages, and the majority lay to the east side of the river. This process went on until there was a village roughly every 5 km along the river.

At least three other processes complicate the

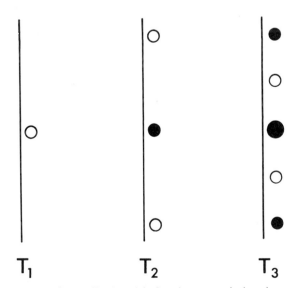

Figure 6.8 Idealized model of settlement evolution along the Atoyac River in the Etla region of the Valley of Oaxaca during three temporal phases.

model. One was an additional proliferation of very small hamlets around the original (T_1) village, San José Mogote. Some of these hamlets might more accurately be considered outlying *barrios* of the latter village, as if it were growing too fast to maintain the normal segmentation rate of its contemporary villages. Some of these outlying *barrios* survived into later periods, while others—perhaps located too near larger villages, or at inconvenient fords or crossing places on the river—disappeared after only a few centuries.

The second of these three additional processes was the colonization of localized resource areas, already mentioned in Chapter 4. Salt-making hamlets may serve as a convenient example. Some, such as Las Salinas in the eastern piedmont, lasted for only a brief part of the Early Formative. Others, like Fábrica San José, were sporadically visited during Early Formative times and became permanent settlements during the Middle Formative. Whether they are to be considered outlying *barrios* or separate communities is frequently hard to answer.

The third additional process is the colonization of major tributary streams in areas where they actually provide more water or alluvium than the main Atoyac. This process was in fact more important in the Tlacolula region of the Valley of Oaxaca during the period we are considering, and did not become a major factor in the Etla region until the Middle Formative.

For the purposes of this chapter, we will consider only those sites involved in the first process mentioned, that is, the evolution of a regularly spaced linear series of villages along the Atoyac River. As suggested earlier in this chapter, this can probably be conceptualized as a gradual reduction in the territory "owned" by each village. The original village at T_1 had available to it a strip of floodplain perhaps 30 km long. At T_2, three villages each had available a strip perhaps 10 km long. At T_3, six villages each had available a strip perhaps 5 km long, and so on.

If we examine six sites of the Late San José phase (1000–850 B.C.) between Santa Marta Etla and Tierras Largas (Figure 6.9), it will be seen that they form a north–south line with remarkably even spacing. The actual intersite distances are as follows:

Santa Marta Etla to San Lázaro Etla*	4.8 km
San Lázaro Etla to San José Mogote	5.5 km
San José Mogote to San Lorenzo Cacaotepec	4.4 km
San José Mogote to Hacienda Blanca	5.3 km
San Lorenzo Cacaotepec to Tierras Largas	5.5 km
Hacienda Blanca to Tierras Largas	4.9 km

The only pair of villages whose intervening distance deviates widely from 5 km is San Lorenzo Cacaotepec–Hacienda Blanca, and since these two villages were on opposite sides of the river at what may not have been a convenient ford, their nearness in airline kilometers may not be important (see p. 179).

We may now begin to put some questions to our data. An obvious preliminary question is "Why is spacing of villages so regular? Is it for environmental, agricultural, or social reasons?" If it is for environmental or agricultural reasons, we might expect to find some relationship between the spacing of villages and the width of the alluvial valley; that is, sites might be closer together where the alluvium is wide, and farther apart where the alluvium is narrow. If social distance is involved, we might expect uniform spacing regardless of the width of the alluvium.

Unfortunately, a sample of six sites is too small to serve as a base for any rigorous statistics. Simple inspection of Figure 6.9, however, suggests that intersite spacing remains uniform despite considerable variation in the width of the high alluvium

(from 1 km near Santa Marta Etla to more than 4 km between San Lázaro and San José Mogote).

Let us examine three of these sites in more detail: San José Mogote, Hacienda Blanca, and Tierras Largas. We will make the simplifying assumption that a line drawn across the valley midway between each pair of sites reasonably divides the alluvium into the lands "owned" by each village. It leaves each village with a strip of alluvium extending roughly 2.5 km to the north and south (see Figure 6.9). We can then calculate the number of hectares of high alluvium available to each village, as follows:

San José Mogote	± 1430 ha
Hacienda Blanca	± 400 ha*
Tierras Largas	± 645 ha

From these figures, it will be clear that spacing is uniform in spite of great disparities in hectares of land available per village.

A further calculation that can be made is the conversion of hectares into kilograms of Formative maize. For this, we will use Anne Kirkby's linear regression diagrams to obtain an estimated yield in kilograms per hectare for maize of the Late San José phase (Kirkby 1973: Figures 48a,b). According to Kirkby's figures, maize at 1000 B.C. would have had a mean cob length of about 6 cm, and a consequent yield on first-class land of about 300 kg per hectare (see also Chapter 4, this volume). This gives us the following estimated maximum productivity (assuming no fallowing) for each of our villages:

San José Mogote	± 429 metric tons
Hacienda Blanca	± 120 metric tons
Tierras Largas	± 193.5 metric tons

Finally, we can compare these figures with an estimated maize consumption of 1 metric ton per

---

*The stream running from Santa Marta to San Lorenzo is nominally a tributary of the Atoyac, but, for our purposes, it can be considered as important as the main river.

*The additional assumption made here is that the ±800 ha in this strip of alluvium was evenly divided between Hacienda Blanca and San Lorenzo Cacaotepec.

TABLE 6.1   Three Late San José Phase Villages Compared with Regard to Available Alluvium, Potential Maize
Production, and Estimated Population

Village	Hectares of alluvium available	Metric tons of maize that could be grown	Number households this could support	Actual number households estimated
San José Mogote	1430	429	429	80–120
Hacienda Blanca	400	120	120	8?
Tierras Largas	645	193.5	193	8

household (Susan Lees, personal communication) and, with our estimates of the size of these three Oaxaca villages (Marcus, Chapter 3, this volume), to produce Table 6.1.

The figures in Table 6.1 are revealing indeed, and in fact provide our most convincing argument for the primacy of social factors in the spacing of villages along the Atoyac River. Even if one assumes that, in any one year, 50% of the alluvium was fallow, no village was even close to the productive limits of its land. San José Mogote, by far the largest site in its region, probably could have survived on one-third the alluvium available to it. When one descends to hamlets of more typical size, such as Tierras Largas, it is clear that even 10% of their alluvial land would have been enough to leave them with a "ceremonial surplus." Clearly, if environmental or agricultural factors had been uppermost, these hamlets could have been spaced much closer together than they were.

I conclude, therefore, that early villages along the Atoyac River were regularly spaced for predominantly social reasons, and that 5 km approximates some minimal distance—perhaps measured in travel time—that was usually maintained between communities. My conclusion is strengthened by the fact that Robert Reynolds, in the section that follows, has discovered a similar tendency for neighboring villages to occur at modal distances along the Grijalva River during the Early Formative. The phenomenon may therefore be one that was widespread during the early village period.

It would be hasty, however, to discount environmental factors entirely. Given a modal distance of 5 km, there was still enough latitude (say, from 4.4 to 5.5 km) so that communities could take local environmental factors into account when selecting an actual site for house construction. A suitable piedmont spur, a gentle slope, the presence of a spring or a convenient flint outcrop—all these environmental factors went into site selection, but they operated at the *site catchment* level. This, then, is the point we have tried to make in Chapters 4 and 6: Social factors may set the approximate distance one must settle from his neighbors, but factors of site catchment are called into play in the selection of the exact location for settlement. Moreover, even the social factors may play a frequently unrecognized ecological role—as, for example, by causing villages to locate so far apart that they are in no danger of approaching the productive limits of their available land.

Riverbank Choice

A glance at Figure 6.9 shows that four of our six sites (including the three northernmost) are to the east of the river. South of Cacaotepec, the pattern changes, and two of three sites are to the west. Why should this be? Following Burghardt, we might propose that, agricultural factors being equal, the side of the river chosen will reflect the more distant hinterland of the site in question. This "sustaining hinterland" might include piedmont areas for wild plant collecting, mountain areas for hunting, important tributary valleys, or localized resources such as salt, flint, and pottery clay.

Such a proposal can be supported by our data.

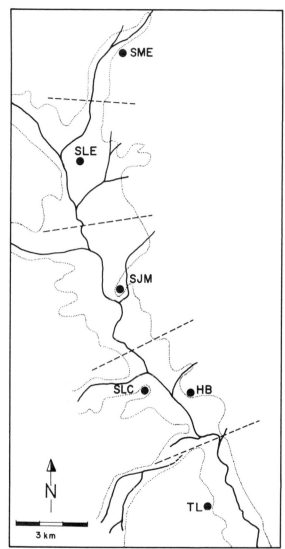

Figure 6.9 The Etla region of the Valley of Oaxaca, showing linear pattern of villages along the Atoyac River during the late San José phase (1000–850 B.C.). Dotted line indicates limit of alluvium.

From Santa Marta Etla south to Hacienda Blanca, the eastern piedmont is by far the broadest (up to 5 km) and the east bank tributaries carry the most water. The piedmont was a source of hackberry, mesquite, prickly pear, organ cactus fruit, and cottontail rabbit. Still farther to the east lies the high Sierra Juárez, a source of pine (for construction

material and firewood), acorns, black walnut, wild avocado, black zapote, white-tail deer, and collared peccary. It is a much longer trip to comparably high and forested mountains from the west side of the river. Moreover, the major salt resources of the Etla region are springs in the eastern piedmont at places like Fábrica San José, Viguera, and Las Salinas (Figure 4.6). Hence, given the broad stretches of first-class corn land on both sides of the Atoyac, the east side of the river gives best access to piedmont and mountain hinterland.

These conditions change as one passes south of San Lorenzo Cacaotepec. Here the eastern piedmont narrows drastically (to under 1 km in places) while the western piedmont expands, and major tributaries enter from the west. The Sierra Juárez swings away from the Etla region and is replaced by rocky cliffs. In addition, the important pottery clay beds of the Atzompa–Cacaotepec area are all west of the river. Good corn land being available to either side of the Atoyac, the west side now has the most desirable hinterland.

This illustrates yet another of the multivariate aspects of settlement systems. To be sure, early villages settled near rivers to have access to humid bottom land. Yet their choice of *bank* may have been related to other factors, such as hunting or wild plant collecting, which will not appear in a model based solely on agriculture.

Opposite-Bank Nearest-Neighbor Pairs

What are we to conclude about pairs of sites, such as Cacaotepec and Hacienda Blanca, whose nearest neighbor lay just across the river? Unfortunately one single, definitive answer cannot be given to this question. In the case of the two sites just mentioned, I suspect that the river was a sufficiently effective barrier (at least during the rainy season) so that, in terms of *travel time*, they may not have been "nearest neighbors" at all. The major ford for the Atoyac well may have been at San José Mogote, in which case Cacaotepec and Hacienda Blanca may simply coincide in their distance from that ford.

In other cases, where the river was a means of transportation, small sites that are opposite-bank nearest neighbors of large villages may simply be outlying *barrios* or dependent hamlets related to the larger site. Indeed, in the study that follows, Robert Reynolds discovers an interesting cyclical pattern for opposite-bank neighbors along the Grijalva River in Chiapas.

Summary

Our Etla Valley example, although illustrating many of the characteristics of a linear settlement pattern, cannot be statistically analyzed because it involves too few sites as yet. For this reason, it falls short of providing us with the set of rules that generated the pattern in the first place. However, if I had to guess at what some of those rules might eventually turn out to be, this would be my guess:

1. The first settlement in the region will locate near a good ford on the river near the center of the valley.
2. Expansion of settlement will be symmetrical upstream and downstream.
3. The first stage of expansion will take the form of daughter communities along the river, midway between the original community and the limits of the valley; the second stage will involve new villages spaced midway between the previously founded daughter communities; and so on.
4. The pattern will continue to fill in until some socially determined spacing is reached (in the Etla case, about 5 km).
5. Given that spacing, however, villages will have a latitude of perhaps .5 km upstream or downstream in order to select a suitable place for settlement.
6. Other factors being equal, villages will locate on that side of the river which affords them the best catchment area with respect to mountain hunting lands, piedmont wild plant collecting areas, and special resources like salt, flint, or pottery clay.
7. As the pattern begins to fill in, some villages may place outlying *barrios* at or near some of these special resources.
8. Through time, some of those outlying *barrios* may grow to be villages in their own right.

When the sample of sites in the Etla region is larger, it may be possible to test the validity of these "rules" by statistical means. There are a number of ways this could be done. For an example of the kind of analysis that can be carried out on a linear settlement pattern with a larger sample of sites, I refer the reader to the section by Reynolds, which follows.

Linear Settlement Systems on the Upper Grijalva River: The Application of a Markovian Model

ROBERT G.D. REYNOLDS

Introduction: Randomness and Directional Models

It is perhaps part of our inheritance from the days of astronomer-mathematician Gauss that we continue to pay homage to the great god Randomness. That elusive oracle, provided sufficient methodological sacrifice, often enables archeologists to gaze into the future via the techniques of statistical inference, in order to make predictions about the past. This is surely a tantalizing offer, one that is very hard to resist. Such predictions, so-called "tests of significance," serve in part to detach the responsibility for an error in inference from the experimenter, and reassign it to the capricious musing of Randomness. Indeed, the compulsion to seek shelter under his broad wings (while avoiding the tails) is so great that inferential statistics are often employed when the conditions upon which their validity depends are not satisfied, even in the broadest sense.

Of the many brands of inferential statistics currently on the market, the most frequently used, and consequently the most commonly misapplied, are those labeled as parametric. Since many parametric statistics were developed for use within other fields, notably astronomy, they embody assumptions that are often incompatible with the experimental frames within which they are used by anthropologists (Gould 1970). For example, Gauss developed the theory of least-square errors to analyze certain directional measurements in astronomy. However, owing to the inspired meddling of Randomness, a situation was produced in which the various small observational errors tended to cancel out each other. As a result of this divinely mediated "historical accident," Gauss proceeded to make a linear approximation that ultimately resulted in his development of a linear, rather than directional, theory of error. To quote the statistician R. A. Fisher (1953:295):

> The theory of errors was developed by Gauss primarily in relation to the needs of astronomers and surveyors, making rather accurate angular measurements. Because of this accuracy it was appropriate to develop the theory in relation to an infinite linear continuum .... The actual topological framework of such measurements, the surface of a sphere is ignored in the theory which is developed with a certain gain in simplicity.
>
> It is, therefore, of some little mathematical interest to consider how the theory would have had to be developed if the observations under discussion had had to be taken into account. The question is not however entirely academic,

for there are in nature vectors with such large natural dispersions.

As a result, techniques like this fail to implicitly take into account the directional character of the data. This distinction, perhaps, is of little consequence if orientation is not an important aspect of data to be analyzed. However, it is not uncommon to see archeologists employing these techniques in situations where methods that exploit the directional nature of the data would be eminently more suitable (Mardia 1972).

As a case in point, it would be useful to isolate directional differences in organizational structure as they are reflected in the spatial patterning of occupational units and related material remains. Directional differences, if they exist in a particular situation, can provide substantial information about the direction of population movements as well as about the forces, both cultural and environmental, that produced them. It is the purpose of this study to apply a particular type of probability model, the *double dependent Markov chain*, to the analysis of a linear Formative settlement system along the upper Grijalva River in Chiapas, Mexico, in an effort to isolate certain directional differences in settlement organization and expansion over time.

The Upper Grijalva River

The Central Depression of Chiapas is a long, irregular trough, running for 150 miles (250 km) through the center of that Mexican state. The trough is partly the result of faulting, as well as the downcutting of its soft marine limestones by the Grijalva River and its tributaries. Lying in the rain shadow of higher mountains on either side, the Depression is characterized by tropical deciduous vegetation and a marked winter dry season.

From the standpoint of Formative agriculture, the best opportunities are offered by the flat terraces of fertile alluvium along the Grijalva and its principal tributaries. Frequently the lowest terrace is permanently humid soil, and such terraces are featured prominently in the site catchments of early villages (see Chapter 4). Frost is not a problem, because no part of the river floodplain exceeds an elevation of 1800 feet (550 m) about sea level. However, the local topography is such that the river course is divided into subregions of good alluvium, separated from each other by stretches where low, thorn-forested hills come down almost to the river.

The study area selected is a 40-mile stretch where the river runs straight, and Formative settlements exhibit a striking linear pattern. From the standpoint of catchment area, of course, these early villages often were found in locations with large concentrations of humid alluvium. This study, however, addresses itself to the observed spacing between villages. Did villages along this section of the Grijalva, for example, exhibit certain directional regularities in spacing between sites; and, if so, did the nature and extent of these regularities change between the Early and Late Pre-Classic periods?

The Double Dependent Markov Process

Initially, let us assume that we are given a series of *M* observations made sequentially over time, where the value for any one observation comes from a finite set of *n* mutually exclusive and exhaustive values or states. If this sequence is purely random or unstructured, then each of the *n* states would be equally likely at every point in time. Since, by our definition, the sequence must always be in one of the *n* different states, the probability that it will be in any *one* particular state at a time *t* is always $1/n$. Consequently, a random sequence behaves as if it has no recollection of past actions, and can be described as possessing a *zero order memory*.

It is often the case, however, that the series is not a purely random one: *The value for any one observation in the sequence may be in part predictable from knowledge of the values for certain prior positions along the chain*. This situation reflects the presence of certain organizational ten-

dencies within the system generating the sequence, that place restrictions on the type of output sequences that the system can produce. As a result, a more structured or organized pattern is generated than would be expected if every observation were independent of every other. Sequences having this characteristic are said to exhibit the *Markov property* if, in addition, the sum of the probabilities of an observation being in any one of the *n* states is always equal to 1. This property is so named after the Russian mathematician A. A. Markov, who originally defined it (Kemeny and Snell 1960:1).

To illustrate, let us suppose that a Paleolithic hunter returns to camp either with or without game of some sort. In other words, we will assume that he returns in one of two states, as a success or as a failure. If we were in a position to observe the results of a subsequent number of future hunts, it would then be possible to model his hunting success in terms of a simple Markovian model. This model can be formally described in terms of a well-defined *state set* A, where

$$A = \{ \text{success, failure} \},$$

and by a *transition matrix*. The transition matrix describes the specific probabilistic relationships that hold between the states of the model. For each state in the model, it gives the probability, determined over the entire sequence of observations, that the state will be succeeded in the next time step by another of the possible model states. In our example, the specific transition matrix might look like the following:

		The state at time = $t + 1$	
		success	failure
The state at time = t	success	.79	.21
	failure	.10	.90

Note that the sum of the probabilities over each row is equivalent to 1. This is consistent with our assumption that the simplified system can be described completely by the states of the model. If this is not the case, the system exhibits behavior that cannot be described in terms of the states of the existing model. Probability models of this latter type are generally referred to as *non-Markovian*.

Given a specific Markovian transition matrix, what can it tell us about the system that it supposedly describes? In the present case, for example, the matrix might suggest to us whether or not there is a discernible pattern in either the hunter's successes or his failures. If the sequence of states is random, then each state has an equal chance of being succeeded by any other state. It corresponds here to a .5 probability in every cell. The extent to which the observed probabilities differ from those expected theoretically for a random process provides us with a measure of the deterministic aspects of the system's structure. However, the precise algorithm that will be employed to measure these differences will be described in a later section. It is left as an exercise for the reader to discern what patterns the transition matrix in our example might suggest.

The general Markov model can be subdivided into several categories designed to reflect differences in the extent and complexity of the observed Markovian behavior. For example, the state of a sequence may depend upon values at more than one previous position. The *double dependence Markov process*, as the name would suggest, applies to instances where the number of previous positions is equal to two. Employing this model, we assume that *the system's behavior is dependent upon its state at two previous points in time or space, each associated with a particular step length*. The step length of a process is therefore an indicator of the extent to which the system's present behavior is influenced by its past. If, for example, its performance at any time t was found to depend upon its behavior at times $t-1$ and $t-7$, it would be described as a double dependence Markov process, with step lengths of 1 and 6, where the length of the second step is described as an increment to the first. To state this in arche-

ological terms, the presence of a Formative village at a given point along a river system might be in part dependent on the presence of villages at distances of roughly 1 and $1 + 6$ (= 7) miles either upstream *or* downstream (where the *or* is exclusive).

In order to test the assumption that the transition probabilities characteristic of a particular sequence of events actually exhibit a significant double dependence structure, Anderson and Goodman (1957) have suggested the following test statistic:

$$\gamma = 2 \sum_{i=1}^{m} \sum_{j=1}^{m} \sum_{k=1}^{m} N_{ijk} \, log_e\left(\frac{P_{ijk}}{P_{jk}}\right)$$

where

m	=	the number of distinct states in the sequence
i	=	the state for the second-order step
j	=	the state for the first-order step
k	=	the state of the reference cell*
N_{ijk}	=	the number of times that the state of the second-order cell had a particular value i, the state of the first-order cell was j, and that of the reference cell was k.
P_{jk}	=	the observed probability that the state of the first-order cell was a particular value j, and that of the reference cell was a certain value k.
P_{ijk}	=	the observed probability that the state of the second-order step had a certain value i, while the first-order step was in state j and the reference cell had a specific value k.

This formula is ultimately related to a statistic called the *entropy function*, a measure of the information content of a system. The null hypothesis for the test is that the chain is a singly dependent process, in which case γ is distributed

*For the nature of the "cells" used in this analysis, see discussion on p. 186.

approximately as chi-squared with $m\ (m-1)^2$ degrees of freedom. The single-order Markov process can then be considered as a special case of the double dependence or second-order process. In this instance, knowledge of the state for the second-order step provides us with no more information about the behavior of the system at these step lengths than we would have gotten by observing only the state of each cell and its first-order neighbor. Thus, mathematically

$$P_{1jk} = P_{2jk} = \ldots = P_{mjk} = P_{jk}$$

for any combination of values for j and k, and the corresponding value for γ in this case would equal zero. However, to the extent that knowledge of the value for the second-order step tells us something about the states of the other two cells, the value of γ will *not* be zero.

If the calculated value deviates significantly from zero, we would accept the alternative hypothesis that the process exhibited a significant double dependence memory for the particular combination of first- and second-order step lengths tested. In other words, for linear riverine settlement systems, we would be able to say that, if γ equals zero for a second-order step length of 4 miles and a first-order step length of 1 mile, knowledge of the state of a cell 5 miles downstream, for instance, will provide us with no information about the condition of the other two cells.

It should be noted that, although significance tests provide useful guidelines in analyzing the dependence structures present within a system, one should always plot the computed values of γ against the length of the second-order step. We will refer to the resulting graph as the second-order settlement profile where extensions of this terminology to models of differing order should be obvious.

One advantage of this graphic approach lies in the realization that our Markovian paradigm is a discrete model of a continuous system. As such, by displaying our results as a connected series of discrete observations, we can readily approximate the trends for the underlying continuous system. Another advantage of a settlement profile is that, with small sample sizes (less than 50), tests of significance often will tend to produce erroneous results for a variety of reasons. Graphic analysis, however, even in the case of small samples, will still provide a useful source of information regarding the system's structure. For these reasons, we will stress the graphic approach here.

With this general framework in mind, the several limiting assumptions implicit with the syntactical structure of any Markovian model should become apparent. One critical assumption is stationarity, by which we mean that each transition probability, regardless of the number of steps, remains constant over time and space. This suggests that the Markovian model, if it is to be used as a descriptive tool, should be applied to regions where stationarity can be safely assumed. The Formative villages of the Grijalva satisfy this requirement. In addition, the model is valid only to the extent that the states or categories employed are relevant reflections of the process it is designed to describe.

Bearing in mind the basic syntactical structure of the model and its attendant limitations, how might we apply it to the study of linear settlement patterns? Although there are several more mathematically sophisticated ways in which this problem might be approached, the analysis in the following section will, like the other studies in this volume, seek the most simple and straightforward approach in order to illustrate the potential of the technique.

The Formative Settlements of the Grijalva

The New World Archaeological Foundation surveyed extensively along the Grijalva River during the 1950s, and their results have been synthesized and published by Gareth W. Lowe (1959: Figure 64). The survey does not pretend to be complete

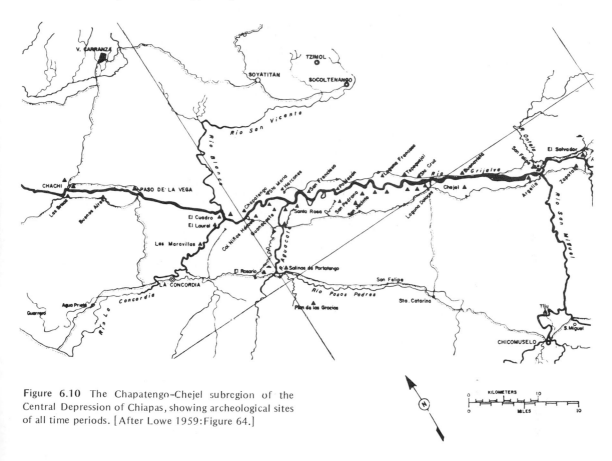

Figure 6.10 The Chapatengo–Chejel subregion of the Central Depression of Chiapas, showing archeological sites of all time periods. [After Lowe 1959:Figure 64.]

or intensive in the way that Sanders', Parsons', or Blanton's surveys in the Valley of Mexico have been (cf. Parsons 1971). Undoubtedly, many small hamlets without visible mounds remain to be discovered. However, it is unlikely that any major sites were missed. Therefore, we will take Lowe's map as a reasonable approximation of the pattern of large and medium-sized villages along the Grijalva River during the Formative.

The most extensive linear pattern of sites occurs along a 40-mile segment of the Grijalva, from Las Brisas upstream to Laguna Dolores (Figure 6.10). This 40-mile segment, from which the data was taken, corresponds roughly (though not exactly) to Lowe's Chapatengo–Chejel subregion, which he treats as partly distinct from other subregions upstream and downstream. It is within this geographical subregion that we wish to apply our Markovian model in an attempt to detect directional regularities in the observed settlement pattern.

Lowe used only two chronological periods in his 1959 paper. His "Early Pre-Classic" (1000–500 B.C.) corresponds to the phases now called Chiapa I–III, and his "Late Pre-Classic" (500 B.C.–A.D. 300) corresponds to Chiapa IV–VII. Obviously, it would help if this finer chronology had been available at the time of Lowe's paper, although a number of sites were occupied through many consecutive phases of the sequence. Seven sites in the 40-mile strip were occupied in Lowe's

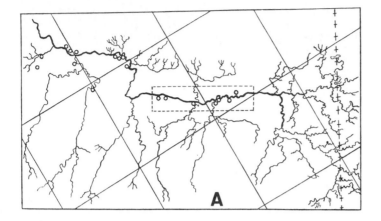

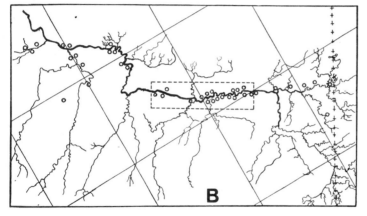

Figure 6.11 Pre-Classic villages along the Grijalva River in central Chiapas. (A) Early Pre-Classic; (B) Late Pre-Classic. The area studied by means of the Markov model is outlined. [After Lowe 1959:Figures 3–4, with modifications as indicated in the footnote on p. 186 of this chapter.]

Early Pre-Classic, while 18 (including the previous 7)* were occupied during his Late Pre-Classic (Figure 6.11). In spite of the unrefined chronology, directional patterns do exist in the data and can be isolated via the Markov model. This allows us to contemplate how much richer the results

would have been, given a more complete and intensive survey using a finer chronological sequence.

Having initially located the sites, the study area was then partitioned into 40 distinct cells, each 1 mile long. The number of sites for each period, as well as the side of the river on which they were situated, was then recorded for every cell. Two distinct classification systems based upon these variables were used to generate several linear sequences, each of which described a somewhat different aspect of the settlement system.

At first, for example, each 1-mile-long cell was coded as 0 if it contained no sites; as a 1 if it contained one site; and so on. In the second classification scheme, the side of the river on which the site was located was incorporated into the classi-

*Lowe's original maps (1959: Figures 3–4) do show two Early Pre-Classic sites (Las Brisas and El Cuadro) as unoccupied during Late Pre-Classic. This was, however, before the ceramic sequence was as well-known as it is now. Flannery (personal communication) reports that, in subsequent conversations with members of the New World Archaeological Foundation, he was given the impression that there is sufficient (albeit greatly reduced) later occupation at these sites so that they should be taken into account in terms of the "memory of the system" for the purposes of this analysis. I have followed Flannery's suggestion in this regard.

fication. If the cell had one site located to the south of the river, it was designated by a 1. In those instances where the site was found to the north of the river, the cell was designated with a 2, and so on. It should be noted that the values of γ (and therefore the results of the analysis) are independent of the specific numbers employed to designate categories.

Since the double dependence model, as we have described it, is essentially undirectional, we can use this to our advantage in the following way. Each sequence was examined twice for the double dependence property. In the first pass, the initial step (α) was fixed at -1, and the second step (β) was set to vary between -1 and -12, where the minus sign refers to the downstream direction. A more complete double dependence model would consist of $-\alpha$ for the first step, and $-(\alpha + \beta)$ for the second, where both α and β are allowed to vary. However, the present model obtained by setting α equal to -1 was considered sufficient at this level of investigation.

The analysis was then repeated where the signs of the step lengths were changed from negative to positive, such that $\alpha = +1$ and β varied from $+1$ to $+12$. Here, the plus sign refers to the upstream direction. Thus, while the first approach measures the average degree of association between the state of each 1-mile-long cell and the corresponding states of its neighboring cells at differing distances downstream, the latter measures its average association with sites upstream. If the location of all villages within a settlement system is influenced to the same degree by their neighbors in either direction, then the respective γ's for the two analyses should be approximately equivalent. This situation is often, but not always, characteristic of initial agricultural settlement within a region. However, as certain sites emerge as dominant regional centers, new settlements are more apt to align themselves relative to them, inducing certain asymmetries into the settlement structure. More generally, asymmetries are likely to arise as a result of any factor that favors or necessitates alignment relative to existing sites or environmental features.

Early Pre-Classic

The settlement sequence for the Early Pre-Classic, generated by assigning to each 1-mile-long cell a state equivalent to the number of sites found within it, was analyzed initially using the γ formula. The results, given in Figure 6.12, indicate that the associational patterns for both the upstream and downstream regions were almost equivalent. In neither case was γ large enough to indicate the presence of a major double dependence structure for any second-order step. In other words, the sequence of states generated by observing only the spacing between existing sites in the Early Pre-Classic does not appear to exhibit any notable double dependence properties.

The situation is altered somewhat if we classify our cells in terms of both (*1*) the number of sites present, and (*2*) the side of the river on which they are located. The results of the analysis for this sequence in the Early Pre-Classic are given in Figure 6.13. Again, no major directional differences (upstream versus downstream) were observed. However, owing to the addition of the sidedness criteria to our classificatory scheme, we now have evidence of a marked double dependence process at second-order steps of both 3 and 10 miles, with a lesser peak at 6 miles. However, these values alone do not tell us what the patterns are. The value for each second-order step refers to the entire transition matrix for that step. Inspection of this matrix will allow us generally to determine exactly what portion is nonrandom and, therefore, what pattern is important in producing the high value of γ observed. It should be noted here as well that, in *all* the observed patterns, the first-order neighbor (adjacent cell) was never occupied. Since the results differ then only in terms of the length of the second-order step, we will compare them only on this basis. The length of the second-order step also will be implicitly taken to represent the distance from one colonized site to another, since the major patterns also were all consistent in this regard.

Whereas spacing between sites alone did not sug-

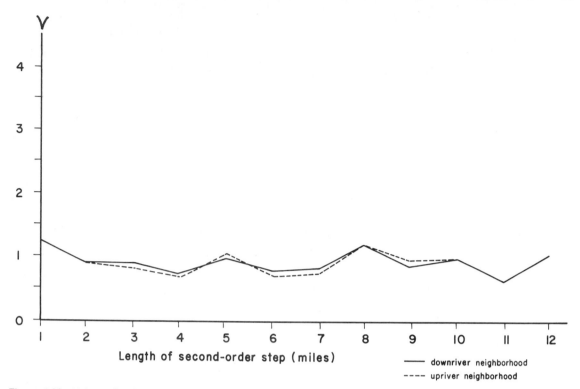

Figure 6.12 Values of γ for the Early Pre-Classic settlement sequence where the side of the river on which settlement occurred is ignored. The length of the first-order step is set equal to 1, with the second varied sequentially from 1 to 12 miles.

gest any patterned nonrandom behavior, the sidedness criteria incorporated into the model the fact that the majority of Early Pre-Classic sites were found on the south side of the river where "the plain lands are the widest" (Lowe 1959:45). As a result, Early Pre-Classic settlements seem to be found generally on the south side of the river at predictable frequencies. Occupied villages were bordered on both sides by unoccupied 1-mile-long cells, but there was likely to be another village on the same side of the river at a distance of either 4, 7, or 11 miles (7, 12, or 19 km). This pattern might represent, in part, a systematic adaptation to certain cyclical patterns in the natural environment and/or an attempt to regulate interaction between sites. The latter explanation seems more likely in this case, since the riverine environment is

reasonably homogeneous along this 40-mile section of the Grijalva.

It should be clear at this point that our approach need not be thought of as a statistical tool per se but, rather, as a translating device—one that takes a sequence or string of symbols written in an unfamiliar language and breaks it down into a set of basic spatial patterns. In doing so, informationally redundant aspects of the string are removed as well. For example, it was found that the dependence structure was equivalent for both the upstream and downstream regions of the Grijalva. This symmetry makes it possible to describe the entire sequence in terms of the spatial relations found in only one of the regions.

It also can be noted here that the basic patterns detected by the double dependence model are not

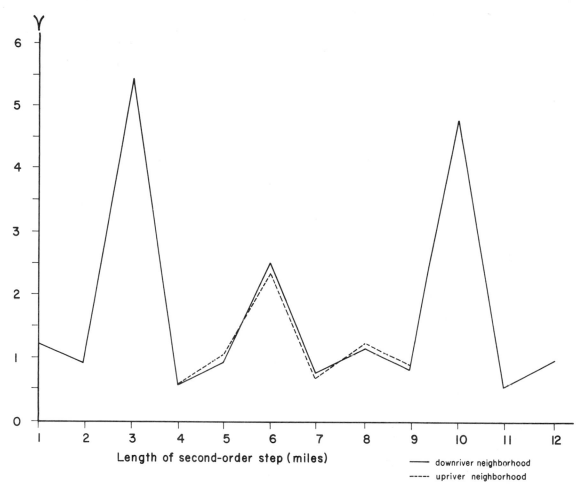

Figure 6.13 Values of γ for the Early Pre-Classic settlement sequence where the side of the river on which sites were located is incorporated into the model. The length of the first-order step is set equal to 1, with the second varied sequentially from 1 to 12 miles.

necessarily the only type to be found in the string. The model is designed to check for a specific type of spatial relation, one in which the state of a cell is associated with the states of two neighboring cells. It is similar, then, to a device that searches an English sentence for a specific phoneme or morpheme. To isolate all of the phonemes within the sentence, it might be necessary to execute a complementary search through the space, using several different devices. Analogously, a more thorough

study of settlement pattern would entail the sequential application of several Markov models of different order, in addition to that of double dependence.

Late Pre-Classic

Given the results for the Early Pre-Classic, the same techniques were employed to analyze the spatial distribution on the 11 new sites added to the system in the Late Pre-Classic. Since these sites

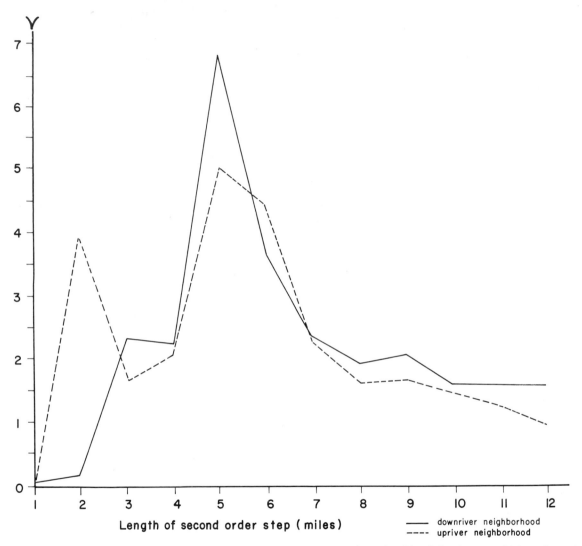

Figure 6.14 Values of γ for the Late Pre-Classic settlement sequence where the side of the river on which settlement occurred is ignored. The length of the first-order step is set equal to 1, with the second varied sequentially from 1 to 12 miles.

were being embedded into a preexisting system, certain directional asymmetries or preferred orientations might be expected. Indeed, for the first sequence where each cell was assigned a state equal to the number of new sites found within it, this is exactly what occurs.

As illustrated in Figure 6.14, two prominent double dependence processes were manifested for the upstream region, and one for its downstream counterpart. While both the upstream and downstream regions exhibited peaks at a second-order step of 5 miles, the former had an additional peak at a step length of 2 miles. In archeological terms, new villages were more likely than not to be bordered by an unoccupied area 1 mile long on either side, and by another new village at approx-

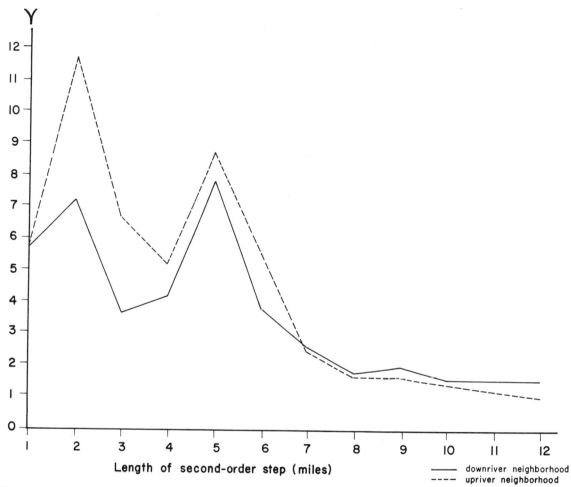

Figure 6.15 Values of γ for the Late Pre-Classic settlement sequence where the side of the river on which sites were located was incorporated into the model. The length of the first-order step is set equal to 1, with the second varied sequentially from 1 to 12 miles.

imately 6 miles upstream or downstream. This recalls similar trends in the Early Pre-Classic, when villages were likely to occur at approximately 6–7-mile intervals on the same side of the river.

As indicated earlier, not only did the patterns of new settlements in the Late Pre-Classic retain aspects of the earlier period, but new spatial relationships also became apparent. In particular, new villages often were associated with adjacent new settlements 3 miles upstream on either side of the river. This suggests not only closer packing of new

sites but a general upstream movement of population as well.

Considering only the number of sites per cell, this closer packing of new sites was observed only with reference to the upstream neighborhood. However, analysis of the sequence, produced by incorporating the side of the river on which the sites were located into the model, demonstrated the presence of a corresponding downstream peak at a second-order step length of 2 (see Figure 6.15). This pattern is much weaker than its upstream counterpart in that it is side-specific. In particular, these downstream sites were found predominantly on the opposite side of the river. This suggests that more restrictions, either cultural or environmental, were placed upon downstream as opposed to upstream colonization during this period.

Conclusions

Early Pre-Classic settlement along the Grijalva River in the Chapatengo–Chejel subregion of the Central Depression of Chiapas displays several patterns characteristic of a phase of initial agricultural settlement within a region: Expansion probably was symmetrical upstream and downstream from a core area, suggesting that neighboring villages to either side were of equal influence. No major directional trends were noted at this stage of development, but some possible spacing rules emerged. No new village was ever founded within a mile of an existing village, and there were likely to be neighboring villages on the same side of the river (south) at distances of 4, 7, and 11 miles, both upstream and downstream.

Although several of the spacing relations exhibited in the Early Pre-Classic also were evident in the spacing of new sites in the Late Pre-Classic, certain new patterns became apparent. These include closer packing between villages, as well as settlement on alternate sides of the river. These new patterns were perhaps responses to increased population density in the region. Any tendency for such close packing to produce strained relations between neighboring communities was perhaps offset partly by a corresponding tendency for those closely spaced sites to be located on alternate sides of the river.* This is true especially for the downstream neighborhood. New villages also were likely to be associated with another new vil-

*Cf. Flannery's discussion of Hacienda Blanca and San Lorenzo Cacaotepec, Oaxaca, in the previous section (pp. 177–179).

lage approximately 3 miles upstream, located on either side of the river; finer chronology might show one member of each of these pairs to be the daughter community of the other.

It also is apparent that fewer restrictions were placed on the packing of sites in the upstream neighborhood. This is perhaps the result of movement into previously unsettled areas, and suggests an actual upstream movement of population, a trend that also is supported by Lowe's maps of the Upper Tributaries subregion (Lowe 1959: Figures 4 and 64), which was virtually uncolonized until Late Pre-Classic times. In sum, the double dependence Markov processes revealed by this analysis indicate that the pattern of new Late Pre-Classic villages is the result of the incorporation of several new patterns of spatial behavior into the system's existing locational repertoire. These new patterns are perhaps external manifestations of the changing intervillage relations brought about by an expanding population.

The reader, at this point, should be forewarned. Given the incomplete nature of the data, these results can be classified as only tentative. As a more detailed specification of the settlement system is produced, certain new patterns may appear while others might be discarded altogether. The point of this exercise, after all, is not to provide a conclusive and final explanation for Formative settlement along the Grijalva, but to demonstrate a methodology using "real" archeological data. In addition, we hope to suggest that it is not always necessary to pay methodological tribute to the dictates of Randomness in order to analyze statistically a data set. Randomness, although a beneficent deity when provided with the proper sacrifice, is often too vain to realize when he is not needed.

Evaluation of the Method

This research has tried to illustrate only one of several ways in which particular types of probability models might be used to describe settlement patterns. In doing so, certain inherent advantages associated with this type of approach were emphasized. In general, it provides a fairly rigorous formal framework within which trends in settlement patterns for different areas might be described, and in turn compared. It is applicable even when the surveys that generate these patterns are less than ideal. Yet the framework is flexible enough to allow for the elimination of descriptive redundancy and for the incorporation of directional considerations into the model as well.

References

Anderson, T. W., and L. A. Goodman
    1957   Statistical inference about Markov chains. *Annals of Mathematics and Statistics* 28:89–110.

Blanton, R. E.
    1972   Prehispanic settlement patterns of the Ixtapalapa peninsula region, Mexico. *Occasional Papers in Anthropology* No. 6. Dept. of Anthropology, Pennsylvania State University, University Park.

Burghardt, A. F.
    1959   The location of river towns in the central lowland of the United States. *Annals of the Association of American Geographers* 49:305–323.

Bylund, E.
    1960   Theoretical considerations regarding the distribution of settlement in inner north Sweden. *Geografiska Annaler* 42:225–231.

Christaller, W.
    1933   *Die zentralen orte in Süddeutschland*. Jena: Karl Zeiss.

Coe, M. D.
    1961   La Victoria: An early site on the Pacific coast of Guatemala. *Papers of the Peabody Museum of Archaeology and Ethnology* Vol. LIII. Harvard University, Cambridge, Mass.

Coe, M. D., and K. V. Flannery
    1967   Early cultures and human ecology in south coastal Guatemala. *Smithsonian Contributions to Anthropology* No. 3. Washington, D.C.

Fisher, R. A.
    1953   Dispersion on a sphere. *Proceedings of the Royal Society of London* A 217:295–305.

Flannery, K. V.
    1972a   The origins of the village as a settlement type in Mesoamerica and the Near East: A comparative study. In *Man, settlement, and urbanism*, edited by P. J. Ucko, R. Tringham, and G. W. Dimbleby. London: G. Duckworth. Pp. 23–53.
    1972b   The cultural evolution of civilizations. *Annual Review of Ecology and Systematics* 3:399–426.

Flannery, K. V., M. Winter, S. Lees, J. Neely, J. Schoenwetter, S. Kitchen, and J. C. Wheeler
    1970   Preliminary archeological investigations in the Valley of Oaxaca, Mexico, 1966–1969. Mimeographed preliminary report. Ann Arbor, Mich.

Gould, P. R.
    1970   Is *Statistix inferens* the geographical name for a wild goose? *Economic Geography* 46:439–448.

Green, D. F. and G. W. Lowe
    1967   Altamira and Padre Piedra: Early preclassic sites in Chiapas, Mexico. *Papers of the New World Archaeological Foundation* No. 20, Provo, Utah.

Haggett, P.
    1965   *Locational analysis in human geography*. London: Edward Arnold.

Johnson, G. A.
    1972   A test of the utility of central place theory in archaeology. In *Man, settlement, and urbanism*, edited by P. J. Ucko, R. Tringham, and G. W. Dimbleby. London: G. Duckworth. Pp. 769–785.

Kemeny, J. G., and J. L. Snell
    1960   *Finite Markov chains*. New York: D. Van Nostrand.

Kirkby, A. V. T.
    1973   The use of land and water resources in the past and present Valley of Oaxaca, Mexico. *Memoirs* No. 5. Museum of Anthropology, University of Michigan, Ann Arbor.

Lowe, G. W.
    1959   Archaeological exploration of the upper Grijalva River, Chiapas, Mexico. *Papers of the New World Archaeological Foundation* No. 2 (Pub. no. 3). Provo, Utah.
    1966   Current research in southeastern Mesoamerica. *American Antiquity* 31(3):453–463.

Lorenzo, J. L.
    1955   Los concheros de la costa de Chiapas. *Anales del Instituto Nacional de Antropología e Historia* 7(36):41–50. Mexico, D.F.

Lösch, A.
    1954   *The economics of location*. New Haven, Conn.: Yale University Press.
MacNeish, R. S.
    1964   Ancient Mesoamerican civilization. *Science* 143:531–537.
    1969   Comments delivered at symposium, "The Origins of the Village," Annual Meeting of the Society for American Archaeology, Milwaukee, Wisconsin, May 1969.
MacNeish, R. S., F. A. Peterson, and K. V. Flannery
    1970   *The prehistory of the Tehuacán Valley*. Vol. 3. *Ceramics*. Austin: University of Texas Press.
Marcus, J.
    1973   Territorial organization of the lowland Classic Maya. *Science* 180:911–916.
    1974   An epigraphic approach to the territorial organizaton of the lowland Classic Maya. Unpublished Ph.D. thesis, Harvard University, Cambridge, Mass.
Mardia, K. V.
    1972   *Statistics of directional data*. New York: Academic Press.
Parsons, J. R.
    1971   Prehistoric settlement patterns in the Texcoco region, Mexico. *Memoirs* No. 3. Museum of Anthropology, University of Michigan, Ann Arbor.
    1972   Archaeological settlement patterns. *Annual Review of Anthropology* 1:127–150.
Sanders, W. T.
    1956   The central Mexican symbiotic area: A study in prehistoric settlement patterns. In *Prehistoric settlement patterns in the New World*, edited by G. R. Willey. *Viking Fund Publications in Anthropology* No. 23. New York: Wenner–Gren. Pp. 115–127.
Tolstoy, P., and S. K. Fish
    1973   Excavations at Coapexco, 1973. Mimeographed preliminary report. Dept. of Anthropology, Queens College (C.U.N.Y.), New York.
Vita-Finzi, C., and E. S. Higgs
    1970   Prehistoric economy in the Mt. Carmel area of Palestine: Site catchment analysis. *Proceedings of the Prehistoric Society* 36:1–37.
Willey, G. R., W. R. Bullard, Jr., J. B. Glass, and J. C. Gifford
    1965   Prehistoric Maya settlements in the Belize Valley. *Papers of the Peabody Museum of Archeology and Ethnology* Vol. LIV. Harvard University, Cambridge, Mass.

Chapter 7

ANALYSIS ON THE REGIONAL LEVEL: PART II

Introduction

In the preceding chapter, we discussed the distribution of early Mesoamerican villages along linear river courses, such as the Atoyac and the Grijalva. We introduced the notion that sociopolitical factors, as opposed to environmental variables, played a primary role in establishing the spacing intervals between these villages. At the same time, we conceded that, once the spacing interval was set, environmental factors presumably helped to determine the location of the village within its catchment area. Finally, we suggested a difficult but necessary search for the rules on which Formative settlement systems were based.

Of course, not all early Mesoamerican villages developed along linear streams. Outside of the great sluggish river drainages of the tropical lowlands—the Pánuco, Papaloapan, Coatzacoalcos, Grijalva, Usumacinta, and Belize, to mention a few—such "ribbon strip" settlements were probably the exception rather than the rule. Scores of

highland valleys had settlement patterns in which the villages lay dispersed in every direction. Moreover, even in the riverine lowlands, settlement hierarchies can violate the linear pattern: Although the hamlets and villages follow stream courses, the regional administrative centers can form patterns that are independent and nonlinear.

In this chapter, Timothy Earle explores one way of analyzing such nonlinear Formative settlement patterns. The technique he uses is nearest-neighbor analysis, a method borrowed from ecologists and human geographers. In Chapter 5, Stephen Plog touched briefly on the utility of nearest-neighbor analysis for determining the overall tendency for sites in a newly surveyed region to be clustered, random, or evenly spaced. But nearest-neighbor analysis becomes an even more effective tool once the survey has been done and the sites have been classified by time period and settlement type. At that point, one can begin to speak of the nearest-neighbor coefficient for "Early Formative villages," "Toltec hamlets," or "Late Classic administrative centers." Such analysis points up changes through time which may not be apparent from simple, inductive, "eyeball" inspection of the data. With nearest-neighbor analysis, we may be able to see that, in a given area, for example, early settlements are randomly located with regard to each other, but with the pattern becoming increasingly more evenly spaced as time goes on. Or we may be able to observe a pattern form among the dependencies of a major regional center, where, in previous periods, there was little regularity in the data.

In the section that follows, Earle applies nearest-neighbor analysis to two areas with early Mesoamerican villages. The first is the Texcoco-Ixtapalapa-Chalco region of the Valley of Mexico, which has been intensively surveyed by J. R. Parsons (1971) and R. E. Blanton (1972). In this area, the "total universe" of sites was recovered insofar as humanly possible, allowing very interesting analyses to be made. Earle starts with the pattern at 850 B.C., clearly within the time period of our interest, and traces it to the Terminal Formative (250 B.C.–A.D. 100). Villages of the latter period do not really qualify as "early," but this extension into later times is essential to Earle's analysis of the trends through time, and hence justified.

To contrast with the high, cool, and semiarid Valley of Mexico, Earle chooses as his second region the hot, humid, tropical lowlands of the southern Gulf Coast. In this area, sometimes lovingly referred to as the "Olmec heartland," the entire chronological span covered by Earle falls within the period of our interest (1500–500 B.C.). In contrast to the Valley of Mexico, the Olmec region has been subjected to only one intensive and systematic published survey, that of Edward Sisson (1970). In other parts of the southern Veracruz-Tabasco region, only incomplete surveys and isolated "major sites" have been published. However, by using Sisson's survey as a clue to hamlet and village level settlement, and analyzing the major regional centers in their own right, Earle succeeds in showing some interesting patterns. Indeed, he finds some indications of the same principles that operated in the far distant and environmentally different Valley of Mexico during a somewhat later period.

Because of the "boundary effect" mentioned in Earle's definition of nearest-neighbor statistics, the kind of analysis he employs for the Valley of Mexico requires recovery of the total universe of sites within large blocks of territory. In Chapter 8, Elizabeth Brumfiel subjects the same region to a different form of analysis, which can be done even with quadrat samples.

A Nearest-Neighbor Analysis of Two Formative Settlement Systems

TIMOTHY K. EARLE

Introduction

This study examines Formative settlement patterns in two contrasting environmental regions in Mesoamerica, the Valley of Mexico and the southern Veracruz-Tabasco lowlands. In both regions, the settlement pattern seems to have been generated by a hierarchical settlement system: The founding and spacing of hamlets and small villages followed one set of rules, the growth and spacing of large villages or regional centers followed another. Some of the similarities are so striking as to suggest a set of general rules for hierarchical settlement systems, rules that are not restricted to any one environment. The existence of these similarities, in turn, makes it easier to detect contrasts that probably are related to differences between environmental zones, with different agricultural practices as an intervening variable.

Before examining the archeological data, we will consider briefly the methodology used, its strengths and its shortcomings, and the theoretical framework in which the results are to be interpreted. Of particular relevance to settlement pattern studies are various models from locational geography and ecology which generate distributions that deviate from random. A random distribution means simply that all individuals have an equal probability of occurring at any given point on a surface plane. Deviation from random can be of two types: (*1*) Individuals can be more clustered than expected in a random distribution, with the extreme case occurring when all individuals are located at one point; and (*2*) Individuals can be more regularly spaced than expected, with maximum regularity occurring when straight lines drawn between all individuals form hexagonal patterns (see Figure 7.1). Clustered distribution is a possible result of the mutual attraction of individuals toward a strategic (necessary and localized) resource, or the nature of the generative process where new individuals originate from one or more parent individuals already located in space. In contrast, regular distribution is usually caused by the mutual antagonism of individuals upon each other's location. It is evident that a wide range of models based on varying assumptions of causal factors can be used to generate nonrandom spacing. The purpose of this study is not to examine any specific model but, rather, to investigate a means by which to describe site distribution so that the applicability of a given model can be tested in an archeological case.

Figure 7.1 Models for three types of distributions. (a) Regular; (b) random; (c) clustered. [Redrawn from Haggett 1965:Figure 4.1.]

The Nearest-Neighbor Statistic

One method of analyzing distributions that deviate from random is by the use of the *nearest-neighbor statistic*. This statistic originally was developed by ecologists to discover nonrandom distributions of individuals in plant and animal populations. Nearest-neighbor is a descriptive statistic, and therefore cannot itself offer an explanation. It simply describes a scatter of points as being either random or nonrandom. If nonrandom, it measures the degree and direction of nonrandomness.

As originally described by Clark and Evans (1954), the distance to nearest neighbor (closest individual in any direction to a given individual) is a direct measure of spacing. The nearest-neighbor statistic expresses departure from randomness as the ratio (R) of the mean distance observed $(\bar{r}_A)$ for the study population, to the mean distance expected $(\bar{r}_E)$ for a randomly distributed population of a given density:

$$R = \frac{\bar{r}_A}{\bar{r}_E}$$

The factor $\bar{r}_E$ is derived from the *Poisson distribution*, which gives the probabilities with which randomly spaced events or objects will occur 0, 1, 2, 3, 4 (and so forth) times within a given period of time or unit of space. These probabilities are calculated using as a parameter only the average number of occurrences per unit time or space. For example, a given valley may experience an average of one flood per year and have an average of three villages per square kilometer. The Poisson distribution then allows the calculation of the probabilities of having a year with 0, 1, 2, 3, etc. floods, or of surveying a square kilometer and finding 0, 1, 2, 3, 4, 5, etc. villages. It is assumed in these calculations that the spacing of floods through time, and of villages over the area, are random. As the average number of events or objects becomes large, the Poisson distribution approaches the form of a normal distribution.

As derived from the Poisson distribution, $\bar{r}_E$ is determined entirely by density (*rho*):

$$\bar{r}_E = \frac{1}{2\sqrt{\rho}}$$

The density used to determine $\bar{r}_E$ should be derived in some independent manner, like quadrat sampling, from the study population. This density can be measured in any specified units, but these units must correspond to those used to measure distance to nearest neighbor (r).

As derived, the nearest-neighbor ratio has a definite and limited range of continuous variability from 0.0 to 2.1491. For the case of maximum aggregation, where all individuals are located at one locus, distance to nearest neighbor will be zero ($R = 0$). For a randomly distributed population, expected and observed will be identical by definition ($R = 1$). For maximum spacing, all individuals will be arranged in an even, hexagonally spaced pattern, and, as shown by Clark and Evans (1954, Appendix), $R = 1.0746/\sqrt{\rho} = 2.1491$. Therefore, $R = 1$ is a watershed, with values less than 1 showing aggregation and those greater than 1 showing regular spacing. For a more detailed discussion of the nearest-neighbor statistic and various tests for significance of results, the reader is referred to Clark and Evans' original paper (1954).*

---

*For example, Clark and Evans recommend the use of an *F* distribution to test significance of differences between values of *R* of several populations, and the use of a normal curve to test significance of difference between $\bar{r}_A$ and $\bar{r}_E$ of a single population.

Selected Applications of Nearest-Neighbor Analysis

Plant Studies

The object of Clark and Evans' (1954) pioneer work was to study the distribution of three grassland plant species in an abandoned field of several acres in lower Michigan. Earlier ecological studies often had assumed that individual plants of a species would be randomly distributed within a uniform area. This, however, proved not to be the case. The R for all three species showed a statistically significant trend towards aggregation. In contrast, individual trees from a closed canopy, oak–hickory woodlot nearby showed a more regular than random distribution. As a final check of the method, Clark and Evans also determined the ratio for a synthetic random distribution obtained by plotting points whose coordinates were selected from a table of random numbers. As predicted, the synthetic random sample showed no significant departure from random expectation.

Clark and Evans concluded that the causes of aggregation in the grassland species lay in the nature of plant reproduction and dispersal, as well as minor but significant variations in ecological condition within the study area. The regular spacing observed for trees would be the result of competition in the canopy for light.

There have been various attempts to extend the method in plant studies (Clark and Evans 1955; Clark 1956; Evans 1969), but results have not been adequately reported. Pielou's (1959, 1961) work with distance from randomly selected points to nearest neighbor, and between a plant and nearest neighbor of a different (but specific) species, will just be mentioned in passing since

TABLE 7.1   Results of Clark and Evans (1954) Pioneer Study

Statistic	Synthetic random	*Solidago*	*Liatris*	*Lespedeza*	Forest trees
R	.9635	.7266	.5541	.4885	1.371

TABLE 7.2 Grocery Store Spacing in Lansing, Michigan[a]

Time period	1900	1910	1920	1930	1940	1950	1960
R	1.074	.673	.658	.772	.792	.841	.998

[a]From Getis 1964.

they are important studies but not of immediate relevance to the work here.

Animal Studies

In animal studies, the application of the nearest-neighbor statistic has given some provocative results. Following a suggestion by Clark (1956:374) that wider than expected spacing in the distribution of burrows was "a consequence of the social behavior of prairie dogs," Hansen and Remmenga (1961) studied the distribution of individuals within a population of pocket gophers. Since this species is strongly territorial, it was suggested that the pattern of distribution might be more regular than expected in a random distribution. Although the overall distribution did not deviate remarkably from a random expected pattern, it was shown that "the tendency towards regular spacing was indicated where densities were highest and a tendency towards contagious distribution at the lowest density" (Hansen and Remmenga 1961:813).

Miller and Stephen's (1966) study of sandhill cranes is an ingenious use of the nearest-neighbor statistic. Flocks of the cranes were photographed from an airplane as they fed in open agricultural fields. It is obvious even to the casual observer that, during feeding, cranes do not distribute themselves randomly over an area, even though cultivated fields may represent a simple, uniform habitat. Cranes show marked aggregation into flocks. But of more interest is the pattern *within* the flock. These birds maintain a standard distance of 5 to 6 feet to nearest neighbor, regardless of flock size. In all cases but one, departure from randomness was toward regular spacing. In 26 of 29 flocks, this departure is statistically significant. This trend toward regular spacing, however, varies in strength inversely with flock size. As flocks increase in size, density decreases and R approaches 1. Miller and Stephen conclude that this is the result of subgroups forming within the flock. These results show variation in pattern at three distinct levels of analysis: (*1*) the flock within the total feeding zone; (*2*) the large flock consisting of subflocks; and (*3*) small flocks equivalent to subflocks. From Level 1 to Level 3, there is observed a definite increase in regular spacing.

Locational Geography

Nearest-neighbor analysis was introduced into geography in the early 1960s as a measure of the spacing of human activities. The work of Dacey (1962) and King (1962) stand out as innovative in their field, but they both have been more interested in studying new variations of the method than investigating actual problems of distribution. For a review of this work, see King (1969).

Of greater use to archeologists is Getis' (1964) study of grocery store spacing in Lansing, Michigan, between 1900 and 1960. The development of store location shows a striking trend (see Table 7.2). Getis interprets this table as showing an initial period of random location, before clear economic patterns became established during the next 20 years. The marked trend away from aggregation after the 1920s is seen as a result of better transportation, which would allow service centers to decentralize. This study demonstrates the potential for applying nearest-neighbor analysis to the investigation of patterns that change through time.

The Archeological Potential of
Nearest-Neighbor Analysis

Explicit in the concept of archeological settlement pattern studies is the assumption that a pattern does exist, if one can detect it. Nearest-neighbor analysis offers a high degree of objectivity for the description of distributions that may be mapped as points. Such phenomena include a wide array of human activities that occur at discrete loci—work areas, houses, communities, specialized service centers, cities, and so forth. The distribution of such activity loci can be described for a functional level, or even for the relationship between levels (see Pielou 1961). It is crucial in any kind of research to be able to describe an observed phenomenon on an objective scale so that it can then be compared with a particular model representing some theoretical statement.

The basic difficulty with nearest-neighbor analysis is that the expected mean distance to nearest neighbor ($\bar{r}_E$) is derived for an *infinite* and *uniform* plane. These assumptions should be met if the ratio is to be meaningful. Areas of all natural distribution are, of course, bounded. Therefore, the strategy should be to select in some objective manner a sample area within the boundaries of distribution. Within this selected area, the density of individuals should be computed and, for the points in the sample, the distance to nearest neighbor (whether within or outside the sample area) should be measured. In cases studied by archeologists, the total area that is intensively surveyed is usually quite small. In order to increase sample sizes, there is a desire to use all sites located in the survey. By using sites found near the periphery of the survey area, however, distance to nearest neighbor may be artificially increased. As a result, the nearest-neighbor ratio will show sites to be more regularly spaced than is actually the case.

Let it be assumed that, in many cases, a sample can be selected and its nearest-neighbor ratio computed. As noted in the original paper by Clark and Evans, a standard result is to show an aggregation of individuals. This can be the result of either the mutual attraction of sites on each other, or the attraction of sites independently toward an unevenly distributed resource. In order to test these alternative hypotheses, the survey area should be stratified by environmental or resource zones. This is an attempt to approximate a uniform plane, but, in the process, it reduces the sample sizes. Sample sizes will always affect the reliability of the ratio. The exact effect, however, has not yet been adequately tested.

A final potential problem is the familiar one of "missing data." Especially with the small sample sizes normal in archeology, the inability to locate even a few sites of a given hierarchical level may have dramatic effects on the nearest-neighbor ratio. Where surveys are not uniform, the problem becomes accentuated. For example, a normal result with such discontinuities is a high "aggregation" of lower-level sites. Regrettably, because of this problem with nearest-neighbor analysis, data gathered by quadrat sampling cannot be used. Any attempt to apply nearest-neighbor analysis to isolated quadrats would merely result in an extreme case of the "boundary effect." Note that Plog (Chapter 5, this volume), in his tests of sampling strategies, calculates his nearest-neighbor statistic for large survey blocks of up to 55 sq km, but *not* for the individual quadrats (squares .5 to 1.0 km on a side) in his 10% samples.

Nearest-Neighbor Analysis in the
Mesoamerican Formative

The Valley of Mexico

Introduction. The Valley of Mexico has been the object of intensive archeological survey, starting with the Teotihuacán area (Sanders 1965) and moving southward into the regions of Texcoco (Parsons 1971), Ixtapalapa (Blanton 1972), and Chalco (Parsons 1970). The eastern side of the former lake system has now received nearly total coverage for an area about 60 km long and 20 km wide (Figure 7.2).

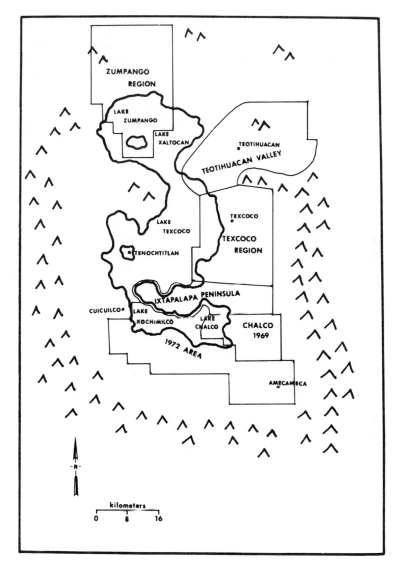

Figure 7.2 The Valley of Mexico, showing areas of intensive survey. [Courtesy, Jeffrey R. Parsons.]

Natural Environment. The Valley of Mexico's climate is characterized by Palerm and Wolf (1960:13) as Central Highland Type I, Variant B: "Cold. Dry for the better part of the year, with abundant rain in summer." To summarize briefly the environment as described by Parsons (1971) and Sanders (1965), the Valley of Mexico is an internally drained, elliptical basin measuring 130 km north–south and 60 km east–west. The area is high, with a minimum altitude of 2240 m above sea level. The volcanic mountain range which bounds the Valley on the west, south, and east rises rapidly to altitudes occasionally exceeding 4000 m. Before the Spaniards drained much of the area, the lake system covered about 1000 sq km. The mean average annual rainfall is about 750 mm, but this is restricted mostly to the summer months. There is considerable spatial variation in rainfall, both from north (often under 600 mm) to south (1000 mm for Chalco) and from low to high altitude (up to 1500 mm on southeastern slopes). Frost also is a critical factor; because cold air settles, "low areas are more subject to frost damage than hill slopes" (Parsons 1971). The combined effects of rainfall and frost thus play major roles in determining the distribution of the Valley's vegetation zones.

Analysis of All Sites. Three contiguous subregions of the Valley of Mexico will be studied by the nearest-neighbor method. The two southern regions (Ixtapalapa and Chalco) have been surveyed totally. In Texcoco, the area was, however, surveyed in three discontinuous sections. The southernmost section borders on the Ixtapalapa region, but the two northern sections are each separated by short interstitial strips. (The largest of these two strips has been surveyed to the extent that all sites larger than hamlets can be assumed to have been located; the other strip has received no survey.) Survey data from the Teotihuacán Valley was not included, because the preliminary nature of its presentation made it hard to compare with the data from other subregions.

Ixtapalapa and Chalco and the three sections of Texcoco were all analyzed, both separately and as a unit. For each unit, the density of sites was determined by dividing the number of sites located by the area surveyed. For example, if nine sites are located in a survey area of 100 km^2, this would yield a density (*rho*) of .09/km^2. From the formula ($r = \frac{1}{2\sqrt{\rho}}$), the expected distance to nearest neighbor in a random distribution of such density

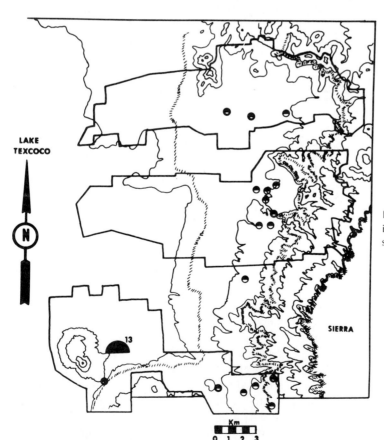

Figure 7.3 Middle Formative settlement in the Texcoco region (for key to symbols, see Parsons 1971:Map 5).

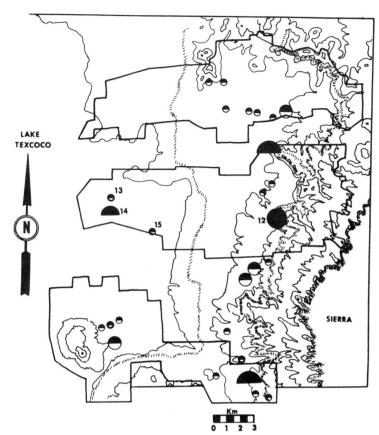

Figure 7.4 Late Formative settlement in the Texcoco region (for key to symbols, see Parsons 1971:Map 6).

would be $\dfrac{1}{2\sqrt{.09}}$ or 1.667 km. If observed distance to nearest neighbor is greater than this "expected" value, the ratio will be above 1 and indicate regular spacing; if less, the ratio will be below 1 and indicate aggregation. When all units were analyzed together, the interstitial strips in the Texcoco region were included so that measurements across gaps would not artificially increase the nearest-neighbor ratio. The mean distance to nearest neighbor was determined in all cases by measuring the distance from each site to its nearest neighbor, whether inside or outside the study unit.

First Analysis: Aggregation by Zone. For the first analysis, all habitation sites, regardless of size, were used. The simplifying assumptions made were that (*1*) all such sites were permanent communities rather than camps, and that (*2*) during a given time period they all were occupied contemporaneously. The nearest-neighbor ratio was computed on a regional basis for the sites of the three main Formative periods in the valley (Figures 7.3, 7.4, 7.5). These phases are designated by Parsons (1971) as: (*1*) Middle, 850–550 B.C. (MF); (*2*) Late, 550–250 B.C. (LF); and (*3*) Terminal, 250 B.C.–A.D. 100 (TF) (see Table 7.3). Unfortunately, the Early Formative could not be included because of inadequate sample size.

TABLE 7.3 Regional Nearest-Neighbor Ratio by Period[a]

Period	Middle Formative	Late Formative	Terminal Formative
Ratio	.7141	.7953	.9128

[a]For sample sizes $\bar{r}_A$, see Table 7.7.

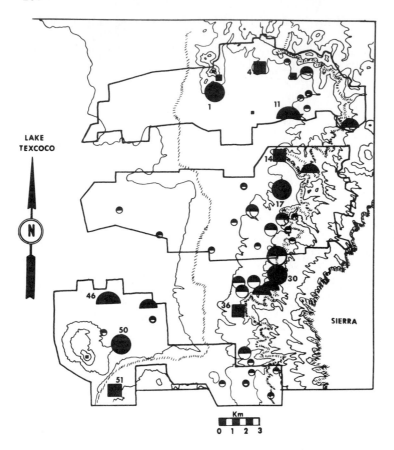

LAKE
TEXCOCO

SIERRA

Km
0 1 2 3

Figure 7.5 Terminal Formative settlement in the Texcoco region (for key to symbols, see Parsons 1971:Map 7).

Since the ratio during all three phases is less than 1, there is a slight tendency toward aggregation on a regional scale. We might hypothesize that such aggregation could be the result of either (*1*) the independent attraction of villages toward an unevenly distributed resource, or (*2*) the mutual attraction of villages toward each other.

As a test of the first hypothesis, it can be postulated that *the dominant environmental zone in such an area will show less aggregation than the area as a whole*. Such an effect from different scales of analysis already has been discussed for social behavior of sandhill cranes (p. 199); while the birds show a strong aggregation into flocks, they retain regular spacing within flocks. For Texcoco, it was determined by simple inspection of the survey maps that most sites con-

centrated in the zone called the Lower Piedmont (2250–2500m), and even more specifically in the Lower Piedmont above the 2300 m contour line. If the aggregation noted in Table 7.4 is due to the strong attraction of resources in the latter zone, the nearest-neighbor ratios should rise away from zero as the more restricted zones are examined.

TABLE 7.4   Regional Nearest-Neighbor Ratio by Topographic Zones and Periods

	Middle Formative	Late Formative	Terminal Formative
All Zones	.7141	.7953	.9128
Lower Piedmont	.6210	.9257	.9755
Lower Piedmont above 2300 m	.6900	1.0913	1.1856

In both the Late and Terminal Formative periods, the expected trend away from aggregation can be seen clearly in Table 7.4. In the Middle Formative, however, although there is the expected trend away from aggregation in the relationship between the Lower Piedmont and the Lower Piedmont above 2300 m, both these restricted zones show greater (rather than less) aggregation than the area taken as a whole. Thus, for the Middle Formative, the hypothesis of attraction toward the Lower Piedmont zone cannot be supported. Regrettably, the hypothesis (suggested by Parsons 1971) that villages might have been attracted to a lower zone cannot be tested with nearest-neighbor analysis because of a limited sample size for the Middle Formative.

An alternative hypothesis, that village aggregation results from mutual attraction, should be considered for the Middle Formative. Since the Middle Formative was a period of colonization for much of the area, the process by which an area is first populated must be considered. If, in this process, new villages are formed by "budding off" from established communities, the new village would perhaps tend to locate nearer to its parent community than expected in a random distribution. The result would be an initial pattern of site aggregation. The fact that this pattern broke down during Late and Terminal Formative times (cf. Table 7.4) could be seen as evidence for the attraction of the Lower Piedmont resources above the 2300-m contour, following an initial period of colonization.

Second Analysis: Competition within Zones. There are other changes through time which remain to be analyzed. For the Formative period, Sanders (1965), Parsons (1971), and (to a lesser extent) Blanton (1972), describe a large increase in population and cultural complexity. Related to this is a definite (though not dramatic) temporal trend in the overall nearest-neighbor ratio away from an initial aggregation. This trend suggests three alternative hypotheses: (1) As villages begin to fill an area, the relationship between a new village and its parent community becomes more tenuous; (2) with increased specialization of communities in a more complex social system, villages locate in more diverse areas; or (3) as villages increase in number, competition for necessary resources causes a trend toward regular spacing. The first hypothesis is difficult to evaluate without some simulation model of site expansion into an unoccupied area. The second hypothesis is strengthened by the increased occurrence of sites along the lakeshore and in the Upper Piedmont (above 2500 m), in areas where the villages probably could not be as agriculturally self-sufficient. This hypothesis could be tested by excavations at possible specialized sites.

The third hypothesis can be tested by the nearest-neighbor ratios in the following way. If the trend away from aggregation is a result of competition for necessary resources, this trend should be most pronounced in the zones of most crucial resources. As can be seen in Figure 7.6, the Lower Piedmont above 2300 m (and to a lesser degree, the whole Lower Piedmont) show a steeper up-trend in R values than do all zones together. In a previous discussion, it was demonstrated on the basis of inflated R values that the Lower Piedmont had probably become a dominant resource zone by at least the Late Formative. It can then be asked logically whether or not this increase in R for the Lower Piedmont can be justified merely by the assertion of zone dominance. For the Lower Piedmont, this could be the case, but, for the Lower Piedmont above 2300 m, the explanation is not adequate. Although both the "all" and "LP" lines could be approaching 1, the "LP (2300)" is well above 1. As set forth in the theoretical section on nearest-neighbor analysis, 1 is the watershed value between aggregation and regular spacing. If village location is determined solely by resource location, a theoretical maximum value for R is 1. Values above 1 can be caused only by the mutual antagonism of villages upon each other's location. Since this mutual antagonism can be demonstrated only for the dominant environmental zone, the

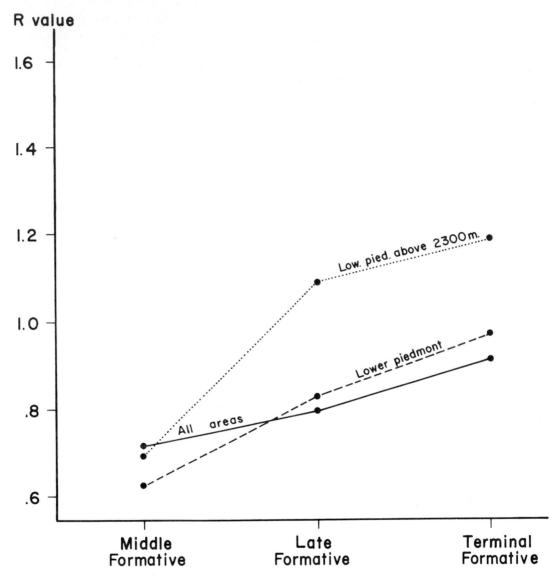

Figure 7.6 Uptrend in *R* values for three zones of the eastern Valley of Mexico: all zones, the Lower Piedmont, and the Lower Piedmont above 2300 m.

probable cause is competition for the agricultural resources of that zone.

To conclude this section: By the Late Formative period at least, village locations were strongly influenced by the dominance of the Lower Piedmont, especially above 2300 m. Sites are "clus-

tered" in this zone relative to the area as a whole, yet *within* the zone, they become regularly spaced by competition.

Third Analysis: Site Hierarchies. Altering the strategy used in the previous section, this analysis is based on habitation site hierarchy. In his study of the Texcoco region, Parsons arranged settlements into a hierarchy on the basis of site size, sherd density, and architectural complexity. Various qualitative elements in this typology made it impossible for me, as an outsider, to extend it to the Ixtapalapa and Chalco data. A new typology was devised, therefore, based entirely on site size. From data on the various subregions, histograms were constructed for the numbers of sites in each size class (defined as 1 ha intervals from 1–130 ha). Possible discontinuities in the distributions were noted at 7, 25, and 50 ha. These were used to define the following site types: hamlets, .5–7 ha; small villages, 8–24; large villages, 25–49; towns, greater than 50. For the Texcoco Formative data, the new typology disagreed with Parsons' (1971) in only 7 out of 89 cases. Whether or not discrete levels of a hierarchy actually existed for the Formative Period in the Valley of Mexico must be tested further, and the typology used here should be viewed merely as an initial analytical tool.

An assumption used in my analysis of the habitation site hierarchy is taken from what human geographers call *central place theory* (Haggett 1965:121): Each level in a hierarchy is typified by some distinctive feature, but the level also possesses all the features typical of the lower levels. For example, a possible site hierarchy for a midwestern American state might be like that shown in Table 7.5. The town would be characterized by having a clothing store, but also would have at least one tavern and one post office. The village would have a tavern and post office, but no clothing store. The hamlet would have only a post office. For the

analysis of the Valley of Mexico, Level 1 in the hierarchy would include all sites; Level 2, all sites greater than 7 ha; Level 3, all sites greater than 25 ha; and Level 4, all sites greater than 50 ha. The same subregions will be used in this analysis as were used in the previous analysis of all sites (Level 1). Analysis by various zones is, however, impossible because of the problem of small sample sizes. In this analysis of hierarchy, site specialization within a level is not studied.

In the previous work in the area (Sanders 1965; Parsons 1971; Blanton 1972), there has been an initial attempt to understand the functions of the various suggested hierarchical levels. Parsons summarizes the development of settlement patterns in the Texcoco area during the Formative period as follows:

> It is in the Late Formative that we have the first impression of three or four discrete regional centers (Tx-LF-9, Tx-LF-12, TX-LF-22, and perhaps TX-LF-29) in the Texcoco Region, each with a hinterland of dependent, dispersed rural population. This contrasts with the Middle Formative situation where there was a single large community, in a prime ecological niche, with only scattered occupation over the rest of the area. This changing settlement configuration suggests the replication, in Late Formative times, of small, independent political entities—which can probably be conceptualized as related chiefdom units—from a Middle Formative base in which large areas (Including the Teotihuacán Valley and most of the Texcoco Region) existed in an essential demographic vacuum outside the limits of any effective socio-political sphere.
>
> We can thus visualize the Late Formative as a transitional era in the Valley of Mexico in which small, relatively independent regional centers were becoming established as foci of small political entities, each associated with a discrete territory. Such replication of an existing cultural pattern was possible only so long as there was adequate vacant land and access to strategic resources so that demographic pressure did not build up to, or beyond, the point where there would have been strong selection for a basic structural re-organization. As we will presently see, the culmination of this basic

TABLE 7.5 Hypothetical Midwest American Site Hierarchy

Level	Distinctive feature
Hamlet	Post office
Village	Tavern
Town	Clothing store

Formative pattern was attained during the subsequent Terminal Formative period.

The conceptualization of the Tezoyuca–Patlachique horizon [Terminal Formative] as an era of intensive competition, at several levels, between separate political entities, seems particularly attractive as it lends itself well to understanding the socio-political implications of the rather abrupt and startling changes in regional settlement configuration which began to take place early in the first millenium A.D. [Parsons 1971:184]

Important to this conceptualization is intense competition between units on all levels of the hierarchy. Town-size sites, called "regional centers," are viewed as demographic foci for independent political units equivalent to separate chiefdoms or city-states. Competition should increase through time as population gains on land resources.

TABLE 7.6   Nearest-Neighbor Ratio for Hierarchical Levels during Formative Periods[a]

	Middle Formative	Late Formative	Terminal Formative
Level 1			
All areas	.7141	.7953	.9128
Texcoco	.6831	.7469	1.1419
Ixtapalapa	.9724	.9391	.9526
Chalco	.9298	1.0211	.9110
Level 2			
All areas	1.070	1.203	.8892
Texcoco	—	1.132	.8978
Ixtapalapa	1.447	1.492	.8811
Chalco	1.173	1.237	1.068
Level 3			
All areas	1.072	.9995	1.045
Texcoco	—	1.109	.9760
Ixtapalapa	—	1.092	1.3644
Chalco	—	1.006	1.004
Level 4			
All areas	—	1.371	.8149
Texcoco	—	—	1.677
Ixtapalapa	—	—	—
Chalco	—	.9491	1.067

[a] — represents insufficient sample size

Since severe competition would be represented by "antagonism" between individual units on a given level, it is possible to predict an increase through time in R for all levels, *but especially for Level 4 (towns)*. The R values are represented in tabular form (Table 7.6) and graphic form (Figures 7.7, 7.8). These are computed from data presented in Tables 7.7 and 7.8.

The only level that shows a definite trend toward increasing R through time is Level 1 (all sites taken together). Parson's hypothesis concerning the relationship between a population expansion through time and increased competition, therefore, is not confirmed.

The observed distribution for Level 4 sites still remains very interesting. On a regional basis, there is a definite movement toward aggregation that would directly contradict Parsons' hypothesis. This is not true, however, *within* the two subregions for which adequate data is available. Although Chalco shows only a minor trend toward regular spacing, Texcoco yielded the unusually high nearest-neighbor ratio of *1.677* for the Terminal Formative period.

In Texcoco, certain functionally distinct sites, also dating to the Terminal Formative, have been located. These sites, typed as "segregated elite districts" (Parsons 1971), are characterized by their isolated hilltop or ridge location and distinctive architectural elaboration. The nearest-neighbor ratio for the larger of these sites (those greater than 8 ha) is *1.618*. This strong trend toward regular spacing is comparable to the spacing of Level 4 sites just described. From simple inspection of site distributions, Parsons believes that, for the Terminal Formative, the Texcoco region was divided into four clusters of sites with a major population center (Level 4 site) and a "segregated elite district" articulated as a focus for each. He concludes: "These four principal demographic clusters represent separate socio-political entities—territorial statelets or perhaps chiefdoms" (Parsons 1971:192). For the Teotihuacán Valley, Sanders already had come to a similar conclusion for the early Terminal Formative (Sanders 1965).

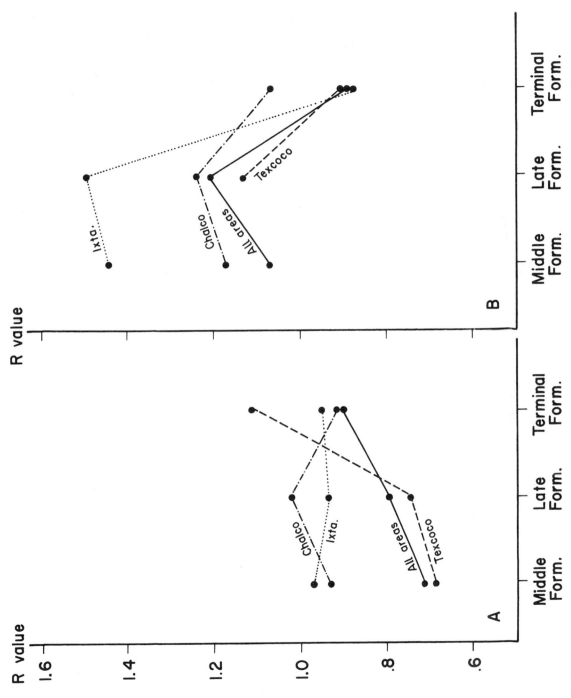

Figure 7.7 Trends in *R* values during three stages of the Formative period for the lower two levels of the site hierarchy, eastern Valley of Mexico. (A) Level 1 sites; (B) Level 2 sites.

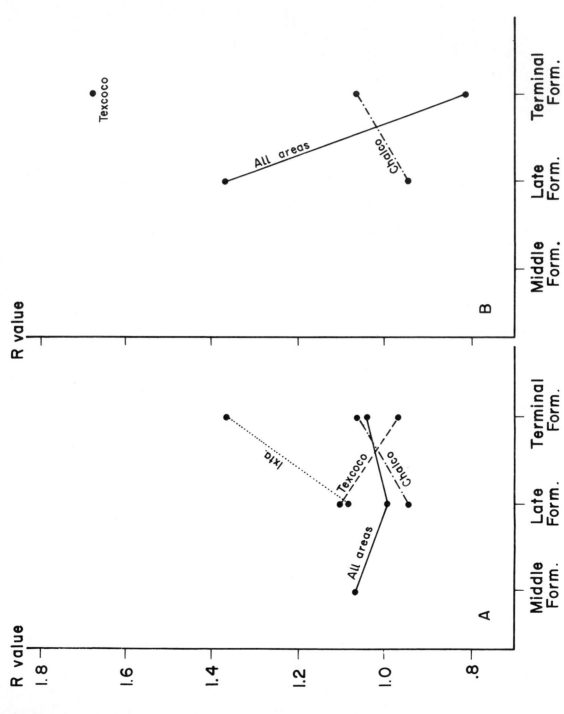

Figure 7.8 Trends in *R* values during three stages of the Formative period for the upper two levels of the site hierarchy, eastern Valley of Mexico. (A) Level 3 sites; (B) Level 4 sites.

TABLE 7.7 Nearest-Neighbor Data for the Eastern Valley of Mexico: Measurements in Kilometers of Mean Distance to Nearest Neighbor by Level in Hierarchy[a]

| | | Level 1 | | | | |
	All	LP[b]	LP (2300)[b]	Level 2	Level 3	Level 4
Middle Formative						
Texcoco	1.39 (18)			— (1)	— (0)	— (0)
Ixtapalapa	3.92 (4)			8.25 (2)	— (1)	— (0)
Chalco	2.09 (9)			3.23 (6)	— (2)	— (1)
All	1.92 (31)	1.12 (26)	1.16 (21)	5.34 (9)	9.27 (3)	— (1)
Late Formative						
Texcoco	1.29 (25)			4.39 (7)	6.57 (3)	— (1)
Ixtapalapa	2.10 (13)			5.38 (5)	4.40 (4)	— (1)
Chalco	1.67 (17)			2.78 (9)	2.77 (6)	3.20 (4)
All	1.55 (59)[c]	1.46 (34)	1.51 (31)	3.93 (21)	4.15 (13)	8.38 (6)
Terminal Formative						
Texcoco	1.47 (45)			1.92 (22)	3.54 (8)	8.60 (4)
Ixtapalapa	2.13 (13)			2.90 (6)	5.50 (4)	— (0)
Chalco	1.01 (37)			1.86 (15)	2.56 (7)	3.60 (4)
All	1.34 (104)[c]	1.08 (69)	1.12 (62)	2.03 (43)	3.59 (19)	6.10 (8)

[a]From Parsons (1970, 1971); Blanton (1972). Sites placed on a regional base map (scale, 1 cm = 1 km). Sample size in parentheses.

[b]LP = Lower Piedmont. LP (2300) = Lower Piedmont above 2300 m.

[c]Sites from B–C separation included.

Both the regular spacing of "Level 4" sites and "segregated elite" sites (and the apparent articulation between these site types) would argue for the presence of political units. The independence of these political units must, however, be questioned because of their *regional* tendency to aggregate. Millon (1966:60) has shown that a definite urban development already was underway at Teotihuacán early in the Terminal Formative. It has been suggested by Parsons (1971) that a competitive urban center also was developing at Cuicuilco, along the southwestern side of the lake. If this is true, Ixtapalapa falls approximately on the frontier between the two centers. While all other subregions studied showed definite population increases from Late to Terminal Formative, Ixtapalapa showed a decline. This population decline is particularly noticeable in the eastern section of the Ixtapalapa area and the southeastern section of the Texcoco area. The regional aggregation of Level 4 sites might therefore be caused by a Terminal Formative split into northern and southern regions, each affiliated with one of the two developing urban centers.

TABLE 7.8 Nearest-Neighbor Data for the Eastern Valley of Mexico: Measurement of Areas in Square Kilometers[a]

	All zones	LP[b]	LP(2300)[b]
Texcoco A	97.8	68.9	38.9
Texcoco A–B	41.4	31.9	12.5
Texcoco B	115.5	53.4	38.8
Texcoco B–C	81.3	38.3	28.4
Texcoco C	85.0	17.0	15.5
Ixtapalapa	260.0	26.2	18.1
Chalco	181.9	102.6	85.2
Other	33.6	0.0	0.0
Totals	896.5	338.3	237.4

[a]From Parsons (1970, 1971); Blanton (1972). Sites placed on a regional base map (scale, 1 cm = 1 km).

[b]LP = Lower Piedmont. LP(2300) = Lower Piedmont above 2300 m.

The regular spacing between Level 4 sites in the Terminal Formative should, therefore, not be viewed as a result of lower-level competition, which would certainly have tended to eliminate regional aggregation. Instead, it might be the result of a resettlement of people around the regularly spaced administrative centers to which they were dependent. This might explain Parsons' dilemma:

> Despite the general trends of population expansion and increase in site size, the three Late Formative sites (Tx-LF-9, Tx-LF-12, and TX-LF-22) were largely or wholly abandoned by the Terminal Formative (as were the two largest Late Formative communities in the Teotihuacan Valley). We are presently at a loss to explain this site abandonment in both areas. The largest Terminal Formative sites grew up in areas of scanty Late Formative settlement (as was also the case in the Teotihuacan Valley). [Parsons 1971:190]

In our analysis of the functional significance of village hierarchies, it will be postulated that the nearest-neighbor ratio is an index of the political significance of a hierarchical level. From the theoretical discussion, it is known that values of R greater than 1 can result only from mutual "antagonism" of sites. This antagonism can be caused by either competition or state planning, but, in either case, this would designate a politically meaningful group.

Level 1 already has been discussed; the main conclusions were that the attraction of sites to a dominant resource zone, plus minor competition within that zone, resulted in some tendency toward regular spacing. In contrast, *Level 2* distribution shows higher R values and hence more regular spacing (see Table 7.6), at least in the Middle and Late Formative; in the Terminal Formative, these values dramatically decline. *Level 3* sites show near-random distribution in all but the Terminal Formative period in the Ixtapalapa peninsula. During that period, no higher-level sites were located on the peninsula. The even spacing of *Level 4* sites has just been discussed for the Terminal

Formative. They were, however, already showing that trend in the Late Formative as indicated by the fairly high regional R of *1.371.*

Summary and conclusions. Little can yet be said about the Middle Formative distribution of the eastern Valley of Mexico. Level 2 sites (minimum size, 8 ha) do show regular spacing and probably represent focal points for competitive social units of some kind—perhaps still composed of locally based lineages, although this is not known. In the Late Formative, Level 2 sites retain their importance, but Level 4 sites now have become dominant. This may represent the loosely held dominance of a central village over several neighboring and related villages. Such a pattern might result from the kind of organization Service (1962) refers to as a "chiefdom," featuring a ranked (but not stratified) society.

A radical shift in the Terminal Formative shows the complete loss of Level 2's importance on both a local and regional basis. Level 4 also loses its importance on a regional basis, but retains it on a local basis. The simplest interpretation of this stage is that it reflects the establishment of a strong early state at Teotihuacán: Level 4 sites become subordinate to the latter, but are still the foci for local organization. Level 2 sites, which perhaps once represented organizational foci for local kin groups, become politically irrelevant. Nearest-neighbor analysis of the eastern Valley of Mexico data may thus document a classic example of the breakdown of lower (kin-based) hierarchical levels during the evolution of the state, although obviously other lines of evidence are necessary to confirm this.

We will temporarily leave the Valley of Mexico at this point to extend the same type of analysis to a much more scantily surveyed area, the Gulf Coast. In a later section, using the same Texcoco survey data I have used, Elizabeth Brumfiel tests hypotheses of population growth and land pressure. The variety of tests that can be run on such data points up the high desirability of having intensive surveys of the "total universe" of sites for large areas of Mesoamerica.

The Southern Gulf Coast

Introduction. Although the "Olmec" art style has attracted a great deal of attention (Coe 1965), archeological survey in the southern Gulf Coast lowlands has been limited. The early extensive surveys of Stirling (1957) or Drucker and Contreras (1953) located many sites, but published insufficient information to date or estimate accurately the size of the sites. The main regional ceremonial–civic centers—La Venta, San Lorenzo, Tres Zapotes, and to a lesser degree Laguna de los Cerros—have been described well. For La Venta and San Lorenzo, there are even discussions of the possible support area, based on the ethnography of modern local populations (Heizer 1960; Coe 1969; Rossmann, Chapter 4, this volume). Intensive archeological survey in these postulated areas has, however, never been attempted.

Edward B. Sisson's (1970) survey in the Chontalpa district, about 60 km east of La Venta, provides the only extensive information on Formative village settlement patterns in the Olmec region. Thus, while it may be assumed that all or most of the primary centers in the Olmec area have been located, knowledge of secondary centers is minimal, and the only useful sample of hamlet-size sites is restricted to Sisson's survey area. This general lack of specific information on small site locations is unfortunate, since it will greatly restrict the level of analysis attempted here.

Natural Environment. The "Olmec heartland" is defined as the coastal lowlands in the modern Mexican states of Veracruz and Tabasco (Figure 7.9). It is bordered roughly on the west by the Papaloapan River and on the east by the Grijalva River (Bernal 1969). The land is mostly flat, except for the volcanic Las Tuxtlas Mountains in the northwest. Through the flat land flow many rivers. They are important transportation routes, and their natural levees are the preferred agricultural land. Soil is entirely alluvial (except in the Tuxtlas)—recent in the lower zones, and Pleistocene in the higher.

The best description of the area can be found in a monograph by West, Psuty, and Thom (1969) on the Tabasco lowlands. They characterize the climate as "tropical monsoon" (p. 15). Rainfall is variable (increasing inland), but averages about 2000 mm per year. There is a double maximum in the summer (June and September) and a single spring minimum (April). Droughts are occasional near the coast. In back of a zone of beach dune and mangrove swamp vegetation, a broad zone of tropical rain forest is intermixed with areas of tropical savanna. These savannas are located mainly on poorly drained soils, but recently have been extended by fires for pasturage. The land is definitely not uniform in natural vegetation or agricultural potential, but no clear zonal pattern is evident. With certain reservations, the area can be considered a uniform plane for the purposes of spatial analysis.

Analysis of Hamlet and Village Level Sites. Sisson's (1970) survey in the Chontalpa district of western Tabasco is unique to Olmec area studies because he attempted an intensive study of a restricted area, identifying sites of all sizes and time periods (Figure 7.10). Since the Mexican government has deliberately converted the Chontalpan vegetation to pasture, Sisson was able to locate even small sites, a nearly impossible task in tropical rain forest. For the Formative period, Sisson defined five phases on the basis of pottery associations (Table 7.9). Sites located for all these phases are considered "small, probably a cluster of houses on a natural levee." In Phase 3 (Puente), two sites possess "small planned groups of large mounds" (p. 45). Mound groups may have existed during

TABLE 7.9 Chontalpa District, Formative Period Phases[a]

Phase	Dates	Number of sites
1. Molina	1350–1150 B. C.	8
2. Palacios	1050–900 B. C.	10
3. Puente	900–500 B. C.	11
4. Franco	500–300 B. C.	9
5. Castañeda	"Late Pre-Classic"	6

[a]Sisson (1970).

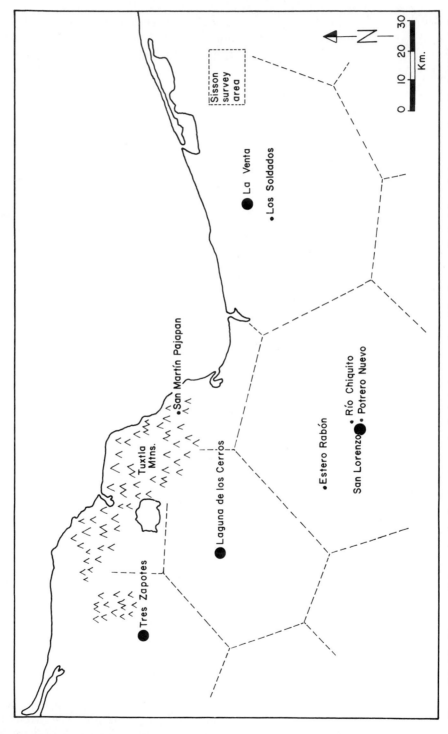

Figure 7.9 The Veracruz–Tabasco lowlands, showing archeological sites mentioned in the text. Dashed lines (---) suggest hypothetical boundaries between territories served by each major ceremonial–civic center.

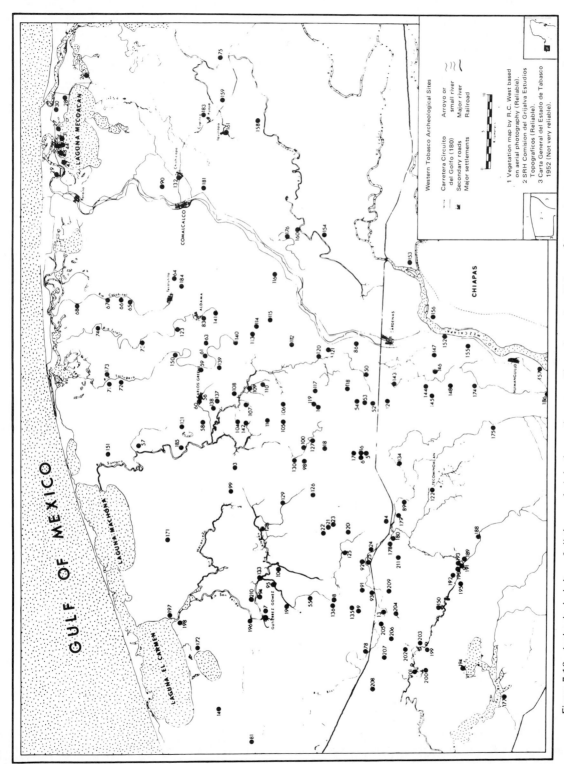

Figure 7.10 Archeological sites of all time periods in the northwestern Chontalpa region, Tabasco. [Survey by E.B. Sisson, 1970:Figure 1.]

TABLE 7.10 Nearest-Neighbor Ratios for the Chontalpa District

Phases	1	2	3	4	5
R_1	.5627	.7120	.9169	.7831	.9213
R_2	.5163	.6347	.9048	.8907	.9827

other phases, but Sisson views the association as still doubtful.

As can be noted from Sisson's (1970) study, sites of the Formative period cluster in the western part of his survey area. On this one level at least, villages are highly aggregated. The cause of such apparent aggregation could be among the following: (1) close intervillage association; (2) microenvironmental variation; or (3) differential preservation. Close intervillage association could result either from the relationship of new villages to their parent communities, as described for the Valley of Mexico, or from the mutual attraction of villages by some phenomenon like a secondary regional center just outside Sisson's survey area. Although microenvironmental variation also could cause a similar pattern, it seems unlikely that the Tabasco environment would feature a localized resource of such importance. The third explanation is a distinct possibility: Since alluviation is heaviest in the areas where no sites have been located, some small Formative hamlets may simply be deeply buried. Because these hypotheses are all possible, and cannot be evaluated without new data, the analysis here will deal with the more limited area of actual distribution.

The main problem encountered by reducing the scale of analysis is the definition of the new area. Since the size of the area directly affects the expected distance to nearest neighbor in a random distribution, this should not be done arbitrarily. For purposes of analysis, the size of the area is defined by a circle with the radius equal to the mean distance to the farthest neighbor $(\overline{r}_n th)$:

$$A = \pi \, (\overline{r}_n th)^2$$

This estimate should be used only in cases where an area cannot be defined by either survey limits or environmental zones. Before it is used extensively, it should be checked against synthetic random samples. In general, the problems of using small populations of very restricted distribution need more analysis than is possible in this chapter.

In the actual analysis, two nearest-neighbor ratios were determined by defining the area using the mean distance to farthest neighbor, first for each specific phase, and then for all phases together. In the first case (R_1), the size of area would vary slightly by phase. In the second case (R_2), it would remain constant. Results did not vary remarkably between the two techniques (see Table 7.10). Mean distances to nearest-neighbor are listed in Table 7.11.

In all phases, R values show aggregation. Assuming that differential site identification is not important on this scale of analysis, the probable factors causing such aggregation are the mechanism of village propagation and microenvironmental variation.

As suggested in the section on the Valley of Mexico, aggregation resulting from the process of village propagation (the budding off of daughter communities from parent communities) should decrease in importance as an area is populated. In

TABLE 7.11 Measurements of Mean Distance to Nearest Neighbor for Sites of Five Formative Phases in the Chontalpa District, Tabasco[a]

	Nearest neighbor (km)
Period 1 (Molina)	4.0 (8)
Period 2 (Palacios)	4.4 (10)
Period 3 (Puente)	5.9 (11)
Period 4 (Franco)	6.6 (9)
Period 5 (Castañeda)	8.9 (6)

[a]Sisson (1970). Sample size in parentheses.

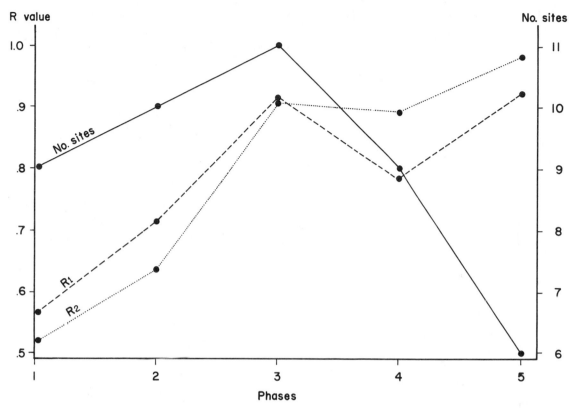

Figure 7.11 Changes in numbers of sites during five Formative phases in the Chontalpa of Tabasco, compared with nearest-neighbor ratios for each phase (see text).

contrast, microenvironmental factors should remain constant unless there is a demonstrated shift in subsistence patterns. As can be seen in Figure 7.11, the graph of the nearest-neighbor ratio parallels the graph of site counts for Phases 1–3. For Phases 4 and 5, there is no observed relationship. This trend supports the hypothesis of the relationship of aggregation to the colonizing of an area. To summarize this analysis, during the initial phases, the process of fully colonizing an area causes an initial aggregation to tend increasingly toward random spacing. The minor aggregation retained in the last three phases may be the result of a constant microenvironmental variation. No competition for resources can be noted from the nearest-neighbor ratios.

Analysis of Higher-Level Sites. The highest-order site category for the Olmec region consists of the major ceremonial-civic centers—La Venta, San Lorenzo, and Tres Zapotes. The elaboration of monumental art and architecture from these sites is described well in numerous volumes (see for example, Drucker, Heizer, and Squier 1959; Coe 1968; Bernal 1969; Medellín Zenil 1960). Their importance as socio-political centers is unquestionable. Although all three sites varied in importance during their occupation (Coe 1968), they all were occupied during the period 1000–600 B.C. For purposes of the analysis here, these sites will be treated as broadly contemporaneous and of roughly equal importance. Laguna de los Cerros presents a more difficult problem (Coe 1971). Al-

TABLE 7.12 Nearest-Neighbor Statistic for Major Olmec
Ceremonial Centers

	Map estimate	$\bar{r}_n th$ estimate
Excluding Laguna de los Cerros	2.065	1.495
Including Laguna de los Cerros	1.504	1.129

though it consists of 95 mounds on some 94 acres of land, no monumental basalt heads have yet been identified there (Bernal 1969). Its equivalence to the other major centers in both date and function therefore still remains uncertain.

In addition to the sites already mentioned, one or more levels of sites intermediate in importance between the major centers and Sisson's hamlets seem to be indicated. Sites like Los Soldados and Estero Rabón (Figure 7.9) are likely candidates for such intermediary positions (Coe 1971). These sites contain some monumental art and have mound groups, but not on the scale of the major centers. Regrettably, since no comprehensive work has been done on this intermediary level, there is too little data for analysis by the nearest-neighbor statistic.

The analysis of the major ceremonial centers will be run both excluding and including Laguna de los Cerros. Since there are no easily discernible natural boundaries, the area will be determined in two ways: First using map-estimated boundaries, and then using the mean distance to farthest neighbor as described in the previous section (but eliminating ¼ as a compensation for the nearness of the ocean on one side) (Table 7.12).

The results show variation (as might be expected from the different estimates), but a tendency toward regular spacing is clear and definite. The importance of missing data is clearly observable in Tables 7.12 and 7.13. If Laguna de los Cerros is to be included, R values are decreased greatly. The effect of area also is important, but the values probably represent extremes. It can, therefore, be concluded that major Olmec ceremonial-civic centers do show regular spacing. The cause of this must be the mutual antagonism of the centers, re-

sulting either from carefully planned location or from intersite competition. At present, there is no clear evidence for site dominance among the major centers. Since site planning directed over such considerable distances (for example, 86 km between San Lorenzo and La Venta) seems unlikely at this stage of the Formative period, intercenter competition may be the most economic explanation for the regular spacing.

To summarize: A trend toward competition between major Olmec ceremonial-civic centers probably is demonstrated by the regular spacing of such centers. On the hamlet or village level, sites show no competition. Location seems to be random, after a period of initial colonization. The articulation between levels in the settlement hierarchy cannot be studied empirically because of a lack of adequate data for sites of the intermediate levels.

Conclusions on Site Hierarchies

In this short discussion of site hierarchies, I will attempt to reconstruct the structural and functional relationships between Formative communities of different size and complexity. In our analysis of data from the Valley of Mexico, the nearest-neighbor ratio was used as an index of the political significance of four hierarchical levels. It was shown that Level 2 sites were important during the Late Formative, and to a less pronounced degree during the Middle Formative. Level 4 was important on a regional basis for the

TABLE 7.13 Measurements of Mean Distance to Nearest and Farthest Neighbor for Major Olmec Ceremonial–Civic Centers in Southern Veracruz and Tabasco

	Nearest neighbor (km)	Farthest neighbor (km)
Excluding Laguna de los Cerros	92.3 (3)	137.7
Including Laguna de los Cerros	58.2 (4)	133.5

TABLE 7.14 Analysis of Site Aggregates in the Eastern Valley of Mexico: Step 1—Computing the Area of Territories

Middle Formative	Late Formative		Terminal Formative
$\bar{r}$ of Level 2 = 5.34	$\bar{r}$ of Level 4 = 8.38	$\bar{r}$ of Level 2 = 3.93	$\bar{r}$ of Level 4 = 6.10
$\frac{1}{2}\bar{r}$ = 2.67	$\frac{1}{2}\bar{r}$ = 4.19	$\frac{1}{2}\bar{r}$ = 1.96	$\frac{1}{2}\bar{r}$ = 3.05
area = 22.40 km^2	area = 55.16 km^2	area = 12.07 km^2	area = 29.23 km^2

Late Formative, and on a local basis for the Terminal Formative.

If it can be assumed that a high R designates that sites of a given level function as focal points for aggregates of sites of smaller sizes, several parameters of these aggregates can be determined.

1. Minimum size of territory (T) associated with an aggregate will equal the area of a circle with a radius one-half the mean distance to nearest neighbor ($T = \pi (\frac{1}{2}\bar{r})^2$) (Table 7.14).
2. The composition of sites making up an aggregate is equal to the proportion of lower-level sites to significant higher-level sites (converted to a standardized *1*) (Table 7.15).
3. Approximate population range for the aggregate can be computed by multiplying the number of sites for a given hierarchical level (rounded to nearest whole number), times the range in site size of the aggregate in hectares, times 10 (an estimate of the minimum number of people per hectare from Parsons 1971) (Table 7.16).

The following is a synthesis of Table 7.17. During the Middle Formative, aggregate sizes were small—under 1000 persons living at about three communities. A large or small village acted as the focal point for the group, and there is no evidence of more than one level of site hierarchy. This probably reflects some kin-based organization, perhaps on a "tribal" level (Service 1962). By the Late Formative, group sizes had expanded to about 1000–2000 persons, living at about five sites. A town now acted as the focal point of the group. During this period, however, Level 2 sites still retained an important role in the hierarchy. They

would represent subgroups of 1000 persons or less, perhaps analogous to the aggregates of the Middle Formative. Social organizaton still would be kinship-based, but the two-tiered hierarchy suggests a chiefdom level of organization (Service 1962). The Terminal Formative groups were very similar to, though a little larger than, the town-dominated Late Formative groups. The subsidiary level of dominance (Level 2) is, however, no longer significant. Instead, the regional aggregation of these large groups suggests their integration into a larger state organization, perhaps that developing at Teotihuacán. During the Formative Period in the Valley of Mexico, there thus appears to be a marked process by which social organization evolves. More complex organizational units are built by the integration of existing units, with one such unit becoming dominant.

In the Olmec area, the lack of comprehensive data makes any conclusions concerning hierarchies much more tenuous. The hamlet level sites (as

TABLE 7.15 Analysis of Site Aggregates in the Eastern Valley of Mexico: Step 2—Computing Proportion of Lower-Level Sites to Significant Higher-Level Sites[a]

	Level			
	1	2	3	4
Middle	26	9	3	0
Formative	1.89	*1*		
Late	34	21	13	6
Formative	2.17	1.33	1.17	*1*
	.62	*1*		
Terminal	69	43	19	8
Formative	3.25	3	1.38	*1*

[a]Highest level converted to *1*.

TABLE 7.16   Analysis of Site Aggregates in the Eastern
Valley of Mexico: Step 3—Computing
Population Ranges for Each Aggregate

	Minimum		Maximum	
Middle	1 x 8 x 10 =	80	1 x 50 x 10 =	500
Formative	2 x .5 x 10 =	10	2 x 7 x 10 =	140
		90		640
Late (a)	1 x 51 x 10 =	510	1 x 120 x 10 =	1200
Formative	1 x 26 x 10 =	260	1 x 50 x 10 =	500
	1 x 8 x 10 =	80	1 x 25 x 10 =	250
	2 x .5 x 10 =	10	2 x 7 x 10 =	140
		860		2090
(b)	1 x 8 x 10 =	80	1 x 120 x 10 =	1200
	1 x .5 x 10 =	5	1 x 7 x 10 =	70
		85		1270
Terminal	1 x 51 x 10 =	510	1 x 120 x 10 =	1200
Formative	1 x 26 x 10 =	260	1 x 50 x 10 =	500
	3 x 8 x 10 =	240	3 x 25 x 10 =	750
	3 x .5 x 10 =	15	3 x 7 x 10 =	210
		1025		2660

represented by Sisson's study) show a near-random distribution after a period of initial colonization. Since there is no competition between these sites (as noted by R's less than 1), it can be suggested that they are subsidiary to some higher-level site. If Sisson is correct in concluding that his Formative period hamlets were small (let us estimate 25–75 persons), this would give a very low population density. During the Puente phase (900–500 B.C., contemporary with the major development at La Venta), population density reached its maximum with 11 sites in 93 km^2, yielding an estimated density of 3–9 persons per km^2.

In an interesting paper, Heizer (1960) has calculated that the construction of La Venta required a periodic work force of 1850 people. Assuming that one individual from an average family of 5 would be recruited, and that the population density of the southern Veracruz–Tabasco area averaged about 6/km^2 as calculated earlier, such a ceremonial-civic center would require a territory of 1542 km^2. If this territory were represented in circular form, it would have a radius of 22.2 km.

Assuming that each major Olmec center was located at the midpoint of its territory, the minimum spacing between ceremonial-civic centers would be twice the radius just mentioned, or 44.4 km. From this calculation alone, Laguna de los Cerros is still a potential major center, since its distance to nearest neighbor (Tres Zapotes) is 41 km. In addition, these figures suggest that additional centers still might be discovered in areas toward the Gulf, west from San Lorenzo, or south, east, and west of La Venta.

Relationships between the major centers and their surrounding minor communities need still to be examined. The center would require a fairly

TABLE 7.17   Summary of Site Aggregate Analysis,
Eastern Valley of Mexico

Middle Formative	significant level = Level 2
	area = 22.40 km^2
	composition = 1 small or large village, 2 hamlets
	population range = 90–640 persons
	density = 4.02–28.57 persons/km^2 (mean, 16/km^2)
Late Formative	(a) significant level = Level 4
	area = 55.16 km^2
	composition = 1 town, 1 large village, 1 small village, 2 hamlets
	population range = 860–2090 persons
	density = 15.59–37.89 persons/km^2 (mean, 27/km^2)
	(b) significant level = Level 2
	area = 12.07 km^2
	composition = 1 small village–town, 1 hamlet
	population range = 85–1270 persons
	density = 7.04–105.22 persons/km^2 (mean, 56/km^2)
Terminal Formative	significant level = Level 4
	area = 29.23 km^2
	composition = 1 town, 1 large village, 3 small villages, 3 hamlets
	population range = 1025–2660 persons
	density = 35.01–91.00 persons/km^2 (mean, 63/km^2)

large but *periodic* work force. Heizer estimates that the 1850 workers would be required only every *50 years*. Smaller numbers would be required at shorter intervals, but there is no reason that necessitates our conceiving of a continuous relationship between highest- and lowest-level sites. Even the major ceremonial centers had a relatively small population (Coe [1968] estimates San Lorenzo at around 1000 persons) and may have been self-sufficient in food production. Because of the periodic nature of the labor demand and the diffuse distribution of hamlets, secondary centers probably mediated any relationship between highest and lowest levels. These secondary centers also would have had periodic labor requirements for construction of mounds and so forth, and therefore each would require a subregion as its support area. If it can be assumed (in accordance with central place theory) that each major center would function as a secondary center to its own subregion, and therefore require a similar support area, secondary sites should be located two-thirds of the way from the major center to its territorial border, or about 15 km from a major center. To check this against two probable secondary centers—Los Soldados is 10 km south of La Venta, and Estero Rabón is 24 km west of San Lorenzo.

In the future, the distribution of these secondary centers should be studied more closely. If these secondary sites show regular spacing on a regional basis, they can be considered partially independent of the major center. If, however, they group around the centers, such firmer control might suggest the presence of a kind of nonurban "state." As a final comment, sites like Tenochtitlán and Potrero Nuevo—lying only a few kilometers from San Lorenzo—as well as similar small mound groups near Tres Zapotes and Laguna de los Cerros, well may be related to the secondary center functions of the major center. This could represent a spatial isolation of hierarchical roles for which there is no evidence at other sites of the 1000–600 B.C. period.

Though sketchy, the preceding data on the Olmec area may be synthesized into the following model. Major competing ceremonial–civic centers show a regular distribution, with minimum spacing between sites being about 44 km. Secondary sites should be located two-thirds the distance to the territorial border, or 15 km from a major center. Both levels well might show regional regular spacing when more secondary centers are studied. This would be interpreted as an overlapping pattern of dominance, where secondary centers retained a definite degree of independence. The major center would have control over the underlying population *only* through the secondary center. As already described, such an organization would fit the model for a kin-based chiefdom. Controls would never be direct, as expected in a state. The centers would require labor for monumental work, and offer services in the form of cyclical ceremonies, among other things. Food and most other forms of production would be organized on a very localized level, with no hierarchical controls necessary or suggested.

In some ways, the Middle Formative level of organization in the Gulf Coast lowlands could be viewed as analogous to the Late Formative organization in the Valley of Mexico. Although the Olmec regional aggregate would include a larger population (probably near 10,000 individuals versus less than 2000), the system of organization would be called into operation only at periodic intervals. The extensive nature of the Olmec system, with its low population densities, contrasts sharply with the Late Formative for the Valley of Mexico. While the distance from the center to the periphery of an Olmec territory is estimated at 22 km, the same distance in the Valley of Mexico would be only 4 km. This may be a partial answer to a perennial archeological dilemma concerning the apparent inability of the Olmec to develop an urban state organization. Development of the primary state may require a much more compact population, perhaps in a more nearly continual condition of interaction. Certainly state formation and population density must be interrelated in some system of mutual causation; but rather than tackling it here, I direct the reader to Elizabeth Brumfiel (Chapter 8 of this volume).

References

Bernal, I.
1969 *The Olmec world*. Berkeley: University of California Press.

Blanton, R. E.
1972 Prehispanic settlement patterns of the Ixtapalapa peninsula region, Mexico. *Occasional Papers* No. 6. Dept. of Anthropology, Pennsylvania State University, University Park.

Clark, P. J.
1956 Grouping in spatial distribution. *Science* 123:373–374.

Clark, P. J., and F. C. Evans
1954 Distance to nearest neighbor as a measure of spatial relationships in populations. *Ecology* 35:445–453.
1955 On some aspects of spatial pattern in biological populations. *Science* 121:397–398.

Coe, M. D.
1965 The Olmec style and its distribution. In *Handbook of Middle American Indians*, vol. 3, edited by R. Wauchope and G. R. Willey. Austin: University of Texas Press. Pp. 739–775.
1968 San Lorenzo and the Olmec civilization. In *Dumbarton Oaks Conference on the Olmec*, edited by E. P. Benson. Washington, D.C.: Dumbarton Oaks. Pp. 41–78.
1969 Photogrammetry and the ecology of the Olmec civilization. Paper read at Working Conference on Aerial Photography and Anthropology, Cambridge, Mass., 10–12 May 1969. Mimeograph.
1971 Unpublished correspondence with T. K. Earle.

Dacey, M. F.
1962 Analysis of central place and point pattern by a nearest neighbor method. *Lund Studies in Geography, Series B, Human Geography* 24:55–75.

Drucker, P., and E. Contreras
1953 Site pattern in the eastern part of Olmec territory. *Journal of the Washington Academy of Science* 43:389–396.

Drucker, P., R. F. Heizer, and R. J. Squier
1959 Excavations at La Venta, Tabasco, 1955. *Bulletin* No. 170. Bureau of American Ethnology, Smithsonian Institution, Washington, D.C.

Evans, F. C.
1969 Spatial relations in ecology: An overview. *Michigan Academician* 2:69–76.

Getis, A.
1964 Temporal land-use pattern analysis with the use of nearest neighbor and quadrat methods. *Annals of the Association of American Geographers* 54:391–399.

Haggett, P.
1965 *Locational analysis in human geography*. London: Edward Arnold.

Hansen, R. M., and E. E. Remmenga
1961 Nearest neighbor concept applied to pocket gopher populations. *Ecology* 42:812–814.

Heizer, R. F.
1960 Agriculture and the theocratic state in lowland southeastern Mexico. *American Antiquity* 26: 215–222.

King, L. J.
1962 A quantitative expression of the pattern of urban settlements in selected areas of the United States. *Tijdschrift voor Economische en Sociale Geografie* 53:1–7.
1969 *Statistical analysis in geography*. Englewood Cliffs, N.J.: Prentice-Hall.

Medellin Zenil, A.
1960 Monolitos inéditos olmecas. *Palabra y Hombre* 16:75–98.

Miller, R. S., and W. Stephen
1966 Spatial relationships in flocks of sandhill cranes. *Ecology* 47:323–327.

Millon, R.
1966 Extensión y población de la ciudad de Teotihuacán en sus diferentes períodos: Un cálculo provisional. In *Teotihuacán, XI Mesa Redonda*. Sociedad Mexicana de Antropologia, Mexico, D.F. Pp. 57–78.

Palerm, A., and E. Wolf
1960 Ecological potential and cultural development in Mesoamerica. In *Social science monographs*. Vol. 3. *Studies in human ecology*. Washington, D.C.: Pan American Union. Pp. 1–37.

Parsons, J. R.
1970 Settlement pattern surveys of the Chalco region, Valley of Mexico. Unpublished maps.
1971 Prehistoric settlement patterns in the Texcoco region, Mexico. *Memoirs* No. 3. Museum of Anthropology, University of Michigan, Ann Arbor.

Pielou, E. C.
1959 The use of point-to-point distances in the study of pattern. *Journal of Ecology* 47: 607–613.

1961   Segregation and symmetry in two-species pop-
       ulations as studied by nearest neighbor rela-
       tionships. *Journal of Ecology* 49:255–269.
Sanders, W. T.
  1965   The cultural ecology of the Teotihuacán valley.
         Dept. of Anthropology, Pennsylvania State Un-
         iversity, University Park. Mimeograph.
Service, E. R.
  1962   *Primitive social organization*. New York: Ran-
         dom House.
Sisson, E. B.
  1970   Settlement patterns and land use in the north-
         western Chontalpa, Tabasco, Mexico: A pro-
         gress report. *Cerámica de Cultura Maya*
         6:41–54.
Stirling, M. W.
  1957   An archaeological reconnaissance in south-
         eastern Mexico. *Bulletin* No. 164:213–240.
         Bureau of American Ethnology, Smithsonian
         Institution, Washington, D.C.
West, R. C., N. P. Psuty, and B. G. Thom
  1969   The Tabasco lowlands of southeastern Mexico.
         Technical Report No. 70. Coastal Studies
         Institute, Louisiana State University, Baton
         Rouge.

Chapter 8

ANALYZING PATTERNS OF GROWTH

Introduction

Few processes are as characteristic of the Formative period as population growth. As William Sanders and Barbara Price (1968:29) have pointed out, during the Formative, "a continuous and rapid population growth took place, as is evidenced by the greater numbers of sites, their large size, and the increasing evidence of socioeconomic complexity within and between them." The same authors add that, from a developmental standpoint, "all over central and southern Mesoamerica shortly after 1500 B.C. population growth had reached a level that permitted and encouraged the development of a chiefdom level of social structure" (p. 120).

So indisputable is the evidence for growth in Mesoamerica as a whole that it has provided the Real Mesoamerican Archeologist with one of the most overworked weapons in his arsenal: "popula-tion pressure." This pressure—along with trade and religion—explains almost everything. The origins of agriculture? Population pressure on wild plant resources brought it about. The origins of irrigation? Population pressure on early dry farming brought it about. Ranked society? Population pressure on strategic resources brought it about. Urban civilization? Population pressure on "the human ecosystem" of the Late Formative brought it about. The collapse of urban civilization? Population pressure on the same ecosystem, 1000 years later, brought it about. No question about it: Planned Parenthood could have nipped Mesoamerican civilization in the bud.

Since population pressure has become such an indispensable tool, one would expect that R.M.A. would have a consistent and standardized means of studying and measuring it. On the contrary, he has no means at all. The pressure is simply there, like the force of gravity or the barometric pressure of

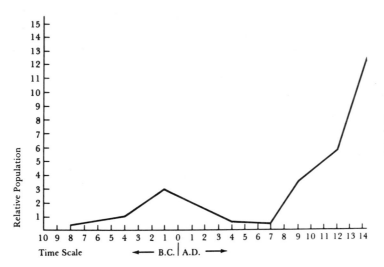

Figure 8.1 Population growth in the Texcoco region, Valley of Mexico. [After Sanders 1972:Figure 5.3.]

the San Jacinto drainage. Moreover, when R.M.A. talks of population growth, he rarely distinguishes between the growth of an individual community, the growth of a small subregion, the growth of a larger region, or the growth of Mesoamerica as a whole.

In a recent paper, Sanders (1972) has presented a series of graphs showing the growth of "relative population" in a dozen regions of Mesoamerica.

We have reproduced two of these, as Figures 8.1 and 8.2. Both graphs clearly indicate the complexity of growth on a regional level in Mesoamerica. Even though Mesoamerica *as a whole* shows population increase during the Formative, individual regions may show an actual decrease, or a sequence of peaks and valleys. The smaller the region studied, the less likely it is to show anything resembling a steady population increase.

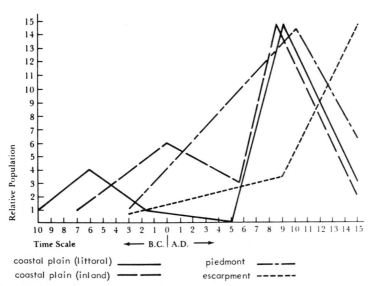

Figure 8.2 Population growth in four regions of the Pacific Coast of Guatemala. [After Sanders 1972:Figure 5.10.]

Indeed, as Sanders' graphs point out, in several parts of Mesoamerica, "civilization" arose during a period of regional population *decline*.

We feel that Chapters 3 through 7 provide some methodological support for the study of population growth and population pressure on two levels: the community and the region. In one of the sections that follow, Marc Winter discusses community growth (or lack of it) in the area he knows best, using the results of a random sampling program at a small hamlet and an intensive systematic surface collection at a large nucleated village. In the other section, Elizabeth Brumfiel evaluates the effect of "population pressure" in the intensively surveyed eastern Valley of Mexico. Brumfiel uses site-catchment analysis (see Chapter 4) coupled with linear regression analysis to study the relationship between population and agricultural land. Both Winter's and Brumfiel's results raise serious doubts about some of R.M.A.'s most treasured beliefs. In fact, they make me wonder if anything we Mesoamerican archeologists believe could stand up to really rigorous scrutiny. But then, with any luck, their studies will probably never be followed up.

Differential Patterns of Community Growth in Oaxaca

MARCUS C. WINTER

Most archeologists analyzing multiperiod sites eventually deal in some way with the problem of community growth. In Mesoamerica, a frequent assumption made is that villages are small when founded, undergo growth during subsequent periods, and then—after reaching their maximum extent—shrink gradually until they are finally abandoned. Of course, there are exceptions. But the fact remains that the basic assumption itself has never been tested. In part, this is because of the difficulty of obtaining reliable population estimates for any period in a community's life cycle.

In this section, I will compare the growth patterns of two communities in the Valley of Oaxaca, which were specifically studied with this problem in mind. The two communities show very different patterns. Tierras Largas, a hamlet in Parsons' (1971a) typology, was occupied for seven subphases of the Early and Middle Formative.

Throughout this period, in spite of fluctuations in the numbers of square meters covered, the community showed essentially no growth in terms of households. Data from nearby hamlets like Fábrica San José (Drennan 1972) show a similar pattern. During the same seven subphases, however, the site of San José Mogote grew to more than 20 times its original size. It seems likely that these two different patterns have something to do with the "strongly discontinuous" site size distribution described by Marcus in Chapter 3 (this volume).

Tierras Largas: A Hamlet

One objective of the excavations carried out at Tierras Largas (see Chapter 3) was to gather data on the layout of a Formative hamlet, and to ascertain whether or not spatial organization of the community changed during Early and Middle Formative times. In this section, I will try to describe briefly how community layout and change at Tierras Largas were studied, using the "household cluster" as the basic unit of analysis (see p. 25 for the definition of a household cluster).

Excavations indicated that most Early and Middle Formative household clusters could be bounded roughly by a circle 20 m in diameter, or by a 20-by-15-m rectangle. In other words, cultural features comprising a single household cluster occur within an area of about 300 sq m. This pattern seemed to remain constant for approximately 1000 years (from around 1400 to 400 B.C.), although some of the Middle Formative (Guadalupe phase) data do not support this generalization. It should be noted that most of the surface area in household clusters excavated at Tierras Largas did not yield primary deposits. In fact, calculations indicate that, in most cases, only from 3% to 10% of the surface area within a household cluster yielded primary deposits.

It was possible to estimate the number of household clusters present at Tierras Largas using (1) an estimate of the area covered by deposits and features in a household cluster, and (2) the household cluster evidence found in the randomly selected, excavated sample squares. Predictions for any given Early to Middle Formative phase seem within reason for a village of that size. However, in some cases, the statistical confidence interval was large, so that the estimated number of household clusters fell within a range of, for example, about 5–30. Obviously a smaller range is desirable, and could have been obtained if we had excavated even more sample squares.

Estimates based on sample excavation results were modified with data on spacing between household clusters (Table 8.1). Early Formative household clusters at Tierras Largas seem to be spaced about 20–40 m apart, although we found two Late San José phase clusters that were closer together, which may represent parts of an extended household or a social unit larger than the

nuclear family. The Middle Formative spacing pattern is somewhat different from the Early Formative pattern. The Guadalupe phase evidence from Tierras Largas is ambiguous, but slightly later Rosario phase household clusters (Table 8.1) were spaced some 35 m apart, which is half again the San José phase spacing.

Best estimates of the number of household clusters at Tierras Largas were calculated by combining the previously mentioned factors of (1) household cluster size, (2) predictions from the sample excavations, and (3) considerations of spacing (Winter 1972). In this respect, it should be noted that the random sampling program and statistical procedures alone did not provide simple solutions to research questions. The sampling program and statistics were helpful only when taken in conjunction with additional considerations, based more on common sense than on mathematical formulas.

Ten household clusters are estimated for the first half of the Early Formative (Table 8.1). If the average household were composed of 5 people, a

TABLE 8.1 Estimated Size (in Hectares) and Population (in Households) at Tierras Largas, Oaxaca, for Seven Consecutive Subphases[a]

Subphase and estimated date	Estimated size in hectares	Estimated number of households
Early Tierras Largas (1400–1300 B.C.)	1.58	10
Late Tierras Largas (1300–1150 B.C.)	2.24	10
Early San José (1150–1000 B.C.)	.95	5
Late San José (1000–850 B.C.)	1.59	8
Early Guadalupe (850–750 B.C.)	3.0	9–10
Late Guadalupe (750–650 B.C.)	3.0	9–10
Rosario phase (650–500 B.C.)	3.0	9

[a]After Winter (1972).

population of 50 is estimated for the community. After the end of the Tierras Largas phase, the number of households may have declined to about half of the previous estimate. It quickly increased again to the previous level, and probably remained at 9–10 households throughout the Middle Formative period.

Despite the apparent continuity in terms of number of households and population size, some changes took place at Tierras Largas during the Early and Middle Formative periods. At the time of the initial occupation in the Early Tierras Largas phase, household clusters seem to have been present in two discrete parts of the site—one group of clusters to the north edge, and another to the southwest. Perhaps the site was settled initially by two different families or groups, though this has not been demonstrated. Following the early occupation, the site seems to have become a single spatial unit, with household clusters over an area of more than 2 ha. At the end of the Early Formative period, household clusters were concentrated in the north part of the site in an area somewhat greater than 1 ha. Thus the earlier Tierras Largas phase occupation was scattered over an area roughly twice the size of the later San José phase occupation (Figures 8.3 and 8.4).

The Middle Formative occupation was distributed over an area of perhaps 3 ha, or a somewhat larger one than the Tierras Largas phase occupation. By the Rosario phase (see Table 8.1), there is some evidence that a major change had occurred at the site, with the appearance of a high-status residence in the center of the occupation area (Figure 8.5). More excavation will be necessary to confirm this possibility, but we did find a prepared earth floor, a concentration of postholes, three large ovens, and a number of artifacts that may indicate the presence of a high-status residence. This might increase the Middle Formative population estimate of 50 people by 5–10 or so, depending on the size and nature of the high-status household. As Figure 8.5 shows, common or low-status Rosario phase households are dispersed around the center of the

site where the probable high-status residence is located.

The relation between estimated population size and site area during the Formative at Tierras Largas is shown in Figure 8.6.

San José Mogote: A Large Nucleated Village

The pattern of community size and growth at Tierras Largas (Figure 8.6) holds for many Early and Middle Formative hamlets in the Valley of Oaxaca. Drennan's (1972) excavations at Fábrica San José suggest that population there remained at 10–12 households throughout the Middle Formative. Nearly a dozen more hamlets throughout the Valley remained between 1 and 3 ha in size during Early and Middle Formative times.

The pattern at San José Mogote, on the other hand, is considerably different (Figure 8.7). Late in the Tierras Largas phase, San José Mogote was only slightly larger than Tierras Largas. By 1150 B.C., it was growing enormously, and, by 900 B.C., it was 10 times the size of Tierras Largas. San José Mogote continued to pull away, growing to 15 times the size of Tierras Largas by 550 B.C. During this entire period, San José Mogote seems to have been more internally differentiated than Tierras Largas, and a substantial part of its growth lay in the proliferation of public buildings. After reaching a second peak in the Proto-Classic, it slowly declined until abandonment.

Summary Comments

In the community growth patterns of the Valley of Oaxaca, we see some of the dynamics that produced the "monster sites" of which Marcus (Chapter 3, this volume) speaks. Nearly half the *regional population growth* of the Valley of Oaxaca between 1500 and 500 B.C. can be attributed to the growth of a single large nucleated village. That village added 5 ha to its size every century for roughly 700 years.

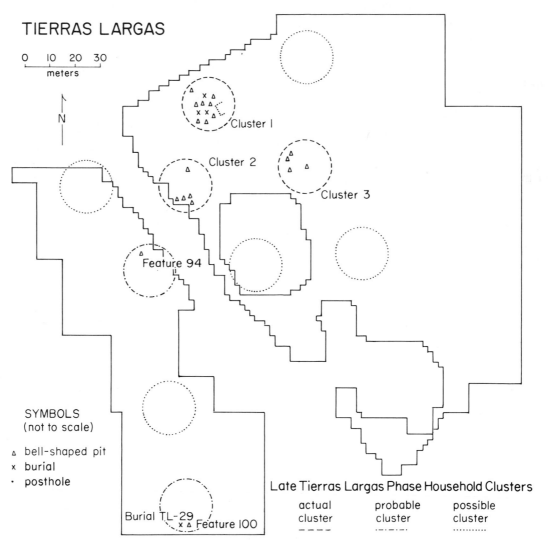

Figure 8.3 Spatial distribution of known Late Tierras Largas phase household clusters, other primary deposits, and possible household clusters at Tierras Largas. [After Winter 1972:Figure 9.]

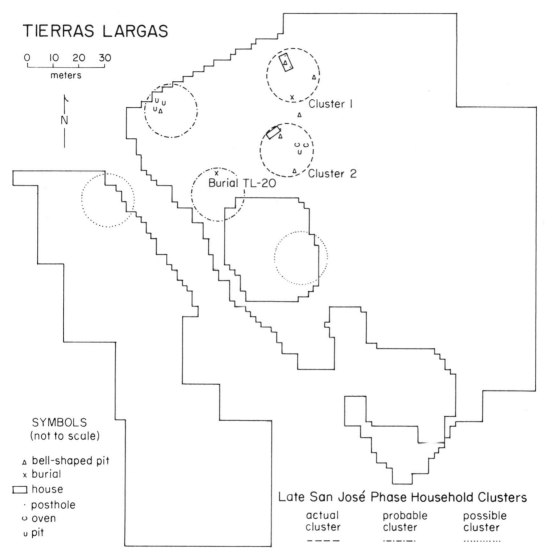

TIERRAS LARGAS

0 10 20 30
meters

N

Cluster 1

Cluster 2

Burial TL-20

SYMBOLS
(not to scale)

△ bell-shaped pit
x burial
▭ house
· posthole
∪ oven
∪ pit

Late San José Phase Household Clusters

actual   probable   possible
cluster   cluster   cluster
- - - -   -·-·-·-   ············

Figure 8.4 Spatial distribution of known Late San José phase household clusters, other primary deposits, and possible household clusters at Tierras Largas. [After Winter 1972: Figure 11.]

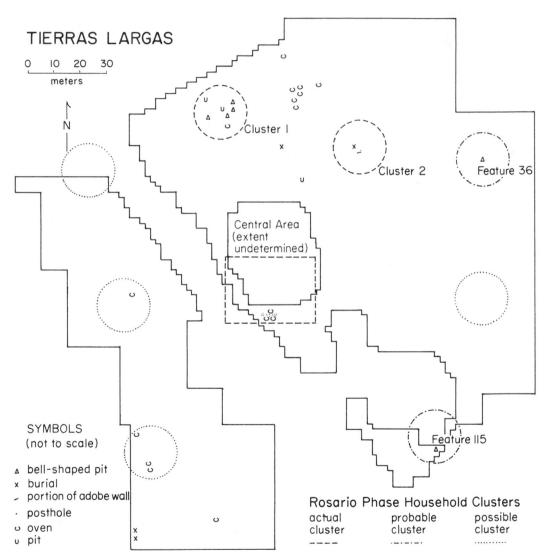

Figure 8.5 Spatial distribution of known Rosario phase household clusters, other primary deposits, and possible household clusters at Tierras Largas. [After Winter 1972:Figure 13.]

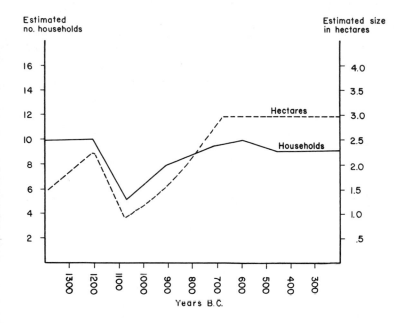

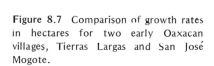

Figure 8.6 Changes in the estimated area (in hectares) and population (in households) through time at Tierras Largas, Oaxaca. [Data from Winter 1972.]

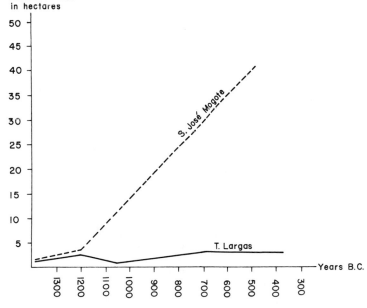

Figure 8.7 Comparison of growth rates in hectares for two early Oaxacan villages, Tierras Largas and San José Mogote.

On the other hand, most hamlets—including Tierras Largas and Fábrica San José—showed relatively little change in size and estimated households during the same millenium. In fact, granting all our possible sources of error in household estimation, it would be reasonable to say that most hamlets, once they had reached 8–12 households, remained stable at that size. This fact, coupled with the high number of 1–3-ha sites located on survey, suggests that there may be a modal size for Early and Middle Formative hamlets.

On the other hand, there were some significant changes in Tierras Largas late in the Middle Formative period. The first probable high-status residence made its appearance. Household clusters became larger and were spaced farther apart, so that, even though the hamlet covered more area than previously, it probably consisted of the same number of households as before. Clearly, these changes cannot be attributed to "population pressure" at Tierras Largas itself; probably we must turn to intercommunity relations and to valley-wide processes to understand them (cf. Brumfiel, this chapter).

Finally, the Tierras Largas data suggest that a pattern of growth, climax, and decline cannot simply be assumed for Formative hamlets. Indeed, that pattern may fit only large nucleated villages like San José Mogote, San Lorenzo, or Chiapa de Corzo. The 1–3-ha hamlet may be a very stable unit with a very predictable population range, at least for areas like the Valley of Oaxaca.

Regional Growth in the Eastern Valley of Mexico: A Test of the "Population Pressure" Hypothesis★

ELIZABETH BRUMFIEL

Introduction

In recent years, a number of studies have dealt with the origins of complex sociopolitical systems (Steward 1949; Fried 1960; Adams 1966; Sanders and Price 1968; Carneiro 1970). Though differing in the intermediate causal variables they emphasize (irrigation, trade, warfare, etc.), all these works, with the possible exception of Adams', ultimately trace back the origins of the state to an original condition in which a human population began pressing the productive capabilities of its environment. Steward (1949:19), for example, states:

> As population increased, new clusters evidently budded off and established themselves on unsettled lands. In the course of time, as flood plains became densely settled and as need arose to divert water through canals to drier land, collaboration on irrigation projects under some coordinating authority became necessary.

*I wish to thank Kent V. Flannery, Richard I. Ford, Jeffrey R. Parsons, Edwin N. Wilmsen, Robert E. Whallon, Jr., and Henry T. Wright for reading earlier drafts of this paper and offering valuable comments on them. I am especially indebted to Parsons for his generous aid in evaluating the topography of site catchment areas in the eastern Valley of Mexico, and to Wright who greatly facilitated the statistical analysis of the accumulated data.

And Carneiro (1970:735) writes:

> With increasing pressure of human population on the land ... the major incentive for war changed from a desire for revenge to a need to acquire land.... Through the recurrence of warfare of this type, we see arising in coastal Peru integrated territorial units transcending the village in size and in degree of organization.

Sanders and Price (1968:74) summarize their own ideas as follows:

> We cite three basic processes which have played a major role in the evolution of New World civilizations: population growth, competition, and cooperation. Population growth may be considered as a primary process in the cause-and-effect network with competition and cooperation as derivative processes.

All these statements share one basic assumption: that human populations tend to grow until they reach the productive limits of the subsistence systems that support them.

This assumption has its attractions. As Binford (1968) has pointed out in another context, it enables the investigator to assume that population exerts a constant pressure on human cultural systems. If state organization is viewed as a response to population pressure, and if all human populations are subject to population pressure, then it can be postulated that the state *will* occur wherever it *can* occur, and the problem of explaining the origins of the state is reduced to one of isolating the variables that permit cultural evolution to run its natural course. Thus, Steward (1949) can focus on arid and semiarid lands with the potential for irrigation agriculture, Sanders (1956) can isolate regions of economic symbiosis, and Carneiro (1970) can stress the importance of areas of circumscribed agricultural productivity.

But certain investigators have questioned the validity of such an assumption. Wynne-Edwards (1962) has presented the argument in general theoretical terms: If any animal population expanded

to the maximum limits of its food supply, it would be caught up in a downward spiral of overexploitation and diminishing returns. Thus, selection would constantly favor an animal population that established a demographic equilibrium well below the maximum limits set by its food supply. On a more empirical level, Wagley's (1973:154) investigation of population dynamics in two Tupi tribes led him to conclude that human populations can, and do, stabilize beneath the limits set by their subsistence systems: "While population potentials are certainly limited by food supply ... and other material factors, social institutions and culturally derived values are influential in determining trends in population size within the limits set by such 'natural' factors."

A number of other ethnographic studies have suggested that many human populations practicing subsistence agriculture have not grown to the numbers that their agricultural systems could support. Brookfield and Brown (1963) claim that the Chimbu population density of 288 per square mile represents only 64% of the density that could be supported if the agricultural system were expanded to its limits. Turner (1957) states that Ndembu densities are no more than 20% of those which could be maintained. And Carneiro (1960) estimates that the Kuikuru agricultural system is capable of supporting villages 14 times larger than those observed in the Kuikuru area today.

These challenges to the assumption that population will grow to the limits imposed by its food supply have been countered in a number of different ways. Some authors claim that the populations just cited have been studied while in a state of demographic disequilibrium. Carneiro (1961), for example, feels that Amazonian groups like the Kuikuru were expanding at the time of contact, and eventually would have grown to the limits set by their subsistence systems. Others (cf. Sanders and Price 1968) argue that estimates like those just cited are not valid because they are based only on the caloric productivity of food crops, whereas, in fact, populations may be limited by shortages of critical nutritional elements that have not been taken into account. Washburn (1968) has pointed out that a population consuming only 20–30% of the food normally available to it may actually be limited by the amount of food available in occasional years of poor productivity.

Despite the merits of these counterarguments, it seems to me that archeologists can no longer assume that prehistoric cultural evolution invariably took place under conditions of population pressure. Whenever population pressure is called upon to explain the origins of the state, archeologists must demonstrate that such a condition did, in fact, exist. It is essential, then, to develop some method of testing for population pressure in prehistoric populations. The purpose of this section is to present one such method and to use it to test for population pressure in an actual case of primary state formation.

The Procedure

The Valley of Mexico will provide the test case; it is suitable for several reasons. First, the pattern of increasing social complexity within the valley is fairly well defined. The large, densely occupied, architecturally complex communities dating from the Late Formative suggest to Parsons (1971a) that chiefdoms were functioning within the valley by 550 B.C. State formation generally is considered to have coincided with the dramatic growth of Teotihuacán, an urban center on the northeastern margin of the valley, at about A.D. 100 (Millon 1967). Second, intensive surveys of the eastern half of the valley by Parsons (1971a,b) and Blanton (1972) have provided data from which reasonable relative population estimates can be made. Finally, these data do suggest that increasing population may have been a problem for the Formative inhabitants of the valley. Parsons (1971c) estimates that, from a base population of 10,000 in the Middle Formative (850–550 B.C.), the total population of the eastern Valley of Mexico grew to 70,000 in the Late Formative (550–250 B.C.)

and to 110,000 in the Terminal Formative (250 B.C.–A.D. 100). Furthermore, the changing pattern of village placement within the valley makes tenable the supposition that competitive relationships between political units of increasing size and complexity existed throughout the Formative period (Earle, Chapter 7, this volume).

Population pressure is a relative term, referring to the relationship between the needs of a population and the productivity of the resources it possesses. Both these factors are determined, in part at least, by the cultural system of a given population. Boserup (1965) has pointed out that the agricultural productivity of an environment varies greatly with the productive system used to exploit it, and Wolf (1966) argues that the cost of social and ceremonial payments must be included in the calculation of subsistence minima. It is for this reason that investigators like Carneiro (1960) and Allan (1964) evaluate carrying capacities using levels of productivity and consumption as they exist in the cultures examined. These culturally determined aspects of population pressure present considerable difficulties for the archeologist wishing to evaluate the status of prehistoric populations. Though the productivity of Formative period crops and agricultural techniques has been estimated for some areas of Mesoamerica (cf. Kirkby 1973), no estimates have yet been made for the Valley of Mexico. Formative levels of consumption are a completely unknown factor. Therefore, it has been necessary to formulate a somewhat indirect means of measuring the intensity of population pressure in the case to be considered.

Population pressure may be defined as occurring whenever the total needs of a population approach the maximum output that its subsistence system will produce. Therefore, if we compare several communities, all of which are under population pressure, we should find a high positive correlation between their needs and their productive capabilities. The needs of communities with very productive subsistence systems should be quite numerous and the needs of communities with less productive subsistence systems should be correspondingly fewer. If all these communities shared a uniform culture, then the culturally determined aspects of population pressure—such as levels of consumption and subsistence technology—would be the same for each community. The needs of each community would vary only in proportion to the size of its population, and all variation in the subsistence productivity of the various communities would be a function of the amounts and fertility of the resources available to them.

If we make the assumption of cultural uniformity for all villages in the eastern Valley of Mexico dating to a single time period, we could expect a situation of population pressure to be expressed in a simple correlation between *the relative number of inhabitants at each village* and *the relative productive potential of agricultural land available to each village*. If, on the other hand, we examined the populations and productive potentials of Formative villages in the eastern Valley of Mexico and found that they did *not* covary, we would be forced to conclude that population pressure was not a factor of any importance during the Formative period.

In this investigation, site area has been used as an indicator of population size. Thus, when one site covers twice the area of a second, it is assumed to have contained twice the number of inhabitants. Although the site areas of regional administrative centers might be somewhat inflated by the utilization of some land for nonresidential purposes (temples, market places, storehouses, and so on), it is also possible that populations were more densely packed in large centers; thus these two factors might more or less balance each other. The productive potential of each site has been scored on the basis of two factors: the amount of agricultural land available to the occupants of each site, and the relative fertility of the land.

Estimates of available agricultural land have been made by performing a *site-catchment analysis* for each of the Formative villages considered. Since site catchment has been defined in Chapter 4 of this volume, I will not describe it in detail except

to say that the methodology used resembled the catchment analysis of David Rossmann (this volume) rather than the chi-square method of Fred Plog (1968) or Alan Zarky (this volume). It applied Vita-Finzi and Higgs' (1970) suggestion that agriculturalists will cultivate land up to 5 km from their residences. Although the method employed is most useful in regions which have been totally surveyed (such as Parsons and Blanton have provided), it also can be used with quadrat samples from areas where total survey is impossible (see Chapter 5 of this volume).

Figures for available agricultural land were obtained by measuring the number of hectares of land suitable for digging-stick cultivation lying within a 5-km radius of each Formative village (see Figures 8.8 and 8.9). Variation in the amount of agricultural land available to different villages was a function of three factors. *Site Size* accounted for some slight variation. Since the 5-km catchment radius was extended from the peripheries of the sites in question, the catchment areas of larger villages were potentially greater than those of smaller villages.

Site packing provided a major source of variation. Whenever two villages lay within 10 km of each other, their catchment areas overlapped. In these cases, a line joining the two points of intersection of the overlapping circles established the boundary between the catchment areas of the two villages. The catchment areas of villages with many neighboring communities nearby were consequently quite small.

Catchment topography provided the final source of variation. Land falling within the bed of former Lake Texcoco, or above the 2750-m contour (the upper limit of maize cultivation in the area), or along steep-sided barrancas or mountain ridges, was considered unarable. It was therefore excluded in the calculation of available agricultural land. The catchment areas of four Late Formative communities diagrammed in Figures 8.8 and 8.9 show the effects of some of these sources of variation.

Figures on the relative fertility of agricultural land in various parts of the Valley of Mexico were

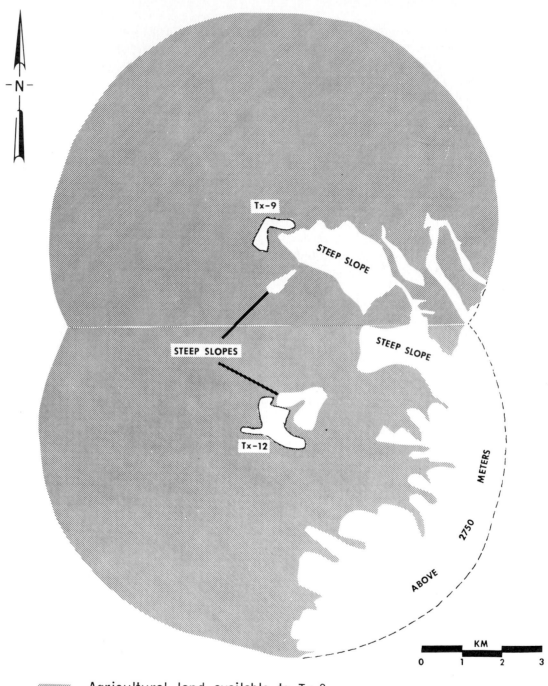

Figure 8.8 Catchment areas of Late Formative sites Tx-9 and Tx-12.

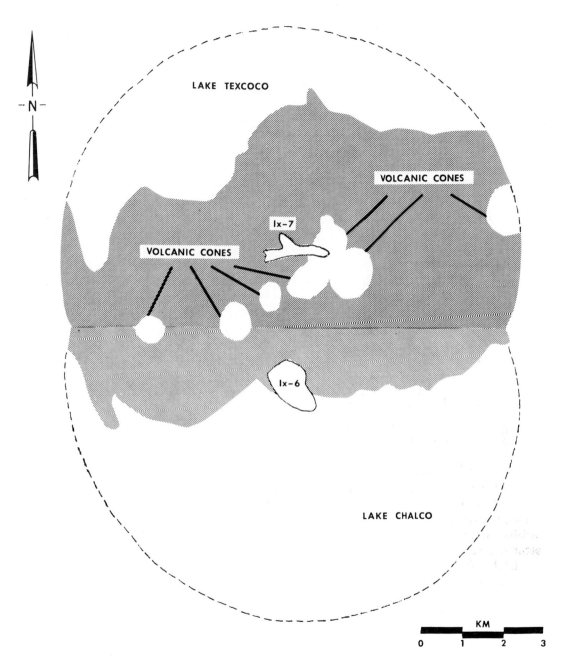

Figure 8.9 Catchment areas of Late Formative sites Ix-7 and Ix-6.

obtained from a recent agricultural census of the valley (Mexico 1960). This census lists the number of hectares of land planted in maize in each *municipio** in the eastern Valley of Mexico, and the number of metric tons of maize this land produced. Tons of maize produced per hectare planted provided an indicator of the relative fertility of the agricultural land available to occupants of various Formative villages. In the census, the figures on hectares planted and maize produced are broken down by the size of the land holdings (for example, *ejido*† lands; private holdings of 5 ha or less; private holdings larger than 5 ha) and by the presence or absence of irrigation. In most cases, the relative fertility ratio was computed using the figures for nonirrigated *ejido* land, since agricultural techniques used today on this land are thought to resemble most closely the agricultural technology of Formative inhabitants of the area. However, the dense packing and linear arrangement of large Formative villages in the southeastern corner of the valley suggested that these lands had been irrigated. Therefore, Late Formative sites Ch-7 and Ch-8, and Terminal Formative sites Ch-14, Ch-25, Ch-26, and Ch-27 were assigned fertility ratios based on the output of irrigated small holdings in the Chalco area. The output of irrigated land in the eastern Valley of Mexico is roughly twice that of unirrigated land. This accounts for the high fertility ratios assigned each of these sites.

Multiplication of the amount of agricultural land available to each village (as determined by site-catchment analysis) times the relative fertility of that land (on the basis of its present-day productivity) yielded a score of the productive poten-

---

*The Mexican *municipio* is an administrative and political unit, similar to an American county but endowed with greater political autonomy.

†*Ejido* lands are communally owned by the *municipio*. They are divided into small plots and worked by individuals who enjoy usufructuary rights to the land. *Ejido* plots and small private holdings are practically identical, except that the former cannot be sold (Lewis 1951).

tial of each Formative village. These scores indicate the productive potential of each Formative village relative to every other Formative village in the eastern Valley of Mexico. Thus, the Late Formative inhabitants of site Tx-9 (which has a productive potential of 60.8) were capable of producing twice as much maize as the Late Formative inhabitants of site Ch-4 (which has a productive potential of 30.4). Similarly, the Terminal Formative inhabitants of Ix-5 (with a productive potential of 14.1) could produce only one-third as much maize as the Terminal Formative inhabitants of Ch-29 (with a productive potential of 42.1). Relevant data for all sites analyzed are presented in Table 8.2.

The analysis involved only large communities, those covering an area of 30 ha or more. It seemed reasonable to assume that large communities would be the first to fully exploit all arable land within a 5-km radius. Therefore, a correlation between community size and productive capacity would be more likely to appear among a sample of large communities than among a group of smaller communities. In addition, it was felt that using villages of a uniformly large size would strengthen the assumption of cultural uniformity among villages analyzed. Since there were only two large villages in the eastern Valley of Mexico dating from the Middle Formative, this period was not analyzed. Maps showing the locations of sites included in the analysis are provided in Figures 8.10 and 8.11.

The Statistical Analysis

The relationship between village size and productive potential was investigated statistically by means of a *linear regression analysis*. Roughly speaking, a linear regression analysis tells us with what degree of accuracy the value of Y can be predicted, if the value of X is known; for instance, how accurately can we predict a man's weight if the only thing we know about him is his height? If

TABLE 8.2 Raw Data Used in Site Catchment Analysis for the Eastern Valley of Mexico

Site number	Size of site in hectares	Available agricultural land (km^2)	Relative productivity (see text)	Agricultural potential (see text)	Area covered by lake (km^2)	Topographically unarable (km^2)	Land lost to other sites (km^2)
Tx-MF-13	45.0	53.0	1.1	58.3	45.2	3.3	none
Ch-MF-5	57.7	95.9	.96	91.7	1.4	7.2	none
Tx-LF-9	33.0	72.5	.84	60.8	none	4.8	20.2
Tx-LF-12	86.0	61.2	.84	51.4	none	21.2	17.6
Tx-LF-22	45.0	73.3	1.1	80.6	none	26.8	3.6
Ix-LF-2	37.0	17.6	.85	15.0	42.0	5.3	16.4
Ix-LF-6	65.0	17.9	.73	13.1	46.1	.3	28.9
Ix-LF-7	30.0	39.1	.73	28.5	21.6	5.0	15.5
Ch-LF-2	59.7	35.4	.96	33.8	7.0	none	46.5
Ch-LF-3	67.0	29.0	.96	27.8	.8	none	56.4
Ch-LF-4	34.8	31.8	.96	30.4	none	4.3	60.1
Ch-LF-7	86.0	21.6	1.92	41.5	none	.5	73.1
Ch-LF-8	130.0	34.8	1.92	66.9	none	29.7	44.4
Ch-LF-12	43.2	66.8	.82	54.8	none	2.7	32.8
Tx-TF-1	74.0	89.9	.90	80.9	none	15.2	9.2
Tx-TF-17	118.0	54.2	.84	45.5	none	12.3	28.4
Tx-TF-30	50.0	50.8	.84	42.6	none	26.4	17.0
Tx-TF-50	52.0	51.0	1.1	56.1	40.2	5.3	2.5
Ix-TF-4	37.0	21.4	.85	18.2	43.8	5.7	5.7
Ix-TF-5	32.0	19.6	.73	14.1	16.7	2.5	25.0
Ix-TF-10	32.0	34.0	.73	28.9	21.8	4.6	22.7
Ch-TF-5	54.5	54.7	.96	52.3	1.7	none	33.1
Ch-TF-14	75.0	29.4	1.92	56.4	4.6	.3	60.9
Ch-TF-18	38.4	24.8	.96	23.7	none	10.3	53.1
Ch-TF-25	35.2	6.0	1.92	11.5	none	none	95.6
Ch-TF-26	90.5	12.7	1.92	24.4	none	.3	82.5
Ch-TF-27	129.0	26.4	1.92	50.7	none	23.9	52.5
Ch-TF-29	43.1	51.4	.82	42.1	none	2.7	49.6

we can predict a man's weight quite accurately from his height, then we must conclude that weight and height are strongly correlated. In similar fashion, if we can predict the size of a village fairly accurately on the basis of its productive potential, we can conclude that village size and productive potential are correlated. The accuracy of the prediction is phrased in terms of "variance explained." If X is a perfect predictor of Y, then X will "explain" 100% of the variance in Y. If X explains only 2% of the variance in Y, we would have to conclude that X is a poor predictor of Y, that is, that the two variables are probably not

correlated. The regression analysis actually was performed for the logarithm of site size on productive potential, since this increased the linearity of the regression (Table 8.3).

The Results

As a first step in analysis, the size of each site was plotted against the productive potential of its catchment area. The plots for Late Formative and Terminal Formative sites are presented in Figures 8.12 and 8.13. Visual examination of these scatter

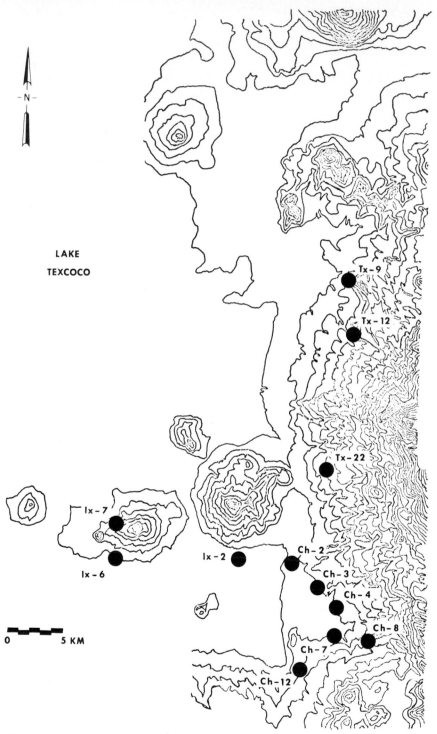

Figure 8.10 Late Formative sites of over 30 ha in the eastern Valley of Mexico. (Contour interval, 50 m)

242

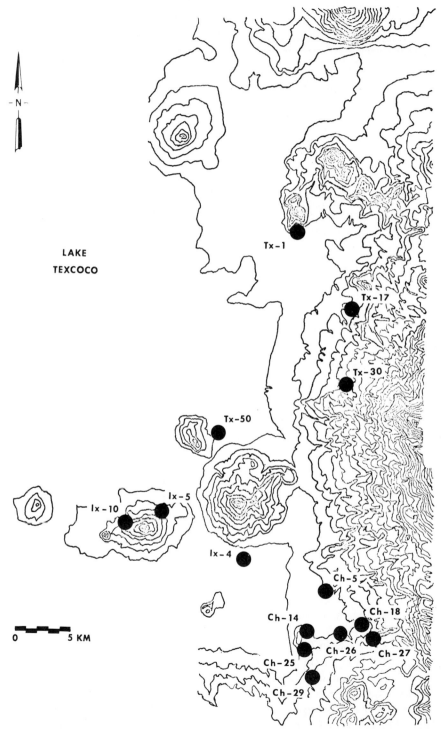

Figure 8.11 Terminal Formative sites of over 30 ha in the eastern Valley of Mexico. (Contour interval, 50 m)

TABLE 8.3 Data Used in the Linear Regression Analysis

Site	(1) Size (ha)	(2) Log_{10} of site size	(3) Arable land (km^2)	(4) Relative fertility	(5) Productive potential (3 × 4)	(6) Ratio of population to productive resources (1:5)
Late Formative sites						
Tx-9	33	1.52	72.5	.84	60.8	.54 : 1
Tx-12	86	1.93	61.2	.84	51.4	1.84 : 1
Tx-22	45	1.65	73.3	1.10	80.6	.56 : 1
Ix-2	37	1.57	17.6	.85	15.0	2.46 : 1
Ix-6	65	1.81	17.9	.73	13.1	4.96 : 1
Ix-7	30	1.48	39.1	.73	28.5	1.05 : 1
Ch-2	60	1.78	35.4	.96	33.8	1.76 : 1
Ch-3	67	1.83	29.0	.96	27.8	2.41 : 1
Ch-4	35	1.54	31.8	.96	30.4	1.14 : 1
Ch-7	86	1.93	21.6	1.92	41.5	2.07 : 1
Ch-8	130	2.11	34.8	1.92	66.9	1.94 : 1
Ch-12	43	1.63	66.8	.82	54.8	.78 : 1
MEANS	60	1.78	41.8	1.05	42.0	1.79 : 1
Terminal Formative sites						
Tx-1	74	1.87	89.9	.90	80.9	.92 : 1
Tx-17	118	2.07	54.2	.84	45.5	2.62 : 1
Tx-30	50	1.70	50.8	.84	42.6	1.17 : 1
Tx-50	52	1.72	51.0	1.10	56.1	.93 : 1
Ix-4	37	1.57	21.4	.85	18.2	2.03 : 1
Ix-5	32	1.50	19.6	.73	14.1	2.27 : 1
Ix-10	32	1.50	34.0	.73	28.9	1.11 : 1
Ch-5	54	1.73	54.7	.96	52.3	1.04 : 1
Ch-14	75	1.88	29.4	1.92	56.4	1.33 : 1
Ch-18	38	1.58	24.8	.96	23.7	1.62 : 1
Ch-25	35	1.54	6.0	1.92	11.5	3.06 : 1
Ch-26	90	1.95	12.7	1.92	24.4	3.71 : 1
Ch-27	129	2.11	26.4	1.92	50.7	2.54 : 1
Ch-29	43	1.63	51.4	.82	42.1	1.02 : 1
MEANS	61	1.78	37.6	1.17	39.1	1.81 : 1

diagrams suggested that there was no *single* relationship between the size and the productive potential of prehistoric settlements during either the Late or Terminal Formative period. Instead, *separate* relationships between site size and productive potential were positively correlated for Late Formative sites larger than 50 ha (log 50 = 1.70) but were not correlated at Late Formative sites smaller than 50 ha. Site size and productive potential were positively correlated for all Terminal Formative sites, but the sites lined up in two

tiers: a higher tier composed of the three sites larger than 80 ha (log 80 = 1.90), and a lower tier composed of sites smaller than 80 ha. On the basis of these observations, the decision was made to subject the data to four separate regression analyses, one each for large and small Late Formative and Terminal Formative sites.

The regression analyses confirmed these observations made on the scatter diagrams. The regression of site size on productive potential for the larger Late Formative sites explained over 78% of the

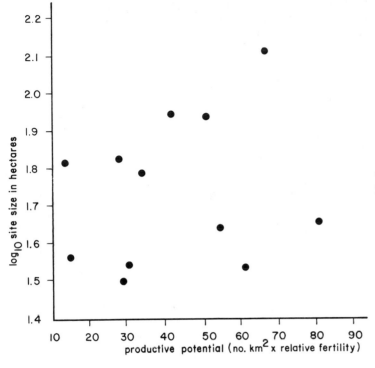

Figure 8.12 Plot of productive potential versus site size, Late Formative sites (550–250 B.C.).

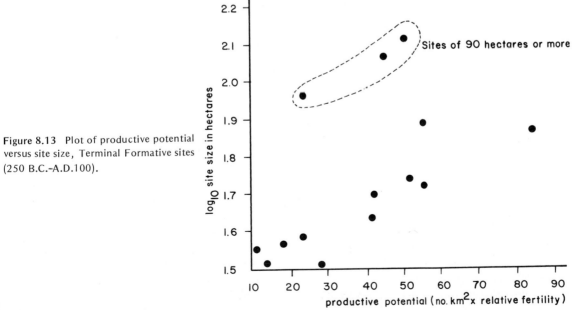

Figure 8.13 Plot of productive potential versus site size, Terminal Formative sites (250 B.C.–A.D.100).

Sites of 90 hectares or more

variance in site size, and was significant at the .02 level. The regression of site size on productive potential for the smaller Late Formative sites explained less than 58% of the site size variance, significant only at the .24 level. In other words, site size and productive potential were positively correlated at the larger, but not significantly correlated at the smaller, Late Formative sites.

The regression of site size on productive potential for the larger Terminal Formative sites accounted for over 99% of the variance in site size, but, because there were so few (three) large Terminal Formative sites, this was significant only at the .03 level. The regression for the smaller Terminal Formative sites accounted for more than 82% of the variance in site size, significant at better than the .01 level. These analyses indicate that site size and productive potential are positively correlated at both the larger and smaller Terminal Formative sites.

If it is true, as argued earlier, that population pressure will be reflected in a correlation between site size and productive potential, then these data suggest that an important transition occurred between the Late and Terminal Formative periods in the eastern Valley of Mexico. During the Late Formative, population pressure occurred on a *localized* basis only, at some but not all Late Formative sites. Population pressure affected Late Formative settlements larger than 50 ha in size but seems not to have significantly affected smaller Late Formative settlements. I would argue that this expresses a tendency toward maximal nucleation at large Late Formative sites, but does not reveal a general pattern of overpopulation. In contrast, the data from Terminal Formative sites suggest that the inhabitants of *all* settlements over 30 ha in size were, to a greater or lesser extent, experiencing population pressure. Population pressure thus had become a more universal condition.

Three discrete factors, operating in combination or alone, conceivably could account for population pressure during the Terminal Formative. Population growth is the most commonly cited cause of population pressure. But population pressure could be produced as easily either by decreases in subsistence system productivity (i.e., a decrease in soil fertility, a deterioration of climatic conditions, etc.) or by increases in per capita needs (i.e., the level of consumption). Let us consider the possible role of each of these factors in producing the generalized condition of population pressure that existed during the Terminal Formative period.

Our figures do record substantial population growth. The total occupied area of sites analyzed increases from 716 ha in the Late Formative to 857 ha during the Terminal Formative. Thus, it is possible that the correlations between the size and productive potential of Terminal Formative sites was the result of increased numbers of people. The population of each settlement might have grown until it reached some fixed ratio of the site's productive resources, that is, until the carrying capacity of the settlement's catchment area was approached. Or the growing population might have budded off, filling in adjacent areas until the amount of agricultural land available to each settlement was reduced to the minimum that would support its population. Either process would imply a significant increase in the ratio of population to available resources or, in terms of our variables, the ratio of site size to productive potential. The mean ratio of site size to productive potential does increase slightly from 1.79:1 in the Late Formative to 1.81:1 in the Terminal Formative, but this increase is minimal, significant only at the .6 level. Therefore, it may be concluded that population growth alone cannot account for the population pressure we have recorded for the Terminal Formative.

It is more difficult to assess possible changes in subsistence system productivity from the Late to the Terminal Formative. On the one hand, the productivity of crops probably increased. Kirkby's (1973: Figure 48) analysis of prehistoric corncobs from Tehuacán and the Valley of Oaxaca suggests that the yields of Mesoamerican maize varieties probably improved steadily throughout the Formative period. On the other hand, conditions for agriculture may have been less favorable. Parsons (1971a,b) and Blanton (1972) found both Late and Terminal Formative sites lying below the Aztec-period level of Lake Texcoco. The lake was evidently smaller at this time, possibly indicating that drier conditions prevailed during the Late and Terminal Formative periods. However, such a drop in lake level could have been caused by an alteration of drainage patterns in the tectonically unstable Mexican Altiplano. In any case, there is no evidence that the level of the lake was lower during the Terminal Formative than it had been during the preceding Late Formative period.

Moreover, changing climatic conditions are unable to account for the curious two-tiered character of population pressure which is evident in the scatter diagram of the size and productive potential of Terminal Formative sites. It is difficult to imagine any configuration of climatic conditions that would permit three large sites to maintain an average population-to-productive-potential ratio of 2.95:1 while creating population pressure at 10 smaller sites with the much lower ratio of population to productive potential of 1.50:1. I would suggest that the two-tiered nature of population pressure during the Terminal Formative is better explained by sociopolitical factors than by demography or by the conditions of agricultural production. Modifying the assumption of cultural uniformity for the Terminal Formative data, I would suggest that the larger and smaller Terminal Formative sites followed different regimes of production and consumption, and that these differences were based on the ability of the large "secondary regional centers" to draw produce from the smaller settlements in the form of taxes, tribute, or payment for special services rendered. The collection of such tribute by a regional center would constitute a kind of "productive activity," the yields of which would be unrelated to the agricultural productivity of the catchment area immediately surrounding the center. The rendering

of payments by smaller sites would constitute a new means of disposing of produce, an added component in the regime of consumption. The resultant increase in the per capita level of consumption at smaller sites well may have created the condition of population pressure which finds expression in the lower tier correlation between site size and productive potential.

Thus, population pressure in the eastern Valley of Mexico during the Terminal Formative period was quite possibly a sequel to changes in the political structure of society which enabled the occupants of certain larger sites to extract payments from the occupants of smaller sites on a larger, more systematic basis. Such changes would normally attend the inception of a state-like political organization.*

Our data clearly contradict the idea that population growth caused the emergence of the state in the eastern Valley of Mexico. Until a more adequate picture of rainfall levels in the Valley of Mexico during the Formative period is available, reduced subsistence system productivity cannot be totally eliminated as a possible cause of state formation. But our data do suggest an alternative explanation. It is evident that, during the Late Formative period, there was a tendency for some settlements to grow to the maximum size permitted by their local productive systems. Whatever the reasons for this tendency, it is quite possible that the difficulties of maintaining large, nucleated populations at regional centers during the Late Formative generated the kinds of pressures that brought tribute relationships (and perhaps also state organization) into being during the Terminal

---

*Earle's nearest-neighbor analysis of Terminal Formative sites in the eastern Valley of Mexico (this volume) led him to a similar conclusion. "The regular spacing between Level 4 (large) sites in the Terminal Formative...," Earle writes, "might be the result of planned resettlement of people around regularly spaced administrative centers.... Such regular resettlement points to a strongly developed state organization for the Valley of Mexico well before it had been expected."

Formative. A *general* condition of overpopulation in the Valley of Mexico during the Formative period may never have been a factor.

Conclusions

It has been suggested by many anthropologists that population pressure, resulting from population growth, is the driving force behind the evolution of the state. The data presented here do not support this proposition. Population pressure, expressed in terms of a correlation between settlement size and productive potential, apparently did exist in the eastern Valley of Mexico during the Terminal Formative. But since the mean ratio of population to productive resources remains virtually constant from the Late through Terminal Formative periods, population pressure cannot be regarded as a consequence of population growth in this particular case. Although information on climatic conditions in the Valley of Mexico during the Formative period is scanty, there is no evidence that would suggest that the climate actually deteriorated from the Late to the Terminal Formative. Thus, population pressure was probably not a consequence of reduced subsistence system productivity during the Terminal Formative. The two-tiered nature of the correlation between site size and productive potential among the smaller Terminal Formative settlements suggests that population pressure in the Valley of Mexico was brought about by changes in the sociopolitical sphere rather than in the material conditions of existence. Terminal Formative population pressure probably should be regarded as an effect, rather than a cause, of the evolution of the state.

References

Adams, R. Mc.
  1966   *The evolution of urban society*. Chicago: Aldine.
Allan, W.
  1965   *The African husbandman*. New York: Barnes & Noble.

Binford, L. R.
  1968   Post-Pleistocene adaptations. In *New perspectives in archeology*, edited by L. R. Binford and S. R. Binford. Chicago: Aldine. Pp. 313–341.
Blanton, R. E.
  1972   Prehispanic settlement patterns of the Ixtapalapa peninsula region, Mexico. *Occasional Papers in Anthropology* No. 6. Dept. of Anthropology, Pennsylvania State University, University Park.
Boserup, E.
  1965   *The conditions of agricultural growth*. Chicago: Aldine.
Brookfield, H. C., and P. Brown
  1963   *Struggle for land*. Melbourne, Australia: Oxford University Press.
Carneiro, R. L.
  1960   Slash-and-burn agriculture: A closer look at its implications for settlement patterns. In *Men and cultures*, edited by A. F. C. Wallace. Philadelphia: University of Pennsylvania Press. Pp. 229–234.
  1961   Slash-and-burn cultivation among the Kuikuru and its implications for cultural development in the Amazon Basin. *Antropologica*, Suppl. 2:47–67.
  1970   A theory of the origin of the state. *Science* 169:733–738.
Drennan, R. D.
  1972   Excavations at Fábrica San José, Oaxaca, Mexico. Mimeographed preliminary report. Ann Arbor, Mich.
Fried, M.
  1960   On the evolution of social stratification and the state. In *Culture in history*, edited by S. Diamond. New York: Columbia University Press. Pp. 713–731.
Kirkby, A. V. T.
  1973   The use of land and water resources in the past and present Valley of Oaxaca, Mexico. *Memoirs* No. 5. Museum of Anthropology, University of Michigan, Ann Arbor.
Lewis, O.
  1951   *Life in a Mexican village*. Urbana: University of Illinois Press.
Mexico: Dirección General de Estadística
  1960   *IV Censo agrícola y ganadero del estado de México*. México, D.F.
Millon, R.
  1967   Teotihuacán. *Scientific American* 216:38–48.
Parsons, J. R.
  1971a   Prehistoric settlement patterns in the Texcoco region, Mexico. *Memoirs* No. 3. Museum

of Anthropology, University of Michigan, Ann Arbor.

1971b Prehispanic settlement patterns in the Chalco region, Mexico. Mimeographed preliminary report. Ann Arbor, Mich.

1971c Prehispanic settlement patterns in the Valley of Mexico. Unpublished proposal to the National Science Foundation. Ann Arbor, Mich. Mimeograph.

Plog, F. T.
1968 Archaeological survey—a new perspective. Unpublished Master's thesis, Dept. of Anthropology, University of Chicago.

Sanders, W. T.
1956 The central Mexican symbiotic region: A study in prehistoric settlement patterns. In *Prehistoric settlement patterns in the New World*, edited by G. R. Willey. *Viking Fund Publications in Anthropology* No. 23. New York: Wenner-Gren. Pp. 115–127.

1972 Population, agricultural history, and societal evolution in Mesoamerica. In *Population growth: Anthropological implications*, edited by B. Spooner. Cambridge: M.I.T. Press. Pp. 101–153.

Sanders, W. T., and B. J. Price
1968 *Mesoamerica*. New York: Random House.

Steward, J. H.
1949 Cultural causality and law. *American Anthropologist* 51:1–27.

Turner, V. W.
1957 *Schism and continuity in African society*. Manchester, Eng.: Manchester University Press.

Vita-Finzi, C., and E. S. Higgs
1970 Prehistoric economy in the Mt. Carmel area of Palestine: Site catchment analysis. *Proceedings of the Prehistoric Society* 36:1–37.

Wagley, C.
1973 Cultural influences on population: A comparison of two Tupi tribes. In *Peoples and cultures of native South America*, edited by D. R. Gross. Garden City: Doubleday/The Natural History Press. Pp. 145–156.

Washburn, S. L.
1968 The central Eskimo: A marginal case? In *Man the Hunter*, edited by R. B. Lee and I. de Vore. Chicago: Aldine. P. 84.

Winter, M. C.
1972 Tierras Largas: A Formative community in the Valley of Oaxaca, Mexico. Unpublished Ph.D. dissertation, Dept. of Anthropology, University of Arizona, Tucson.

Wolf, E. R.
1966 *Peasants*. Englewood Cliffs, N.J.: Prentice-Hall.

Wynne-Edwards, V. C.
1962 *Animal dispersion in relation to social behavior*. London: Oliver & Boyd.

Chapter 9

ANALYSIS OF STYLISTIC VARIATION WITHIN AND BETWEEN COMMUNITIES

Introduction

The Real Mesoamerican Archeologist loves to work with pottery, but if there's one thing he can't stand, it's "whispering potsherds." This is a term he borrowed from his colleague, Donald Lathrap, and it refers to sherds that whisper gently into your ear, "The potter who made me was a 43-year-old mother of four, born into a matrilineal, matrilocal clan of the Raven moiety, who used Crow kinship terms and was taught pottery making by an Anglican Missionary."

R.M.A., in other words, supports the "thumbs down" view of a volatile debate that has rocked American archeology since publication of the still controversial ceramic studies of James F. Deetz (1965), William A. Longacre (1970), and James N. Hill (1970) in the American West. All three studies were based on the assumption that there is some

relationship between the extent to which two potters interact and the degree to which their works show shared stylistic attributes. Further—and this was a result of the fact that they chose to work with the Arikara and Pueblo Indian regions of North America—all three relied on the assumption that women were the recent prehistoric potters of the area, and that women learned pottery making from their mothers. In matrilocal societies, so the argument goes, subconscious preferences for certain design elements should be passed on from grandmother to mother to daughter, and so on. Thus, residential wards where certain design elements tend to cluster could indicate the location of specific matrilineages within a pueblo, and lack of such clustering could show the breakdown of matrilocal residence.

Needless to say, not all archeologists accept these assumptions. Perhaps the most energetic criticism has come from Michael Stanislawski (1973), who insists that Pueblo potters do not always learn through their matriline; in addition, he argues, sherds do not always wind up in the part of the Pueblo where the pot originally was made.

The Real Mesoamerican Archeologist loved every minute of the "antimicrostyle backlash," and he mentions the "whispering potsherd people" with great annoyance and just a little bit of fear. The fear has stuck with him from an earlier time, when he believed that Deetz, Longacre, and Hill might be right—and was afraid that he, too, might be expected to come up with an exact provenience for all his decorated sherds. Now that they've been attacked, he feels a lot more relaxed and has been much easier to live with. I really enjoy him most when he's his old self, arguing theory with me over a beer in the plaza, or trying to figure out where an unlabeled bag of sherds under the back seat of his Jeep might have come from.

For his Skeptical Graduate Student, on the other hand, an unlabeled bag of sherds is a nonexistent bag of sherds. "A sherd without provenience is scientifically useless," he proclaims.

"That's nonsense," says R.M.A. "Some of the finest studies in Mesoamerican archeology have been done on material whose provenience is unknown. Did Miguel Covarrubias know the provenience of every Formative figurine he studied? Did Caso and Bernal know the provenience of every Oaxacan urn? Did Joralemon know the provenience of every Olmec pot?"

"Publicizing stolen goods by such studies," says S.G.S., "is antithetical to science. By convincing collectors that even looted pots are useful, it encourages buying and selling of artifacts."

"You're too idealistic," says the Real Mesoamerican Archeologist. "Given the right price, anyone will sell. It's like the old story about George Bernard Shaw."

S.G.S. always sighs at this point.

"Shaw asked this lady at a party if she'd go to bed with him for $10,000. She said yes. Then he asked if she'd go to bed with him for $1. She said 'No! What do you take me for?'

" 'We've already established that,' said Shaw. 'Now we're just haggling about the price.' Did I ever tell you that story?"

"Yes," says S.G.S., "but the last time you attributed it to Oscar Levant instead of Shaw."

All of which is a roundabout way to introduce their argument on "whispering potsherds"—an argument that took place after their second field season on the Río San Jacinto. R.M.A. wanted to produce a giant seriated ceramic sequence relating the Río San Jacinto to neighboring regions. S.G.S. wanted to analyze all the decorated sherds by square and level, in an attempt to figure out where each prehistoric lineage had resided, how many lineages there were, and whether each villager tended to marry his mother's brother's daughter.

"You can't *use* Mesoamerican potsherds that way," R.M.A. protested. "Unilineal descent is rare to absent in Mesoamerica; women are potters in some areas, men in others; residence rules are quite variable; and besides, I don't really believe there's any relationship between designs and kin groups."

"What would *you* like to do with the pottery?" asked S.G.S.

"Something a little more useful. We calculate the percentages of one type to another for each level, and seriate all the levels from the various pits based on the changing percentages through time. Then we relate our sequence to the Valley of Mexico."

"How do we do that?"

"Easy. Our earliest phase has white pottery with incised parallel lines and 'double-line-break' motifs. That means they were in contact with the Altica phase potters of the Teotihuacán Valley. Our later levels have cylindrical tripod vessels with hollow slab feet, which means they're in contact with Teotihuacán. During the Post-Classic, the area has Mixtec polychrome and stamped bowl-bottom designs, which means it's more closely in contact with Puebla and Oaxaca than with the Aztecs."

"Because of those pottery types, they're more closely in contact with Puebla than the Aztecs?"

"Of course," said R.M.A. "If they were more closely in contact with the Aztecs, I'd expect more Aztec III pottery, more black-on-reds, and so on."

"So you *do* believe," said S.G.S., "that there is a relationship between the degree to which two groups are in contact and the degree to which they share ceramic styles and decoration."

"Of course."

"But you don't believe there's any relationship between the degree to which members of two lineages interact and the degree to which they share ceramic styles and decoration."

"Of course not," said R.M.A.

"It seems to me, then," said S.G.S., "that you're a little like the lady in the George Bernard Shaw story. We've established the principle you believe in. What we're haggling about now is the depth of your commitment."

I have tried to set down R.M.A.'s and S.G.S.'s words just as they spoke them, for it seems to me that this is the crux of the "whispering potsherd" controversy. For decades, all Mesoamerican archeology has been based on the principle that two areas that do share the same pottery decoration are more closely related than some third area that does not. Even within a single valley, some Mesoamerican archeologists are prepared to argue that one end of the valley shows "ties with the Gulf" while the opposite end shows "ties with the Central Highlands." But carry the same principle one notch lower on the scale of analysis—say "these six houses are more closely related to each other than either is to those six over there, and therefore they represent two different segments of the community"—and the Real Mesoamerican archeologist begins to drag his feet.

On the basis of similar pottery decoration, our friend R.M.A. feels it perfectly likely that a storm-tossed boatload of Japanese fishermen washed up on the coast of Ecuador and initiated the Formative there. On the basis of similar iridescent paint, he believes that pottery making on the Pacific Coast of Guatemala began when a boatload of visitors from Ecuador arrived. These he considers to be conservative positions. This same archeologist believes it wildly irresponsible that, on the basis of similar pottery decoration, Hill and Longacre should attempt to discover different residential groups at a late prehistoric southwestern Pueblo.

It is true that the precise type of study done by Hill and Longacre probably cannot be applied to Early Mesoamerican villages, because many of the assumptions on which it rests (matrilocal residence, female potters, and so on) are inappropriate for Mesoamerica. We believe, however, that Mesoamerican archeologists have largely ignored a whole range of design-element studies that could be used on the subregional or even subvillage level, where sufficient controls are present. We strongly urge, however, that highly complex statistical techniques should be used only with great caution, since we still know so little about the sources of decorative variation that to use complex techniques might only compound the errors already inherent in the material.

In the sections that follow, Stephen Plog and Nanette Pyne explore two avenues of microstyle analysis. Plog tries to see if a simple gravity model will accurately predict the amount of interaction between villages within a single valley. Pyne uses a simple matrix of chi-squares to discover that, even within a single Formative village, specific designs with ritual significance may be associated more closely with certain groups of households than with others. Both studies are cautious. Either could be greatly modified by future discoveries. We believe they are worth the attempt because, should they prove reliable, they give us a closer look into the workings of Formative villages than we have ever had before.

As both Pyne and Plog discovered, one of the thorniest problems in design-element analysis is

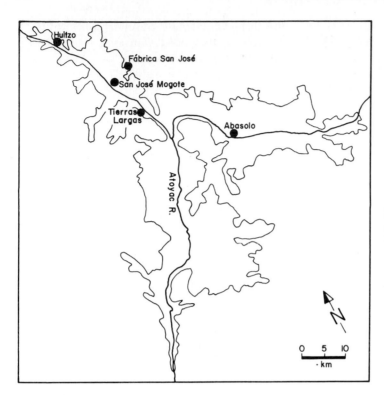

Figure 9.1 Map of the Valley of Oaxaca, showing the locations of the Formative villages mentioned in Chapter 9.

temporal change. No design study can be trusted unless one can show that the variation in decoration between two houses, two villages, or two valleys is not wholly due to style change through time. Even in the most carefully controlled situations, where one knows from other criteria that two provenience units are essentially contemporary, a small and unspecified percentage of the stylistic difference is probably temporal. This fact has not discouraged Mesoamericanists from distinguishing regional style areas, and it should not discourage us from attempting to distinguish intravillage microstyle areas. All we can do is try to hold the temporal variation to a minimum, insofar as our data permits. About this, Pyne and Plog have been very frank.

Measurement of Prehistoric Interaction between Communities *

STEPHEN PLOG

Introduction

Many anthropologists have argued that culture change must be understood in terms of a society's adaptation to its physical and social environment. Yet, as Kushner (1970) and Flannery (1972) have pointed out, emphasis by archeologists on the natural environment has exceeded emphasis on the social environment. This is probably, in part, a result of the scarcity of methods that archeologists have developed to obtain information on the relationships between prehistoric societies. Because of this scarcity, it is important that reliable new methods be developed. Some of the most innovative research in the past decade has been directed toward the development of such methods (Longacre 1964, 1970; Connor 1968; Leone 1968; Whallon 1968; Cook 1970; Hill 1970; Tuggle 1970; Wiley 1971). However, the methods these researchers have developed are based on several untested assumptions, so that their reliability remains an important question. The purpose of this section is to discuss one of the procedures that has been developed to measure one aspect of the social environment: the intensity of interaction between communities. I will first outline the way this variable has been measured. Next, I will set forth a means of testing its reliability. Finally, a test will be made, and the results of the test and the implications of the results for future research will be discussed.

Measuring and Predicting Interaction Intensities

Archeologists have attempted to measure the intensity of interaction among rooms within a prehistoric community (Longacre 1964, 1970; Hill 1970) and among communities (Longacre 1964; Tuggle 1970; Cook 1970; Wiley 1971) by quantifying the degree of similarity of stylistic attributes—pottery designs in particular—on artifacts from these units. (It should be noted that others have measured interaction by focusing on the degree of intravillage stylistic variation rather than intervillage similarity [Connor 1968; Leone 1968; Whallon 1968]. This paper will not discuss that method.) These studies have been based on the assumption that the degree to which designs are shared by social segments or communities is directly proportional to the amount of interaction between the units. (A number of secondary assumptions have been made also. See Hill [1970:15–16] for a discussion of these.) *Interaction* has been defined as the movement of individuals between communities (Wiley 1971:4), the exchange of women in marriage (Tuggle 1970), the exchange of pottery and other economic goods (Tuggle 1970; Wiley 1971), or as "social interaction along kin-based, religious, and political lines" (Longacre 1970:38).

The major problem with this method is that the relationship between interaction intensity and stylistic similarity has been assumed rather than

*The research in Oaxaca described in this section was made possible by a National Science Foundation Undergraduate Research Participation Grant (GY-9015) to the University of Michigan in 1971. I wish to thank Richard I. Ford, the grant administrator, for the research opportunity. The ceramics from Chevelon Canyon were collected while I was a participant in the Chevelon Archeological Research Project, which was supported by the National Science Foundation. These sherds were analyzed during my tenure as a National Science Foundation Graduate Fellow. This support is gratefully acknowledged.

demonstrated. Some ethnographic studies have been made to test the assumption. Friedrich's (1970) study of a Tarascan village in Mexico suggested that some stylistic attributes do indicate intensities of communication between potters, whereas others do not. Stanislawski's (1969a,b, 1973) studies of the Hopi villages in Arizona have not supported the assumption. However, the relevance of these studies to simpler prehistoric societies is questionable. The Hopi manufacture pottery primarily for sale to tourists, while, in the Tarascan village, pottery is made, at least in part, for sale in local markets. Foster's (1965) review of ethnographic studies of pottery making in Mexico suggests that the market, whether for local villages or tourists, is a powerful determinant of the innovation in, and diffusion of, design styles. He states:

> The stimulus of the market . . . can easily be seen, and it is fairly well documented. In most parts of the peasant world, pottery is sufficiently plentiful so that the buyer has great choice. . . . Obviously, the successful potter is the one who satisfies the customer. [1965:52]
>
> The stimulus of the market can explain much of the process of innovation in pottery styles, and perhaps also in productive techniques [1965:52].

Bunzel's (1929) study of Hopi pottery making has supported these statements. In describing the innovative efforts of one potter, Nampeyo, in reviving a pottery style in the Hopi villages, Bunzel notes:

> There is no doubt that it was Nampeyo and not the traders and ethnologists who was responsible for the revival of the Sikyatki style. *Its rapid adoption by other potters was, of course, due to its commercial success,* but the complete assimilation and subsequent efflorescence of the style point to something more than commercial expediency in its adoption [1929:83; emphasis mine]

The existence of conditions such as these in many simpler prehistoric societies, particularly in those in which stylistic similarities have been used as a measure of interaction intensity, is doubtful.

While not denying that additional ethnographic information could be valuable, I would argue that archeologists can test the reliability of the interaction measure themselves, using data from prehistoric communities. The critical problem in carrying out such a test is finding some method, independent of design similarities, of predicting prehistoric interaction. Interaction in general is emphasized, rather than the movement of individuals or goods, simply because it seems reasonable to ask first whether design similarities measure interaction of any kind. If such a relationship is demonstrated, the question of what type or types of interaction are being measured then becomes important.

The Gravity Model

The geographical literature dealing with the prediction of interaction between communities is extensive. A variety of models have been formulated to predict interaction, or have been designed to fit actual interaction data. A discussion of these models will not be given here (see Morrill 1963; Haggett 1965:35-40; or Olsson 1965a). Instead, I wish to deal only with one of the simpler and more commonly discussed of these models, the *gravity model.* This model proposes that *the amount of interaction between two communities is directly proportional to their populations and inversely proportional to the distance between them.* It is sometimes expressed by the formula:

$$I_{ij} = \frac{P_i P_j}{D_{ij}^b}$$

where

I_{ij} = the amount of interaction predicted between place i and place j
P_i and P_j = the populations of the two places
D_{ij} = the distance separating the two places
b = an exponent of some chosen value (see Haggett 1965:35, Olsson 1970:227).

Data from contemporary societies suggest that this model is valid for a wide range of types of interaction. Zipf (1949) has shown that bus, train, and plane travel; telephone calls; and newspaper circulations conform to the expectations of the model. The study of marriage data from American communities has shown an inverse relationship between the frequency of marriage between individuals and the distance between their homes (Abrams 1943; Davie and Reeves 1939; Marches and Turbeville 1953). A study by Chisholm (1968) has supported an inverse relationship between the distance of farming plots from villages and the frequency and intensity with which these plots are cultivated. Schiffer (1971) has found an inverse relationship between the frequency of movements among activity complexes in a research center and the distances among these complexes. A direct relationship between population size and the length of migrations also has received empirical support (Olsson 1965b:20).

In his evaluation of the gravity model, Olsson (1970:227–228) found that the correlation coefficients between the predictions of the gravity model and actual interaction data are high and statistically significant, but the regression coefficients vary. Because of this, he concluded that the predictive power of the gravity model is high, but "its explanatory power is dubious" (Olsson 1970:228). Morrill (1963:82) has stated that the gravity model "has been fitted to many observed sets of distributions of [migration] distances sufficiently well to be statistically reliable."

I would argue that, if the gravity model is valid in the present, then there is little reason to believe it will not be valid in the past. This should be true particularly for the relation between interaction and distance. If distance has a dampening effect on interaction today, with modern transportation systems, its effect on interaction in the past, when travel was by foot, should be even greater. Furthermore, there are some data that support this statement. Renfrew (1969:157) has published data on obsidian distribution in the Near East which show a decrease in the proportion of obsidian in the lithic assemblage of a site as the distance of the site from the obsidian source increases. Pires-Ferreira's (1973:19, and Chapter 10 of this volume) analysis of obsidian exchange in Mesoamerica suggested that "obsidian exchange was related to population density and distribution (Wright and Zeder 1973), since the amount moving in any direction was partly a function of the number of villages in that area; and to distance, since the amount in any village was partly a function of its distance to the nearest source." Deetz and Dethlefsen's (1965) study of gravestone styles in New England, while not prehistoric evidence, is from a period without modern means of transportation. Their study of a style carved by one stonecutter in eastern Massachusetts showed that its popularity during the period from 1720 to 1760 decreased with increasing distance of the graveyards from the stonecutter's residence (p. 203). Finally, Warren (1969) has studied the distribution of the pottery of a single pueblo during the fifteenth century in the Rio Grande Valley. The wares of Tonque Pueblo could be distinguished through petrographic analysis of the tempering material, and by the paste and surface color. Included in Warren's paper is a map that shows the relative percentage of Tonque wares of all pottery at a number of sites in the valley. The map shows that the proportion of Tonque wares decreases with increasing distance away from Tonque Pueblo.

These data support the validity of the gravity model in prehistoric times, although most of the evidence concerns the relationship between interaction and distance. Wright and Zeder (1973) have argued for a direct relationship between population and interaction. It should be noted, however, that population sizes are held constant in Warren's and Renfrew's analyses (assuming that the size of artifact assemblages is directly related to site population sizes) since the percentage of imported items, not the number of imported items, in the site assemblage was measured.

Although it has been suggested that the gravity model seems to be a reliable model of human interaction, there are several problems in applying it prehistorically. One problem concerns the measurement of distance. First, a person's conception of distance does not always coincide with physical distance (Haggett 1965:38). Olsson (1965b:26) has noted that, although one of the assumptions of the gravity model is that the intensity of interaction will decline symmetrically in all directions with distance, very asymmetrical migration fields have been found. He has argued that a migrant's perception of distance is a function of the central place hierarchy (1965b:39). In his study of Swedish migration data, he used "functional" distance, which was measured by the number of intervening regions between two places rather than by physical distance (1965b:9).

If the migrant's perception of distance is a function of the central place hierarchy, there probably is no problem in using the data, to be analyzed later, from the Grasshopper, Hay Hollow Valley, and Chevelon Canyon areas of Arizona, because it is unlikely that any central place hierarchy existed in these places. This problem may be more important in regard to the data from Oaxaca, Mexico, where it is likely that an administrative site hierarchy was in existence during the time period from which data was obtained. If a person's perception of distance is a function of factors other than, or in addition to, the central place hierarchy (such as social influences), the problem is more difficult to deal with. Archeologists have tried to measure what they have called "social distance" (Cook 1970; Leone 1968) between archeological communities, but, as Tuggle (1970:45) has noted, this concept "refers essentially to the intensity of interaction between groups." Therefore, the method they have used to measure social distance has been the same method used to measure interaction intensity, the similarity of stylistic elements.

A second problem with the measurement of distance is that the straight-line distance between archeological sites may give an inaccurate measure of the travel effort required to walk from one

community to another. For instance, a walk of 1 mile over an area characterized by rapid variations in topography requires more effort than a walk of 1 mile over flat terrain. The effect of this factor can be seen particularly in Warren's (1969:40) map of the distribution of Tonque trade wares. The rate of decrease in the amount of trade wares with increasing distance is high as one moves into the higher elevations on the east or west of the pueblo, whereas there is a lower rate of decrease with distance as one moves north or south along the Rio Grande, or along the Jemez River. For all the areas from which the data sets discussed later were collected, physical distance should be a valid measure of travel effort. None of these areas is characterized by terrain rugged enough to affect travel.

A second problem with the use of the gravity model is that, within a certain area close to a community, distance seems to have no effect on interaction intensity. This has been called the "plateau effect" (Olsson 1966:17). For example, Renfrew's data (1969:157) show that the decrease with distance of the proportion of obsidian in assemblages occurs at distances greater than 300 km from the source. Other studies, however, suggest that the plateau effect occurs primarily within distances less than 5 miles (Abrams 1943; Chisholm 1968; Davie and Reeves 1939; Marches and Turbeville 1953; Warren 1969).

A third problem in applying the gravity model is that interaction intensities are influenced by a number of variables in addition to population and distance. For instance, the rate at which interaction intensity changes with distance has been found to vary with factors such as the occupation group of migrants, the level of the migrant's community in the central place hierarchy, the time period of the interaction, and the purpose of the trip (Olsson 1965b:31–32; 1966:16).

Flannery's (1968) model of Olmec exchange has suggested additional factors that may influence interaction intensity. He proposes that those areas that traded with the Olmec were not simply those close by, but were those with local elites who could enhance their status through interaction with the Olmec. The areas most likely to have local elites would be areas with high agricultural and demographic potential (1968:106). In regard to exchange involving such high-status goods, the assumption of the gravity model that all communities "are populated by 'standard' people with identical needs, tastes, and contacts" (Olsson 1965b:26) does not hold, since all people do not have equal access to these goods. Therefore, the distribution of these goods is not a function of distance from their source when all communities or areas are considered. However, the relationship with distance still may hold if the universe is redefined to include only communities or areas with local elites.

On the basis of this data, I would suggest that archeologists could test the reliability of design similarities as a measure of interaction by using the predictions of the gravity model. The test would be based on the assumption that the gravity model is valid. The hypothesis would be that, if design similarities do measure community interaction, then *the similarity coefficients should vary directly with the populations of the communities and inversely with the distance between them.* Problems in applying this model archeologically have been discussed, but some of these problems can be controlled. For example, only stylistic attributes on artifacts to which all individuals have equal access should be considered. Also, the test should be valid only when the average distance between communities is greater than 5 miles. In any case, geographers have found the model to be statistically reliable despite these problems. At the same time, however, it seems reasonable to expect only a statistically significant positive correlation between the observed similarities and the predicted interaction intensities, and not to require any particular level of correlation, since other factors do influence interaction intensity.

One argument against the use of the gravity model in the manner I have suggested has been made

previously. Cook (1970:34, 47) has proposed that the inverse relationship between distance and interaction intensity should hold when no social boundaries are crossed when traveling between communities, because of the free flow of information within culture areas. I would suggest that the evidence just presented shows that this relationship does hold within culture areas. While it seems reasonable to expect that the effect of distance on interaction within culture areas may be less than the effects of distance when cultural boundaries are crossed, this would not invalidate the use of the gravity model. There still would be a decrease in interaction intensity with distance, but the decrease would be greater than expected in instances where social boundaries were crossed in moving between two communities. This might result in greater variation in the amount of interaction between a set of communities separated by some given distance, but it would not change the general tendency for interaction intensity to decrease with increasing distance.

An examination of the relationship between stylistic similarities and physical distance has been made in two previous studies. However, I would suggest that the results of these studies should not be used to assess the validity of design similarities as an interaction measure, for reasons which will be given later.

Some Tests of Community Interaction: The Southwestern United States

A test similar to that which I have proposed has been carried out with ceramic data from Hay Hollow Valley in east-central Arizona. Cook (1970) calculated the similarity of frequencies of color categories on three types of plainware pottery from a group of sites in this area. He plotted the similarity coefficients against physical distance and found no statistically significant relationship between the two (1970:47). One of the problems with using this test to evaluate the hypothesis outlined earlier is that the maximum distance between any of the sites was 4.18 miles (1970:51). As noted before, physical distances this low often may have no effect on interaction intensity. A second problem with Cook's study is his use of color frequencies to measure stylistic similarity between sites. A single plainware pot in the Southwest often may have more than one shade of color. Shepard (1953:180–181) has discussed a number of variables, such as clay source, insufficient oxygen, length of firing, and firing temperature, that can cause variation in the color of pottery. A potter only can control the variables of the firing process within a certain range, so that differential frequencies of color categories may be only a result of random variation.

A second study dealing with the relationship between stylistic similarities and physical distance is Wiley's (1971). She measured the similarity in design elements on black-on-white pottery from another set of sites in the Hay Hollow Valley. Plotting the coefficients against distance for three time periods between A.D. 900 to 1200, she found little relationship between the variables. However, the maximum distance between sites was 3.7 miles, even less than in Cook's study.

Other data sets from design studies are better suited for carrying out the proposed test, primarily because they were obtained from sites separated by larger distances than those in Cook's and Wiley's studies. Data from three areas of the southwestern United States will be discussed briefly, and these data will be used in testing the hypothesis outlined earlier. I will then present a more detailed discussion of an additional data set collected from the Valley of Oaxaca in Mexico. This data set also will be used to test the hypothesis.

Hay Hollow Valley, Arizona

Data from two groups of sites with contemporaneous estimated dates were collected for Longacre's (1964) design analysis of black-on-white ceramics from the Hay Hollow Valley. The average distance separating the 5 sites dating to A.D. 900–1100 was approximately 5.7 miles, with a standard deviation of 3.1 miles. The previous discussion of the "plateau effect" suggests that distances of this magnitude should have effects on interaction intensities. For the 5 sites with dates from A.D. 900–1300, these values were 9.4 miles and 6.3 miles, respectively. A third set of sites dating from A.D. 700–1100 was not included in this analysis, because population estimates were not given for 3 of the 5 sites. The number of design-element occurrences per site for the first set ranged from 62 to 303, with an average of 128. For the second set of sites, these values were 43 to 160, and 116. Tuggle (1970:80–81) has found that, below 75 to 100 element occurrences, Pearson's r tends toward a value of zero, and the Brainerd–Robinson coefficient tends to be related to the number of element occurrences.* However, even though sample sizes of less than 75 to 100 element occurrences are included in Longacre's data, neither coefficient is significantly correlated with sample size for either data set.

Chevelon Canyon, Arizona

A third group of data was collected in the Chevelon Canyon area of east-central Arizona by myself (unpublished). Only sherds from a single pottery type were analyzed, with the type defined by the presence of mineral paint and angular and subangular gray temper fragments in a white paste. The analysis was limited to body sherds, and bowl and jar sherds were analyzed separately. Colton and Hargrave's (1937) classification of design elements was used. This classification was chosen simply because it consisted of elements that have been recognized in a number of other design studies of pottery from various areas of the Southwest (Kidder and Shepard 1936; Beals, Brainerd, and Smith 1945; Carlson 1970). It thus seems likely that studies based on this classification could be replicated by other workers. (The impor-

---

*For definitions of Pearson's r and the Brainerd–Robinson coefficient, see p. 261.

tance of such replication will be discussed later.)
The average distance between the 8 sites with jar
design elements was 5.0 miles, with a standard
deviation of 3.2 miles, while the corresponding
values for the 7 sites with bowl design elements
were 5.4 miles and 3.2 miles. These sites all have
very similar pottery type frequencies, and it is
estimated that they all date to the same 100-year
period. The number of element occurrences for
the sites with jar elements ranged from 9 to 56
with an average of 31. For the sites with bowl
designs, these values were 17 to 39, and 27.
Neither similarity coefficient is significantly correlated with sample size for the sites with bowl
elements. However, both coefficients are significantly correlated (at the .05 level) with sample size
for the sites with jar design elements.

Grasshopper, Arizona

Tuggle (1970) provides similarity coefficients between the sites of the Late Mogollon 3 period in
the Grasshopper area of east-central Arizona that
are based on design frequencies on two types of
pottery, Pinedale Black-on-white and Fourmile
Polychrome. Sites with less than 90 design-element
occurrences were excluded from the analysis. Distances between sites were measured from a map
provided in the text (Tuggle 1970: Figure 3), and
the relative sizes of site populations were obtained
from Tuggle (1970: Figure 4). Some sites for
which coefficients were available had to be excluded from the analysis because they were not on
the map. The average distance between the sites
with coefficients for Pinedale Black-on-white designs was approximately 5.5 miles, with a standard
deviation of 2.4 miles. The average distance between sites with Fourmile Polychrome was 5.4
miles, with a standard deviation of 2.1 miles.

In order to test the hypothesis, *Brainerd–
Robinson* and *Pearson's r similarity coefficients*
were calculated between the sites in each data set
from the Hay Hollow Valley and from Chevelon
Canyon. Tuggle gives only the values of Pearson's *r*
for sites in the Grasshopper area.

To compute the *Brainerd–Robinson coefficients*
(Brainerd 1951; Robinson 1951), the percentages
of each design category at each site were calculated. The figures then were placed in a matrix in
which the percentages for each site were compared
and contrasted with every other site. Resem-
blances were expressed as a figure that represents
the sum of the differences in percentages for all
categories between any two given sites; the coefficient was then calculated by subtracting this sum
from 200. The coefficient thus ranges from 0 to
200, with a value of 200 representing maximum
similarity (identical percentages for all design categories at two different sites), and 0 indicating
maximum dissimilarity.

The second similarity coefficient, *Pearson's r*, is
a measure of the degree to which two variables
covary linearly. It ranges in value from -1.0 to
$+1.0$. A value of $+1.0$ indicates a perfect direct
relationship between the variables (that is, as
variable X increases, variable Y increases propor-
tionally). A coefficient of -1.0 indicates a perfect
inverse relationship, and a value of 0.0 indicates
the absence of any relationship between the
variables.* The formula is:

$$r = \frac{\Sigma (X_i - \overline{X})(Y_i - \overline{Y})}{\sqrt{\Sigma (X_i - \overline{X})^2 \, \Sigma (Y_i - \overline{Y})^2}}$$

where

Σ = the sum for all cases

$\overline{X}$ = the mean of all values of variable X

$\overline{Y}$ = the mean of all values of variable Y

X_i = the value of X for each case

Y_i = the value of Y for each case

*It should be emphasized that different coefficients
measure similarity in different ways. The Brainerd–
Robinson and Pearson's *r* coefficients are the two most
commonly used in stylistic analyses, which is why I have
chosen to use them in this study. However, I would suggest that the degree of fit between the type of similarity
specified in theoretical discussions of style and the manner in which various coefficients measure similarity are
topics that deserve greater consideration in the future.

In this case, the variables used were the two sites in each pair being compared, and the values were the frequencies of design categories.

Once the similarity coefficients were computed, I then calculated the rank correlation, or *Spearman's r coefficient*, for two pairs of variables: (*1*) the similarity coefficient (Brainerd–Robinson or Pearson's *r*) versus distance between sites, and (*2*) the same similarity coefficient versus the interaction predicted by the gravity model. Because the rate at which interaction decreases with distance will vary with a number of factors, and because the rate itself may change with distance, I have chosen to use the Spearman rank correlation coefficient rather than Pearson's *r*, which requires a linear relationship between the variables. Also, because ranks were used, it was not necessary to decide on a value for the distance exponent, *b*, in the gravity formula.

Like Pearson's *r*, Spearman's *r* is a measure of the degree to which two variables covary. However, the ranks of the values for each variable are used in computing the coefficient, in contrast to Pearson's *r* for which the original values are used in the calculations. The coefficient ranges in value from −1.0 to +1.0. A value of +1.0 indicates a perfect agreement between the ranks of the variables for all cases, while a value of −1.0 indicates completely opposite rankings. The formula is:

$$r_s = \frac{6(\Sigma d_i{}^2)}{N\,(N^2 - 1)}$$

where

$\Sigma d_i{}^2$ = the sum of all cases of the squares of the differences between the rank of variable *X* and the rank of variable *Y*

N   = the number of cases

For this analysis, then, the variables used to calculate Spearman's *r* were the ranks of the similarity coefficients, the ranks of the distances between sites, and the ranks of the interaction intensities predicted by the gravity model. The highest value of each variable for each data set was ranked "1," the second highest "2," and so on.

The values of Spearman's *r* are shown in Table 9.1. It was suggested earlier that, if design similarities do measure interaction, the similarity coefficients should vary inversely with the distance between sites and should vary directly with the interaction intensities predicted by the gravity model. A significant negative correlation between the distances and the similarity coefficients was found in none of the data sets, using either similarity coefficient. A significant positive correlation between the similarity coefficients and the predicted interaction intensities was found in two of four cases with the Brainerd–Robinson coefficients, and in one of six cases with Pearson's *r*. The hypothesis is therefore not confirmed.

Interaction between Formative Villages in the Valley of Oaxaca

Studies of intersite design similarities like those just described have not generally been attempted in Mesoamerica. For the later periods in Mesoamerica, it is suspected that much of the pottery was made in craft centers, from which it was distributed to local villages. Such a pattern would tend to affect the differences between sites. This problem probably does not apply to the Early and Middle Formative, however, where it is believed on the basis of all currently available data that each village made most of its own pottery. Of course, even at this early time period, there were a few "export wares" (see Pires-Ferreira, Chapter 10 of this volume) circulating between regions. However, they are rare compared with the thousands of sherds of locally made pottery.

In 1971–1972, I was able to study ceramic designs from five villages in the Valley of Oaxaca, Mexico, which already have been mentioned in Chapters 2 and 3 of this volume. The villages, whose geographic locations are given in Figure 9.1, were as follows:

> Barrio del Rosario, Huitzo
> San José Mogote

TABLE 9.1   Spearman's Rank Correlations Calculated for Design Similarity Coefficients (Brainerd–Robinson and Pearson's r) versus Intersite Distance, and Design Similarity Coefficients versus Predictions from the Gravity Model[a]

| Data set | N | Spearman's r using distance alone | | Spearman's r using gravity model | |
		Brainerd–Robinson coefficient	Pearson's r	Brainerd–Robinson coefficient	Pearson's r
Hay Hollow Valley, A.D. 900–1100	15	.7096[b]	.5487[b]	–.3893	–.4571[c]
Hay Hollow Valley, A.D. 900–1300	15	–.2208	–.2693	.4607[c]	.4107
Grasshopper, Pinedale B/W	9	—	.4333	—	–.4000
Grasshopper, Fourmile Polychrome	10	—	.1394	—	–.1636
Chevelon Canyon, Jars	28	–.2229	–.2842	.6170[b]	.5984[h]
Chevelon Canyon, Bowls	21	.1300	.0234	.0935	.0312

[a] Data from the southwestern United States.
[b] Statistically significant at the .05 level.
[c] Statistically significant at the .10 level.

Tierras Largas
Fábrica San José
San Sebastián Abasolo

The average distance separating these villages is 13.1 miles, with a standard deviation of 7.3 miles. (Miles were used instead of kilometers in order to facilitate comparisons with the southwestern U.S. studies already mentioned.)

The type of pottery used in the Oaxaca analysis was Atoyac Yellow-white, a common household ware used mainly in the production of bowls of various shapes, and unquestionably locally made. The clay used for the body of the vessels derives from weathered Pre-Cambrian gneiss, which is available over hundreds of square miles in the vicinity of each village. The white clay slip is available at kaolinite deposits near thermal springs in the mountains ringing the valley (unpublished technical studies by William O. Payne, personal communication). Atoyac Yellow-white is the

Oaxaca variety of a widespread pottery type whose local varieties include Canoas White in the Valley of Tehuacán, Puebla (MacNeish, Peterson, and Flannery 1970); Altica phase white ware from the Teotihuacán region (Sanders 1965); Conchas White-to-buff from the Guatemalan Pacific Coast (Coe and Flannery 1967); and many other white wares of the period 1150–500 B.C. In Oaxaca, this type begins in low frequency during the San José phase (1150–850 B.C.), reaches its peak between 900 and 700 B.C., and declines during the later part of the Guadalupe phase (850–600 B.C.). Two main types of vessels with incised designs were made with this pottery—cylindrical bowls with exterior incising, and open bowls with incising on the interior. Both of these vessels most likely were used for serving food, and most are the right size for one individual serving. Because of the small sample of cylinders, only the open bowls (with flat bases and outleaned walls) were used in the analysis. This further restricts the time span of the collection, since such bowls were used mainly between 900 and 600 B.C. In the local chronology, this represents the later part of the San José phase and all of the Guadalupe phase (Flannery *et al.* 1970).

Over 90% of the pottery from each village came from excavations rather than surface collections. However, the area excavated at each site was less than 10% of the total site area, and may have been much smaller in some cases, especially for the site of San José Mogote. Part of one site, Tierras Largas, was excavated by simple random sampling (see Chapter 3).

Atoyac Yellow-white, flat-based, outleaned-wall bowls are frequently decorated with incised designs. The most common design is a panel of parallel lines running around the inside just below the rim. At intervals, one line may turn up or down to meet the others, or the lines may be separated by a small free-standing motif. This is the so-called "double-line-break" decoration (Coe 1961) so widespread in Mesoamerica at this time period, which had literally hundreds of variations. In this study, I used only rim sherds and designs that did not appear to extend down the body of the bowl. In part, this was done because it is usually the only part of the vessel decorated. However, it was done also because Friedrich (1970) has found that different designs may be used on different parts of vessels. In order to ensure that any similarities between villages in their choice of design elements would not be affected by differential numbers of body designs versus rim designs, it seemed best to restrict the analysis to the latter.

I divided the double-line-break designs on Atoyac Yellow-white bowls into 183 categories, the most common of which (nos. 1–92) are shown in Figures 9.2 and 9.3 by way of example. During 1971, I classified all such sherds from Huitzo, San José Mogote, Tierras Largas, and Abasolo according to these categories; Nanette Pyne classified Fábrica san José in 1972, using the same design categories. The similarity in design choices between sites was then measured by means of the Brainerd–Robinson coefficient and Pearson's *r* as was done for the data from the southwestern United States. The values of these coefficients for the Oaxaca sites are shown in the last two columns of Table 9.2. In the Valley of Oaxaca study, the two villages showing the greatest similarity in design choices were San José Mogote and Fábrica San José (3 miles apart; B–R coefficient, 83.67). The two villages showing least similarity were Huitzo and Abasolo (28.2 miles apart; B–R coefficient, 12.41).

The next step in the analysis was to assign rough population estimates to each of the five Oaxaca villages so the gravity model could be used. The figures used were estimates of the average number of households at each village during the periods when Atoyac Yellow-white pottery was in use. These were based on M. C. Winter's observations of the numbers of households per hectare at the village of Tierras Largas, and on R. D. Drennan's estimates for the numbers of households at Fábrica San José (cf. Chapters 3 and 8, this volume). In the end, I decided to use a standard estimate of 10 households for all villages in the 1–3-ha range. One site, San José Mogote, was so much larger than all the others that it was assigned an estimate of 280 households. The gravity model would predict that interaction with such a large village would be greater than with a 1–3-ha village a comparable distance away. This seems especially likely since San José Mogote had a complex of public buildings unlike anything found at Fábrica San José, Tierras Largas, or most smaller villages. Thus, San José Mogote presumably performed a range of services that the smaller villages periodically needed or desired, encouraging interaction.

Another step in the analysis was to rank the similarity coefficients, the distances between sites, and the predicted interaction intensities. These ranks are shown in Table 9.3. The covariation of the similarity coefficients with distances between sites and with predicted interaction intensities was then measured using Spearman's *r*. These values are shown in Table 9.4.

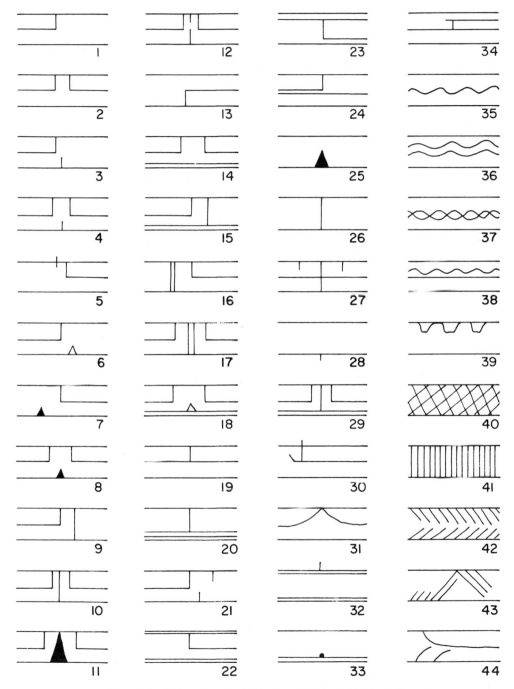

Figure 9.2 Design elements 1–44, Atoyac Yellow-white pottery.

265

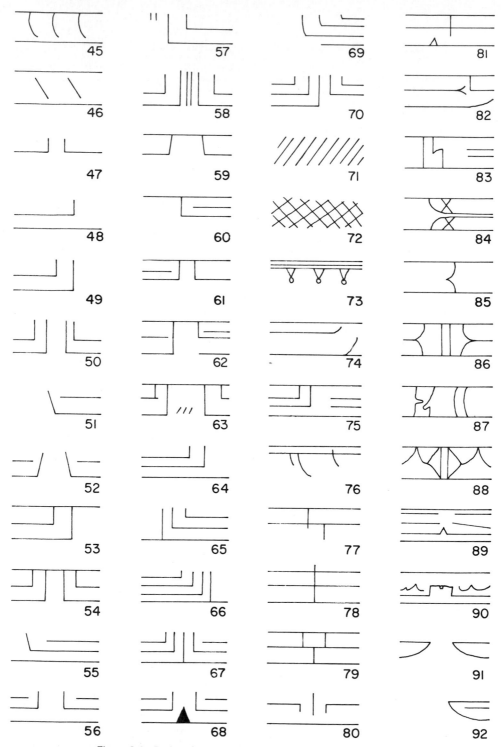

Figure 9.3 Design elements 45–92, Atoyac Yellow-white pottery.

TABLE 9.2 Brainerd–Robinson and Pearson's *r* Coefficients for Shared Design Elements on Atoyac Yellow-White Pottery for Five Oaxacan Villages

Site pairs	Number of element occurrences per site pair	Distance between site pairs in miles	Population estimate per site pair in households	Brainerd–Robinson coefficient	Pearson's *r* coefficient
Fábrica San José–San José Mogote	264–94	3.0	10–280	83.67	.6364
Fábrica San José–Huitzo	264–274	10.8	10–10	46.47	.2532
Fábrica San José–Tierras Largas	264–143	7.2	10–10	42.72	.2948
Fábrica San José–Abasolo	264–13	17.6	10–10	42.42	.5984
San José Mogote–Huitzo	94–274	9.9	280–10	39.40	.1535
San José Mogote–Tierras Largas	94–143	6.4	280–10	66.39	.5648
San José Mogote–Abasolo	94–13	18.4	280–10	42.55	.6428
Huitzo–Tierras Largas	274–143	16.1	10–10	19.89	−.0083
Huitzo–Abasolo	274–13	28.2	10–10	12.41	.0024
Tierras Largas–Abasolo	143–13	13.0	10–10	39.16	.3538

TABLE 9.3 Predicted Interaction Intensity Compared with Similarity Coefficients on Design Elements for Five Oaxacan Villages[a]

Site pair	Rank by distance	Predicted interaction intensity	Brainerd–Robinson	Pearson's *r*
Fábrica San José–San José Mogote	10	1	1	2
San José Mogote–Tierras Largas	9	2	2	4
Fábrica San José–Tierras Largas	8	5	4	6
San José Mogote–Huitzo	7	3	7	8
Fábrica San José–Huitzo	6	6	3	7
Tierras Largas–Abasolo	5	7	8	5
Huitzo–Tierras Largas	4	8	9	10
Fábrica San José–Abasolo	3	9	6	3
San José Mogote–Abasolo	2	4	5	1
Huitzo–Abasolo	1	10	10	9

[a]Column one ranks the site pairs by distance in miles; Column two ranks them by intensity of interaction predicted by the gravity model. Columns three and four rank the site pairs in terms of shared designs on Atoyac Yellow-white pottery as measured by Brainerd–Robinson and Pearson's *r* coefficients.

TABLE 9.4   Spearman's *r* Values (r_s) Measuring Covariation between Variables Shown in Table 9.3
            for Five Oaxacan Villages[a]

r_s for distance compared with Brainerd–Robinson rank order:	-.7455[b]
r_s for distance compared with Pearson's *r* rank order:	-.1879
r_s for predicted interaction intensity compared with Brainerd–Robinson rank order:	.7697[b]
r_s for predicted interaction intensity compared with Pearson's *r* rank order:	.4788

[a]Distance between site pairs, and interaction between site pairs predicted by the gravity model, are compared with
rank orders of site pairs based on shared designs on Atoyac Yellow-white pottery, as determined by Brainerd–Robinson
and Pearson's *r* coefficients.
[b]Statistically significant at the .05 level.

Although only the rank correlations using the Brainerd–Robinson coefficient as a similarity measure are statistically significant at the .05 level, both coefficients are positively correlated with the predicted interaction intensities based on the gravity model, and are negatively correlated with absolute distances between sites. Fábrica San José and San José Mogote, lying only 3 miles apart, are ranked as highly similar (1 by Brainerd–Robinson, 2 by Pearson's *r*). Huitzo and Abasolo, 28 miles apart, are ranked as highly dissimilar (10 by Brainerd–Robinson, 9 by Pearson's *r*). Village pairs in the middle distance ranges, however, occur somewhat out of rank. The most striking discrepancy is the Huitzo–San José Mogote coefficient, which is eighth highest by both measures, although it was predicted to be third. There are perhaps two reasons for this, one statistical and one cultural.

The statistical reason is that rank position may be misleading when compared with the actual coefficients in Table 9.2. For example, the pairs Fábrica San José–Tierras Largas, San José Mogote–Abasolo, and Fábrica San José–Abasolo must be ranked 4, 5, and 6 simply because their respective Brainerd–Robinson coefficients are 42.72, 42.55, and 42.42. Considering the full range of coefficients (from 12.41 to 83.67), these three village pairs could be regarded as in a dead heat for fourth. The actual coefficients thus give a better idea of degree of similarity than a simple ranking from 1 to 10.

The possible cultural reasons for the discrepancy are even more intriguing, although they remain to be tested. To illustrate them, we have prepared a series of diagrammatic "maps," which are shown in Figures 9.4–9.6.

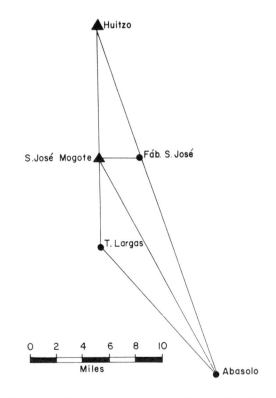

Figure 9.4   Diagram showing actual distances in miles between five Oaxacan villages.

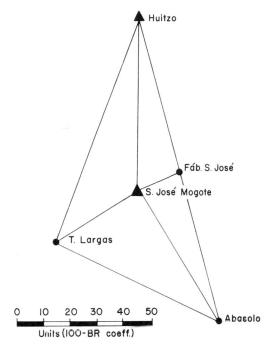

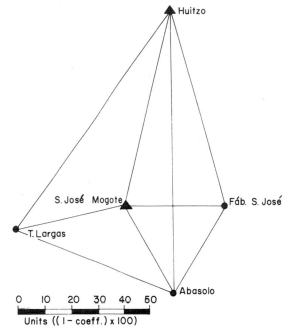

Figure 9.5 Diagram showing nearness of relationship between five Oaxacan villages, using units derived by subtracting the Brainerd–Robinson coefficient from 100 (see text).

Figure 9.6 Diagram showing nearness of relationship between five Oaxacan villages, using units derived by subtracting the Pearson's *r* coefficient from 1 and multiplying the result by 100 (see text).

Mapping of Intersite Coefficients

There are three steps in our investigaton of possible cultural factors affecting the similarity coefficients. First, in Figure 9.4, we have drawn a diagram indicating the actual distances between villages in miles. Huitzo and San José Mogote, both "ceremonial-civic" centers with public buildings, are shown as triangles; the other villages are drawn as dots.

In Figure 9.5, we have diagrammed the same villages but, instead of miles, we have used a figure derived by subtracting from 100 the Brainerd–Robinson coefficient for each village pair. In Figure 9.6, we have done the same thing, but using a figure derived by subtracting from 1.0 the Pearson's *r* coefficient for each village pair, and then

multiplying the result by 100. These latter two maps, in other words, indicate how "far apart" pairs of villages are in terms of shared design-element frequencies. This can then be compared with the actual distances between villages in miles given in Figure 9.4.

A comparison of Figures 9.4–9.6 shows that two general factors might account for most of the discrepancy between the predicted and observed rank orders of site pairs. First, the two ceremonial-civic centers (Huitzo and San José Mogote) are consistently placed "farther apart" on the basis of design elements than they actually are in mileage. Second, most small villages are placed "closer" to San José Mogote than they actually are in mileage. If it could be demonstrated that the Brainerd–Robinson and Pearson's *r* coefficients are measuring interaction, then the following hypotheses could be advanced: (1) *Huitzo and San José Mogote were competing ceremonial-civic centers and hence had less interaction than would be predicted by the gravity model*; and (2) *Fábrica San José, Tierras Largas, and Abasolo used the services provided by San José Mogote in its role as ceremonial-civic center, and hence had even more interaction with it than would be predicted*.

Possible Weaknesses in the Data

Two possible weaknesses in the Oaxaca data should be discussed. First, the sample from one site (Abasolo) is extremely small, consisting of only 13 design-element occurrences. All the other sites have at least 94 element occurrences, with the mean 158 and the maximum 274. The Pearson's *r* coefficients are significantly correlated with sample size (at the .05 level), although the Brainerd–Robinson coefficients are not. Thus, when future excavations at Abasolo have raised the number of element occurrences, the statistics might be recalculated to see if there are significant differences in the placement of Abasolo. Actually, it seems unlikely that its placement as "most different from Huitzo" would change.

A second problem is that temporal variation is known to exist in the data. Most of the Atoyac Yellow-white sherds from the sites of Huitzo and Fábrica San José date from the Guadalupe phase (850–600 B.C.), while most of those from San José Mogote are from the later part of the San José phase (1000–850 B.C.), although there is some overlap. The sherds from Tierras Largas are from the whole span of both phases. However, this weakness seems not to be as great as I had expected; the ranks of the coefficients which one might predict if only temporal variation were operating do *not* correspond with the ranks of the actual coefficients. For example, if temporal variation were the most important variable involved, one would expect Huitzo and Fábrica San José to be the most closely related, and expect San José Mogote and Fábrica San José to be dissimilar. In

fact, the latter two sites are consistently the most closely related, while Huitzo and Fábrica San José are not close at all.

Indeed, if one sets aside questions of interaction for the moment, and takes the empirical data at face value, it appears that regional patterning in design elements was stronger than chronological variation in the same elements for nearly 400 years. This is surprising, and it may tell us something about differences in rate of design change between Mesoamerica and the Southwest (see p. 272). I cannot believe that many areas of the Southwest would show such consistency in element occurrences for so long a period.

An Evaluation of Design Similarities as an Interaction Measure

For all the data sets considered in this section, the expected significant negative correlation with distance was found in only one case using either type of similarity coefficient. The expected significant positive correlation with interaction intensity predicted by the gravity model was found in three cases using the Brainerd–Robinson coefficient, and in one case using Pearson's *r* as a similarity measure. The results of these analyses suggest that one cannot simply calculate a similarity coefficient, using design frequencies at two sites, and assume the coefficient measures the intensity of interaction between the sites; it may, in fact, be measuring some other unspecified variable or variables. Also, although this study was based on the analysis of intersite design similarities, it should be noted that past analyses of intrasite design distributions (Hill 1970; Longacre 1970) also have been based on the assumption that design similarities measure interaction intensities. Therefore, many conclusions that have been drawn in both intrasite and intersite analyses concerning community social organization and intervillage interaction may be erroneous.

However, these conclusions must be qualified by

TABLE 9.5 Average, Standard Deviation, and Range of
Distance between Sites for All the Data
Sets Analyzed

| Data Set | Distance between sites (miles) | | |
	Average	Standard deviation	Range
Hay Hollow Valley, A.D. 900-1100	5.7	3.1	1.2-10.5
Hay Hollow Valley, A.D. 900-1300	9.4	6.3	.1-22.8
Grasshopper, Pinedale B/W	5.5	2.4	2.0-8.9
Grasshopper, Fourmile Polychrome	5.4	2.1	2.5-8.7
Chevelon Canyon, Jars	5.0	3.2	.1-11.4
Chevelon Canyon, Bowls	5.4	3.2	.1-11.4
Valley of Oaxaca	13.1	7.3	3.0-28.2

two additional statements. First, while design similarities were used to measure interaction in all the studies from which these data were taken, the specific methods varied from study to study. For example, in my analyses of design variation in the Valley of Oaxaca and in Chevelon Canyon, designs on different vessel forms and on different parts of a single vessel form were analyzed separately. This was not done in the other studies. Given that the methods that have been used are not uniform, it is possible that there may in fact be a relationship between community interaction and design similarity which has been obscured in some data sets by the particular method used.

Second, it should be noted that, for two of the three data sets for which there was found a negative relation between intersite design similarities and distance, and for which there was revealed a significant positive correlation between design similarities and predicted interaction intensities, the average distances and the range of distances between sites was much greater than in other data sets. These distances are shown in Table 9.5. It is thus possible that I have underestimated the radius of the area around a community within which distance has little or no effect on interaction intensities (see p. 258).

The question of just what design variation can be used to measure has been an important one in archeology. In addition to using designs to measure interaction, past workers have used them to date sites and delineate culture areas. Thus, design variation has been used to measure different things by different archeologists.

I would suggest that three things need to be done if we are going to learn which, if any, aspects of design variation may be associated with social phenomena and which can be used to date sites. First, methods of classifying designs must be improved. All the design classifications on which the foregoing analysis was based, including my own classification of the Oaxaca designs, were created on the basis of intuitive notions as to what constitutes a discrete design element. This subjectivity must be replaced by a more objective method, so that different people working with the same pottery can classify the designs in the same way, and thus obtain the same results from a given body of data. Otherwise, results may vary, depending on who does the design classification. The utility of any method that cannot be replicated exactly by different archeologists is questionable.

Second, statistical methods must receive greater consideration. For example, most design studies use some type of coefficient to measure the design similarity between the units being analyzed. However, different coefficients measure similarity in different ways. The degree of fit between our concept of design sharing, and the manner in which the degree of sharing is measured in computing a similarity coefficient, should be made as close as possible.

Finally, we must attempt to learn which factors cause design variation, rather than assuming that we know the causes. These factors may vary from area to area. For example, we know little about what design elements meant to the various prehistoric people who made them. Having worked in both the Southwest and Mesoamerica, I am struck by the much slower chronological change in elements in Oaxaca (see p. 270) compared with the Southwest. I cannot explain this difference, but will offer one possible line of reasoning. Flannery (personal communication) has suggested that some "double-line-break" motifs on Atoyac Yellow-white pottery actually represent a stylization or degeneration of the "U"-motifs associated with the Olmec fire-serpent (see Pyne, this chapter). Still others show the kind of "brackets" or cross-hatching often used to depict the were-

jaguar (see Pyne, this chapter). If these designs do in fact have some religious or iconographic significance, it might help explain their longevity when contrasted with more secular forms of decoration. Factors like this must be investigated in future analyses. Only after the explanation of design variation has been achieved will we be able to use this variation to measure reliably aspects of the archeological record.

The Fire-Serpent and Were-Jaguar in Formative Oaxaca: A Contingency Table Analysis ★

NANETTE M. PYNE

Introduction

In 1971, I undertook a stylistic analysis of 595 examples of decorated pottery from the period 1150–650 B.C. in the Valley of Oaxaca. Unlike the repetitive panels of rim decoration analyzed by Stephen Plog (this chapter), the designs I studied were free-standing motifs which usually occur only once on each vessel. In all, I distinguished 18 motifs, 14 of which fall stylistically and iconographically within the so-called "highland Olmec" style (Coe 1965). In fact, they include stylized representations of at least two mythological creatures regarded as Olmec "deities" by Joralemon

(1971) in his catalogue of Olmec iconography.[†] We suspected, therefore, that pottery bearing these free-standing, nonrepetitive motifs might have some ritual or cognitive significance.

Through no fault of the authors, much of the pottery illustrated by Coe and Joralemon was recovered by looters, and it is usually not known from where the piece came within a given site; frequently, in fact, even the exact site is not known with certainty. The 595 examles in the present study were chosen because the exact provenience was known—usually to house floor, burial, or feature within the site. They come from three sites—Barrio del Rosario Huitzo, San José Mogote,

*The research described in this section was made possible by a National Science Foundation Undergraduate Research Participation Grant (GY-9015) to the University of Michigan in 1971. I wish to thank Richard I. Ford, the grant administrator, for the research opportunity.

[†]Several Mesoamerican iconographic specialists, including Joyce Marcus (personal communication) remain unconvinced that the fire-serpent and were-jaguar were "deities." I will therefore keep the term in quotation marks whenever it is used.

and Tierras Largas—all of which were occupied during the 500-year period of 1150–650 B.C., and all of which occur along a 25-km stretch of the Atoyac River in the northern Valley of Oaxaca (Flannery *et al.* 1970).

Because the exact provenience was known, simple nonparametric statistics could be used to answer the following questions:

1. Do Olmec motifs tend to occur more frequently on pottery from public buildings or on the ceremonially oriented central areas of sites?
2. Are certain motifs more closely associated with certain houses, certain villages, or certain parts of the valley?
3. What are the relationships among the motifs—do they tend to occur together, or are they antagonistic or mutually exclusive?

The Individual Motifs

Of the 18 motifs I distinguished, numbers 1 through 7 are considered to be variants of the Olmec "fire-serpent" or "sky-dragon"; this is considered by Coe (personal communication) to be one of Mesoamerica's oldest identifiable mythico-religious beings (Figures 9.7a,b, 9.8a). Fire-serpents are depicted by the use of certain characteristic symbols: large, broad horizontal excised bars; upside-down "U-elements" which Coe identifies as the serpent's gums; flames that rise from his eyebrows; and the "paw-wing" symbol (cf. Coe 1965).

Motifs 8 through 14 are considered to be variants of the Olmec "were-jaguar," thought by the Olmecs to be the offspring of an ancestral male jaguar–female human pair (cf. Coe 1965:14). He is depicted by the use of the cleft-head symbol which probably represents the sagittal furrow on the jaguar's head; by "music brackets"; and by vertical bars that look like oversized chemical

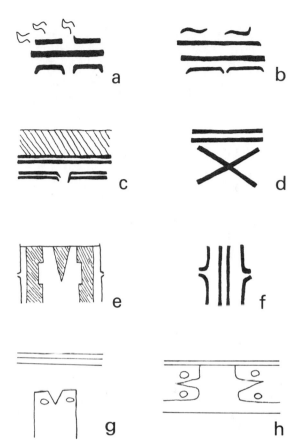

Figure 9.7 Examples of some of the free-standing motifs used in the contingency table analysis. (a, b) Variants of Motif 1 (the most common representation of the fire serpent); (c) Motif 3; (d) Motif 7 ("crossed bands"); (e) Motif 8 (the most common representation of the were-jaguar); (f) Motif 11; (g) Motif 13; (h) Motif 14.

brackets (see Figures 9.7c,d, 9.8b). Iconographically, these two Olmec "deities" are almost mutually exclusive; that is, symbols used to depict the fire-serpent (such as U-elements) are not used to depict the were-jaguar, and vice versa. These artistic conventions, which make each mythological creature readily identifiable even on fragments of vessels, made the "antagonistic" spatial distribution of these motifs (see p. 278) no surprise.

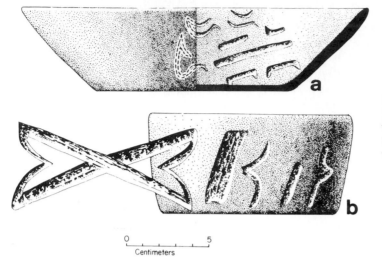

Figure 9.8 Pottery vessels from San José Mogote, Oaxaca, with examples of free-standing motifs. (a) Motif 1 on gray bowl; (b) Motif 11 on cloudy black-and-white cylinder.

Four remaining motifs, numbered 15 through 18, occur frequently on the same pottery types but cannot at present be fitted into Olmec iconography. Since they were treated in many of the same ways as motifs 1 through 14, however, the possibility that these motifs had indigenous ritual or religious significance should not be dismissed.

The Statistical Program

The analysis of this pottery was done using an already available (or "canned") computer program known as the BMDO2-S Contingency Table Analysis.* A *contingency table analysis* begins with a crosstabulation of the two classes of items whose relationship is to be studied. For example, in the section on p. 275, the two classes of items to be studied are motifs and kinds of provenience units.

*Version of July 1, 1968, written by the Health Science Computing Facility of U.C.L.A. (Dixon 1968) and revised and adapted by the Statistical Research Laboratory of the University of Michigan. I am grateful to Robert D. Drennan of the University of Michigan for running the program, advising me on the interpretation of the statistical output, and providing the following brief description of how the program works.

A table similar in form to Table 9.6 is drawn up, and the appropriate numbers are counted and entered into the corresponding positions. From such a table, a variety of statistics can be calculated. One of the most common, and the one used in this study, is the *chi-square statistic*. This statistic is based on the difference between the observed counts in each position of the table and the counts that would be expected in each position if the distributions of the two items were completely independent of one another. If the observed count is greater than the expected count, a positive association is indicated; if the observed count is less than the expected count, a negative association is indicated. Since probability values are associated with chi-square scores, these scores provide a way of determining how likely it is that such an association is owing merely to chance rather than resulting from some patterned activity.

One of the problems with the chi-square statistic, however, is that it is unreliable if the expected counts in the contingency table are low. This study concerns tables with many positions, and it was always the case in such large tables that several of the positions had very low expected values. In order to provide reliable statistics, therefore, the analysis was carried out as a series of smaller tables. Each category of each class of item was considered by itself, and was crosstabulated with each category of the other class of item individually. This resulted in a series of tables of the same form as Table 9.6, but with only two rows and two columns. Thus, a table was drawn up whose rows, for example, were "Houses" and "All other proveniences" and whose columns were "Fire-Serpent motif 1" and "All other motifs." In most cases, the expected values of such tables were large enough to provide reliable statistics.

The results of these two-by-two crosstabulations are contained in Tables 9.6–9.12. If the crosstabulation given in the above-mentioned example had resulted in a positive association with a probability of less than .05 that it was owing to chance alone, a "+" would have been entered into Table 9.6 in the position corresponding to Fire-Serpent 1 and Houses. If that crosstabulation had resulted in an expected count of less than 5 for one or more of the four positions in the table, the "+" would have been followed by a "*". If the probability that the association was owing to chance alone was between .05 and .08, the "+" would have been followed by a "?".

If the result had been a negative association with a probability of less than .05 that it was owing to chance alone, a "−" would have appeared instead of a "+". The same considerations would have applied in following the "−" with a "*" or a "?". If the probability of the association's being a result of chance alone had been greater than .08, then nothing at all would have been entered into that position in Table 9.6. The cutoff point of 5 for expected counts is the usual rule of thumb for chi-square (see, for example, Siegel 1956:111).

The cutoff points of .05 and .08 for significance levels were chosen arbitrarily.

Results of the Contingency Table Analysis

Associations with Provenience Units

Olmec motifs occurred with four main types of provenience units in the Oaxaca sites: houses, bell-shaped storage pits, burials, and platforms that had once supported public buildings. Among other things, we wanted to see if pottery with Olmec designs was more common around religious, ceremonial, or administrative structures. We therefore ran two contingency table analyses involving these four provenience units—first, using all 18 of the design motifs, and, second, using lumped fire-serpents and lumped were-jaguars. The results are given in Tables 9.6 and 9.7.

The chi-square scores showed no tendency for Olmec motifs to occur with platforms for public buildings. Indeed, there were very few highly probable associations, and most of those are probably spurious. For example, the association between were-jaguars and storage pits is easily explained by the very high number of such pits (about 100) found at Tierras Largas, a site where were-jaguar motifs predominated (see p. 277).

In fact, as further analyses (later) will suggest, all these motifs probably were associated more with residential units and the people occupying them than with public institutions. This is perhaps in significant contrast to later Oaxacan societies, organized on a state level, much of whose art was

TABLE 9.6 Association of Free-Standing Motifs with Types of Provenience Units, Oaxaca[a]

	Fire-serpent motifs				Were-jaguar motifs				Non-Olmec motifs			
	1	2	3,4,5	6,7	8,9	10	11	12,13,14	15	16	17	18
House or household cluster					+			−				+?
Storage pit	−		−*		+							
Burial	+?*			+*								
Platform						+*						

[a]See text for explanation of symbols.

TABLE 9.7 Association of Fire-Serpents and Were-Jaguars with Types of Provenience Units, Oaxaca[a]

	All fire-serpents	All were-jaguars
House or household cluster	–?	+?
Storage pit	–	+
Burial	+?*	
Platform		

[a]Fire-serpent motifs 1–7 lumped; were-jaguar motifs 8–14 lumped.

intimately connected with state institutions and tended to occur around public buildings (Marcus 1974:89–91).

Associations with Individual Households

Eight individual Early Formative houses or household clusters—six from San José Mogote* and two from Tierras Largas—were excavated extensively enough to yield an adequate sample of decorated sherds for contingency table analysis. As usual, the houses were run first against the full range of 18 motifs, and then against lumped fire-serpents and lumped were-jaguars. There were a

*The six houses or household clusters from San José Mogote come from two different areas. Houses 2 and 9 are part of a residential area on the west edge of the site; Household Clusters C1 through C4 occurred as a superimposed stratigraphic sequence near the eastern limits of Early Formative occupation (Flannery *et al.* 1970:38–58).

number of associations with a probability value less than .05, and many between .05 and .08. The results are shown in Tables 9.8 and 9.9.

Several households at San José Mogote showed positive associations with fire-serpent motifs, and negative associations with the were-jaguar. The two houses at Tierras Largas—judged to be contemporary with those at San José Mogote on the basis of all other ceramic criteria—showed positive associations with the were-jaguar motif and negative associations with the fire-serpent. Such associations are typical of the two sites as a whole (see p. 277), although there also may be some houses at San José Mogote where the most probable association is with a "non-Olmec" motif. Those houses with the highest proportion of fire-serpents also have more *Spondylus* shell, pearl oyster, mica, and magnetite than any house at Tierras Largas, and some of them occur not far from areas of public architecture. At least one burial near

TABLE 9.8 Association of Free-Sampling Motifs with Individual Houses at San José Mogote (SJM) and Tierras Largas (TL), Oaxaca[a]

	Fire-serpent motifs				Were-jaguar motifs				Non-Olmec motifs			
	1	2	3,4,5	6,7	8,9	10	11	12,13,14	15	16	17	18
SJM, H.C. C1			+*									+*
SJM, H.C. C2			+*						+*			
SJM, H.C. C3			+*		–*							
SJM, H.C. C4										+*	+*	
SJM, House 2												
SJM, House 9		+			–*							
TL, Area A, House 1		–			+		+					+*
TL, Area D, House 3	–		–?*		+	+*						

[a]H.C. = household cluster.

TABLE 9.9 Association of Fire-Serpents and Were-Jaguars with Individual Houses at San José Mogote (SJM) and Tierras Largas (TL)[a]

	All fire-serpents	All were-jaguars
SJM, H.C. C1		
SJM, H.C. C2		
SJM, H.C. C3	+	–
SJM, H.C. C4		–
SJM, House 2		
SJM, House 9	+	
TL, Area A, House 1	–	+
TL, Area D, House 3	–	+

[a]H.C. = household cluster. Fire-serpent motifs 1–7 lumped; were-jaguar motifs 8–14 lumped.

Houses 2 and 9 at San José Mogote was an adult male accompanied by a cylindrical bowl with a fire-serpent motif.

The observed tendency for certain houses to be positively associated with one "deity" and negatively associated with another is striking. The differences are not temporal, and cannot simply be explained as sampling error; the samples are too large and the results too consistent within a given residential area (cf. Household Clusters C1–C3 at San José Mogote). It therefore seems to be the case that certain Olmec mythological beings are associated in some way with specific households, and that households in any one residential area tend to share the same association.

Associations at the Community Level

The final level of analysis was to total up the number of occurrences of Olmec and non-Olmec motifs from all three sites—Barrio del Rosario Huitzo, San José Mogote, and Tierras Largas—and see to what extent the motifs associated with specific villages. As usual the chi-square scores were calculated first for the 18 motifs, then for lumped fire-serpents and lumped were-jaguars. The results are given in Tables 9.10 and 9.11.

There are many highly probable associations in these tables, but perhaps the most significant are those resulting from the lumping of various representations of each "deity." Here we have the same pattern of positive and negative association seen in the previous analysis. At both Huitzo and Tierras Largas, were-jaguars show a high positive association and fire-serpents a high negative association. At San José Mogote, the reverse is true. Because Huitzo lies to the north of San José Mogote, and Tierras Largas to the south, the differences cannot be simply regional. Areas A and C at San José Mogote—the largest, most complex and centrally located of all three villages—are highly associated with the fire-serpent and negatively associated with the were-jaguar during the Early Formative.

Some slight bias may be introduced by the fact that a small proportion of the motifs from Huitzo are from early Guadalupe phase levels. This problem was also confronted by Plog (this chapter), who found evidence that such temporal differences probably had not seriously affected his results. Similarly, in my study, temporal differences cannot be invoked to explain the differences between, for example, Houses 1 and 3 at Tierras Largas and House 9 at San José Mogote. I therefore suspect that temporal variation is a minor problem, but one whose effects should be more fully investigated in the future when a larger sample is available.

Possible Interpretation of the Associations

Contingency analysis tells us only that certain items are positively or negatively associated; it

TABLE 9.10   Association of Free-Standing Motifs with Three Different Formative Villages, Oaxaca

	Fire-serpent motifs				Were-Jaguar motifs				Non-Olmec motifs			
	1	2	3,4,5	6,7	8,9	10	11	12,13,14	15	16	17	18
Barrio del Rosario Huitzo								−				
San José Mogote	+		+	+	+							
Tierras Largas	−		−		+	+						

does not tell us why. To answer the latter question, further tests must be designed. In the meantime, let us propose a tentative model to account for the associations just discussed.

The were-jaguar and the fire-serpent are supernatural, mythological beings in whose iconography both Coe (1965) and Joralemon (1971) see relationships to later Mesoamerican deities. Our first contingency table analysis, however, showed that they are no more associated with public or "ceremonial" structures than with private residences. Further analysis showed that they were associated with groups of houses in particular residential areas, and that, when a house is positively associated with one "deity," it is often negatively associated with another. Thus, during the same time period, certain families or groups of families used predominantly pottery decorated with fire-serpents; others, predominantly pottery decorated with were-jaguars. Thus, the distribution of the two motifs is antagonistic, though not mutually exclusive.

Here, we may introduce two additional lines of evidence. First, Marcus Winter's analysis of more than 50 Formative burials in the Valley of Oaxaca (Winter 1972) suggests that decorated "Olmec" pottery definitely occurs with adult male burials, but rarely or never with female burials. Second,

Flannery's work at San Sebastián Abasolo, Oaxaca (Flannery et al. 1970:72) shows that cylindrical bowls with carved fire-serpents occur even with infant burials. The association between certain households and the fire-serpent therefore may have been (1) hereditary, and (2) predominantly through the male line.

Most ethnographically known Mesoamerican groups had bilateral descent, and most Formative societies may have had as well. We are most emphatically not proposing here that they were "patrilineal" or, for that matter, unilineal at all. We are merely pointing to circumstantial evidence that primary affiliation to a given Olmec mythico-religious being may have been through the male line. This in no way precludes bilineality.

If the were-jaguar and the fire-serpent were the symbols used for sodalities—such as the clown societies, medicine societies, or dance societies of the Southwestern Pueblos (Ford 1968)—one would expect to find such pottery only with initiated adults. If they were associated only with certain "strata" of society, one would expect to find them with women as well as with men. If they were associated only with "religious specialists," we would expect them mainly in the ceremonial center of the community; instead, they occur throughout.

TABLE 9.11   Association of Fire-Serpents and Were-Jaguars with Three Different Formative Villages, Oaxaca[a]

	All fire-serpents	All were-jaguars
Barrio del Rosario Huitzo	−	+
San José Mogote	+	−
Tierras Largas	−	+

[a]Fire-serpent motifs 1–7 lumped; were-jaguar motifs 8–14 lumped.

TABLE 9.12 Raw Counts of Free-Standing Elements from All Proveniences Used in the Contingency Table Analysis

	Fire-serpent 1	Fire-serpent 2	Fire-serpent 3,4, or 5	Fire-serpent 6 or 7	Were-jaguar 8 or 9	Were-jaguar 10	Were-jaguar 11	Were-jaguar 12,13, or 14	Other 15	Other 16	Other 17	Other 18
SJM, Area A: H.C. C1	3	2	3	0	0	1	1	0	0	1	0	3
SJM, Area A: H.C. C2	4	3	4	2	3	0	1	0	2	0	0	1
SJM, Area A: H.C. C3	13	7	6	2	0	0	3	0	0	0	0	1
SJM, Area A: H.C. C4	12	2	0	2	1	1	0	0	1	2	4	1
SJM, Area C: House 2	7	5	1	0	1	2	1	2	0	0	0	1
SJM, Area C: House 9	14	11	2	1	0	0	1	0	0	0	0	2
SJM: All houses	63	38	20	8	7	2	7	5	4	3	4	9
SJM: All bell-shaped pits	0	0	0	0	0	0	0	0	0	0	0	0
SJM: All burials	0	0	0	0	0	0	0	0	0	0	0	0
SJM: All platforms	0	1	1	1	0	2	1	0	1	0	0	0
SJM: *Total*	*102*	*48*	*28*	*13*	*9*	*4*	*12*	*8*	*5*	*7*	*9*	*9*
Huitzo: All houses	0	0	0	0	0	0	0	0	0	0	0	0
Huitzo: All bell-shaped pits	0	0	0	0	0	0	0	0	0	0	0	0
Huitzo: All burials	0	0	0	0	0	0	0	0	0	0	0	0
Huitzo: All platforms	3	0	0	0	0	0	0	0	0	0	0	0
Huitzo: *Total*	*9*	*1*	*2*	*0*	*2*	*0*	*2*	*3*	*0*	*1*	*0*	*0*
TL: House 1	15	4	3	0	18	2	9	0	2	0	0	5
TL: House 3	6	10	1	2	26	7	2	0	2	0	1	1
TL: All houses	21	14	4	2	44	9	11	0	4	0	1	6
TL: All bell-shaped pits	8	8	0	0	13	2	5	3	1	0	0	3
TL: All burials	2	0	0	3	0	0	0	0	0	0	0	0
TL: All platforms	0	0	0	0	0	0	0	1	0	0	0	0
TL: *Total*	*80*	*66*	*17*	*7*	*65*	*13*	*25*	*13*	*9*	*4*	*5*	*13*

Coe (1965) points out that the were-jaguar was the offspring of a male jaguar and a human female, depicted in a stone monument from San Lorenzo in the Gulf Coast; the descendants were "the jaguar's children." If the Olmec believed (as Coe argues they did) that long generations of humans had descended from such mythological creatures, it may be that many of Formative Mesoamerica's kin groups claimed descent from, or affiliation with, specific "deities" of the type Joralemon has argued for.

The pattern of association we have observed in the Oaxaca data may reflect the presence of *at least* two major descent groups (with the fire-serpent and were-jaguar as mythical ancestor or patron), and perhaps also a few groups whose patrons cannot at present be fitted into Olmec iconography. At the moment, there is no clear evidence to suggest that any of these descent groups were ranked with regard to each other.

Since this paper was written, additional data have come to light at San José Mogote, as yet unanalyzed and too recently discovered to add to the argument presented here. Joyce Marcus and Kent Flannery (personal communication) report that, during the San José phase, the site was composed of at least four residential wards, roughly corresponding to the cardinal directions north, south, east, and west. Throughout the whole of the phase, fire-serpent motifs on black or gray pottery dominate in the east and west wards (Areas A and C), while were-jaguars on white or yellow pottery dominate the south ward. Future analyses will be aimed at showing whether or not a demonstrable relationship existed between Tierras Largas, Huitzo, and the south residential ward at San José Mogote; and between Tomaltepec, Abasolo, and the east and west wards at San José Mogote. Whether or not such work will indeed map out networks of descent, spanning many villages, is of course open to debate. At the very least, it should demonstrate the considerable amount of data that is lost when the context and provenience of an Olmec motif are not known.

References

Abrams, R. H.
   1943   Residential propinquity as a factor in marriage selection: fifty year trends in Philadelphia. *American Sociological Review* 8. 288–294.
Beals, R., G. Brainerd, and W. Smith
   1945   Archaeological studies in northeast Arizona. *University of California Publications in American Archaeology and Ethnology* 44(1).
Brainerd, G. W.
   1951   The place of chronological ordering in archaeological analysis. *American Antiquity* 16: 301–313.
Bunzel, R.
   1929   *The Pueblo potter: A study of creative imagination in primitive art*. New York: Columbia University Press.
Carlson, R.
   1970   White Mountain redware: A pottery tradition of east-central Arizona and western New Mexico. *Anthropological Papers of the University of Arizona* No. 19. Tucson, Arizona.
Chisholm, M.
   1968   *Rural settlement and land use*. Chicago: Aldine Press.
Coe, M. D.
   1961   La Victoria: An early site on the Pacific Coast of Guatemala. *Papers of the Peabody Museum of Archaeology and Ethnology* Vol. LIII. Harvard University, Cambridge, Mass.
   1965   *The jaguar's children: Pre-classic central Mexico*. New York: Museum of Primitive Art.
Coe, M. D., and K. V. Flannery
   1967   Early cultures and human ecology in south coastal Guatemala. *Smithsonian Contributions to Anthropology* No. 3. Smithsonian Institution, Washington, D.C.
Colton, H., and L. Hargrave
   1937   *Handbook of northern Arizona pottery wares. Museum of Northern Arizona Bulletin* No. 11. Flagstaff, Ariz.
Connor, J.
   1968   Economic independence and social interaction: Related variables in culture change. Department of Anthropology. Field Museum of Natural History, Chicago. Mimeograph.
Cook, T.
   1970   Social groups and settlement patterns in Basketmaker III. Unpublished Master's Thesis, Dept. of Anthropology, University of Chicago.

Davie, M., and R. J. Reeves
1939 Propinquity of residence before marriage. *American Journal of Sociology* 44:510–518.

Deetz, J. F.
1965 The dynamics of stylistic change in Arikara ceramics. *Illinois Studies in Anthropology* No. 4. Urbana: University of Illinois Press.

Deetz, J. F., and E. Dethlefsen
1965 The Doppler effect and archaeology: A consideration of spatial aspects of seriation. *Southwestern Journal of Anthropology* 21: 196–206.

Dixon, W. J.
1968 BMD: Biomedical computer programs. *University of California Publications in Automatic Computation* No. 2. Berkeley: University of California Press.

Flannery, K. V.
1968 The Olmec and the Valley of Oaxaca: A model for interregional interaction in Formative times. In *Dumbarton Oaks Conference on the Olmec*, edited by E. P. Benson. Pp. 79–110. Washington, D.C.: Dumbarton Oaks.
1972 The cultural evolution of civilizations. *Annual Review of Ecology and Systematics* 3: 399–426.

Flannery, K. V., M. Winter, S. Lees, J. Neely, J. Schoenwetter, S. Kitchen, and J. C. Wheeler
1970 Preliminary archeological investigations in the Valley of Oaxaca, Mexico, 1966–1969. Mimeographed preliminary report. Ann Arbor, Mich.

Ford, R. I.
1968 An ecological analysis involving the population of San Juan Pueblo, New Mexico. Unpublished Ph.D. thesis, Dept. of Anthropology, University of Michigan, Ann Arbor.

Foster, G.
1965 The sociology of pottery: Questions and hypotheses arising from contemporary Mexican work. In *Ceramics and Man*, edited by F. R. Matson. *Viking Fund Publications in Anthropology* No. 41. New York: Wenner-Gren. Pp. 43–61.

Friedrich, M. H.
1970 Design structure and social interaction: Archaeological implications of an ethnographic analysis. *American Antiquity* 35: 332–343.

Haggett, P.
1965 *Locational analysis in human geography*. London: Edward Arnold.

Hill, J. N.
1970 Broken K Pueblo: Prehistoric social organization in the American Southwest. *Anthropological Papers of the University of Arizona* No. 18. Tucson, Arizona.

Joralemon, P. D.
1971 A study of Olmec iconography. *Studies in Pre-Columbia Art & Archaeology* No. 7. Washington, D.C.: Dumbarton Oaks.

Kidder, A. V., and A. Shepard
1936 *The pottery of Pecos*. Vol. 2. New Haven, Conn.: Yale University Press.

Kushner, G.
1970 A consideration of some processual designs for archaeology as anthropology. *American Antiquity* 35:125–132.

Leone, M.
1968 Neolithic economic autonomy and social distance. *Science* 162:1150–1151.

Longacre, W. A.
1964 Sociological implications of the ceramic analysis. In *Chapters in the prehistory of Eastern Arizona*. Vol. II. Chicago: Field Museum of Natural History. Pp. 155–167.
1970 Archaeology as anthropology: A case study. *Anthropological Papers of the University of Arizona* No. 17. Tucson, Arizona.

MacNeish, R. S., F. A. Peterson, and K. V. Flannery
1970 *The prehistory of the Tehuacán Valley*. Vol. 3. *Ceramics*. Austin: University of Texas Press.

Marches, J., and G. Turbeville
1953 The effect of residential propinquity on marriage selection. *American Journal of Sociology* 58:592–595.

Marcus, J.
1974 The iconography of power among the Classic Maya. *World Archaeology* 6(1):83–94.

Morrill, R.
1963 The distribution of migration distances. *Papers and Proceedings of the Regional Science Association* 11:75–84.

Olsson, G.
1965a *Distance and human interaction: A review and bibliography*. Philadelphia: The Regional Science Research Institute.
1965b Distance and human interaction: A migration study. *Geografiska Annaler* 47B:3–43.
1966 Central place systems, spatial interaction, and stochastic processes. *Papers and Proceedings of the Regional Science Association* 18: 13–45.
1970 Explanation, prediction, and meaning variance: An assessment of distance interaction models. *Economic Geography* 46:223–233.

Pires-Ferreira, J. W.
    1973   Formative Mesoamerican exchange networks. Unpublished Ph.D. dissertation, Dept. of Anthropology, University of Michigan, Ann Arbor.
Renfrew, C.
    1969   Trade and culture process in European prehistory. *Current Anthropology* 10:151–169.
Robinson, W. S.
    1951   A method for chronologically ordering archaeological deposits. *American Antiquity* 16:293–301.
Sanders, W. T.
    1965   The cultural ecology of the Teotihuacán Valley. Dept. of Anthropology, Pennsylvania State University, University Park. Mimeograph.
Schiffer, M.
    1971   The economy of social interaction: A proxemic view. *Anthropology UCLA* 3:74–83.
Shepard, A.
    1953   Appendix I: Notes on color and paste composition. In *Archaeological studies in the Petrified Forest National Monument,* by Fred Wendorf with others. *Museum of Northern Arizona Bulletin* No. 27:177–193. Flagstaff, Ariz.
Siegel, S.
    1956   *Nonparametric statistics for the behavioral sciences.* New York: McGraw-Hill.
Stanislawski, M.
    1969a   The ethno-archaeology of Hopi pottery making. *Plateau* 42:27–33.
    1969b   What good is a broken pot? *Southwestern Lore* 35:11–18.
    1973   Review of "Archaeology as anthropology: A case study." *American Antiquity* 38:117–121.

Tuggle, H. D.
    1970   Prehistoric community relations in east-central Arizona. Unpublished Ph.D. dissertation, Dept. of Anthropology, University of Arizona, Tucson.
Warren, H.
    1969   Tonque: One pueblo's glaze pottery industry dominated middle Rio Grande commerce. *El Palacio* 76:36–42.
Whallon, R.
    1968   Investigations of late prehistoric social organization in New York State. In *New Perspectives in archeology,* edited by S. R. Binford and L. R. Binford. Chicago: Aldine Press. Pp. 223–244.
Wiley, C.
    1971   Social interaction and economic exchange in the Hay Hollow Valley, 900–1200 A.D. Dept. of Anthropology, Field Museum of Natural History, Chicago. Mimeograph.
Winter, M. C.
    1972   Tierras Largas: A formative community in the Valley of Oaxaca, Mexico. Unpublished Ph.D. thesis, Dept. of Anthropology, University of Arizona, Tucson.
Wright, H. T., and M. Zeder
    1973   The simulation of a linear exchange system under equilibrium conditions. Paper presented at the Annual Meetings of the Society for American Archaeology, San Francisco, May 1973. Unpublished manuscript. Museum of Anthropology, University of Michigan.
Zipf, G.
    1949   *Human behavior and the principle of least effort.* New York: Addison-Wesley Press.

Chapter 10

INTERREGIONAL EXCHANGE NETWORKS

Introduction

Previous chapters in this volume have explored the study of early Mesoamerican villages at the regional level: regional settlement systems, the growth of linear and nonlinear patterns, the evolution of regional hierarchies. It is time now to consider a still broader unit of analysis—the *interregional networks* of trade, exchange, sacred lore, and ritual paraphernalia which linked all the regions of Mesoamerica into a single complex culture area. Religion will be the topic of Chapter 11. In this chapter, we will touch briefly on networks of trade and exchange.

We have alluded frequently to the theoretical chasm between the Real Mesoamerican Archeologist and his Skeptical Graduate Student. On no subject are they farther apart than the subject of trade. R.M.A. thinks in terms of "trade wares" and "trade items"; for S.G.S., trade is the King Kong of all prime movers.

In May of 1970, the annual meetings of the Society for American Archaeology were held in Mexico City. R.M.A. and S.G.S. presented a joint paper on "Prehispanic trade in the Río San Jacinto drainage." Assuming that S.G.S. would stick to the typed version, R.M.A. let him read the paper "to improve his stage presence a little; after all, he'll have to stand up in front of 100 undergraduates someday, and explain patrilateral cross-cousin marriage." It wasn't long before R.M.A. discovered that it was not stage presence S.G.S. was most in need of.

The talk opened with color slides of "trade items" from the Mound 1 excavation at San Jacinto: three jade beads, a small pile of obsidian blades, a chunk of red ocher, four sea shells, a stalactite, two teeth with pyrite inlays, and a piece of "amber" that looked suspiciously like a sherd from an old Carta Blanca beer bottle. By far the most interesting, however, was a series of dinosaur gastroliths, obviously from some undiscovered

Jurassic deposit. These had been polished by the villagers at San Jacinto "for use as charm stones, talismans, or gaming pieces," according to R.M.A. And R.M.A.'s section of the joint paper concluded:

> Since only a few such artifacts have been found in the valleys to the east and west, we conclude that the main Gastrolith Route leading from the highlands to the Gulf Coast must have passed along the Río San Jacinto. The presence of this route may in fact have been one of the major attractions that drew settlers to the spot. San Jacinto's strategic location along the route undoubtedly explains the strong ceramic influences from Morelos, Puebla, and the Gulf; and this, in turn, may help to explain the curious, "mixed" appearance of some parts of our ceramic sequence.

Here S.G.S. paused, cleared his throat, and took a drink of water from a glass on the podium (in spite of the fact that R.M.A. had told him not to drink the water).

"I'm going to deviate from our prepared paper," said S.G.S. to the assembled crowd, "because the farther I read the less I agree with it."

I glanced through the darkened auditorium at R.M.A., but his facial expression was mercifully not visible.

"I don't really believe there was a Gastrolith Route. At least, I don't think we have rigorous data with which to test the hypothesis of such a route," S.G.S. went on. "In addition, it's a tautology. The San Jacinto people are supposed to have settled along a trade route. But what would the route be doing in an area that didn't have people in it already? Trade routes aren't like asphalt highways, built along the easiest grade. They go where people already are, people who want what's being traded.

"An alternative hypothesis, based on the unusually high numbers of gastroliths, would be that San Jacinto was a center for their redistribution. Such a hypothesis would be wholly consonant with ethnographic data on groups at a 'chiefdom'

level of development. Suppose, for example, that gastroliths were a strategic resource desired by the elite of the San Jacinto drainage to reinforce their status. Their control of this strategic resource would put them in a position of advantage. Consider the bargaining power the Paramount would have over lesser chiefs if it were only through him that gastroliths could be obtained.

"Indeed, our data enables me to generate a testable hypothesis for the origins of the state in the San Jacinto drainage. Gastroliths are probably the one strategic resource the area really lacks. By controlling their redistribution, the elite of Mound 1 would have been able to escalate the process of stratification by putting themselves at the head of an overarching macrosystem of prestige goods exchange." S.G.S. sat down to thundering applause.

I didn't really want to watch R.M.A.'s reaction to S.G.S.' ad lib conclusions, so I ducked out at the coffee break. It was not until very late that evening that I caught up with the two of them again. A little before midnight, Richard Gomez and I came across them arguing in a booth at the infamous Barba Negra, a cabaret on Calle Bolívar.

With all due respect to the Barba Negra, it was not really the best place to carry on a serious conversation. Even if you could hear above the music of the Conjunto Tropical, you were in constant danger of a collision with one of the mammoth taxi dancers, known affectionately as "Los Tanques de General Sherman." Moreover, the upstairs of the Barba was so dark that a waiter made the rounds every 30 minutes, shining a flashlight under the tables to make sure nothing was going on. At 11 P.M. on a Saturday night, the place was so crowded that if one more person walked in the front door, someone else was automatically pushed out the back. In fact, Gomez claims that he saw a man shot one night when the dance floor was so crowded that the unfortunate victim could not even fall. Pressed like a sardine between the bodies of the dancers, the corpse was cha-cha'd from one end of the dance floor to the other until it disappeared, to be discovered hours later sitting in the third stall of the ladies' room. But that's another story.

"Can we break up the argument?" said Gomez, as he slid bravely into the booth between R.M.A. and S.G.S.

"Did you see what Little Einstein did to our joint paper this afternoon?" R.M.A. demanded. "He totally shafted me. He forgot the cardinal maxim: 'Quiet is the sound of a well-made graduate student'."

"I couldn't stand there propagating that Old Archeology," said S.G.S.

"All you proved," said Gomez, "is that bad New Archeology is as bad as bad Old Archeology."

"Worse," said R.M.A. "When the Old Archeologists wrote something bad, you could ignore their theory and use their raw data. When the New Archeologists write something bad, it doesn't even have any data you'd want to use."

"It's a perfectly defensible model," insisted S.G.S. "It accounts for all our 'trade items', as you call them, and it generates law-like propositions for the role of trade in the rise of the state."

"Let me get this straight," I said. "You're arguing that the San Jacinto elite escalated the process of stratification by controlling the trade in Jurassic charm stones?"

"It's comparable to the Olmec case," said S.G.S. "The Olmec arose in an area with nothing: no jade, no obsidian, no granitic rock for *metates*, no serpentine, no magnetite or ilmenite, no decent chert, no rock crystal or chalcedony. They had to trade for it, right? And how did they trade for it? By setting up an incredible trade network that had to be tied into their chiefly lineage, or it never would have worked."

"If their area had nothing, what were they doing there?" asked R.M.A.

"Growing three metric tons of maize per hectare," muttered Gomez, who had worked on the levees of the Coatzacoalcos River.

"And what were they trading for all this jade, and serpentine, and obsidian, and magnetite?"

R.M.A. demanded.

"Ideas," said S.G.S.

"I don't think I heard you right," said R.M.A. "Ideas?"

"Sure. The Olmec were in the process of working out the greatest intellectual and artistic tradition in early Mesoamerica, weren't they? Isn't that what you and Michael Coe keep telling me? The 'great tradition' in the sense that Robert Redfield used the term: calendrics, writing, monumental art, the concept of social rank, cosmology, the cult of the were-jaguar. Wasn't that worth selling? You once told me that list of items 'constituted Olmec culture'."

"You got any more good ideas?" asked Gomez. "I might want to buy one myself."

The Real Mesoamerican Archeologist held his head in his hands for a minute, and we listened to the Conjunto Tropical. Finally he said, "You know, it makes me think of a Just-so Story. You want to hear it?"

"Why not?"

"Do you remember reading about that 200-lb jade boulder they found under a stairway at Kaminaljuyú?" asked R.M.A.[*]

"Sure. A huge boulder, partly sawed up for artifacts."

"Following Little Einstein's theory, I know how it got there."

"Enlighten us," said Gomez.

"It was back in the seventh century B.C., O Best Beloved," said R.M.A. "Two Indians met on a jungle trail at the Isthmus of Tehuantepec. One was an Olmec from La Venta. The other was a guy from the Motagua Valley, carrying a 200-lb jade boulder with his tumpline.

" 'Hey, soul brother', says the Olmec. 'What'll you take for that jade boulder?'

" 'What have you got?' says the guy from Motagua.

" 'Ideas', says the Olmec.

" 'Let's hear one.'

---

[*] This boulder is described by Coe (1966:79).

" 'If you put a seed of maize in the ground and water it, by August a whole plant will come up.'

" 'We've known that since the El Riego phase, my friend,' says the guy from Motagua.

" 'And if you select it carefully, the cob will get bigger and the glumes will get softer.'

" 'We've known that since the Coxcatlán phase.'

" 'Try planting it by means of a calendar of 18 months of 20 days each.'

" 'We've been doing that since 3113 B.C. Try another idea.'

" 'Our chief is descended from a jaguar who mated with a human female.'

" 'So is ours.'

" 'If you'd let me have that jade boulder, I think we could make our chief into a king.'

" 'What's that mean?'

" 'That means he'd be semidivine, and have life-and-death power over his subjects; he'd have a monopoly of force, and the power to conscript soldiers, levee taxes, and exact tribute.'

" 'If *our* chief tried that, we'd whip his ass.'

"The Olmec sighs.

" 'That's all the ideas you got?' says the guy from Motagua.

"' 'That's all I'm authorized to trade.'

" 'In that case,' says the Motagua Indian, 'if you don't mind, I'll head on up to the Kaminaljuyú area, where the chief is offering 10, maybe 12 girls from elite lineages for every hundredweight of jade.' And that, O Best Beloved, is how the Great Jade Boulder got to Kaminaljuyú."

The Skeptical Graduate Student stared critically at R.M.A.

"The trouble with that," he said, "is that that jade boulder was found in an Esperanza phase deposit—Early Classic. That's at least 1000 years too late to have had anything to do with the Olmec." He stood up, slid past Gomez, and went to find the waiter.

"He took it seriously," said Gomez with amazement. "Or is he putting us on?"

R.M.A. smiled sadly. "There is one thing—just one thing—for which I will never forgive the New Archeology. And that is for taking all the fun out of archeology."

Ethnographic Models for Formative Exchange

JANE W. PIRES-FERREIRA and
KENT V. FLANNERY

Introduction

When contrasted with the preceding preceramic era, the Early and Middle Formative periods in Mesoamerica (1500–500 B.C.) witnessed many significant changes in population growth, architecture, settlement patterns, and artifact categories. One of the most striking changes, however, was in the enormously expanded volume of material, both raw and finished, traveling between cultural regions. Interregional movement of pottery, obsidian, jade, turquoise, iron pigments, iron ores, mica, mollusk shell, turtle shell, fish and stingray spines, shark teeth, and other commodities often reached impressive proportions. Many of these items were of ritual use and, as pointed out by Drennan (Chapter 11, this volume), probably reflect an increasing role for rituals of sanctification on the part of Formative peoples. Others were "utilitarian" in nature, although the line between utilitarian and nonutilitarian is often hazy (see p. 290).

Primitive Exchange

In this chapter, we use the term "exchange" in preference to "trade," in much the same manner that Sahlins (1965) used it in his classic article "On the sociology of primitive exchange." The term "trade" has been used in so many different contexts—many of them associated with state societies, and the kinds of formal trade engaged in by Western states—that we prefer not to use it. The kind of "primitive exchange" described by Sahlins is more appropriate for the level of sociopolitical evolution we assume, on the basis of all available archeological evidence, to have characterized the Early and Middle Formative periods. In such societies (corresponding roughly to the ideal types originally defined by Service [1962] as "tribes" and "chiefdoms," and by Fried [1967] as "egalitarian" and "rank" societies), exchange frequently takes the form of gift giving, with the unstated assumption that the gift will be reciprocated at some time in the future, though not necessarily in the form of the same commodity. Equivalences between commodities are generally not fixed, nor are the rates of exchange standard, although Sahlins (1972) has shown that participants do have ideas about the relative values of goods exchanged. Apart from Sahlins' work, superb models for the operation of primitive exchange systems can be found in Rappaport's (1968) work on the Maring of New Guinea, Harding's (1967) work on the Siassi Islanders, and Leach's (1954) work on the Kachin of Burma.

Varieties of Formative Exchange

If we turn to the kind of ethnographic literature just mentioned, we feel that we can distinguish at least six different kinds of exchange that probably are archeologically detectable in the Formative

data at our disposal. And here is the important part: Each of these kinds of exchange is so different that it requires a different model to describe it. When Mesoamerican archeologists lump together such commodities as obsidian, shell, magnetite, and exotic pottery as "trade items," they may be obscuring the fact that all these items had somewhat different mechanisms of exchange, each of which needs to be understood in its own right. For example, in the Valley of Oaxaca, obsidian moved at the level of every household; shell moved at the level of the regional craft specialist; and magnetite may have moved mainly between elites. All were "trade goods" but, as we hope to show in this chapter, each must be analyzed separately. To do this, we need quantified data which are missing in most Formative site reports.

Let us briefly consider six kinds of primitive exchange that are probably documented both in the ethnographic and archeological records.

1. *Exchanges of subsistence items (that is, basic foodstuffs) between villages in different environmental zones.* Examples would be the arrival of humid-zone products such as white zapote, black zapote, and coyol palm fruits in the arid, highland Tehuacán Valley during the Formative (Smith 1967:233). Some of these "imported" foodstuffs were later grown by irrigation in Tehuacán (Woodbury and Neely 1972:93), but they probably came initially from nearby Veracruz. Presumably, early maize from Tehuacán moved in the opposite direction. Such exchange perhaps was analogous to the ethnohistorically documented movement of coca and maize from the Amazon lowland Indians to the highland Peruvian llama herders in exchange for *charqi* (dried meat) and *chuño* (freeze-dried potatoes) (Murra 1972).

2. *Reciprocal exchange of utilitarian commodities (excluding foodstuffs) to which every single villager had access.* An example of such exchange would be the movement of obsidian flakes and chunks during the Early Formative period. In spite of the abundance of native flints, cherts, or silicified tuffs in highland Mesoamerica, hardly a

household that has been carefully excavated there is without obsidian; while some lowland villages, lacking local flint deposits, used obsidian exclusively.

Obsidian exchange was probably related both to (*1*) *population density and distribution*, since the amount moving in any direction was partly a function of the number of villages in that area (Wright and Zeder 1973); and to (*2*) *distance*, since the amount in any village was also partly a function of its distance to the nearest source. This exchange was probably analogous to the ethnographically documented obsidian exchanges of the Siassi Islanders, in which the resource decreased in amount and increased in value as distance from the source increased (Harding 1967:42).

In the Early Formative, obsidian trade was probably an egalitarian form of exchange in which all villages participated. In the Valley of Oaxaca, where house-by-house data on obsidian are available, variation in the sources used and the percentage of obsidian from each are usually so great as to suggest that each household obtained its obsidian on an individual basis. Unfortunately, comparable data cannot be provided for areas where only one source was used. Another important phenomenon is that the amount of obsidian found from village to village appears to decrease in rough proportion to distance from the source (see p. 299).

3. *Pooling of utilitarian commodities for later distribution to all members of the community*. An example of such exchange would be the movement of prismatic obsidian blades, beginning on a serious scale around 1000–900 B.C. in Mesoamerica. Although the quantity of prismatic blades exchanged was presumably related to the same population and distance factors affecting reciprocal exchange of utilitarian commodities, the type of exchange was different. In contrast to the variation in source utilization from household to household characteristic of reciprocal exchange, uniform distribution of obsidian from several sources among households in some residential wards at large ceremonial–civic centers like San José

Mogote, Oaxaca, suggests pooling of obsidian by some central agency prior to distribution to households.

Evidence of such pooling first appears around 1000 B.C., and is probably associated with the introduction of imported prismatic obsidian blades. Through time, as blades became more and more the object of exchange (and certain sources become more important as a result), such pooling became more the rule than the exception. By the Middle Formative, this pattern of obsidian distribution seems to be true even of small Oaxacan hamlets (Winter 1972; and see Winter and Pires-Ferreira, this chapter).

4. *Exchanges of unworked nonutilitarian commodities for conversion by part-time specialists, with most villagers having access to the finished product*. Unmodified shell was moved from the Pacific Coast and tidewater estuaries to households at certain villages in Oaxaca (for example, San José Mogote and Tierras Largas) where it was converted into ornaments. The range of artifacts on the house floors where the shell was found suggest that their occupants were farmers with a part-time specialty, not full-time shell workers. Finished ornaments, on the other hand, have been found at small neighboring sites (such as Abasolo) where no evidence of shell working was found. Neither the mechanism by which the raw material reached the shell workers, nor the mechanism by which the finished products reached their users, is fully understood. But the situation may be similar to that described for some Siassi Islanders who work raw material traded to them by another island, which they use themselves and pass on to still a third island (Harding 1967).

5. *Conversion of exotic raw material into even more exotic commodities for exchange between chiefly elites*. The production of magnetite mirrors during the Early Formative period at one residential ward of one site in Oaxaca, evidently for exchange with sites in Morelos, Nochixtlán, and Veracruz, provides an example of this type. The distribution of these mirrors indicates an exchange

that is *not* a function of distance from source. A very restricted number of sites (and households within these sites) had access to mirrors that, based on evidence from certain figurines, may have been worn on the chests of elite individuals. Analogous ethnographic situations might be the manufacture of tortoise-shell combs in Truk for wearing by members of highly ranked lineages (David M. Schneider, personal communication) or the exchanges of jade in Burma between Kachin chiefs and Shan aristocrats (Leach 1954). The mechanism for such exchanges may have been gifts between elites, perhaps sometimes set up by marriage alliances (Flannery 1968).

6. *Exchanges of items that function in ceremonial context or public ritual, some of which probably were considered community property*. Examples would be the circulation of turtle-shell drums and conch-shell trumpets in the Mesoamerican Formative, discussed by Robert D. Drennan in Chapter 11 (this volume). The mechanisms that moved such products—evidently indispensable in the ceremonial life of the early Mesoamerican village—from lowland supply areas to highland villages is unknown. Just as lowland Mesoamerica depended heavily on the highlands for obsidian, the highlands depended heavily on the lowlands for ritual paraphernalia. In much the same way, highland herders on the altiplano of Peru today find it impossible to celebrate an important ritual without the use of *chicha*—the fermented beverage from a plant (maize) that cannot even be grown at that altitude (Webster 1971; Murra 1972).

These are the six modal types of commodity exchange we have outlined for Early and Middle Formative Mesoamerica. Although each of these types can be defined and examined as a distinct entity, eventual understanding of exchange processes must come from examination of the variation within, and interrelation between, the various types of commodity exchange. Utilitarian and nonutilitarian goods are assigned differential standing within the networks in which they move

(Sahlins 1972:277), so that a commodity moved by our Type 2 exchange in one valley may, in fact, be handled by Type 3 exchange in the next. By examining the relative position of each commodity in relation to other commodities within the exchange sphere, it becomes possible to propose hypotheses about which products acted as "regulatory mechanisms" serving to maintain the system in spite of long-term fluctuations in population or its distribution.

Before proceeding to a series of individual studies of traded Formative commodities, let us briefly consider two kinds of exchange—reciprocity and redistribution—that are widely mentioned in the literature. Although archeologists constantly refer to these two types of exchange, they have rarely designed tests to show which was operating in a given archeological situation, or why. We believe that such tests are possible, within limits, because the house-to-house patterns of distribution of a commodity should vary with the two types of exchange.

Exchange under Conditions of Reciprocity

Rappaport's (1968) study of the egalitarian Maring tribesmen of New Guinea illustrates the mechanisms of exchange under conditions of reciprocity. Trade among the Maring is effected through direct exchanges between individuals on a reciprocal basis, and each trader or local group acts as one link in a "chain-like" structure (Rappaport 1968:106–107). The producers and consumers of a particular commodity may be separated from each other by so many links that they are unknown to each other, just as the prehistoric village of Beidha in Jordan probably had no knowledge of the Çiftlik obsidian source in Turkey, and the village of Tierras Largas in Oaxaca no real knowledge of the Barranca de los Estetes obsidian source in the Valley of Mexico. In such a situation, the material passes from kinsman to kinsman, or from valley to valley, through "trade partnerships" established by fictive kin ties. These ties are necessary because, as Sahlins (1972) points out, at a prestate level, people generally do not like to trade with (and do not deal fairly with) non-relatives. As yet, however, we do not have a convincing methodology for archeologically demonstrating trade partnerships.

In the Maring system described by Rappaport, the two main locally produced exchange items are salt (from saline springs in the Simbai Valley) and stone axes (from quarries in the Jimi Valley). Both are "utilitarian" items, but they are circulated in the same "sphere of conveyance" (Bohannan, quoted by Rappaport 1968:106) with "nonutilitarian" goods such as ornamental feathers (from bird-of-paradise, parrot, and eagle), shells, and animal furs (used to decorate shields, headbands, and loincloths). (The ascription of "nonutilitarian" status here is perhaps arbitrary, because many of these latter items are used as bride wealth by the Maring, and hence are of great economic importance; but this fact need not concern us for the moment.)

Bird-of-paradise plumes and fur enter the Simbai Valley from the north. The local villagers keep some and trade others south to the Jimi Valley, along with Simbai Valley salt. Shells of three types (gold lip, sea snail, and cowrie) enter the Jimi Valley from the south. The local villagers keep some and trade the rest north to the Simbai Valley, along with Jimi Valley axes.

Such a chain-like reciprocal exchange structure, as Rappaport points out, has a number of weaknesses. First, the number of axes produced by the Jimi quarries is a function, not of the demand for axes, but the Jimi Valley's need for salt. And if the Simbai Valley people have an adequate supply of axes, they may simply say, "We don't want any more," whereupon the Jimi Valley suffers a salt shortage. So many links separate the quarries from the salt springs that the Jimi axe makers cannot shame, cajole, or wheedle the Simbai salt makers into making more salt. Second, trade in "subsistence" items is related to population density anyhow; if population in the Jimi Valley drops, it will need less salt, and the Simbai probably will be

left with an axe shortage. Thus, "it may be questioned whether a direct exchange apparatus that moves only two or three items critical to subsistence would be viable" (Rappaport 1968:106).

For these weaknesses, Rappaport offers a tentative solution: "It may be suggested that the inclusion of both the nonutilitarian valuables and utilitarian goods within a single 'sphere of conveyance' . . . stimulated the production and facilitated the distribution of the utilitarian goods." Bird-of-paradise plumes fade, fur perishes, and the pressure for spectacular generosity in bride wealth is so great that demand for these items is constant, and they "could be freely exchanged for stone axes and native salt" (1968:106). Thus, so-called "nonutilitarian" or "exotic" exchange might act as a *systemic regulator*, which perpetuates trade in subsistence products even when the balance of trade or demographic stability is in doubt. If this is the case, it is possible that, in the case of Formative Mesoamerica, such exotic items as Pacific Coast pearl oyster shells, macaw plumes, and lumps of magnetite ore moved north from Oaxaca through the Valleys of Nochixtlán and Morelos along the same chain-like route through which Barranca de los Estetes obsidian blades moved south to Oaxaca.

In a reciprocal economy where individual households negotiate for their own obsidian, we would expect a great deal of variation between households, both in the sources used and the proportions of obsidian from various sources. The source for this variation would be differences from one household or kin group to another in terms of their trade partnerships or contacts in areas nearer to the sources. This kind of variation is what Winter and Pires-Ferreira's households in Formative Oaxaca seem to show (this chapter). We also would expect to see widespread evidence of long-distance trade in exotic, "nonutilitarian" items, both as a form of "foreign relations" (Ford 1972) and to provide regulators for the subsistence items moving in the same "sphere of conveyance." Long-distance networks of this type are in fact documented in this chapter and in Chapter 11.

Exchange under Conditions of Redistribution

As Rappaport points out, systemic regulators are needed because of the unsophisticated nature of reciprocal exchange and of "chain-like" structures. In redistributive economies, where trade is coordinated by a chief or some managerial agency, "supralocal authorities may demand production and enforce deliveries" (Rappaport 1968:108). In this case, exchange might continue in spite of demographic shifts in chain-like systems. "They might even work in 'reciprocal systems' in which the parties to the transactions are *groups* in which production might be commanded by a local authority who might, conceivably, take into consideration the requirements of other groups" (1968:108).

In redistributive economies, materials coming into a valley might be "pooled" by some administrative authority—either a paramount chief at the largest village, or a "head man" or high-status family at smaller villages. The pooler might then redistribute the material to his kinsmen or followers, according to their needs and the amount of pressure they are able to put on him. In the case of obsidian in Formative Oaxaca, the introduction of prismatic obsidian blades from the Barranca de los Estetes and Zinapécuaro source areas, beginning around 1000 B.C., is associated with a reduction of variation in source usage by households—suggesting that some form of pooling, probably associated with the rise of a managerial elite and reinforced by the increased value of prismatic blades over unstandardized flakes, was being practiced.

Eventually, if the redistribution of utilitarian items also came to be based on chiefly power, we would expect the authorities to "demand production and enforce deliveries," as Rappaport suggests. In this case, the exchange system would no longer need the "exotic" or "nonutilitarian" items as regulators. One might expect long-distance trade in exotic ores, shells, and plumes to diminish, except insofar as the elite needed these to enhance their status. The administration of a highly developed chiefly authority should have been able to demand levels of production that would make it possible to derive most "utilitarian" items from within their own sphere of influence, or negotiate for them with the elites of other regions. One would therefore expect *more regionalization* and *less long-distance trade in exotica on the level of the individual household*. This does seem to be reflected in our Middle Formative data (see p. 325).

While some Mesoamerican Formative societies were egalitarian, others were complex chiefdoms or emergent chiefdoms, almost certainly with redistributive economies (Flannery 1968). Whereas in egalitarian society, most goods are equally available to all members of the community, at the chiefdom level, some goods are amassed by paramount chiefs for redistribution according to a hereditarily defined rank order (Service 1962; Sahlins 1972). The position of chief is an institutionalized office conferred by birth order within the ruling lineage, and often associated with the concept of divine descent from the gods. This exclusive chief-god relationship serves to legitimize the right of chiefly stewardship over the land, its people, and their produce. But concomitant with the chiefly right to demand community support and tribute is chiefly responsibility for accumulation, storage, and redistribution of the produce. Negligence of these responsibilities may lead to the overthrow of a chief. Exclusive control over the exploitation and distribution of rare resources, ensured by the power of chiefly *tabu*, further underwrites the position of the paramount chief in relation to his followers. Transformation of such rare resources into luxury goods is usually accomplished by craft specialists attached to the chiefly household; their products, together with the raw material itself, provides the paramount with a basis for negotiating exchange with other chiefs. Such exchanges lead to the acquisition of both utilitarian and exotic sumptuary goods, which again are used to reinforce and legitimize chiefly status and power. Abstractly then, a chiefdom can be pictured as a sphere where lines of redistribution radiate from the central paramount, according to social rank order, to integrate dependent villages. Two or more such spheres may be linked in an exchange network as a result of exchange between their respective elites. In Formative Mesoamerica, magnetite mirrors may have been so exchanged.

Archeologically, it is a difficult matter to identify chiefdoms. Improved evidence has since come from bone strontium analysis of burials, which detects dietary differences (present by the Middle

Formative) that probably have a basis in hereditary rank (Brown 1973). Such evidence of hereditary ranking is diagnostic of chiefdoms, but since most chiefdoms have a redistributive economy, we also can look to artifact distributions for evidence of redistribution. The exchange of obsidian in Formative Mesoamerica (to be discussed in the following section) has provided some evidence for the development and growth of redistributive systems.

Obsidian Exchange in Formative Mesoamerica★

JANE W. PIRES-FERREIRA

Introduction

Obsidian has become one of the most frequently studied prehistoric exchange items, owing to its widespread archeological occurrence and to the fact that it can usually be identified to source by means of trace elements. Optical spectroscopy, x-ray fluorescence, and neutron activation all have been used to trace obsidian artifacts to the volcanic flows where it occurs naturally (see, for example, Cobean et al. 1971). The present study summarizes a more extensive report (Pires-Ferreira n.d.) on the neutron activation analysis of some 600 samples from 20 geological sources in Mesoamerica and 422 archeological samples of Early

and Middle Formative date in Mesoamerica. The methodology used was an automated technique for calculating the percentage of sodium (Na) and manganese (Mn) by neutron activation, which previously has been described in detail by Gordus and his co-workers (1967) and is further documented in Pires-Ferreira (n.d.).

Obsidian is a volcanic glass created by rapid cooling of extrusive lava, widely used by Mesoamerican Indians to make chipped-stone tools. Mesoamerican obsidians occur primarily in the east-west neovolcanic chain of central Mexico and in the highlands of Guatemala. Samples collected from 20 of these obsidian source were examined in this study. Every geological source and archeological sample was irradiated and its resultant radioactivity counted a minimum of five times, and the final Na and Mn percentage calculations resulting from this process represent an average of the five results. Multiple analyses ensure an accuracy of better than ±2.0% at a .95 confidence level. The calculated percentages are plotted

★So many archeologists supplied me with obsidian samples that it is impossible to thank all of them here. I am especially thankful to Paul Tolstoy (Valley of Mexico), Jörg Aufdermauer and Heinz Walter (Puebla), Michael Coe and Robert Cobean (Veracruz), David Grove (Morelos), Edward Sisson (Tabasco), and Gareth Lowe and Thomas Lee (Chiapas).

against each other on a graph with the percentage of Na scaled from 2.00 to 4.12 along the abscissa and the percentage of Mn $\times 10^2$ scaled from .00 to 14.40 along the ordinate. All sources thus analyzed and plotted produced a roughly elliptical cluster of data points on the graph.

Boundaries for each source cluster were calculated in a standard manner. Utilizing a computer-controlled digital plotter, a *confidence ellipse with a probability level of .95* was drawn, based on the distribution of data points for each source containing 20 or more samples (Figure 10.2, Cerro de las Navajas). When fewer than 20 samples were available for a source, the ellipse was determined from the degree of inclination and spread of the available points and the known *maximum* variations in the Na and Mn content for Mesoamerican obsidians (Figure 10.3, Altotonga). Adoption of the .95 probability level ellipse provides a standardized definition of source boundaries, elimination of erroneous data points, and a reasonably accurate tool for distinguishing between sources. Of the 20 geological sources analyzed, only 9 were found to have been utilized during the period 1500–500 B.C. (Figures 10.1–10.4). These were:

1. Zinapécuaro, Michoacán
2. Barranca de los Estetes, Valley of Mexico
3. Cerro de las Navajas, Hidalgo
4. Tulancingo, Hidalgo
5. Guadalupe Victoria, Puebla
6. Altotonga, Veracruz
7. "Unknown Oaxacan source," probably near Tlaxiaco*
8. El Chayal, Guatemala
9. Other Guatemalan source (unnamed).

Archeological samples were analyzed and plotted

*While this source is verbally reported by geologists of Plan Oaxaca, a United Nations development project, I was unable to reach the area because of poor road conditions. Twenty-one obsidian samples from Nochixtlán in the Mixteca region of Oaxaca strongly suggest that the source is not far away.

as outlined earlier. Transparent overlays, on which the .95 confidence ellipses for all sources had been drawn to the standard plot scale, were used to determine the source origin of archeological samples. Those artifacts which did not fall within the area of any source ellipse were recorded as indeterminate, and set aside for reanalysis. Where two ellipses overlapped a cluster of archeological data points—as sometimes happened with the Barranca de los Estetes and Tulancingo ellipses—it was found that the samples generally would be distributed throughout the entire area of one or the other ellipse. For example, 75 samples from the site of Moyotzingo, Puebla, were densely packed within the Barranca de los Estetes ellipse, including an overlap zone with the Tulancingo ellipse; but not one sample fell in any other part of the Tulancingo ellipse. Though obviously we cannot be 95% confident of the ascription, in such cases, all samples were recorded as having come from the one source whose ellipse was completely filled. The use of additional trace elements might achieve a neater separation.

Obsidian as a Function of Distance from Source

One of the most interesting uses of prehistoric obsidian exchange data is Renfrew, Dixon, and Cann's (1968) linear regression analysis of the relationship between quantity of obsidian traded and distance to the source (see Table 10.1). Utilizing optical spectroscopic analysis, they identified 12 Neolithic villages in the Near East whose obsidian came from the Çiftlik flow in central Turkey. The percentage of imported obsidian versus locally available flint or chert in the lithic inventory was recorded, and the distance to Çiftlik from each site was calculated. This was then recorded on lognormal graph paper, with percentage of obsidian on the logarithmic (Y) axis and distances from source on the arithmetic (X) axis. A linear regression line relating (*1*) distance from the source to (*2*) the percentage of the total chipped-stone in-

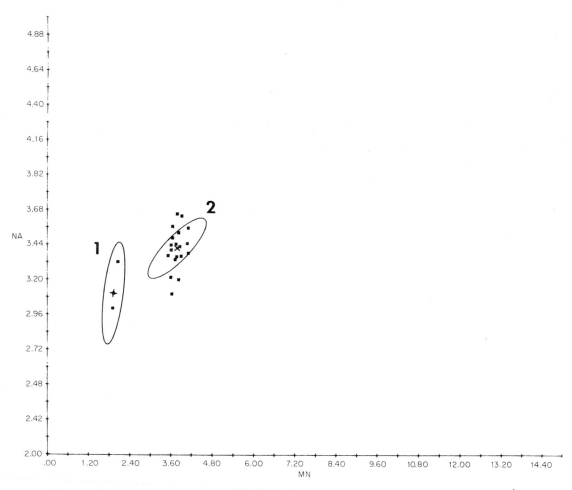

Figure 10.1 Confidence ellipses with a probability level of .95 for obsidian samples from sources at Zinapécuaro (1) and Barranca de los Estetes (2).

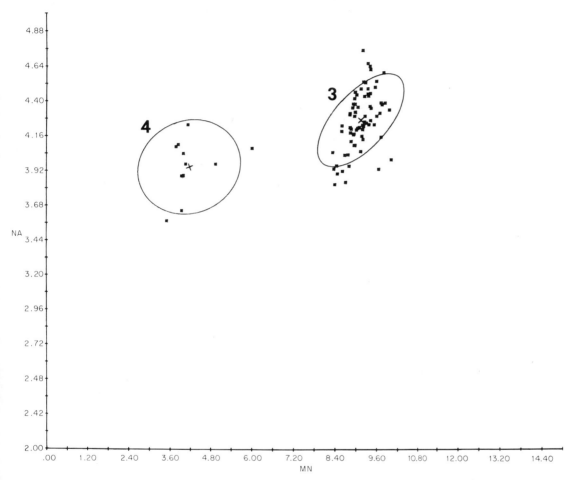

Figure 10.2 Confidence ellipses with a probability level of .95 for obsidian samples from sources at Cerro de las Navajas (3) and Tulancingo (4).

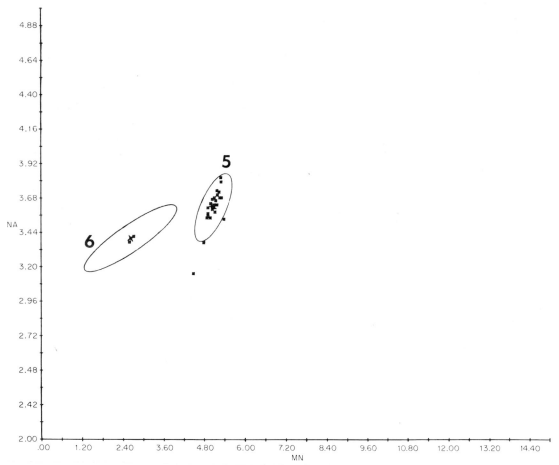

Figure 10.3 Confidence ellipses with a probability level of .95 for obsidian samples from sources at Guadalupe Victoria (5) and Altotonga (6).

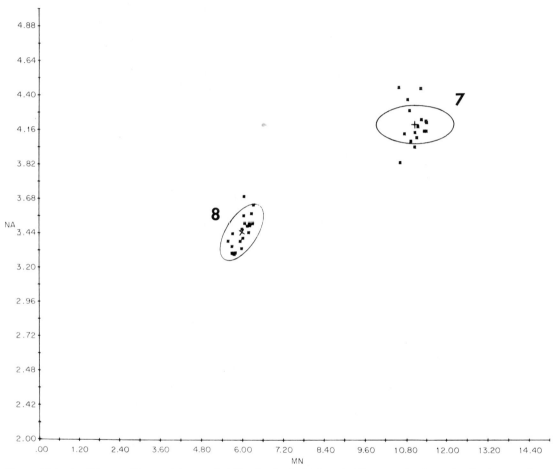

Figure 10.4 Confidence ellipses with a probability level of .95 for obsidian samples from the "unknown Oaxacan" source (7) and El Chayal (8).

TABLE 10.1 Sources of Obsidian at 19 Early and Middle Formative Villages as Determined by Neutron Activation Analysis [a]

Region	Site	Zinapécuaro, Michoacán	Barranca de los Estetes, Mexico	Cerro de las Navajas, Hidalgo	Tulancingo, Hidalgo	Guadalupe Victoria, Puebla	Altotonga, Veracruz	Unknown Oaxacan	El Chayal, Guatemala	Other Guatemalan	Indeterminate, to be reanalyzed	Total sample size
Early Formative												
Chiapas	Altamira								7			7
	Angostura-el Carmen								2			2
Morelos	San Pablo		42				2	2			4	50
Oaxaca	Huitzo						1					1
	San José Mogote	14	19			5	2	1	1	2		44
	Tierras Largas	8	20			26	6	1	1		4	66
Puebla	Las Bocas		7									7
Tabasco	Campo Nuevo					49			2	1		52
	Gamas					3						3
	Nerio Hernández					7						7
	Rancho Guadalupe					10			3	1		14
Valley of Mexico	Tlapacoya		2									2
											Subtotal	255
Middle Formative												
Morelos	Cerro Chacaltepec		3							2		5
Oaxaca	Huitzo		1	1	3							5
	Tierras Largas	4	8	1	1	7		8		2		31
Puebla	Acatepec		9				1	1			1	12
	Moyotzingo		75								17	92
Valley of Mexico	El Arbolillo	1	7	2	1			1		1		13
	Zacatenco		3		1			2		3		9
											Subtotal	167
											Total	422

[a] Figures are actual numbers of pieces, not percentages.

ventory that obsidian had contributed was then plotted.

Within 100 to 300 km of Çiftlik, most chipped stone found at Neolithic sites is obsidian: at least 80%, as against 20% flint or chert. Outside this "supply zone," the proportion of obsidian decreases exponentially with distance. At Tabbat al-Hammam in Syria, 400 km away, the percentage of obsidian is down to 5%; at Beidha in southern Jordan, almost 900 km away, the percentage is only .1%. The authors suggest such a pattern would result if, for example, "villages were spaced at 90 kilometers apart, and . . . each village would pass to its neighbors down the line one half of the total it received" (Renfrew, Dixon, and Cann 1968:329). Of course, there are many more villages than that, and a good deal of variation to either side of the regression line; but the model ("percentage of obsidian is partly a function of distance to source") is useful (see Figure 10.5).

The model works in the Near East because there are sources only in the north, so the percentage of obsidian decreases as one moves south. In Mesoamerica, where obsidian sources form a mosaic pattern, the situation becomes more complicated: As one moves south, away from the Valley of Mexico sources, he comes gradually closer to the Guatemalan sources. Moreover, there are some coastal areas—such as, for example, the Ocós region of Guatemala (Coe and Flannery 1967)—where there is no available chert source, and thus 100% of the chipped stone is traded obsidian regardless of distance to source. All these problems, coupled with the fact that most Mesoamerican excavators have not published the percentage of obsidian in their total chipped-stone assemblage, makes application of the Renfrew–Dixon–Cann model difficult at present.

The few figures we have, however, suggest that it might be applicable if sufficient data were available. For example, in Table 10.2, we give the percentage of obsidian from all sources versus flint, and the distance in kilometers to the nearest *primary* obsidian source known to have been used

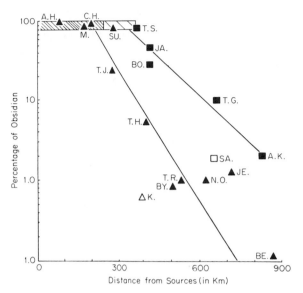

Figure 10.5 Percentage of obsidian in the total chipped-stone industry plotted against distance from source for Early Neolithic sites in the Near East, 6500 to 5000 B.C.

Triangles indicate sites in Central Anatolia and the Levant (supplied by the Cappodocian sources), squares those in the Zagros area (supplied by Armenian sources). Percentages are plotted on a logarithmic scale. Shaded areas indicate the supply zones, the straight lines show approximately exponential fall-off in the contact zones.

Key to sites: Zagros: T.S., Tell Shemsharah; JA., Jarmo; BO., Bouqras; T.G., Tepe Guran; A.K., Ali Kosh; SA., Sarab. Levant, etc: A.H., Asilkli Hüyük; C.H., Catal Hüyük; M., Mersin; SU., Suberde; T.J., Tell al-Judaidah; T.H., Tabbat al-Hammam; T.R., Tell Ramad; BY., Byblos; N.O., Nahal Oren; JE., Jericho; BE., Beidha; K., Khirokitia.

[After Renfrew, Dixon, and Cann 1968:328.]

by each site. Data on the percentage of obsidian versus flint is very scanty for the Early Formative. For the Middle Formative, the sites of El Arbolillo and Zacatenco in the Valley of Mexico, only 30 km from the source, have obsidian percentages of 80% and 86% relative to "quartz."* Las Canoas in the Valley of Tehuacán, at approximately 100 km distance, has 50% obsidian to flint; Barrio

*This is the term Vaillant (1935) used for flint or chert.

TABLE 10.2   Obsidian as a Function of Distance: Distance from Primary Obsidian Source, Compared with the Percentage Obsidian (versus Flint or Chert) Used at Various Formative Villages[a]

	Distance in kilometers to primary source	Total obsidian from all sources versus flint	Percentage of Barranca de los Estetes obsidian in total obsidian	Percentage of Barranca de los Estetes obsidian versus flint
Middle Formative Sites				
El Arbolillo I–II[c]	30 (1)	80.20%	53.84%[b]	43.31%
Zacatenco[c]	30 (1)	86.60%	30.00%[b]	28.90%
Las Canoas[d]	100 (1?)	50.00%	?	?
Cerro Chacaltepec[e]	135 (1)	?	60.00%[b]	±56.00%
Huitzo[f]	230 (3)	15.00%	20.00%[b]	3.00%
Tierras Largas[f]	400 (1)	16.00%	25.80%	4.10%
Early Formative Sites				
Tlapacoya[g]	40 (1)	?	100.00%[b]	?
Gualupita[c]	90 (1)	57.60%	?	?
Las Bocas[f]	120 (1)	?	100.00%[b]	?
San Pablo[e]	130 (1)	?	90.70%	±80.00%
Tierras Largas[f]	245 (2)	15.00%	30.30%	5.00%
San José Mogote[f]	390 (1)	18.50%	43.18%	6.80%

[a]Primary sources: (1) Barranca de los Estetes; (2) Guadalupe Victoria; (3) Tulancingo. [b]This percentage based on small number of analyzed samples. [c]Vaillant 1935. [d]Flannery 1964. [e]Grove 1970. [f]Pires-Ferreira n.d. [g]Tolstoy and Paradis 1970.

del Rosario, Huitzo, and Tierras Largas in the Valley of Oaxaca, at about 240 km, have 15% and 16% respectively. These figures seem sufficient to suggest that Mesoamerica also may have had "supply areas" within which the obsidian percentage is close to 80%, and beyond which the proportion drops exponentially with distance.

Determination of Regional Exchange Networks

By the use of matrix analysis, it is possible to break down Formative obsidian exchange into a series of *regional exchange networks*—groups of sites whose pattern of utilization of a given source is so similar as to suggest that they were among the links in a "chain-like" network like that described earlier in this chapter. The raw data used consisted of some 396 obsidian fragments identified to source from a variety of Early and Middle Formative sites.

The method of analysis used was a *Q-type sample-to-sample correlation matrix*, produced by means of an already available (or "canned") computer program, the "Midas Statistical Package" of the University of Michigan Statistical Research Laboratory. This method is based on the *Pearson's r* statistic, which is described in Chapter 9 (p. 261) by Plog. For example, a matrix can be set up (see Figure 10.6) in which there are seven *variables*, representing the seven regions involved (Valley of Mexico, Puebla, Morelos, Oaxaca, Tabasco, Veracruz, and Chiapas). Each of these variables is then compared with all other variables, on the basis of seven *observations*—namely, the number of pieces of obsidian from each of the seven obsidian sources identified from Early Formative sites in each region. Pearson's r is then calculated for the degree to which any two regions share the same sources in roughly the same proportions. As described in Chapter 9, perfect positive correlation would be +1.0; no correlation, 0.0; and perfect negative correlation, −1.0.

Each separate geological source observation was first computed against the archeological data and cells of high correlation, suggesting the degree of

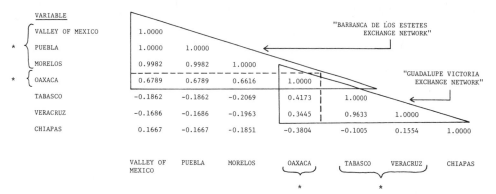

Figure 10.6 Q-type correlation matrix for Early Formative obsidian samples. Seven observations = obsidian sources; (*) = local exchange sphere.

participation in the "exchange sphere" for each source under consideration, were noted. Subsequently, the archeological site data were grouped according to geographic area, and matrices including all the obsidian source observations were calculated. The composition of exchange networks determined by the grouped data matrix (graphically shown in Figure 10.8) matches almost exactly the composition of exchange spheres previously determined through the individual source–archeological site matrices. Where obsidian from a given source amounts to more than 20% of the total obsidian supply for a given site, some

degree of regularity in the supply, possibly involving an exchange network, is suggested.

Early Formative Networks

1. *The Guadalupe Victoria Exchange Network.* The Guadalupe Victoria obsidian source, located adjacent to the village of the same name in the eastern part of the state of Puebla, is characterized by an extensive stream-laid deposit of weathered obsidian boulders. Guadalupe Victoria obsidian is quite brittle, and experimental attempts to produce prismatic blades from the boulders were not

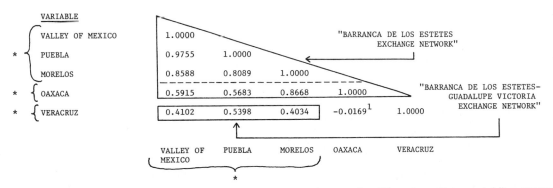

Figure 10.7 Q-type correlation matrix for Middle Formative obsidian samples. Nine observations = obsidian sources; (*) = local exchange sphere; (1) = note the change from .3445 in the Early Formative, indicating a significant realignment in obsidian exchange networks.

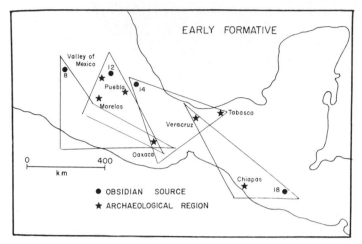

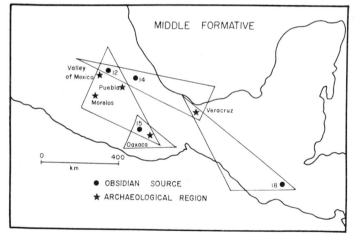

Figure 10.8 Early and Middle Formative obsidian exchange networks as determined through correlation matrix analysis. The large triangles enclose the sites and sources linked in exchange networks, and do not represent actual geographic boundaries. The sites in each archeological region which have contributed samples are listed in Table 10.1. The obsidian sources on which the exchange networks are based are 8, Zinapécuaro; 12, Barranca de los Estetes; 14, Guadalupe Victoria; 15, "unknown Oaxacan"; and 18, El Chayal.

successful. Core preparation was difficult, as the flakes consistently assumed anomalous and irregular forms due to the inclusions and generally poor quality of this obsidian. The fact that this source was a poor one for prismatic blades is important in understanding the shifts in exchange networks subsequent to 1000 B.C. (see p. 303).

Our obsidian sample from Las Bocas, Puebla, approximately 100 km to the west (and one of the closest known early sites to the source) contained no Guadalupe Victoria obsidian. Approximately 300 km to the south, at the major Early Formative site of San Lorenzo, Veracruz, Guadalupe Victoria was found to be the source of 62.2% of the total

obsidian sample. At Edward Sisson's four smaller sites of Campo Nuevo, Gamas, Nerio Hernández, and Rancho Guadalupe, located in the Chontalpa region of Tabasco some 450 km southeast of Guadalupe Victoria, 90.8% of the obsidians sampled came from that source. And finally, 36.5% of the obsidians examined for the sites of Huitzo, San José Mogote, and Tierras Largas in the Valley of Oaxaca were found to come from the approximately 200-km-distant Guadalupe Victoria source.

2. *The El Chayal Exchange Network*. Of the Early Formative San Lorenzo (Veracruz) obsidian sample, 21.7% was found to have come from the El Chayal source in Guatemala, some 580 km to

the southwest. This source, located in the central highlands near Guatemala City, is noted for its extensive deposits of high-quality grey obsidian. Early Formative sites are known from nearby highland areas, and Shook and Proskouriakoff (1956:96) report Middle Formative (Las Charcas Phase) obsidian workshops from Kaminaljuyú, approximately 35 km southwest of El Chayal. Unfortunately, however, no analyses of obsidian from Formative Guatemalan sites were available to me, and the networks of exchange through which San Lorenzo obtained El Chayal obsidian are not known.

Grove (in press) has suggested a Pacific coastal exchange route for the El Chayal obsidian. In fact, the exclusive presence of El Chayal obsidian at the New World Archaeological Foundation's Early Formative site of Altamira, Chiapas (and even inland as far as Angostura-el Carmen), suggests that this source may have been the only one serving the abundant Early Formative sites of the Guatemalan and Chiapas Coast.

Secondary distribution of El Chayal obsidian after it reached San Lorenzo (Veracruz) is also of interest because it evidently followed the linkages of the Guadalupe Victoria exchange network. El Chayal obsidian represents 5.6% of the sample at the small Tabasco sites, and 2.0% of the sample in Oaxaca. No El Chayal obsidian has yet been identified from any site located outside the linkages of the Guadalupe Victoria and El Chayal exchange networks.

3. *The Barranca de los Estetes Exchange Network*. The Barranca de los Estetes obsidian flows are located in the Teotihuacán Valley, near the village of Otumba in the State of Mexico. These deposits are extensive and contain a highly silicified grey obsidian of uniform quality. Experimental knapping with Barranca de los Estetes obsidian shows that its flaking properties are ideally suited for controlled pressure-flaking and prismatic blade production. The distribution of Barranca de los Estetes obsidian during the Early Formative is densest in the central highlands region of Mexico. Although no Early Formative

period sites have been reported from the Teotihuacán Valley proper, they are numerous elsewhere in the Valley of Mexico.

When the percentage of Barranca de los Estetes obsidian in the total obsidian sample is calculated (setting aside for the moment the percentage of flint), it suggests a "supply zone" extending up to 130 km from the source, and including the sites of Tlapacoya, Valley of Mexico (with 100% Barranca de los Estetes obsidian), Las Bocas, Puebla (with 100% Barranca de los Estetes obsidian), and San Pablo, Morelos (with 90.7% Barranca de los Estetes obsidian). Beyond the "supply zone," Early Formative obsidian samples from the Valley of Oaxaca, approximately 375 km to the south, contain 36.5% Barranca de los Estetes obsidian. Similar proportions of Barranca de los Estetes obsidian in the central highlands continue during the Middle Formative, and indeed are characteristic of all periods except, perhaps, the Aztec era (unpublished data). The reasons for this almost unique homogeneity in obsidian exploitation patterns during central highlands prehistory probably lie in the richness of the source and its suitability for blade making.

Considerable exchange between the central highlands and Oaxaca is indicated by the presence of 36.5% Barranca de los Estetes obsidian (with a +.67 average matrix correlation) found in the Early Formative Oaxacan samples. Barranca de los Estetes obsidian also was found at San Lorenzo, Veracruz, but comprised only 4.8% of the total obsidian industry. The −.17 average matrix correlation for San Lorenzo suggests that San Lorenzo may have received Barranca de los Estetes obsidian only indirectly, as a by-product of its established Guadalupe Victoria exchange linkages with Oaxaca.

Increasing movement of Barranca de los Estetes obsidian to distant regions in subsequent periods probably reflects an increasing demand for prismatic blades. In Morelos, in Oaxaca, and along the Gulf Coast, the earliest known prismatic blades date to about 1000–900 B.C. and are made of Barranca de los Estetes obsidian. The rare blade cores found at these sites are insufficient in size and number to have produced the quantities of blades that were recovered. This permits the hypothesis that much of the Barranca de los Estetes obsidian was exported from the Central Highlands in the form of finished blades. Certainly this was the case in later periods; MacNeish (personal communication) reports finding obsidian blades wrapped in bark cloth, presumably to prevent breakage during transportation, in one Tehuacán cave.

4. *The Zinapécuaro Exchange Network.* The Zinapécuaro, Michoacán, flows produce a cloudy grey obsidian of high quality. The area surrounding the source is poorly known archeologically, so that the network of sites through which Oaxaca obtained 20.2% of its total obsidian supply from this source (located at a distance of approximately 530 km) cannot be determined. A suggestion of the possible importance of the Zinapécuaro source area as a second center of prismatic blade manufacture and export is seen in the equal proportions of Barranca de los Estetes and Zinapécuaro prismatic blades in Oaxaca.

Middle Formative Networks

During the transition from the Early to Middle Formative, some of the existing obsidian exchange networks broke down, others were modified, and new ones were established as new villages rose to prominence. The "pan-Mesoamerican" aspect of the Early Formative long-distance exchange was reduced, and a period of increasing insularity and regionalization followed. Perhaps paradoxically, this regionalization took place during a period of great political evolution in the highland regions of Mexico.

For example, despite the premier position of La Venta as the dominant Gulf Coast center succeeding San Lorenzo (a position reflected in monumental construction and amassed luxury items), La Venta remains a regional site. The excavators have suggested that the bulk of the raw material found at La Venta was probably obtained within 100 miles of the site (Heizer 1961). A similar

trend toward regionalization has been noted for Middle Formative sites in the Valley of Mexico (Tolstoy and Paradis 1970), Morelos (Grove 1970), and the Valley of Oaxaca (Winter 1972). Four obsidian exchange spheres have been identified for this period.

1. *The Guadalupe Victoria–Barranca de los Estetes Exchange Network.* The most significant modification of exchange network patterns from the Early Formative to the Middle Formative period was the breakdown and realignment of the Early Formative Guadalupe Victoria exchange system. A dissolution of traditional exchange ties between the Gulf Coast and the Valley of Oaxaca followed the destruction of monuments at San Lorenzo and the rise of La Venta to political dominance. The San Lorenzo–Oaxaca Q-type matrix correlation drops from an Early Formative +.38 average to a −.01 average during the Middle Formative, clearly reflecting the weakening of ties between these spheres. Unfortunately, obsidian percentage data for La Venta are not available,* and we can only guess what its role in the Middle Formative obsidian exchange networks might have been.

The second important change in obsidian exchange during the Middle Formative involves an increase of obsidian moving between the Valley of Mexico and Gulf Coast. Barranca de los Estetes obsidian jumps from 4.8% to 26.3% of the total at San Lorenzo, and the average correlation coefficient between the two areas changes from −.17 to +.47. The increase of direct contact between these two areas may in part reflect the weakening of Oaxaca–San Lorenzo exchange relations; but a

---

*Only 12 excavated obsidian samples from La Venta have been analyzed (Jack and Heizer 1968). Of the samples, 3 were identified as Cerro de las Navajas obsidian, 2 as "unknown source B," 6 as "unknown source C," and 1 as possibly coming from El Chayal. Unknown sources B and C are grey obsidians, and may possibly represent the same Barranca de los Estetes and Guadalupe Victoria sources found in the Middle Formative samples from San Lorenzo.

more compelling factor is that, by the Middle Formative, well-made prismatic blades were in great demand throughout Mesoamerica, thus increasing the importance of the Barranca de los Estetes source. Our first Middle Formative obsidian exchange network thus links the Gulf Coast (San Lorenzo and probably La Venta) with the Guadalupe Victoria and Barranca de los Estetes sources. The Guadalupe Victoria–Barranca de los Estetes exchange network included a one-way movement of obsidian from Barranca de los Estetes to the Gulf Coast which, while it represented a change in patterns of obsidian utilization for the coast, does not seem to have involved a comparable change in the patterns of distribution within the Central Highlands.

2. *The El Chayal Exchange Network*. The percentage of El Chayal obsidian at San Lorenzo increased from 21.7% to 31.6% during the Middle Formative. At La Venta, 1 of the 12 excavated obsidians analyzed by Jack and Heizer (1968) was identified as coming from this source. Although a series of Chiapas Pacific coastal sites near Aquiles Serdán, Izapa, and Pijijiapan flourished during this period, this region is poorly understood because no obsidians from Middle Formative sites in the Guatemalan highlands or the Pacific Coast are included in our sample.

3. *The Original Barranca de los Estetes Exchange Network*. The original network of Mexican central highland sites associated with the Barranca de los Estetes during the Early Formative remained essentially intact during the Middle Formative period. The predominant importance of Barranca de los Estetes obsidian in the central highlands continued; 85.7% of the obsidian at Cerro Chacaltepec, Morelos, and 97.6% of the obsidian of Acatepec and Moyotzingo, Puebla, came from this source. In the Valley of Mexico, however, an interesting diversity of sources was seen at El Arbolillo and Zacatenco. Although these sites are the closest to the Barranca de los Estetes of all the sites analyzed, they contain only 45.5% Barranca de los Estetes obsidian. Small amounts of

obsidian from other sources comprise the balance: Zinapécuaro, 4.5%; Cerro de las Navajas, 9.1%; Tulancingo, 9.1%; "unknown Oaxacan," 13.7%; and Guatemalan (other than El Chayal), 18.2%.

Of the obsidian samples from Middle Formative levels in Oaxaca, 25% were of Barranca de los Estetes obsidian, indicating a continuity of exchange ties with the central highlands from the Early to the Middle Formative periods. The average correlation coefficient between the two areas changes only slightly, from +.58 to +.50. A diversification of source utilization, similar to that in the Valley of Mexico, also is seen in Oaxaca at this time. It is in this period that pooling of obsidian by some central agency, seen only at major villages during the Early Formative period, spreads to include even the small hamlets (see Winter and Pires-Ferreira, this chapter).

4. *The "Unknown Oaxacan" Exchange Network*. Although obsidian from eight geological sources is found in the Middle Formative of Oaxaca, five of the sources could have been obtained through contact with the already established Barranca de los Estetes exchange system; two suggest some continued contact with the Gulf Coast, and one source is a local one. (Definition of the "unknown Oaxacan" source is discussed on p. 293). The obsidian is consistently green in color, and the irregular shape of the artifacts suggests it may not be of very high quality. It represents 22.2% of the total Oaxacan obsidian, 13.7% of the Valley of Mexico obsidian, and 1.2% of the Puebla Middle Formative obsidian. The source had been known already during the Early Formative (1.1% in Oaxaca and 4.6% in Morelos), but was not extensively exploited at that time. The reasons for this may lie partly in the apparent poor quality of the source, and partly in Oaxaca's position as "middleman" in the exchange of obsidian from higher-quality sources. Increased use of this Oaxacan source is probably further evidence for the Middle Formative regionalization already mentioned.

Indeed, during the Middle Formative, for the

first time, each of the major settlement areas we have mentioned—the central Mexican highlands, the Gulf Coast, highland Guatemala, and Oaxaca— apparently concentrated most heavily on its own local obsidian source. Individually negotiated long-distance trade, a form of "foreign relations" characteristic of simpler societies like the previously described Maring and Siassi, was gradually replaced by more intensive regional exploitation, and by regional specialization in blade making. In the case of the latter, Barranca de los Estetes and El Chayal rose to prominence because of their suitability. In later times, Teotihuacán and Kaminal-juyú were to monopolize blade making in those areas.

Distribution of Obsidian among Households in Two Oaxacan Villages

MARCUS C. WINTER and
JANE W. PIRES-FERREIRA

Introduction

Previous sections in this chapter have discussed the "chain-like" networks of villages by which obsidian from various natural flows reached distant communities in Formative Mesoamerica. In this section, we deal with the way obsidian was distributed among households within communities after it had arrived. We will use obsidian from the Valley of Oaxaca because it is one of the few areas in which we have house-by-house data. The two villages involved, Tierras Largas and San José Mogote, are discussed in Chapters 2, 3, and 8 of this volume.

As suggested by Winter (1972) in an earlier report on Tierras Largas, in a reciprocal economy where individual households negotiate for their own obsidian, we would expect a good deal of variation between households, both in the sources used and the proportions of obsidian from various sources. Conversely, in an economy where the flow of obsidian is controlled by an elite or by important community leaders, who pool incoming obsidian for later distribution to their relatives, affines, or fellow villagers, we would expect less variation and more uniformity from one household to another. Let us now see how this model fits the data from Oaxaca.

Tierras Largas: A Small Village

Winter's sample of obsidian from Tierras Largas consists of 107 pieces from a total of 8 Early and Middle Formative "household clusters" (see Chapter 2) from which all chipped stone was saved. The 107 fragments analyzed were drawn at random by Pires-Ferreira from the total collection of 249 pieces from those clusters. In addition, Winter calculated the percentage by piece that obsidian contributed to the total chipped-stone assemblage at these household clusters. On the average, locally available cherts constituted 85% of the assemblage and obsidian only about 15% (see Table 10.3).

TABLE 10.3 Percentages, by Piece, of Obsidian among All Chipped Stone from Selected Proveniences at Tierras Largas

Time period	Pieces of obsidian	Percentage of obsidian
Rosario phase	41	20.00
Guadalupe phase	46	15.65
Late San José phase	13	16.05
Early San José phase	51	16.50
Late Tierras Largas phase	95	13.57
Early Tierras Largas phase	3	7.50
Total	*249*	*14.88*

There were three types of information provided by this sample. One was the percentage of obsidian versus chert in each cluster. The second was the relative contributions of the various sources represented at a given time period. The third was the variation between households at a given time period with respect to source usage. Winter analyzed the household clusters according to the following periods and subperiods:

Middle Formative:
Rosario phase (650– 500 B.C.)
Guadalupe phase (850– 650 B.C.)

Early Formative:
Late San José phase (1000– 850 B.C.)
Early San José phase (1150–1000 B.C.)
Late Tierras Largas phase (1300–1150 B.C.)
Early Tierras Largas phase (1450–1300 B.C.)

Although more households at more villages will have to be analyzed to confirm the patterns suggested by our results, the following statements can be tentatively advanced.

1. *All households within the village probably had equal access to obsidian.* A comparison of the percentage of obsidian to other chipped stone from two Late San José phase house floors, House 1 in Cluster LSJ-1 and House 2 in Cluster LSJ-2, shows a remarkably even distribution of 18.91% and 18.61% respectively. These figures are

somewhat higher than the figure of 16.05% for all Late San José phase deposits combined, and may indicate that obsidian was used more frequently in houses than elsewhere in the occupation area. A sample of house floors excavated at San José Mogote also yielded relatively higher frequencies of obsidian in comparison to non-house-floor deposits (unpublished data). In general, however—at least at Tierras Largas—obsidian is quite evenly distributed in excavated deposits of any given Formative period. There is no evidence from the site for wide differences in amounts of obsidian between households of a given period, such as might be expected if obsidian were a luxury item.

2. *There is an apparent increase in the amount of obsidian reaching the village during the course of the Formative.* Table 10.3 shows the percentage, by piece, of obsidian among all chipped stone at Tierras Largas. This may not be a particularly accurate expression of amounts of obsidian at the site, because (*1*) the Early Tierras Largas phase figure may be skewed by the small sample size, that is, only three pieces of obsidian; (*2*) possible functional variation between provenience units is not considered; and (*3*) differences in size and weight of obsidian and other chipped stone are not taken into account. Despite these problems, Table 10.3 suggests that the amount of obsidian at Tierras Largas increased through time, with three major periods of change. The amount of Late Tierras Largas phase obsidian is nearly double the amount of Early Tierras Largas phase obsidian. A slight increase occurred in the Early San José phase, and the amount then remained approximately the same until the Rosario phase, when another increase brought the percentage to almost three times what it had been during initial occupation of the site. It is worth noting that a good deal of the increase results from an increase in finished prismatic blades (see Table 10.3).

3. *In the Early Formative, more sources are represented, and they apparently were used differentially by various households.* Table 10.4, which presents information on the sources of the Tierras

TABLE 10.4   Sources of 107 Pieces of Obsidian Found in Various Household Clusters at Tierras Largas[a]

Time Period	Provenience	G.V.	B.E.	Zin.	U.S.	Alto.	El Ch.	Total	Number of sources
Rosario phase	Cluster R–1	9	7	3	7			26	4
Guadalupe phase	Cluster G-3		2	2	2			6	3
All Middle Formative		9	9	5	9			32	4
Late San José phase	Cluster LSJ-1	2	4	12		1		19	4
	Cluster LSJ-2	4	5	2				11	3
Early San José phase	Cluster ESJ-1	3	3	1	1	1		9	5
Late Tierras Largas phase	Cluster LTL-1	21	3			1		25	3
	Cluster LTL-2	1						1	1
	Cluster LTL-3	2	7				1	10	3
All Early Formative		33	22	15	1	3	1	75	6
Total		42	31	20	10	3	1	107	

[a]Sources are abbreviated as follows: G.V. = Guadalupe Victoria, Puebla; B.E. = Barranca de los Estetes, Valley of Mexico; Zin. = Zinapécuaro, Michoacán; U.S. = Unknown Oaxacan Source; Alto. = Altotonga, Veracruz; El Ch. = El Chayal, Guatemala.

Largas obsidian, illustrates this point. A wider range of sources is documented for the Early Formative Period (six sources) than for the Middle Formative Period (four sources). Most of the Early Formative obsidian derives from two sources to the north and northwest of the Valley of Oaxaca, but there is also one piece of obsidian from El Chayal, Guatemala, to the southeast of the Valley. All Middle Formative obsidian apparently derives from the north and west, since the "unknown Oaxacan" source is thought to be to the west of the valley (see discussion earlier in this chapter). Middle Formative sources are nearly equally represented, which is not true for the Early Formative.

If the number of obsidian sources represented is any indication, interregional contact seems to have been at a peak in the Early San José phase, when five sources are represented. At that time, material from Zinapécuaro and the unknown Oaxacan source first appears at Tierras Largas. Both these sources go on to be represented well by the Middle Formative period.

The Late Tierras Largas phase and Late San José phase data are particularly interesting, because a fairly large number of obsidian pieces were sampled for two different household clusters within each time period. In both cases, sources are *not* equally represented in the obsidian from the two household clusters, and there is a good deal of variation among houses. We assume that these distributions are not simply a result of chance in selection of obsidian pieces for neutron activation analysis. Specifically, in the Late Tierras Largas phase, obsidian from Household Cluster LTL-3 is mostly from Barranca de los Estetes. In the Late San José phase, obsidian from Household Cluster LSJ-1 is mostly from the Zinapécuaro source, while obsidian from Household Cluster LSJ-2 is mostly from Guadalupe Victoria and Barranca de los Estetes (see Table 10.4 for exact figures). These data suggest that contemporaneous Early Formative households at Tierras Largas may have had differential exchange relationships with different areas, and perhaps that obsidian was obtained directly by individual households.

4. *Although the sample is probably insufficient, it tentatively appears that fewer sources were used, but used more uniformly, in the Middle Formative.* As Table 10.4 suggests, only two Middle Formative household clusters were analyzed, which

makes our conclusions somewhat suspect. However, in both these clusters, the amounts of obsidian from various sources are more uniform than in previous periods. In Guadalupe phase Cluster G-3, identical amounts from Barranca de los Estetes, Zinapécuaro, and the unknown Oaxacan source were present. In Rosario phase Cluster R-1, similar amounts were present from Guadalupe Victoria, Barranca de los Estetes, and the unknown Oaxacan source. It would be interesting to know more about the amount of variation from one household to another during the Middle Formative, but this cannot be derived from a sample of two houses.

If future analysis of a larger sample of Middle Formative households confirms this lessened variation between households and more uniform use of a smaller number of sources, it may be that, during that period, there was some kind of "pooling" of obsidian coming into the valley before distribution to individual households. This pooling might have been done by the important Middle Formative families whose houses occupy the centers of villages like Tierras Largas (see Chapter 8). Analyses of variance between households and between sites may answer these questions in the future.

5. *Changes in the use of specific sources through time may be partly a function of increased trade in blades*. This is a conclusion reached already by Pires-Ferreira (this chapter), who states that, while the Barranca de los Estetes source is suitable for blade making, the Guadalupe Victoria source is not.

Obsidian associated with the Tierras Largas phase occupation at Tierras Largas consists only of flakes, flake fragments, and chunks. Blades appear initially in the Early San José phase but constitute less than 5% of the total obsidian. Significant quantities of blades first appear in the Late San José phase. A similar pattern is reported on the Gulf Coast at San Lorenzo (Cobean *et al.* 1971: Figures 1 and 2) and in Morelos (Grove 1971:40), where obsidian blades appear in quantity at about 1050 B.C.

San José Mogote: A Large Village

While the data from Tierras Largas remains ambiguous, owing to the small size of the Early Formative sample, it is strengthened by Pires-Ferreira's data from the larger village of San José Mogote. Obsidian from a sample of 11 houses or household clusters from that site seem to show evidence for the same kind of "pooling" suspected by Winter to have occurred at Tierras Largas, and the San José Mogote sample comes from a somewhat earlier time period. Thus, though neither sample is as large as we would like, both seem to show the same phenomenon.

As Table 10.5 reveals, sources used and the proportions of obsidian from each source are remarkably uniform for Household Clusters C1, C2, C3, and C4 in Area A, a residential ward occupied throughout the San José phase. Our sample from Area C, a contemporary residential ward some 400 m distant, is unfortunately too small to be conclusive. However, one could at least tentatively propose that incoming obsidian from various sources was being pooled before distribution to various households in Area A during the San José phase.

The four household clusters in Area A also show a number of stratigraphic continuities in shell working, mica working, and other craft activities over four "generations" of house construction in one residential ward (Flannery *et al.* 1970). They contain a wide variety of exotic items, as well as evidence of manufacture of small flat magnetite mirrors which were exchanged with communities as far away as Morelos, Nochixtlán, and the Gulf Coast (see Pires-Ferreira, this chapter). The evidence for pooling suggests that the part-time craft specialists whose handiwork is seen in Area A may have been affiliated with an important individual or family from whom they received their obsidian. We are struck by the fact that this earliest evidence of obsidian pooling is also contemporary with the earliest importation of prismatic blades from the Barranca de los Estetes and Zinapécuaro sources,

TABLE 10.5 Sources of 44 Pieces of Obsidian Found on Various House Floors (Area C) or in Various Household Clusters (Area A) at San José Mogote, Oaxaca[a]

Provenience	Zin.	B.E.	G.V.	Alto.	U.S.	El Ch.	O.G.	Total
San José phase								Total
Area A								
H.C. C1	2	2	2			1		7
H.C. C2	3	3						6
H.C. C3	3	3	1	1				8
H.C. C4	2	2						4
Area C								
House 1		1					1	2
House 2		1						1
House 5	1	1						2
House 6		1						1
House 8	1	3					1	5
House 9	2		2	1				5
House 10		2			1			3
Total	*14*	*19*	*5*	*2*	*1*	*1*	*2*	*44*

[a]Abbreviations are as follows: Zin. = Zinapécuaro, Michoacán; B.E. = Barranca de los Estetes, Valley of Mexico; G.V. = Guadalupe Victoria; Alto. = Altotonga, Veracruz; U.S. = Unknown Oaxacan source; El Ch.= El Chayal, Guatemala; O.G. = other Guatemalen source; H.C. = household cluster.

beginning about 1000 B.C. A causal relationship between the two events could be suggested; perhaps elite control of obsidian was not worthwhile until the more valuable prismatic blades were involved, although the evidence from San José Mogote suggests that flakes and chunks were being pooled as well.

The absence of pooling at Tierras Largas during the Early Formative (and its somewhat different source percentages) suggests that it did not obtain its obsidian from San José Mogote, in spite of its probable dependence on the latter for a variety of ceremonial-civic services. Thus, pooling at San José Mogote may have been restricted initially to a few important individuals or families who brought in obsidian for distribution to their affines or dependents.

By the Middle Formative period, however, some evidence of pooling of obsidian is found even in small hamlets. At Tierras Largas, the aforementioned analyses suggest that pooling may have been practiced in the Guadalupe and Rosario phases. This phenomenon is associated with the probable establishment of a resident elite household at the site (Winter 1972:121, and Chapter 8, this volume) and an increasing demand for high-quality prismatic blades. Thus, the pooling of imported obsidian probably should be seen as a gradual process, beginning in the Early Formative among important families at the largest sites and spreading as the demand for prismatic blades grew. By Middle Formative times, elite families probably controlled, pooled, and "redistributed" obsidian to their affines or dependents even at hamlets (Figure 10.9). This suggestion needs to be checked in other regions and, needless to say, this will require house-by-house data on obsidian source variation.

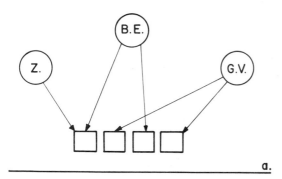
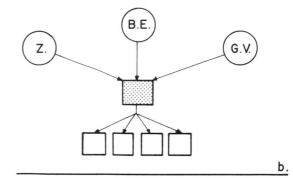

Figure 10.9 Tentative models to explain the observed differences in distribution of obsidian between households in Formative Oaxaca. (a) At Early Formative Tierras Largas, it appears that each household negotiated individually for its obsidian, resulting in considerable variation between houses in the percentage of obsidian from each source; (b) in Area A at San José Mogote, and at Middle Formative Tierras Largas, it appears that incoming obsidian from various sources was pooled by some central agency like an elite household (stippled square) before distribution to individual households, resulting in less variation. Sources shown are Zinapécuaro (Z.), Barranca de los Estetes (B.E.), and Guadalupe Victoria (G.V.).

Shell and Iron-Ore Mirror Exchange in Formative Mesoamerica, with Comments on Other Commodities

JANE W. PIRES-FERREIRA

At the beginning of this chapter, we listed six kinds of primitive exchange that we felt could be documented for Early and Middle Formative Mesoamerica. Previous papers have discussed both reciprocal exchanges and local "pooling" of obsidian, a commodity to which all households had access. In this section, I will deal with exchanges of Types 4 and 5 (see pp. 288–289), involving commodities for part-time craft specialization to which not all households had access.

Shell Exchange Networks in Formative Mesoamerica

The tropical waters of coastal Mesoamerica are rich in mollusk species, many of which were used for food by the earliest villagers in the area. A few of these species have shells suitable for ornament manufacture, and these were eagerly sought by the Formative peoples of the highlands, three of the most popular being pearl oyster (*Pinctada* sp.), spiny oyster (*Spondylus* sp.), and pearly fresh-water mussel (*Barynaias* and other genera).

Examples of long-distance trade in marine shell are frequent in the ethnographic literature. For example, we alluded earlier in the chapter to the exchange of gold lip, sea snail, and cowrie shells among villages in highland New Guinea (Rappaport 1968). The use of such shells in building up bride wealth or dowries, or simply for personal adornment, is widespread. In the case of Formative Mesoamerica, it is interesting that the final conversion of this shell into ornaments (presumably further increasing their value) was not always done by the coastal villagers who had the easiest access to the shell; for example, unmodified *Spondylus* shells were traded intact to the Valley of Oaxaca where local part-time craftsmen cut, ground, and drilled them into pendants.

Shells: Methodology and Raw Data

The identification of shell materials from Early and Middle Formative Mesoamerican sites was completed by Joseph R. Morrison and the author, using the former's extensive collections of Meso-american mollusks at the Smithsonian Institution. Shells were identified from San José Mogote, Tierras Largas, Huitzo, Abasolo, and Laguna Zope, Oaxaca; Gamas, Tabasco; Nexpa and San Pablo, Morelos; and El Arbolillo in the Valley of Mexico. To this we added previously published identifications from La Victoria (Coe 1961) and Salinas la Blanca (Coe and Flannery 1967) in Guatemala, and Zacatenco (Vaillant 1930) and El Arbolillo (Vaillant 1935) in the Valley of Mexico. As the analysis proceeded, it became clear that two major categories of shell material were to be found in Early and Middle Formative sites—Pacific Coast marine and estuary shells, and Atlantic drainage freshwater shells. These categories are tentatively regarded as reflecting two different networks. The results of this analysis are more fully reported in Pires-Ferreira (n.d.), and will be only briefly summarized here.

The Early Formative:
Tentative Shell Exchange Networks

Precise identification of shell exchange networks is not possible, owing to the limited amount of data available from Early Formative sites and to the nonspecific nature of information on the areas inhabited by various mollusk species. We are usually limited to generalizations such as "Pacific marine" or "Atlantic drainage." Despite these limitations, certain patterns of shell species distribution in the available data do admit the tentative definition of two regionally distinct exchange networks: one transporting a small variety of Atlantic freshwater species for simple ornament manufacture, and one transporting a greater variety of Pacific marine species, including some for the manufacture of more complex ornaments (Table 10.6). However, the presence of both kinds of shell on sites at the Isthmus of Tehuantepec suggests that both networks may have converged there on their way to the highlands.

1. *The Pacific Coast Shell Exchange Network.* Seventeen species of Pacific Coast shells (including marine and estuary forms) have been recovered from 3 Early Formative sites (Abasolo, San José Mogote, and Tierras Largas) in the highland Valley of Oaxaca, while 29 species come from 3 sites (Laguna Zope, La Victoria, and Salinas la Blanca) on the Pacific Coast. Of the species, 11 represent mollusks used for food at the coastal sites (and not occurring elsewhere); many of the others are found at both highland and coastal sites. It is the latter that provide the main basis for our discussion.

Of the shell species found at both Pacific Coast and highland Early Formative sites, *Pinctada mazatlanica* (the Pacific pearl oyster) is the most frequent. Commonly found in shallow offshore water from lower California to Peru (Keen 1958:58), these shells were one of the favored materials used by Early Formative shell workers in the Oaxaca highlands. The shells of an adult animal are sufficiently thick and durable to permit cutting,

TABLE 10.6 Pacific Coast Shells Imported by Early
Formative Villages in the Valley of
Oaxaca[a]

Mollusk	Village
Agaronia testacea	Tierras Largas
Anachis sp.	San José Mogote
Anomalocardia subrugosa	San José Mogote
	Tierras Largas
Arca cf. *labiata*	Tierras Largas
Busicon cf. *columella*	Tierras Largas
Cerithidia mazatlanica	San José Mogote
Cerithium stercus-muscarum	San José Mogote
	Tierras Largas
Chione sp.	San José Mogote
Neritina cassiculum	San José Mogote
Ostrea chilensis	Tierras Largas
Pinctada mazatlanica	Abasolo
	San José Mogote
	Tierras Largas
Spondylus calcifer	San José Mogote
Spondylus cf. *pictorem*	Tierras Largas
Strombus galeatus	Abasolo
	San José Mogote
	Tierras Largas
Strombus cf. *galeatus*	Tierras Largas
Pyrene sp.	San José Mogote
Thais biserialis	San José Mogote
Tivela cf. *gracilior*	Tierras Largas

[a]After Pires-Ferreira (n.d.).

grinding, and drilling into elaborate forms. The
shape of these shells provides a relatively large flat-
tish working surface, with waste limited to the
marginal valve area. These characteristics differ
from those exhibited by the fragile Atlantic freshwater shells, which could be drilled but not cut or
ground into decorative forms (unpublished experimental data). At the sites of San José Mogote and
Tierras Largas in the Etla region of the Valley of
Oaxaca, abundant evidence of the working of *Pinctada mazatlanica* shells was found; at Abasolo in
the Tlacolula region, a finished pendant of pearl
oyster was recovered with a burial, but no evidence of shell working was discovered.

The exchange links through which the unworked
shell reached the Oaxacan craftsmen are not

known. The possibility that they may have passed
through the Tehuantepec region is raised by surface shell material identified at the site of Laguna
Zope near Juchitán, Oaxaca. This large Early and
Middle Formative site was reported first by
Delgado (1961, 1965). A surface survey of the site
in 1968 located quantities of shell in association
with Early and Middle Formative period ceramics
(Flannery, personal communication). Included
among the shells were both worked and unworked
Pinctada mazatlanica fragments. The most frequent worked form was a shell with the heavy
valve section cut away. This indicates the existence
of local shell working and/or the preparation of
shell "blanks" for long-distance exchange. Examination of this hypothesis must await the analysis
of more recent excavation at Laguna Zope by
Robert and Judy Zeitlin (personal communication). So far, the Zeitlins report abundant shell but
no actual areas of ornament manufacture.

Two other Pacific marine shells found less frequently at both highland Mexican and Pacific
coastal sites are *Spondylus calcifer* and *Strombus
galeatus*. Both species are commonly found just
below the low-tide line on beaches from California
to Peru (Keen 1958:336). The spiny oyster *Spondylus calcifer* was found among the shells at
Laguna Zope and in association with shell-working
areas of Early Formative households at San José
Mogote. Unlike *Pinctada mazatlanica*, however, it
appears that these shells were imported whole and
trimmed to be used as large pendants, but not cut
or worked into smaller ornaments. Also imported
whole were conch shells, most commonly *Strombus galeatus* but also including *Malea ringens*. Fragments of presumed conch shell trumpets have been
found in shell-working areas on house floors at San
José Mogote and in association with public buildings at San José Mogote and Barrio del Rosario
Huitzo (see Chapter 11). Fragments of *Strombus*
also have been found at Laguna Zope, La Victoria,
and Salinas la Blanca on the Pacific Coast.

Surface materials from Laguna Zope contain
abundant shells, including four of the Pacific

marine genera found at both highland and lowland sites and the Atlantic freshwater genus *Barynaias*. Future excavations here and at other sites in the Tehuantepec region may show this area to be an important crossroads for the Pacific and Atlantic shell exchange networks. Once in the highlands, access to the imported raw shell appears to have been limited—especially in the case of *Pinctada mazatlanica*—to shell-working villages or residential wards in villages, which in turn passed on their finished shell ornaments to other villages. Pacific shell may have moved through the same "sphere of conveyance" that brought El Chayal obsidian to the Oaxaca highlands, the Isthmus, and the Gulf Coast, but full evaluation of this hypothesis must await future excavations.

2. *The Atlantic Drainage Freshwater Shell Exchange Network.* While Atlantic drainage *freshwater* shells were widely exchanged as ornaments during the Early Formative period, Atlantic *marine* and *estuary* shells were rarely traded or modified, although the marine mollusks were exploited for food. The most widely distributed of the Atlantic mollusks found at sites outside their native drainage area are the pearly freshwater mussels (*Barynaias* sp. and *Barynaias* cf. *pigerrimus*). Native to the large river systems from Tampico to the Laguna de Términos, these mussels have been identified at the sites of San José Mogote and Tierras Largas in the Valley of Oaxaca; at Laguna Zope on the Pacific Coast of the Isthmus of Tehuantepec; at El Arbolillo in the Valley of Mexico; and at San Pablo in Morelos. Apparently because of their fragility, these shells were not cut up into smaller ornaments; rather, when utilized, they were perforated for suspension as pendants. Three other taxa also found at the sites in the Valley of Oaxaca include *Actionaias* sp., *Anadara incongrua*, and *Anadonta globosa*. The native distribution of these mollusks is the same as for *Barynaias*.

The exchange of Atlantic drainage freshwater mussel shells is poorly understood, owing to the widespread natural range of these five species and the total absence of shell data from Early Formative Gulf Coast sites. It is possible that these shells were moved into the highlands along the same "sphere of conveyance" that brought Guadalupe Victoria obsidian to the Gulf. Moreover, there are differences in the distribution of Atlantic freshwater and Pacific marine shell among households at San José Mogote and Tierras Largas. These are commented on later, but can probably not be fully explained without further excavation.

The Middle Formative: Tentative Shell Exchange Networks

Among the shells identified for 7 Middle Formative sites, more than 30 species were recorded. In Oaxaca, only 6 Pacific species were found, as compared with 17 at Early Formative sites; similarly, the freshwater Atlantic drainage total drops from 6 species to 1 for the Middle Formative.

1. *The Pacific Coast Shell Exchange Network.* Pacific Coast shells from seven Middle Formative sites were considered. Five of the sites are located in the Mexican highlands—Huitzo and Tierras Largas in the Valley of Oaxaca; El Arbolillo and Zacatenco in the Valley of Mexico; and Nexpa in Morelos (Table 10.7). Two are on the Pacific Coast of Guatemala, namely, La Victoria and Salinas la Blanca. Nine marine and nine estuary species were found *only* at the coastal sites, and probably represent food refuse. The traded shells include five marine and five estuary species found so far at highland sites. This is a reduction in overall numbers of traded species compared to the Early Formative.

Only 3 of the 13 Pacific Coast shell species found at highland Early Formative sites in Oaxaca continued to appear in Middle Formative layers. *Strombus galeatus*, found at La Victoria, Salinas la Blanca, and Tierras Largas, is the only marine species so far found at both coastal and highland sites during both Early and Middle Formative periods. Presumably the importance of conch shell

TABLE 10.7 Pacific Coast Shells Imported by Various Middle Formative Villages in Highland Mexico[a]

Mollusk	Village
Amphichaena kindermanni	Huitzo, Oaxaca
Malea cf. *ringens*	Huitzo, Oaxaca
Melogena cf. *patula*	El Arbolillo West, Valley of Mexico
Neritina (Theodoxus) luteofasciata	Zacatenco, Valley of Mexico
Neritina usnea	El Arbolillo East, Valley of Mexico
Pinctada mazatlanica	Zacatenco, Valley of Mexico
	Nexpa, Morelos
	Huitzo, Oaxaca
	Tierras Largas, Oaxaca
Spondylus sp.	Huitzo, Oaxaca
Strombus galeatus	Tierras Largas, Oaxaca
Turitella jewettii	Huitzo, Oaxaca

[a]After Pires-Ferreira (n.d.).

trumpets accounts for this. Other Pacific marine species exchanged during both periods include *Pinctada mazatlanica* (found at Middle Formative Zacatenco, Nexpa, and Tierras Largas) and *Spondylus* sp. (found at Huitzo). The sample size for this period is small, and no evidence concerning the relation between shell import and shell ornament production is available.

2. *The Atlantic Drainage Freshwater Shell Exchange Network*. A decrease, similar to that seen in the number of traded Pacific Coast species, also is recorded for Atlantic drainage shells during the Middle Formative period. Only four shells of *Barynaias* sp. (from Huitzo and Tierras Largas) have been identified in our sample of seven Middle Formative sites. This reduction in the exchange of freshwater clam shell is evidently not made up by the substitution of other Atlantic species, for only one fragment of Atlantic marine shell, *Cassis* sp., or cameo shell, has been identified (at El Arbolillo). The cause for the drop-off in the exchange of Atlantic drainage shell is probably also to be found in the trend toward regionalization during the Mid-

dle Formative, noted in our earlier discussion of obsidian.

Distribution of Shell among Formative Households: An Example from Oaxaca

As mentioned in Chapter 2 of this volume, Tierras Largas and San José Mogote are unique among Early Formative villages so far excavated in Oaxaca: Every house of that period at both sites contains some shell, and usually evidence of shell working. Similar evidence has not appeared at Huitzo, Abasolo, Fábrica San José, or Tomaltepec. It would thus appear that a very high proportion of the shell ornaments made during the Early Formative were turned out by part-time craftsmen in this one localized area of the Valley of Oaxaca.

Evidence from three house floors of the Tierras Largas phase at the site of Tierras Largas indicates that the importation of Pacific marine shell goes back to before 1300 B.C. (Winter 1972:181). The shell appears to be evenly distributed among all the houses, and no Atlantic drainage shells are found.

The importance of Pacific Coast shell, both marine and estuary, grew during the San José Phase (1150 to 850 B.C.). Data from 13 house floors or household clusters at San José Mogote suggest that Pacific Coast shell (especially pearl oyster) was the primary object of local shell ornament production (Table 10.8). Twenty-three Pacific Coast shell ornaments and finished pieces are present, compared to 2 Atlantic drainage freshwater shell ornaments; 23 Pacific Coast shell unfinished pieces or waste products are present, compared to 16 Atlantic drainage shells in this same category. However, the numbers of unmodified shells are approximately equal, with 24 from the Pacific Coast and 26 from the Atlantic drainage.

There are variations in shell content of the 13 household areas at San José Mogote which are intriguing, but the samples are too small to be con-

TABLE 10.8 Sources and Utilization of Mollusk Shells on House Floors and in Household Clusters at Early Formative San José Mogote, Oaxaca[a]

	Ornaments and finished pieces, including fragments			Unfinished pieces and waste products			Unworked shell fragments			Unworked whole shells			Shell tools			Subtotal			Total
	P	A	U	P	A	U	P	A	U	P	A	U	P	A	U	P	A	U	Total
Area A																			
H.C. C1	2		1	1												3		1	4
H.C. C2	1				2			1	4							1	3	4	8
H.C. C3	3	1	1	3	9		4	1	2							10	11	3	24
H.C. C4			2	2	3		1	3								3	6	2	11
Area C																			
House 1	2						1		1							3		1	4
House 2	6			5	1			6	2	2						13	7	2	22
House 4	3	1		10			7	2		4			1			25	3		28
House 5				1			2									3			3
House 6							2									2			2
House 7	1									1						2			2
House 8	2		1	1			5	2					1		1	9	2	2	13
House 9	2		1		1	1	2	11	2							4	12	4	20
House 10	1															1			1
Total	23	2	6	23	16	1	24	26	11	7			2		1	79	44	19	142

[a]H.C. = household cluster; P = Pacific marine and estuary; A = Atlantic drainage; U = Unidentified.

clusive, usually because whole houses were rarely recovered. Tentatively, it appears that some houses may have worked primarily Pacific shell while others worked primarily Atlantic shell—perhaps indicating different networks of trade partners. Extensive concentrations of Atlantic Coast waste products or unworked shell fragments occurred in House 9 (Area C) and Household Cluster C3 (Area A); House 4 (Area C) had a similar concentration of Pacific Coast waste products.

One can also cite households that had finished ornaments from one coast but primarily waste products from the other coast. House 9 had 2 elaborate finished Pacific shell products, including a pendant with an Olmec paw-wing motif, but there was no evidence for Pacific Coast shell working; the householders were mainly involved in working Atlantic freshwater mussel. Similarly, Household Cluster C3 had 3 finished Pacific Coast products including a fragment of a mother-of-pearl mirror holder for a magnetite mirror, while its waste products were mainly from *Barynaias*. On the other hand, the residents of House 4 clearly had been working Pacific shell (10 unfinished pieces or waste products), but there was little to indicate the working of Atlantic drainage mussel, although 4 unworked whole shells were present. House 2 had 6 finished products and 5 unfinished fragments or waste products of Pacific Coast shell, accompanied by scantier evidence for Atlantic drainage mussel working. In Household Cluster C4, the working of shells from both regions was well-documented. Less variation from house to house in shell ornament manufacture was found at the smaller site of Tierras Largas, where Winter (1972: 181) notes an even distribution of shell and shell-working evidence among the three San José phase household clusters he excavated.

Iron-Ore Mirror Exchange in Formative Mesoamerica

One of the most interesting discoveries made at La Venta, Tabasco, was a series of large, parabolically concave mirrors made of three types of iron ore: magnetite, ilmenite, and hematite (Drucker, Heizer, and Squier 1959). Garniss Curtis (1959), who determined the gross petrological characteristics of the mirrors, placed their probable point of origin somewhere in the "metamorphic and granitic province" of the state of Oaxaca (Curtis 1959: Figure 80).

In 1966, Flannery (1968) excavated a residential ward at San José Mogote in Oaxaca which was producing small, flat iron-ore mirrors. Michael Coe's discovery of identical mirrors at San Lorenzo, Veracruz (Coe 1968), led Flannery to suggest an exchange relationship between the two areas, based in part on San Lorenzo's importation of Oaxaca mirrors (Flannery 1968:106). That suggestion, however, remained to be confirmed by physicochemical studies on the sources of iron. Moreover, it dealt only with the small flat mirrors, all of which date to the Early Formative (San José phase in Oaxaca, and San Lorenzo and Nacaste phases in Veracruz). The large concave mirrors, which have been found only on the Gulf Coast, date mainly to the Middle Formative (construction phases II-IV at La Venta), although there is one small concave mirror from pyramid fill at Early Formative San Lorenzo.

My study, briefly described next (and more fully documented in Pires-Ferreira n.d.), confirms the fact that small flat mirrors from Valley of Oaxaca sources were traded over great distances during the Early Formative, although access to the mirrors may have been restricted to an elite. The large concave mirrors, however, seem to be largely a Gulf Coast development, which reached its peak in the Middle Formative. Indeed, the small flat specimens and the large parabolic specimens may have had very different functions, a point perhaps obscured by lumping tham all together under the name "mirror."

Mössbauer Spectrum Analysis

Recent developments in the instrumentation for Mössbauer spectroscopy, and the large number of carefully executed fundamental studies of magnetites (Evans 1968), ilmenites (Greenwood and Gibb 1971; Shirane *et al*. 1962), and hematites (Artman, Muir, and Wiedersich 1970) using this technique made conditions rather propitious for the application of Mössbauer spectroscopy to a study of the iron-ore sources and mirrors from archeological sites in Mesoamerica. Mössbauer spectral analysis of 25 geological sources and 38 archeological iron-ore samples was completed in collaboration with B. J. Evans of the Department of Geology and Mineralogy, University of Michigan. A report by Evans on the techniques and procedures used in analysis of these samples is included in Appendix II of Pires-Ferreira (n.d.).

A systematic survey of all potential iron-bearing geologic zones in the Valley of Oaxaca was completed during a 5-month period in 1967; surveys in the Isthmus of Tehuantepec, the Central Depression of Chiapas, and the Valley of Morelos also were completed in 1968 and 1970. In the Valley of Oaxaca, 36 major surface exposures of iron ore were discovered, but only sources that were suitable for mirror production were analyzed (Figure 10.10).

In order to simplify the referencing of spectra, the iron ores studied by Mössbauer analysis were divided into the following five general groups: I, samples composed mainly of magnetite; II, samples of relatively pure hematite; III, samples of ilmenite; IV, samples containing a mixture of magnetite and ilmenite; and V, samples composed of a mixture of magnetite and hematite. In the case of the archeological samples, these groups were later subdivided (e.g., I-A, I-B) according to the geologic source from which they most probably had come.

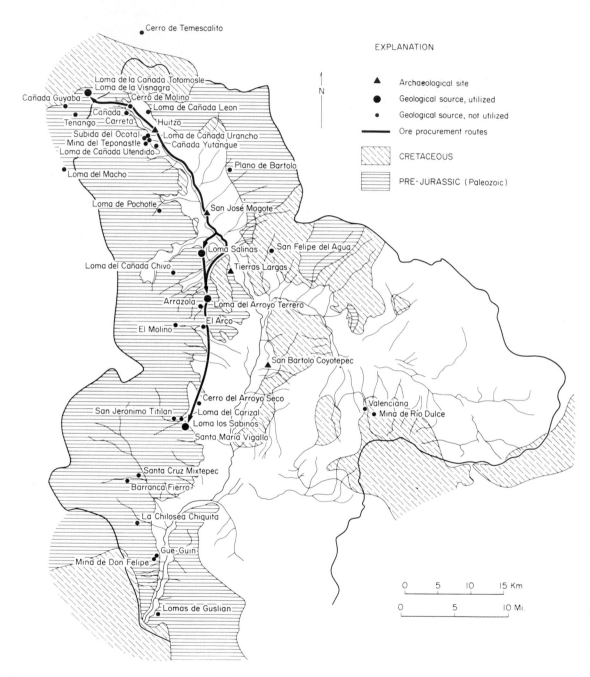

Figure 10.10 Geological sources of iron ore in the Valley of Oaxaca and probable Early Formative procurement routes.

Our sampling studies show that there is virtually no variation in the major phase composition of ore throughout a geological source. Once this was established, the probability of accurately identifying the geologic origin of mirror ores was greatly increased.

Archeological samples from the Early Formative sites of San José Mogote (Figure 10.11), San Bartolo Coyotepec, and Tierras Largas in the Valley of Oaxaca; Etlatongo in the Valley of Nochixtlán; San Pablo, Morelos; and San Lorenzo, Veracruz, were analyzed. Middle Formative samples come only from La Venta, Tabasco; Las Choapas, Veracruz; and Amatal, Chiapas. Several spectral details were used in matching the archeological and geological source samples. For the magnetite samples, the relative intensity and separation of the doublet structure of the peaks in the extreme negative velocity region were used to distinguish between the various sources that make up this group. For mirrors containing hematite and ilmenite, the spectra are so distinctive that the choices are obvious. For the mixed magnetite and ilmenite group, the presence of magnetite is evidenced by the doublet structure in the region of the high channel numbers. In some cases, a significant amount of titanium has dissolved in the magnetite, and the doublet structure has been reduced to a strong outer peak and a weak inner peak. The relative intensity of these two peaks, however, serves to distinguish sources (see Figure 10.12).

All groups defined by my study are discussed in detail in Pires-Ferreira (n.d.). In this chapter I will briefly summarize the most important groups, as follows.

Group I-A is a quite pure magnetite which presents inclusion-free faces ideally suited for mirror making. It includes 10 Early Formative ore lumps or mirror fragments from San José Mogote, Oaxaca, and 1 Early Formative ore lump traded to San Pablo, Morelos. The spectrum matches ore from the twin sources of Loma de Cañada Totomosle–Loma de la Visnagra, near Santiago Ten-

Figure 10.11 Magnetite mirrors and mirror fragments from San José Mogote, Oaxaca. Scale in cm.

ango, 27 km north of San José Mogote (Figure 10.13).

Group I-B is a magnetite with slight ilmenite contamination, very compact and suitable for mirror making. Its spectrum matches the source at Loma los Sabinos, near Zimatlán, 33 km south of San José Mogote. The group include five Early Formative lumps or mirror fragments from San José Mogote, one sample from Coyotepec in the Valley of Oaxaca, and one mirror traded to Etlatongo in the Valley of Nochixtlán, Oaxaca (Figure 10.13).

Group I-C consists of a single large, concave, scalloped-edge magnetite mirror from Middle Formative La Venta, whose spectrum does not match any source we have collected.

Group II-A is a dense, compact hematite ideally suited for mirror making, and tentatively identi-

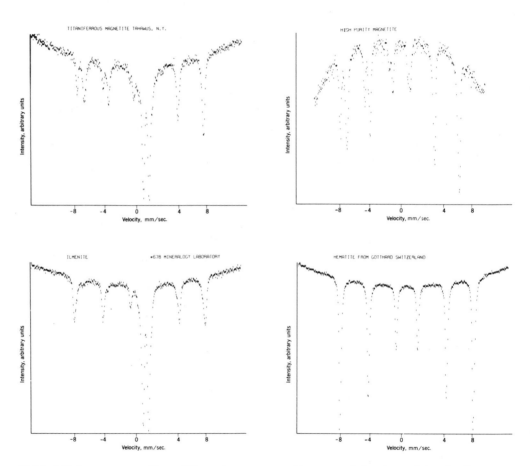

Figure 10.12 Mössbauer spectra of four different iron ore types. From upper left to lower right: titaniferrous magnetite; high purity magnetite; ilmenite; and hematite. [Courtesy, B.J. Evans.]

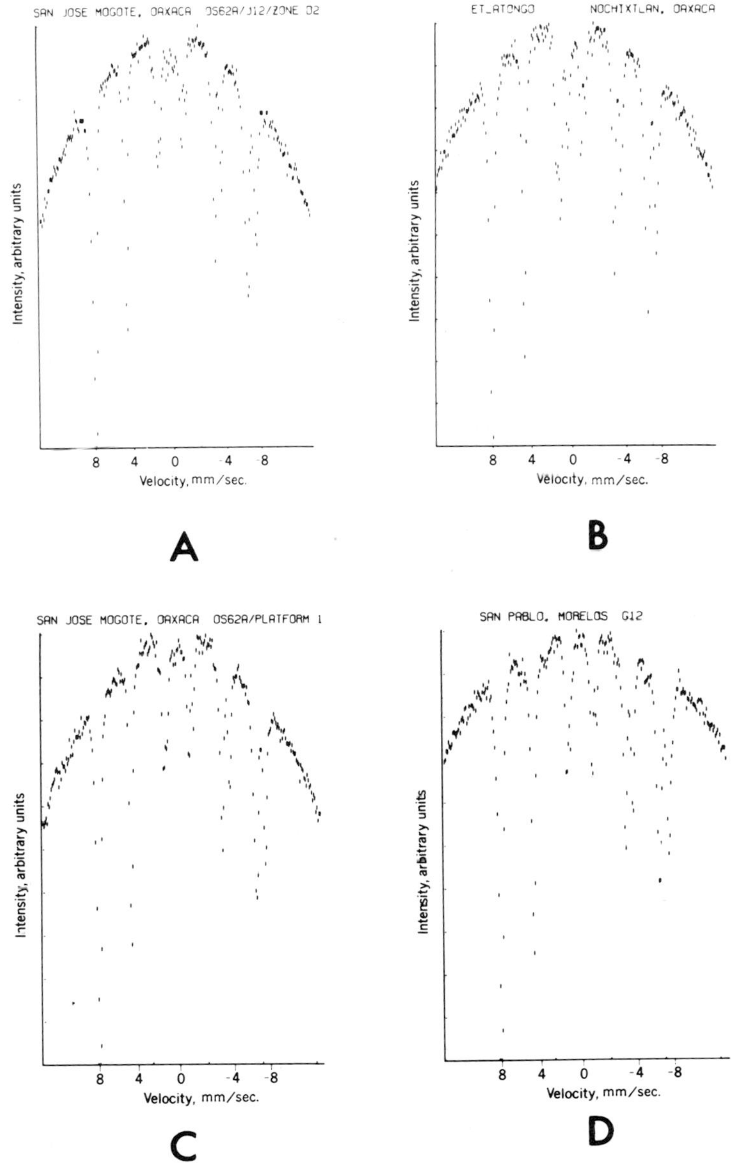

Figure 10.13 Mössbauer spectra of magnetite samples from Early Formative villages. (A and B) Group I-B (source: Loma los Sabinos, Valley of Oaxaca); (C and D) Group I-A (source: Loma de Cañada Totomosle–Loma de la Visnagra, Valley of Oaxaca). A and C are from San José Mogote; B is a small mirror traded to Etlatongo, Nochixtlán Valley; D is an ore lump traded to San Pablo, Morelos.

fied as coming from the source at Cerro Prieto, near Niltepec, Oaxaca, in the Isthmus of Tehuantepec. The group includes two thick flat mirrors from Nacaste phase levels at San Lorenzo, Veracruz, and two large concave mirrors from Middle Formative La Venta (Figure 10.14).

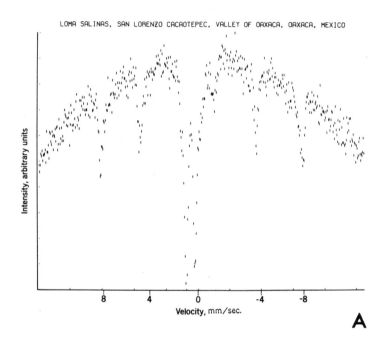

A

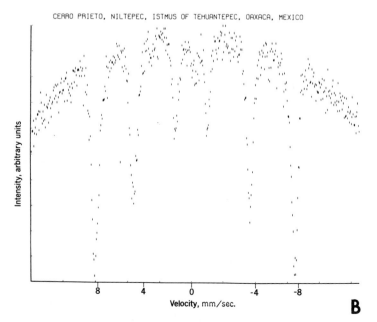

B

Figure 10.14 Mössbauer spectra of iron ore from source areas. (A) Ilmeno-magnetite from Loma Salinas, Valley of Oaxaca. Mirrors of this ore (Group IV-B) were traded as far as San Lorenzo, Veracruz. (B) Hematite from Cerro Prieto, near Tehuantepec. This is the probable source for the Group II-A mirrors used at San Lorenzo and La Venta.

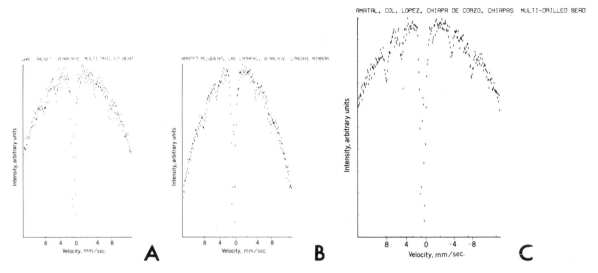

Figure 10.15 Mössbauer spectra of ilmenite artifacts from Group III-A. (A) Multidrilled bead from San Lorenzo, Veracruz; (B) concave mirror from Arroyo Pesquero, Veracruz; (C) multidrilled bead from Amatal, Chiapas. The source for Group III-A ilmenite has not yet been located.

Group III-A is an ilmenite whose geological source is as yet undiscovered, although it was widely used. Two small flat mirrors and one small concave mirror from San Lorenzo were made of this ilmenite. Two large mirrors from La Venta and a third from Arroyo Pesquero near Las Choapas, Veracruz, probably all date to the Middle Formative. Finally, this source was used for two unusual, multidrilled ilmenite beads, one from an Early Formative cache associated with a colossal head (Monument 17) at San Lorenzo, and another from an undated cache at Amatal near Chiapa de Corzo, Chiapas (Figure 10.15).

Group IV-A is a mixed magnetite–ilmenite of low quality, probably from a source at Loma del Arroyo Terrero near Arrazola, just off the western slope of Monte Albán in the Valley of Oaxaca. Lumps of this ore were carried to San José Mogote, but apparently not converted into mirrors; a single lump also occurred at Tierras Largas, only 8 km from the source.

Group IV-B is a mixed magnetite–ilmenite whose spectrum matches the source exposed on the surface and in arroyo profiles at Loma Salinas near San Lorenzo Cacaotepec, only 7 km southwest of San José Mogote, Oaxaca. The group includes a partly worked ore lump from San José Mogote and two small flat mirrors evidently traded to San Lorenzo, Veracruz, during the Nacaste phase (Figure 10.14).

The Early Formative: Magnetite Mirrors as an Item for Elite Exchange

By far the majority of the Early Formative archeological samples were either magnetites or mixed magnetite–ilmenites from sources in the Valley of Oaxaca. The bulk of the samples examined came from San José Mogote, the largest site in the Valley of Oaxaca during this period. A surface survey of the site revealed a striking, 1-ha concentration of iron ores—more than 500 pieces which had evidently been collected from various iron sources in the valley. Excavations within this area (Area A) exposed a series of four superimposed household clusters (numbered C1 through C4) and associated midden deposits. Whole and broken magnetite mirrors, unfinished mirrors, and worked and unworked lumps of iron ore were found together in these household clusters. Comparative examination of the finished and unfinished mirrors reveals a similarity in size, shape, and grinding technique. The typical products are thumbnail-size, flat-surface mirrors of various geometric forms, highly polished on one or both sides. Traces of multidirectional grinding are discernible on the unfinished and roughly finished sides of the mirrors. Closer examination of the mirror surfaces reveals some traces of ochre in surface irregularities, indicating that this substance may have been used to obtain the high polish of the finished products. It is not known for what the mirrors served, but evidence from figurines at Tlatilco and La Venta suggests they were worn on the chest, possibly by individuals of some special status. Some of the Oaxaca mirrors may have been worn as inlays in ornaments of pearl oyster shell, judging by some broken specimens found at Area A of San José Mogote (Figure 2.14h).

Considering the restricted distribution of the San José Mogote mirrors both within that site and within the valley, and their possible association with individuals of some social rank, it was proposed by Flannery (1968) that the mirrors were part of an elite exchange that linked Oaxaca with San Lorenzo and the Gulf Coast, as well as to other regions of Mexico. This proposal is supported by two mirrors of Oaxaca ore which reached San Lorenzo during the Nacaste phase, although the mechanisms of the exchange are unknown. We also have been able to demonstrate that mirrors or lumps of Oaxaca ores were traded toward the northwest, possibly as a form of exchange between elites. One lump of high-quality Oaxaca ore was found at the site of San Pablo, Morelos, 320 km northwest of San José Mogote. The possible links between these two sites in the exchange of Barranca de los Estetes obsidian blades are discussed earlier in this chapter. A finished mirror of Oaxaca ore with a presumed

Early Formative date came from what appears to be an eroded public building at the site of Etlatongo in the Valley of Nochixtlán, some 50 km north of San José Mogote. Thus, although the limits of Oaxacan iron ore distribution cannot be defined on the basis of present evidence, they apparently exceeded 300 km to the northwest and 200 km to the northeast.

All of the small iron-ore mirrors recovered *in situ* in Oaxaca date to the second half of the San José phase, or roughly 1000–850 B.C. Many ore lumps, however, occurred in early San José phase context (1150–1000 B.C.), suggesting that earlier mirrors will eventually be found. All the flat mirrors recovered at San Lorenzo, including the two from a source in the Valley of Oaxaca, date to the Nacaste phase (900–750 B.C.). A single concave mirror at San Lorenzo appeared in pyramid fill with mixed sherds of the San Lorenzo A and B phases, and thus cannot with certainty be dated as earlier than San Lorenzo B (1000–900 B.C.). It therefore seems reasonable to assume that the major period for exchanges of small flat mirrors was roughly 1000–800 B.C.

The Middle Formative: Localized Mirror Production on the Gulf Coast

Sometime prior to 800 B.C., mirror production seems to have come to an end in the Valley of Oaxaca. Extensive excavation of Middle Formative (Guadalupe and Rosario phase) levels at the sites of Huitzo, San José Mogote, Fábrica San José, and Tierras Largas have failed to recover even one lump of ore. This same time period saw the defacement of monuments at San Lorenzo and the concomitant rise of La Venta. The small, flat magnetite mirrors disappeared from the archeological inventory of the Gulf Coast, and were replaced by large concave mirrors, which are most frequently made of ilmenite and hematite. These large mirrors often occurred in caches or offerings, in evident ceremonial context.

Evidence of Middle Formative iron-ore mirror production and exchange is incomplete, but the restricted Gulf Coast distribution of large concave mirrors suggests that they are a local product. Both the change in ore and the form of the mirrors reflect a localized development, distinct from the Early Formative iron ore exchange which extended over hundreds of kilometers and spanned many different culture areas.

Summary and Conclusions

It was argued at the start of this chapter that the varieties of Formative exchange were such that one model will not explain them all: Each commodity must be studied in its own right. Obsidian, a commodity to which all villagers had access, was originally moved by long-distance reciprocal trade in which quantity was partly a function of distance from source. With the advent of trade in prismatic blades, distribution of obsidian apparently took the form of "pooling" by some central agency before dispersal. Pacific Coast marine shell traveled to part-time craftsmen at certain villages, where it was converted into ornaments for local distribution. Magnetite was converted into small mirrors by one localized residential ward at a regional ceremonial–civic center and was traded to a limited number of distant regional centers, probably as a form of elite exchange. Other commodities on the move included Xochiltepec White pottery (probably of Gulf Coast manufacture) and Delfina Fine Gray pottery (of Oaxacan manufacture).

During the Early Formative, utilitarian goods and ceremonial items may both have circulated in the same "sphere of conveyance" (see discussion on p. 290). Consider, for example, the network of villages through which obsidian from Guadalupe Victoria, Puebla, was moved. Other products that may have circulated in the Guadalupe Victoria network were Xochiltepec White ceramics, turtle shell drums, pearly freshwater mussels, stingray spines, shark teeth, and conch shell trumpets, many of which probably reached Oaxaca from the Gulf Coast. Oaxaca in turn may have passed some of these on to the central highlands through the Barranca de los Estetes network. In this latter network, Delfina Fine Gray ceramics probably also circulated, since they reached Tlapacoya in the Valley of Mexico (Weaver 1967:29–30; Flannery *et al.* 1970:55). This Oaxacan pottery also reached Aquiles Serdán on the Chiapas Coast (unpublished data), perhaps by indirect linkage with the El Chayal exchange network. Other Pacific Coast items that may have accompanied the El Chayal obsidian to Oaxaca include pearl oyster, *Spondylus,* and other shell (see Figure 10.16).

During the Middle Formative, there were breakdowns and realignments of these networks. The number of shell species traded declined, and obsidian sources changed in value as prismatic blades became more important and local pooling or redistribution more common. Production of small, flat magnetite mirrors ceased, while the Gulf Coast went on to develop local production of large concave mirrors of ilmenite or hematite. The regionalization that set in was accompanied by great political evolution, reflected in elite residences and public buildings as well as increasing pooling or redistribution of goods. Following Rappaport's model, discussed earlier in the chapter, we might propose that the chiefdoms or incipient states of the Middle Formative had greater power to "demand production and enforce deliveries," signaling the end of an era in which circulation of ritual items was needed to sustain and regulate long-distance trade. Exchange continued, but with its character altered in response to the new sociopolitical systems of the later Formative.

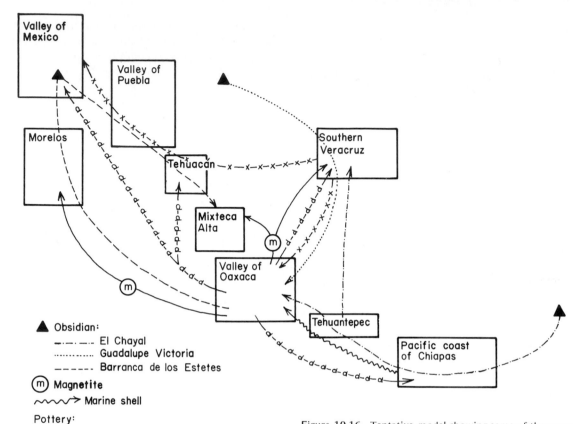

Figure 10.16 Tentative model showing some of the commodities that linked regions of Early Formative Mesoamerica in exchange networks.

References

Artman, J. O., A. H. Muir, Jr., and H. Wiedersich
  1970 Determination of the nuclear quadrupole moment of Fe^{57m} from $\alpha-Fe_2O_3$ data. *Physical Review* 173:337–343.
Brown, A. B.
  1973 Bone strontium content as a dietary indicator in human skeletal populations. Unpublished Ph.D. dissertation, Dept. of Anthropology, University of Michigan, Ann Arbor.
Cobean, R. H., M. D. Coe, E. A. Perry, Jr., K. K. Turekian, and D. P. Kharkar
  1971 Obsidian trade at San Lorenzo Tenochtitlán. *Science* 174:666–671.
Coe, M. D.
  1961 La Victoria: An early site on the Pacific coast of Guatemala. *Papers of the Peabody Museum of Archaeology and Ethnology* Vol. LIII. Harvard University, Cambridge, Mass.
  1966 *The Maya*. New York: Praeger.
  1968 San Lorenzo and the Olmec civilization. In *Dumbarton Oaks Conference on the Olmec*, edited by E. P. Benson. Washington, D.C.: Dumbarton Oaks. Pp. 41–78.
Coe, M. D., and K. V. Flannery
  1967 Early cultures and human ecology in south coastal Guatemala. *Smithsonian Contributions to Anthropology* No. 3. Smithsonian Institution, Washington, D.C.
Delgado, A.
  1961 La secuencia arqueológica en el Istmo de Tehuantepec. In *Los Mayas del sur y sus relaciones con los Nahuas meridionales, VIII Mesa Redonda*. Sociedad Mexicana de Antropología, Mexico, D.F. Pp. 93–103.

1965   Archaeological research at Santa Rosa, Chiapas, and in the region of Tehuantepec. *Papers of the New World Archaeological Foundation* No. 12 (Pub. no. 13).

Curtis, G. H.
   1959   The petrology of artifacts and architectural stone at La Venta. Appendix 4 in Excavations at La Venta, Tabasco, 1955 by P. Drucker, R. F. Heizer, and F. J. Squier. *Bulletin* No. 170. Bureau of American Ethnology, Smithsonian Institution, Washington, D.C. Pp. 284–289.

Drucker, P., R. F. Heizer, and R. J. Squier
   1959   Excavations at La Venta, Tabasco, 1955. *Bulletin* No. 170. Bureau of American Ethnology, Smithsonian Institution, Washington, D.C.

Evans, B. J.
   1968   Order, disorder, and hyperfine interactions in spinel ferrites. Unpublished Ph.D. thesis, Dept. of Geology, University of Chicago.

Flannery, K. V.
   1964   The Middle Formative of the Tehuacán Valley. Unpublished Ph.D. thesis, Dept. of Anthropology, University of Chicago.
   1968   The Olmec and the Valley of Oaxaca: A model for inter-regional interaction in Formative times. In *Dumbarton Oaks Conference on the Olmec*, edited by E. P. Benson. Washington, D.C.: Dumbarton Oaks. Pp. 79–110.

Flannery, K. V., M. Winter, S. Lees, J. Neely, J. Schoenwetter, S. Kitchen, and J. C. Wheeler
   1970   Preliminary archeological investigations in the Valley of Oaxaca, Mexico, 1966–1969. Mimeographed preliminary report, Dept. of Anthropology, University of Michigan, Ann Arbor.

Ford, R. I.
   1972   Barter, gift, or violence: an analysis of Tewa intertribal exchange. In *Social exchange and interaction*, edited by E. N. Wilmsen. *Anthropological Papers* No. 46:21–45. Museum of Anthropology, University of Michigan, Ann Arbor.

Fried, M. H.
   1967   *The evolution of political society*. New York: Random House.

Gordus, A. A., W. C. Fink, M. E. Hill, J. C. Purdy, and T. R. Wilcox
   1967   Identification of the geologic origins of archaeological artifacts: An automated method of Na and Mn neutron activation analysis. *Archaeometry* 10:87–96.

Greenwood, N. N., and T. C. Gibb
   1971   *Mössbauer spectroscopy*. London: Chapman and Hall.

Grove, D. C.
   1970   The San Pablo Pantheon mound: A middle preclassic site in Morelos, Mexico. *American Antiquity* 35:62–73.
   1971   Archaeological investigations along the Río Cuautla, Morelos, 1969 and 1970. Mimeographed preliminary report, Dept. of Anthropology, University of Illinois, Urbana.
   in   The Mesoamerican Formative and South
   press   American influences. In *Primer Simposio de Correlaciones Antropológicas Andino-Mesoamericanas, 1972*. Salinas, Ecuador.

Harding, T. G.
   1967   *Voyagers of the Vitiaz Strait: A study of a New Guinea trade system. Monograph* No. 44. The American Ethnological Society, Seattle, Wash.

Heizer, R. F.
   1961   Inferences on the nature of Olmec society based upon data from the La Venta site. *Kroeber Anthropological Society Papers* 25:43–57. Berkeley, California.

Jack, R. N., and R. F. Heizer
   1968   "Finger printing" of some Mesoamerican obsidians. *Contributions of the University of California Archaeological Research Facility* 5:81–99.

Keen, A. M.
   1958   *Sea shells of tropical west America*. Palo Alto: Stanford University Press.

Leach, E. R.
   1954   *Political systems of highland Burma*. The London School of Economics and Political Science. London: G. Bell & Sons.

Murra, J. V.
   1972   El "control vertical" de un máximo de pisos ecológicos en la economía de las sociedades andinas. In *Visita de la provincia de León de Huánuco (1562)*. Vol. II, Huánuco, Peru: Universidad Hernulio Valdizan. Pp. 429–476.

Pires-Ferreira, J. W.
   n.d.   Exchange networks in Formative Mesoamerica, with special reference to the Valley of Oaxaca. *Memoirs* No. 7. Museum of Anthropology. University of Michigan, Ann Arbor. In press.

Rappaport, R. A.
   1968   *Pigs for the ancestors: Ritual in the ecology of a New Guinea people*. New Haven, Conn.: Yale University Press.

Renfrew, C. A., J. E. Dixon, and J. R. Cann
   1968   Further analysis of Near Eastern obsidians. *Proceedings of the Prehistoric Society* **34**: 319–331. Cambridge, England.
Sahlins, M. D.
   1965   On the sociology of primitive exchange. In *The relevance of models for social anthropology*, edited by M. Banton. *ASA Monographs* No. I. London: Tavistock. Pp. 139–236.
   1972   *Stone age economics*. Chicago/New York: Aldine–Atherton.
Service, E. R.
   1962   *Primitive social organization*. New York: Random House.
Shirane, G., D. E. Cox, W. J. Takei, and S. L. Ruby
   1962   A study of the magnetic properties of the $FeTiO_3$–αFe_2O_3 system by neutron diffraction and the Mössbauer effect. *Journal of the Physical Society of Japan* **17**(10).
Shook, E. M., and T. Proskouriakoff
   1956   Settlement patterns in Meso-America and the sequence in the Guatemalan highlands. In *Prehistoric settlement patterns in the New World*, edited by G. R. Willey. *Viking Fund Publications in Anthropology* No. 23. New York: Wenner–Gren. Pp. 93–100.
Smith, C. E., Jr.
   1967   Plant remains. In *The prehistory of the Tehuacán Valley*. Vol. 1. *Environment and subsistence*, edited by D. S. Byers. Austin: University of Texas Press. Pp. 220–255.
Tolstoy, P., and L. I. Paradis
   1970   Early and middle preclassic culture in the Basin of Mexico. *Science* **167**:344–351.

Vaillant, G. C.
   1930   Excavations at Zacatenco. *Anthropological Papers* Vol. 32: Part 1. American Museum of Natural History, New York.
   1935   Excavations at El Arbolillo. *Anthropological Papers* Vol. 35: Part 2. American Museum of Natural History, New York.
Weaver, M. P.
   1967   Tlapacoya pottery in the museum collection. *Indian Notes and Monographs, Miscellaneous Series* No. 56. Museum of the American Indian (Heye Foundation), New York.
Webster, S. S.
   1971   Una comunidad Quechua indígena en la explotación de multiples zonas ecológicas. *Waita* Nos. 4–5:55–64. Cuzco, Peru.
Winter, M. C.
   1972   Tierras Largas: A Formative community in the Valley of Oaxaca, Mexico. Unpublished Ph.D. thesis, Dept. of Anthropology, University of Arizona, Tucson.
Woodbury, R. B., and J. A. Neely
   1972   Water control systems of the Tehuacán Valley. In *The prehistory of the Tehuacán Valley* Vol. 4. *Chronology and irrigation*, edited by F. Johnson. Austin: University of Texas Press. Pp. 81–153.
Wright, H. T., and M. Zeder
   1973   The simulation of a linear exchange system under equilibrium conditions. Paper presented at the Annual Meetings of the Society for American Archeology, San Francisco, May 1973.

Chapter 11

INTERREGIONAL RELIGIOUS NETWORKS

Introduction

Religion was another phenomenon that linked Mesoamerica, region by region, into one giant sphere of interaction. Indeed, it often seems that, for Early Formative Mesoamerica, there was only one religion—one touched on by Nanette Pyne in her study of fire-serpents and were-jaguars (Chapter 9, this volume). It was a religion in which dancers, summoned by conch shell trumpets and accompanied by turtle shell drums, dressed in macaw plumes and equipped with gourd and armadillo shell rattles, performed in the disguises of mythical half-human, half-animal creatures. All this is suggested archeologically; what eludes us is the underlying structure.

We have saved religion for the last chapter in this book because it is perhaps the one subject that has been most disastrously handled by the Real Meso-american Archeologist. Compared to his handling of Formative religion, all his other efforts—in excavation, stratigraphy, settlement patterns, sampling, economics, trade, and social organization—look like acts of divine inspiration. As usual, I must fall back on a parable to make my point. But what could be more appropriate in a chapter on religion?

In 1968, I visited the Real Mesoamerican Archeologist during his Río San Jacinto project. He was digging the remains of a small Formative hamlet, SJ-12, and virgin soil was nearly in sight. As he cleaned the profile of his center trench, a figurine head popped from the uppermost 20 cm of Post-Classic overburden that covered the Formative remains. It was a representation of Huehueteotl, the Old God, one of the oldest recognizable deities in Mesoamerica.

"Ugly," said R.M.A., cleaning the figurine head on his sleeve.

Poor old Huehueteotl, I thought, and I was reminded of H. L. Mencken's "Memorial Service":

> Where is the graveyard of dead gods? What lingering mourner waters their mounds? There was a time when Jupiter was the king of the gods, and any man who doubted his puissance was *ipso facto* a barbarian and an ignoramus. But where in all the world is there a man who worships Jupiter today? And what of Huitzilopochtli? In one year—and it is no more than five hundred years ago—50,000 youths and maidens were slain in sacrifice to him. Today, if he is remembered at all, it is only by some vagrant savage in the depths of the Mexican forest. Huitzilopochtli, like many other gods, had no human father; his mother was a virtuous widow; he was born of an apparently innocent flirtation that she carried on with the sun. When he frowned, his father, the sun, stood still. When he roared with rage, earthquakes engulfed whole cities. When he thirsted he was watered with 10,000 gallons of human blood. But today Huitzilopochtli is as magnificantly forgotten as Allen G. Thurman. Once the peer of Allah, Buddha and Wotan, he is now the peer of Richmond P. Hobson, Alton B. Parker, Adelina Patti, General Weyler and Tom Sharkey.
>
> Speaking of Huitzilopochtli recalls his brother Tezcatlipoca. Tezcatlipoca was almost as powerful: he consumed 25,000 virgins a year. Lead me to his tomb: I would weep, and hang a *couronne des perles*. But who knows where it is? Or where the grave of Quitzalcoatl is? Or Xiehtecutli? Or Centeotl, that sweet one? Or Tlazolteotl, the goddess of love? Or Mictlan? Or Xipe? Or all the host of Tzitzimitles? Where are their bones? Where is the willow on which they hung their harps? In what forlorn and unheard-of Hell do they await the resurrection morn? [Mencken 1949: 95–96]

"I wonder who *their* gods were—the Formative people, down below," I ventured.

"We'll never know," said R.M.A. "There's no way we can handle Formative religion systematically. It was in their heads, and it's gone. Like Levi-Strauss says, it was a 'code' in their minds, and we can't predict it or produce it again. What do we find in sites like this? Sherds, chunks of wattle and daub, maybe a few burnt corncobs and broken animal bones. We can say that they lived in houses, grew corn, hunted deer, maybe traded pots with the Indians in the next valley. These are the things we can deal with. Their religion is out of reach—it didn't survive the ravages of time."

That's R.M.A., I thought: the ultimate inductivist. He sticks to what we can really say on the basis of hard data, and leaves the rest to the science fiction writers.

One year later, I again visited R.M.A. in the San Jacinto drainage. This time he was excavating SJ-1, the major Formative ceremonial center for the whole region. Twelve pyramidal mounds of earth and adobe covered the ridge top, and his pit in the central plaza was 4 m deep when I arrived. R.M.A. had found a pavement of green stone celts, broken in four places by burials with smudged-white pots bearing carved were-jaguar designs. The burials formed a row which continued the alignment of the pyramids before them. R.M.A. was literally dancing from one workman to the other as each one uncovered a burial.

"What·have you got here?" I asked as I got out my camera.

"A Middle Formative cult center," he beamed. "Look. The whole ceremonial complex is laid out to face Sirius, the dog star, on the longest day of the year. The pavement of celts, if you look at it from here—over here, where I'm standing—can be interpreted as representing a giant Star of David. And the four burials—that number is no accident either. They represent the four cardinal directions, each associated with a color, just like the Maya. See, Burial 1 is in a sort of red clay; Burial 2 is in white ash; Burial 3 is sort of—well, in an area of big yellow stains—"

"Big yellow stains, huh? He must have been scared. Maybe they were burying him alive."

"—and Burial 4 is in an area of black charcoal flecks. Look how his jaw has slumped away from the skull. Look at that expression. He must have died in a visionary trance. He knew he was going to meet that Big Were-Jaguar in the Sky, the were-jaguar who had sent him out from Veracruz to missionize the people of the San Jacinto basin."

"You think these burials are actual Olmec missionaries?" I asked, incredulous.

"Got to be. Don't you see the cleft skull on this one?"

"I think one of your workmen may have done that."

"I suppose my workman left these flames rising from his eyebrows?" he demanded triumphantly. I had to admit, he had me there. In fact, to this day I've never been able to explain how those flames got there.

The foregoing parable illustrates the split personality of my friend the Real Mesoamerican Archeologist. Give him a simple Formative hamlet and he displays the conscience of a conservative. Give him the slightest hint of a ceremonial feature and he's off to the theoretical stratosphere, with cults, missionaries, rituals, converts, sacrifices, anthropophagy, and hallucinogenic mushrooms. The reasons for this wide range of responses are not hard to find: *Mesoamerican archeology has absolutely no coherent and consistent theoretical framework by means of which ritual or religious data can be analyzed and interpreted.* This being the case, it's every man for himself, and R.M.A.'s guesses are as good as anyone's.

As R.M.A. has pointed out, a good deal of the "code" in the Formative villager's mind is gone beyond recall. In view of this, is there any hope of developing a useful theoretical framework for Formative religion? We believe that one is already in the process of development, and has been elaborated over a period of 8 years by ethnologist Roy A. Rappaport (1968, 1969, 1971a,b). While Rappaport's framework for religion was not worked out with archeologists in mind, it is admirably suited for archeology, as Robert D. Drennan attempts to demonstrate later in this chapter. One of the reasons it is suitable is that it ties religion to social organization, politics, and subsistence, rather than leaving it on the ephemeral plane of mental activity. Another reason for its utility is

that it breaks down religious phenomena into classes that are functionally different and have different contexts. The archeologist, therefore, can look to the contexts of his ritual or religious discoveries for clues to their function in the overall system (Flannery, this chapter). Moreover, Rappaport's framework makes possible deductive models in which the presence or absence of certain ritual or religious features in archeological contexts can be predicted. In this way, perhaps it can contribute to more reliable and universally acceptable interpretations of the religious behavior of Formative villagers.

As Levi-Strauss and countless of his ethnographic colleagues have shown us, all human societies act on the basis of "cognized models" of the way the world is put together. In Rappaport's scheme, part of this cognized model consists of what are called *ultimate sacred propositions*— "completely unverifiable beliefs that are held as unquestionable truths by the faithful," as Drennan describes them. As an indication of the kinds of ultimate sacred propositions that Formative Mesoamerican peoples might have believed unquestioningly, we may examine Michael Coe's (1972) reconstruction of Mesoamerica's primeval origin myth, one he feels can be traced back to Early Formative times and reconstructed from Olmec iconography and Aztec and Maya cosmology:

> This myth can be summarized as follows. Originally, the world consisted of nothing but an ocean, in which two creatures resided: the male–female Fire God and the Feathered Serpent. Out of this opposition the dry land was produced. Then, the old father god and mother goddess contained in the dual Fire God produced four offspring who were also gods. These were the four Tezcatlipocas, each assigned to a color direction; the third of these was the Feathered Serpent, while at least to the Aztec the fourth was Huitzilopochtli, their tribal Sun God. These last two created the Death Gods and Water Gods, as well as fire. Most importantly, they created the first pair of commoners or macehualli, thus announcing for all time the separate origin of the divine Tezcatlipoca lines and that of the plebians.

Eventually, since there was only a half-sun giving faint light, the four Tezcatlipocas initiated a series of four consecutive "suns" or creations, each of which ended in destruction. These were also conceived of as the result of a never-ending opposition between Tezcatlipoca and Quetzalcoatl. At the end of the First Sun, Tezcatlipoca was knocked from the sky by the Feathered Serpent, fell into the sea, and was changed into a great jaguar, which form he apparently retained throughout the entire cycle of suns.

At the end of the Fourth Sun, which was destroyed by floods, the sky fell to the earth. Just after the start of the Fifth Sun, it was raised again by the four Tezcatlipocas, who created the four world trees to help in the gigantic task; this part of the myth is also found in the Book of Chilam Balam of Chumayel, where the identity of these gods with the four Bacabs of the Maya becomes clear.

The remainder of the origin myth describes the creation of the Sun (the Fifth, the one in which we live) and the Moon and deals with other divine and astral matters. It then moves into the world of demigods and heroes who are the ancestors of all the Mesoamerican dynasties. Finally we come down to the world as we know it. [Coe 1972:8–9]

Obviously, not all archeologists will agree with Coe's reconstruction of this myth, or his projection of it back to the Formative; but that is not the issue here. The point is that, given the iconography of the Formative, something *like* it must have been believed strongly enough so that it communicated various ultimate sacred propositions.

In Rappaport's scheme, ultimate sacred propositions are interpreted on a less sacred level in a body of theology that directs the faithful to perform *rituals* of various kinds. These are relatively standardized religious acts which, if performed sufficiently often during the occupation of a site, will appear in the archeological record as patterned behavior. Some rituals are ad hoc—occurring at the birth or death of an individual, or at times of unpredictable abundances of food (Yengoyan 1972). But even more characteristic of agricultural village societies like those of Formative Mesoamerica are

calendric rituals—ceremonies that occur on roughly the same date each year. Such calendric rituals often coincide with the planting or harvesting of crops, and may be accompanied by ceremonial redistribution of crop surpluses which "even out" the difference in yield between various parts of a village's landholdings (Ford 1971). Formative Mesoamerica had a 260-day ritual calendar composed of 20 day signs and 13 numbers, which probably evolved together with such calendric rituals; this calendar can be detected as far back as 500 B.C. in the Oaxaca region (Caso 1928; Marcus n.d.).

Ad hoc rituals in early Mesoamerica include infant sacrifice and cannibalism accompanying the burials of important adults (see Drennan, this chapter), and adult sacrifices accompanying the construction of "public" (possibly ceremonial) buildings (Flannery *et al*. 1970:36). Calendric rituals are harder to detect, but there are numerous artifacts found in Formative sites which, in later periods of Mesoamerican history, we know to have been used at annually recurring rituals. These include the stingray spines and pottery masks mentioned later by Drennan, to which we may add figurines of masked persons who are almost certainly dancers at some recurrent ceremony. Figurines of dancers masked to resemble jaguars may relate some of these ceremonies to the ultimate creation myth reconstructed by Coe.

To return to Rappaport's scheme, one of the major functions of ritual is to induce an awe-inspiring or "numinous" *religious experience* (see discussion by Drennan, this chapter). This awe-inspiring experience verifies for the believer the ultimate sacred propositions—by experiencing the numinous, he knows it is true. Peter Furst (1968) believes that the impact of these ancient Mesoamerican religious experiences was heightened by the use of hallucinogens like the morning glory, or alcoholic beverages like pulque. Either is plausible, but archeological evidence for it is notoriously hard to come by.

Finally, religion and ritual cycles in Rappaport's framework are seen as having adaptive functions far beyond increasing group solidarity. In highland New Guinea, he sees one ritual cycle as regulating man-land ratios, adjusting domestic pig population densities, and spacing out incidents of warfare (Rappaport 1968). Various rituals function to transmit information about human population densities—by observing the manpower one village can muster for a mass dance display, a second village can evaluate its potential as an ally or enemy in warfare. Still other rituals function to redistribute foodstuffs where no chiefly apparatus for redistribution is present. And some—like ritual infanticide—serve as a check on population where birth rates are high and agriculture primitive. All these adaptive functions have some relevance for the interpretation of Formative Mesoamerican ritual.

Contextual Analysis of Ritual Paraphernalia from Formative Oaxaca

KENT V. FLANNERY

Methodology of Contextual Analysis

Any archeologist who works extensively in Formative villages finds features or artifacts that probably functioned in ritual. If one function of ritual is to "transmit useful information in an atmosphere of unquestioned religious truth" (see discussion by Drennan, this chapter), a reasonable question for each archeologist to ask would be: What information was this ritual feature or artifact designed to transmit?

If the archeologist is lucky, the answer may lie somewhere in the context of his discovery. Does the item occur only in the context of public buildings? If so, it may be associated with rituals performed for the community or the region as a whole, perhaps transmitting information at that level. Does the item occur mainly with elite households or burials? If so, it may be designed to communicate their elite status. Does the item occur with great frequency in ordinary households? If so, two more questions should be asked. First, on the basis of ethnographic analogy, is it likely to reflect the activities of a sodality that crosscuts many households? Or second, on the same basis, is it likely to reflect an act of personal ritual by an individual or his household? Depending on how these last two questions are answered, we might be able to determine whether the transmitted information concerns individual religious commitment or group commitment. If the latter, it could refer to calendric ceremonies (regulating planting time, harvest time, food or land redistribution), ad hoc ceremonies (preparation for raiding, initiation, or emergency communal action of some kind), and so forth.

The trouble is that, for most ritual items, we have little contextual data, since houses or household clusters are so rarely distinguished. Museums are full of fascinating ritual paraphernalia from illegal excavation, with no provenience data at all. In fact, one reputable Mesoamerican archeologist of my acquaintance insists that he would not know any more about such objects if he *did* have the contextual data. I hope to prove in this chapter that that is untrue (except, possibly, in his case). Restricting myself to one region, the Valley of Oaxaca, I will give the contextual data on those "ritual" structures, features, and artifacts we have been able to recover as of this writing. I feel that contextual analysis does allow one to distinguish between ritual paraphernalia functioning at the level of the individual, the household, the sodality, the community, and beyond, although obviously some items functioned on several levels. I shall discuss, therefore, (1) *structures, features, and artifacts that probably functioned in public ritual at the level of the community or beyond*; (2) *features and artifacts that probably functioned in ritual on the level of household or sodality*; and (3) *artifacts that probably functioned in personal ritual*.

Once having answered the question of context, the archeologist might ask himself, "What adaptive function could the transmission of information in that context have provided?" Still harder to answer is the next question, "What ultimate sacred proposition dictated the ritual and was verified by it?"—for not all Formative cultures have the iconographic richness on which Coe drew in his reconstruction of Mesoamerica's primeval creation myth. Whatever the problem, however, these questions bring us closer to a coherent interpretive framework than Formative archeology has had in the past. Some day, when such information is

available for several related regions, we will be in a position for a real network analysis of Formative religious systems.

Public Ritual

Public Buildings

Certain Oaxacan villages, but not others, had evidence of structures that were evidently public buildings rather than residences. As yet, we have no idea what *specific* public activities were carried out at these buildings. Nor do we know what percentage of this public activity was "ceremonial" as opposed to "secular," if indeed such a distinction can be made for the Formative.

The earliest such buildings, dating to the Tierras Largas phase (1400–1150 B.C.), are known from only one village, San José Mogote, where they occupy an area of at least 300 sq m (see Figure 11.1). These buildings were rectangular and oriented 8° west of true north. They were built of heavy pine posts, with a plaster floor set on a platform of crushed volcanic tuff, lime, and sand. The walls were built of similar material, then faced with true lime plaster in which multiple layers can sometimes be detected. The floors, in contrast to

Figure 11.1 Remains of a public building of the Early Tierras Largas phase (1350 B.C.) at San José Mogote, Oaxaca. The building, 5.4 by 4.4 m, featured pine posts and cane wattle plastered with white stucco. A poorly preserved altar or step was found against the south wall (to the left in the photo). In the center of the floor was a plastered storage pit, filled with powdered lime for making stucco. (Masons are shown constructing a protective stone wall outside the area of the Formative building.)

Figure 11.2 Public building of the Guadalupe phase (ca. 700 B.C.) at Barrio del Rosario Huitzo, Oaxaca. The building is of earthen fill with retaining walls of planoconvex adobes and a surface of white stucco.

those of ordinary residences, were swept clean of debris (Flannery *et al.* 1970:49-51).

By the Guadalupe phase (850-600 B.C.), several villages, including San José Mogote and Barrio del Rosario Huitzo, had public buildings of earth and adobe construction (see Figure 11.2). At Huitzo, such structures occupied just under 3500 sq m, or about 13% of the village. One building—thought to be the southernmost of a group of three or four arranged around a common patio—was oriented 8° west of true north like contemporary buildings of Complex A at La Venta, Tabasco (Drucker, Heizer, and Squier 1959). Its basal platform, built

of earth held in place by retaining walls of plano-convex adobes, was faced with a thick coating of mud plaster, followed by white lime plaster or stucco. Its front facade, 11.5 m wide, had a three-step stairway 7.6 m long which led from the patio up to a massive wattle-and-daub structure that had once crowned the platform. Similar buildings are known from many parts of Mesoamerica at the same time period. However, they are apparently absent at most villages in the Valley of Oaxaca, such as Tierras Largas and Fábrica San José.

Conch Shell Trumpets and Turtle Shell Drums

Two artifacts that probably functioned in community-level ritual are the conch shell trumpet and the turtle shell drum. Both came from the coastal lowlands, most likely from the Gulf Coast. Both were still in use when the Spanish arrived in the Valley of Oaxaca. In fact, carved conch shell trumpets are still used in some Zapotec-speaking villages in Oaxaca to summon participants in *tequio*, a kind of obligatory communal work for the village. The trumpets, usually of *Strombus* shell, are associated with a public office rather than an individual, and are kept in the *municipio* for generations. Turtle shell drums are invariably made from the shell of *Dermatemys mawii*, an occupant of the large sluggish rivers of the Isthmian lowlands like the Coatzacoalcos, Grijalva, and Papaloapan. Pottery sculptures from the Classic period show the drums being played with a deer antler, just as they were when the Spanish arrived.

Contextual data on our specimens (Table 11.1) shows that such drums and trumpets are relatively rare, as might be expected. One fragment of carved conch occurred in a midden associated with a series of Guadalupe phase public buildings. Another conch, possibly broken in the process of carving, occurred in a shell-working area on a house floor—suggesting that shells were imported unmodified, then carved by local craftsmen before going into public service. Fragments of *Dermatemys* shell occur in or between household clusters, but it is clear that very few households had

TABLE 11.1   Contextual Data on Possible Conch Shell Trumpet and Turtle Shell Drum Fragments
from Early Oaxacan Villages

Object	Provenience	Context	Period and estimated date
Frag. conch (*Strombus*), possibly broken in process of carving	San José Mogote, Area A, Household Cluster C4	Shell-working area in household cluster	San José phase (1100–1000 B.C.)
Frag. conch (*Strombus*), possibly broken in process of carving	San José Mogote, Area C, House 4	On house floor, in shell-working area	San José phase (1150–1000 B.C.)
Frag. conch (*Strombus*)	Abasolo, Area A, Zone D	Midden, possibly part of relatively high-status household cluster	San José phase (1000–900 B.C.)
Frag. conch (*Strombus*)	San José Mogote, Platform 1, Stage II east	Debris around public building	Late San José phase (900 B.C.)
3 frags. conch (*Strombus*)	Tierras Largas, Various test squares	Debris in open area between houses	2 frags., San José phase; 1 frag., Guadalupe phase (850–650 B.C.)
2 frags. conch (*Malea* sp.), carved, probably from trumpet	Huitzo, Area C, Zone D2	Midden associated with series of public buildings	Guadalupe phase (700–650 B.C.)
Plastron of turtle (*Dermatemys*), probably drum fragment	Tierras Largas, Area B Feature 75	In bell-shaped storage pit, in Household Cluster 1 of Late Tierras Largas phase	Late Tierras Largas phase (1300–1200 B.C.)
Frags. turtle plastron (*Dermatemys*), probably drum fragments	Fábrica San José, Area A, Zone I	Debris in open area between houses, possibly high-status residences	Guadalupe phase (850–650 B.C.)

them. They may have been used *both* in the contexts of community ritual and sodality-level ritual.

Household or Sodality Ritual

Possible Household "Shrines"

Very few features found in household context can be interpreted even tentatively as ritual in function. In Area A at San José Mogote, we discovered parts of two enigmatic features in stratigraphic Level C3, which dated to the middle of the San José phase (ca. 1100–1000 B.C.). The presence of a hearth, a bell-shaped pit, and abundant shell and mica debris suggests that our excavations had exposed part of the courtyard in a household cluster, very near the house itself. *Feature 3* (see

Figure 11.3) was a circular area, 120 cm in diameter and recessed 5 cm into the courtyard, which had been mud-plastered and then painted red with specular hematite. *Feature 8* was a similar circle, only partly exposed by our excavation, and possibly painted yellow. We cannot imagine what function these features served, but it seems unlikely that it was utilitarian. No other household cluster so far investigated has produced such painted circles, and they are very different in conception from features called "altars" in other Formative sites (Figure 11.4).

Figurines of Dancers

In the introduction to this chapter, we alluded to the likelihood that Early and Middle Formative

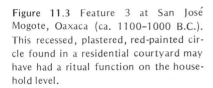

Figure 11.3 Feature 3 at San José Mogote, Oaxaca (ca. 1100–1000 B.C.). This recessed, plastered, red-painted circle found in a residential courtyard may have had a ritual function on the household level.

cultures had "dance societies," or sodalities that performed dances on certain occasions during the year. Such dances were still performed when the Spanish arrived, and are now performed for the benefit of tourists in many areas. Mesoamerican Indian dancers made great use of feathers, animal fur and gourd and shell rattles in their costumes. They also wore masks, many of which were so small as to cover only the lower half of the face.

Included in the thousands of Early and Middle Formative figurines from Oaxaca are many that seem to represent dancers wearing costumes and masks (Figure 11.5). Some are dressed as fantastic animals, others as birds, jaguars, or pumas. Similar figurines are reported from Tlatilco or Tlapacoya in the Valley of Mexico, some wearing small masks over the lower face (Coe 1965b: Figures 157–158; Piña Chán 1955: Figure 11). Since many of the illustrated specimens are from illegal excavations, contextual data are hard to come by. In the case of Oaxaca, contextual data can be stated quite simply: With the exception of one obviously arranged group (see Drennan, p. 352), figurines and figurine fragments are broadly coextensive with potsherds. They occur in domestic refuse, and wherever sherds are abundant, so usually are figurines. Most of the "costumed dancers" are Early Formative in date and, whatever their function,

Figure 11.4 Middle Formative altar (or "throne") of carved stones at Chalcatzingo, Morelos. An Olmec cacique serves as scale. [Courtesy, D.C. Grove.]

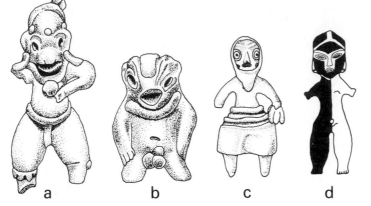

Figure 11.5 Pottery figurines from Formative villages in Mesoamerica, showing masked or costumed individuals who may be dancers. (a) From Tierras Largas, Oaxaca; (b) from San José Mogote, Oaxaca; (c) from Tlatilco, Valley of Mexico; (d) also from Tlatilco, shows body painting rather than costume. [(c) and (d) are redrawn from Piña Chán 1955:Figures 10, 11.]

they belong contextually with the household cluster. Perhaps some dances were accompanied by the turtle shell drums mentioned earlier, which also may have functioned in a sodality context.

Pottery Masks

Excavations in many parts of Mesoamerica have recovered the actual masks used by the dancers just mentioned. The most famous are the pottery masks from Tlatilco (Piña Chán 1955:Lám. 20; Coe 1965b:Figures 161, 163), where some were found with burials. In this case, one suspects the buried individual was a member of a dance sodality, whose mask was buried with him. Other beautiful examples come from illegal excavations at Tlapacoya in the Valley of Mexico and Las Bocas, Puebla (Coe 1965b:Figures 162, 164). Most are small—perhaps 10–15 cm in height—and would have covered only the lower face.

Table 11.2 gives contextual data on 12 pottery masks from Oaxaca (See Figure 11.6A). Note that most are Middle Formative in date, only two being earlier. Where undisturbed, the context is invariably one of domestic refuse: on a house floor, in a household cluster, or in the debris between houses. Note also that pottery masks were much more abundant than conch shell trumpets or turtle shell drums, occurring in many more households. This is

what one would expect if they were associated with widespread sodalities linking households rather than with public rituals conducted only by community leaders.

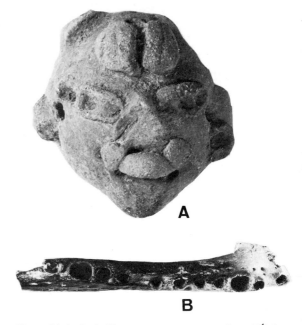

Figure 11.6 Probable costume components from Fábrica San José, Oaxaca. (A) Pottery mask; (B) fragment of crocodile mandible. Not to same scale. [Courtesy, R.D. Drennan.]

TABLE 11.2 Contextual Data on Pottery Masks from Early Oaxacan Villages

Object	Provenience	Context	Period and estimated date
Pottery mask	San José Mogote, Area A, Household cluster C3	Found in household cluster (near red-painted, circular "ritual feature")	San José phase (1100–1000 B.C.)
Pottery mask frag.	San José Mogote, Area C, N215, depth 195 cm	In slope wash, downhill from San José phase household cluster	San José phase (1100–900 B.C.)
Pottery mask frag.	Fábrica San José, Area F, Zone F	Midden associated with possible high–status household	Guadalupe phase (850–650 B.C.)
Pottery mask	Fábrica San José, scraping profile	?	Probably Guadalupe phase
Pottery mask frag.	Fábrica San José, Area A (II), Zone C	Mixed, disturbed deposit	Guadalupe or Early Rosario phase
Pottery mask frag.	Fábrica San José, Test Pit 14	Debris in open area between houses	Terminal Guadalupe or Earliest Rosario phase
Pottery mask frag.	Fábrica San José, House 6	On floor of ordinary house	Terminal Guadalupe or Earliest Rosario phase
Pottery mask frag.	Fábrica San José, Area H, Zone G	Debris in open area between houses	Early Rosario phase (600 B.C.)
Pottery mask frag.	Fábrica San José, Test Pit 49	Debris in open area between houses	Early Rosario phase (600 B.C.)
Pottery mask frag.	Fábrica San José, Area A(IV), Zone F	Mixed, disturbed deposit	Early Rosario (600 B.C.) or Monte Albán Ic (ca. 300 B.C.)
Pottery mask frag.	Fábrica San José, Area F, Zone C	Mixed, disturbed deposit	?

Mask or Costume Components

Pottery masks are preserved because of their imperishable nature. But hundreds of masks may have been carved of wood or made of animal hide, feathers, or vegetal material that have long since perished. For example, the Huave Indians of Tehuantepec are famous for masks of wood, bark, deer and peccary hair, and feathers of various kinds (Varner and Brown 1972). Fortunately, a

TABLE 11.3 Contextual Data on Possible Mask or Costume Components from Early Oaxacan Villages

Object	Provenience	Context	Period and estimated date
Macaw bones, with wing bones cut so as to preserve feathers	Tierras Largas, Area B, Feature 116 (but at juncture with intrusive pit, Feature 195)	In bell–shaped storage pit (F.116) in Household Cluster 1 of Late Tierras Largas phase, disturbed by Rosario phase pit (F. 195)	Probably Late Tierras Largas phase (1300–1200 B.C.); but could be intrusive from ca. 600 B.C.
Macaw bones	Tierras Largas, Area G, Feature 184	In bell–shaped storage pit, in Household Cluster 2 of Late Tierras Largas phase	Late Tierras Largas phase (1300–1200 B.C.)
Macaw bones	Tierras Largas, Area B, Feature 141	In bell–shaped storage pit, in Household Cluster 1 of Early San José phase	Early San José phase (1150 B.C.)
Armadillo shell frags. (2)	San José Mogote, Area A, Zone C2	In household cluster (near shell and magnetite-working areas)	San José phase (1100–1000 B.C.)
Armadillo shell frags. (3)	Fábrica San José, Area H, Zone F	In debris in open area between houses	Early Rosario phase (600 B.C.)
Crocodile mandible	Fábrica San José, Area H	In mixed refuse in open area	Mixed, Early Rosario phase (600 B.C.) and Monte Albán II (100 B.C.-100 A.D.)

few of those substances do leave archeological traces.

Table 11.3 gives contextual data on three types of faunal remains from Oaxacan villages which may represent mask or costume components. None are native to the Valley of Oaxaca, and all could have been traded from the Isthmus of Tehuantepec. In Chapter 2, we mentioned that bones of macaw (*Ara* cf. *militaris*) were more common at Tierras Largas than elsewhere; the context was usually a bell-shaped storage pit in a household cluster. The blue-green plumes of the military macaw were widely used in ancient Oaxaca.

Armadillos are unknown in the Valley of Oaxaca, but their shell fragments occur in or between household clusters, in Early or Middle Formative context. Such fragments may come from armadillo shell rattles or from mask components. Finally, a crocodile mandible which might have been part of a spectacular Middle or Late Formative costume came from a refuse area at Fábrica San José (Figure 11.6B). All in all, the contextual data from Tables 11.2 and 11.3 suggest that costumes were made, stored, and finally discarded around the house. Moreover, they occurred with both "high-status" and "ordinary" households.

Personal Ritual

Stingray Spines

One of the most widespread personal rituals in Pre-Columbian Mesoamerica was self-mutilation or bloodletting. The rite could be an act of individual penance, or a ritual of propitiation carried out by an individual priest on behalf of a larger segment of society. Priests drew blood from tongue, lips, ear-lobes, or sexual organs, using stingray spines, obsidian blades, *Agave* spines, or knotted strings of thorns (Nuttall 1904). Among the Aztec at the time of the Spanish Conquest,

> the letting of one's own blood was [a] way to ensure divine favor, and people did horrible self-penances such as mutilating themselves with knives or drawing through their tongues a string on which were threaded maguey spines. The higher the social position of the individual and the more he consequently knew of ritualistic observance, the more arduously he performed the fasts, penances and tortures imposed by the religion. The priests, therefore, were strongly cognizant of their social responsibility and by the rigor of their own lives strove to ensure the well-being of the tribe. [Vaillant 1941:206]

The sharp, serrated spine of the stingray was a favored artifact for ritual bloodletting (Borhegyi 1961). Contextual data on such items is given in Table 11.4 (see also Figure 11.7). A *true* stingray spine occurred in a midden associated with Middle Formative public buildings—the same midden that produced the carved conch shell trumpet fragment mentioned earlier. An *imitation* stingray spine, carved from a deer bone splinter, was found in a bell-shaped storage pit in a Middle Formative household cluster. It is possible, therefore, that, during the Middle Formative, there was a tendency for village leaders to have access to real stingray spines, while ordinary householders sometimes used imitations.

Fish Spines

Spines from marine fish imported to the Valley of Oaxaca were far more common than stingray spines, especially in the Early Formative. Table

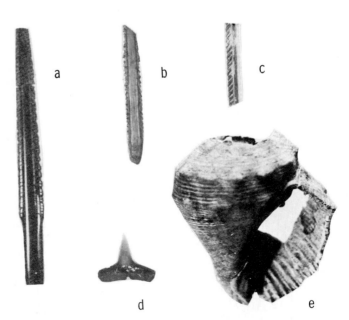

Figure 11.7 Ritual paraphernalia from Formative sites. (a) Jade stingray spine from La Venta [after Drucker 1952]; (b) true stingray spine from Huitzo, Oaxaca; (c) imitation stingray spine carved from deer bone splinter, Tierras Largas, Oaxaca; (d) shark tooth, San José Mogote, Oaxaca; (e) conch shell trumpet, also from San José Mogote. Not all to same scale.

a   b   c

d   e

TABLE 11.4 Contextual Data on Fish Spines, Stingray Spines, and Shark Teeth from Early Oaxacan Villages

Object	Provenience	Context	Period and estimated date
Marine fish spine (species unknown)	San José Mogote, Area A, Platform 1 east, Stage II	On steps to stone-faced public bldg.	Late San José phase (900 B.C.)
Vertebra of marine fish (sp. unknown) with spine trimmed off; and ceratohyal bone	San José Mogote, Area A, Platform 1 east, Stage II	On surface of stone-faced public bldg.	Late San José phase (900 B.C.)
Vertebra of marine fish (sp. unknown) with spine trimmed off	San José Mogote, Area A, Household cluster C3	In household cluster (near shell- and magnetite-working areas)	San José phase (1100–1000 B.C.)
Articular bone from jaw of marine fish (sp. unknown)	San José Mogote, Area A, Zone D2	Midden associated with house of magnetite worker	San José phase, (1100–1000 B.C.)
Marine fish spine (Pomadasidae)	Tierras Largas, Area C, House 2	Floor of house, in Household Cluster 2 of Late San José phase, but near disturbed area	Probably Late San José phase (900 B.C.)
Otolith from marine fish (Sciaenidae)	Tierras Largas, Area A, House 1	Floor of house, in ·Household Cluster 1 of Late San José phase	Late San José phase (900 B.C.)
Marine fish spine (Sciaenidae)	Tierras Largas, Area E	In debris in open area between houses	Mixed debris, predominantly late San José phase
Marine fish spine (Sciaenidae)	Tierras Largas, Area A, House 1, Feature 1	In trash inside oven, but possibly redeposited from house floor	Oven (Guadalupe phase) is intrusive into Late San José phase house
Sea catfish spine (Ictaluridae)	Fábrica San José, House 14	Floor of probable high-status residence	Guadalupe or Early Rosario phase (650 B.C.)
Marine fish spine (Lutjanidae)	Fábrica San José, Area C, Zone J	Midden, possibly associated with high-status residence	Early Rosario phase (600 B.C.)

Table 11.4 (Continued)

Object	Provenience	Context	Period and estimated date
Marine fish spine (Lutjanidae)	Huitzo, Area C, Feature 4	Intrusive pit in area near public buildings	Late Rosario phase
Stingray spine	Huitzo, Area C, Zone D	Midden, near area of public buildings	Guadalupe phase (700 B.C.)
Imitation stingray spine made from deer bone splinter	Tierras Largas, Area D, Feature 157	Bell-shaped storage pit in Household Cluster 1 of Guadalupe phase	Pit (850–650 B.C.) could contain some redeposited Late San José phase material (900 B.C.)
Imitation fish spine, made from dog(?) bone	Fábrica San José, Test Pit 43	In area of mixed, disturbed deposits	Undateable; can be no earlier than ca. 300 B.C.
Shark tooth	San José Mogote, Area A, Zone D	Midden associated with house of magnetite worker	San José phase, (1100–1000 B.C.)

11.4 gives contextual data on 11 marine fish fragments from Oaxacan villages. Assuming these fish spines also served in ritual bloodletting, the distribution of fragments is very interesting. Actual spines occur on the steps to a public building, on the floors of both high-status and ordinary residences, in ordinary household refuse, and in a refuse pit near a public building. The vertebrae from which some spines were trimmed occur on the surface of a public building, and in a household cluster. A few other discarded fragments from marine fish occur in the context of household clusters. We might therefore propose that (*1*) marine fish spines often arrived in the Valley of Oaxaca still attached to vertebrae or other parts of the skeleton; (*2*) the trimming off of the spine and the discarding of the rest usually took place in the household cluster; (*3*) the spines were usually kept in the home; (*4*) the spines were sometimes taken to a public building to be used.

We might also propose, on the basis of Table 11.4, that bloodletting began as a personal ritual carried out by members of most, if not all, households in each village. So far as we can tell, all households probably had access to fish spines, which were traded into the Valley of Oaxaca from the coast. The spines are from four families—marine catfish (Ictaluridae), snappers (Lutjanidae), grunts (Pomadasidae), and drums (Sciaenidae)—all of which occur along both coasts at the Isthmus of Tehuantepec. By Middle Formative times, when stingray spines also were traded to Oaxaca villages, there may have been some differences in access based on social status. Ordinary villagers sometimes whittled imitation spines from mammal bone. The presence of a true stingray spine near a Middle Formative public building suggests that some persons, perhaps community leaders, had access to genuine goods. An additional bit of evidence to suggest that social differences were involved comes from a basalt-column tomb in Mound A-2 at La Venta, Tabasco (Coe 1965a: 689–690; Drucker 1952), whose offerings included a "stingray spine" carved out of jade. Obviously, access to such an artifact must have been still more restricted. To repeat Vaillant's observation, "the higher the social position of the individual . . . the more arduously he performed the fasts, penances, and tortures." Perhaps the continuum from imitation, to genuine, to jade spine reflects the fact that the autosacrifice of the elite was important for his whole lineage or community, and not merely for himself or his household.

Shark Teeth

Shark teeth (Figure 11.7), also probably used for bloodletting, were related to stingray spines in the cosmology of Mesoamerican peoples for an interesting reason. According to Borhegyi (1961), Mesoamerican Indians most often recovered stingray spines when fishing for sharks. It seems that, when sharks eat the rays, the spines frequently become lodged between the shark's teeth; washed constantly by sea water, they are cleaned of poison by the time the fisherman recovers them from the shark's mouth. A single shark's tooth occurred in household cluster context at San José Mogote (Table 11.4).

Summary and Conclusions

Formative villagers in the Valley of Oaxaca participated in ritual on at least three levels: personal, household–sodality, and community–region. On the personal level, villagers performed acts of ritual bloodletting with fish spines which were imported from the coastal lowlands for that purpose. Kept in the home until needed, the spines were sometimes taken to public buildings for the ritual. The pain involved in such acts may have contributed to the numinous experience defined by Rappaport (see Drennan, this chapter). In the Early Formative, such bloodletting was probably an egalitarian

ritual; by the Middle Formative, it was adapted to an increasingly ranked society, with chiefly individuals using jade spines, community leaders using true stingray spines, and ordinary villagers sometimes whittling imitation spines from mammal bone splinters.

Sodalities, or fraternal organizations, evidently crosscut many households. One of the activities of such sodalities were dances, whose performers were drawn from many homes. Each performer probably prepared his own costume, often with articles like macaw plumes and armadillo shell which had to be imported from the lowlands. By the Middle Formative, many had their own pottery masks, which were kept in the home until needed. (Elsewhere in Mesoamerica, these masks were sometimes buried with their owners.) Perhaps in the heat and excitement of the dance, more numinous experiences occurred.

Finally public buildings were built and maintained at certain Oaxacan villages, presumably to serve not only that community but neighboring hamlets as well. We have little evidence of the rituals carried on at such buildings, but conch shell trumpets were used at some of them. And since the buildings share an astronomical orientation with ceremonial–civic structures hundreds of miles away on the Gulf Coast, their use was probably founded on a series of ultimate sacred propositions believed in by dozens of regional cultures over much of southern Mexico and adjacent Guatemala.

In the section that follows, R. D. Drennan provides a more wide-ranging application of Roy Rappaport's theoretical framework to Formative Mesoamerica. In the process, he suggests that Formative Mesoamerica's need for *rituals of sanctification* promoted an extensive interregional exchange, not only of symbolic conventions but also of physical paraphernalia like conch shell trumpets, turtle shell drums, stingray spines, shark teeth, and the like. Many of these products were of lowland origin—and so, if Coe (1972) is correct, was much of the origin myth to which they were related. On the other hand, that origin myth may go back much farther than the Olmec. Stripped of

its elite–plebian aspects, it may go back to the
preceramic societies that preceded them—societies
that, as MacNeish's data show, already had some
elaborate ideas about ritual, cannibalism, and

infanticide. At any rate, the pan-Mesoamerican
aspects of Early Formative religion certainly qualify Drennan's paper for inclusion in any discussion
of interregional relationships.

Religion and Social Evolution in Formative Mesoamerica★

ROBERT D. DRENNAN

Introduction

Archeologists have taken into account a wide
variety of phenomena in their efforts to explain
such major transformations in social organization
as the emergence of a sedentary agricultural way
of life, or of institutionalized authorities regulating
human affairs. The "seasonality" and "scheduling"
of hunting-and-gathering societies have been explored, together with changes implied by the shift
to agriculture (Flannery 1968a). Population pressure in zones of marginal productivity has been
advanced as a selective pressure for the origins of
agriculture (Binford 1968). Wittfogel (1938 and
1956) has proposed that the coordination requirements of large-scale irrigation systems are the
major cause of the emergence of discrete administrative authorities. Carneiro (1970) has discussed
the role played in this process by warfare. "Economic symbiosis" also has been assigned an important place (Sanders 1968; Sanders and Price 1968).
Others have declined to emphasize single causes,
but have attempted to weave together a large
number of factors (Adams 1966).

*This paper has benefited from the suggestions of K. V.
Flannery, R. I. Ford, and R. A. Rappaport, who have read
various versions of the manuscript. I remain responsible
for any misuse to which their ideas may have been put.

Such explanatory propositions deal with the effects and functions of new forms of social organization. This section is an attempt to elucidate the
operation of these new forms of social organization with respect to the understandings and motivations of those who participate in them. In
seeking to explain sociocultural phenomena, anthropologists rely on what Rappaport (1968:237–
239) has called "operational models." These
models deal with phenomena in terms of a set of
understandings belonging to the analyst. They may
be contrasted with "cognized models," which
comprise the sets of understandings belonging to
the people whose behavior is being studied by the
anthropologist. It is in the realm of the cognized
model that the motivations and understandings
necessary to the actions of men in a society are
provided. It is important to consider not only the
selective pressures for new forms of social organization, but also the development of the cognized
models that provide the motivations and understandings necessary to the successful operation of
these new social forms. Operational models must
be developed to deal with cognized models. Such
an operational model is the subject of this section
of Chapter 11.

In terms of cognized models, the effect of such a
transformation of social organization as the emer-

gence of administrative authorities is to create a new set of social conventions. This set of social conventions deals with broad principles of social organization, as well as with principles of communication concerning the regulation of social, economic, and ecological variables. This latter aspect is important, since one of the major changes in the emergence of administrative authorities involves communication within the social group (cf. Wright 1969).

In order that a social system operate, it is necessary that the participants accept these social conventions and pattern their activities accordingly. What is it that motivates the participants to accept the social conventions? Even if, for example, an explanation centered on economic symbiosis is accepted to explain the emergence of administered society, it fails to explain the emergence of the cognized models that enable such a system to operate. It seems highly unlikely that the natives of highland Mesoamerica accepted the social conventions granting higher status to a restricted set of individuals (and requiring that their directives be obeyed) because they realized that this was necessary in order to maintain a system of economic symbiosis, which in turn enabled them to enjoy various economic advantages of specialization.

The social conventions maintaining such a social system include many relatively specific directives for behavior, the relation of which to the overall maintenance of the social system is not intuitively obvious to the participants. Neither are the large-scale social, economic, or ecological advantages of a particular form of social organization apt to be apparent to the participants in it. Such large-scale advantages are, in fact, the subject of wide disagreements among anthropologists. Thus, since there is a large number of possible alternative social conventions, the social, economic, or ecological advantages of which are not apt to be perceived by the participants, "social conventions are arbitrary," as Rappaport (1971b:32) has noted.

It is perhaps preferable to say that social conventions *seem* arbitrary to the participants in a given

social group, since each set undoubtedly has its own particular adaptive advantages. The degree of apparent arbitrariness of social conventions varies, a topic which is dealt with later in reference to specific cases. Social conventions that seem arbitrary to members of a social group are not likely to be universally accepted. But, unless there is a high degree of acceptance of social conventions and the specific messages concerned with them, the responses of members of a social group are unpredictable. The successful operation of the social group, however, depends on "some minimum degree of orderliness" or predictability (Rappaport 1971a:68). Just what degree of orderliness is required depends on a number of factors, another topic dealt with later in reference to specific cases. Thus, to the extent that social conventions seem arbitrary, and to the extent that orderliness is necessary to the successful operation of the social system, some mechanism for assuring the acceptance of the social conventions and the messages concerned with them is necessary.

Wittfogel's derivation of "despotism" from canal irrigation is based on the assumption that physical coercion is the mechanism most likely to be employed (Wittfogel 1957). Carneiro's (1970) formulation involves a related role for coercion. The successful application of physical coercion as a primary means to ensure the acceptance of social conventions, however, implies the existence of an administrative structure capable of wielding a certain amount of power. Following Rappaport's (1971a,b) lead, we can apply Bierstedt's definition of power to this situation. Bierstedt (1950) defines power as *the mathematical product of men* × *resources* × *organization*. There is a long period of human history during which there was no administrative structure of suffucient *organizational capacity* to mobilize large numbers of men, and during which the *technology of force* was not sufficiently advanced to render large numbers of men a truly effective coercive body, even if they could be mobilized. During the stage of social evolution considered here, the availability of the organization and resources called for in Bierstedt's formulation was so limited as to make coercion not viable as a primary mechanism for ensuring predictability in people's actions.

The belief systems generally subsumed under the headings of "religion" or "ideology," however, can ensure the acceptance of social conventions, and thus the requisite degree of predictability in the operation of a social system. Rappaport (1969, 1971a,b) has suggested that religious systems can assure the acceptance of social conventions and messages by means of *sanctification*. It is this suggestion that is pursued later with reference to Mesoamerica during the Formative Period.

Religion

Rappaport (1971a) has divided the operation of religion into three categories: "ultimate sacred propositions," ritual, and religious experience. Ultimate sacred propositions are the highest-level doctrines or dogma of a religious system. They are a set of completely unverifiable beliefs that are held as unquestionable truths by the faithful. These ultimate sacred propositions are interpreted on a substantially less sacred level in a body of theology which, among other things, directs the faithful to perform certain kinds of religious acts in particular ways. These acts are called "rituals." A major function of many rituals is to induce religious experience. The term "experience" is used here as James (1903) used it, meaning feeling as opposed to thought. Religious experience is nondiscursive and involves an immediate grasp of things emotionally, rather than a rational, discursive form of knowledge. In some ways, religious experience is like esthetic experience.

Otto (1914) speaks of religious experience in terms of contact with the numinous, or supernatural. The numinous is described by Otto as awe-inspiring, overpowering, urgent, "wholly other," and fascinating. One result of this contact with the numinous in religious experience is to support the ultimate sacred propositions. This occurs because of the intense feeling of reality

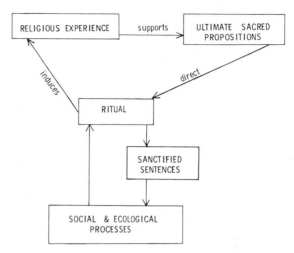

Figure 11.8 Circular relationship linking ultimate sacred propositions, ritual, and religious experience in Rappaport's scheme (see text). In turn, ritual serves as a point of articulation between religion and socioenvironmental processes.

engendered in religious experience. Those things felt in religious experience are felt to be intensely real—in a sense, even more real than those things apprehended in an ordinary discursive, rational manner. "The holy ... not only induces intellectual assent, it enforces emotional commitment" (Geertz 1957:421).

We thus have a circular sequence of the three aspects of religion which are of central importance to the concerns of this paper (see Figure 11.8). Ultimate sacred propositions direct ritual, which induces religious experience, which in turn supports the ultimate sacred propositions. Ritual serves as the point of articulation between religion and the social processes with which we are concerned.

One of the simplest and most direct ways in which this articulation may manifest itself is the aspect of religion noted by Durkheim (1912:474–475): "upholding and reaffirming at regular intervals the collective sentiments and the collective ideas which make its [the social group's] unity and its personality." Thus religion, through ritual, strengthens the bonds uniting members of a single local social group.

A more complex way in which ritual can enter into a social group's regulation of ecological and economic variables is described by Rappaport (1968) in the case of the Tsembaga Maring of highland New Guinea. The ritual cycle of these people directly regulates pig population and distribution of people over land, among other things. An instance of calendric or time-dependent regulation of ecological and economic variables by ritual cycles has been described for the Tewa Indians of the southwestern United States (Ford 1971). In this case, unpredictable inequalities of food production between households are evened out by ritual redistribution of food.

Religion also can be articulated with social processes through *rituals of sanctification*. Rituals of sanctification ensure the acceptance of important messages or conventions, by imparting to these messages or conventions some of the unquestionable nature of the ultimate sacred propositions. To the extent that a message is sanctified, it will be accepted unquestioningly as true. As Rappaport (1971b:30) has noted, to the extent that people accept messages as true, "their responses . . . tend to be predictable." It thus follows that messages likely to be sanctified are those which function to elicit responses that must be predictable so as to permit the orderly operation of society. These messages include both *directives* and several kinds of more general propositions. The importance of the acceptance of directives emanating from some kind of authority is obvious, especially in societies where actual political power is weakly developed, such as the Early Formative cultures of Mesoamerica.

One kind of proposition likely to be sanctified concerns general attitudes, and serves as a general guide to behavior; such propositions are often called *values*. The sanctification of this kind of proposition has long been recognized by anthropologists and sociologists studying religions.

Weber's (1930) elaboration of the "Protestant ethic" involves the sanctification of a particular set of values. Parsons (1966:11) discusses the "legitimation" of this kind of proposition, as well as the kind we discuss next. It is precisely this which Geertz (1957:426–427) is discussing when he says, "Religion, by fusing ethos and world-view, gives a set of social values what they perhaps most need to be coercive: an appearance of objectivity. In sacred rituals and myths values are portrayed not as subjective human preferences but as the imposed conditions for life implicit in a world with a particular structure."

Closely related to the sanctification of values is the sanctification of *persons* and *institutions*. For example, when a chief is said to be descended from a god, he is associated with the ultimate sacred propositions, and some of their unquestionable nature of legitimacy is imparted to his person. Thereafter, whatever statements he may issue also partake of this legitimacy.

Also likely to be sanctified are *messages* containing information that either is unverifiable or requires some special competence for verification. Thus, for example, statements of fact the receiver cannot verify at all (or cannot verify until after he has made his response) are likely to be sanctified.

One of the most important types of message that is apt to receive sanctification concerns social conventions dealing with economic matters—for example, the ways in which goods are distributed among members of a social group. This sort of social convention may seem highly arbitrary, as mentioned earlier. The acceptance of these conventions, however, is crucial to the orderly operation of society. Thus, messages concerning such conventions are very likely to be sanctified, since the effect of sanctification is to "transform the arbitrary into the necessary" (Rappaport 1971b:35). Such messages may be either propositions concerning the social conventions, or directives involved in the execution of the conventions. The nature of these messages varies, depending on the level of control from which they are emanating.

Rappaport (1971b:34) contends that messages emanating from higher levels of control are more abstract. They are thus likely to seem more arbitrary to those who receive them than those emanating from lower levels of control. This comes about since "the range of differences possible in the regulation of the components of a low-order system, such as a production system, is probably narrower than in higher-order systems" (Rappaport 1971b:31). It was noted earlier that a major source of the seeming arbitrariness of social conventions is the recognition of apparently equally feasible alternatives.

The emergence of administration can be viewed as an overlaying of progressively higher-order controls on a basic series of lower-order ones. Thus, as administration emerges, there come to be messages concerning ever-higher orders of control. These messages must seem increasingly arbitrary, and yet their acceptance is increasingly important to the maintenance of orderliness in the operation of the society. It also may be true that the amount of orderliness required by more complex societies is greater. This would be due to an increased dependence upon the actions of others, thus making unpredictable actions more disruptive at the same time as the tolerance for disruption decreases. Thus, the flow of messages likely to be sanctified grows as administration becomes more complex and more comprehensive.

These considerations of religion can be applied profitably to some important social changes that took place before and during the Formative Period in Mesoamerica. These changes include (1) the shift from a migratory way of life to a sedentary one, in which an agricultural base was more important; (2) the emergence of specialized occupational groups on both the intracommunity and the intercommunity levels; (3) dramatic population increase; and (4) a substantial widening of the range of social statuses available for occupation by

members of the society. All these phenomena are touched upon by previous authors in this volume.

The Transition to Sedentary Life

The best data concerning the shift from migratory hunting and gathering to sedentary agricultural village life in Mesoamerica come from the Tehuacán Valley. MacNeish (1964) has proposed a series of hypothetical stages leading to the establishment of permanent villages during the Ajalpan phase (1500–900 B.C.). His scheme involves "wandering microbands" which came together periodically to form "macrobands." These macrobands eventually became "semisedentary," later founding "semipermanent villages." By the end of the Ajalpan phase, substantial numbers of people seem to have lived year-round in permanently established villages. A similar transformation took place in the Valley of Oaxaca by the time of the Tierras Largas phase (1400–1150 B.C.).

A major social change implied by the shift to sedentary village life is a loss of social fluidity. Bands, which are often on the move and are subject to the seasonal coalescing and fragmenting of microbands and macrobands, are socially flexible. This has been reported ethnographically by Woodburn (1968) and Turnbull (1968), to mention only two. Turnbull notes a positive function for such flexibility in a situation where the major decision-making process is one of consensus formation. If the necessary consensus fails to form, the potential for disruption is "defused" by the simple expedient of the separation of the dissenting groups.

In sedentary villages, however, such group fissioning is more difficult. Once sedentary life becomes the rule, each family acquires a greater investment in material goods, which are difficult to move. Once dependence on agriculture has increased to the point that sedentary villages are established, each family also acquires a substantial investment in growing crops. It is not really free to move away at any time as the result of a dispute; it may be forced to remain until after the harvest. Thus, moving away from disruptions can no longer serve as a very effective immediate solution to the problem of maintaining group unity and harmony. New social conventions must evolve concerning the acceptance of decisions affecting the social group and its members. There also must be mechanisms to ensure that these conventions be accepted.

As outlined earlier, such acceptance can be ensured by rituals of sanctification, giving an aura of necessity to conventions that otherwise might seem arbitrary. In the fluid migratory band situation, refusals to accept group decisions are no handicap. A perfectly viable response to a decision with which one disagrees is to move away from it. When this response is rendered less practicable, however, strong mechanisms for ensuring acceptance of group decisions become necessary. Rituals of sanctification are such mechanisms.

A further implication of the switch to sedentary life involves the process of "microenvironment reduction" formulated by Coe and Flannery (1964). In a later paper, they defined two forms of this process. In one case, "the choice made by the band is to concentrate all its exploitive effort on the one resource area which it deems most productive, largely ignoring the others" (Flannery and Coe 1968:270). Flannery (1968a) has since preferred to focus on the "procurement system" rather than the "microenvironment" or "resource area." We can, however, revise his previous formulation in these terms. Thus, the choice just referred to would be to concentrate exploitive effort on a single procurement system, or on a very few procurement systems. The dramatic increase in the proportion of maize in recovered plant remains indicates that such a shift occurred during the Ajalpan phase in Tehuacán (Smith 1967). Although the number of villages is very small, their restriction to the Río Salado floodplain (Mac-Neish, Peterson, and Flannery 1970:239) apparently conforms to the "contagious distribution"'

described by Flannery and Coe (1968). Settlement pattern data from the Valley of Oaxaca are similar. The first sedentary villages, established in Oaxaca by the Tierras Largas phase (1400–1150 B.C.), occur almost exclusively in or adjacent to a riverine alluvium zone where water is available within 3 m of the ground surface. (See Flannery *et al.* 1967; Flannery and Schoenwetter 1970.)

This increased dependence on a reduced number of procurement systems gives increased importance to the regulation of those systems. When a large number of procurement systems are in use, the disruption of a single one is readily counteracted by increased reliance on the others. Such a situation is cited by Lee (1968) for the !Kung Bushmen. During periods of scarcity, their reliance on food sources otherwise not preferred increases. The existence of a stable sedentary way of life, however, necessitates strong mechanisms for preventing the disruption of the reduced number of procurement systems.

This is not to imply that the alternative of foraging to prevent starvation is no longer available after permanent villages have been established; it is simply that, if permanent villages are to remain established, there must be mechanisms that make it seldom necessary to resort to this alternative. Not only specific mechanisms of ecological regulation are involved, but also mechanisms to ensure that these means of ecological regulation will be accepted by all members of the social group. Either direct ritual regulation (of the kind described by Rappaport 1968), or rituals of sanctification ensuring the acceptance of regulatory decisions made by or for the group, can fulfil this need.

These considerations suggest that the establishment of sedentary villages in the Tehuacán and Oaxaca Valleys should have been accompanied by certain changes in the religious system. Although data on ritual in the preceramic hunting-and-gathering era are limited, MacNeish's excavations at Coxcatlán Cave near Tehuacán, Puebla, have provided some examples. Level XV at that site, dating to late in the El Riego phase (ca. 5500–5000 B.C.) yielded a group burial with suggestions that a child might have been sacrificed at the death of an adult:

> During their stay, three extended burials were placed in a pit in the east end of the cave. The burials were those of a child underneath an adult male placed next to a young adult female. Since the chances are slim that all of this "family" of slightly different ages would die naturally at exactly the same time and, further, that the child's skull would be badly smashed, one suspects that there was some sort of dirty work afoot. Is this not perhaps evidence of human sacrifice? The burial further hints that some fairly elaborate burial ritual may have taken place during this twelfth occupation. The pit was lined with grass, and perhaps vegetal food. Remains of some sort of net and cloth wrapping were found with each body. Baskets had been placed both above and below the head and chest regions of each. There is evidence that red paint was sprinkled on the female. The upper portion of the body of the adult male was partially burned after it was laid in the grass-lined pit. [MacNeish 1962:8–9]

Level XIV at the same site, also dating to before 5000 B.C., yielded apparent evidence of child sacrifice and ritual cannibalism:

> In the east end there were two child burials which hint at elaborate burial rituals. Here a large pit had been dug; in it was put the extended body of a child wrapped in a blanket and net. Next, a basket or baskets were placed over the body. The head, a few cervical vertebrae and a string of beads, in a basket covered by another basket, were placed near the shoulders of the headless body. The pit was then partially filled (perhaps mainly with vegetal remains) and a second headless body placed on it. This body was wrapped in a blanket and the legs were flexed or bound inside a net. Baskets were placed over the chest and nine baskets were placed below the feet just above the first burial. The skull (perhaps also in a basket) was then placed in the pit near the right shoulder. Previous to interment, the skull was scraped to remove the flesh, the occipital

> region broken in and the skull burned or roasted—perhaps to boil the brains so they would be more palatable. [MacNeish 1962:9]

The plant and animal remains in Levels XIV and XV date both occupations to the late "wet" or early "dry" season, August–October (Flannery, personal communication). Since this is usually a peak season for wild plant availability, it is of course distinctly possible that these rituals had something to do with wild plant harvests. However, it seems unlikely that they were regular, calendric rituals; for one thing, no similar burials occur in the scores of additional preceramic harvest-season living floors in MacNeish's caves. For another, ethnographic data on hunter–gatherers suggest that such sacrifices are more likely to be ad hoc rituals, possibly related to birth-order rules (say, female infanticide until a male child is born) or propitiatory rites during lean years. What the El Riego phase burials do show is that even preceramic Mesoamerica probably had a substantial body of ritual out of which the great ceremonialism of the Formative could evolve.

Such ad hoc rituals may have contributed to the regulation of population growth (or any number of variables) during the hunting–gathering era, but they do not seem wholly adequate for the cyclic regulation of sedentary agricultural societies. The scheduling of rituals of regulation must be based on the scheduling of the variables they regulate. Rituals taking place at the natural death of some individual are clearly inappropriate. The killing of individuals for the purpose of the rituals we envision would also seem to be precluded, since the nature of the variables to be regulated in early sedentary villages would require rather frequent rituals. Rituals of sanctification also must be thoroughly embedded in the regular cycle of life in the social group (although death rituals can certainly play an important part in rituals of sanctification). In either case, the rituals must involve members of the social group at large. Thus, although the kind of ritual activity known for the El

Figure 11.9 Group of four pottery figurines, deliberately arranged so as to form a scene, buried below the floor of a shed or lean-to attached to an Early Formative house at San José Mogote, Oaxaca. [Excavator: J.W. Rick.]

Riego phase could continue to play a role in sedentary village life, one would expect evidence from the time of the establishment of sedentary villages of increased ritual activity of a kind that would involve the social group at large, and whose occurrence was more frequent and more integrated into the regular life patterns of the social group.

One artifact possibly of use in ritual context is the ceramic figurine. Unfortunately, figurines of the period 1500–1000 B.C. rarely have been found in contexts that would clarify their function. One case that can be cited is Feature 63 from House 16 at San José Mogote, Oaxaca, discovered in 1974 by J. W. Rick (unpublished). In this case, four figurines, apparently forming a scene, had been buried under the floor of a shed or lean-to attached to a house of the San José phase (see Figure 11.9).

Another group of Formative figurines (Figure 11.10) found in what appears to be ritual context comes from a later period. A group of 16 *stone* figurines appeared in Offering 4 at La Venta,

Tabasco, dating to Middle Formative Phase III (Drucker, Heizer, and Squier 1959:152–161). These figurines, along with 6 jade celts, had been set upright in a "hump of reddish-brown sand" under a courtyard floor near the Northeast Platform. They were evidently arranged in such a way as to represent a scene:

> The long slender celts, all of jade, were stood upright edge to edge along the east and southeast edge of an ellipse 20 inches along its north–south diameter, and 14 inches east–west. The figurines were also standing upright. One of them, typically Olmec stylistically, but of very unusual material [granite—Figurine 7], was placed so that it stood with its back against the row of celts. The other 15 figurines, two of which were jade and the rest of serpentine, were placed in front of this figure. A file of four [Figurines 8, 9, 10, 11] was set up as though passing in review from north to south. The 11 other figurines are arranged in a semicircle along the western side of the ellipse, watching. [Drucker, Heizer, and Squier 1959: 152]

The authors of the La Venta report offer several possible interpretations of this scene, but cannot decide between them without more data. Even in the case of the four figures "passing in review," there is no way to decide "whether they are priests who are performing some ritual, or whether they are dancers, or perhaps candidates for some sacrificial rites" (Drucker, Heizer, and Squier 1959:156).

Ethnographic data so far have been of limited utility in interpreting Formative figurines, but the ritual use of pottery figurines by modern lowland Maya and Mixtec peoples has been interpreted as a survival of ancient practices (Villa Rojas 1969: 242; Ravicz and Romney 1969:394).

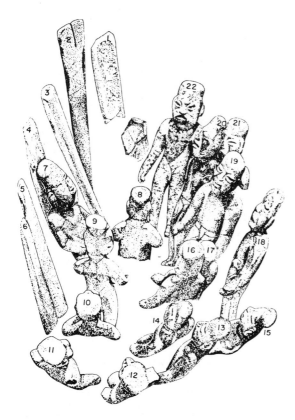

Figure 11.10 Group of 16 stone figurines, deliberately arranged so as to form a scene, buried under a Middle Formative courtyard floor at La Venta, Tabasco. [After Drucker, Heizer, and Squier 1959: Figure 38.]

Although a single clay figurine is known from "preceramic" deposits dating to 2300 B.C. at Zohapilco (Tlapacoya) in the Valley of Mexico (Niederberger 1969), figurines do not become really abundant until after 1500 B.C. Figurines first appear in the Tehuacán Valley during the Ajalpan phase, and in the Valley of Oaxaca during the Tierras Largas phase. Thus, it seems that they first appear in quantity at the time of the establishment of sedentary villages, although it must be noted that the period immediately preceding this is one of the least known in all of Mesoamerican prehistory.

There are nearly four figurine fragments for every thousand sherds recorded by MacNeish, Peterson, and Flannery (1970) from Early Ajalpan deposits. The presence of figurines in relatively large quantities and in deposits of all kinds (at all kinds of sites) indicates that the activity in which they were used was not infrequent, and was of such a nature as to involve all households in a social group. It is this kind of ritual whose increase was predicted for this time period.

Further evidence for an increase in the kind of ritual activity predicted would be the appearance of religious areas or structures within sites from this time period. Once again, we are handicapped by a lack of data on possible ritual areas or structures from the preceding era of hunting and gathering. A single "structure" from the preceramic site of Gheo-Shih in the Valley of Oaxaca, dating to 5000–4000 B.C., provides one possible example (Figure 11.11). Here excavator Frank Hole discovered

> two parallel rows of boulders about 20 meters long. The space between them, which was 7 meters wide, was swept clean and contained virtually no artifacts. To either side of the parallel lines of boulders, however, artifacts were abundant. The boulder lines ended without turning a corner, and their function is unknown. What they most resemble are the borders of a cleared "dance ground," such as characterized macro-band camps of some Great Basin hunting-gathering Indian groups. [Flannery *et al.* 1970:23-24]

Figure 11.11 Gheo-Shih, Oaxaca. Double line of boulders flanking a cleared "dance ground" or possible "public" area 7 by 20 m in extent. Preceramic, 5000–4000 B.C.

Assuming the boulder lines at Gheo-Shih do frame a dance ground, they elicit a conclusion much like the one we have given for the burial rituals of the El Riego phase. The "dances" performed by most hunting–gathering groups are ad hoc affairs, held when unpredictable abundances of wild foods are available (cf. Yengoyan 1972). While undeniably important, such rituals probably would not be adequate for the permanent integration of large sedentary villages.

The lime-plastered, north-oriented buildings already described by Flannery (this chapter) for Tierras Largas phase levels at San José Mogote in the Valley of Oaxaca are a different story (Figure 11.1). Such buildings apparently were replastered (and even rebuilt) over a considerable

time period, and they eventually were replaced by still more substantial adobe structures. They unquestionably differ in form from the ordinary Tierras Largas phase houses. It is possible that they were buildings for public and/or ritual activity, although their various functions have not yet been established conclusively.

In sum, although data on the transition to sedentary life are less adequate than one would like, we can single out two phenomena that probably reflect an evolutionary advance in ritual associated with the integration of large permanent villages. One is permanent "ceremonial" architecture, which does seem to be present from as early as 1400–1300 B.C. Another is the enormous proliferation of ceramic figurines during the period 1500–

500 B.C. Both represent striking innovations when compared with the child sacrifices and possible "dance grounds" of the hunting–gathering era.

The Role of Religion in Social Ranking and Specialization

During the period following the establishment of sedentary villages, the social systems of the Formative continued to become more complex. Data from the Valley of Oaxaca suggest that, during the period 1150–850 B.C., there was a substantial increase in social ranking and in specialization on both intersite and intrasite levels. Burials from this period show decided differences in the quantity of goods included, although the elaborateness of the offerings does not approach that of later times. Part-time craft specialization likely included the working of magnetite, hematite, mica, quartz, and many kinds of marine shell (see Chapter 2). By 1000 B.C., the site of San José Mogote was substantially larger than, and apparently functionally differentiated from, other contemporary sites. San Lorenzo, Veracruz (Coe 1968a,b), was even larger and perhaps more differentiated at the same time period.

To the extent that these social changes indicate the presence of discrete administrative authorities, it is possible that the society of this period was administered, although true statehood is not indicated. Some attention has been devoted by others to the question of whether or not the existence of such specialized subgroups within a single society necessitates direction by discrete authorities. Sanders (1956, 1968) discusses this problem under the heading of "economic symbiosis." He stresses the importance of a stable framework within which goods can be exchanged between specialized groups, especially between those with some degree of geographic separation. Wright (1969) has suggested that an administrative system is the best solution to problems of information processing in a society composed of specialized subgroups.

Some confirmation that these problems may have been met by the institutionalization of administrative authorities during the period 1150–850 B.C. is the size and internal diversity of the site of San José Mogote. This village was substantially larger than any of its neighbors, indeed substantially larger than any other village known in the Valley of Oaxaca for that time period (see Chapter 3). It also seems to have been involved in a much wider range of craft activities than other sites (see Chapter 2). It seems likely that it was an administrative center of some sort for a substantial number of other villages during the time period under consideration. The social changes to be dealt with during this period, then, include increased social ranking, intersite specialization, intrasite specialization, and perhaps also discrete administration.

It was noted earlier that the emergence of discrete administration substantially increases the number of messages flowing within a society which are likely to be sanctified. Interdependence of specialized subgroups increases the dependence upon each other of different segments of the population, and thus increases the importance of predictability in social behavior. Social ranking must increase the apparent arbitrariness of social conventions; surely the designation of high-ranking individuals would seem arbitrary unless sanctified. Thus, all the major social changes that have been discussed for the period 1150–850 B.C. would point to an increased role for rituals of sanctification.

An indication that this, in fact, took place during this period would be an elaboration of structures serving ritual functions. Platforms for public buildings do seem to become more common and more complex after 1000 B.C. They are larger and sometimes stone-faced, as Platforms 1 and 2 at San José Mogote (Figure 11.12) or Platform 4 at Huitzo (Flannery *et al*. 1970). These large adobe platforms with stairways supported massive structures that were almost certainly "temples" in the sense of those described by the Spanish on their arrival in Mexico. The inhabitants of San Lorenzo

Figure 11.12 Dry-laid stone masonry platform with stairway at San José Mogote, Oaxaca. Early Formative, 1000–900 B.C.

and La Venta carried out monumental construction of earthen mounds on an even greater scale. The frequent alignment of such constructions to true north or 8° west of north, depending on the time period involved, is further support for their ceremonial function. Such buildings reflect institutions that must have involved the participation not only of whole villages but also of neighboring communities without public buildings.

In addition to the public buildings that occupied 10–15% of some Early and Middle Formative villages in Oaxaca, one residential household cluster at San José Mogote also had some "painted circles" of possible ritual function (Flannery, this chapter, Figure 11.3). If these unusual features are indeed ceremonial in nature, it raises the question of how their function differed from that of the

public buildings or "temples" in the same village. Actually, ethnographic parallels for household altars in Mesoamerica are abundant (cf. Vogt 1969:83; see discussion in Chapter 2 of this volume). In societies with ranking, members of chiefly lineages may have more elaborate household shrines; a convenient example is provided by the *mdai dap* described by Leach (1954:108) for highland Burma. The *mdai dap* is a shrine to a special spirit to whom the chief is believed to have particular access; the access of the common people to this spirit is through their chief. The effectiveness of this arrangement as a ritual of sanctification is immediately apparent. As Pyne's data suggests (Chapter 9, this volume), Formative people had no shortage of mythological spirits, including the fire-serpent and were-jaguar.

Before examining the ritual artifacts of this period, it will be necessary to consider briefly the nature of ritual artifacts in general. We can expect artifacts used in religious ritual to be objects that would be helpful in inducing religious experience. This applies to artifacts used in rituals of sanctification as well, since, by evoking religious experience, the persons manipulating the artifacts or the messages transmitted in such an event are sanctified. The terms cited earlier, in which Otto (1914) described religious experience, involved contact with something mysterious, awe-inspiring, and "wholly other."

Two categories of physical objects that might help to induce such experience suggest themselves. The first kind includes objects inherently mysterious, different, and foreign to the experience of their observers. This is to say, such objects may be made of strange materials from far away, with properties unlike those of more familiar materials.

The second kind includes objects that, although not necessarily inherently mysterious, are given the required characteristics during their manufacture. They are made into symbolic shapes or decorated with symbols, and thereby take on the mysterious and esoteric properties of the referents of these symbols. If such objects are made into recognizably representational forms, it would be expected that these forms would be something mysterious and awe-inspiring derived from the local mythology. This has been noted, for example, for religious idols in Polynesia which seem "adapted to excite terror rather than inspire confidence in the beholder" (Ellis 1853, Vol. 4:428). Vastokas (1967) has noted that sacred Eskimo spirit masks are formally more abstract than the naturalistic secular masks. Stylized representations, derived from the more literal depictions, also are apt to be used. In this case, certain motifs may stand for the entire concept. The esoteric nature of such stylized symbols makes them ideal for use in rituals of sanctification.

In the preceding section, Flannery presents in tabular form the contextual data on ritual paraphernalia in Oaxaca; such paraphernalia included both naturally exotic and deliberately modified objects. It appears that, as far back as 1150–850 B.C., several regions in Mesoamerica were drawn into a network of exchange, involving the first category of ritual objects just discussed. Exotic material arriving in Oaxaca included lowland turtle shell, fish and stingray spines, shark teeth, and marine shell. Small black mirrors of magnetite were being manufactured in Oaxaca, some of them exported to Veracruz, Morelos, and Nochixtlán (see Pires-Ferreira, Chapter 10, this volume). Ethnographic and early post-Conquest sources also suggest ritual uses for these materials. The Aztec god Tezcatlipoca was identified with a black mirror, although most depictions of that late period suggest the mirror was obsidian (Garibay K. 1958:253–254; Sahagún 1950–, Book 2, Part III:161). Early post-Conquest sources also report ritual bloodletting (Sahagún 1950–, Book 2, Part III:76, 124, 138, 152, 156, 184–185, 203, and illustration 41) for which sharks' teeth and stingray (and other fish) spines evidently were used (Tozzer 1941:113–114; Borhegyi 1961). Turtle shell drums also were used in Aztec rituals (Sahagún 1950–, Book 2, Part III:137), and figurines from the Classic period in the collection of Howard Leigh of Mitla, Oaxaca, show the use of drums made from turtle shell. Conch shells were used as trumpets by Aztec priests (Sahagún 1950–, Book 2, Part III:21, 76–78, 119, 124, 130, 132, 202, 205, and illustration 22) and, in modern times, by the Zapotec of Oaxaca (Nader 1969:355).

Some of these exotic raw materials, such as marine shell, were arriving in the Valley of Oaxaca at least as early as 1350 B.C. While an occasional sea shell reached Oaxaca during the preceramic hunting-and-gathering era, it was not until village life was established that substantial amounts began to arrive. And the flow of exotic goods increased dramatically after 1150 B.C. (Pires-Ferreira, Chapter 10, this volume), perhaps reflecting the increased need for rituals of sanctification.

Also at this time period, several regions within Mesoamerica were drawn into a network involving the use of certain shared symbols. Many of these symbols are featured in the so-called "Olmec" art style of the period 1150–850 B.C. Much attention has been devoted to discussions of the point of origin of the Olmec style (Covarrubias 1957, Coe 1965c, and Wicke 1971, to cite only a few). The argument over exactly where the style originated will not be continued here, since it is not important to the questions raised in this section. Rather, here it is assumed that the *focus* of the Olmec style during the Formative period was the southern Gulf Coast. This assumption is reasonable, since its greatest elaboration seems to have occurred in the Gulf Coast region at precisely this time. The most impressive and largest-scale building projects and the most monumental stone sculpture of the period seem to have occurred at sites in southern Veracruz and Tabasco.

Most of the "Olmec" objects from the Valley of Oaxaca well may have been of ritual use. Some figurines during the period 1150–850 B.C. showed the "baby face" characteristic of the Olmec style. Other aspects of this style are the highly abstracted free-standing motifs of the same period, discussed by Pyne (Chapter 9). These motifs are suited perfectly for use in rituals of sanctification, as noted in the second category of ritual objects discussed earlier. Joralemon (1971) has shown that these very abstract motifs are derived from much more realistic representations of the Olmec "were-jaguar." Discussions of this part-human, part-jaguar being have been central in considerations of the iconography of Olmec art (Coe 1965c). Furst (1968) has dealt with the shaman/jaguar transformation and the question of jaguar ancestry common in ethnographic accounts of the mythology of Mesoamerican and South American Indian groups. He sees strong evidence of such beliefs in Olmec art. Particularly interesting here is his interpretation of the distorted expressions often found on those were-jaguar representations as ecstatic experiences. To him, they convey "the feeling of

some emotional stress almost beyond bearing" (Furst 1968:151). Such a feeling is criterial of religious experience.

Evidence also has been found in Olmec art for the mating between a jaguar and a human female: for example, Monument 1 at Tenochtitlán and Monument 3 at Potrero Nuevo, Veracruz (Stirling 1955). Stirling has suggested that this is the depiction of an origin myth involving the offspring of such a mating. Grove (1970:32) interprets an Olmec-style painting in Guerrero in the same way. Coe (1965c) accepts this notion, and further suggests (Coe 1972) that Olmec "kings" were believed to have descended from the creatures thus created. Although the use of the term "king" is surely an overstatement of the social complexity of the Early Formative period, the utility of such an origin myth in terms of sanctification of authority is obvious. The social position of a highly ranked individual would be secure if this convention were sanctified by his descent from this original human–jaguar mating. Likewise, statements he might issue would be sanctified by partaking of the unquestionable legitimacy of this ultimate sacred proposition. Such a system of sanctification based on descent myths seems to be operating today among the Tzotzil of highland Chiapas (Holland 1964).

We have suggested that social changes in the Valley of Oaxaca in the Early Formative led to an increased need for sanctification by the beginning of the San José phase. An efficient way to meet this need would be a connection with the ultimate sacred propositions of the religious system that apparently was functioning already in this way on the Gulf Coast. This could be accomplished by using the symbols of the Gulf Coast religious system. By the San José phase (1150–850 B.C.), pottery from the Valley of Oaxaca shows extensive usage of symbols derived from the Olmec were-jaguar. Flannery (1968b) has discussed the use of these borrowed symbols as marks of status. Our suggestion here is that some of these symbols functioned to connect those who were entitled to use them to the ultimate sacred propositions of Olmec religion, that is, some individuals were connected to the descendents of the primal jaguar-human pair or perhaps to descendents of other deities such as the fire-serpent. As such, any social conventions establishing these people as high-ranking individuals, and likely administrative authorities, were sanctified. As noted in Pyne's analysis, the fire-serpent and were-jaguar both were important in the San José phase, but in different residential areas. If both were, in fact, used in rituals of sanctification, this fact would tend to support the notion that the need for such rituals increased during this period.

Considerations of religion thus lead us to suggest that a major reason for the sudden diffusion of the Olmec art style throughout Mesoamerica was the increased need for mechanisms of sanctification in various regions owing to internal social evolution. The entire model is summarized in Figure 11.13. Such an explanation seems more coherent with the possible sociopolitical structure of the Early Formative period than the militaristic empire sometimes suggested (Covarrubias 1957:77, 83; Coe 1965c:771, and 1968a:63, 65). It accounts for the nature of the artifacts through which this diffusion is traced. Further, it provides an explanation for why this interregional circulation of ritual paraphernalia should flourish at this particular time, by grounding it in the evolution of social systems in the various regions. Such a causal mechanism is altogether lacking in explanations that rely on the founding of Olmec colonies or the expeditions of an Olmec *pochteca* (Coe 1965b:122–123). Nor does saying that this interregional interaction was due to trade provide such a causal mechanism: It says nothing about why trade in certain kinds of materials suddenly became so important at this particular time. And, finally, the model proposed here provides us with a possible insight into the reasons for the end of this interregional interaction as well (see later discussion).

Desanctification and the Olmec Collapse

The three major centers in the southern Gulf Coast region where the greatest elaboration of the Olmec style took place are San Lorenzo, La Venta, and Tres Zapotes (see Earle, Chapter 7, this volume). The peak of the Olmec development at San Lorenzo seems to have occurred during the Early Formative between 1150 and 900 B.C.; following this phase, the use of the Olmec style came to an abrupt and apparently violent end, with considerable defacement of monuments (Coe 1968a, 1970).

Agreement on the chronology at La Venta has been difficult to reach (see Drucker, Heizer, and

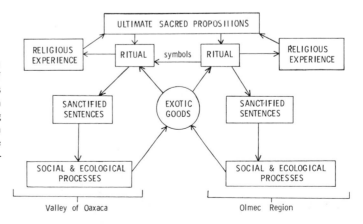

Figure 11.13 Religious interaction between Oaxaca and the Gulf Coast Olmec. Because of shared ultimate sacred propositions, various ritual symbols originating in the Olmec region could be rapidly adopted in Oaxaca. Drawing on its very different environment, each region developed exotic goods (magnetite, marine shell) which were featured in the ritual subsystem of the other region.

Squier 1959; Coe and Stuckenrath 1964; Heizer 1964; Drucker and Heizer 1965, with ensuing "Comment" by Coe and Stuckenrath, and "Final Comment" by Heizer). Redating of radiocarbon samples (Berger, Graham, and Heizer 1967) and more recent excavation (Heizer, Drucker, and Graham 1968; Heizer, Graham, and Napton 1968) have been unable to resolve this controversy, and modern encroachment on the site makes it seem unlikely that further extensive excavation can be successfully carried out there. What does seem clear, however, is that the Olmec development at La Venta reached its peak in the Middle Formative, and that it, too, came to a violent end (Drucker, Heizer, and Squier 1959:229–230). While there is no evidence of violence, Tres Zapotes seems to have reached its climax during the Late Formative or Early Classic, after which the site was abandoned (Drucker 1943:117–123). The Tres Zapotes sequence is much more difficult to integrate with those from other sites (see, for example, Coe 1965a). We can, however, consider the end of Olmec development at San Lorenzo and La Venta in terms of rituals of sanctification and desanctification.

Rappaport (1971b:28) notes that a system of ritual is very "expensive." While rituals of sanctification do ensure the acceptance of social conventions and important messages, those rituals consume a considerable amount of goods and labor. The artifacts used in the rituals of sanctification themselves must be acquired (often from some distance away, as noted before) and/or manufactured. Even more time-consuming is the maintenance of the overall ritual system necessary to support the ultimate sacred propositions upon which the rituals of sanctification depend. Large numbers of ritual artifacts must be produced or acquired, specialized structures must be built, part- or full-time ritual specialists must be supported. As Brumfiel points out in Chapter 8, the demands of administrative specialization may be sufficient to create actual pressure on the land at the village level. Ritual specialization can have the same ef-

fect. Pressures for greater intensity or efficiency of production in turn produce a larger flow of the kind of messages we have identified as likely to be sanctified, as well as greater pressure on the social conventions involved in this production. In the absence of some qualitative change in human motivation, this would imply an increased load on the system of rituals of sanctification, which in turn implies still greater expense. Thus, the circle is complete with increased production requirements leading, by way of increased ritual expense, to still further increases in production requirements.

It may be that, for some technologically limited systems, this is a fatal spiral. So that production can be increased, ritual expenditures are increased, leading to still further increased production requirements. Such a spiral can be fatal because any given environmental or agricultural system has productive limits. The only escape from such a spiral comes in innovation. Two possible forms of such innovation are transformations that render the environment or agricultural technology more productive and/or efficient, and transformations that can ensure the requisite degree of societal orderliness without increasing ritual expenditure. In this latter context, as noted at the outset, application of the coercive political power of a true state government can serve as an alternative to rituals of sanctification. How do these considerations apply to the Gulf Coast during the Formative Period?

Numerous speculations, as well as some serious data, have been applied to the ability of the region surrounding La Venta to support the population necessary to build the structures there (Drucker 1961; Drucker and Heizer 1960; Heizer 1960, 1961, 1962). These data suggest that the immediate environs of La Venta were capable of supporting only a tiny fraction of the number of laborers required to build and maintain the structures. No comparable estimates have been made for the manpower necessary to build the earthen mounds and platforms at San Lorenzo. Coe (1968a:57–58; 1968b:7) estimates the population of San Lorenzo as on the order of 1000 persons, which might include only 200–300 able-bodied men. He further suggests that "it would have required, according to our own experience in moving large monuments, more than 1000 men to have dragged Monument 20 to its present resting place" (Coe 1968a:59). Coe goes on to conclude: "These centers were drawing upon a vastly larger support area with an untold number of inhabitants, a conclusion also reached by Heizer and Drucker in their study of La Venta" (1968a:59). Even if Coe's figures are overestimates, it seems likely that major Olmec centers depended on a rather large hinterland from which considerable travel time was required in order to reach La Venta or San Lorenzo.

It is therefore possible that two conflicting demographic processes, one centrifugal and the other centripetal, were operating on major Olmec centers. Despite the rich, localized cropland available on river levees near San Lorenzo (see Rossmann, Chapter 4), much of its hinterland was tropical forest. The centrifugal tendency of tropical forest cultivators has long been noted in the literature (e.g., Meggers 1954:807). Thus, while the Coatzacoalcos levees probably enabled 1000 persons to nucleate at San Lorenzo, most of the hinterland villages on which it depended for labor must have been subject to the centrifugal forces of tropical forest agriculture. We say this with the caveat offered by Ferdon (1959), that any generalization about the tropical forest must be modified by consideration of the subsistence system(s) actually in use.

This centrifugal tendency, dispersing population from San Lorenzo, would have been directly opposed to the centripetal tendency generally associated with complex social systems. The centripetal "pull" of San Lorenzo, with its massive labor requirements, might have been as great as that seen in Late Formative highland centers, where increased population density and nucleation occurred (see Chapters 3 and 8). The increasing amounts of labor required for public construction and ritual might tend to concentrate people more

and more heavily in the immediate environs of major centers. There is some reason to believe that this happened at San Lorenzo: Three nucleated villages totaling 80 ha, with an estimated population of 2500 persons, all occurred within 2–8 km of each other. This complex of three sites—San Lorenzo, Tenochtitlán, and Potrero Nuevo—represents the largest single concentration of population known from Early Formative Mesoamerica (Marcus, Chapter 3, this volume).

Even in an area of rich levee soils, such a concentration of population might reach levels that are maladaptive in ecological terms. The food requirements of such an 80-ha complex alone would give it little or no reserve against environmental fluctuation. Coe (1969) cites catastrophic flooding in the San Lorenzo area which may periodically, unpredictably, and substantially reduce the amount of prime agricultural land in a given year.

For this reason, control hierarchies dependent on sanctification may, by their own tendency to concentrate population, render themselves incapable of regulating the very social, economic, and environmental variables in terms of which their function was originally defined. "The willingness, indeed the ability, of the members of a congregation to affirm through religious experience the ultimate sacred propositions which sanctify the control hierarchy may be in considerable measure a function of the effectiveness of the hierarchy in maintaining equilibria in and among those variables which define their material well-being in the long run" (Rappaport 1969:43). Thus, if the sanctified Olmec hierarchy, through its tendency to concentrate population, exposed that population to calamity induced by periodic environmental fluctuation, the population may have been rendered periodically unable to support the entire ritual system.

The Effects of Cognitive Inconsistency

In order to examine further the mechanisms of such an eventuality, some psychological implications of sanctification may be considered. The direct effect of an environmental calamity such as that just described would be to prevent the carrying out of certain ritual activities, the prescriptions for which were derived from the ultimate sacred propositions. For example, it might be impossible to come to the ceremonial center for some ritual due to the increased amount of labor required to secure food.

Cognitive consistency theories are relevant to the effects of such an action. Cognitive consistency theories

> postulate a basic "need" for consistency. Some stress a basic "need" for everyone to be personally consistent; others emphasize the maintenance of consistency between attitudes, between behaviors, and among attitudes and behaviors; and still others emphasize the perception of the world in a consistent, unified manner. Usually most of the theorists further assume that the presence of inconsistency produces "psychological tension," or at least is uncomfortable, and in order to reduce this tension, one "rearranges" his psychological world to produce consistency. [Kiesler, Collins, and Miller 1969:155]

Gerard (1968:456) stresses the behavioral implications of cognitive consistency theory and the need to "maintain an unequivocal behavioral orientation." Inconsistency thus arises when a person does something inconsistent with his beliefs. The failure to perform some ritually specified action, for example, can give rise to cognitive inconsistency.

That this inconsistency can be quite intense is indicated by considerations of cognitive ramification dealt with by Weick (1968). A system of religious beliefs would seem almost the ultimate case of a "maximally interconnected" or "highly ramified" cognitive system. By "highly ramified," Weick means the various beliefs that make up the system have numerous links to each other; they form a group of beliefs with a very high degree of interdependence. Weick (1968:513) notes that "highly ramified systems are relatively immune to

inconsistent elements, but once they intrude, the system is vulnerable and discomfort is substantial." Thus, the economic necessity of performing in contradiction to some ritual prescription would be a source of cognitive inconsistency on a grand scale.

Festinger (1957:18–24) outlines three ways in which "cognitive elements" may be modified so as to eliminate or reduce inconsistency resulting from a disconformity between belief and behavior. First, a cognitive element relative to the behavior may be changed. This involves either changing the behavior or refusing to believe that it has occurred. In the case of the Gulf Coast, the former may have been impossible; the latter involves a breach with reality which sometimes occurs (Festinger, Riecken, and Schacter 1956), but only very rarely. Second, a new cognitive element may be added to the system to account for the inconsistent behavior. This is, however, exceedingly difficult in a highly ramified system, since any new element must fit into the entire complex pattern of interlinked beliefs. Thus, this alternative may be a logical impossibility. Third, the inconsistent beliefs may be changed. If this occurs, it seems almost inevitable that the complete collapse of the highly ramified belief system must ensue.

If, for example, the socioeconomic system upon which San Lorenzo depended were contingent upon rituals of sanctification, the collapse of the belief system would entail the collapse of the socioeconomic system as well. The abrupt stoppage in monumental works at San Lorenzo at the end of the San Lorenzo phase (Coe 1968a, 1970) indicates that such a collapse may, in fact, have occurred. If the alternative chosen to eliminate the cognitive inconsistency (resulting from failure to perform a ritually specified activity) involved the collapse of the belief system, the elimination would not be complete as long as elements of this belief system remained. The continued presence of such monumental artifacts of the old rituals of sanctification as the huge stone sculptures of San Lorenzo would serve as a continued source of cognitive inconsistency. The destruction of these monuments would, in itself, be a ritual act communicating the final demise of the belief system upon which their existence was contingent.

A similar destruction of religious sculpture following massive desanctification in Hawaii in 1819 has been noted by Ellis (1853, Vol. 4:15–16):

> In our travels among the islands, we have seldom passed any steep or dangerous paths, at the commencement or termination of which we have not seen these images, with heaps of offerings lying before them.... The natives who accompanied us in our excursions ... usually overturned the idols, battered them with stone, or rolled them down the precipice or passage which they were supposed to defend.

Since Ellis was a missionary, it is relevant that he also notes that "this action was never the consequence of our directions, and seldom received our approbation, for we were not anxious to become iconoclasts" (1853, Vol. 4:16). In the light of cognitive consistency and sanctification, such destruction of religious sculptures by the inhabitants of chiefdoms in Hawaii or the Formative Gulf Coast is not unexpected.

After the collapse of San Lorenzo, it is possible that La Venta underwent a similar cycle of development (Table 11.5). Major building programs at La Venta seem to have reached their peak after the collapse at San Lorenzo, and there is evidence of an eventual violent collapse at La Venta as well, including similar mutilation of monumental sculptures (Drucker, Heizer, and Squier 1959:229–230).

Although La Venta rose to prominence mainly after the demise of San Lorenzo, it is not simply a case of replacement. Other forces were at work which suggest further social evolution during Middle Formative times. Changes in the relationship between Oaxaca and the Gulf Coast can serve as a convenient example. The period 1150–850 B.C. was one of considerable long-distance trade between the two areas, in magnetite, pottery, and possibly obsidian (Pires-Ferreira, Chapter 10, this volume).

TABLE 11.5 Relative Chronology of Phases at San Lorenzo, Veracruz, and La Venta, Tabasco[a]

Date B.C.	San Lorenzo	La Venta
400—		
		* * * * * *
500—	Palangana	
		Phase IV
600—		
	(Hiatus in occupation)	Phase III
700—		
800—	Nacaste	Phase II
900—	* * * * * * *	
	San Lorenzo B	Phase I
1000—	- - - - - - - - - - - - - - -	
	San Lorenzo A	
1100—		
1200—	Chicharras	

[a]After Coe (1970). Asterisks indicate periods of defacement of stone monuments according to the excavators.

Olmec motifs on Oaxaca pottery reached their peak at this time, with considerable emphasis on the fire-serpent and were-jaguar. In addition to these references to Coe's "reconstructed" ultimate origin myth (see the introduction to this chapter), the black iron mirrors may be referable to one or all of the four Tezcatlipocas in the same primeval myth.

The situation changed drastically between 850–500 B.C. As La Venta rose to prominence, long-distance trade dwindled. Magnetite became unimportant, although the Olmec now made large parabolic mirrors of local ilmenite and hematite. Jade and serpentine appeared for the first time in quantity. Olmec motifs rapidly disappeared from Oaxaca pottery. At the very time of La Venta's apogee, the Olmec ritual impact on the Valley of Oaxaca lessened. The implication is that far-reaching changes, perhaps affecting even the ultimate sacred propositions, now separated the two areas. The Valley of Oaxaca went on to achieve true statehood, based on increased use of actual power, during the period 500–100 B.C. (Flannery *et al.* 1967).

Concluding Remarks

It has thus been proposed that the circular process of increased production requirements and rituals of sanctification led to a maladaptive concentration of population near San Lorenzo. The decreased resistance of this population to environmental fluctuation led eventually to massive desanctification, which resulted in the sudden and violent end to the manufacture of ritual artifacts and structures. It should be noted that there is no suggestion here that some "natural" catastrophe caused the collapse of San Lorenzo or La Venta. The suggestion is rather that the control hierarchy whose function was the regulation of social, economic, and ecological variables malfunctioned to such an extent that normal long-term environmental fluctuation set in motion a *social* catastrophe.

If this hypothesis is correct, settlement pattern data should show increasing concentration of population in the San Lorenzo area up through the San Lorenzo B phase, with subsequent dispersal. Likewise, settlements should tend to congregate around La Venta up through Phase IV and then shift outward. In the case of San Lorenzo, there is evidence for dense settlement (an estimated 2500 persons in 3 sites only a few kilometers apart) during the San Lorenzo phase. In the case of La Venta, Sisson (1970) has noted a southward and eastward shift in settlement (away from La Venta) in the Chontalpa region at approximately the right time. Further surveys are needed, however, especially in the areas surrounding both La Venta and

San Lorenzo, and the ceramic sequence must be refined on an area-wide level so that all sites can be dated more accurately. If such a concentration and later dispersal of settlements emerges from survey data, comparison with land productivity figures and site-catchment analyses might indicate whether or not this concentration had reached such an intensity as to render the population vulnerable to sudden environmental fluctuation. Desanctification, under these circumstances, might be one harbinger of the rise of later societies with integrative mechanisms of greater capacity.

References

Adams, R. McC.
    1966   *The evolution of urban society*. Chicago: Aldine.
Berger, R., J. A. Graham, and R. F. Heizer
    1967   A reconsideration of the age of the La Venta site. *Contributions of the University of California Archaeological Research Facility* No. 3:1–24.
Bierstedt, R.
    1950   An analysis of social power. *American Sociological Review* 15:730–738.
Binford, L. R.
    1968   Post-Pleistocene adaptations. In *New perspectives in archeology*, edited by S. R. Binford and L. R. Binford. Chicago: Aldine. Pp. 313–341.
Borhegyi, S. F.
    1961   Shark teeth, stingray spines, and shark fishing in ancient Mexico and Central America. *Southwestern Journal of Anthropology* 17:273–296.
Carneiro, R. F.
    1970   A theory of the origin of the state. *Science* 169:733–738.
Caso, A.
    1928   Las estelas zapotecas. *Monografías del Museo Nacional de Arqueología, Historia y Etnografía*. Mexico, D.F.
Coe, M. D.
    1965a   Archaeological synthesis of southern Veracruz and Tabasco. In *Handbook of Middle American Indians*, vol. 3, edited by R. Wauchope and G. R. Willey. Austin: University of Texas Press. Pp. 679–715.

1965b *The jaguar's children: Pre-classic central Mexico*. New York: Museum of Primitive Art.

1965c The Olmec style and its distribution. In *Handbook of Middle American Indians*, vol. 3, edited by R. Wauchope and G. R. Willey. Austin: University of Texas Press. Pp. 739–775.

1968a San Lorenzo and the Olmec civilization. In *Dumbarton Oaks Conference on the Olmec*, edited by E. P. Benson. Washington, D.C.: Dumbarton Oaks. Pp. 41–78.

1968b Map of San Lorenzo, an Olmec site in Veracruz, Mexico. Dept. of Anthropology, Yale University, New Haven, Conn.

1969 Photogrammetry and the ecology of the Olmec civilization. Paper read at Working Conference on Aerial Photography and Anthropology, Cambridge, Mass., 10–12 May 1969. Mimeograph.

1970 The archaeological sequence at San Lorenzo. *Contributions of the University of California Archaeological Research Facility* No. 8:21–34.

1972 Olmec jaguars and Olmec kings. In *The cult of the feline*, edited by E. P. Benson. Washington, D.C.: Dumbarton Oaks. Pp. 1–12.

Coe, M. D., and K. V. Flannery
1964 Microenvironments and Mesoamerican prehistory. *Science* 143:650–654.

Coe, W. R., and R. Stuckenrath
1964 A review of La Venta, Tabasco and its relevance to the Olmec problem. *Kroeber Anthropological Society Papers* No. 31:1–43.

Covarrubias, M.
1957 *Indian art of Mexico and Central America*. New York: Alfred A. Knopf.

Drucker, P.
1943 Ceramic sequences at Tres Zapotes, Veracruz, Mexico. *Bulletin* No. 140. Bureau of American Ethnology, Smithsonian Institution, Washington, D.C.

1952 La Venta, Tabasco: A study of Olmec ceramics and art. *Bulletin* No. 153. Bureau of American Ethnology, Smithsonian Institution, Washington, D.C.

1961 The La Venta support area. *Kroeber Anthropological Society Papers* No. 25:59–72. Berkeley, Calif.

Drucker, P., and R. F. Heizer
1960 A study of the milpa system of La Venta island and its archaeological implications. *Southwestern Journal of Anthropology* 16:36–45.

1965 Commentary on W. R. Coe and Robert Stuckenrath's review of "Excavations at La Venta, Tabasco, 1955." *Kroeber Anthropological Society Papers* No. 33:37–70. Berkeley, Calif.

Drucker, P., R. F. Heizer, and R. J. Squier
1959 Excavations at La Venta, Tabasco, 1955. *Bulletin* No. 170. Bureau of American Ethnology, Smithsonian Institution, Washington, D.C.

Durkheim, Emile
1912 *The elementary forms of the religious life*, translated by J. W. Swain. New York: Free Press edition, 1965.

Ellis, W.
1853 *Polynesian researches during a residence of nearly eight years in the Society and Sandwich Islands*. London: Henry G. Bohn.

Ferdon, E. M.
1959 Agricultural potential and the development of cultures. *Southwestern Journal of Anthropology* 15:1–19.

Festinger, L.
1957 *A theory of cognitive dissonance*. Palo Alto: Stanford University Press.

Festinger, L., H. W. Riecken, and S. Schacter
1956 *When prophecy fails*. Minneapolis: University of Minnesota Press.

Flannery, K. V.
1968a Archeological systems theory and early Mesoamerica. In *Anthropological archeology in the Americas*, edited by B. J. Meggers. Washington, D.C.: Anthropological Society of Washington. Pp. 67–87.

1968b The Olmec and the Valley of Oaxaca: A model for inter-regional interaction in Formative times. In *Dumbarton Oaks Conference on the Olmec*, edited by E. P. Benson. Washington, D.C.: Dumbarton Oaks. Pp. 79–110.

Flannery, K. V., and M. D. Coe
1968 Social and economic systems in Formative Mesoamerica. In *New perspectives in archeology*, edited by S. R. Binford and L. R. Binford. Chicago: Aldine. Pp. 267–283.

Flannery, K. V., A. V. T. Kirkby, M. J. Kirkby, and A. W. Williams, Jr.
1967 Farming systems and political growth in ancient Oaxaca. *Science* 158:445–454.

Flannery, K. V., and J. Schoenwetter
1970 Climate and man in Formative Oaxaca. *Archaeology* 23:144–152.

Flannery, K. V., M. Winter, S. Lees, J. Neely, J. Schoenwetter, S. Kitchen, and J. C. Wheeler
1970 Preliminary archeological investigations in the Valley of Oaxaca, Mexico, 1966–1969. Mime-

ographed preliminary report. Ann Arbor, Mich.

Ford, R. I.
1971   An ecological perspective on the eastern Pueblos. In *New perspectives on the eastern Pueblos*, edited by A. Ortiz. Albuquerque: University of New Mexico Press. Pp. 1–17.

Furst, P. T.
1968   The Olmec were-jaguar motif in the light of ethnographic reality. In *Dumbarton Oaks Conference on the Olmec*, edited by E. P. Benson. Washington, D.C.: Dumbarton Oaks. Pp. 143–174.

Garibay K., A. M.
1958   Veinte himnos sacros de los Nahuas. *Fuentes Indígenas de la Cultura Náhuatl, Informantes de Sahagún* No. 2. Univ. Nacional Autónoma de Mexico.

Geertz, C.
1957   Ethos, world-view and the analysis of sacred symbols. *Antioch Review* 17:421–437.

Gerard, H. B.
1968   Basic features of commitment. In *Theories of cognitive consistency: A sourcebook*, edited by R. P. Abelson, E. Aronson, W. J. McGuire, T. M. Newcomb, M. J. Rosenberg, and P. H. Tannenbaum. Chicago: Rand McNally. Pp. 456–463.

Grove, D. C.
1970   The Olmec paintings of Oxtotitlan Cave, Guerrero, Mexico. *Dumbarton Oaks Studies in Pre-Columbian Art and Archaeology* No. 6. Washington, D.C.: Dumbarton Oaks.

Heizer, R. F.
1960   Agriculture and the theocratic state in lowland southeastern Mexico. *American Antiquity* 26:215–222.
1961   Inferences on the nature of Olmec society based upon data from the La Venta site. *Kroeber Anthropological Society Papers* No. 25:43–57. Berkeley, Calif.
1962   The possible sociopolitical structure of the La Venta Olmecs. *Proceedings, International Congress of Americanists, Vienna, 1960*, Vienna: Verlag Ferdinand Berger, Horn. Pp. 310–317.
1964   Some interim remarks on the Coe-Stuckenrath review. *Kroeber Anthropological Society Papers* No. 31:45–50. Berkeley, Calif.

Heizer, R. F., P. Drucker, and J. A. Graham
1968   Investigations at La Venta, 1967. *Contributions of the University of California Archaeological Research Facility* No. 5:1–34.

Heizer, R. F., J. A. Graham, and L. K. Napton
1968   The 1968 investigations at La Venta. *Contributions of the University of California Archaeological Research Facility* No. 5:127–205.

Holland, W. R.
1964   Contemporary Tzotzil cosmological concepts as a basis for interpreting prehistoric Maya civilization. *American Antiquity* 29:301–306.

James, W.
1903   *The varieties of religious experience*. New York: Mentor edition, 1958.

Joralemon, P. D.
1971   A study of Olmec iconography. *Dumbarton Oaks Studies in Pre-Columbian Art and Archaeology* No. 7 Washington, D.C.: Dumbarton Oaks.

Kiesler, C. A., B. E. Collins, and N. Miller.
1969   *Attitude change: A critical analysis of theoretical approaches*. New York: John Wiley.

Leach, E. R.
1954   *Political systems of highland Burma*. Boston: Beacon Press edition, 1964.

Lee, R. B.
1968   What hunters do for a living, or, How to make out on scarce resources. In *Man the hunter*, edited by R. B. Lee and I. DeVore. Chicago: Aldine. Pp. 30–48.

MacNeish, R. S.
1962   *Second annual report of the Tehuacán archaeological-botanical project*. R. S. Peabody Foundation for Archaeology, Andover, Mass.
1964   Ancient Mesoamerican civilization. *Science* 143:531–537.
1967   A summary of the subsistence. In *The prehistory of the Tehuacán Valley*. Vol. 1. *Environment and subsistence*, edited by D. S. Byers. Austin: University of Texas Press. Pp. 290–309.

MacNeish, R. S., A. Nelken-Terner, and I. W. Johnson
1967   *The prehistory of the Tehuacán Valley*. Vol. 2. *Nonceramic artifacts*. Austin: University of Texas Press.

MacNeish, R. S., F. A. Peterson, and K. V. Flannery
1970   *The prehistory of the Tehuacán Valley*. Vol. 3. *Ceramics*. Austin: University of Texas Press.

Marcus, J.
n.d.   The iconography of militarism at Monte Albán and neighboring sites. In *The origins of religious art and iconography in Pre-Classic Mesoamerica*, edited by H. B. Nicholson. In press.

Meggers, B. J.
 1954 Environmental limitation on the development of culture. *American Anthropologist* 56:801-824.
Mencken, H. L. (Editor)
 1949 *A Mencken chrestomathy*. New York: Alfred A. Knopf.
Nader, L.
 1969 The Zapotec of Oaxaca. In *Handbook of Middle American Indians*, vol. 7, edited by R. Wauchope and E. Z. Vogt. Austin: University of Texas Press. Pp. 329-359.
Niederberger, C. V.
 1969 Paleoecología humana y playas lacustres post-Pleistocénicas en Tlapacoya. *Boletín* No. 37:19-24, Instituto Nacional de Antropología e Historia, Mexico, D.F.
Nuttall, Z.
 1904 A penitential rite of the ancient Mexicans. *Papers of the Peabody Museum of American Archaeology and Ethnology* Vol. I, no. 7. Harvard University, Cambridge, Mass.
Otto, R.
 1914 *The idea of the holy*, translated by J. W. Harvey. London: Oxford University Press edition, 1958.
Parsons, T.
 1966 *Societies: Evolutionary and comparative perspectives*. Englewood Cliffs, N.J.: Prentice-Hall.
Piña Chán, R.
 1955 *Las culturas preclásicas de la cuenca de Mexico*. Fondo de Cultura Económica, Mexico, D.F.
Rappaport, R. A.
 1968 *Pigs for the ancestors: Ritual in the ecology of a New Guinea people*. New Haven, Conn.: Yale University Press.
 1969 *Sanctity and adaptation*. Paper read at Burg Wartenstein Symposium No. 44, "The Moral and Ethical Structure of Human Adaptation." New York: Wenner-Gren Foundation (multilith).
 1971a Ritual, sanctity, and cybernetics. *American Anthropologist* 73:59-76.
 1971b The sacred in human evolution. *Annual Review of Ecology and Systematics* 2:23-44.
Ravicz, R., and A. K. Romney
 1969 The Mixtec. In *Handbook of Middle American Indians*, vol. 7, edited by R. Wauchope and E. Z. Vogt. Austin: University of Texas Press. Pp. 367-399.

Sahagún, B. de
 1950- *Historia general de las cosas de Nueva España*, translated by A. J. O. Anderson and C. E. Dibble. Santa Fe, N.M.: The School of American Research and the University of Utah.
Sanders, W. T.
 1956 The central Mexican symbiotic region: A study in prehistoric settlement patterns. In *Prehistoric settlement patterns in the New World*, edited by G. R. Willey. *Viking Fund Publications in Anthropology* No. 23. New York: Wenner-Gren. Pp. 115-127.
 1968 Hydraulic agriculture, economic symbiosis, and the evolution of states in central Mexico. In *Anthropological archeology in the Americas*, edited by B. J. Meggers. Washington, D.C.: Anthropological Society of Washington. Pp. 88-107.
Sanders, W. T., and B. J. Price
 1968 *Mesoamerica: The evolution of a civilization*. New York: Random House.
Sisson, E. B.
 1970 Settlement patterns and land use in the northwestern Chontalpa, Tabasco, Mexico: A progress report. *Cerámica de Cultura Maya et al.* No. 6:41-54.
Smith, C. E., Jr.
 1967 Plant remains. In *The prehistory of the Tehuacán Valley*. Vol. 1. *Environment and subsistence*, edited by D. S. Byers. Austin: University of Texas Press. Pp. 220-255.
Stirling, M. W.
 1955 Stone monuments of the Río Chiquito, Veracruz, Mexico. *Bulletin* No. 157 (*Anthropological Paper* No. 43). Bureau of American Ethnology, Smithsonian Institution, Washington, D.C.
Tozzer, A. M. (Editor)
 1941 Landa's Relación de las cosas de Yucatán. *Papers of the Peabody Museum of American Archaeology and Ethnology* Vol. XVIII. Harvard University, Cambridge, Mass.
Turnbull, C. M.
 1968 The importance of flux in two hunting societies. In *Man the hunter*, edited by R. B. Lee and I. DeVore. Chicago: Aldine. Pp. 132-137.
Vaillant, G. C.
 1941 *Aztecs of Mexico*. New York: Doubleday, Doran.
Varner, D. M., and B. A. Brown
 1972 Mexican Indian masks of Oaxaca. *The Mus-*

tang 14(6):1–6. Texas Memorial Museum, Austin.

Vastokas, J. M.
1967   The relation of form to iconography in Eskimo masks. *The Beaver, Magazine of the North* 298 (Autumn no.):26–31.

Villa Rojas, A.
1969   Maya lowlands: The Chontal, Chol, and Kekchi. In *Handbook of Middle American Indians*, vol. 7, edited by R. Wauchope and E. Z. Vogt. Austin: University of Texas Press. Pp. 230–243.

Vogt, E. Z.
1969   *Zinacantan: A Maya community in the highlands of Chiapas*. Cambridge, Mass.: Belknap Press (Harvard University).

Weber, M.
1930   *The Protestant ethic and the spirit of capitalism*. New York: Scribner's.

Weick, K. E.
1968   Processes of ramification among cognitive links. In *Theories of cognitive consistency: A sourcebook*, edited by R. F. Abelson, E. Aronson, W. J. McGuire, T. M. Newcomb, M. J. Rosenberg, and P. H. Tannenbaum. Chicago: Rand McNally. Pp. 512–519.

Wicke, C. R.
1971   *Olmec: An early art style of Precolumbian Mexico*. Tucson: University of Arizona Press.

Wittfogel, K. A.
1938   Die theorie der Orientalischen Gesellschaft. *Zeitschrift für Sozial Forschung* 7:90–122. (Revised and reprinted in English in *Readings in Anthropology*, edited by M. Fried. Vol. II. New York: Thomas Y. Crowell. Pp. 94–113.

1956   The hydraulic civilizations. In *Man's role in changing the face of the earth*, edited by W. L. Thomas. Chicago: University of Chicago Press. Pp. 152–164.

1957   *Oriental despotism: A comparative study of total power*. New Haven, Conn.: Yale University Press.

Woodburn, J.
1968   Stability and flexibility in Hadza residential groupings. In *Man the hunter*, edited by R. B. Lee and I. DeVore. Chicago: Aldine. Pp. 103–110.

Wright, H. T.
1969   The administration of rural production in an early Mesopotamian town. *Anthropological Papers* No. 38. Museum of Anthropology, University of Michigan, Ann Arbor.

Yengoyan, A. A.
1972   Ritual and exchange in aboriginal Australia: An adaptive interpretation of male initiation rites. In *Social exchange and interaction*, edited by E. M. Wilmsen. *Anthropological Papers* No. 46:5–9. Museum of Anthropology, University of Michigan, Ann Arbor.

Chapter 12

A PRAYER FOR AN ENDANGERED SPECIES

KENT V. FLANNERY

Let him who is without sin cast the first stone. [John 8:7]

The time has now come to conclude our parable of the Real Mesoamerican Archeologist, the Great Synthesizer, and the Skeptical Graduate Student. If at times I have seemed too harsh in my treatment of them, let me repeat what I said at the outset: All three characters reside in all of us. In earlier and more innocent years, I happily committed every sin I have attributed to them. Rolling out of the Jeep every morning to take another biased sample, sticking a phone booth into an unknown site, removing an endless stream of arbitrary 20-cm levels, bad-mouthing the very professors from whom I had learned the most. And archeology has never been more fun.

I did not want to submit this book to a publisher until R.M.A., his student, and the Great Synthesizer had read it over and given me their constructive criticism. I got a copy of the manuscript to them in time for the anthropology meetings in Mexico City. We met in the G.S.' room in the

María Isabel. I had not been so nervous since my thesis defense.

The Great Synthesizer put me right at ease. "It's splendid," he said. "I've weighed the manuscript, and it must be a full 7 lb. There are only two or three spelling errors, and they're minor. You know, under different circumstances, it would have made an acceptable library dissertation."

The Skeptical Graduate Student shuffled his feet. "I liked some of the papers, like Plog's on sampling and Reynolds' on Markov processes," he said, "but your editing is really heavy-handed. A good editor never lets his own style intrude."

I looked at the Real Mesoamerican Archeologist. "And what did *you* get out of it?" I asked. "What did it tell you about Formative villages?"

"Well, to be honest with you . . . you know, I've been so busy this term—" R.M.A. explained—"to tell you the truth, I only read the funny parts."

"What funny parts?" asked S.G.S., with genuine

bewilderment.

R.M.A. glared at him. "I think you've just put your finger on the major problem with the New Archeology," he muttered.

The Great Synthesizer cleared his throat.

"If I may," he said, "I'd like to run through what I got out of the book. Sort of a trial balloon."

There was a respectful silence.

"If I understand young Winter correctly," said the Great S., "the nuclear family was the basic unit of residence, production, storage, and consumption in the early Mesoamerican village. There was a sexual division of labor which, as you suggest, may be reflected in a division of the house into men's and women's work areas. All households did some agriculture, some hunting or fishing or gathering, but crafts varied tremendously from house to house and village to village. The household area included a lot of open space outdoors, and there may have been courtyards shared with other households.

"Linking households within a village were things like dance societies, which crosscut families. And there were descent lines of some sort, perhaps tracing ancestry from mythical beings like the were-jaguar or fire-serpent. Children, young girls, and some adults were buried around the house, but most adults were buried in cemetery areas. If we knew more about why some were extended east–west and some north–south, among other things, we might know more about the groups they belonged to after initiation. As Ms. Pyne suggests, certain residential areas may have been more strongly associated with a given mythical being than others, and some descent groups probably spanned several villages. That there may have been some degree of ranking among descent lines seems clear from the differences in houses, access to exotic goods, and participation in ritual—consider the difference between jade stingray spines, real stingray spines, and imitations. Yet the houses of higher-status residents could at first occur anywhere in the village, according to Whalen.

"Most exchange was reciprocal, and there was a whopping amount of long-distance trade. But your people seem to have evidence for several different types of exchange, including some pooling and redistribution of obsidian. I was struck by the way long-distance trade in some products dwindled, though, as redistribution increased. It gives some support to Drennan's view that the social hierarchy was at first supported by rituals of sanctification that required great quantities of exotic goods, labor, cannibalism, autosacrifice, public architecture, and so on, some of which was to change with the evolution of real political power.

"That brings us to the macrostructure, the overall settlement pattern. If your people are to be believed, there were whole networks of villages that used a common ceremonial–civic center, and shared a great deal of ceramic design for hundreds of years. At the same time, the villages in those networks spaced themselves at intervals in excess of what agricultural considerations required, apparently in response to some rules of 'social distance' we don't fully understand. Those rules, however, allowed a certain leeway so that villages could take advantage of local environmental factors in picking a location. Each village seems to have used a series of concentric catchment circles, the inner ones largely agricultural and exclusive, the outer ones largely for wild products shared with neighboring villages. And virtually all villages were underproductive in terms of local carrying capacity.

"If we add some quantitative flesh to the qualitative skeleton I've just given you, here's the spatial model we come up with. Individual households were kept about 20–40 m apart. A typical 1–3-ha hamlet might have 8–12 households. A village of 20 ha was large; a village of 50 ha was huge. Such huge communities had a growth pattern very different from the typical hamlet, and they were usually at one end of a very discontinuous size distribution. Evidently, they provided a whole range of services not available in smaller villages.

"Rarely did villages settle within a kilometer of a

neighbor, except in the case of really tiny settlements, like those on the Guatemalan Coast (and those may have been little more than extended households). Unless one village was an outlying *barrio* of another, it was more common for sites to lie at least 3 km apart. For example, Early Formative communities in the Valley of Oaxaca were usually 5 km apart. Those in central Chiapas tended to have neighboring villages at intervals of 4, 7, and 11 miles, which suggests a 7-km spacing. Each of those settlements probably did most of its farming within 1 km of the village, but maintained exclusive rights to a larger area with a 2-3-km radius.

"As population grew, the settlement system became complex, with a hierarchy of settlement types like hamlet, village, regional center, and so on. Most settlements had less than 100 persons, and even the largest had only a few thousand until Middle Formative times. The sites on the upper tier of the hierarchy, as some of your studies show, obeyed spacing rules different from the hamlets. They showed a kind of regular spacing which suggests competition—perhaps competition for tribute to support the ritual, ceremonial, and administrative services they provided. In some cases, the demand for tribute may have produced a kind of 'land pressure' on the smaller villages where none had appeared before. When that pressure was too great, there were revolts, iconoclasm, 'desanctification', and population shifts. Such pressure apparently could occur even at what we would consider relatively 'low' population densities.

"To give you an idea of the kind of density I'm referring to, consider some of Earle's estimates. For the Middle Formative of the southern Gulf, primary centers or 'paramount chiefs' villages' were located some 44 km apart, at the center of territories with a 22-km radius. Each of these territories might have included 10,000 persons, for a density of less than 7 persons per square kilometer. This is not a particularly high overall density, but, as Drennan suggests, the labor

requirements of some of the major centers may have created maladaptive concentrations of population in their vicinity.

"In the Valley of Mexico, Early Formative densities were very light. But, between the Middle Formative and the Terminal Formative, the average local site aggregate grew from 1 village and 2 hamlets (with a population range of 90–640 persons) to a town, 1 large and 3 small villages, and 3 hamlets (with a population range of 1025–2660 persons) in 29 sq km. In other words, a population density of 35–91 persons per square kilometer.

"Stripped to its essentials, that's how your people seem to see it," concluded the G.S. "I'd say it was anything but a static and stable period. I see it as continually in disequilibrium, responding to constant, asymmetrical growth."

The Real Mesoamerican Archeologist spoke in a hushed voice. "My God, is that what the book said? G.S., that's formidable. As usual, none of it really made sense to me until I heard you pull it all together. You ... I guess I don't need to tell you, you've done it again. You really ought to put that in print."

"I have every intention of doing so," said the Great S., returning my manuscript to his briefcase. "Of course, I have other irons in the fire at the moment, but—one somehow finds time."

He took the watch out of his vest and looked at it.

"Almost time for the Executive Committee Meeting," he said, and with one graceful move he was gone.

"I don't believe it," said the Skeptical Graduate Student. "No one has talked that long without stopping for breath since Marlow told the whole story of *Heart of Darkness* from the deck of his ship while it rode at anchor on the Thames."

R.M.A. glowered. "I hope you listened as carefully as Marlow's audience did," he said. "You might learn something about how to draw anthropological conclusions from archeological data."

"From *that*?" said S.G.S. incredulously. "That wholly inductive, totally normative bedtime story?

It didn't even sound as if he'd read the same book I did."

"I suppose all you read was the part that had numbers, Greek letters, and giant summation signs," said R.M.A.

"Right on," said S.G.S.

"And what did *you* get out of the book?" I asked hopefully.

"That there's been a lot of rotten archeology done in Mesoamerica."

"And some good archeology," said R.M.A. defensively.

"The average Mesoamerican archeologist couldn't get a job doing salvage archeology in Illinois," said S.G.S.

"The average Mesoamerican archeologist," said R.M.A. pointedly, "wouldn't want one."

There was a moment of silence while the Skeptical Graduate Student stared moodily into space. Perhaps he was mentally picturing Sylvanus G. Morley applying for a contract to put a few test pits in the Kaskaskia Reservoir, and being turned down.

"I'll tell you what I got out of the book," said S.G.S. suddenly. "I'd like to go back to the San Jacinto drainage now and stratify it by natural environmental zones. I'd either survey it all, or I'd sample it by transects or small quadrats. On each site, I'd do a controlled surface pickup, and I'd use a Brainerd–Robinson matrix or Pearson's *r* to define groups of related sites sharing lots of design elements. I'd construct a site typology: towns, villages, hamlets, camps. I'd test one site of each type, the shallow ones by random quadrats and the deep ones by transects. Each site would be excavated by natural levels, and I'd use house floors, storage pits, activity areas, and so on as my units of collection. We'd sample a series of houses for tools, seeds, pollen, and bones, and set up a contingency table to compare them; search for craft areas, to get a handle on specialization and divisions of labor; get age, sex, and burial association on every skeleton, and the context of every ritual item. We'd quantify the data on traded goods, and study the context to see which mechanisms were moving it. A catchment analysis would be performed on each site, using chi-square to see which environmental factors were being selected for. Each level of the settlement hierarchy would be studied by the nearest-neighbor method to see what the spacing was, and changes in the pattern over time would be studied with a Markov model to see if we could detect any of the rules."

"Beautiful dreamer," said R.M.A. "How long do you think that would take?"

"At least a couple of years."

"A person could make quite a dissertation out of it, couldn't he?" said R.M.A. There was something in his tone that caught S.G.S. short. The Real Mesoamerican Archeologist reached into his jacket pocket. "A person who had that as a dissertation topic would really have to put up or shut up, wouldn't he?" And he poked a check and an airline ticket dramatically at S.G.S.

S.G.S. unfolded the travel advance as if he were unwrapping the Nobel Prize. "You'll want to come, too, won't you?" he said, in an unusually subdued tone.

"Later in the season," said R.M.A. "I have to teach Winter Term."

S.G.S. took a newspaper-wrapped cylinder out of his briefcase. "You'll probably need this in Winter Term," he said. "I was going to give it to you later, but if I'm going back through Customs . . ."

R.M.A. slowly unwrapped the newspaper.

"It's the kind with the worm inside the bottle," said S.G.S.

"Eight years old," said R.M.A. thoughtfully.

A look passed between them. Fleeting. To me it looked like love, but it might just have been *détente*. I walked out onto the mezzanine floor and pressed the button on the elevator. The Real Mesoamerican Archeologist and I rode down together.

"He's a real little smart-ass," said R.M.A. And then, as an afterthought, "But he's *my* little smart-ass."

It was the third day of the meetings, and I had

had as much physical punishment as I could take. I had one last drink in the María Isabel, tried unsuccesfully to hail a cab, and walked back to my hotel. For a while, I just lay on my bed with the lights out, watching the green archeological mounds of the San Jacinto drainage pass before my eyes. R.M.A., that old son-of-a-gun, must have drawn that travel advance for S.G.S. out of his own grant funds. Would the kid remember that? Or would he use R.M.A. as the straw man for his polemic dissertation? Would his work be a tour de force of analytical method that would reduce R.M.A. to a single paragraph, entitled: Previous (Bad) Work in the Region?

The green mounds of the San Jacinto are a resource we cannot afford to lose, but there are laws that protect them. There are no laws protecting the Real Mesoamerican Archeologist; he faces obsolescence, the most pitiless looter of them all. Suddenly, I realized it was not the early village that was the real endangered species: It was me.

Is it too late for salvation? If not, please let me have the analytical expertise of the New Archeology—and the humility and common sense of the Old.

SUBJECT INDEX

STUDIES IN ARCHAEOLOGY

Consulting Editor: Stuart Struever

Department of Anthropology
Northwestern University
Evanston, Illinois

Charles R. McGimsey III. **Public Archeology**

Lewis R. Binford. **An Archaeological Perspective**

Muriel Porter Weaver. **The Aztecs, Maya, and Their Predecessors: Archaeology of Mesoamerica**

Joseph W. Michels. **Dating Methods in Archaeology**

C. Garth Sampson. **The Stone Age Archaeology of Southern Africa**

Fred T. Plog. **The Study of Prehistoric Change**

Patty Jo Watson (Ed.). **Archeology of the Mammoth Cave Area**

George C. Frison (Ed.). **The Casper Site: A Hell Gap Bison Kill on the High Plains**

W. Raymond Wood and R. Bruce McMillan (Eds.). **Prehistoric Man and His Environments: A Case Study in the Ozark Highland**

Kent V. Flannery (Ed.). **The Early Mesoamerican Village**

Charles E. Cleland (Ed.). **Cultural Change and Continuity: Essays in Honor of James Bennett Griffin**

Michael B. Schiffer. **Behavioral Archeology**

Fred Wendorf and Romuald Schild. **Prehistory of the Nile Valley**

Michael A. Jochim. **Hunter-Gatherer Subsistence and Settlement: A Predictive Model**

Stanley South. **Method and Theory in Historical Archeology**

Timothy K. Earle and Jonathon E. Ericson (Eds.). **Exchange Systems in Prehistory**

Stanley South (Ed.). **Research Strategies in Historical Archeology**

John E. Yellen. **Archaeological Approaches to the Present: Models for Reconstructing the Past**

Lewis R. Binford (Ed.). **For Theory Building in Archaeology: Essays on Faunal Remains, Aquatic Resources, Spatial Analysis, and Systemic Modeling**

James N. Hill and Joel Gunn (Eds.). **The Individual in Prehistory: Studies of Variability in Style in Prehistoric Technologies**

Michael B. Schiffer and George J. Gumerman (Eds.). **Conservation Archaeology: A Guide for Cultural Resource Management Studies**

Lewis R. Binford. **Bones: Ancient Men and Modern Myths**

Richard A. Gould and Michael B. Schiffer (Eds.). **Modern Material Culture: The Archaeology of Us**

Muriel Porter Weaver. **The Aztecs, Maya, and Their Predecessors: Archaeology of Mesoamerica, 2nd edition**

Arthur S. Keene. **Prehistoric Foraging in a Temperate Forest: A Linear Programming Model**

Ross H. Cordy. **A Study of Prehistoric Social Change: The Development of Complex Societies in the Hawaiian Islands**

C. Melvin Aikens and Takayasu Higuchi. **Prehistory of Japan**

Kent V. Flannery (Ed.). **Maya Subsistence: Studies in Memory of Dennis E. Puleston**

Dean R. Snow (Ed.). **Foundations of Northeast Archaeology**

Charles S. Spencer. **The Cuicatlán Cañada and the Rise of Monte Albán**

Steadman Upham. **Polities and Power: An Economic and Political History of the Western Pueblo**

in preparation

Vincas P. Steponaitis. **Ceramics, Chronology, and Community Patterns: An Archaeological Study at Moundville**

Michael J. O'Brien, Robert E. Warren, & Dennis E. Lewarch (Eds.). **The Cannon Reservoir Human Ecology Project: An Archaeological Study of Cultural Adaptations in the Southern Prairie Peninsula**

Carol Kramer. **Village Ethnoarchaeology: Rural Iran in Archaeological Perspective**

Merrilee H. Salmon. **Philosophy and Archaeology**